Criminal Conduct and Substance Abuse Treatment

Dedication

*To our spouses,
Dottie Wanberg and Meredith Fogg,
for their patience and support.*

Kenneth W. Wanberg ■ Harvey B. Milkman

Criminal Conduct and Substance Abuse Treatment

Strategies for Self-Improvement and Change
The Provider's Guide

SAGE Publications
International Educational and Professional Publisher
Thousand Oaks London New Delhi

For information:

SAGE Publications, Inc.
2455 Teller Road
Thousand Oaks, California 91320
E-mail: order@sagepub.com

SAGE Publications Ltd.
6 Bonhill Street
London EC2A 4PU
United Kingdom

SAGE Publications India Pvt. Ltd.
M-32 Market
Greater Kailash I
New Delhi 110 048 India

Printed in the United States of America

Library of Congress Cataloging-in-Publication Data

ISBN 0-7619-0945-1 (hardcover)

ISBN 0-7619-0946-X (paperback)

98 99 00 01 02 03 04 7 6 5 4 3 2 1

Acquiring Editor:	Margaret Zusky
Editorial Assistant:	Renée Piernot
Production Editor:	Wendy Westgate

TABLE OF CONTENTS

SECTION III

Consent for Release of Confidential Information

Full Disclosure Statement Sample

Notice of Federal Requirements Regarding Confidentiality of Alcohol and Drug Abuse Patient Records

Personal Data Questionnaire (PDQ)

Provider Session Evaluation Summary (PSES)

Referral Evaluation Summary (RES)

LIST OF FIGURES

LIST OF TABLES

FOREWORD

This project was developed under Contract Number 957230 and 960671 with the Colorado Alcohol and Drug Abuse Division, Department of Human Services and under Contract Number 94-DB-15A-58-1 and 95-DB-15A-58-2 with the Division of Criminal Justice, Colorado Department of Public Safety from the Edward Byrne Memorial State and Local Law Enforcement Assistance Program, Drug Control and System Improvement Program Formula Grant to Colorado from the U.S. Department of Justice.

This was a two-year, broad-based project that included a number of efforts. Providers of service to both substance abuse and criminal justice clients in Colorado were surveyed with respect to different methods used in client treatment and intervention. A bibliographical search was made of relevant treatment approaches to individuals with the dual problem of substance abuse and criminal conduct. The manual was written. A statewide training effort was launched to train a cadre of service providers in both the public and private sector. Pilot delivery sites were established, and service delivery was monitored at these sites. The authors consulted with a variety of service providers throughout the State of Colorado in providing services to offenders with substance abuse problems. Funding for this project was $91,368 (72%) Federal funds and $36,327 (28%) State funds from the Offender Surcharge Fund.

Kenneth W. Wanberg, Th.D., Ph.D., is a private practice psychologist and the Director of Center for Addictions Research and Evaluation (CARE), Arvada, Colorado. Harvey B. Milkman, Ph.D., is Professor of Psychology at Metropolitan State College of Denver and Director of the Center for Interdisciplinary Studies, Denver, Colorado.

Criminal Conduct and Substance Abuse Treatment is a project of
The Center for Interdisciplinary Studies, Inc.

Correspondence should be sent to:

The Center For Interdisciplinary Studies
899 Logan Street, Suite 207
Denver, Colorado 80203
(303) 830-8500, Fax (303) 830-8420

ACKNOWLEDGMENTS

The authors have drawn upon numerous resources, documents and publications in developing this manual. A number of experts in the field were interviewed as to what they felt were important components for a cognitive-behavioral program for substance abusing offenders. About 20 experts working in substance abuse and correctional programs in the State of Colorado reviewed the manual.

A number of treatment manuals were also reviewed. These included manuals developed by Bush and Bilodeau (1993), Kadden and associates (1992), King et al., (1994), Miller, Zueben, DiClemente and Rychtarik, Rener, Schmidtz, Stipetich and Woldsweth (1994), Monti, Abrams, Kadden and Cooney (1989), Monti, Rohsenow, Colby and Abrams (1995), Ross and Ross (1995), and Ross, Fabiano and Ross (1986). The program content, concepts and process described in these manuals were helpful in developing the Strategies for Self-Improvement and Change (SSC) treatment curriculum.

The clinical, research and academic experience of the authors provided the most substantive basis for the development of the treatment curriculum. Kenneth Wanberg, Th.D., Ph.D., has 35 years experience in the evaluation, treatment and research of substance abuse problems and criminal conduct, both within public and private agencies and in private practice. Harvey Milkman, Ph.D., has 25 years of experience in developing multidisciplinary perspectives on the causes, consequences and solutions for addictive behaviors. The combined skills of the authors provided a substantial basis for the development of the content, skill practice and exercises of the treatment curriculum.

Finally, the reviews of the manual by Brad Bogue, M.A., Reid Hester, Ph.D., Alan Marlatt, Ph.D., George Parks, Ph.D, Robert Ross, Ph.D. and David Timken, Ph.D., provided valuable input in and review of the development of the program structure and process and curriculum content. Katie Smyth is credited with the design and layout of this volume.

The authors, are especially appreciative of Alan Marlatt's sagacious consultation with the authors and his review, in collaboration with George Parks, of the materials presented in this book. His unprecedented contribution to the field of addictions and particularly his work in the area of relapse prevention became invaluable resources for this manual.

PREFACE

I know of no more encouraging fact than the
unquestionable ability of man to elevate his
life by conscious endeavor.

Henry David Thoreau

Alcohol and other drug (AOD) abuse is commonly found among individuals with a history of criminal conduct. Surveys show that from 50 percent to 80 percent of offenders have a history of problems with AOD use and substance abuse. A review of the literature indicated that there were limited comprehensive resources, with a manual-driven model, available for the treatment of this dual-occurring disorder. A number of manual-determined treatment programs have been developed for AOD abuse clients or for criminal justice clients. A few short-term treatment approaches have been developed for individuals with both problems. The purpose of this project was to utilize as many of the relevant resources available in developing a long-term, comprehensive, manual-based intervention and treatment program for bringing about self-improvement and change within the substance abusing offender (SAO).

A review of the literature, the professional practice of the authors and formal and informal interviews with providers indicated that there have been seven important developments in recent years in the area of implementing improvement and change in substance abuse and criminal justice clients. These are briefly summarized.

Multi-dimensional assessment as a platform for implementing change: Research over the past 30 years has clearly indicated that there is a significant degree of variance found among individuals with AOD problems. Even within alcoholism clients, the variance is significant and various types and patterns are found. This finding has called for a multi-dimensional, differential assessment approach to both the evaluation and the diagnosis of AOD clients. Effective assessment is multi-dimensional, not based on a unitary or single-condition concept of alcoholism or drug abuse and clearly identifies the multiple conditions of the client's life adjustment problems. This approach provides a basis for applying different treatment approaches to different types and patterns of addictions.

Cognitive-behavioral therapy or treatment (CBT) as a key approach for implementing change: CBT approaches are indicated to be effective in the intervention of AOD abuse and criminal conduct. These approaches vary from a strong focus on behavioral therapy, a strong focus on cognitive therapy or a focus on the combination of the two. Although many CBT approaches are described in the literature in the treatment of these two groups (AOD abusers and offenders), cognitive restructuring and coping and social skills training seem to be the two most commonly applied.

Relapse and recidivism prevention are essential components of treatment: The research and clinical literature are clear that effective treatment must build specific programs and approaches to address relapse and recidivism. Over the past 20 years, clear and distinct treatment protocols have been developed to formally address these issues in treatment.

Individuals go through stages when making changes in their life adjustment problems: Research during the 1980s and 1990s in the area of the *psychology of change* has indicated that individuals go through relatively identifiable stages when changing psychosocial and behavioral patterns and problems. Individuals differ with respect to this change process, particularly as to the degree of readiness and motivation to engage in a formal change process. Drawing upon the concepts of change in the literature, the authors have developed a model for change upon which the treatment program presented in this manual has been built.

The implementation of change is based on the key principles of therapeutic support and motivation, therapeutic confrontation and therapeutic reinforcement: Efforts to bring about change begin with developing a climate of rapport, trust and openness. Change is further enhanced through the methods of therapeutic feedback and confrontation. Change is strengthened through methods of therapeutic reinforcement.

The integration of therapeutic and correctional approaches: When working with substance abusing offenders, providers are called upon to integrate the methods and concepts of therapeutic and correctional treatment approaches. Effective treatment of the SAO will integrate the concepts of therapeutic and correctional confrontation. Thus, effective SAO treatment is both client-centered and society-centered. Treatment addresses both the agenda of the client and the agenda of society with respect to behavioral change and correction.

Effective treatment capitalizes on the strengths of diversity: Treatment is culturally responsive and sensitive and addresses the client's cultural values, competencies and strengths. Treatment utilizes these strengths and competencies to enhance growth and change. Treatment acknowledges that strengths are found in the diversity of gender, age, ethnic group and life-span experiences.

With these concepts and principles in mind, the authors developed *Strategies for Self-Improvement and Change* for the substance abusing offender. The program utilizes the principles of differential assessment, the key concepts and approaches of CBT, and the principles of the psychology of change in the development of the process, structure and content of the program. The program is client-oriented but provider-directed.

The authors reduced the psychology of change to a three-stage model: *Challenge to Change, Commitment to Change* and *Ownership of Change.* It is our premise that individuals must first be challenged to make changes and improvement in their lives. This challenge may be from within, from without or a combination of both. For many of our clients, it will be the legal sanctioning system. Once challenged, the goal is to reduce ambivalence and to get the commitment of the client to make change. Once change takes place, those individuals who maintain their changes are those who feel a sense of ownership of that change. *"It's mine."*

Finally, as you proceed in your work with the substance abusing offender, we would like you to reflect on these thoughts. Our clients, individuals with substance abuse problems and a history of criminal conduct, are human and have the same human needs as all people in our society. It is important that we approach our SAO clients with respect and as persons who deserve to have the benefits of what we know and have learned about the psychology of change. Society typically "looks down" upon our clients and often views them as hopeless with respect to rehabilitation and change. As we hear this message and at times feel the discouragement ourselves, let us remember two important facts.

First, the most human quality we have is the ability to *think.* All persons have this unique and human capacity—different from all other species on earth. Our greatest hope for improving ourselves and becoming better persons is to use our mind and capacity to think. *Everyone can capitalize on the strengths of this unique capacity—including individuals with substance abuse problems and a history of criminal behavior.* This program capitalizes on this strength. It takes the capacity to think and makes it the fulcrum for change. It is through our thinking that we have the most hope for change. That hope for change is just as great with the substance abuser and the offender as with any other person. The challenge is to capitalize to the fullest extent on this capacity. We have only begun to discover how we can use the human mind to bring about change and improvement in the lives of people.

Our second basis for hope is that *change is natural.* Change is built into nature. Nothing remains the same. "Everything has its season." The most real aspect of living is change. The fact of change becomes the basis of our hope. If change is natural, then it is natural for the substance abusing offender to change. The challenge is to use all of our skills and knowledge to capitalize on and direct the inherent capacity of change in positive, constructive and healthy directions.

Some Guidelines and Concerns

This manual is designed to deliver a long-term (nine months to one year) intensive, cognitive-behavioral oriented treatment program to *adult substance abusing offenders*. The recommended client age is 18 years or above. However, some older adolescents may benefit from portions of the curriculum. The program is sensitive to the diverse needs across gender, race, culture and age. Although sessions do not address specific diversity topics, providers should strive to be culturally sensitive and competent and to help clients capitalize on their cultural strengths. Guidelines for enhancing cultural competence are provided in Chapter 8 of the Provider's Manual. Providers should address these differences according to the special needs of individuals and groups. The broad range of topics covered in the treatment curriculum provides ample opportunity to capitalize on the strengths of diversity within clients and the providers themselves.

Although it was designed to be delivered in an outpatient setting, it can easily be delivered to offenders within an incarcerated setting. Some providers may find it difficult to extend a particular treatment program over a period of nine months to one year. Modifications may be made to shorten the time period of treatment. For example, following Phase I, where sessions are delivered twice a week, providers may continue to deliver sessions on a twice-a-week basis. This would shorten the formal presentation by three months.

Modification can also be made on the basis of not delivering some materials because clients have had exposure to some portions of the curriculum. For example, if a group of clients have had the basic alcohol education services, then the portion in Module 3 dealing with this area could be eliminated. However, for the full effectiveness of this program, it is recommended that the treatment curriculum be followed as closely as possible, and that the period of time not be less than six months.

This *Strategies for Self-Improvement and Change* (SSC) manual provides a standardized, structured and well-defined approach to the treatment of the SAO client. However, the personal and unique style and approach of each provider are important variables in effective treatment of the SAO. Modifications, changes and enhancements of approach and curricula are to be expected, based on the experiences, skills and training of each provider.

There are many methods of and approaches to treatment for individuals with substance abuse problems and a history of criminal conduct. No one approach of treatment for the SAO has been shown as effective for all SAO clients. Although a blending of many approaches was used in this manual, SSC represents one of many approaches that can be used with SAO clients.

The authors make no claims or guarantees regarding the effectiveness of the *Strategies for Self-Improvement and Change* program for the SAO provided in this manual. The principles of differential assessment, the psychology of change, of CBT, upon which the treatment program in this manual is based, are well grounded in clinical practice and research. Many of the proposed treatment strategies and methods have been documented as being effective in bringing about improvement and change in helping individuals with substance abuse problems and individuals with a history of criminal conduct. The efficacy of the specific SSC program in this manual is yet to be tested with respect to the relevant treatment outcome expectations such as relapse into drug use or recidivism into criminal behavior. To date, the program has been effectively delivered to a number of substance abusing offender groups providing clear evidence of the service delivery feasibility.

INTRODUCTION

This manual is designed as a guide for all persons involved in the treatment and education of individuals with substance abuse problems and a history of criminal conduct—substance abusing offenders (SAOs). During the past decade, the most significant advances in treating both individuals with criminal involvement and individuals with problems of drug abuse—as

> *In fact,*
> *the criminal justice system*
> *is awash with drug users.*
> C. G. Leukefeld and F. M. Tims, 1992

separate populations—have been in the field of cognitive-behavioral psychology. The overall goal of this manual is to bring together effective cognitive-behavioral treatment approaches for changing the behaviors of individuals who have both problems of substance abuse and criminal behavior.

The term "cognitive-behavioral therapy" or "cognitive-behavioral treatment" (CBT) is used quite broadly to refer to treatment and rehabilitation approaches that focus on the interplay between thought, emotion and action in human functioning and more specifically in psychopathology (Freeman, Pretzer, Fleming & Simon, 1990). Although there are varying forms of CBT (e.g., problem-solving skills, social skill development), most would agree with Hollen and Beck (1986), who define cognitive-behavioral therapies as "those approaches that attempt to modify existing or anticipated disorders by virtue of altering cognitive processes" (p. 443).

Traditional ways of treating clients with substance abuse problems focus mainly on helping them to identify and take ownership of their own symptoms and patterns of maladaptive use of substances. Then, within the context of a non-judgmental therapeutic relationship, clients are expected to learn and commit to lifestyle changes that will establish abstinence from the use of substances.

In more recent times, alcohol and other drug (AOD) abuse treatment has integrated the CBT model in helping clients develop new thinking skills. These thinking skills help clients to reorganize their drug-related beliefs and automatic thoughts that promote urges and cravings. Then, behavioral treatment methods are used to change clients' behaviors which, in turn, changes and reinforces the new thinking skills.

Although a variety of methods and approaches have been used to treat the adult offender (e.g., Andrews & Bonta, 1994; Ross et al., 1986; Ross & Ross, 1995), traditional treatment of the individual with criminal behavior has been correctional in nature. That is, the main goals of treatment are to "correct" the behavior of the offender, to bring the offender's behavior into compliance with the laws of society and to prevent recidivism.

We have identified a number of underlying assumptions that are basic to integrating effective CBT approaches in the treatment of the substance abusing offender (SAO).

1 A substance abusing offender (SAO) treatment program must be *deliverable by a variety of personnel* having direct responsibility of providing substance abuse counseling and services to rehabilitate offenders. There are not enough psychologists, psychiatrists and social workers to help the multitude of substance abusing offenders.

2 Although the term *treatment* is used in various portions of this manual, SAO service providers are seen as *educators and skill trainers,* rather than traditional treatment providers as narrowly defined by the disciplines of psychiatry, psychology, social work and substance abuse counselors.

3 Although we refer to the substance abusing offender (SAO) in order to be brief, our assumption is that it is more meaningful to think in terms of an *individual with a history of criminal conduct* or an individual with *substance abuse behavior.* Instead of referring to an individual as alcoholic or as a criminal, we refer to the individual as engaging in criminal conduct or as having a particular alcoholic pattern. This view separates the person from the problem. It allows us to focus on changing the person's thinking and behavior. It sees the person as having the power to change behaviors or thoughts and not necessarily as having to change his or her very self.

4 Our fourth assumption is that effective SAO treatment must integrate the principles of both the *therapeutic and correctional treatment models.* AOD treatment has been based mainly on the former; criminal offender treatment has been based mainly on the latter.

5 Self-improvement and change involves, first and foremost, *developing the motivation to change.* Gaining the client's cooperation and preventing dropout from treatment are vital to the successful treatment of SAOs. Clients with greater character problems and antisocial histories are most likely to drop out of treatment. Once a therapeutic alliance is forged, self-regulating skills may then be learned through motivational counseling, therapeutic confrontation and reinforcement of life-enhancing behavior. Sobriety and stability are maintained through effective relapse-prevention strategies.

6 Assessment and treatment must be based on the idea that origins, expressions and continuation of criminal conduct and substance abuse are *multidimensional* in nature (Wanberg & Horn, 1983). Individuals will vary according to how they fit the different patterns of substance abuse and criminal conduct. There are many causes and patterns of criminal conduct and substance abuse disorders, fulfilling different needs at different times in an individual's life. Factors contributing to criminal conduct and addictive behavior are many. They may be linked to the individual, family, peer group, community and society at large. Thus, effective SAO treatment depends not only on developing standard approaches which are applied to all SAOs but also on the development of individualized treatment strategies drawn from comprehensive and ongoing assessment practices.

7 Recent advances have shown that people with addictive disorders go through a *series of stages* as they make changes in their use and abuse of substances. These stages of change are also relevant to persons with a history of criminal conduct. Treatment strategies for achieving increased self-regulation for AOD abuse and criminal conduct must be made to fit the individual's level of awareness, cognitive development and determination to change disruptive patterns of thought and behavior. Effective treatment will use the right strategies at particular stages of each client's process of change.

8 Treatment must engage the client's *significant others* and the client's primary social unit. Treatment needs to enlist the support, understanding and reinforcement power of the family and significant others in the person's effort to make change.

9 The principles of *relapse prevention* must be utilized in order to assure long-term maintenance of positive treatment outcomes. In the case of the SAO, relapse and recidivism must be seen within the context of both criminal conduct and AOD abuse. In many cases, the two are closely related. Relapse into AOD use and abuse can lead to recidivism into criminal conduct, and vice versa.

10 Effective treatment makes the most of the *strengths of diversity*. Treatment is culturally responsive and sensitive and addresses the client's cultural values, competencies and strengths. It utilizes these strengths and competencies to promote growth and change. These strengths are found in the client's gender, age, ethnicity, culture and life-span experiences.

11 Finally, an important philosophical assumption of this CBT program is that *healthy thinking and behavior* are based on the learning of key lessons of life. Often, we have been taught that experience is the best teacher. Someone once said that experience is not a good teacher. In fact, experience is a poor teacher. Why? Because experience gives the test before the lesson. What good teacher will give you the test before the lesson? The SAO clients have only too often not learned the important lessons in life which will allow them to handle critical life experiences. The overriding purpose of this program is to provide clients with the necessary lessons to pass the tests of living—to handle the experiences they encounter. Thus, we see each of the sessions in this program as a lesson designed to help the client pass the crucial tests of living.

How This Program and Manual Are Organized

Building on these assumptions, we have organized this manual into the following three sections.

Section I provides a historical perspective and theoretical foundation of the issues relevant to the development of this manual—*Strategies for Self-Improvement and Change: A Cognitive-Behavioral Approach for Treatment of the Substance Abusing Offender*. This section provides the reader with a theoretical and empirical justification for integrating cognitive-behavioral treatment (CBT) for the individual dually affected by substance abuse and criminal conduct. It also provides an understanding of the theory of self-improvement and change and addresses concerns about the impact of diversity on treatment implementation.

Chapter 1 provides the historical roots, underlying principles, common features and key focuses of Cognitive-Behavioral Treatment (CBT).

Chapter 2 addresses the treatment of substance abuse. The characteristics of the substance abuser are summarized. The broad variable domains of treatment are outlined, and the recent work in the area of treatment matching is discussed. A review of AOD treatment efficacy and outcome is provided with a focus on which treatment approaches have been most effective. As well, the key cognitive-behavioral (CBT) areas of focus and the key CBT interventions used with AOD abusers are summarized.

There is a substantial and unique history of cognitive-behavioral treatment of the criminal offender. *Chapter 3* summarizes the approaches to correctional intervention with particular focus on treatment efficacy, risk factors and dynamic predictors as a basis for determining treatment needs.

The focus of this manual is on the substance abusing offender. Thus, it is important that the link between substance abuse and criminal conduct is established. *Chapter 4* provides the evidence for this linkage.

Treatment readiness, motivation to change and the change process have become important elements in contemporary substance abuse and offender treatment. *Chapter 5* provides a grounding for the reader with respect to the theories and approaches to treatment motivation and the change process.

Chapter 6 provides a model for integrating substance abuse and offender treatment. The integrated model is built around the concepts of relapse and recidivism prevention and best approaches as found in our literature review.

Effective assessment is critical to establishing the treatment plan. *Chapter 7* provides an historical perspective of assessment in AOD use, criminal conduct and cognitive processes.

Chapter 8, "Understanding and Enhancing Cultural Competence," provides an understanding of the impact of culture, ethnicity, life span and life experiences on treatment and the change process. Issues related to gender-specific treatment needs are addressed.

Section II of this manual addresses the essential elements of the treatment platform for *Strategies for Self-Improvement and Change: A Cognitive-Behavioral Approach for Treatment of the Substance Abusing Offender*.

Chapter 9 provides the philosophical and conceptual framework and treatment structure of the program. It gives the SAO treatment provider the conceptual basis for integrating the concepts of therapeutic communication and change with correctional treatment in order to produce positive treatment outcomes. The CBT conceptual framework to be used in this manual is summarized.

Chapter 10 outlines what we view as the traits and characteristics of the effective SAO service delivery provider. This chapter also addresses the issue of seeing SAO service providers as educators and skilled trainers as well as providers in the more traditional counseling role.

Effective treatment is based on a comprehensive and accurate assessment of the problems, vulnerabilities and resiliency factors that exist for each client. Multifactorial assessment, conducted in an atmosphere of empathy and concern, provides a basis upon which we can plan for self-improvement and change. *Chapter 11* provides the rationale, methods and approaches for screening clients into the program and for doing the in-depth differential assessment of the client. The in-depth assessment provides the basis upon which the client *Master Profile* (MP) is developed. The MP is then used to develop the client's *Master Assessment Plan* (MAP) which is used as a guide for the client's in-depth treatment.

Chapter 12 outlines the operational procedures and methods of the treatment program. It provides guidelines for group facilitation, recommended ground rules and guidelines to be used with clients. It also discusses issues pertaining to client admission, consent for treatment, counselor full disclosure and client confidentiality.

Section III of this manual provides the treatment curriculum. This section is presented in three phases of treatment activity: 1) *Challenge to Change* or the reflective-contemplative phase; 2) *Commitment to Change* or the determination and action phase; and 3) *Taking Ownership of Change* or the stabilization and maintenance phase of treatment. Each treatment phase is broken into specific modules built around a particular treatment theme. A series of lesson experiences called sessions are utilized to achieve the objectives and goals of the module themes.

The *Challenge to Change* phase involves the client in a reflective-contemplative process. A series of lesson experiences is utilized to build a working relationship with the client and to help the client develop motivation to change. Sessions are also directed at providing basic information on how people change, the role of thought and behavior in change and basic information about substance abuse and criminal conduct. A major focus of Phase I is helping the client develop self-awareness through self-disclosure and receiving feedback. The client is confronted with his or her own past and then challenged to bring that past into a present change-focus. The goal is to get the client to define the specific areas of change and to commit to that change. This phase includes a review of the client's current AOD and criminal conduct with the results of this review becoming a focus of the reflective-contemplative process.

The *Commitment to Change* or action phase involves the client in an active demonstration of implementing and practicing change. Each client undergoes an in-depth assessment of his or her life situation and problems and looks carefully at the critical areas that need change and improvement. Targets of change are identified. Then, a series of sessions is provided to strengthen basic skills for change and help the client to learn key CBT methods for changing thought and behavior which contribute to substance abuse and criminal conduct. Focal themes of these sessions include coping and social skills training with an emphasis on communication skills; managing and changing negative thoughts and thinking errors; recognizing and managing high-risk situations; managing cravings and urges that lead to AOD use and criminal conduct (CC); developing self-control through problem solving and assertiveness; managing thoughts and feelings related to anger, aggression, guilt and depression; understanding and developing close relationships; understanding and practicing empathy pro-social values and moral development.

The *Ownership of Change* or the stabilization and maintenance phase involves the client's demonstration of ownership of change over time. This involves treatment experiences designed to reinforce and strengthen this commitment and established changes. The concepts of relapse and recidivism prevention are reviewed. This phase includes sessions on critical reasoning, conflict resolution and establishing and maintaining a healthy lifestyle. Change is strengthened though helping the client become involved in a variety of auxiliary methods including mentoring and role modeling, self-help groups and other community-based recovery maintenance resources.

The treatment curriculum is built around the treatment modules, which are structured around the three phases of treatment outlined above. Each module provides an overall statement of purpose, contextual explanation and a series of discrete sessions (lesson plans) with specific learning objectives and strategies to achieve those objectives. Each module with its discrete session plan is taught in a logical sequence with basic topics covered first, serving as the foundation for more difficult concepts covered later.

The session plan is prefaced by a clear statement of measurable objectives. Clear and detailed content is spelled out for each session. This content is presented in a language format that is readable for the client. Much of the content sections of each session are included in the Participant's Workbook. Group exercises are provided. Classroom and homework exercises and tasks are spelled out in detail. The workbook exercises are integrated into the session plan. Methods are outlined for the provider to evaluate the effectiveness of each session and the level of client participation.

The treatment program is delivered primarily in group format and is structured around the three phases of treatment. Phase I, *Challenge to Change*, comprises six treatment modules with 18 two-hour group sessions to be held over a period of nine weeks (two-hour sessions twice a week). The completion of this phase and admission into Phase II will depend upon the client's response to the program.

Phase II, *Commitment to Change* or *Taking Action*, involves three modules comprising 22 sessions to be held once a week or a period of six months (22 weeks). Again, the completion of Phase II will depend on the client's demonstration of change and ownership of that change.

Phase III, *Taking Ownership of Change* represents the maintenance and aftercare component of the program. This phase involves three modules comprised of sessions to be held over a period of two months. The Strengthening Change phase allows the client to demonstrate change maintenance and ownership of that change. Following this, the client will demonstrate voluntary participation in an ongoing maintenance group or experience. Opportunities for mentoring will be made available for those who wish to participate in this part of the program.

Individualized Treatment Protocols

The Individualized Treatment Protocol provides guidelines for individualized treatment plans determined through the differential assessment process. These individual needs are addressed through both in-program resources and by referring the client to outside service providers. The individualized treatment may include family, relationship and marital treatment sessions provided within the context of cognitive-behavioral techniques (e.g., reciprocity marriage counseling). These resources may also include the use of urine and breath analyses in monitoring the client's goals of maintaining drug-free living. Pharmacologic treatments may also be available, depending on the resources of the service provider. These would include antabuse, blocking AOD effects (naltrexone), treating abstinence syndromes, and the use of adjunct pharmacologic treatment for anxiety, mood or thought disorders (e.g., lithium, prozac, thorazine).

A separate Participant's Workbook provides in-session skill development exercises and homework assignments carefully designed to complement each session plan. The workbook, which has a Spanish translation, has been carefully reviewed to ensure cultural appropriateness, sensitivity and optimal responsivity.

The Participant Workbook was written to accommodate a reading level of about seventh grade. Clients with reading levels below grade seven may need assistance in understanding some portions of the workbook. When it is suspected that a client may not have the reading and comprehension skills to negotiate the workbook, it is recommended that the provider perform a skills-level check by asking the client to read and explain portions of the workbook text.

HISTORICAL PERSPECTIVE
AND
THEORETICAL FOUNDATIONS

The greates discovery of my generation is
that a human being can alter his life
by altering his attitude

William James

The purpose of this section of the Provider's Manual is to provide you with historical and theoretical background of the issues related to the use of cognitive-behavioral therapy (CBT) in the treatment of the substance abusing offender (SAO). An overview of CBT and its key principles is provided. The use of the principles of CBT in the understanding and treatment of alcohol and other drug (AOD) problems is then summarized. Approaches to correctional treatment and the relationship between criminal conduct and AOD use and abuse are discussed. *Section I* also provides a review of some of the important aspects of assessment as it applies to individuals who are involved in patterns of AOD use and involved in criminal conduct. Since treatment, motivation and compliance are important components of AOD abuse treatment, research findings and theory in this area are also reviewed. We then integrate these various historical perspectives into an overall working model of cognitive-behavioral treatment of the substance abusing offender. Since the population of offenders with substance abuse problems is very diverse with respect to age, ethnicity, life-span experiences and gender, we will look at how the strengths of diversity can be captured in SAO treatment.

C H A P T E R ①
OVERVIEW OF COGNITIVE-BEHAVIORAL THERAPY

Historical Roots of Cognitive-Behavioral Therapy

Since the focus of this manual—*Strategies for Self-Improvement and Change* (SSC)—is the treatment of the substance abusing offender through the theory and practice of cognitive-behavioral therapy, it is important that the reader understand the historical roots of this approach and how the two paths of behavior therapy and cognitive therapy joined.

The development of behavioral therapies of the late 1950s and 1960s provided the evolutionary foundation of the behavior component of cognitive-behavioral therapy. Franks and Wilson (1973) note that behavioral therapy has a long past but a short history. This long past is found in the work of the behaviorist and learning theorists in the first half of this century (Glass & Arnkoff, 1992). Pavlov's work in classical conditioning (Pavlov, 1927), the behaviorism of Watson (1913) and the operant conditioning models of Skinner (1938) in the early part of this century provided the theoretical foundations of behavioral therapy.

During this same period, the work of Thorndike (1931), Guthrie (1935), Hull (1943) and Mowrer (1947) in the psychology of learning also added to the theoretical grounding of behavioral therapy. As these theories emerged, so did the number of efforts to apply them clinically (Glass & Arnkoff, 1992). Most noteworthy was Dunlap's (1932) use of negative practice involving the repetition of undesirable behavior such as tics, the Mowrers' (Mowrer & Mowrer, 1938) "bell and pad" method of treating bed wetting, Jacobson's (1938) method of progressive relaxation and Salter's (1949) method of directly practicing a behavior in a particular situation.

Emerging methods such as systematic desensitization (Wolpe, 1958) to help patients manage anxiety and the applications of contingency reinforcement (Skinner, 1953) in behavioral management spelled the beginning of modern behavioral therapy in the 1950s and 1960s. Eysenck (1960) was the first to use the term "behavioral therapy" in a book title, and he, along with Rachman, founded the journal *Behavioral Research and Therapy*. Behavioral therapy gained a strong foothold in psychology with the introduction of the concepts and applications of modeling (Bandura (1969), anxiety management through flooding, behavioral self-control and self-monitoring (Goldiamond, 1965; Kanfer, 1970) and social skills training (Lange & Jakubowski, 1976), which is an important component of contemporary cognitive-behavioral therapy.

The historical roots of the cognitive component of cognitive-behavioral therapy (CBT) are found in the literature of philosophy and psychology and in the studies on self-change (Arnkoff & Glass, 1992). The concept that our view of the world shapes the reality that we experience is found in Greek thinking and in Plato's concept of the ideal forms (Leahy, 1996). Plato saw these forms as existing within the mind and represent what is real in the world. Philosophers of the 17th and 18th centuries built their view of the world around the idea that the mind determines reality. This is particularly found in Descartes' concept that "I think, therefore I am" and Kant's idea that the mind makes nature (Collingwood, 1945).

Arnkoff and Glass (1992) note that there are differing opinions as to whether cognitive therapy evolved within modern behavioral therapy or whether it emerged as a new and independent movement. Whichever the case, it seems fair to conclude that the cognitive approach was a reaction to the more narrow view of behavioral psychology which did not attend to, and even rejected, the importance of internal mediating cognitive responses and processes, such as attribution, problem solving and expectancy. Bandura's classic work *Principles of Behavior Modification* (1969) challenged the traditional view of non-mediational behavioral psychology. Bandura stressed the importance of internal mental processes in the regulation and modification of behavior.

Arnkoff and Glass (1992) see modern cognitive restructuring therapies as emerging out of the mid-1950s with the work of Ellis (Ellis & Harper, 1961) and his development of rational-emotive therapy

(RET), presented in *A Guide to Rational Living*. The work of Ellis is seen as an important precursor to the work of Beck (1963, 1964), who is commonly seen as the founder and developer of cognitive therapy emerging out of his work with depression at the University of Pennsylvania in the early 1960s (Arnkoff & Glass, 1992; Beck, 1995; Leahy, 1996). Leahy (1996) credits Kelly (1955) in his development of cognitive constructs as "the early founder of cognitive therapy," p. 11). Beck (1996) made it clear that he borrowed from Kelly's cognitive constructs when he first applied "the concept of negative cognitive schemas to explain the 'thinking disorder' of depression" (p. 1). The work of Kelly of Piaget (1954) in his study of the structure of thinking provided a firm foundation for the development of the cognitive restructuring therapies.

Following the work of Beck (1963, 1970, 1976) in applying the cognitive model to the treatment of depression, other cognitive restructuring therapies began to emerge. These different forms of cognitive therapy began to blend the elements of behavioral therapy with cognitive restructuring therapy.

Meichenbaum (1975, 1977) developed self-instructional training, stress inoculation and coping skills training. This approach had a strong behavioral therapy flavor. Goldfried, Decenteceo and Weinberg. (1974) implemented systematic rational restructuring, which teaches the individual to modify internal sentences (thoughts) and then to practice the rational reanalysis of these thoughts through role playing and behavioral rehearsal. Cautela (1966, 1990) conceived covert sensitization (1966) as a method for cognitive-behavioral change. Problem solving therapies and training became prominent features of cognitive-behavioral treatment (Spivack & Shure, 1974; Shure & Spivack, 1978; D'Zurilla & Goldfried, 1971). The coping skills and stress inoculation training approaches were developed to help clients deal with problem and stressful situations (Meichenbaum, 1977, 1985). The stress inoculation method involves teaching the individual coping skills and then practicing these skills when deliberately exposed to a stressful situation.

Although behavioral therapies and cognitive restructuring approaches seemed to develop in parallel paths, over time the two approaches merged into what we now call cognitive-behavioral therapy. As Arnkoff and Glass (1992) note, "the line distinguishing behavior therapy from cognitive therapy has become blurred, to the point that cognitive-behavioral is a widely accepted term" (p. 667). The behavioral component is of crucial importance particularly in the treatment of children (Arnkoff & Glass, 1992) but also in the treatment of alcohol and other drug abuse problems and of criminal conduct. Alan Marlatt has noted (personal communication, 1995) that "cognitive therapy á la Ellis and Beck has over the years become progressively more behavioral and that behavioral therapy á la Bandura, Goldfried, Kanfer, Mahoney, Michenbaum, etc., has over the years become progressively more cognitive—together creating contemporary CBT."

Cognitive-Behavioral Therapy (CBT): An Integration of Cognitive and Behavioral Principles and Approaches

Contemporary behavioral therapy focuses on current determinants of behavior with an emphasis on overt behavior change guided by specific treatment objectives (Kazdin, 1978). It involves the application of principles that come from learning theory and social and experimental psychology. It involves environmental change and social interaction using approaches that enhance self-control (Franks & Wilson, 1973-1975). It is further characterized by a focus on client responsibility and the therapeutic relationship (Franks & Barbrack, 1983). The common intervention approaches used in behavioral therapy are coping and social skills training, contingency management, modeling, anxiety reduction and relaxation methods, self-management methods and behavioral rehearsal (Glass & Arnkoff, 1992).

The underlying principle of cognitive therapy is that disturbances in behaviors, emotions and thought can be modified or changed by altering the cognitive processes (Hollen & Beck, 1986). In simplistic terms, "cognitive therapy is based on the simple idea that your thoughts and attitudes—and not external events—create your moods" (Burns, 1989, p. xiii). The fundamental idea of the cognitive model of emotion as outlined by Beck (1976) is that "emotions are experienced as a result of the way in which events are interpreted or appraised. It is the meaning of the event that triggers emotions rather than the events themselves" (Salkovskis, 1996a, p. 48). The role of the cognitive therapist is to help the individual see the alternative ways of thinking about and appraising a situation, to check the relative merits and accuracy of the alternatives against past, present, and future experiences, and then help the individual "identify any obstacles to thinking and acting in this new, more helpful way" (Salkovskis, 1996a, p. 49). The goal is not to convince the individual that his or her view of the situation is wrong, right, negative or irrational but rather to help the person discover other ways of looking at the situation.

Yet, this does not necessarily mean a straightforward cause and effect (thinking being the cause and emotions and action the results). Cognitive psychology assumes an interplay between thought, emotion and action. As Freeman and colleagues (1990) note, "the cognitive model is not simply that 'thoughts cause feelings and actions'" (p. 6). Emotions and moods can change cognitive processes. Actions can have an influence on how one sees a particular situation. Emotions can prompt behaviors. There are a number of studies to indicate how moods and emotions influence cognition, as in memory or perception (Freeman et al., 1990).

The common intervention approaches used in cognitive therapy are the cognitive restructuring methods of *Rational Emotive Therapy* (RET), restructuring of cognitive distortions of negative schemas, maladaptive assumptions and automatic thoughts (Leahy, 1996), self-instructional training, problem solving, coping skills, relaxation therapy, modeling strategies, thought stopping and covert conditioning (Arnkoff & Glass, 1992; Kendall & Bemis, 1983; Leahy, 1996).

Contemporary CBT, then, is an integration of the key components of behavioral and cognitive therapy. Even though prominent recent publications have titles containing *Cognitive Therapy,* (e.g., Beck, 1995; Leahy, 1996; Salkovskis, 1996b), the descriptions of the methods and approaches of cognitive therapy in these texts clearly integrate the behavioral therapy counterpart. In 1983, Kendall and Bemis argued that behavioral influences were predominant in the practice of cognitive therapy. Even though there appears to have been an evolutionary merging of the two approaches over the past 20 to 25 years, there has been some resistance to integration, particularly from behavior therapists (Arnkoff & Glass, 1992). During the 1990s, there has been a strong movement toward the integration of all forms of contemporary psychotherapy (Arnkoff & Glass, 1992; Goldfried, 1995).

The underlying principle of this treatment manual is that both cognitive and behavioral approaches bring combined strengths to the implementation of self-improvement and change in the substance abusing offender. Alan Marlatt (personal communication, 1995) states "I believe the strength of CBT is in its combined emphasis on aspects of both cognitive and behavioral approaches to change."

Our review of the literature leads us to believe that the combining element of cognitive and behavioral approaches is found in the principle of *self-reinforcement*. This concept simply states that cognitive and behavioral changes reinforce each other. When cognitive change leads to changes in action and behavior, there occurs a sense of well-being which strengthens the change in thought patterns, which leads to changes in action. In turn, the changes in thinking reinforced by the changes in behavior further strengthen those behavioral changes. This self-reinforcing feedback process is a key principle which becomes the basis for helping clients understand the process and maintenance of change.

As is obvious from the above discussion, there are many forms and variations of cognitive-behavioral therapy. Yet, among all of the variations, there are a number of common features of CBT (Arnkoff & Glass, 1982; Beck; 1995; Clark & Steer, 1996; Dobson & Block, 1988; Kendall & Bemis, 1983; Kendall & Hollon, 1979; Leahy, 1997; Mahoney & Arnkoff, 1978). Some of these principles are premised on behavior therapy, others on cognitive therapy. All are important in the understanding of and effective implementation of CBT. Table 1.1 shows common elements of the CBT approach.

Table 1.1

Common Features and Underlying Principles of the CBT Approach

- ◆ Individuals are actively involved in the construction of their realities;
- ◆ individuals can know about and get in touch with their mental and cognitive world;
- ◆ people respond to their mental interpretation of the environment rather than the environment itself;
- ◆ feelings, thoughts and behaviors are interactive and interrelated;
- ◆ learning is mediated by cognitive processes;
- ◆ disturbances in emotions and behaviors are a result and function of disturbances in the thinking, seeing and feeling processes;
- ◆ changes in behavior and emotions occur through changes in thinking;
- ◆ assessment of psychological and emotional problems is based on the identification of attitudes, expectancies and attributions;
- ◆ treatment initially places emphasis on the present and the here and now;
- ◆ the counselor and client work together in a partnership in evaluating, assessing and developing solutions to problems; CBT is based on a sound therapeutic alliance;
- ◆ there is a strong focus on relapse prevention;
- ◆ there is an emphasis on changing overt behaviors as well as thinking patterns;
- ◆ there is an emphasis on identifying and changing dysfunctional beliefs and thoughts;
- ◆ changes in thinking and action need to be reinforced with self-reinforcement as the most powerful determinant of maintaining change;
- ◆ it is an educational process;
- ◆ counselors and treatment providers fulfill the roles of evaluator, educator and consultant in understanding disturbed and maladaptive thought processes and in developing, with the client, life-response changes.

Key Focuses of CBT

An important underlying assumption of the cognitive-behavioral model is that mental or cognitive events cause emotions and behavior. Rosenhan and Seligman (1995) summarize the mental or cognitive events that are the focus of CBT. They indicate that these events can be broken into short-term and long-term processes. They identify the short-term cognitive processes that become the focus of treatment as *expectations, appraisals and attributions*. The long-term processes are *beliefs* and *attitudes*.

Expectancies become an important focus of CBT. The mental expectation that a certain behavior will bring pleasure will often lead an individual to engage in that behavior. If that behavior does fulfill the expectation, then the behavior is reinforced. Bandura (1978) calls these *outcome expectations*. An important part of expectancy theory is self-efficacy. If a person believes that he or she can perform a particular behavior, than most likely that individual will engage in that behavior. Bandura (1978) calls these *efficacy expectations*. This concept is of particular importance in the treatment of the substance abuser. Helping the client develop the skill of coping with anxiety in ways other than AOD use will build the efficacy expectation so that conditions that produce stress can in fact be handled in ways other than drinking.

Appraisals represent another category of cognitive events that lead to action and feelings (Rosenhan & Seligman, 1995). This is the cognitive process that continually evaluates what individuals are experiencing and their responses to their experiences. Our mental appraisals often come quickly and without deliberate thought. These are called *automatic thoughts* (Beck, 1976; Beck, Wright, Newman & Liese, 1993; Freeman et al., 1990; Leahy, 1997) or errors in thinking or logic and become a primary focus in CBT. For example, an automatic thought of the depressed person who experiences rejection might be "I'm no good."

Another mental event that becomes the focus of CBT is *attribution*. This is the individual's explanation of why things happen to him or her. An important part of attribution theory is where the individual sees the source of his or her life problems or successes or one's *locus of control* (Rotter, 1966). This locus of control might be internalized ("I'm responsible for the accident") or externalized ("If they would have locked their car doors, I wouldn't have ripped off their stereo").

Rosenhan and Seligman (1995) identify the long-term cognitive processes as less available to our consciousness. These mental processes are more durable and stable and they help determine the short-term mental processes that are in our conscious state. They are our *beliefs* and our *attitudes*. Irrational beliefs become the focus of the cognitive therapist. This is one of the primary target areas in *Rational Emotive Therapy* (RET; Ellis, 1962, 1975).

Freeman and his colleagues (1990) suggest that CBT focuses on four major areas that are basic to bringing about change in maladaptive and dysfunctional cognition and behavior. These are:

- automatic thoughts;
- underlying assumptions;
- cognitive distortions; and
- the influence of emotions and mood on cognition.

They suggest that treatment starts with helping the client to identify her or his automatic thoughts and cognitive distortions. Then, intervention moves to address the underlying assumptions and maladaptive beliefs associated with these automatic and cognitive distortions.

Finally, the reinforcement of change and self-improvement is a key factor in CBT. As discussed above, self-reinforcement is the sine qua non of the maintenance of long-term change.

Recent Developments

One recent development in CBT is the emergence of constructivist cognitive therapies (Arnkoff & Glass, 1992) as found in the works of Guidano (1987), Guidano and Liotti (1983) and Mahoney (1990). The underpinnings of this CBT approach are found in constructivism philosophy as expressed in the works of Kuhn (1970), Hanson (1958), Toulmin (1972) and also found in Cicourel's (1974) cognitive sociology, the phenomenological social theories of Schultz (1932/1967) and the personal construct theory of Kelly (1955). Constructivism and phenomenology hold that individuals construct and create their own realities. Thus, the therapist cannot necessarily assume to know what is going on with the client through logical observation, as is the belief of most CBT approaches. This model has increased CBT therapists' awareness of the importance of understanding how the client constructs his or her reality and how that reality brings about disturbed thinking and actions.

As CBT therapies have evolved, this approach has given more attention to emotions and/or the importance of the therapeutic relationship (Arnkoff & Glass, 1992). The importance of building rapport and trust and focusing on motivational methods and techniques have also become important factors in the evolution of CBT (Beck et al., 1993; Miller & Rollnick, 1991).

SUBSTANCE ABUSE AND THE COGNITIVE-BEHAVIORAL APPROACH

Overview

The purpose of this manual is provide a detailed guide for an extended and intensive outpatient treatment program for the substance abusing offender built around the principles of cognitive-behavioral treatment. The foundation for such a program is found in the key assumptions, elements and approaches to cognitive-behavioral treatment that we reviewed in Chapter 1. The building stones for this kind of program must come from the treatment approaches that have been found to be effective in the treatment of substance abuse clients.

Because the design of the treatment program is built around the nature of clients to be treated, we first look at some of the key characteristics and needs of the AOD abusing client. Then we present the broad variable domains that make up the treatment framework. Treatment approaches—the building stones of treatment—represent one of these broad variable domains. We look at treatment efficacy in a general sense, and then more specifically, review the evidence around the effectiveness and efficacy of various treatment approaches. Because this manual is built around the CBT approach, we discuss the cognitive processes that underlie addictive thinking and behavior and upon which CBT of the substance abuse client is premised. A summary of the various interventions used with AOD abusers, which utilize the principles and methods of CBT, is then presented. The implications of these findings for the development of a CBT program for the substance abusing offender is outlined.

Some Key Characteristics of AOD Abusing Clients

There are some key characteristics found among AOD abusers and addictive clients that predispose them to AOD abuse and are primary focal points for the CBT approach to treatment.

1 Vulnerability Factors

Several vulnerability factors have been identified in the literature which can become the focus of CBT treatment. Beck et al. (1993, p. 40) outline characteristics that predispose individuals to AOD abuse patterns. These are:

- Tendency to magnify sensitivity to unpleasant feelings;
- Lack of motivation to control behavior;
- Impulsive acting;
- Excitement seeking and low tolerance to boredom;
- Low tolerance for frustration;
- Lack of prosocial alternatives to achieve pleasurable feelings and a sense of hopelessness in ever achieving this goal.;
- Poor coping skills.

2 Involvement in Addiction Cycles

A common cycle found among AOD abusers is what Wanberg (1990) calls the *psychobehavioral*. The initial phase of this cycle involves AOD use to reduce stress or to turn off unpleasant internal feelings or perceptions of an external threat. This is the use of drugs to cope with stressful life situations. With many individuals, this kind of AOD use never leads to a cycle of dependency. With some individuals, however, AOD use itself leads to life problems (e.g., committing a crime when under the influence of drugs, receiving a citation for driving under the influence). Since the main coping mechanism is that of AOD use, then the obvious response to the problems that come from use is to engage in AOD use. The cycle then reaches full circle when the individual engages in AOD use to deal with the stress that comes from the problems that come from AOD use. For many individuals, this cycle of addiction continues for several years before they seek treatment. The psychobehavioral cycle is premised, in part, on the stress reduction model of AOD use and abuse (Cappell & Greeley, 1987; Lehrer, Carr, Sargunaraj & Woolfork, 1993; Sher, 1987).

Another pattern of addiction is the *psychophysical* dependency cycle (Wanberg, 1990). This is based on the concept of the AOD withdrawal rebound phenomenon (Gitlow, 1970, 1982, 1988; Glenn & Hockman, 1977; Grilly, 1989; Peyser, 1988) or what Gitlow calls the asynchronous relationship between the short-term sedative effect and the long-term agitating effect. This involves using alcohol to treat their drug abstinence syndrome or the symptoms resulting from withdrawal from AOD use. For example, when alcohol is used to excess, the body experiences sedation. When the alcohol blood level approaches zero, the body rebounds into an agitation or neurochemical stimulation phase. The best "cure" for this is to again sedate the system with alcohol. Peyser (1988) notes that the prolonged withdrawal syndrome can produce an agitation effect lasting several weeks to several months.

With cocaine, the opposite effect occurs. Cocaine stimulates the system, and the resulting abstinence symptoms are sedation and depression. Another dose of cocaine is the best "cure" for this depression. Although treatment for this cycle or abstinence syndrome is certainly medically based, CBT can be used to first help the client understand the cycle itself. Then, the client can learn to anticipate this kind of cycle when the urge or craving to use the drug occurs. This leads to the next common characteristic of the AOD addicted person—craving.

3 Cravings and Urges: Feeling Good or Not Feeling Bad

Cravings and urges are seen as key characteristics for many persons with substance abuse problems (Baker, Cooney & Pomerleau, 1987; Beck et al., 1993; Blum & Payne, 1991; Liese & Franz, 1996; Marlatt, 1985a; Newman, 1977). Making the distinction between cravings and urges helps to fine-tune the CBT of the substance abusing client. Most experts agree that *craving* represents a desire or want for the drug; the *urge* represents an internal movement toward acting on that desire or the behavioral intention (Beck et al., 1993; Marlatt, 1985; Marlatt & Gordon, 1985). The craving can be seen as the obsession and the urge as the compulsion to engage in consummatory behavior (taking the drug).

There are two types of cravings and subsequent internal urges. The first is the craving to feel good, to have pleasure, to *"feel wonderful."* As Milkman and Sunderwirth point out, "we spend much of our lives in relentless pursuit of fleeting moments of exalted delight" (1987, p. ix). Although the healthy pursuit to achieving pleasure would be through "natural highs" (Milkman & Sunderwirth, 1993), for many people, AOD use often becomes a primary pathway to both physical and psychological highs. A developed or consistent pattern of AOD use, which becomes the primary if not only "pathway to pleasure," puts a person at risk for developing a pattern of AOD abuse. Such a pattern can be altered by CBT approaches in early intervention therapy, for example, non-AOD alternatives to finding pleasure and feeling good.

The second type of craving is the desire to avoid unpleasant or negative experiences. This can be a desire to avoid psychological discomfort—the need to avoid stress as described in the psychobehavioral addiction cycle outlined above. It also can be associated with a desire to avoid physical discomfort—the need to avoid the pain of the abstinence syndrome or withdrawal as described in the psychophysical cycle outlined above.

Although clients may describe "uncontrollable cravings for drugs," certain irrational thoughts or self-defeating beliefs tend to feed these negative feeling states. For example, the person may have an uncontrolled craving for a drug because he or she believes (based on experience) that stopping drug use will produce incapacitating side effects and unbearable physical discomfort. This may lead to a feeling of helplessness—the only alternative is to use drugs to avoid the pain.

Not all individuals who abuse substances experience cravings and urges. This may represent a unique pattern of substance abuse, based in part on the type of substance used. One pattern is represented by sustained, continuous users who "rarely experience strong cravings because they take drugs before their level of craving has an opportunity to escalate" (Liese & Franz, 1996).

Using the CBT approach, we try to help the client understand the craving as the thought that precedes the urge and then look at alternative ways of thinking about the event that is related to the craving. The goal is to restructure those thoughts associated with the craving so that the craving does not lead to the urge. The cognitive-behavioral outcome is that the desire for pleasure or the need to reduce discomfort is met by alternative thoughts and alternative outcome behaviors. These alternative thoughts and behaviors are then reinforced if they lead to positive outcomes (the need for pleasure is met; the need to reduce discomfort is met).

For those who do experience cravings and urges, there may be a therapeutic window of opportunity in which to apply the CBT approach. Beck et al. (1993) describe this as "the delay between the experience of craving and the implementation of the urge" (p. 40). While cravings and urges tend to operate automatically, the challenge of effective therapy is to provide voluntary means for self-regulation. Clients often equate powerful cravings and urges with imperative needs. "Increasing the ratio of the subjective power of control to the subjective power of the urge may be used as a guide for intervention" (Beck et al., 1993, p. 4).

4 Limited Coping Abilities and Social Skills

Cognitive behavioral therapists take the position that people who are AOD abusers have limited competencies for coping with the problems and conflicts of everyday life and problems in managing interpersonal expectations and conflict (Chaney, 1989; Curry & Marlatt, 1987; Riley, Sobell, Leo, Sobell & Klajner, 1987). They have difficulty identifying and expressing a range of emotions in relationships. It is difficult for them to assertively handle interpersonal conflicts or the need to say "no" to social pressure to participate in self-destructive behaviors. They often lack the skills to achieve gratification through healthy activities such as games, sports or aesthetic involvement. Such behavioral deficits may interact with biological, social and mental processes to increase the likelihood of AOD abuse.

The AOD abuser's coping abilities and social skills are particularly put to test in high-risk situations that lead to AOD use relapse (Annis & Davis, 1989; Daley & Marlatt, 1992; Dimeff & Marlatt, 1995; Marlatt & Gordon, 1985). Persons who lack social skills and coping abilities have a higher probability of relapse (Marlatt & Gordon, 1985). When individuals with substance abuse problems use these abilities and skills to prevent relapse, they feel an increase of self-confidence and self-efficacy (Marlatt & Gordon, 1985).

5 Automatic Thoughts

A mainstay of concentration for cognitive-behavioral therapists is the client's interpretation of a given situation. As discussed in a previous section, these are called *automatic thoughts* (Beck et al., 1993; Beck, 1995; Freeman et al., 1990). These are thoughts that pop up quickly, are evaluative in nature and are not based on cognitive deliberation. Automatic thoughts are usually based on one's core beliefs. For example, the automatic thought of the AOD abusing client may be "have a drink or two, it will relax you," and it may be based on the belief that the "only way I can relax is to have a few drinks." The decision to use a substance may be based upon the client's automatic thoughts concerning questions such as Will I be able to "get over" this situation without drugs or alcohol? Or if I snort, hit-up or drink, etc. a small amount of substance, what effect will this have on my mood and subsequent actions? Answers to these and other questions are likely to be found during childhood and adolescence, with some conclusions drawn before any AOD abuse occurs (Goldman, Brown, and Christiansen, 1987).

6 AOD Use Expectancies and Benefits

The perceived benefits and *expectancies* derived from AOD use powerfully reinforce continued use (Marlatt, 1985a). Expectancy theory has gained an important role in understanding and treating AOD users (Goldman et al., 1987). The whole area of perceived benefits and expectancies also incorporates tension reduction theories (Cappell & Greeley, 1987) and stress response dampening theories (Sher, 1987).

Traditional behavioral treatment holds that the outcomes of a particular behavior determine the likelihood of the behavior repeating itself. That is, if a behavior is reinforced by an outcome that gratifies some need, that behavior will increase in frequency. CBT theory views the expected outcome of a behavior as another powerful factor in determining whether the behavior will be repeated.

Both positive and negative expectancies motivate the individual toward and away from specific actions because of the predicted outcomes. If a person believes that a drink will help to lower anxiety, then this increases the desire (craving) to drink. On the negative side, a person who anticipates horrible or intolerable feelings upon withdrawal from heroin will avoid quitting.

Research has shown that heavy drinkers have different expectations for alcohol use than light drinkers or non-drinkers. This is a good example of how alcohol outcome expectancies influence behavior. Problem drinkers, for example, have been found to have strong expectations that alcohol will enhance sexual and aggressive behavior (Brown, Goldman, Inn & Anderson, 1980). They have also been found to expect more stimulation and pleasurable loss of inhibitions and to develop a perception of themselves as being more dominant and in control when moderately drunk (Southwick, Steele, Marlatt & Lindell, 1981).

Alcohol expectancies also increase the belief that one is more competent. A substance-abusing offender, for example, may believe that a criminal act such as a burglary or a robbery may be committed more effectively if properly dosed with a particular alcoholic beverage, such as tequila. George and Marlatt (1983) have identified several sources of "alcohol efficacy expectations."

- Experience in which performance was effective while drinking (e.g., the offender succeeds at carrying off a crime when under the influence of AOD).

- Observations of others behaving effectively while using AOD (e.g., others succeed at achieving desired outcomes).

- Encouragement and reinforcement from others for drinking or drugging (e.g., the AOD abusing offender is told that s/he was awesome while under the influence).

- Reduction of anxiety through AOD use, which results in a temporarily more effective use of coping skills (e.g., the offender, while under the influence of AOD, lies his/her way out of a near bust with relative ease).

Horn, Wanberg and Foster (1987) have measured three very reliable expectancy or benefit factors in their *Alcohol Use Inventory* (AUI): Social Benefit, Mental Benefits and Mood Change. These factors clearly indicate that individuals perceive themselves as deriving certain benefits from the use of alcohol. Yet it is important to keep in mind that not all AOD clients fit these patterns. In fact, research done through the use of the Alcohol Use Inventory (AUI) indicates that only about 20 percent of alcohol abuse clients would score high on the factor measuring the improvement of mental functioning through the use of alcohol (Wanberg & Horn, 1983).

7 Behavioral Justification-Attribution Theory

Closely related to expectancies are *attributions*. These are an individual's explanations for his/her behavior. There is considerable literature in cognitive psychology on the need to maintain consistency of self-view (consistency or balance theory, Heider, 1958; Lecky, 1961). Such theory holds that we need to attribute (or explain) our behavior to certain logical causes (attribution theory, Kelley, 1971) and that we have a need to reduce dissonance between our view of ourselves and experiences of the real world (cognitive dissonance, Festinger, 1957). Berglas (1987) uses these theories as the basis of his self-handicapping alcohol use theory.

These theories hold that there is a strong need to maintain a consistent and rational view of self. If that view is challenged, efforts may be made to explain, attribute or deny the view or behaviors which are seen as not consistent with that view of self. This is certainly the psychological basis for the concept of denial so often used (and misused) in dealing with disruptive or unacceptable behavior associated with AOD use.

For example, a person who commits a crime may explain the behavior in a number of ways. The criminal act may be attributed to external factors (such as being pressured into doing it by friends) or internal (such as a lack of morality or conscience). The crime may be attributed to factors that are uncontrollable, such as an intolerable drug craving and withdrawal. Or the crime may be attributed to factors which are controllable, such as a special opportunity the offender decided not to pass up. The action may be attributed to more general factors such as a lack of willpower or factors that are specific such as a period of intense financial need because of losing one's job.

Finally, attributions may be stable or unstable (as in fluctuations in mood or circumstances). The explanations that are given for one's behavior, whether in relationship to AOD abuse, criminal conduct, or both, will influence if, when, where, how much and how often the behavior will recur.

8 Social Influences and Modeling

Identifying with role models and peers is a powerful determinant of the development of AOD use and abuse patterns (e.g., Botvin & Botvin, 1992; George & Marlatt, 1983; Miller & Hester, 1995). Bandura (1969, 1977, 1986) provided the first thorough treatment of social reinforcement theory and modeling. He spoke specifically about how modeling affects learning AOD use. "Alcoholics are people who acquired, through differential reinforcement and modeling experiences, alcohol consumption as a widely generalized dominant response to aversive stimulation" (Bandura, 1969, p. 536). There is a lot of evidence that modeling is a powerful factor in establishing the cultural norms that influence people. More specific to our focus, it is clear that modeling promotes the development and continuation of AOD use behaviors (for a thorough treatment of social learning theory and modeling as it applies to AOD use, see Abrams & Niaura, 1987).

George and Marlatt (1983) have given us a useful way to see the differences between types of AOD modeling. They refer to *imitative* modeling as passively observing another person using alcohol or other drugs. Subsequently, the observer responds by imitating the user. *Co-active* modeling is the simultaneous interaction with someone else who is engaging in the behavior. George and Marlatt (1983) found that for adult drinkers, coaction rather than imitation best describes the modeling effects. During childhood and early adolescence, however, imitative modeling effects may be more potent. Co-active modeling is a powerful reinforcer of criminal conduct in that the model sanctions the criminal behavior at the same time that the immediate positive outcomes reinforce the criminal behavior.

9 Relapse

A common characteristic of AOD treatment clients is relapse. In its broadest sense, relapse is defined as a failure to maintain initial changes in behavior. As will be discussed later in this chapter, outcome studies indicate that a high percentage of individuals treated for AOD problems experience relapse. An important focus of this manual is on relapse and relapse prevention.

10 Biological Contributions

Up to this point, we have mainly described the psychological and social risk factors and key characteristics associated with substance abuse. In biology, broad physical characteristics such as genetics, the biochemistry of the brain, irregularities in metabolism, and neuroadaptation also need to be considered. Blum and Payne (1991) focus on the concepts of somatopsychic syndromes which involve the interaction of the brain, emotion and behavior. They note "we are now beginning to understand that genetic defects leading to deficiencies and imbalances in neurotransmitters, enzymes, and receptors may give rise to compulsive diseases and a wide range of behavioral disturbances" (p. 247).

For many years, numerous molecular genetics research centers have made a concerted effort to discover the genetic factors associated with substance abuse, particularly alcoholism. Although some studies have been misinterpreted to indicate that there is an "alcoholism gene," Blum, Cull, Braverman and Comings, (1996) make it clear that to date, "there is no such thing as a specific gene for alcoholism" (p. 132). What has become apparent and most promising in molecular genetic studies is that there is an association between genes and various behavior disorders.

Blum and associates (1996) have pursued this association, and they conclude that there is a link between the addictive disorders (substance abuse) and the biological part of the brain that provides pleasure in the process of rewarding certain behavior. They have labeled this the *reward deficiency syndrome.* They connect this syndrome with a reduction of dopamine D2 receptors in the part of the brain that is directly related to the activation of the brain's pleasure centers. If the activity of the D2 receptor is deficient, then the individual experiences unpleasant emotions or cravings for substances that can provide temporary relief by releasing dopamine in the brain. Alcohol, nicotine and cocaine have been identified as agents that release dopamine in the brain.

According to Blum and associates (1996), a higher percentage of persons with addictive problems have a reduction in the dopamine D2 receptors. This depletion has been associated with a unique variation in the dopamine D2 receptor gene called the A1 allele. Individuals having the A1 allele have about 30 percent fewer D2 receptors. A greater percentage of individuals with addictive disorders tend to have the A1 allele variation. For example, Blum and associates found that of 35 persons diagnosed as alcoholic, 69 percent had the A1 allele whereas 31 percent had the A2 allele and only 20 percent of persons determined to be nonalcoholic had the A1 allele. With cocaine addicts, 52 percent had the A1 allele variation compared with 21 percent of nonaddicts.

The above findings illustrate that there are biological and biogenetic variations characteristic of a significant percentage of individuals with AOD addiction problems. Blum and associates (Blum & Payne, 1991) conclude that biological risk factors are interactive with psychological and social risk factors. For example, acquiring a particular drinking pattern can be explained through social learning concepts. The continuation of the pattern can be explained by stress-reduction concepts. However, the prolonged, excessive use of alcohol may be explained, in part, by the idea of physical dependence and the fear and pain of alcohol withdrawal. In some cases, when these biological factors kick in, the original purpose or value of drinking may have been lost. Continued drinking is now done independently of the original reason for acquiring the behavior (Abrams & Niaura, 1987).

11 AOD Clients are Variable and Different

Even though there are some key traits and features among AOD abusers, not all fit these common features. In fact, what is evident in the research literature is that there is a great degree of variation among individuals considered to be AOD abusers. AOD use and abuse are multidimensional in nature, and there is no unique pattern of alcoholism or AOD abuse. Research shows that there are a number of independent patterns and types found among individuals who have AOD problems (Horn & Wanberg, 1969; Horn et al., 1987; Wanberg & Horn, 1983, 1987). These different patterns and types have different etiologies, different paths of development, different treatment needs and different treatment outcomes. Once these different patterns and types are reliably defined, it is quite likely that they will show different biogenetic characteristics. Effective assessment of AOD problems must be *multidimensional,* and specific treatment approaches must be developed for different patterns and types of AOD problems.

Broad AOD Treatment Variable Domains

There are several broad variable domains that have been used to define the treatment services provided to substance abusing clients (see Wanberg, 1990, for a detailed discussion of these variables).

One broad domain is *treatment structure* (or what has been called level of intervention, Miller, 1989), which varies across a number of variables including inpatient care, medically managed hospitalization, therapeutic community, concentrated outpatient structure and traditional outpatient (see Lowinson, Ruiz, Millman & Langrad, 1992, for a detailed discussion of some of these structures).

A second broad treatment variable domain is the *modality or mode* through which treatment approaches and methods are delivered. Variables in this domain would include individual, group, lecture or didactic formats, couples and family and multifamily groups. Sometimes, the treatment structures as defined in the above paragraph are considered as modalities.

A third broad variable domain is *level of treatment intensity.* Intensity can vary at the interpersonal level, or the degree of confrontation by and involvement with the therapist or group peers. It can vary at the intrapersonal level, or the degree to which the client confronts him or herself. Intensity can also vary as to type of methods used. At the individual level, a supportive-reflective approach would be less intense than a confrontive-direct approach. A program may be high structure, using mainly group modality but low intensity.

A fourth broad variable domain are *general theories not specific to AOD use and abuse* which underlie various treatment methods. These theories are usually identified as

- biomedical;
- psychodynamic;
- behavioral;
- existential-humanistic;
- cognitive-behavioral;
- systems approach;
- eclectic.

Another broad variable domain are *general theories or conceptual models specific to AOD use and abuse.* Brickman and associates (1982) identified four models of addiction based on etiological and behavioral change determinants. These are the moral model, disease model, spiritual or "enlighten-ment" model and compensatory model. They see the latter as holding the individual responsible for the change process. Marlatt and colleagues see the compensatory model as more congruent with relapse prevention approaches (e.g., Dimeff & Marlatt, 1995; Marlatt & Gordon, 1985; also see Dimeff & Marlatt, 1995, for a thorough discussion of the Brickman and associates' development of these four explanatory models of addiction and behavioral change).

Miller and Hester (1989, 1995) provide a comprehensive discussion of the various explanatory models of alcoholism. Some of these include

- moral models;
- disease models;
- spiritual models;
- conditioning models;
- cognitive models;
- social learning models;
- general systems model;
- public health model.

Another broad variable domain is the *methods or approaches* (or what others have called strate-gies) used to treat substance abuse clients. Some of these approaches are exclusively designed for the treatment of drug use disorders; others are premised on general theories whose boundaries are much broader than substance abuse treatment. These approaches have been discussed in detail in a num-ber of sources (Blane & Leonard, 1987; Cox, 1987; Frances & Miller, 1991; George, 1990; Hester & Miller, 1989, 1995; Lowinson et al., 1992). Those that are considered to be AOD focused or that emerged out of efforts to develop effective AOD treatment strategies are

- aversion therapies;
- antidipsotropic medications (antabuse);
- 12-step approaches;
- relapse prevention;
- self-control training.

Approaches developed outside the addictions and substance abuse field and utilized in AOD treatment are

- brief therapies and interventions;
- solution focused approaches/strategies;
- motivational strategies;
- psychodynamic therapy;
- marital and family systems treatment;
- various cognitive-behavioral strategies;
- psychotropic medications;
- community reinforcement;
- group process therapy.

Treatment Matching

The purpose of treatment matching is simple: differentiate AOD types and patterns and find the best treatment for a particular pattern or type. Treatment matching brings together the complex set of broad treatment domain variables described above with clinically or empirically determined descriptions of client types.

The concept of treatment matching has a long history. Horn and Wanberg (1969), in their classic factor analytic study of the dimensions and symptom patterns of alcoholism clients, conclude: "the results provide a challenge to discover the extent to which the patterns indicate distinct underlying dynamics or call for different kinds of treatment" (pp. 56-57). Later, in their description of the *Alcohol Use Inventory* (AUI), they state that the description of clients through the AUI profile "can lead to a more personalized approach to treatment planning. The eventual goal of this effort will be to determine which kind of treatment is most effective for which kind of profile or alcoholism typology" (Wanberg, Horn & Foster, 1977, p. 541).

Over the past ten years, client matching has become a primary focus in AOD research and treatment, particularly with alcoholism clients (Allen & Kadden, 1995; Donovan & Mattson, 1994; Litt, Babor, DelBoca, Kadden & Cooney, 1992; Miller, 1989; Rohsenow et al. 1991; also see *Journal of Studies on Alcohol Supplement,* No. 12, 1994). A conclusion from The Institute of Medicine's (1990) review of outcome literature was not whether alcoholism treatment worked, but what kind of treatment for what kind of client? Responding to that challenge, the National Institute on Alcohol Alcoholism and Alcohol Abuse has sponsored a large study—Project MATCH—to evaluate this hypothesis. Initial results have recently become available and will be discussed below (Project MATCH Research Group, 1997).

Allen and Kadden (1995) provide a comprehensive summary of treatment matching studies. This summary certainly provides evidence that a client-treatment matching approach does yield promising results in terms of increasing treatment efficacy.

Review of AOD Treatment Outcome and Implications for the Treatment of the Substance Abusing Offender

1 Background and Early Findings

Alcohol and drug abuse treatment have been available during most of the 20th century. It was not until the mid-1960s that formalized treatment systems began to develop as part of the public health system in the United States (Hubbard, 1992). It was not until the early 1970s that AOD treatment follow-up studies began in earnest. As data came in from these studies over the next 10 years, the general results did not favor positive outcome. These studies indicated that relapse rates across addictions range from 50 to 90 percent (Catalano, Howard, Hawkins & Wells, 1988; Emrick, 1975; Hunt, Barnett & Branch, 1971; Hunt & Matarazzo, 1973; Marlatt & Gordon, 1980; Miller & Hester, 1980, 1986a). The

Armor, Polich and Stambul, (1978) study indicated that less than 10 percent of patients remained totally alcohol free over a two-year posttreatment period. The Riley et al. (1987) review of 68 studies involving a sample of over 14,000 clients indicated 34 percent were able to remain alcohol-free or engage in non-problem drinking after treatment. Other studies report between 40 and 60 percent abstinence rates in the first year after treatment (Institute of Medicine, 1989). For the chronic severe patient, 93 percent relapsed within a year following admission (Wanberg, Fairchild & Bonn, 1977). That same study found that among the less severe, first admissions, 75 percent went back to some drinking within one year following a two week residential care program.

2 Treated Clients Overall Do Better than Untreated Clients

The good news from these outcome studies clearly indicated that those clients who did receive AOD treatment overall do better than clients who are untreated and that treated clients show greater reduction of the negative effects of continued drinking than the untreated clients (e.g., see Emrick's review, 1975). Even relative brief intervention is more effective than no treatment with respect to changing drinking patterns (e.g., Chick, Ritson, Connaughton, Stewart & Chick, 1988; Harris & Miller, 1990; Holder, Longabaugh, Miller & Rubonis, 1991). Other studies have indicated that methadone maintenance and therapeutic community programs are effective in reducing drug abuse during and after treatment and in reducing criminal activities in clients during treatment (DeLeon, 1984; Holland, 1982; Nash, 1976; Sells, 1979; Smart, 1976; Tims & Ludford, 1984).

A number of studies using both quasi-experimental and clinical trial designs during the 1980s provided strong evidence that "treatment contributes significantly to change in client behavior during and after treatment" (Hubbard, 1992). These studies, summarized in major reviews (Anglin & Hser, 1990; Gerstein & Harwood, 1990; Sisk, Hatziandren & Hughes, 1990; Fuller, Branchey & Brightwell, 1986), conclude that drug abuse treatment is effective. Miller, Brown and associates' (1995) comprehensive review of 211 alcoholism treatment outcome studies indicated that 69 percent of these studies reported a significant positive outcome effect.

3 Residential Versus Outpatient, Long-Term Versus Short-Term

Having established that treatment was effective, research programs were designed to test the efficacy of traditional inpatient treatment. Several studies and reviews (Annis, 1986; Miller & Hester, 1986b; Saxe et al., 1983) showed that longer term, more intensive alcoholism treatment is no more effective than short-term, less intensive treatment, particularly when abstinence is seen as a primary measure of outcome. As well, Miller and Hester (1986b) concluded that length of stay, whether residential or outpatient, had little if any effect on alcohol abstinence outcome and that no difference was found between minimal intervention programs (thorough assessment and a guide for self-directed change) and weekly outpatient programs with similar content. Chick et al., (1988), however, found that extended treatment regimens versus brief or minimal treatment approaches tend to show less deleterious effects from alcohol use on follow-up, even though the diverse treatment regimens do not show differential abstinence rates.

The *Treatment Outcome Prospective Study* (TOPS) of residential care and outpatient alcohol and drug clients during cohort years 1979 to 1981 indicated quite different findings from the studies of alcoholism treatment. The TOPS client makeup varied across all drug use categories; however, over half of the outpatients were methadone clients who also used other drugs. Residential patients were fairly evenly distributed across the primary drug types. Clients who remained in treatment for at least 3 months had more positive outcomes and showed half the pretreatment rate of drug use (Hubbard et al., 1984). Clients who stayed in treatment for more than 12 months indicated major changes in behavior (Hubbard, et al., 1989). Hubbard (1992) concluded that his reviews of the findings "provide comprehensive and convincing evidence that long-term treatment is effective" (p. 600). Other studies (McLellan, Luborsky, Woody, O'Brien & Druley, 1983; Orford, Oppenheimer & Edwards, 1976) found that more intensive treatment is more effective for clients with more severe levels of AOD use and social adjustment disruption and that the more socially stable clients do better in less intensive treatment settings.

4 What Works Best?

Treatment studies then began to address what treatment strategies work best. Pertinent to the goal of this manual, how effective are treatment approaches based on the principles and techniques of CBT?

The most thorough review of alcoholism treatment outcome thus far was done by Miller, Brown and associates (1995). They gave efficacy ratings to 211 studies categorized into 30 different treatment methods and 11 specific alcoholism treatment approaches. Treatment approaches with the highest efficacy ratings included brief intervention approaches (including motivational enhancement), skill training strategies, marital/family therapy (including cognitive-behavioral marital/family) and cognitive-behavioral approaches.

Monti and colleagues' (1995) review provides convincing evidence of the efficacy (reduction of drinking, fewer severe relapse episodes, abstinence, etc.) of a wide variety of communication skills and cognitive behavioral training. The specific skills training and approaches included

- rehearsal of communication skills;
- assertiveness training modeling;
- behavioral rehearsal of assertiveness skills;
- refusal skills;
- enhancing expression of feelings;
- problem analysis and production of adaptive responses;
- role-playing, modeling, and video feedback;
- cognitive-restructuring.

Therapist style and particularly therapist empathy have significant impact on treatment outcome (Luborsky, McLellan, Woody, O'Brien & Auerbach, 1985; Miller & Rollnick, 1991). As much as two thirds of the variance in six-month outcome data could be attributed to the degree of empathy shown by therapists during treatment (Miller, Taylor & West, 1980), and therapist empathy accounted for half the variance in outcome at one year and one fourth of the variance in outcome at 24 months.

5 Project MATCH

Having established that some treatment approaches may do better than others, the next logical step in the research of AOD treatment efficacy and outcome was to tackle the issue of client matching. Project MATCH, which represents the largest publicly funded, national, multisite study ever launched, addressed this issue. Using a hindsight (Miller & Cooney, 1994) model, clients were randomly assigned to three treatment approaches (Miller et al., 1994; Nowinski, Baker & Carroll, 1992; Kadden et al., 1992).

- *Cognitive-Behavioral Therapy:* based on principles of social learning, emphasis placed on helping the client build social and coping skills to deal with problems rather than using alcohol;
- *Motivational Enhancement Therapy:* employs motivational strategies to mobilize client's self-resources, uses structured feedback and reinforcement of client progress, provides change advice, enhances therapist empathy and builds client self-efficacy;
- *12-Step Facilitation:* grounded in the concept of alcoholism being a spiritual and medical disease, the client is brought through the 12 steps of Alcoholics Anonymous with emphasis on AA being the best chance for recovery; it focuses on personal alcohol history, negative consequences of drinking, tolerance, loss of control, self-monitoring of use, urges and slips.

Results of the posttreatment drinking outcomes have been reported (Project MATCH Group, 1997). Significant and sustained improvements were achieved across all three treatment groups with respect to drinking outcomes, indicating all were effective in producing change in clients. Drinking outcome measures did not differ across the three treatments. Only 1 of 10 matching variables—psychiatric severity—demonstrated a significant attribute by treatment result. Clients low in this attribute did better in the 12-step model. Several factors about the study are important to note, relevant to this treatment manual. Individuals whose probation or parole requirements might interfere with protocol participation were excluded from the study; the treatment modality was individual; the sessions extended over a twelve-week program; alcohol had to be the principal drug of abuse; clients with a diagnosis of dependence on stimulants, cocaine, opiates or sedative/hypnotics were excluded; and clients could have no intravenous use for six months prior to admission.

6 Antisocial and Criminal Justice AOD Clients

There are a number of studies that support the efficacy of the treatment of the SAO (Annis, 1988; Field, 1989; Inciardi, 1995; Vigdol & Stadler, 1992; Weekes, 1997; Weekes, Moser & Langevin, 1997; Wexler, Falkin & Lipton, 1990). Several studies have shown that criminal justice clients do as well as if not better than other clients in drug abuse treatment and that the criminal justice system involvement helps clients stay in drug abuse treatment (Collins, Hubbard, Rachal & Cavanaugh, 1988; Collins & Allison, 1983; Hubbard, Collins, Rachal & Cavanaugh., 1988). Clients with more severe sociopathy and psychopathology receiving CBT (versus interactional therapy) had slower relapse rates; however, clients with little sociopathy and psychopathology did better in interactional therapy (Kadden, Cooney, Getter & Litt, 1989). Coping skills training and therapies are more effective than interactional-interpersonal therapies with alcohol clients who have antisocial or sociopathic patterns (Cooney, Kadden, Litt & Gerter, 1991; Kadden et al., 1989).

7 Implications for the Treatment of the Substance Abusing Offender

The above findings of AOD treatment efficacy have several important implications for developing a treatment program for the substance abusing offender utilizing the principles, methods and procedures of cognitive-behavioral treatment.

First, AOD treatment in general has a positive impact with respect to changing AOD use patterns.

Second, people with alcohol and drug problems probably benefit more from longer-term treatment structures, even though this may not be necessarily true for alcohol-specific clients.

Third, the findings certainly support the broad-spectrum application of cognitive-behavioral treatment as an effective approach in changing AOD abuse patterns. Broad-spectrum CBT refers to the utilization of all the treatment approaches relevant to the principles of CBT outlined in Chapter 1. Those specific approaches will be summarized below.

Fourth, there is evidence that AOD clients with a criminal justice and antisocial history respond well to AOD treatment programs.

What are the implications of the initial findings of Project MATCH for developing a treatment program for the SAO? The most important is that *motivational enhancement* should be an integral part of any CBT program for the SAO. Second, it means that such a CBT program should encourage and support the client's use of community self-help and 12-step programs such as Alcoholics Anonymous. Third, a salient component of CBT for SAOs should be social/coping skills training.

But most important are the salient differences between the Project MATCH protocols and clients and the CBT we have developed in this manual for the SAO. These are that

- the target treatment group is dually affected: AOD and criminal conduct;
- the target treatment group is high risk with respect to overall social adjustment and possibly AOD abuse;
- length of treatment is one year;
- there is a strong integration of motivational enhancement methods and CBT principles and methods;
- group treatment is the primary modality;
- clients are quasi-voluntary with the program being a required part of probation or parole for many clients;
- correctional treatment approaches are integrated with therapeutic approaches.

Key Focuses in the Cognitive-Behavioral Treatment of Addictive Thinking and Behavior

The cognitive-behavioral approach to substance abuse assumes that people with addictive problems "are able to compensate for their difficulties by assuming responsibility for changing their behavior" (Marlatt & Gordon, 1985, p. 14). The goal of CBT of the person with substance abuse problems is to "teach the client to eventually become the agent of change" (Marlatt & Gordon, 1985, p. 15). Or, more specifically, "the role of the therapist is...one of teaching clients how to alter maladaptive cognitive processes and environmental contingencies" (Brickman et al., 1982, p. 380). In this regard, the therapist serves as an educator who expects substance abusing clients to "set their own standards, monitor their own performance and reward or reinforce themselves appropriately" (Brickman et al., 1982, p. 380). The therapist's goal is to assist substance abusing clients in becoming their own therapist.

In Chapter 1, we identified several mental processes that become the focus of cognitive-behavioral treatment. Marlatt (1985a) identifies four of these processes which relate to or underlie addictive thinking and behavior. (Also see Beck et al., 1993 and Emrick and Aarons for further discussion of these focus areas.)

1. One of these key cognitive processes relevant to the addictions is *self-efficacy*. This is the individual's perceived ability to deal with situations or events that can lead to substance use. Low levels of self-efficacy predict relapse. Individuals with high levels of self-efficacy are able to establish and maintain sobriety (Marlatt, 1985a).

2. *Attributions:* As discussed above, these can be either internal or external. The individual may either externalize the reason for drinking: "I drink because of the terrible marriage I am in;" or internalize the reasons for drinking ("I can't deal with life without drinking"). These kinds of thoughts tend to strengthen the client's drinking behavior. CBT focuses on such attributions and the beliefs and attitudes that underlie them.

3. *Outcome Expectancies:* Substance users usually have rather clear expectations of AOD use. If those outcome expectancies are positive, then the thinking that precedes AOD use behavior will be reinforced.

4. Underlying AOD use and abuse is a *decision making process.* A number of choice points or decisions may go into a particular AOD use event. The decisions are often more deliberate than what the individual wants to believe. But the point is, the person chooses to use or to relapse.

Key Cognitive Behavioral Methods Used with AOD Abusers

The treatment experience of the authors of this manual over the past 25 years and a review of the literature have identified a number of CBT approaches and interventions that have been used with AOD abusers, either in an individual treatment or a structured group programmatic modality. Numerous literature sources were used for this review (Beck et al., 1993; Cox, 1987; Daley & Marlatt, 1992; Hester & Miller, 1995; Kadden et al., 1992; Liese & Franz, 1996; MacKay, Donovan & Marlatt, 1991; Miller & Rollnick, 1991; Monti et al., 1989; Wanberg, 1990; Wright, Beck, Newman & Liese, 1993). This summary is considered to be a broad-spectrum perspective of CBT approaches for AOD clients. Only those approaches and methods relevant to the development of this treatment manual are reviewed.

1 Treatment Preparation: The Therapeutic Relationship and Motivational Enhancement

Although the methods of developing rapport and trust with the client may not be seen as specific CBT approaches, they are basic to the application of CBT. Rapport and trust are established in CBT when the therapeutic relationship is collaborative and based on *warmth, trust, empathy* and *genuineness* (Beck et al., 1993; Liese & Franz, 1996). The basic skills of therapeutic communication (Wanberg, 1974, 1983, 1990), motivational interviewing (Miller & Rollnick, 1991) and awareness of the client's stage of change (Prochaska, DiClemente & Norcross, 1992) are essential components in building the therapeutic relationship, enhancing client motivation and preparing the client for CBT treatment.

Miller and Rollnick (1991) stress the use of five principles of motivational interviewing which prepare the client for treatment:

- Express empathy;
- Develop discrepancy;
- Avoid argumentation;
- Roll with resistance; and
- Support self-efficacy.

A more detailed description of the client-counselor relationship and the process of preparing the client for treatment is outlined in Chapter 10 of Section II of this manual.

2 Providing Information and Knowledge About Drugs and the Process of Cognitive-Behavioral Change: Changing AOD Related Beliefs

A core knowledge about substance abuse, the cycles of substance abuse and about the cognitive-behavioral model as it applies to substance abuse will provide the client with a platform for change. This core knowledge also provides a common language in the collaborative relationship between client and counselor. It provides the basis upon which beliefs and attitudes about drug use can be changed and how drug abuse influences our lives.

Building this knowledge base is a *cognitive-structuring method*. It structures the client's thinking about drug use and abuse and provides the basis for changes in core beliefs and attitudes. It also socializes the client to the cognitive model (Liese & Franz, 1996). This involves teaching the client about the cognitive-behavioral change model and how to integrate that model into daily thinking and behaving patterns. Helping the client to build a knowledge base fits in with the contemplative and preparation stages of change (Prochaska, DiClemente, & Norcross, 1992) or the authors' *Challenge to Change* where one important goal is to give the client information about substance abuse and the cycles of abuse.

3 Feedback of AOD Use Patterns and Appraisals Revealed in Assessment

A basic assumption of this manual is that change is premised on self-awareness. Feedback enhances the self-awareness process. Assessment is the basis upon which the counselor develops a database for feedback to the client about his or her drug use pattern. An important component of the assessment and feedback process is *appraisals*. Appraisals "serve as the mediating link between perception and action (Sanchez-Craig, Wilkinson & Walker, 1987). Part of the assessment process is to evaluate the client's appraisals, efficacy, and outcome expectations and beliefs about substance use.

Feedback on the results of the AOD assessment can help the client gain a preliminary view of his or her AOD use and abuse patterns. Feedback on how the client fits the various patterns of alcohol use can provide the client and counselor with valuable information to help them, as partners, in developing solutions to the client's AOD use problems. Feedback on the assessment of expectations (e.g., through the measurement of perceived benefits of use as provided, for example by the Alcohol Use Inventory) can help the client to have a better understanding of his or her expectancy patterns.

Feedback is an important component of motivational enhancement and is an ongoing process in treatment (Liese & Franz, 1996; Miller & Rollnick, 1991). It keeps the client centered in the change process and is a way of reinforcing change. It is a two-way process in that the client also feeds back to the counselor his or her experiences and expectations of treatment.

4 Coping and Socials Skills Training

Skills training may represent the broadest and most comprehensive of the CBT approaches to treating individuals with AOD abuse patterns (Chaney, 1989; Curry & Marlatt, 1987; MacKay et al., 1991; Monti et al., 1995; Riley et al., 1987). Many AOD clients lack the interpersonal, social, expressive and communication skills to handle relationships, thoughts and emotions. Skills training is an integral part of most CBT programs for substance abusing clients.

Some skills training approaches focus on helping the client develop coping skills to handle life problems. Another approach is to use skills training to modify or eliminate the drinking behavior itself (Riley et al., 1987). For non-addicted drinkers, skills training has been used to teach a non-abusive drinking pattern; for alcohol and drug dependent clients, AOD refusal skills training is used. Other approaches include teaching skills to cope with stress, communication skills and assertiveness training, teaching relationship skills, mood management training, and enhancing family management and parenting skills. Behavioral rehearsal and role play are useful tools in implementing skills training (Beck et al., 1993).

Monti and colleagues (1989, 1995) and Kadden and colleagues (1992) have developed a skills training program for alcohol-dependent individuals. Their material focuses on three primary areas:

- *Interpersonal* (basic communication and assertion skills, giving and receiving criticism, drink-refusal skills, conflict resolution, and enhancing social support networks);
- *Intrapersonal* (cognitive coping with maladaptive thoughts, relaxation training, managing anger and other negative moods, problem solving and planning for emergency situations associated with relapse risk, urge coping skills and cue exposure training);
- *Community responsibility and productivity training* (job seeking skills; family involvement and parenting skills).

Skill development in the interpersonal and intrapersonal domains are effective in improving self-regulation and reducing relapse among alcohol-dependent individuals.

5 Problem Solving

Problem solving therapy or problem-solving training has its roots in the work of Spivack, Platt & Sure, (1976), and Kendall et al. (Kendall & Bemis, 1983; Ingram & Kendall, 1987). Although this skill therapy is often considered to be part of coping and social skills training (Monti et al., 1995), it warrants special stand-alone treatment. Individuals with AOD problems are often poor problem solvers. Problem solving therapy teaches clients to address stressful and problem events in a systematic manner. This is an essential intervention for persons with substance abuse problems (Beck et al., 1993). The steps to problem solving have been outlined in numerous documents (e.g., Beck et al., 1993; D'Zurilla & Goldfried, 1971; Nezu, Nezu & Perri, 1989). These are

- developing orientation to the problem and gathering information;
- defining the problem;
- identifying and evaluating alternative solutions;
- choosing and implementing one of the alternatives;
- evaluating the outcome.

6 Cognitive Aversive Reaction and Advantage-Disadvantage Analysis

Traditional aversive conditioning attempts to produce a learned response to the taste, sight or smell of a drug. *Cognitive aversive reaction therapy* (Wanberg, 1990) attempts to increase the awareness of a client's negative experiences and consequences which have already occurred as a result of drug use. The client is asked to generate in thought or writing all of the negative consequences s/he has experienced from AOD use, and then to look at the feelings and emotions associated with these negative consequences. This can be done at the one-to-one level, in focus groups or with a journal. Beck et al. (1993) and Liese and Franz (1996) identify this as the *Advantages-Disadvantages (A-D) Analysis* technique. Whereas the cognitive-aversive reaction method places strong emphasis on the negative and aversive consequences of drug use, the A-D approach has the client also look at the advantages of drug use.

7 Relaxation Training and Stress Management

The rationale for this CBT approach is that AOD use is a response to the need to manage anxiety and stress. AOD abuse emerges as a disturbed or pathological response to tension. This rationale is based on tension reduction (Cappell & Greeley, 1987) and stress response dampening (Sher, 1987) theories. Stress management focuses on helping the client change his or her perceptions about external factors that are a source of anxiety, alter lifestyles to reduce stress and use cognitive coping skills to change or replace stress responses (Stockwell, 1995). Relaxation methods commonly used with AOD clients include *muscle relaxation* (Jacobson, 1938, 1970), *autogenic training* (Benson, 1975), *meditation* (Benson, 1975) and *exercise*. Biofeedback can be used in this kind of training in order to provide the client and therapist with direct feedback as to the effect of the relaxation training.

Candidates for relaxation training would be individuals with high scores on the AUI's Anxious Concern scale (Horn et al., 1987) or on other measures of anxiety associated with AOD use. AOD use for such individuals is a way of reducing anxiety or relaxing. Relaxation training provides the client with a safe and drug-free environment in which to relax (Beck et al., 1993). When it works, the client's self-control and self-efficacy are enhanced and reinforced.

8 Community Reinforcement and Contingency Management

Community reinforcement and contingency management involves arranging a client's environment so as to use the social, recreational, family and other community reinforcers to facilitate and reinforce change (Sisson & Azrin, 1989; Smith & Meyers, 1995). The use of these contingencies allows for positive reinforcement to follow a commitment to sustain drug-free living, gain self-control and develop adaptive behaviors (Riley et al.., 1987). This approach works at helping the client replace maladaptive drinking behaviors with effective coping strategies. Thus, coping skills training is an important part of CRA (Smith & Meyers, 1995). It is based on the theory that positive behaviors are reinforced when followed by positive consequences. CRA can be seen as a stand-alone strategy, however, its principles and techniques are usually integrated into a comprehensive CBT program.

9 Expectancy Challenge

This approach attempts to show clients that alcohol or other drugs may not really have the good effects that clients believe they have, especially on their social or sexual performance. Darkes and Goldman (1994) report unique success in reducing the level of alcohol consumption for heavy drinkers by using the method of *expectancy challenge*. Subjects were randomly provided with alcohol or placebo beverages and then asked to rate their own sobriety and that of peers who participated in two conditions of group activity: (1) social activities involving word games and (2) discussion of the attractiveness of women from various photographic presentations. A group leader then facilitated discussion around what subjects had expected and assumed about the effects of alcohol on these activities. Subjects were challenged regarding the inaccuracy of how alcohol affects functioning around social or sexual issues. In this manner, the researchers were able to reduce overall consumption in heavy drinkers.

As in an earlier study by Massey and Goldman (1988), the *expectancy challenge* was the only method that lowered drinking in heavily drinking subjects. Lighter drinking subjects, however, lowered their drinking as a function of both *expectancy challenge* and traditional treatments.

10 Self-Efficacy Training

Training in *self-efficacy* (Bandura & Adams, 1977) means teaching a person the ability to bring about desired changes on his or her own. It strengthens and reinforces the mastery of skills that successfully help the individual achieve his or her goals and expectations. It represents "the final common pathway through which different treatments are considered to produce change" (Kazdin, 1983, p. 279). Although seen as a theory in the broadest sense, the enhancement of self-efficacy can be seen as a method or technique of CBT. Marlatt (1985b) outlines a number of techniques that can be used to enhance self-efficacy (pp. 225-226):

- relating to the client as a colleague;
- instructing the client that change is based on skill acquisition rather than willpower;
- changes take place in stages over time;
- providing the client feedback concerning performance in treatment.

1 Challenging Automatic Thoughts

Identifying and challenging automatic thoughts are central to cognitive therapy (Freeman, et al., 1990). Some techniques that do this include

- Guiding the client to explore his or her own thoughts and feelings in more detail so as to learn more about them;
- Asking candid questions about a client's statements that certain things absolutely are true or false in order to help the client see that those certainties are not necessarily the way they seem (challenging absolutes);
- Helping the client see other explanations for his or her thinking or behavior;
- Directly disputing a client's statement;
- Helping the client see that events and consequences are not necessarily overwhelmingly, hopelessly catastrophic (we call this decatastrophizing);
- Pointing out contradictions in the client's thinking, seeing and doing.

2 Changing Dysfunctional Underlying Assumptions

The first step in changing the assumptions and beliefs that interfere with healthy functioning is to identify those beliefs and assumptions. Once this is done, many of the techniques used to challenge automatic thoughts can be used to change these underlying assumptions. Having the client write out the dysfunctional assumptions and rational alternative assumptions is one approach (Freeman et al., 1990).

3 Imagery Techniques

Klinger (1987) and Beck et al. (1993) hold that imagery techniques can be effective in changing the thoughts, behavior and emotions of AOD clients. These approaches include

- building a mental aversion to alcohol or drugs, such as Cautela's (1966, 1990) covert sensitization;
- helping the client to imagine and practice behaviors at the mental level which can be used to handle urges to use drugs;
- imagining pleasant scenes to enhance the relaxation response;
- *guided affective imagery* (GAI; Klinger, 1987). At its simplest level, GAI helps the client to imagine how he can handle threatening persons or situations so as to handle the emotions and feelings associated with those situations. Other mental imagery techniques include replacement imagery, desensitization and flooding, coping imagery, thought stopping, refocusing and scheduling worries (Freeman et al., 1990);
- helping the client visualize self-control and changing AOD use related beliefs.

4 Managing Drug Cravings

Some argue that there is little support for a biological basis for cravings outside of the desire for a drug to cure the withdrawal from drugs (Baker et al., 1987; Fingarette, 1988). Others (e.g., Blum & Payne, 1991; Blum et al., 1996) argue that there is a biological basis to cravings outside the withdrawal syndrome. Beck et al. (1993) identifies four kinds of cravings:

- response to withdrawal symptoms;

- response to lack of pleasure;

- conditional response to drug cues; and

- response to hedonic desires.

Marlatt (1978) sees cravings as *the anticipation of the reinforcing effects of a drug*. While this expectancy is not based on physiology alone, it has been shown to have an influence on the individual's choice of whether to drink and how much to drink in a given situation, especially for those situations that have been associated with past alcohol use. Research with college students indicates that those drinkers with the highest positive expectancies for the effects of alcohol tend to drink the most.

A number of CBT methods have been used to treat drug cravings. These include cue-exposure treatment where the client is exposed to pictures or drinking situations through guided imagery until the craving is diminished. Baker et al. (1987) and Monti et al. (1995) provide basic guidelines and warnings around the use of this method. Other methods of dealing with cravings are pharmacological therapies including methadone for the opiate-dependent person.

15 Relapse Prevention

Given the fact that the majority of AOD clients relapse within one year of treatment, *relapse prevention* is an obvious logical component of treatment. Curry and Marlatt (1987) conclude, from their review of the literature, that relapse must be considered as one part of the process of recovery and change for many clients. They do not maintain that a full relapse is necessary in the change process, but that it may be part of that process. Some of these arguments are based on the concept of the natural history of alcoholism as represented in the work of Vaillant (1983). His findings suggest that lapses, slips or mistakes do not necessarily lead to the recurrence of the debilitating pattern of addiction. As Riley et al. (1987) note, "we must recognize that most outcomes, even good outcomes, are frequently interrupted by relapses, and we must learn how to help our clients constructively deal with such events" (p. 108).

Relapse prevention is designed to be used with individuals who have made a commitment to change. "It is a self-management program designed to enhance the maintenance stage of the habit-change process" (Marlatt & Gordon, 1985, p. 3).

Daley and Marlatt (1992 have outlined the key themes in relapse prevention (pp. 536-540). These key themes are designed to help the client

- to identify high-risk relapse factors and develop strategies to address them;

- to understand relapse as a process and an event;

- to understand and negate AOD cues as well as actual cravings;

- to understand and handle social pressures to use substances;

- to develop a supportive relapse prevention network;

- to develop methods of coping with negative emotional states;

- to learn methods to cope with cognitive distortions;

- to work toward a balanced lifestyle;

- to develop a plan to interrupt a lapse or relapse.

A more detailed discussion of relapse and relapse prevention will be presented in Chapter 5.

16 Recording and Journaling

There are a number of specific approaches and elements to the process of recording and journaling in CBT of the AOD client (see Beck et al., 1993; Bush & Bilodeau, 1993; Liese & Franz, 1996). These include structured thinking reports, journaling, activity monitoring and scheduling, keeping a daily thought record and structured homework.

Harm Reduction as a Conceptual Framework for Understanding Outcome

As noted above, relapse prevention is a logical treatment method in light of the high rate of relapse among substance abuse clients. Just as logical is harm reduction as a concept to help us understand treatment outcome (Heather, Wodak, Nadelmann & O'Hare; Marlatt, Baer & Larimer, 1995; Martlatt & Gordon, 1996; Marlatt, Larimer, Baer & Quigley, 1993; Mariatt & Tapert, 1993). *Harm reduction* is a model that views change from the standpoint that reducing the harm from substance use is better than no change at all. It is premised on the idea that a baseline harm level is established for the client, and then treatment moves the client in the direction of less harmful involvement in drug use. Harm reduction is not a treatment approach as much as a treatment goal setting framework for individual clients as well as for public policy. Liese and Franz (1996) note that "harm reduction is compatible with cognitive therapy because both place strong emphasis on collaboration, empathy, respect, recognition of individual differences, and attention to personal beliefs" (p. 472).

Individualized Treatment

A treatment plan designed specifically for the individual can help change his or her distorted or dysfunctional expectancies and explanations of behaviors. The counselor needs to examine the individual's thoughts regarding his/her ability to cope with a variety of situations with and without alcohol. Emrick and Aarons (1990, p. 275) identify four broad areas of assessment with respect to developing a comprehensive understanding of the AOD abuser's personal skills and internal resources for coping with stress:

- unpleasant feelings (depression, anxiety, loneliness or anger);
- biological states (hunger, sexual arousal, excitement, tiredness, physical illness, pain);
- social encouragement to drink (at parties or on holiday);
- interpersonal events (conflicts with children, spouse; divorce; separation; or death of a loved one).

By attending to how the AOD abuser thinks about these areas of experience, the counselor may develop a more cognitive-behaviorally oriented assessment. This assessment will focus on the type, amount and frequency of an individual's substance use; the psychological, social, economic and health effects of AOD involvement; the degree of physical dependence involved; and the role of thoughts, beliefs and emotions in AOD use and abuse.

We shall now review the relevant findings and approaches involved in correctional treatment.

C H A P T E R ❸
APPROACHES TO CORRECTIONAL INTERVENTION

Our next step is to look at the area of correctional treatment. This review is guided by several areas of focus. First, we summarize the research regarding treatment efficacy. Second, we review the key risk factors identified as important in the assessment of criminal conduct. Finally, the important components of CBT of the offender are summarized.

Treatment Efficacy: Does It work?

There is a significant body of literature to support the efficacy of the treatment of offenders (Andrews, 1995; Andrews et al., 1990; Izzo & Ross, 1990; Lipsey 1989, 1992; Lipsey & Wilson, 1993; Lipton, 1994; McGuire & Priestley, 1995; Van Voorhis, 1987). Lipsey (1989) showed that 64 percent of 443 studies favored treatment over comparison groups in terms of reducing recidivism. This finding is consistent with Andrews and Bonta's (1994, p. 188) estimate that 40 percent to 80 percent of the studies they surveyed reported reduced recidivism.

In Lipsey and Wilson's (1993) comprehensive review of the efficacy of psychological, education and behavioral treatment meta-analysis studies, they included 10 meta-analysis studies of treatment programs for offenders involving 873 studies. All 10 of these meta-analysis studies showed mean effect sizes indicating positive outcomes or effects of treatment.

A meta-analysis study done by Andrews, Bonta & Hoge (1990) with respect to using severity of official processing and criminal sanctions approaches indicated that "less is better than more" (Andrews & Bonta, 1994, p. 190). That is, when recidivism is studied relative to the type and severity of judicial processing (i.e., official processing versus police cautioning; probation versus informal adjustment; probation versus open custody; closed versus open custody; and probation versus closed custody), "more as opposed to less criminal processing was associated with slightly *increased* recidivism rates" (p. 190). None of the comparisons involved variations in the duration of custody or supervision. These findings indicate that "the mean effect of correctional treatment service, averaged across a number of dispositions, was clearly greater and more positive than that of criminal sanctioning without the delivery of treatment services" (Andrews & Bonta, 1994, p. 190).

Further, in an analysis of punishment "alternatives" or "intermediate" sanctions, including shock incarceration, boot camps, intensive probation supervision, "scared straight," fines, day centers, community services orders, restitution, mandatory arrest of male batterers, Gendreau (1993) concludes "on average, not one of the new range of alternative punishments has been found to be associated with reduced recidivism." And Andrews and Bonta (1994) conclude "Whatever the social role of punishment, there is no evidence that a reliance on just deserts or deterrence-based sanctioning is followed by meaningful reductions in recidivism."

Treatment Efficacy: What Works?

The evidence to date suggests that *clinically relevant* interventions involving treatment services hold the best promise for reducing recidivism rather than interventions based on criminal sanctions only (Andrews & Bonta, 1994). But what is clinically relevant treatment for the offender?

Lipsey (1989) concludes that the most effective interventions are structured and focused. On the average, these kinds of interventions reduced recidivism by about 30 percent. In his review of the studies of treating the individual with criminal conduct history, he identified six major treatment variables associated with reduced recidivism (from Andrews & Bonta, 1994, p. 189):

- Longer duration of treatment and more meaningful contact (except for the continuous contact provided by institutional care);

- services provided outside formal correctional settings and institutions;

- services under the influences of the evaluator;

- behavior-oriented, skill-oriented and multimodal treatment;
- service for higher risk cases; and
- treatment that attends to extrapersonal circumstances, such as family and peers.

Andrews, Bonta, and Hoge (1990) see clinically relevant treatment as that which maintains respect for and attention to diversity in both people and programming. These clinically and psychologically appropriate treatments for criminal conduct clients are

- Structured one-on-one paraprofessional companionship programs (but not non-behavioral friendship companionship programs);
- behaviorally oriented academic/vocational programs (but not weakly structured academic/vocational programs);
- short-term, home-based, behavioral family interventions (but not psychodynamic family therapy);
- structured cognitive-behavioral skills training (for example, self-management skills); and
- matching program intensity to offender's level of risk.

The findings also suggest that treatment benefits are more apt to be derived from focusing on the high-risk offenders rather than the low-risk offenders (Andrews and Bonta, 1994). This conclusion is premised on the idea that the low-risk offender will most likely do well with or without treatment and that if we are to derive maximum benefit from treatment endeavors, then the rate of return will be greater for high-risk offenders.

The literature is reasonably strong and supports vigorous pursuit of ethical, decent, humane and cost-efficient approaches to prevention and rehabilitative programming for higher risk cases under a variety of conditions of just sanctioning. The active and effective human service agency may contribute to a still more powerful knowledge base by building assessment, reassessment and research into the agency (Andrews & Bonta, 1994, p. 236).

Recognizing that clinically relevant and appropriate treatments are more effective than criminal sanctioning alone, the question must be asked: who is most likely to benefit from the application of clinically relevant treatments? The answer to this question is based on understanding the differences found among criminal conduct clients. Such differences can be understood by identifying the risk factors associated with criminal conduct.

Risk Factors and Dynamic Predictors as a Basis for Determining Treatment Needs

There are several ways to organize the risk factors that predict criminal conduct and recidivism:

1 Fixed or Static Risk Predictors

The fixed or static factors are *unalterable* aspects of the offender's criminal life. These include factors that do not change such as having family members who are criminals or being male.

2 Specific Risk Factors That Correlate With Criminal Behavior

A second set of predictors are factors that indicate different levels of risk for *future* criminal activity. These are specific risk factors that correlate with criminal behavior. They are identified through correlation studies, cross-sectional studies or, through what Andrews and Bonta call "single-wave longitudinal" studies.

There are a number of these factors found in adolescents that are associated with involvement in later criminal behavior. These include

- early involvement in deviancy and acting out behavior;
- emotional, psychological and family disruption in childhood and adolescence;
- involvement with an antisocial peer group;

- school problems and failure;
- AOD use during childhood and early adolescence.

These risk factors also have strong association with the development of substance abuse in adolescence (Andrews & Bonta, 1994; Botvin, 1986; Bukstein, 1995; Hawkins, Lishner & Catalano, 1985; Newcomb & Bentler, 1989; Newcomb, Maddahian & Bentler, 1986; Patterson, DeBarsyshe & Ramsey, 1989; Wanberg, 1992; Wanberg, Befus & Embree, 1990).

A review of the risk factor literature would suggest that the following represent the specific risk factors that seem to be most predictive of criminal conduct and recidivism in adults (Andrews, 1994; Andrews & Bonta, 1994; Patterson et al., 1989; Andrews, Wormith & Kiessling, 1985; Rogers, 1981). This list includes the identified risk factors which are found in adolescents and have strong correlations with later criminal behavior. These factors are

- antisocial and procriminal thinking, attitudes, beliefs, affective states, and emotional states;
- involvement with antisocial and criminal associates who reinforce or support criminal conduct;
- a history of and early involvement in deviant, antisocial behavior and criminal behavior;
- poor problem solving, social and self-management skills;
- involvement in and a product of a disruptive, abusive, neglectful family which includes lack of parental attention, caring and supervision;
- lack of achievement and success in school, work, leisure and finances;
- history of substance abuse with onset at early age;
- impulsive and temperamentally aggressive, calloused, and egocentric.

Using these or similar risk factors, research indicates that offenders can be reliably categorized into either low or high risk with respect to recidivism. From the use of these categories, recidivism rates have been predicted with a 70 percent to 80 percent accuracy.

3 Dynamic Predictors

A third set of risk factors is what Andrews and Bonta (1994) call *dynamic predictors*. These are identified from "multiwave longitudinal studies" that focus on changes associated with subsequent criminal behavior and recidivism. This method determines differences between initial assessment and reassessment, then relates this observed difference to a third assessment of predicted future criminal conduct. Andrews and Bonta identify these "dynamic predictors" as *criminogenic need factors*. They find that dynamic predictors provide "a still higher level of empirical understanding"; more important, they become the basis upon which we determine our treatment objectives. "They do more than "simply forecast criminal events. They actually influence the chances of criminal acts occurring through deliberate intervention" (p. 43).

The dynamic predictors are part of the offender's daily experience and are more amenable to change. Gendreau, Little and Groggin, (1996), Andrews (1994), and Andrews and Bonta (1994) concluded that the dynamic risk factors are most predictive of recidivism, are more relevant to prevention and rehabilitation and should become targets for intervention. If these dynamic risk factors, or *criminogenic needs,* undergo change, then criminal behavior may diminish.

Andrews and Bonta provide a list of change targets which are built on these dynamic risk factors or criminogenic needs. For example, the treatment target of developing relationships with prosocial peers is based on the finding that individuals who engage in criminal conduct are those who are more apt to have developed close associations with antisocial peers. The first items in Table 3.1 summarize those listed by Andrews and Bonta (1994, p. 233) as *promising targets for change*. These are most relevent in developing a manual for the treatment of criminal conduct clients. The remaining six targets for change in Table 3.1 are considered by the authors of this manual as relevent in the treatment of offenders when they are addressed within the context of antisocial and criminal thinking and behavior. Andrews and Bonta (1994) see these six targets for change as less promising in the treatment of criminal conduct.

Table 3.1

Targets for Change—Dynamic Predictors

◆ developing and enhancing life management skills, problem solving and self-control skills;

◆ developing associations, relationships and bonding with prosocial and anticriminal peers and with prosocial and anticriminal role models;

◆ enhancing closer family feelings and communication;

◆ enhancing positive family structures to promote monitoring;

◆ managing and changing antisocial thoughts, attitudes and feelings;

◆ managing and/or changing antisocial feelings;

◆ replacing antisocial behaviors (e.g., lying, stealing, aggression) with prosocial alternatives;

◆ changing patterns of AOD use and addiction;

◆ shifting reinforcement and reward potentials away from criminal conduct to noncriminal involvement and conduct;

◆ helping the individual to recognize those situations and areas of involvement that increase risk for engaging in criminal conduct and to provide the client with skills to cope with or avoid those situations;

◆ attenuating the situational and personality barriers to positive involvement in services and programs which can lead to cognitive and behavioral change;

◆ developing self-control skills and problem-solving skills;

◆ change other factors in the life of the criminal conduct client which are based on individual-ized and differential assessment and associated with involvement in criminal conduct (e.g., sense of hopelessness about one's economic condition).

Also found in the review of the literature are other targets for change that are based on dynamic risk factors. Wanberg and Milkman indicate that these are relevant targets for change if they are not addressed within the context of antisocial and criminal thinking and behavior. These include

◆ enhancing self-esteem within the context of prosocial thinking, feeling and noncriminal peer association;

◆ therapeutic focus on discomfort resulting from anxiety and depression particularly as these relate to criminal conduct;

◆ developing skills and attitudes to develop and maintain empathy and understanding in relationships;

◆ developing and enhancing moral values and beliefs which are supportive of a constructive relationship with people and community;

◆ attempting to increase involvement with positive and prosocial peer groups;

◆ focusing on improving the individual's living conditions while addressing the criminogenic needs of high-risk individuals

Key Components of Cognitive-Behavioral Treatment of the Offender

The findings to date indicate that increased criminal processing, variations in criminal sanctioning and the various types of punishment alternatives (e.g., community service), when administered apart from clinically relevant treatment, are not associated with the reduction of recidivism. There is a well-documented position that punishment in general—even harsh punishment—does not diminish criminal activity.

Our review of the literature clearly suggests that cognitive-behavioral treatment is certainly one of the clinically relevant treatment paradigms that can be effectively used with the offender. Andrews and Bonta (1994) go so far as to conclude that "behavioral, cognitive-behavioral and social learning approaches to treatment provide the greatest likelihood of success" (p. 200).

If CBT approaches provide the greatest likelihood for success in our work with the offender, then what are the components of CBT that seem most relevant, and which have been most salient in the treatment of the offender? In order to address this question, a number of documents were reviewed which had a CBT orientation to the treatment of the person with a history of criminal conduct and behavior (Andrews & Bonta, 1994; Bush & Bilodeau, 1993; Freeman et al., 1990; Gorski, 1993, 1994; Hester & Miller, 1995; Ross et al., 1986; Ross & Ross, 1988, 1995; Ross, Antonowicz, & Dhaliwal, 1995). These documents ranged from textbook type of documents that addressed CBT treatment issues to manuals that provide programmatic structure. Our review is not exhaustive; however, the documents reviewed represent a reasonable sampling of the CBT literature focusing on the treatment of persons with antisocial and criminal conduct.

Our review indicates first, that basic to most of these programs and interventions are the core assumptions of cognitive-behavioral treatment. These common assumptions have been outlined in Chapter 1 and will not be repeated here. We summarize the review around four areas: program structure, program process, characteristics of the offender relevant to CBT, and common content components that structure the treatment program. These are briefly outlined.

1 Common Elements of Program Structure

- programs are from six months to one year long with a minimum of two-hour weekly sessions;
- delivery is best done within a group context, and the group counselor or leader and the group are seen as essential change agents;
- providers are seen as teachers, trainers, counselors and, in some cases, therapists;
- optimal group sizes range from 6 to 15;
- learning is based on group interaction and experiences with didactic presentations seen as secondary to experiential-based sessions;
- programs need to have basic rules and guidelines;
- programs are offered in a variety of settings including incarceration, community corrections settings, day reporting centers and in the community for offenders on parole and probation;
- there is usually a selection and admission protocol and process;
- role playing, structured group sharing, homework, journaling and thinking reports are common methods used in the program.

2 Common Elements of Program Process

- offenders do not come to the program motivated to change, but motivation is something that is developed within CBT program structure; the participant needs to be challenged to change;
- the first step to motivation and treatment involves a process of building trust and rapport with the offender;
- change is based on getting the client to self-disclose in a non-defensive manner;
- when changes in attitudes and beliefs begin to occur and when these changes become translated into behavioral expressions and action, the offender begins to experience a commitment to change;
- having participants keep journals and write thinking reports are helpful in the change process;
- change occurs when it is internalized and when the participant attributes the change to his or her own effort—the participant takes ownership of the change.

3 Common Characteristics of Offenders

- offenders go through basic stages of change;
- offenders put up barriers to and resist change;
- offenders have generic treatment needs and unique treatment needs;
- offenders have a common set of attitudes, beliefs and thinking patterns which underlie their anti-social and criminal behavior;
- offenders have an underlying anger which provides the psychological energy for engaging in antisocial behavior;
- offenders are deficient in problem solving, communication, interpersonal and intrapersonal coping skills;
- offenders lack self-control and self-management skills and are impulsive in their thinking and acting;
- offenders' thinking processes are often based on faulty thinking and errors in thinking, and they lack skills in critical reasoning;
- offenders primary social support and peer influence system is composed of antisocial peers and antisocial role models;
- offenders' have a clear deficit in moral development and values which lead to irresponsible and criminal behavior in the community;
- the process of automatic thought is basic to criminal thinking and behavior;
- offenders have developmental histories which are often abusive, chaotic and disruptive;
- offenders are vulnerable to recidivism and relapse;
- most offenders have multiple problems and many have co-existing disorders.

4 Common Content Components That Structure CBT of the Offender

Our review indicates that there are some common content components to offender CBT. These content components are usually translated into lessons, modules or specific session experiences. The following are the most salient of these components

- Build trust, rapport and cooperative involvement;
- Develop and enhance motivation to change;
- Multiple problems assessment;
- How people change within the CBT framework and learn about attitudes, beliefs and thinking processes;
- Understand the role of thinking, feeling and behaving in criminal conduct and change;
- Learn and experience how attitudes and beliefs are involved in criminal conduct and change;
- Learn, experience and practice the process of self-disclosure;
- Understand the process and stages of change;
- Strong focus on relapse and recidivism prevention;
- Skill building experiences in the following areas:
  - Interpersonal communication;
  - Assertiveness;
  - Problem solving;
  - Managing anger, aggression, guilt and depression;
  - Critical reasoning;

- Conflict resolution;
- Moral and values development;
- Identify cognitive distortions and practice changing those errors or distortions;
- Identify and change antisocial thoughts and feelings;
- Understand what changes are needed to develop prosocial and community-responsible behaviors;
- How to change the thought processes such as automatic thoughts and be in control of thinking;
- Understanding and developing empathy and caring.

Through the CBT approach, important criteria for effective corrective counseling can be met. The offender's criminogenic needs and the dynamic risk factors can be effectively addressed, prosocial and anticriminal modeling and reinforcement can be accomplished, an open and honest relationship based on fairness yet firmness between the provider and offender can be established, and a strong reinforcing environment for noncriminal behaviors can be maintained (Andrews & Bonta, 1994).

Integrating AOD and Correctional Treatment Through Cognitive-Behavioral Treatment

At this point, it would seem clear that there is considerable overlap between the CBT methods and approaches used with substance abuse clients and those used with the offender. This provides an important foundation for developing a relevant CBT program for the substance abusing offender. How else might AOD abuse and criminal conduct be linked? We will look at this in the next chapter of this manual.

C H A P T E R ❹
RELATIONSHIP BETWEEN CRIMINAL CONDUCT AND
AOD USE AND ABUSE

The relationship between AOD use and crime is complex. To the general public, the relationship seems quite simple—drugs lead to crime. Survey data of incarcerated offenders indicate that at least 70 percent have a history of substance abuse (U.S. Bureau of Justice Statistics, 1983a, 1983b; Weekes, et al., 1997). As many as 80 percent of those incarcerated for robbery, burglary or assault committed the offense under the influence of an intoxicant (U.S. Bureau of Justice Statistics, 1987, 1988). In a national survey of 5,000 jail inmates (U.S. Bureau of Justice Statistics, 1991), prisoners were found to be current users of drugs at a rate of seven times as high as the general population. More than one third of the inmates surveyed reported that they were in prison for a crime intended to obtain money to purchase drugs. Considering recidivism in the federal justice system, 61 percent of offenders known to have a history of substance abuse violated the terms of their parole versus only 29 percent of parolees with no known history of AOD abuse who violated the conditions of their parole (U.S. Bureau of Justice Statistics, 1992).

The interaction between substance abuse and criminal conduct is apparent in many ways as we observe the patterns and behaviors of substance abusing offenders. Drugs change or modify mood, thought and behavior. These modifications are often interactive with criminal conduct. Compulsive substance use can result in loss of control and inhibitions—subsequently interacting with criminal conduct. The social, economic and health consequences of drug disruption place a high financial burden on the substance abuser. Criminal conduct which is often viewed by the offender as having economic benefit can fit into these consequences. In contrast to steady employment, criminal lifestyles are far more compatible with the drug abuser's inner world, which is dominated by craving, impulsivity and economic upheaval. The internal results of criminal conduct (e.g., fear of getting caught or guilt) can be relieved with drugs.

In adolescent research findings, there is a strong relationship between criminal conduct and AOD use and abuse (Elliot, Ageton, Huizinga, Knowles & Cantor, 1983; Kandel, Simcha-Fagen & Davies, 1986; Tinklenberg, Murphy, Murphy & Pfefferbaum, 1981; Wanberg, 1991, 1992; Wanberg, Befus & Embree, 1990). Correlations between these two phenomena range from .45 to .60. In a large study of juvenile committed offenders, using reliable deviancy and AOD use measures, the correlations range from .47 to .63 (Wanberg, 1992). Furthermore, there seem to be several possible pathways to criminal behavior, with AOD use an important component.

The AOD and criminal conduct associations, however, are complex. In some patterns, we find that AOD use leads to criminal conduct. In other patterns, criminal conduct results in increased AOD use. Thus, the "chicken and egg" problem cuts both ways. In many cases, the crime may come first. The 1986 U.S. Bureau of Justice Statistics survey found that more than half the inmates who had used a major drug (e.g., heroin, cocaine, methadone, PCP or LSD) and later became regular users did so only after their first arrest. They became substance abusers after crossing the threshold of antisocial activities. To be sure, criminals participate in many forms of illegal and antisocial activity, such as robbery, gambling, prostitution, assault. Drug use and abuse is only one of many.

A similarity between the AOD abuser and the offender is found as we compare the two groups with respect to post-rehabilitation outcomes. With the *AOD abuser,* we refer to this outcome as a return to drinking which may be a lapse or a full relapse. With the *offender* we call it full recidivism or a return to committing criminal acts. In either case, it is the negative outcome of treatment or the failure of recovery following rehabilitation. Research findings indicate that the recidivism rate for crime and for heroin and gambling addictions are quite similar. Between 60 and 80 percent of individuals with AOD addiction relapse within 6-12 months from the onset of attempted abstinence (Milkman, Weiner & Sunderwirth 1984). The recidivism rate for adult offenders has been reported at 50 percent to 80 percent (Andrews & Bonta, 1994, Lillyquist, 1980).

As we think about rehabilitation and recovery for substance abusing offenders, it is necessary to address the issues of drug dependence and addiction. But positive outcomes inevitably involve more penetrating assessment, prolonged counseling and prescriptive treatments. Increasing the length of sentencing seems to have little effect on recidivism of substance abusing offenders (Zinberg, 1990). This conclusion by Zinberg (1990) and the argument presented by Andrews and Bonta (1994) that sanctioning is not effective apart from clinically relevant treatment leads us to the conclusion that rehabilitation requires effective reeducation and treatment. Yet, it is also safe to conclude that prolonged treatment within the criminal justice system will require parallel sentence lengths.

Although the interaction between AOD abuse and criminal conduct is complex, what is simple and straightforward is the fact that there is a distinct group of individuals who are dually affected: they manifest both a history of AOD abuse and criminal conduct. Thus, our best understanding of the interaction between AOD abuse and criminal conduct comes as we evaluate and provide intervention and treatment service for this dually affected group—the substance abusing offender (SAO).

One manner in which we can gain this understanding is found in our attempt to develop multiple classifications and dimensions of SAOs. There is a substantial body of research and literature devoted to developing a multiple classification system for the offender and the AOD abuser separately.

With respect to the juvenile and adult offender, a number of different classification models have been developed. These classifications have focused on *personality types* (Gold & Mann, 1984; Megargee & Bohn, 1979; Quay, 1987), *behavioral classifications* (Quay, 1984; Wanberg, Tjaden, Embree & Garrett, 1986; Wanberg, Tjaden & Garrett, 1990), and *developmental and interpersonal maturity* (I-level) classifications (Palmer, 1971, 1984; Warren, 1971). The criminal statutes also provide a way to classify the offender and the basis for managing the offender in the forensic system.

The literature also supports the theory that there are several patterns, dimensions and types of AOD abusers (see Horn et al., 1987 and Wanberg & Horn, 1983, 1987, for detailed discussions of these findings).

Research in the area of the multiple classification of the substance abusing offender, however, is scant. In an unpublished study (Wanberg, 1994), committed juvenile offenders were classified by their scores on the Deviancy and AOD Disruption scales of the *Adolescent Self Assessment Profile* (Wanberg, 1991b). About 200 offenders were classified into nine groups using a scoring scheme of low, medium or high on the two scales. The frequency distribution of these nine types for the 200 subjects indicated that about 40 percent fell in the three categories of high deviancy-high substance abuse, high deviancy-medium substance abuse or high substance abuse-medium deviancy. Those falling in these categories are considered as juvenile substance abusing offenders.

The differential and multidimensional assessment models which have been developed and applied to AOD abusers (e.g., Wanberg & Horn, 1983, 1987) also need to be further developed and applied to the substance abusing offender (SAO). Weekes and associates (1997) provide clear support for this approach in their paper on the assessment of the SAO presented at the 1997 annual meeting of the International Community Correctional Association.

Without empirical foundation, we can only hypothesize SAO dimensions and types from clinical experience and our assessment of the specific areas of AOD abuse and criminal conduct. A better understanding of this foundation for assessing different dimensions and types of SAO clients will be gained as we explore the assessment aspects of SAO treatment. Chapter 11 provides a framework for developing a *Master Profile* which can be used to describe the individual client across the various dimensions of substance use and abuse and criminal thinking and behavior.

C H A P T E R ⑤
MOTIVATION TO CHANGE AND THE CHANGE PROCESS

In our search for the essential elements of an effective CBT program for the substance abusing offender, two additional factors stood out. One was the importance of developing a readiness and motivation for treatment in the client. The second was evidence supporting the hypothesis that individuals go through patterns or stages when making changes. First we look at the issue of treatment readiness and motivational enhancement. Second, a commonly accepted stages of change theory is reviewed. Finally, the change framework that structures the current treatment program is introduced.

Developing the Treatment Relationship and Motivation for Intervention

The results of Project MATCH provide evidence for the efficacy of motivational enhancement as an important component in implementing treatment readiness and change in alcohol abuse clients (Project MATCH Research Group, 1997). The necessity for the use of motivational enhancement methods is found in *client ambivalence*. Most individuals with addictive behaviors display an ambivalence about changing their lives—or at least, changing the addictive behavior (Miller and Rollnick, 1991). The individual with antisocial traits and criminal conduct history has become accostomed to a lifestyle of impulsivity, irresponsibility, expression of maladaptive anger, interpersonal problems, and illegal behavior. Most of these behavioral patterns are difficult to change. Resolving ambivalence and resistance to change addictive and antisocial patterns, and helping the client to develop an internal sense of readiness, openness and responsiveness to treatment are primary objectives of the early stages of treatment. There are a number of approaches that enhance the readiness and motivation of the AOD and criminal conduct client for treatment.

1 Therapeutic Stance

The therapeutic stance underlying motivational enhancement is based on the core elements of the client-centered therapeutic relationship: Warmth, empathy, genuineness and positive regard (Rogers, 1951, 1957, 1961). Just how the counselor interacts with clients is a critical determinant of treatment outcome. There is a long history to the research finding that the degree of empathy shown by counselors during treatment is a significant predictor of treatment efficacy. Style of relating becomes apparent early in the therapeutic encounter and can impact treatment retention, even in one introductory session. With respect to AOD clients, Miller and Rollnick (1991) show that successful therapy is predicated upon counselors providing clients with three critical conditions: 1) accurate empathy, 2) non-possessive warmth, and 3) genuineness. These effective counselor features are discussed in Chapter 10.

2 Theraputic Alliance

Therapeutic alliance builds on but goes beyond the core elements of the therapeutic stance that underlie motivational enhancement as discussed above. Therapeutic alliance involves a collaborative relationship, affective bonding and a mutual understanding and sharing of the treatment goals between the client and treatment provider (Bordin, 1979; Conners, Carroll, DiClemente, Longabaugh & Donovan, 1997; Raue, Goldfried & Barkham, 1997).

There is a robust relationship between therapeutic alliance and improvement in treatment , regardless of the therapeutic orientation or treatment approach utilized by the treatment provider (Bachelor, 1991; Connors et al., 1997; Gaston, 1990; Harvorth & Symonds, 1991; Krupnick et al., 1996; Raue & Goldfried, 1994; Raue et al., 1997). These studies also indicate that client ratings of therapuetic alliance are more predictive of outcome than therapist ratings; therapeutic alliance scores tended to be higher for cognitive-behavioral sessions than for sessions conducted under a psychodynamic-interpersonal orientation; and that the efficacy of therapeutic alliance is found across various therapeutic modalties.

Most relevant to the development of this manuaal are the findings of Connors and associates (1997) in their examination of therapeutic alliance data gathered in the national multisite study of matching of patients to alcoholism treatment (Project MATCH Research Group, 1993, 1997). Connors and associates found a consistent positive relationship among outpatient alcohol clients between therapeutic alliance and treatment participation and positive drinking-related outcomes, regardless of whether the rating was based on client self-report or a therapist-report. The consistent findings regarding the efficacy of therapeutic alliance across treatment approaches, modalities and different nosological groups clearly indicate the crucial importance of this component in the treatment process.

3 Non-Confrontational Therapies

Confrontational therapy—previously touted as the treatment choice for substance abuse—may actually be damaging to people with low self-esteem (the majority of AOD clients may struggle with this issue). *Coercive intervention* is at odds with the writings of Bill Wilson, one of the co-founders of AA. The program is said to work best on the basis of *attraction and support* (as opposed to compulsion, e.g., court order). "Recovery begins when one alcoholic talks to another alcoholic, sharing experience, strength and hope" (Alcoholics Anonymous, 1976, p. XXII). Wilson advocated that alcoholics be treated with an approach that "would contain no basis for contention or argument. Most of us sense that real tolerance of other people's shortcoming and viewpoints, and a respect for their opinions are attitudes which make us more helpful to others" (Alcoholics Anonymous, 1976, pp. 19-20). Reflecting on the principle of empathy, non-possessive warmth, and genuineness in working with alcoholics, Wilson advised:

> Let him steer the conversation in any direction he likes. You will be most successful with alcoholics if you do not exhibit any passion for crusade or reform. Never talk down to an alcoholic. He must decide for himself whether he wants to go on. He should not be pushed or prodded. If he thinks he can do the job in some other way or prefers some other spiritual approach, encourage him to follow his own conscience. We have no monopoly on God, we merely have an approach that worked with us. (Alcoholics Anonymous, 1976, p. 45)

Aggressively confronting the patient's unwillingness to honestly discuss alcohol or other drug (AOD) problems—denial busting—has been attributed to the Synanon Group (substance abuse) and the Minnesota Model (alcoholism). Although "verbal haircuts"—softened by empathic listening when clients break down—continue as treatment staples in the therapeutic community, this technique is becoming increasingly isolated. According to Miller and Rollnick (1991), research does not support the common belief that people with AOD problems display pathological lying or an abnormal level of self-deception. Nor does self-labelling promote more effective recovery. In fact, Sovereign and Miller (1987) found that problem drinkers randomly assigned to confrontational counseling showed a far greater incidence of arguing, denying or changing the topic than those given a more client-oriented motivational intervening approach.

4 Enhancing Interest in Change

Motivation is a state of readiness, openness or eagerness to participate in a change process. Miller et al. (1994, p. 2) have summarized the research to date on what motivates problem drinkers to change. Their work on Motivational Enhancement Therapy (MET) highlights the effectiveness of relatively brief treatment for problem drinkers. The elements that the authors consider necessary to induce change are summarized by the acronym **FRAMES**:

1. **FEEDBACK** of personal risk impairment;
2. Emphasis on personal **RESPONSIBILITY** for change;
3. **ADVICE**;
4. A **MENU** of alternative change options;
5. Therapist **EMPATHY**;
6. Facilitation of client **SELF-EFFICACY** or optimism.

Therapeutic interventions containing some or all of these motivational elements have been demonstrated to be effective in "initiating treatment and in reducing long-term alcohol use, alcohol-related problems, and health consequences of drinking" (Miller et al., 1994, p. 2).

An important focus in enhancing motivation and interest for change in criminal conduct (CC) clients is that of developing "a more enlightened view of their self-interest and recognize that it is in their own best interest to anticipate the long-term consequences of their actions" (Freeman et al., 1990, p. 229). This model is designed to help the criminal conduct (CC) client to control impulsivity long enough to perceive the consequences of antisocial action as not as rewarding as the long-term consequences of prosocial behavior. In essence, motivation is enhanced by helping the CC client take a long-term view of her/his self-interest. This can only be done when the counselor takes a collaborative approach to treatment (a key component of CBT) and a trust-based working relationship has been developed. These two objectives of treatment—*building a collaborative relationship* and helping the client *take a long-term view of self-interest*—are primary focuses in the treatment sessions of this manual.

Stages of Change

Recent research into addictive disorders has identified stages that individuals go through when making change (Prochaska & DiClemente, 1992; Prochaska et al., 1992; Shaffer, 1992). This is a transtheoretical model of how people change addictive lifestyles. Prochaska and associates describe five stages of change that seem to apply to most clients with addictions, whether the process is self induced or therapy-assisted.

At the *precontemplative stage,* clients are resistive, do not process information about their problems, and give little or no energy to self-evaluation. They are also less open to significant others about their problems. At this stage, the client gives little or no thought to serious change in his/her behavior.

Clients in the *contemplative stage* give some thought to change but take little action to change. Ambivalence around change is a key characteristic of this stage. Clients are more open to consciousness-raising techniques such as information feedback and interpretations and are more likely to respond to educational procedures. Clients in this stage are also more open to what Prochaska et al., (1992) call *dramatic relief experiences.* They become more conscious of themselves and the kind of problems they experience, and are more into self-evaluation processes. They also are more open to how their problems impacted their environment and significant others. Yet, they are still ambivalent about change. For example, clients struggle with such questions as "How do I think and feel about living in a deteriorating environment that places my family or friends at increasing risk for disease, poverty, or imprisonment?" (Prochaska et al., 1992, p. 1109). If the ambivalence about change is resolved, this stage becomes a turning point for the client.

In Shaffer's (1992) stages of change model, which emphasizes the transition from addiction to recovery, "the acceptance of personal responsibility represents the actual turning point" (p. 101). Shaffer posits that psychodynamically oriented therapy may provide the best structure for resolving ambivalence about "letting go." What prevents substance abusers from doing what they already know is their ambivalence. In order to move forward, they must discover what AOD use does *for* them and what it *means* to them (p. 103).

As clients move through the contemplative to the *determination* (or what Prochaska et al. have called the preparation for treatment) *stage* they continue to increase the use of cognitive, affective and valuative processes of change. In the *determination stage,* clients begin to take steps toward using specific techniques to reduce their use of substances and to control their unique situations with methods other than using substances.

In the *action stage,* a sense of self-direction and self-liberation begins to develop. There is greater internalization of self-determination and self-regulation. There is more openness to using reinforcement tools and techniques to change behavior, and there is an increased reliance on support and understanding from significant others and helping relationships (e.g., the counselor). The development of alternative responses to the use of addictive substances is an important part of this stage.

The *maintenance stage* provides a condition where the prevention of relapse is managed through the development and reinforcement of alternative responses. Strategies to reinforce established behavioral change and stimulus control (e.g., urge to drink when with friends) are used. Commitment to strengthening change through therapeutic support and support from significant others and the continuation of the practice of established skills to manage potential relapse into addictive behavior are all important in this phase. In this stage, self takes on a greater value and change supporters are important ingredients in this process.

Prochaska and DiClemente (1992) have postulated a sixth stage—*relapse*—in their scheme. This is the stage where the individual begins to engage in behaviors and thinking which portend engaging in addictive behaviors—or where the individual relapses into the full pattern of use.

Smokers, for example, have been shown to go through these stages three to seven times before permanently quitting, with the average smoker needing to re-visit the change process about four times. From this perspective, relapse is recognized as normal in the recovery process, that is, "each slip brings you closer to recovery." Rather than inviting clients to relapse, the aforementioned phrase may simply prevent patients and staff from demoralization when unsteadiness or backsliding occurs. The motivational model of overcoming resistance or motivational deficits is predicated upon counselors using appropriate intervention strategies during a client's current stage of change.

Effective treatment choices are based on a "determination of which method of care, for which patient should be applied at which specific time during the process of recovery" (Miller & Rollnick, 1991). Shaffer and Gambino (1990) discuss the question of whether therapists should cultivate a broad base of clinical skills to cover the entire continuum of change or direct patients to other clinicians during the course of treatment. The authors find both possibilities acceptable: therapists may function as primary care providers or as case managers who remain sensitive to shifts in patient need throughout the recovery process, providing access to specialty treatments when appropriate.

Integration of Motivational Enhancement and the Change Process

The treatment model developed in this manual integrates the concepts and methods for developing treatment readiness and motivation. Providers are given guidelines for developing treatment readiness and motivation. The program structure is also built around a stages of change concept with treatment phases and experiences congruent with the client's readiness for treatment and the client's stage of change. This model is described in more detail in Chapter 9.

CHAPTER 6
INTEGRATING MODELS AND SELECTING BEST APPROACHES FOR CBT OF THE SUBSTANCE ABUSING OFFENDER

Overview

The purpose of this text is to bring together the best approaches in order to develop an integrative CBT program for individuals with patterns of AOD abuse and a history of criminal conduct—as these phenomena dually exist in selected individuals. From our review of the treatment alternatives, as presented in Chapters 2, 3 and 5, it is apparent that there are many common elements found in the treatment of the two groups (substance abusers and offenders). These commonalities provide the basis upon which we have built our *Strategies for Self-Improvement and Change* (SSC) CBT program for the substance abusing offender.

Evidence was also provided to indicate that there is a robust relationship between drug use and abuse and criminal conduct. Studies indicate that from 60 to 80 percent of offender populations have identifiable histories of substance abuse. This strong relationship between AOD abuse and criminal conduct provides further support for a program focusing on the substance abusing offender.

Another common element that stands out in the treatment of these two populations is the primary concern of preventing the client from backsliding into the thoughts, emotions and actions that originally brought the client into treatment. In the case of the criminal offender, it is the prevention of recidivism to criminal conduct; for the AOD abuser, it is preventing relapse into AOD use. This common factor becomes an important basis for the integration of treatment of the substance abusing offender.

Foundational Approaches for Relapse and Recidivism Prevention

There are a number of models that have been developed over the years to address relapse in AOD abuse clients and recidivism in offenders. Two, however, are foundational. The first is *Marlatt's Relapse Prevention* (RP) model which addresses relapse in the AOD abuse and dependent client (Daley & Marlatt, 1992; Dimeff & Marlatt, 1995; Marlatt, 1978, 1985c; Marlatt & Barrett, 1994; Marlatt & Gordon, 1985). Its counterpart, the *Ross Reasoning and Rehabilitation* model, is directed at dealing with offender recidivism (Ross et al., 1995; Ross et al., 1986; Ross & Ross, 1988, 1995). These two approaches provide the basis for merging effective approaches for criminal justice and substance abuse clients.

Overview of the Marlatt Relapse Prevention (RP) Model

Relapse prevention is a CBT self-management program "that combines behavioral skill training procedures with cognitive intervention techniques to assist individuals in maintaining desired behavioral changes" (Marlatt & Barrett, 1994, p. 285). Skills training and motivational enhancement are central to RP (Dimeff & Marlatt, 1995). Clients are taught new coping responses (e.g., alternatives to addictive behavior), they learn to modify maladaptive beliefs and expectancies concerning their behavior, and they learn to change personal habits and lifestyles. Motivational strategies are based on the compensatory attribution model of treatment (Brickman et al., 1982), which sees the client as having the power to influence change and focuses on building client self-efficacy and responsibility in the change process.

The Marlatt RP model has been used as an adjunct to treatment programs and also as a stand-alone program for the cessation and maintenance phases (Dimeff & Marlatt, 1995). A stand-alone Marlatt RP program is summarized in Dimeff & Marlatt (1995).

In the Marlatt RP model, relapse is defined "as any violation of a self-imposed rule regarding a particular behavior" (Dimeff & Marlatt, 1995). The model stresses that relapse must be reframed from the traditional "all-or nothing" view to the view that it is a transitional process in which *slips* or *lapses* may or may not result in a full return to the level of the pretreatment substance use pattern. A single occurrence is different from a full-blown relapse (Dimeff & Marlatt, 1995).

As a person develops control over the behavior targeted for change, there is an increase in self-control and self-efficacy. The self-efficacy is strengthened over time. Self-control becomes challenged when the person encounters a high-risk (HR) situation—a situation where the person's sense of self-control is threatened. HR situations can be external or internal cues that can set off relapse. If the person copes effectively with the HR situation, self-control and self-efficacy increases. If coping is ineffective, self-efficacy decreases. The first step in RP is to help the client *identify* HR situations. The second step is to help the client *build coping and problem solving skills* to deal with HR situations without returning to the use of substances.

Another important component of the Marlatt RP model is to help the client deal with a lapse so that it does not lead to a full-blown relapse. The model uses the *rule violation effect* (RVE) to explain how lapses can lead to full relapse and help the client manage lapses or slips (Curry & Marlatt, 1987; Dimeff & Marlatt, 1995; Marlatt, 1985a). RVE is the result of violating the individual's rule to change target behaviors and will be discussed in more detail below. When RVE refers specifically to abstinence, then it is appropriate to use the expression *abstinence violation effect* (AVE), a term used earlier in the Marlatt model (personal communication, Marlatt, 1995).

Finally, the Marlatt Relapse Prevention (RP) model focuses on helping the client to deal with lifestyle imbalances that occur between the individual's perceived external demands or "shoulds" and perceived desires or "wants." Strong imbalances in the direction of "shoulds" may lead to strong feelings of being deprived and resulting desire to indulge (even to the point of a craving or urge). The goal is to help the client build a balanced lifestyle which ultimately helps the client deal with HR situations that can lead to relapse. The Marlatt RP model has developed *Global Intervention* procedures aimed at helping the client to build a balanced lifestyle. This includes developing coping skills to effectively manage factors that are precursors to high-risk situations and relapse (Dimeff & Marlatt, 1995). Figure 6.1 provides a flowchart of Marlatt's RP Model (Marlatt, 1985).

Applying the Marlatt Model to the SAO and Recidivism Prevention

Let us now look at how criminal conduct recidivism has much in common with addictive behavior relapse and how the Marlatt RP model can be helpful in understanding recidivism. It is important to remember that the similarities drawn in this text do not assume that the relapse and recidivism processes are identical. Whether recidivism actually occurs along the same processes as defined in the Marlatt model is an empirical question still to be answered. Clinical experience indicates that the processes are similar and that using the Marlatt RP model can be helpful in understanding recidivism. Later we will discuss an area in which the Marlatt RP model (or any substance abuse RP model) has to be altered with respect to its application to recidivism. In our treatment platform and conceptual framework chapter (9), we provide an adaptation of the Marlatt RP model to SAO relapse and recidivism.

From a broad perspective, a common ground for the application of a relapse prevention effort is that both crime and substance abuse include acts that lead to immediate reward, and the experience of immediate reinforcement (the rush, high or relief from participating in the act itself) is followed by delayed negative consequences such as anxiety, guilt, social disapproval or legal sanctions. When an SAO client enters an intervention program, there is an intent to change that pattern. In this context, a relapse prevention model can be viewed as an approach to preventing the substance abusing offender from returning to the lifestyle that led to entry into the criminal justice system. Relapse and recidivism is a violation of the self-imposed rule (RVE) to not return to a destructive lifestyle.

Regarding the application of Marlatt's RP Model to the SAO, we start with describing how high-risk situations in combination with covert (hidden from awareness) predispositions (patterns of thinking and feeling) may set the stage for relapse and recidivism. Intervention strategies are then discussed that can be used to prevent the occurrence of relapse or to cope with the "fallout" should a relapse occur. In Marlatt's Relapse Prevention Model, the relapse process consists of a series of events that may not necessarily be followed by a return to the pretreatment (baseline) levels of target behavior. We will apply the Marlatt model to recidivism using specific examples of thoughts, feelings and behaviors associated with criminal conduct.

Figure 6.1

Marlatt's Cognitive-Behavioral Model of the Relapse Process

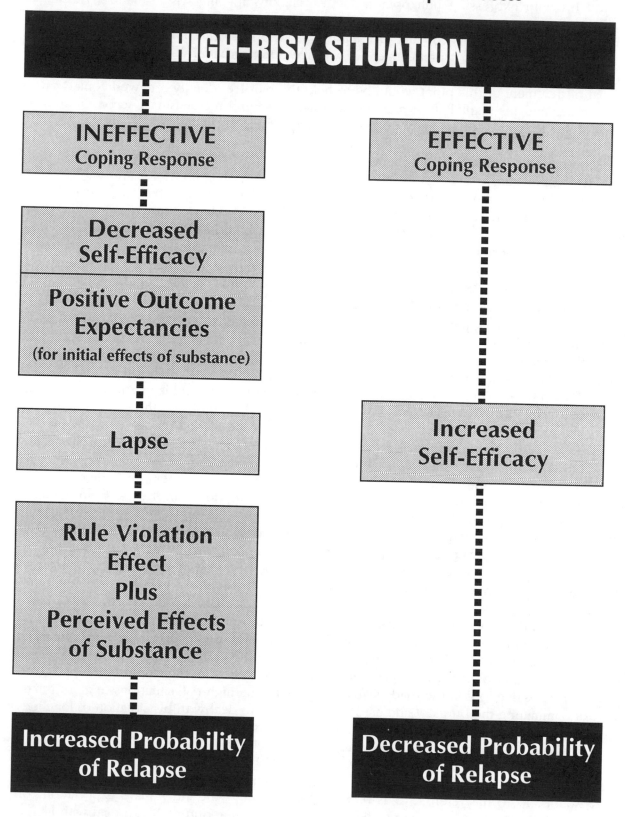

Reprinted with permission of the authors of *Relapse Prevention: Maintenance Strategies in the Treatment of Addictive Behaviors (p. 38)* edited by G. A. Marlatt and J. R. Gordon, © copyright 1985 by The Guilford Press.

A gregarious drinking, married SAO parolee, for example, has been in treatment and has maintained a steady period of not "using" and "going straight." He finds himself unable to make friends and being socially isolated—high-risk situation. He also find himself experiencing stress in his marriage and his wife expressing unhappiness in the relationship—high-risk situation. He subsequently renews contact with criminal associates who use substances. We interpret this regressive excursion, with respect to criminal conduct, as a *lapse* or as an *initial stage of recidivism*. Whether this leads to *full relapse* (returning to a pretreatment destructive drinking pattern) or *full recidivism* (committing a crime) depends to some degree on the attributions and expectations of the person involved.

One goal of treatment at this point would be to help the parolee identify renewed contacts with criminal associates and his marital stress as high risk for relapse and recidivism. A second would be to help the parolee learn the behavioral skills and cognitive strategies to handle the high-risk situation and prevent a slip from progressing into a full-blown episode of relapse or recidivism. Success management of the high-risk situations and maintenance of a drug-free and crime-free pattern increases self-control and self-efficacy.

Marlatt's model views each episode of diminished self-control as a "fork in the road" or a division of a decision tree, with one route returning to the former problem behavior (relapse) and the other continuing in the direction of positive change. Rather than an indication of failure, lapses (e.g., lying, aggressive episodes, associating with drug using and criminal associates) may be viewed more optimistically as "a challenging mistake or error, an opportunity for new learning to occur" (Marlatt & Barrett, 1994). A schematic presentation of some specific intervention strategies suggested by Marlatt's Relapse Prevention Model is shown in Figure 6.2.

Now remember that our parolee has been experiencing a sense of perceived control while complying with the rules of his parole and staying drug free. The longer the period of successful compliance, the greater will be his perception of self-control. This perception of self-regulation continues until the client is faced with the identified "high-risk" situation that threatens to upset the momentum of adaptive coping. Now the parolee experiences more stress in his marriage and his wife informs him she wants a divorce. He feels angry and betrayed, his automatic thoughts are "nothing works out, I did my best, the hell with it." He experiences what the Marlatt model calls P.I.G. (problem of immediate gratification). He begins drinking, spends more time with his criminal associates and then "slips" into thinking about committing a burglary. With some SAOs, the substance use precedes the initial stage of recidivism—thinking about committing a crime. With others, the crime precedes drug use, and then drugs are used to manage the reaction—(rule violation effect)—from failing to maintain his goal of being drug free and "going straight."

In an analysis of initial relapse episodes for clients manifesting various P.I.G. behaviors (e.g., smoking, problem drinking, heroin addiction, compulsive gambling and overeating), three primary high-risk situations were associated with nearly 75 percent of all the relapses reported: 1) *negative emotional states*—35 percent of all relapses in the sample; 2) *interpersonal conflict*—16 percent of the relapses; and 3) *social pressure*—20 percent of relapses (Cummings, Gordon & Marlatt, 1980; Marlatt, 1985c). Note that all three of these high-risk situations apply to our parolee.

The Marlatt RP Model holds that if a client is able to execute an effective coping response in a high-risk situation (does not drink when experiencing stress in the marriage), then the probability of relapse is decreased. Recidivism can be viewed in the same vein. Through program support, our parolee takes the positive fork in the road, is able to deal with the high-risk situations (e.g., resists the temptation of committing the burglary and uses cognitive skills to deal with his situation of loneliness and his feelings of anger about being betrayed by his spouse). The probability of recidivism decreases, as illustrated in Figure 6.1. The individual's sense of self-mastery is likely to improve with the expectation of being able to successfully cope with the next challenging situation.

The feeling of confidence in one's ability to overcome temptation results in what Bandura (1977; Bandura & Adams, 1977) has referred to as *increased self-efficacy*—the individual's expectation concerning the capacity to cope with an impending situation or task—a kind of "I can deal with it" feeling. As the coping responses continue and the client is able to successfully return from an array of high-risk situations, the perception of control is proportionately enhanced and the probability of recidivism would be inversely affected (decreased).

Figure 6.2

Specific Intervention Strategies in Marlatt's Relapse Prevention Model

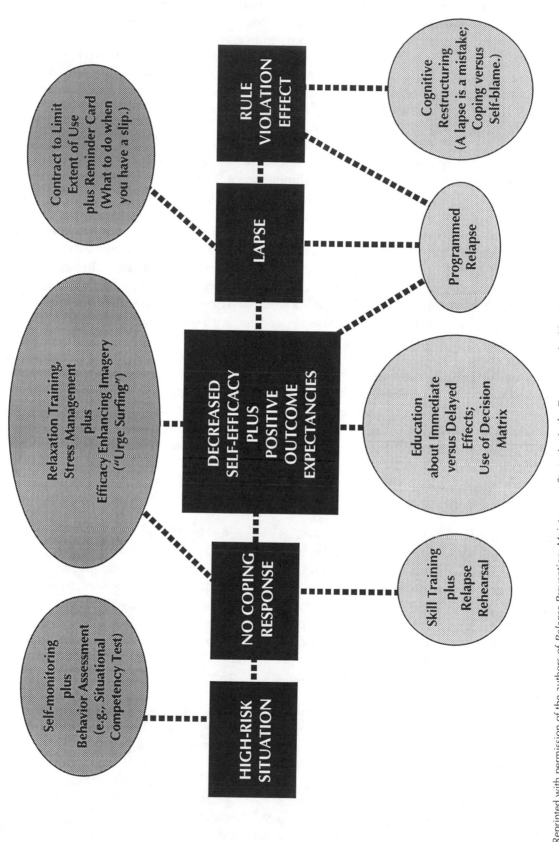

Reprinted with permission of the authors of *Relapse Prevention: Maintenance Strategies in the Treatment of Addictive Behaviors (p. 54),* edited by G. A. Marlatt and J. R. Gordon, © copyright 1985 by The Guilford Press.

Addictive Behaviors Research Center, University of Washington

While the individual who copes effectively with a high-risk situation experiences an increase in self-efficacy, the opposite is true for people who do not perform with effective coping responses. The probability for relapse/recidivism increases if the individual has positive expectancies about the benefits of partaking in what s/he perceives as a need-gratifying act. The alluring fantasies of immediate gratification (P.I.G), spending time with criminal associates to alleviate loneliness, the commission of a crime or indulgence with drugs (or all three), become dominant with increasing inattentiveness to delayed negative consequences. "The combination of being unable to cope effectively in a high risk situation coupled with positive outcome expectancies for the effects of the habitual coping behavior ...greatly increases the probability that an initial lapse will occur" (Marlatt & Barrett, 1994, p. 240). Whether the initial stage of recidivism (e.g., renewing contact with criminal associates) progresses to full-blown relapse/recidivism (reengaging in a criminal lifestyle; going back to the destructive pattern of drug use) depends in large measure upon how the SAO interprets the "causes" of lapsed behaviors.

Jumping the fence into territory that is well known to the SAO as "off limits" (as in the case of our parolee, spending time in the bars with criminal associates, going to their homes where people are getting high) may precipitate a constellation of thoughts and feelings that almost inevitably stage relapse and/or recidivism. *The Rule Violation Effect* provides a conceptual basis for explaining the covert (hidden from awareness) thoughts that unwittingly precipitate relapse or recidivism. The key cognitive-affective components of the *Rule Violation Effect* (RVE) are *cognitive dissonance* (conflict and guilt) and *self-attribution* (blaming oneself for the cause of the relapse). The intensity of the RVE is affected by multiple factors: 1) the degree of prior commitment or effort to abstain from rule violation; 2) the duration of abstinence from the prohibited behavior; and 3) the importance or value placed by the person on the prohibited behavior. An intense RVE may culminate in a motivational crisis—characterized by severe demoralization—whereby commitment to rule compliance is catastrophically eroded.

Undoubtedly some rule violations occur in the context of escalating reactions to unexpected high-risk situations, such as finding oneself at a party where marijuana is offered without advance notice. Many, if not most, relapses, however, occur after a series of cognitive distortions. Denial and rationalization covertly conspire in the destruction of prosocial conduct. An important strategy for circumventing rule violation is to train the SAO to recognize *early warning signals,* that is, cognitive distortions such as dismissing the desire to go to the bar with former criminal associates as "no big deal." These *seemingly irrelevant decisions* (SIDS) may stage a relapse episode whereby the SAO may sidestep personal responsibility by claiming unexpected exposure to overwhelming and irresistible circumstances.

The Marlatt RP Model suggests that P.I.G. is mediated by *lifestyle balance.* As outlined above, balance is defined as the degree of equilibrium between perceived "shoulds" and "wants" in an individual's life. "Wants" are activities for pleasure or self-fulfillment (e.g., playing sports), while "shoulds" are those activities that one experiences as external demands (e.g., paying bills). Let's imagine that our parolee has worked hard in treatment and that his life since entering treatment has been skewed by a preponderance of perceived "shoulds" and "oughts." Adding to that the two high-risk situations of feeling isolated and marital stress, he begins to feel justified in responding to the impulse for pleasure and indulgence. He responds to his automatic thoughts described above, adds to that "nobody really cares," and rationalizes his engaging in "controlled" drinking and spending time with criminal associates as something "I really deserve."

RP practitioners have developed strategies for teaching clients to recognize the elements of self-sabotage and to perform effective coping responses across the continuum from risk-escalating outcome expectancies through lapses, to the full-blown re-emergence of addictive or criminal conduct. Counselors may invoke specific RP intervention strategies to counteract the progression of high-risk micro-situations and attitudes that lead to relapse. Additionally, global RP self-control strategies may be designed to modify the client's lifestyle and to identify and cope with covert determinants of relapse and recidivism. The Marlatt model has the capability of integrating both the specific intervention and skill development techniques and the global self-control lifestyle strategies (Dimeff & Marlatt, 1995; Marlatt & Barrett, 1994).

All of Marlatt RP strategies (specific and global) may be categorized as 1) *skill training,* 2) *cognitive reframing* or 3) *lifestyle intervention. Skill training* procedures offer alternative behavioral and thought responses to high-risk situations. *Cognitive reframing techniques* arm clients with adaptive thoughts concerning the habit change process and introduce coping imagery to cope with craving and urges, and to restructure responses to the initial lapse, thereby preventing further escalation.

Finally, the Marlatt *lifestyle balancing* (maintenance) strategies (e.g., meditation, exercise, nutrition, artistic endeavor) serve the dual purpose of improving a client's global coping capacity while reducing the frequency and intensity of cravings associated with the P.I.G. While it is possible to standardize RP techniques for the purpose of testing the efficacy of RP versus other treatment models, Marlatt and Barrett (1984) encourage practitioners to select particular techniques on the basis of the initial evaluation and ongoing assessment findings.

When abstinence has been identified as the goal of treatment (a very low percentage of SAOs may qualify for controlled drinking as an alternative to abstinence), the overall aim of specific intervention approaches is to instruct clients to identify and cope with situations that may precipitate a slip, and to modify reactions to a single lapse, thereby preventing full-blown regression to drug dependence and criminal conduct. Figure 6.2 diagrams specific RP intervention strategies as they may be applied along the continuum of events leading to abstinence violation or rule violation.

The earlier one identifies his/her position on the continuum, the more effective is the re-establishment of self-regulation by performing an appropriate coping skill. "Remedial skills training necessitated by identification of coping skill deficits is the cornerstone of the RP treatment program" (Marlatt & Barrett, 1994, p. 294).

In the Marlatt model, skill training programs may be individualized with a range of possible CBT intervention topics including assertiveness, stress management, communication skills, marital therapy, and social or dating skills. Teaching methods include behavioral rehearsal, instruction, coaching, evaluative feedback, modeling, role playing and cognitive self-instruction. Regular homework assignments serve as adjunct learning modules that help to reinforce and consolidate individual or group skills training lessons. RP practitioners anticipate the possibility that their clients may slip because of failure to employ adequate coping skills. The post-slip response is critical because it may determine escalation from a single lapse to a full-blown reinstatement of pro-criminal activity. The basic post-lapse intervention strategy is to teach a client how to use cognitive restructuring as an antidote to the rule violation effect (RVE).

Application of the Ross Reasoning and Rehabilitation Cognitive Skills Model to the Substance Abusing Offender

In a *Colorado Specialized Drug Offender Program* (SDOP) (Colorado Department of Public Safety, 1991), offenders with severe drug problems were randomly assigned to a series of group sessions designed to improve cognitive and life skills. Group sessions followed the *Ross Reasoning and Rehabilitation Cognitive Skills Training Model* (Ross et al., 1986; Ross & Ross, 1988, 1995). This cognitive-behavioral model requires a series of 35 small group sessions, each two hours in duration. It is designed to compensate and mitigate cognitive and behavioral deficits characteristic of offenders which are key to recidivism. These include 1) *impulsivity,* 2) *sense of powerlessness,* 3) *conceptual rigidity,* 4) *lack of interpersonal problem solving skills,* 5) *egocentricity* and 6) *low critical reasoning ability (leading to susceptibility to influence by others).* The primary goal of the Ross model is to prvent full recidivism.

The SDOP consists of nine interrelated modules:

1. problem solving;
2. social skills;
3. negotiation skills;
4. managing emotions;
5. creative thinking;
6. values enhancement;
7. critical reasoning;
8. skills in review;
9. cognitive exercises.

Instead of regarding the SAO's antisocial behavior as symptomatic of some lasting character pathology, cognitive training takes the position that offenders are *under-socialized,* that is, they lack the values, attitudes and problem solving and social skills necessary for prosocial adjustment. These skills can be learned just as can many others, such as sports, art or communication. Cognitive training cannot be equated with psychotherapy. The goal is not to achieve massive personality restructuring, but rather to teach skills that enable SAOs to better cope with problems. Hence, a fundamental premise of the cognitive model is that *education* is the best approach to the treatment of offenders—directly and systematically training them in the skills needed to live more effectively.

In the Colorado sample, each sequence spanned 17-18 weeks, that is, 2 sessions/week. Clients were selected for the research pool on the basis of receiving elevated scores (5 or higher) on the *Addiction Severity Index* (ASI) (McLellan et al., 1985). Referred clients who received scores of 5 or higher (on a 9-point scale) were assigned to one of the treatment groups (SDOP Cognitive or Non-Cognitive) or to regular probation. Johnson and Hunter (1992) report significant advantages for extra supervision and Cognitive Group Training.

Overall, the Ross model treatment group showed the lowest rate of revocation. In terms of loss rates (i.e., retention on probation), cognitive-behavioral treatment was found highly beneficial for clients with severe drug or alcohol issues who do not also have serious psychiatric or sociopathic problems. Johnson and Hunter (1992) found that *extra supervision* appeared to be needed for SAOs who have psychiatric and/or sociopathic disorders concurrent with drug dependence. The cognitive behavioral model was found to be particularly effective for male clients age 20 or over (females had a low rate of revocation across all treatment categories).

Integration of Models and Model Alteration

From the above discussion, it seems clear that most of the Marlatt RP Model concepts, methods and procedures can be applied in the prevention of recidivism among substance abusing offenders. Also, the Ross Skills Training Model fits in well with not only addressing the prevention of recidivism but also in addressing the problem of drug use relapse in the SAO.

Recognizing that the SAO faces problems of both relapse and recidivism, we have utilized both the Marlatt and Ross models in developing an integrated model for relapse/recidivism prevention (RRP). That model is presented in Chapter 9.

Even though we have developed two module to formally deal with RRP, we should not see RRP as a stand-alone concept in the treatment of the SAO. In fact, we can conclude that all of the sessions in this manual are directed at RRP. Once a client engages in the program, that client has been challenged to change lifestyles, and there is some degree of commitment to a self-imposed rule of developing a drug-free and crime-free lifestyle. Consequently, all program activity henceforth can be construed RRP.

There is one area of alteration that needs to be made with respect to the integration of relapse and recidivism. This has to do with the goals and outcome of treatment. For AOD use, even though the goal is abstinence from drug use, a full relapse can be tolerated and even seen as a basis for ongoing recovery and change. A full relapse into AOD use will not necessarily result in legal sanctions. With criminal conduct, the case is different. There is zero tolerance into full recidivism. Full recidivism will result in legal sanctions with no "second chance" outside of the criminal justice system. Thus, it is essential that the RRP model be altered in the sense that with criminal conduct, there will be a strong focus on cognitive and affective recidivism with these elements being considered as initial recidivism or lapses (e.g., thinking about committing a crime; spending time with criminal associates). At the cognitive level, we need not have zero tolerance. At the behavioral level, zero tolerance for full recidivism is required.

Best Approaches for CBT Treatment of the Substance Abusing Offender

The purpose of Chapters 1 through 5 of this manual was to review the concepts and evidence that could provide a foundation for selecting the best approaches and most effective elements in developing a CBT program for the substance abusing offender. Chapter 1 provided the essential concepts and principles of CBT creating the foundation for a CBT program for the SAO. Chapter 2 provided evidence for the effectiveness of several treatment approaches for AOD abusers and a conceptual framework for AOD treatment. Chapter 3 provided evidence for the efficacy of using CBT methods and principles in the treatment of the offender, and Chapter 4 gave evidence for the robust relationship between substance abuse and criminal conduct. Chapter 5 discussed the ingredients necessary for forming a productive treatment alliance with the client—recognizing the SAO's position on the continuum of change—to promote optimal treatment outcome.

The present chapter provided arguments for using relapse and recidivism prevention as the "glue" that binds a combined approach to treat the dually affected individual. These findings and reviews provide us with the essential elements and themes that make up an effective treatment program for the substance abusing offender. Table 6.1 lists these essential elements.

Table 6.1

Essential Elements of an Effective Treatment Program for the SAO

- the principles and methods of motivational enhancement therapy in building treatment responsiveness, trust and rapport;

- building treatment readiness;

- people go through identifiable stages when making change;

- importance of self-disclosure in developing self-awareness which opens the doors to self-improvement and change;

- the cognitive-behavioral principles and treatment methods as outlined in Chapter 2 with a special focus on enhancing social and coping skills and self-control training;

- the principles of Marlatt's Relapse Prevention and the Ross Reasoning and Rehabilitation models;

- encouraging the client to utilize community 12-step and self-help programs when indicated.

The evaluation of the SAO offender within the context of CBT includes five areas of assessment:

- AOD use and abuse;
- criminal conduct and patterns;
- cognitive-behavioral sets or styles;
- current life-situation problems;
- motivation and readiness for treatment.

An effective assessment approach recognizes that there is a general influence of a certain problem area on a person's life and within the problem area there occurs a wide variety of differences among people (Wanberg & Horn, 1987). For example, alcohol has a general influence on the life of the alcohol-dependent individual. Yet, individuals who have alcohol problems differ greatly. Some are solo drinkers and others drink at bars; some have physical problems from drinking and others do not; some drink continuously and some periodically.

Assessment, then, should consider these two levels of evaluation: 1) *the general effect of a certain problem area* (e.g., AOD abuse, criminal conduct) and 2) *the specific ways that these problem areas affect the person's life*. Assessment of the general influence is usually the basis of screening. Looking at the more specific influences and problem areas involves the application of a differential or multi-dimensional assessment. This differential and in-depth assessment is usually done after the client has been admitted into a treatment program. There is a rich body of literature that applies to assessment within each of the domains of AOD use, criminal conduct and issues pertinent to the use of cognitive intervention and treatment.

Assessment of AOD Use and Abuse

There are two levels of assessment for the evaluation of alcohol and other drug use problems (Wanberg, 1993b; Wanberg & Horn, 1987). The first level is *screening*. This level of AOD assessment utilizes inclusion criteria to address two simple questions: Does the person have an AOD problem? Is the individual appropriate for treatment referral? Jacobson's (1989) concepts of detection and assessment would fall into this screening or first level of evaluation. Miller, Westerberg and Waldron (1995) also identifiy this as screening. However, the goal of screening is more than just answering yes or no to the question of whether the person has an AOD problem. The goal is also to determine the *degree of involvement* in AOD use and abuse.

Deciding whether the individual is to be included into the category of drug misuse does not mean that one has obtained a valid description of the different conditions associated with AOD misuse or abuse. Thus, the second level of evaluation identifies the distinct conditions associated with the disorder or problem. This level helps you to develop a comprehensive understanding of the progress, process and existing condition of the individual to formulate a treatment plan and approach within the framework of expected outcome. Whereas Jacobson (1989) calls this level of evaluation diagnosis, Wanberg (1992) identifies this level as *in-depth differential assessment*.

Each of these areas of assessment is reviewed. For a comprehensive review of AOD assessment, evaluation methods, and measurement instruments, please see George (1990), Jacobson (1989), Miller, Westerberg and Waldron (1995), Center for Substance Abuse Treatment (1994) and Allen and Columbus (1995).

1 Inclusion Screening Approaches

Clinical screening "is a preliminary gathering and sorting of information used to determine if an individual has a problem with AOD abuse, and if so, whether a detailed clinical assessment is appropriate" (Center for Substance Abuse Treatment, 1994, p. 5). The screening level of evaluation is almost always unidimensional (Jacobson, 1989; Wanberg & Horn, 1987). That is, the goal is to determine whether the individual has a condition indicating drug abuse, drug dependence, alcoholism, a drug use problem, or an alcohol use problem. Several screening approaches have been developed to meet the objective of categorizing individuals with respect to having an AOD use problem, being an AOD abuser, or being AOD dependent (Wanberg & Horn, 1987).

Minimum Symptom Criteria

The most commonly applied approach is the minimum symptom criteria. This approach is represented by the *World Health Organization's* (WHO) cross-cultural criteria (WHO, 1964; Edwards, Gross, Keller & Moser, 1976; Edwards, Gross, Keller, Moser & Room, 1977), the dichotomous indicators used by the *National Council on Alcoholism* (NCA, 1972), and the criteria as outlined in the *Diagnostic and Statistical Manual of Mental Disorders IV: DSM-IV* (American Psychiatric Association, 1994).

The *WHO's* definition is based on two criteria for determining alcohol use problems:

- *Alcohol Dependence Syndrome (ADS):* impaired control, increased tolerance, repeated withdrawal symptoms, drinking to avoid withdrawal, compulsion to drink, reinstatement of symptoms after abstinence and obsession with drinking related activities;
- *Alcohol Related Disabilities (ARD):* loss of behavioral control when drinking, drinking causes problems with work, marriage and family, the law and emotional stability.

The *NCA* definition is based on 86 indicators divided into two tracks:

- *Track I:* physiological dependence (withdrawal symptoms, decreased tolerance and blackouts) and clinical (illnesses associated with alcohol use such as liver disease, Wernicke-Korsakoff syndrome, alcoholic cardiomyopathy);
- *Track II:* disruption in behavioral, psychological and attitudinal functioning and includes the criterion that the individual drinks despite strong medical complications or despite strong social problems (job, marriage, etc.).

The *DSM-IV* criteria for substance dependence are provided in Table 7.1, and the DSM-IV criteria for substance abuse are provided in Table 7.2.

The *CAGE* questionnaire (Allen, Eckardt & Wallen, 1988) is also a simple minimum symptom criteria. It includes the four areas of attempts to **C**ut down, feeling **A**nnoyed when people complain about the individual's drinking, feeling **G**uilt about the drinking, and having an **E**ye-opener.

The minimal symptom criteria approach essentially involves defining AOD problems in terms of a set of diagnostic criteria and requiring that a certain number of these criteria be met for inclusion into the category of AOD problems, abuse or dependence. This approach requires that the evaluator rate the client across these inclusion or diagnostic criteria.

Table 7.1

Diagnostic and Statistical Manual IV Criteria for Substance Dependence

A maladaptive pattern of substance use, leading to clinically significant impairment or distress, as manifested by three (or more) of the following, occurring at any time in the same 12-month period.

1. Tolerance, as defined by either of the following:
   - a need for markedly increased amounts of the substance to achieve intoxication or desired effect
   - markedly diminished effect with continued use of the same amount of the substance

2. withdrawal, as manifested by either of the following:
   - the characteristic withdrawal syndrome for the substance
   - the same (or a closely related) substance is taken to relieve or avoid withdrawal symptoms

3. the substance is often taken in larger amounts or over a longer period than was intended

4. there is a persistent desire or unsuccessful efforts to cut down or control substance use

5. a great deal of time is spent in activities necessary to obtain the substance or use the substance

6. important social, occupational, or recreational activities are given up or reduced because of substance use

7. the substance use is continued despite knowledge of having a persistent or recurrent physical or psychological problem that is likely to have been caused or exacerbated by the substance

Specify if:

With Physiological Dependence: evidence of tolerance or withdrawal (either item 1 or 2 is present)

Without Physiological Dependence: no evidence of tolerance or withdrawal (neither item 1 or 2 is present)

Table 7.2

Diagnostic and Statistical Manual IV Criteria for Substance Abuse

A. A maladaptive pattern of substance use leading to clinically significant impairment or distress, as manifested by one (or more) of the following, occurring within a 12-month period:

- recurrent substance use resulting in a failure to fulfill major role obligations at work, school, or home (e.g., repeated absences or poor work performance related to substance use; substance-related absences, suspensions, or expulsions from school; neglect of children or household)

- recurrent substance use in situations in which it is physically hazardous (e.g., driving an automobile or operating a machine when impaired by substance use)

- recurrent substance use despite legal problems (e.g., arrests for substance-related disorderly conduct)

- continued substance use despite having persistent or recurrent social or interpersonal problems caused or exacerbated by the effects of the substance (e.g., arguments with spouse about consequences of intoxication, physical fights)

B. The symptoms have never met the criteria for Substance Dependence for this class of substance

---

Standardized Psychometric Approaches

Standardized psychometric measurement solves some of these problems. A standardized self-report questionnaire or test always asks the same questions to all persons being evaluated. Such tests are set up so that one area of evaluation, such as social benefit drinking, is measured by several questions. In this way, the risk of an error being made by asking only one question is cancelled out. The more valid aspects of a variety of questions, all of which are answered by the respondent, more accurately measure the particular area of evaluation. By summing up or adding across all of the questions, subjectivity can be reduced. This is the basis of most psychological measurement (Horn et al., 1987).

While these standardized tests can cut down on the subjective influences of ratings made by the clinician or evaluator, they do not eliminate the fact that the self-report measures are still subjective. Subjectivity is inherent in self-ratings. A person can be unaware of her or his own condition or can consciously falsify the condition. It does avoid the double subjectivity found in rater data.

The basic problem with these measures, or what are often called scalograms, has to do with which symptoms we count and how many should be counted. A study of the individual items can help in making this kind of evaluation. A cutoff value can also be helpful, which can be based on the distribution of scores found in a particular normative or reference group.

For adults, there are a number of standardized screening measures that have been developed. A comprehensive summary of screening measures may be found in *Assessing Alcohol Problems: A Guide for Clinicians and Researchers* (Allen & Columbus, 1995). Several screening devices are briefly discussed.

The Michigan Alcoholism Screening Test (MAST) (Hedlund & Vieweg, 1984; Selzer, 1971), is one of the most widely used screening instruments for alcohol problems. The MAST is composed of 25 items which measure common signs and symptoms of what is commonly considered to indicate alcoholism. A raw score of five is often used as a cutoff value to indicate alcohol problems. Studies by Jacobson and his associates (Jacobson, 1989) have found that the cutoff score of five produces between 20 and 35 percent false positives, and that a cutoff value of 12 reduced the false positive rate to an acceptable range.

Horn, Skinner, Wanberg and Foster's (1984) *Alcohol Dependence Scale (ADS)* measures the ADS features of the WHO definition, as well as many of the features of the NCA and DSM-IV (American Psychiatric Association, 1994) criteria. It incorporates several assessment procedures that tend to reduce subjectivity such as that of combining several indicators. Twenty-five of the 29 items in ADS are from the Disrupt1 scale of the *Alcohol Use Inventory* (Horn et al., 1987). Thus, these two measures are really the same. The items in both of these scales measure compulsion to drink excessively, repetitive experiences of withdrawal symptoms, and a loss of control over one's behavior while drinking.

The Adult Substance Use Survey (ASUS) (Wanberg, 1993a, 1993b) also provides a psychometric approach to inclusion screening. This instrument provides a broad measure, not only of multiple-symptoms resulting from the AOD use but also of the degree to which an individual has been involved in ten commonly defined categories of drugs. In addition, the *Adult Substance Use Survey* provides a brief assessment of antisocial behavior and mental health problems and a defensiveness measure. It is currently being used statewide in Colorado by the adult criminal justice system for screening. Users of this manual may use this without cost (see Chapter 11).

Other instruments that provide a screening assessment of drug use include the *Addiction Severity Index* (ASI) (McLellan et al., 1985; McLellan, Luborsky, O'Brien & Woody, 1980), the short *MAST*, the drug-severity index of the *Offender Profile Index* (Inciardi, 1994), the *CAGE* (Allen et al., 1988), the *Drug Abuse Screening Test* (DAST) (Skinner, 1982) and the *Simple Screening Inventory* (SSI) (Center for Substance Abuse Treatment, 1994). Although the fifth edition of the ASI provides a differential assessment across major life functioning areas, the area of AOD use and abuse represents a screening measurement. The ASI is administered in an interview format and is not conducive to self-administration as are the above-mentioned instruments.

Other Inclusion Criteria

There are several other inclusion criteria or rules that can be used in the process of screening. These include utilization of the *impaired control cycle, self-selection into treatment* and the *relationship-identifier*. These criteria are usually used in conjunction with the minimum symptom and standardized psychometric approaches to assessment.

The concept of impaired control and the impaired-control cycle (Wanberg, 1974, 1990; Wanberg & Horn, 1987) can be useful in identifying the presence of an AOD problem. Impaired control occurs when notable negative consequences result from drug use (e.g., loss of job, physical problems, relationship or marital problems, etc.). The cycle begins when drugs are used to solve the very problems that result from their use and continues when the individual continues to use drugs to solve the problems that come from drug use. If we define a drug use problem on the basis of the occurrence of negative consequences, then all persons who develop a negative or disruptive effect from using drugs meet the criteria for inclusion in the drug use problem group. For example, this could include the drug user arrested for possession, the adolescent drinker arrested for alcohol possession or the adult drinker arrested for driving under the influence.

Self-selection is also an important inclusion criterion. An individual can be classified as having problems with drugs through the use of the above inclusion screening methods. It does not necessarily follow that the individual will enter treatment. The client must be aware of having problems related to AOD use and then acknowledge the need for treatment. Such self-selection is enhanced when the individual experiences some emotional concern about the disruptive quality of drug use.

The presence of a *relationship identifier* (RI) (Wackwitz, Diesenhaus & Foster, 1977) is also helpful. A RI is a person who forges a link between life-role disruptions and alcohol. Often the person who makes this connection is not the alcohol user. The RI concludes that the undesirable behaviors of the drug user are a direct consequence of the use of drugs (although the major determinants of the life-role disruptions may be other than drug use). There is a pattern of drug use (e.g., compulsion to use drugs, always having drugs around) and disruptions in life-role functions; a RI links these together. The user often accepts the RI's analysis and requests treatment. In the case of more resistant clients, such as court referrals, the RI may put pressure on the individual or even force the individual into treatment. Until the link between the use of drugs and life disruption problems is established, the user is not likely to enter AOD treatment, no matter how many other indicators of drug abuse may be present.

Inclusion criteria do not necessarily depend on diagnostic criteria as, for example, described in the *Diagnostic and Statistical Manual IV* (American Psychiatric Association, 1994). In fact, it is best not to rely on formal diagnostic criteria for this purpose in that this may cause the individual doing the screening to make a large number of false negative errors. This kind of error occurs when the evaluator concludes that the individual does not have a drug use problem when in fact such a problem does exist. A strict application of formal diagnostic criteria increases the number of false negatives at the screening level of evaluation. Thus, the most effective inclusion screening model might involve the use of all of the above methods and approaches.

2 In-depth Assessment—The Multidimensional Model

The most widely accepted model for the second level of evaluation is the *multidimensional or multiple-condition approach*. This model holds that there are independent and separate multiple causes, patterns and outcomes of psychoactive drug use. These patterns of use require different treatments. In order to have an in-depth understanding of an individual screened into the category of having an AOD problem, then, assessment (and measurement) across these multiple conditions is important. There is strong support in the literature for a multiple-condition theory of assessment (Allen & Kadden, 1995; Caddy, 1978; Hart & Stueland, 1979; Hyman, 1976; Miller, Westerberg & Waldron, 1995; Pattison & Kaufman, 1982; Pattison, Sobell & Sobell, 1977; Wanberg & Horn, 1983).

The *multidimensional* approach to in-depth assessment allows the counselor to develop a treatment plan around the multiple conditions associated with AOD use. A conceptual framework for multiple-condition or multidimensional AOD use assessment is provided in Table 7.3 (Wanberg & Horn, 1987). Five broad dimensions are outlined along with specific factors within these dimensions. From these broad and specific factors, four AOD types are defined (bottom of Table 7.3).

Several psychometrically based instruments have been developed that provide the clinician with a multidimensional approach for assessing adult substance use clients. (See Allen & Columbus, 1995 and Miller, Westerberg & Waldron, 1995, for a list of instruments.)

For alcoholism, one of the most comprehensive instruments is the *Alcohol Use Inventory* (AUI) (Horn et al., 1987; also see Jacobson, 1989, and Miller, Westerberg & Waldron, 1995). For a broader measure of AOD problems, the *Drug Use Self Report* (DUSR) (Wanberg & Horn, 1989a; 1989b) provides an in-depth measure of drug use across ten major drug categories. Users of this manual may use the DUSR as part of the assessment SAO assessment protocol outlined in Chapter 11. The *Comprehensive Drinker Profile* (Miller & Marlatt, 1984), a structured intake interview for assessing AOD problems, provides a differential assessment of adult AOD patterns. The *Addiction Severity Index* (McLellan et al., 1985, McLellan, Luborsky, O'Brien & Woody, 1980) also provides a differential screening assessment across several risk factor domains, including medical, employment, drug use, legal status, family relationships and psychological status.

Table 7.3

Conceptual Framework for Describing Multidimensional Drug Use Patterns and Conditions

BENEFITS	STYLES	CONSEQUENCES	CONCERNS	ACKNOWLEDGMENT
Social	Gregarious	Behavioral control loss	Guilt	Acknowledgment
Mental	Solo	Social role maladaptation		Awareness of problems
Manage depression and stress	Periodic	Psychophysical withdrawal	Prior help to stop	
	Sustained	Psychoperceptual withdrawal		
Coping with losses	Compulsive			Acknowledgment of problems
Coping with relationships	Capricious	Relationship disruption		
			Concern by significant others	Willingness and readiness to seek help
	Drug of choice	Emotional disruption		
	Quality of use	Tissue and organ damage		
SELF-ENHANCEMENT FROM USE	**INVOLVEMENT IN USE**	**DISRUPTION FROM USE**	**ANXIETY FROM USE**	**MOTIVATION TO CHANGE USE PATTERN**

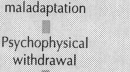

Psychosocial dependence— commitment to drug use   **Physical dependence with impaired control**   **Anxious impaired control with disruption**   **Anxious awareness— commitment not to use**

Assessment of Criminal Conduct

The assessment of criminal conduct must be done within the context of understanding and assessing antisocial problems. Criminal conduct is one dimension of antisocial behavior and the antisocial personality pattern. Even though this manual is focused on the treatment of the criminal offender with AOD problems, it is important to have a *general view* of the overall antisocial personality pattern and disorder.

1 The Antisocial Personality Pattern

At the very broad level, the antisocial personality pattern is represented by a pattern of behavior involving "disregard for, and violation of, the rights of others" (American Psychiatric Association, 1994). Any realistic assessment of antisocial personality patterns must consider the long-term history of the individual, for these patterns are at least foreshadowed if not obvious in the developmental years. "By definition, a personality disorder is an enduring pattern of thinking, feeling, and behaving that is relatively stable over time" (American Psychiatric Association, 1994, p. 632).

At the more specific level of assessment, antisocial patterns are often characterized by the attitudes and behavioral patterns outlined in Table 7.4 (American Psychiatric Association, 1994; Sarason & Sarason, 1995). The characteristics identified in Table 7.4 are similar to what has been identified as psychopathy in abnormal psychology literature (Andrews & Bonta, 1994). *The Psychopathy Checklist* (PCL) developed by Hare (1980, 1986) has many of the items found in Table 7.4. There is a strong argument for the idea that the psychopath represents a discrete personality type or taxon and that psychopaths are different from other criminals (Hare, 1980, 1986; Harris, Rice & Quinsey, 1992). Hart Kropp and Hare (1988) found that offenders with moderate to high scores on the PCL have a much higher rate of recidivism than non-psychopathic offenders (low scores on PCL).

As in the case of all behavioral disorders, antisocial patterns and disorders are *multidimensional*. That is, there are varying patterns of behaviors within the antisocial domain. For example, not all of the antisocial features described in Table 7.4 are found in all individuals with antisocial patterns and disorders. Not all people with antisocial patterns have engaged in criminal behavior. Within offender populations, we will find varying antisocial and psychopathic patterns.

2 Different Assessment Approaches

Offender Types and Classifications

Many assessment approaches involve the classification of offenders into a typology system or distinct groups. As noted in Chapter 4, the multiple classification approaches have focused on personality types, behavioral classifications, developmental and interpersonal maturity, and the criminal statutes that drive the criminal justice system. Such classifications allow for a differential approach to offender treatment. For example, the *Adult Internal Management System* (AIMS) was developed from Quay's (1965) five offender types—aggressive-psychopathic; situational; manipulative; inadequate-dependent and neurotic-anxious types. Using AIMS to manage inmates safely with a prison setting, inmate-staff and inmate-inmate assault rates have been reduced by 50 percent (Levinson, 1988; Quay, 1984).

Risk Factor Assessment

One recent approach has been the development of risk-assessment instruments. These instruments are premised on the theory that criminal behavior is predictable (Andrews & Bonta, 1994). Using various risk-assessment instruments, research strongly suggests that offenders may be reliably grouped into high-or low-risk categories which yield recidivism predictors with 70-80% accuracy.

Very early work in risk assessment was done by Burgess (1928), whose risk-assessment instrument allowed for the prediction of 76 percent recidivism for those with maximum points on the instrument. Other risk-assessment instruments include the *Salient Factor Score* (Hoffman, 1983), the *Wisconsin Risk Assessment Instrument* (Baird, Heinz & Bemus, 1979) and the *Statistical Index for Recidivism Scale* used in Canada (Nuffield, 1982). The latter is reported to indicate that about 85 percent of the individuals falling in the "very good" risk category were considered to be successful with respect to recidivism.

Rogers' (1981) six-item risk scale includes being male, under age 24, prior criminal record, association with antisocial people and offenders, not having a focus in surplus time and coming from a family on public assistance. It is of note that 94 percent of her sample who scored positive on all six of these indicators and about 77 percent of her sample who scored positive on five indicators, reoffended. Additionally, she found that 61 percent of the offenders who reoffended while in treatment or super-

Table 7.4
Characteristics of the Antisocial Personality Pattern

Characteristics of Antisocial Patterns

- repeatedly performing acts which do not conform to social norms with respect to obeying the law and that are grounds for being arrested;

- impulsivity and failure to plan ahead;

- patterns of deceit, lying, conning others for personal gain or pleasure;

- inability to handle anger in adaptive ways;

- low frustration tolerance;

- ineffective problem solving in interpersonal relationships;

- irresponsibility in finances, relationships, and societal obligations;

- reckless disregard for the safety of others and of self;

- inability or unwillingness to delay gratification;

- aggressive and even assaultive behavior;

- denial of personal responsibility and blaming others;

- associating with friends who are antisocial and engage in illegal conduct;

- manipulating and exploiting relationships;

- lack of empathy for others;

- lack of remorse and guilt;

- aggrandizement of self and inflated view of self.

vision ended up being post-program recidivists.

A risk-instrument currently in widespread use and considered to be reliable is the *Level of Service Inventory* (LSI) (Andrews, 1982). This is a rater-determined inventory. However, many of the items are based on facts about the offender (e.g., prior convictions, currently employed). A number of the items in the LSI are rater variables and rely on the subjective assessment of the interviewer.

The LSI provides a measurement of the primary risk factors that contribute to the development of life adjustment problems and that also predict recidivism. These risk factors are very similar to the non-AOD multiple conditions that are outlined by Wanberg and Horn (1987) as important in the assessment of AOD clients. The LSI risk factors are included in Table 7.5.

A number of studies indicate that the LSI has good predictive validity with respect to recidivism (Andrews & Bonta, 1994). For example, 90% of the recidivists had LSI scores which fell outside the minimal supervision range and 100 percent of the multiple conviction cases had scores outside the minimum range. Other findings indicate that as many as 93 percent of the offenders who completed their sentence at a community halfway house were identified as low-risk by the LSI and about 90 percent of the low-risk offenders were free from incarceration one year after completing their halfway house program.

Table 7.5

Level of Service Inventory (LSI) Risk Factors

- ◆ criminal history and deviancy;
- ◆ education, employment and financial adjustment;
- ◆ family and marital relationship problems;
- ◆ leisure time and recreation;
- ◆ emotional and personal adjustment;
- ◆ attitude and orientation toward criminal behavior;
- ◆ social involvement and companions;
- ◆ involvement with alcohol and other drugs;
- ◆ accommodations and living situation.

LSI scores are grouped to reflect three levels of supervision:

- ◆ *maximum*-scores which fall in the upper 15 percent of the distribution;
- ◆ *medium*-scores in the middle 35 percent of the distribution.
- ◆ *minimum*-the lower 50 percent of the distribution.

Risk assessment is pertinent to decisions concerning the commitment of treatment resources. Andrews and associates (1990) found that reduction in recidivism for high-risk offenders occurred only when such offenders received intensive levels of service. However, when the same level of intensity was applied to low-risk offenders, the treatment result was minimal or even negative.

Criminogenic Needs

Another area of assessment is criminogenic needs (Andrews & Bonta, 1994). Criminogenic needs are "dynamic attributes of the offender that, when changed, are associated with changes in the probability of recidivism" (Andrews & Bonta, 1994, p. 176). Such needs are identified as procriminal attitudes and involvement with associates who are deviant and antisocial. Noncriminogenic needs such as anxiety and low self-esteem are considered to be dynamic but do not seem to have predictive validity with respect to recidivism. These dynamic predictors and their respective targets for change have been discussed in more detail in Chapter 3 of this manual.

Self-Reported Antisocial Behavior and Criminal Conduct

Another area of assessment is the client's self-report of involvement in antisocial behaviors, criminal conduct and procriminal attitudes. First, this assessment is important in that it provides a *standardized* self-report measure of the degree of involvement in antisocial and illegal behaviors. Second, self-report measures of criminal behavior and deviancy provide an indication of the *degree to which the offender is willing to be open and honest* about his/her criminal conduct. This in turn provides some indication of the degree to which the client is willing to be involved in treatment. Finally, these self-report measures are important when they are *compared to interviewer ratings* based on uniform criteria and to the *criminal record* of the offender. When the offender has relatively low scores on a self-report measure of antisocial or deviant behavior yet a high risk score with respect to a history of convictions and recidivism, s/he is probably a poor candidate for treatment.

There are several self-administered self-report screening instruments measuring antisocial, deviant and criminal behavior and attitudes. Gough's (1965) Socialization (So) scale of the *California Personality Inventory* clearly differentiates between offenders and non-offenders (Wilson & Hernstein, 1985). The general deviancy scale of the *Adolescent Self-Assessment Profile (ASAP)* significantly differentiates between juvenile offenders and non-offenders (Wanberg, 1991b, 1992). *The Adult Substance Use Survey (ASUS)* (Wanberg, 1993a) has a narrow but reliable measure of deviancy and antisocial behavior. The ASUS defensiveness measure, which indicates the degree to which the individual is willing to be open and honest in responding to the test questions, was found to have a negative .51 correlation with the deviancy scale, as measured among 484 adult offenders. This indicates that those offenders who were more open with respect to admitting a history of deviancy and antisocial attitudes were overall less defensive when approaching the test questions.

A minimum assessment of criminal conduct should include the evaluation of risk levels as measured by the LSI; self-administered, self-report measures of criminal conduct history and attitudes; criminal history; and history of recidivism and reoffending.

Assessment of Cognitive and Affective Processing

Assessment in cognitive treatment refers to "the identification and measurement of a broad spectrum of relevant factors that are necessary to ensure the best possible alteration of a particular individual's maladaptive behavior" (Goldfried, 1995, p. 21). Since the rationale behind cognitive therapy is that emotions and actions are determined by the way an individual structures his/her world, the task of assessment is to understand the way the individual structures that world (McDermott & Wright, 1992). The primary window for such an assessment is that of examining the individual's *cognitions*. Through assessment, understanding, conceptualizing and intervening, treatment helps the client to understand and control emotions and actions which in turn will influence the individual's cognitive world.

In the assessment of the relevant factors of the individual's life and cognitive world, assessment goes beyond the traditional assessment model used in clinical and educational work.

The *traditional or psychodynamic approach* to assessment is directed toward understanding the individual's personality characteristics or traits as a way of predicting behavior. This model assumes that the behavioral expression of these personality characteristics is consistent across independent situations. Thus, traditional personality tests are directed at bringing about responses that point to underlying traits. The traditional model involves "the assessment of personality constructs that, in turn, are used to predict overt behavior" (Goldfried, 1995, p. 49).

In contrast to the traditional model, the CBT approach involves direct measurement and assessment "of the individual's response to various life situations" (Goldfried, 1995, p. 32). Greater emphasis is placed on what a person does or how an individual responds to various situations. Rather than underlying constructs becoming the unit of focus in assessing the behavior determinants, "the basic unit for consideration involves the individual's response to specific aspects of his environment" (p. 36). Thus, the selection of behavioral test responses is based on the situation most relevant to target behaviors or cognitions. Responses given to tests used in assessment are considered to be "samples of the criterion behaviors themselves" (p. 44). Thus, "sampling of the criterion situation and behavior is obtained first, after which an attempt is made to develop efficient measurement procedures for assessing these behavioral-environment interactions" (p. 45). In essence, assessment capitalizes on the similarities "between the actual test response and the criterion measure" (p. 48). There is a direct sampling of the criterion measures themselves.

This is not to say that traditional assessment is not important in the assessment of the client's treatment needs and in the development of an effective treatment plan. Such assessment needs to be an integral part of the overall assessment of the individual's cognitive, affective and behavioral response to real life situations.

Goldfried (1995) suggests a criteria analysis for behavioral assessment. These behaviorally oriented criteria consist of (p. 41):

1. *situational analysis* in which relevant environmental situations are evaluated;

2. *response enumeration* which involves developing a pool of responses for each of the various identified situations;

3. *response evaluation* which involves categorizing each of the various responses in a particular situation according to the degree of effectiveness of those responses in addressing the particular life situation.

Goldfried (1995) suggests the judgment of effectiveness of the various responses needs to be done by *significant others* or individuals the client respects. The assumptions are that 1) there are normative or standardized behaviors for effectiveness in these particular life situations; 2) these standards are stable over time; and 3) scoring criteria are established for the effectiveness of the responses.

The assessment process in the early years of behavioral therapy focused mainly on assessing the individual's responses in a particular situation as the targets for change. (The above material comparing traditional and behavioral assessment comes from Goldfried and Kent's 1972 *Psychological Bulletin* article which was reprinted in Goldfried, 1995.) As cognitive and behavioral approaches were merged into CBT treatment, it became more apparent that the targets for change were not only the specific behaviors, but also—and even more important—the cognitions (thoughts) and emotions involved in the individual's response. Thus, the "target" for change is not the behavioral response, but rather the *thoughts* and *feelings* which are antecedent to the behavioral response. This kind of assessment fits into the overall theory of CBT in that thoughts produce emotions and behavior. This fits into the *dynamic risk-factor model* of Andrews and Bonta (1994). In this sense, thoughts and emotions become the primary targets for change (Goldfried, 1995).

Thus, the task of assessment in cognitive-behavioral treatment involves a need to go beyond behavioral assessment or the gathering of historical information to the assessment of the client's feelings, thoughts, beliefs and underlying assumptions (Freeman et al., 1990). "Cognition, emotion and behavior are the three aspects of human functioning that are of prime importance in Cognitive Therapy and that are the targets of assessment of ongoing therapy" (Freeman et al., 1990, p. 32). Assessment in CBT treatment focuses on these three areas.

A number of techniques are available for assessing the three areas of cognition, affect and action. These include basic methods such as *clinical interviewing, self-report testing,* and *traditional psychological testing.* Most important for CBT are methods that are situationally relevant such as self-monitoring and real life observations.

Assessment in CBT treatment begins with the client's first contact with services that are directed at implementing change in his/her life. However, assessment in CBT treatment is continuous and ongoing. The evaluation of change in cognition, mood and action occurs at each treatment intervention point, between sessions and within the context of the individual's real-life setting. Expectations around this kind of assessment are tied in with the client's readiness for treatment and the stage of change the client is in as s/he progresses in the treatment process. This, then, sets the stage for two important focuses in treatment: 1) motivating the client for change and 2) understanding the stages that people progress through when making change.

Assessment of Life-Situation Problems

There are several areas of assessment, outside of the AOD abuse, legal and criminal conduct area, that need to be addressed at both the screening and more in-depth levels of evaluation. These pertain to current life-problems which the client may be experiencing. These areas are

- *Social-interpersonal adjustment:* problems in establishing supportive social relationships; problems in getting along with people; social isolation; restricted interests; lack of residential stability;

- *Productivity adjustment:* job adjustment problems; inadequate vocational and occupational skills; economic difficulties; income and economic adjustment;

- *Marital, family and relationship adjustment:* marital conflict; family problems; problems in close and intimate relationships; problems in parenting;

- *Health adjustment:* this area includes physician and self-reported medical and physical problems;

- *Psychological-emotional:* assessment for depression, anxiety and phobias, mood fluctuations, anger, levels of self-esteem, distrust of others and unusual and disturbed (psychotic-like) thinking.

At the screening level, criminal justice clients in the state of Colorado are briefly assessed in the areas of education and employment, family and marital problems, and emotional-psychological issues. This is done through the *Level of Supervision Inventory* and the *Adult Substance Use Survey.*

For more in-depth assessment of the above five areas, several instruments are available for use. For the psychological and emotional areas, the *Minnesota Multiphasic Personality Inventory II* (Butcher, Dahlstrom, Graham, Tellegan & Kaemmer, 1989) and the *Symptom Checklist 90* (SCL-90) (Derogatis, 1977) can be used. *The Life Situation Questionnaire* (Wanberg, 1995) can be used to assess the areas above. *The Moos Family Environment Scale* (Moos & Moos, 1981) provides a good assessment of the client's current family environment. More detailed discussion of the assessment of life situations problems for the SOA client will be discussed in Chapter 11, Section 2.

Assessment of Motivation and Readiness for Treatment

The work on *stages of change* (DiClemente, 1991; Prochaska & DiClemente, 1986; Prochaska, et al., 1992) has made it clear that an essential component of assessment is that of determining the client's readiness and motivation for treatment.

The area of treatment motivation and readiness should be assessed during the clinical intake interview. A number of questions and issues can be addressed to evaluate this area:

- willingness to be involved in treatment;

- whether the person feels a need for help at this time;

- whether the client has thought about making changes in particular areas;

- whether the client has actually made deliberate changes;

- degree of problem awareness;

- do others feel that the client should make changes or that the client needs help. There are a number of measures and scales that can be used in assessing this area.

High scores on the acknowledgement of a need for help (AWARENES) and the receptiveness to treatment (RECEPTIV) scales of the *Alcohol Use Inventory* (Horn et al., 1987) provide us with good indication of treatment motivation and readiness.

There are other scales which are directed specifically at measuring readiness for change and motivation for treatment. The *Stages of Change Readiness and Treatment Eagerness Scale (SOCRATES)* (Miller, 1994; Miller & Tonigan, 1996) provides a measure of the five areas of change: precontemplation, contemplation, determination, action and maintenance. The *Adult Self Assessment Questionnaire (ASAQ)* (Wanberg & Milkman, 1993) provides six specific and two broad measures of readiness and change. This test was originally developed and normed on adolescent clients but is currently being normed on adult clients.

Summary

We have provided the reader with some perspectives on the assessment of individuals with substance abuse problems and individuals with a history of criminal conduct. Chapter 11 provides the specific approach to and protocols for the screening and assessing the SAO clients admitted to the treatment program of *Strategies for Self-Improvement and Change (SSC).*

C H A P T E R ⑧
UNDERSTANDING AND ENHANCING CULTURAL COMPETENCE: CAPITALIZING ON THE STRENGTHS OF DIVERSITY[1]

Introduction

Effective CBT providers must consider the client's culture—the shared values, norms, traditions, customs, arts, history and institutions—that belong to his or her heritage and present sense of social belonging. A comprehensive view of culture necessarily includes ethnicity, race, gender and social class (Orlandi, Weston & Epstein, 1992).

The original term *culture* comes from the German word "kultur," which was used to distinguish the "more civilized" from less civilized national groups. Those with culture were viewed as more positive than more "primitive" groups who were viewed as not having culture. The definition has changed over the years, yet the qualitative element has sometimes remained. There have been a variety of definitions of culture. Witkin, Dyk, Faterson, Goodenough and Karp, (1962) defined the relationship between behavior and culture as consisting of standards for deciding what is, what can be, how one feels about it, what to do about it, and how to go about doing it. The *"it"* could be using drugs, seeking counseling or changing your personality.

A broad definition is that culture represents all of the behavioral, intellectual, mental, physical, social and artistic expressions and products of human effort and thought that describe, characterize and are peculiar to a particular group, community, class or society. A more individualized definition would be that culture is the way we, as individuals, make sense of our world. How do we relate to others in socially appropriate ways, how close do we stand, do we make eye contact or look down? In European American[2] culture people are accustomed to positioning themselves at a distance of at least six inches from each other's face—unless they are preparing to fight or make love.

Culture tells us what the rules of behavior are, and what we are to do to be accepted within a given group. These rules implicitly and explicitly relate to a variety of social constructs such as gender roles, perceptions of time, or our ideas regarding how emotional problems begin or change. The rules specify what appropriate gender role behavior is within any given culture. For example, drug use among traditional societies such as Hispanic groups is more frowned upon in women than men, thus making it more difficult for women from these cultures to seek treatment. Therefore, both client and counselor enter the therapeutic relationship with a set of cultural beliefs or, to use cognitive behavioral terminology, with a cognitive schema. What are these schema, and how do they influence the counseling process?

The primary question regarding enhancing cultural competence in treatment is this: *How does the provider enhance the treatment group and the individual client's understanding and utilization of the therapeutic change process, given the impact of unique and different cultural backgrounds and socialization experiences?* Out of these different backgrounds and experiences come basic views of self, psychological and social strengths and weaknesses, different values and beliefs, different role perceptions and different ways to communicate.

Of particular importance to cognitive-behavioral therapy is building self-efficacy and self-competence. Dimeff and Marlatt (1995) pose the question, "How do the internalized effects of race, class, and/or gender prejudice and discrimination interact with efforts to establish and maintain self efficacy?" (p. 178). While the goal of treatment is to heighten the SAO's sense of competence for maintaining a

[1] The authors would like to thank Patricia L. Kirk, M.P.A., Colorado Division of Youth Corrections and Ernest L. Chavez, Ph.D., Triethnic Center for Prevention Research, Colorado State University for their contributions made to this chapter.

[2] The term *European American* refers to people of Anglo and European descent or of the Caucasian group. The term *Anglo* is used interchangeable with European American in this text.

comfortable and responsible life, free of substance abuse and crime, the social portrayal of ethnic minorities, women and working-class individuals is that of "low achievers" (Wallace, 1991). It is a difficult task for the therapist and correctional specialist to help the client overcome the psychological deficits and factors that contribute to negative self-views, poor self-esteem and a sense of failure. It is doubly hard to overcome society's reinforcement of these self-views. The culturally competent provider recognizes that some clients are predisposed to expect failure, a self-fulfilling prophecy of low achievement, including tacit acceptance of impending relapse and recidivism.

The client's motivation to accept the challenge to change, demonstrate commitment to change, and maintain positive treatment effects may wane as he or she longs for the psychological comfort of regaining a recognizable sense of self—reestablishing earlier patterns of thought and behavior— despite social stigma or criminal sanctions. A sense of *learned helplessness* (Seligman, 1974, 1975) may prevail over the counselor's wishes and desires for the client to achieve positive treatment results.

Goals and Objectives of This Chapter

The goal of this chapter is to improve treatment outcomes with SAOs by increasing awareness of diversity and enhancing cultural competence among treatment providers. Culturally competent SSC providers recognize how cultural stereotyping, within and between group members, may undermine treatment objectives and impede personal growth. Equally important, they recognize how to draw upon their own cultural experiences to improve individual and group communication, with a corresponding increase in self-efficacy among group participants. Effective counselors acquire a set of cognitive, intrapersonal and interpersonal skills that facilitate others to increase their comprehension and appreciation of cultural commonalities and differences. "This requires a willingness and ability to draw on community-based values, traditions and customs and to work with knowledgeable persons of and from the community in developing focused interventions, communications, and other supports" (Orlandi et al., 1992). Improved cultural competence among SSC providers should result in more relevant treatment experiences for SAO clients, thereby improving client participation and enhancing treatment outcomes.

This chapter provides a philosophical framework and some practical ideas for improving services to minority groups. It emphasizes the cultural strengths inherent in all cultures and examines how the system of care can more effectively deal with cultural differences and related treatment issues. We explore critical aspects of understanding diversity and enhancing cultural competence. This is followed by a general discussion of issues that pertain to the inclusive category of certain minority populations. We then give consideration to special populations including ethnicity, gender and social class.

Understanding Cultural Competence

The American society is one of the most diverse (if not the most diverse) of all societies. The strength of American society is found in that diversity. Yet, this very diversity has led to limitations and restrictions on the rights and freedom of numerous cultures, particular minority groups.

Minority groups have historically had limited access to economic or political power and have, for the most part, been unable or not allowed to influence the structures that plan and administer programs. Many counseling professionals are beginning to recognize the relevance of culturally responsive treatment strategies. This acknowledgment has been evident by growing interest in recognizing diversity, cultural competency training and policy efforts to improve service delivery and more effectively deal with cultural differences and related service issues.

This movement is not universally embraced. Some professionals feel that it is wasteful, trendy and only "politically correct" to give lip service to developing a culturally competent system of care. Such critics do not seem to value the connection between cultural competency and effective service delivery.

Diversity awareness as outlined in this chapter focuses on enhancing the understanding of real and perceived differences among the many subgroups making up our society. *Diversity awareness* is much broader than a therapeutic or treatment issue. Appreciating the real differences that do exist among people is the essence of the *democratic attitude*. Developing viable programs to ensure equal opportunity regardless of those differences is the essence of a *democratic agenda*. Attenuating and eliminating the stereotypes and prejudicial attitudes based on perceived differences is the essence of the *democratic process*.

The *cultural competence* model explored in this document is defined as a set of congruent behaviors, attitudes and policies that come together in a system or agency or among professionals and enables that system, or those professionals, to work effectively in cross-cultural situations. The word *culture* is used because it implies the integrated pattern of human behavior that includes thoughts, communications, actions, customs, beliefs, values, and institutions of a racial, ethnic, religious or social group. The word *competence* is used because it implies having the capacity to function effectively.

1 The Continuum of Cultural Competence

Cultural competence may be viewed as a goal toward which professionals, agencies and systems can strive. Becoming culturally competent is a developmental process. Cross, Bazron, Dennis and Isaacs (1989) suggest that one may envision responding to cultural difference by imagining a continuum that ranges from cultural destructiveness to cultural proficiency. As shown in Table 8.1, there are at least six possibilities along the continuum:

Table 8.1

The Continuum of Cultural Competence

- Cultural Destructiveness—discriminatory or exclusionary policies;

- Cultural Incapacity—paternalistic/negative attitudes toward people of color and other culturally distinct groups;

- Cultural Blindness—culture viewed as neutral or irrelevant;

- Cultural Pre-Competence—sensitivity to cultural inadequacies in the organization;

- Cultural Competence—recognition of dynamics of cross-cultural interactions, presence of culturally-preferred service models;

- Cultural Proficiency—celebration of diversity, ongoing cultural self-assessment and knowledge building.

2 Essential Elements of a Culturally Competent Care System

The culturally competent system of care is made up of culturally competent institutions, agencies and professionals. Among these entities, there is a clear demonstration of awareness and acceptance of diversity. As shown in Table 8.2, five essential elements contribute to a system's or agency's ability to become more culturally competent (Cross et al., 1989).

Table 8.2

Elements of a Culturally Competent System

- value diversity;

- have the capacity for cultural self-assessment;

- be conscious of the dynamics inherent when cultures interact;

- have institutionalized cultural knowledge; and

- have developed adaptations to diversity.

3 Critical Considerations

In order for professionals to work effectively in cross-cultural situations and for programs and policies to truly head toward cultural competence, there are some critical factors to be kept in mind. These are based on the reality that people center on their own culture. A crucial step in building cultural competence in the provider and in the client is to move out from that center and develop a sense of non-judgmental tolerance. This further involves avoiding stereotype substitutions, understanding the resistance to change and seeing cultural competence as multifactorial. We now look at some of these critical factors relevant to the development of *cultural competence* (Isaacs & Benjamin, 1991).

Universal ethnocentricity

Humans tend to center on their own culture or group. This is true of all diverse groups with cultural identity: African Americans, European Americans, Asian Americans, and Hispanic Americans. All are ethnocentric. We usually value our own group over all others. *Cultural competence* involves the balancing of preserving one's own cultural identity while at the same time accepting and working toward enhancing the strengths and value found in other identifiable cultural groups. Up to recent times, very little attention has been given in American institutional structure to help people achieve that balance. It is that balance that helps us to live harmoniously in a pluralistic and multicultural society. The recent movement of peacemaking training is one effort to create this balance or harmony (e.g., Troester & Kelley, 1991). Therefore, each of us needs to learn and practice from a culturally competent perspective.

Non-judgmental tolerance

One step to creating the balance between preserving one's unique cultural values and enhancing the strengths of other cultures and to bring about a true shift in attitudes and behavior is to accept one's own ethnicity and another's without judgment. To do this, it is not necessary or possible to learn all about the numerous cultural groups and customs in this country. The key attribute to learn is *non-judgmental* tolerance based on the recognition that we all operate from an ethnocentric perspective.

Confusion between ethnicity and poverty

In our society, ethnic cultures are often confused with the culture of poverty or other socioeconomic conditions. Some believe that minority groups do not have cultures that are worth respecting or that the major culture of these groups is a "culture of poverty" (a common stereotype of African Americans) or a "culture of alcoholism" (often a stereotype of Native Americans) (Isaacs & Benjamin, 1991). Culturally aware treatment providers understand that the cultural strengths within many ethnic groups have allowed them to survive and grow in the midst of alien and often hostile environments. Culturally competent providers are fully aware that there are no cultures of "alcoholism," or of "poverty," but that alcoholism and poverty are the result of struggles to adapt, for better or worse, to the required interactions with the dominant society. It is important, therefore, to accept, seek, understand and utilize those cultural values and factors that have provided strength and sustenance to ethnic minority groups over time and incorporate them into treatment interventions and program designs.

Avoiding stereotype substitutions

In our attempts to become more sensitive to other cultures, we must avoid substituting one set of stereotypes for another. For example, the American society shifted from viewing Asian Americans as the *yellow peril* (during World War II) to viewing them as the *model minority* with respect to academic achievement and the exceptional student. For example, the latter stereotype has placed undue pressure on Asian Americans, often at the expense of good mental health. Any stereotype or overgeneralization, whether positive or negative, reflects cultural insensitivity.

Evolution of cultural competence

Cultural competence is a dynamic, developmental process and a state toward which we should strive, but it takes a long-term and consistent commitment to achieve. It is not something that comes to the individual, agency or system at a fixed point in time, or a "one-shot deal." The process is ongoing and continuous and is fraught with, to use our AOD metaphor, *slips and relapses*.

Provocation of strong feelings and resistance to change

Individuals who imbue cultural competence tend to evoke strong feelings and reactions. Although some of these reactions stem from the generalized response to any change, many are related to the historical interactions, hostilities and fears that have often marked relationships between ethnic minority groups and the dominant society. In order to move toward cultural competence, there must be willingness and courage to confront all the feelings and attitudes that cultural competence and change connote for the individual, the agency and society in general. Ongoing sharing, communication and dialogue are essential. Opportunities for such sharing and dialogue must be built into the therapeutic process and the structure of the agency or organization seeking to become more culturally competent.

Cultural competence is multidimensional and multifactorial

The degree of cultural competence that counseling professionals and agencies achieve is not dependent on any one factor. Attitudes, structures, policies and practices are the major arenas where development can and must occur. Attitudes change to become less ethnocentric, patronizing or biased. Policies change to become more flexible and culturally impartial. Practices become more congruent with the culture of the client, from the initial contact through termination. Organizational structures support and enhance the growth of cultural competence. Cultural competence is based on valuing diversity and the belief that it is all right to be different. Like other types of competencies, cultural competence is developed over time through training, experience, guidance and self-evaluation (Isaacs & Benjamin, 1991).

4 Necessary Ingredients for Culturally Competent Programs

There are a number of institutional and individual factors, indicated by the literature, that enhance cultural competency in treatment providers and in treatment programs (Isaacs & Benjamin, 1991). Some of these are reviewed.

Commitment to change

There must be a real commitment to developing programs and services that are strongly based on the needs and strengths of the ethnic minority communities.

Ongoing process and outcome evaluation

Needs assessments and planning are vital activities that must take place in the context of the community and involve the leadership and organizations that are respected in the community. Ethnic minority communities are dynamic and ever-changing, which means that the assessment and planning process is an ongoing one and not just a one-time exercise.

Minority involvement at all levels of service delivery

Agencies must strive to hire ethnic minority professionals at all levels of the agency. At the same time, they must offer the necessary training and skills development to make them effective with clients. Just hiring ethnic minority professionals, many of whom are trained in very traditional programs, is not enough. Ongoing cultural training for all staff must be viewed as a critical component of the service program as well.

5 The Culture of Counseling Versus Traditional Cultures

Psychotherapy and counseling have developed a set of cultural values, many of which are based on dominant European American society. These values represent underlying philosophical elements of counseling.

Sue and Sue (1990) have identified some of the characteristics of the *culture of counseling:* verbal emotional expressiveness, individual orientation, openness and intimacy and a somewhat linear cause-effect orientation. Others include placing responsibility on the shoulders of the client, having the client take the lead in counseling and equality of roles in relationships. One of the most important components of the culture of counseling is self-disclosure.

Dana (1993) also identifies a number of the values and beliefs that underlie the work of Western society's human service providers. These include action orientation, individualism and competition, hierarchical power, controlled communication, Protestant ethic, Western scientific method, progress and history, traditional family structure, a tradition of religion and aesthetics and a scientific orientation toward problem solving.

First, these various values of the *culture of counseling* may be at *odds* with the values of many ethnic minority cultures. The culture and values of counseling will sometimes confuse the client with a different cultural orientation (Dana, 1993). For example, individualism and the scientific method are not as highly valued by a number of cultural groups, Asians and American Indians being distinct examples. In American Indian, Hispanic and Asian culture, the orientation is less individualized and more collective or communal in nature, and when cooperation rather than competition is tied into this orientation, the culturally traditional individual's view of appropriate behavior will be obviously different from that of the majority. With some cultures, self-disclosure to strangers is not acceptable.

These values and culture of counseling can also be at variance with the dominant American culture. For example, American culture is based on rugged individualism, being independent and solving your own problems. Other common values of the American family is "keep your problems to your self" and "don't hang your dirty linen in public." Problem solving in American culture has been based on an adversarial model and blaming someone for the problem. The problem is solved when one can prove one party is right and one party is wrong—a win-lose solution model. Even somewhat paradoxical to the previous American values is the value of not being selfish. Just the opposite, the culture of psychotherapy is premised on seeking help for problem solving, "hanging out your dirty linen" through self-disclosure, working toward a win-win solution with people close to you, taking responsibility for your problems rather than blaming and being selfish in terms of getting your own needs met, but not at the expense of others. These different cultural orientations are some of the reasons why rapport building and trust development in psychotherapy are often hard tasks to accomplish.

Counselors should consider all of these issues when attempting to meet the needs of the culturally different client or of clients whose cultural orientation is in contrast to the culture of counseling and psychotherapy. Culturally competent treatment providers are sensitive to these issues and show flexibility in the counseling process in order to facilitate the therapeutic interaction while at the same time not compromising the values and culture of counseling. An in-depth comprehension of the client's cultural background facilitates this process.

6 Improving Ethnic Focus in Service Delivery

Minority populations are underrepresented in community mental health services, although they experience as much stress, or more, than non-minorities. This may indicate that counseling is not perceived as vital or relevant to their needs. According to Sue and Zane (1987), "the single most important explanation for the problem of service delivery (for ethnic minorities) involves the inability of therapists to provide culturally responsive forms of treatment" (p. 37). Atkinson, Morten and Sue (1993) cite language and cultural differences between clients and treatment providers, lack of training in cultural sensitivity and supervisory failure to confront and challenge racism among white trainees as contributing factors to the large-scale failure of counseling for minority groups (p. 49).

Regarding the hazards of misconstrued language, Scott and Bordovsky (1990) find that cross-cultural counseling may falter when:

- participants misinterpret each other's statements;

- language differences support negative and prejudicial attitudes between participants;

- different styles of communicating are not experienced as positive expressions of the client's identity (p. 167).

Concerning therapist-client communication, it may be presumptuous to assume that all group members—especially the undereducated—have the verbal skills to profit from extensive "talk" therapy, particularly when confronted by a counselor who uses complicated or abstract concepts to facilitate change. Some counselors may have an attitudinal bias against clients who speak with an accent or do not use standard grammatical constructions (Padilla et al., 1991; Sue and Sue, 1990).

If the client is other than English-speaking, or if he or she speaks English but is more comfortable in another language, obviously the counseling must be done in the language of the client. There are times when English-speaking professionals attempt to do counseling in English with a client that speaks some English, but whose skills are far below those needed to comprehend the counseling jargon.

A concern during the mid-1990s developed around different dialects in different cultures or ethnic groups. An example is represented by the focus on Ebonics (a combination of the words "ebony" and "phonics") as a possible "second language" for some African Americans. Whether or not Ebonics is considered as an "official second language" is still in debate (Cose, 1997; Leland & Joseph, 1997). The fact is that this language variation or dialect does exist, and that counselors need to understand the content components and syntax of this variation in order to work effectively and communicate with some African American clients.

Counselors who have themselves received counseling become acculturated to the counseling culture and use terminology from that culture. One example is the use of the term *self-concept*. Some use this term as if everyone has the same definition. A client might have an entirely different definition from the one used by the counselor. Successful counselors must make certain that words are being used in a similar manner by both counselor and client. In consideration of the significant number of SAOs for whom Spanish is their first (or only) language, the *SSC Participant's Workbook* has been translated into Spanish with close attention to nuances in words and concepts.

Pertinent to the issue of the culture of counseling, the use of swear words by the therapist or counselor is a common occurrence. This is particularly true in the language of therapeutic confrontation (Ellis, 1990, *Live Demonstration of Rational-Emotive Therapy)*. To some individuals from some subcultures of religious or moral persuasion, this may be offensive and damaging to building rapport with the client.

Counselors' unfamiliarity with minority body language may result in misunderstanding a client's postures, gestures or inflections (Sue, 1990; Sue & Sue, 1990). European Americans, for example, tend to look away (avoid eye contact) when speaking to another person more often than do African Americans. However, when listening to another person, African Americans are more likely to avoid eye contact while European Americans make eye contact. This may account for the treatment provider's erroneous perception that African American participants are not paying attention to their counseling suggestions or didactic presentations. It has also been reported that teachers or counselors may perceive that African Americans are more angry because of what is perceived as an "intense stare" when speaking (Sue, 1990; Sue & Sue, 1990).

7 | The Counselor's Personal Beliefs and Cultural Bias

Counselors enter the counseling process with sets of beliefs related to the problems faced by clients. They also have cultural backgrounds of their own which to some extent dictate their personal view of the world. The counselor's cultural schema influences his or her perceptions of others, how he or she interacts with others and how change occurs. The competent counselor is aware of his or her cultural schema. Sue and Sue (1990) view one of the elements of a culturally sensitive counselor as someone who has an awareness of his or her own values, assumptions and biases. If counselors have not considered these issues, they will be less apt to deliver appropriate treatment interventions. Counselors may become aware of their cultural schema by doing the following exercise.

Create a list of adjectives that best describe the client they are about to see. Client characteristics to which the counselor should attend are gender, ethnicity or race, and type of problem. For example, make a list of the adjectives you would use to describe this client: A 24-year-old Chicana who has been arrested for physically abusing her six-month-old child. The child was beaten and was hospitalized. After her arrest it is found that the client is addicted to heroin.

What assumptions would you make? How would these assumptions change as we change the client characteristics? For instance, what if the person were a male instead of a female, or a White non-Hispanic, African American, or Asian, not abusing drugs? Each of these client characteristics influences our perceptions of the client. These influences from our own cultural schema affect our behavior in both subtle and obvious ways. The counselor must be aware of these issues so that interventions are not unconsciously and inappropriately affected.

8 Understanding the Client's Cultural Identity

After appreciating one's own biases and stereotypes, the next area to be considered is the client's cultural background. This involves understanding the different *nuances* of the client's cultural background as well as the client's ethnic and racial identity.

There are cultural backgrounds outside of ethnic and racial identities that impact on the treatment process. For example, clients who spent their developmental years in a rural culture or who currently live in a rural culture may have different sets of values than clients from an urban culture (e.g., the Iowa farmer versus the corporate executive). The therapist may be wise to wear informal clothing, even jeans, when providing services within a rural, farming community; whereas the therapist servicing a corporate executive in an urban society may want to wear a coat and tie. Although these may seem to be very obvious factors, many counselors do not tune into these kinds of cultural differences.

More specifically, we need to give careful consideration to the ethnic or racial identity of our clients. Bernal and Knight (1995) outline three components of ethnic or racial identity which are helpful in enhancing provider cultural competence:

- self identification, which is the extent to which an individual perceives him- or herself as a member of any given ethnic or racial group;

- the degree to which the client understands the values, customs and traditions of his or her group; and

- the client's unique perceptions and feelings about his or her group.

When evaluating self-identification, the issue of *acculturation* should be considered. To what extent does this client see him- or herself as a member of a particular ethnic group? For example, the client may have a Spanish surname but not perceive himself as Chicano. This lack of identification could be due to having become acculturated to the dominant culture or due to a general lack of information regarding their own ethnicity. Even if the client does self-identify as a member of a particular ethnic or racial group, to what extent does the client have knowledge of and adhere to her or his own culture's traditions? These data will allow the counselor to adapt the counseling in a culturally appropriate manner increasing the likelihood of positive outcome of any given intervention.

Dana (1993) gives a step-wise typology for assessing multicultural clients. He suggests the assessment of cultural orientation such as *nontraditional, bicultural, marginal and traditional.*

Nontraditional are those who have acculturated to the dominant culture and have little association with their own traditional culture. Some authors would argue that nontraditional will suffer psychological consequences related to denying elements of themselves, but this assumption is controversial.

Bicultural persons are able to function well in both their own traditional culture and in majority culture. Biculturalism can exist as an orthogonal process, which means that the two cultural processes existing within the person are independent: the person can be placed across a continuum of being high, medium or low in each of the two cultures.

Someone who is low in both cultural orientations is much like Dana's *marginal* person. This is an individual who does not have a connection with either the dominant majority culture or his or her traditional culture. These individuals are disconnected from all of their societies and are in a state of *anomie* or isolation from cultural identity or involvement. There is some suggestion that these individuals are more susceptible to psychological disorders and other problem behaviors.

The fourth type is the *traditional* individual, one who is primarily associated with his or her traditional culture. These individuals might well be suffering from culture shock or transcultural difficulties as they attempt to establish themselves in majority culture and still retain their culture of origin.

It is helpful for the provider to understand a particular client with respect to these four types. Such understanding will provide a guideline for developing effective approaches to people of different cultural and ethnic backgrounds.

9 Ethnic Differences Between Counselors and Clients

Many potential clients prefer a counselor who has ethnic similarities. This is often true for African Americans, Native Americans, Asian Americans and Hispanics (Atkinson et al., 1993). Unfortunately, recruitment and graduate training of ethnically diverse human service providers has not been proportional to the ethnic group representation in the population. For example, Russo and colleagues compared enrollment in psychology graduate courses from 1972 through 1980 and found that minority graduates in doctoral programs only increased from 6.7 percent to 8 percent during this period (Russo, Olmedo, Stapp & Fulcher, 1981). Subsequent studies suggest that these findings remain constant through 1990 and may explain the "under-utilization of mental health services" (Atkinson et al., 1993, p. 51). The minority psychologist underrepresentation finding may be similar in other mental health professions (e.g., substance abuse counselors, parole or probation personnel). These authors suggest that there is a tendency for training programs to overlook the strengths of underrepresented applicants and that programs should be more proactive in their recruitment of minority counselors and therapists.

Training programs should not only recruit more ethnic minorities; courses for graduate students also should address the need for sensitivity to stereotyping and racial differences. Changes in training programs, however, would require that those teaching graduate courses *address their own biases and tendencies to stereotype before they can instill new values in their students.*

Research suggests that diagnosis and treatment of minorities may also be different from that of European American clients. Such diagnostic and treatment protocols may be the result of stereotyping on the part of counselors and could contribute to the reluctance of clients to continue in treatment. Further, treatment professionals need to develop an awareness that their values may conflict with those of the minority client. Such inherent difference in values may include such basic issues as "the willingness to make and keep counseling appointments" (Atkinson et al., 1993, p. 52), the willingness to self-disclose, cultural differences in attitudes regarding sexual behavior or a need for more structure in counseling sessions.

Treatment Considerations for Special Populations

According to the 1990a census, one out of every four Americans is non-White (U.S. Bureau of the Census, 1990a), and many of these groups are growing dramatically (Henry, 1990). In this section, we focus on several special population groups, including African Americans, Hispanics and Native Americans. We also focus on gender and economic status as considerations in developing cultural competence within the client and provider. Cultural diversity issues are described for each group with the aim of improving counselor empathy and communication in therapeutic endeavors. The section concludes with additional considerations according to gender and social class.

1 African Americans

Demographic and Socioeconomic Factors

African Americans are the largest minority group in the United States, accounting for 12.1 percent of the American population (U.S. Bureau of the Census, 1990b). There are over 25 million African Americans living in the United States, with the majority living in urban settings. Thirty percent of African Americans are below the poverty line in the 1990 Census, and the average net worth of White families was 13 times that of African American families. Although poverty is certainly a reality in African American culture, there is an increasingly affluent African American middle class. "Since 1967 the number of Black families with incomes of more than $50,000 has quadrupled to more than 1 million, and with this increased wealth has come an increase in education, leisure and interest in arts" (White, 1994).

Substance Use Problems

With respect to substance abuse, a 1985 *National Institute on Drug Abuse* survey estimated that 3.2 million African Americans used drugs in the past year and 1.7 million African Americans used an illicit drug in the past month. The survey indicated that African American men 35 years of age or over were much more likely to abuse illicit substances than European Americans (cocaine—5.5% of African American males had used cocaine in the past year vs. 1.9% of Hispanics and 1.2% of Anglos).

Data collected from the *National Drug and Alcoholism Treatment Utilization Survey* (National Institute on Drug Abuse, 1983) indicate that African Americans and Hispanics are three times as likely as Anglos to be in treatment for substance abuse. Additionally, a significant portion of African American substance abusers have been found to suffer from other forms of psychological problems such as affective or anxiety disorders, antisocial personality disorder, schizophrenia or other substance abuse disorders which make them more resistant to traditional substance abuse or correctional treatment (Kosten, Rounsavalle, Kleber, 1985). An important consequence of intravenous drug use is HIV infection. In the 1980s, African Americans and Hispanics constitute 44 percent of the total IV drug use related AIDS cases and African Americans constitute 50 percent of the cases of AIDS among heterosexual intravenous drug users. Perhaps even more striking is the finding that African Americans and Hispanics constitute 41 percent of the reported cases of AIDS (Centers for Disease Control, 1986).

Within treatment populations, it does not appear that African Americans reflect more severity of alcohol abuse problems than European and Hispanic Americans. In a study of 230 Veterans Administration Patients using the *Drug Use Self Report* (Wanberg & Horn, 1989a, 1989b), there was no difference on mean scores on the DISRUPT scale (scale that measures symptoms and negative consequences resulting from substance use) and the DEPEND scale (scale that measures the nine criteria for substance use dependency in the DSM III-R) across the three ethnic groups. Anglos, compared with African Americans and Hispanic Americans, scored significantly higher on alcohol involvement and significantly lower on cocaine involvement, and African Americans, when compared with Anglos and Hispanics, scored significantly higher on cocaine involvement and significantly lower on alcohol involvement.

In another study comparing the four ethnic groups of European, African, Hispanic and Native Americans across the *negative consequences* and *disruption* scales on the *Alcohol Use Inventory,* no differences were found between the first three ethnic groups, but Native Americans, on the average, scored higher on symptom and disruption scores and significantly higher on poverty level income and significantly lower on years of education (Horn et al., 1987; Wanberg, Lewis & Foster, 1978).

These findings of no appreciable differences across the three major ethnic groups with respect to substance abuse problems was replicated in an adolescent sample (Wanberg, 1992). There were no differences in mean scores on the DSM III-R scale and the disruption scales across the three major ethnic groups.

The Criminal Justice System

With respect to crime, African Americans appear to be more likely to commit crimes than are European Americans. About 45 percent of those arrested for serious crimes are African American. However, there appear to be many more *unfounded arrests* with the greater likelihood of African Americans being jailed before trial, paying on the average twice as much bail as Anglos, and receiving heavier sentences for the same crime ("Crime in America", 1996, p. 25). Although African Americans make up 12 percent of the American population, with 13 percent saying they used drugs in the past month, yet they account for 35 percent of arrests for drug possession, 55 percent of convictions, and 74 percent of prison sentences.

The overrepresentation of African Americans in the criminal justice system may in part be related to a cultural preference for crack and the difference in the legal sanctions between cocaine and crack. The mandatory federal penalty for possessing *five grams of crack* (about two days of supply for an addict) is five years in jail. Possession of *half a kilo of cocaine* would get the same five-year jail sentence. Anglos prefer powder cocaine use over smoking crack ("Crime in America", 1996). What is most important is that a study by Hatsukami and Fischman (1996) concludes that the physiological and psychoactive effects of the different forms of cocaine are so similar as to make the existing discrepancy in punishment "excessive."

A study of sentencing in the 1980s indicated that the largest increase in the prison population was among "non-underclass" Blacks convicted for drug offenses. According to the *Sentencing Project* (a Washington-based penal reform group), one-third of 20 to 29-year-old African American men are on probation, on parole, or in prison; that is, prison is increasingly becoming the cultural norm ("Crime in America," 1996, p. 25).

What is important about the information summarized above is that, although within treatment populations, African Americans probably do not differ from other ethnic groups with respect to the consequences and symptoms resulting from drug use, this ethnic group does receive different criminal sanctioning. Most likely, this difference in criminal justice punishment would impact on treatment outcomes for the African American SAO. Just how is not clear.

Treatment Issues for African Americans

For African Americans, their rich history and culture define unifying experiences that aid in the design and implementation of more effective treatment programs. In the United States, African Americans have developed a worldview that combines their historical experiences with their present striving in which they share a language, values and symbols. As defined by Karenga (1980), *the Black Value System*, the *Nguzo Saba*, consisting of seven principles, guides "functioning in an Afrocentric frame of reference" (Butler, 1992, p. 29). These seven principles, recognized in the African American holiday of Kwanzaa, include *unity, self-determination, collective work and responsibility, cooperative economics, purpose, creativity, and faith*. The core elements of African American culture define the group's individual and collective reality. These core elements include *self-identity, knowledge, emotions* and *behavior*.

By definition, African Americans are group members, and each individual's self-identity is tied to the group. African Americans have been described as highly cohesive and emotionally expressive, often responding spontaneously in a "sense of oneness with life and of harmony with nature" (Butler, 1992, p. 32). Individuals are becoming more consciously aware of their origins, their interdependence and interrelationship on past and present generations. Knowledge comes from a combination of symbols, language and rituals transmitted from elders to the next generation. "Life experiences are given depth and meaning through the realization of their interrelatedness and significance in the life and existence of the group" (Butler, 1992, p. 32). This identity as group members may bode well for treating individual members in a group setting.

Bell and Evans (1981) posit that, because of transgenerational discrimination in the United States, the African American must be understood through a double-consciousness model (p. 28). The model examines two critical racial perspectives, coexistent in African American consciousness: *1) How I see myself as a Black person*—acculturated, bicultural, traditional, culturally immersed? Do other Black people see me in the same way as I view myself? *2) How I see Anglos*—racist, covert racist, culturally ignorant, culturally liberated, color blind? In relationship to Anglos: Do I see myself as inferior, superior, equal, powerful or powerless? How do Anglo people see me in relationship to power and acculturation?

It is important that the provider understand the impact of these perceptions (how I see myself; how I see others) and *meta-perceptions* (how I see others see me) on the effectiveness of the delivery of treatment services to the African American. For example, the strong African American identity factor can become a major strength in SAO treatment. Change is strengthened and reinforced when abstinence from drug use and living a crime-free life is associated with a strong sense of cultural pride.

2 Hispanic Americans

Demographics and Terms

A report issued by the *American Council on Education* (Carter & Wilson, 1992) indicated that Hispanics accounted for over 8 percent of the total American population in 1989. A U.S. Census

Bureau forecaster predicted that Hispanics would surpass African Americans as the largest minority group within the United States by 2015 (Dunn, 1991).

The term *Hispanic* is frequently misunderstood. It was used by the U.S. Bureau of Census in 1980 to designate individuals living in the United States whose cultural origins are in Mexico, Puerto Rico, Cuba, Central America and other Latin American countries. This term, however, was not used as an ethnic label before its introduction in the late 1970s and is not universally accepted by those to whom it refers. Among Hispanics with ties to Mexico, for example, one may find self-references to Mexicano, Mexican American, Chicano or Spanish American. Some deplore the term *Hispanic* because of its association with the Spanish Conquistadors. Terminology aside, there are now more than 20 million Hispanics in the United States (U.S. Bureau of the Census, 1990c). The majority (63%) are of Mexican ancestry who reside primarily in the Southwest and Western regions. In contrast to the widespread perception that Hispanics are agricultural workers, approximately 90 percent live in large urban centers.

Substance Abuse Among Hispanics

According to the National Household Survey on Drug Abuse (National Institute on Drug Abuse, 1987), Hispanics have a lower lifetime rate of illicit drug use in comparison to the general population, with the exception of slightly higher consumption of cocaine (11.0% vs. 10.7%), crack (2.2% vs. 1.3%), and heroin (1.1% vs. 1.0%). Some findings show an inverse relationship between ties to Hispanic culture and illicit drug use. "Of Hispanics born in the United States, 53% reported using some illicit drugs during their lifetime, compared to only 25% of those born in Puerto Rico and 11% of Hispanics born in other Hispanic countries" (Ruiz & Langrod, 1992, p. 869). A parallel finding is that 45 percent of Hispanics who speak primarily English had used illicit drugs during their lifetime, compared to only 8 percent who speak mostly Spanish.

Within adult clinical groups, Hispanics do not differ from Anglos and African Americans with respect to the disruption and negative consequences from alcohol or substance abuse (Horn et al., 1987; Wanberg et al., 1978). The same findings hold up for adolescent criminal justice clients who were identified as having salient AOD problems and issues (Wanberg et al., 1992).

Treatment Issues for Hispanic Americans

Differential treatment for Hispanic clients will not rest on the disruption and results of AOD use (as noted above). Rather, such differences between Hispanic and non-Hispanic substance abuse clients are based on sociocultural factors in which horizontal mobility (foreign or domestic migration) and/or vertical mobility (an upward or downward stress-producing move on the economic totem pole) play an important role. This social whirlpool provokes continuous and cumulative stress leading sometimes to escapism through AOD use and abuse (Gomez & Vega, 1981, p. 717).

Treatment programs developed and operated by European American professionals often have not developed the cultural component and awareness that successfully attract working class and lower socioeconomic Hispanics, nor do they retain these populations in treatment (Ruiz & Langrod, 1992, p. 862). There are *few bilingual* staff in these programs. In many instances non-Spanish speaking staff have difficulty relating to the specific problems confronted by the Hispanic client. Government or treatment regulations are sometimes at odds with the cultural schema of the Spanish-speaking SAO. Compulsory urine testing, for example, with its connotation of disbelieving the client's word, may offend the Hispanic participant's sense of dignity, passionately defended within his or her minority population (Ruiz & Langrod, 1992).

When urine analysis (UA) testing is hooked entirely into criminal justice monitoring, and not into treatment, it will only serve to increase distrust and suspicion. UA testing has its greatest advantage when rapport and trust are established with the client, and when the client understands that UA testing serves to strengthen the trust between client and counselor.

It is widely recognized that family, *la familia*, is of central importance to Hispanic culture. Most research points to the value of involving the family in the treatment process (Ruiz & Langrod, 1992). Hispanic families have strong networking systems which can enhance the treatment process. The provider's respect for and comprehension of the individual roles of all family members should be included in treatment settings. Traditionally, each member of the Hispanic family plays a special role: grandparents are respected for their wisdom, fathers for their authority, mothers for their commitment, children for their promise in the future; and godparents for their availability and support during times of crisis. "To not use these family resources when treating Hispanic American addicts represents not only a poor quality of care, but also negligence" (Ruiz & Langrod, 1992, p. 872).

Geographic mobility and migration often play a negative role in the fight against substance abuse and crime. It can lead to the breakdown of the family network, therefore rendering unbonded family members more vulnerable to deviant associates and escape-oriented activities. Key Hispanic cultural values such as dignity, respect and love (*dignidad, respeto y carino*) can all be used in the therapeutic process. Disenfranchised clients may be encouraged to visit their native country, make telephone calls, and correspond with distant, yet cherished, family members. Group discussions with a skillful focus on historical or patriotic themes may improve participant self-esteem and treatment alliance. It is important to recognize that Mexican Americans may often benefit from recognition and appreciation of their strong Indian heritage derived from the Aztec and Mayan cultures. Further, the tendency to value church affiliations, whether Catholic or other, or non-institutional religious beliefs and practices, including *Spiritism, Santeria, Brujeria,* and *Curanderism,* may play a positive role in increasing client comfort and a sense of belonging and stability.

3 Native Americans

Native Americans have a unique history with respect to the use of alcohol and other drugs in our society. First, they are the only ethnic group in the American society specifically targeted by the United States government to which the sale of alcohol was forbidden—from 1802 to 1953 (May, 1989). This may account for a strong norm of alcohol abstinence across Native American groups (May, 1977). Second, this population has received high attention with respect to intervention and treatment services. Alcohol abuse ranks high as a social and medical problem, if not foremost, among Native American populations (Price, 1975; Snake, Hawkins & La Boueff, 1977; Weibel-Orlando, 1987).

There is a common stereotype that Native Americans are more prone to the effects of alcohol and to alcohol addiction, and that the typical Native American pattern of drinking is to drink rapidly over a long period of time with the main goal of getting drunk (Lurie, 1971; Weisner, Weibel-Orlando & Long, 1984). Yet, studies have failed to show a significant difference in alcohol metabolism among Native Americans (Bennion & Li, 1976; Farris & Jones, 1978; Westermeyer, 1992; Zeiner, Paredes & Cowden, 1976).

There are studies to indicate that Native American clients in treatment do show more severe expressions of alcohol disruptions and symptom patterns. A study by Wanberg and associates (Horn et al., 1987; Wanberg et al., 1978) compared randomly selected samples of European Americans, Native Americans, African Americans and Hispanic Americans from a large population of alcoholism patients. Mean scores on education, married versus not married, family income, unemployment, drinking-related social role disruption, quantity of alcohol use, and a scale measuring deterioration or disruption due to alcohol use were compared across the four groups. In all measures except one, the Native American group scored in the direction of being more socially, economically, vocationally and alcohol-related disrupted. Native Americans ranked third (and Hispanic Americans fourth) with respect to fewer years of education. As well, Native Americans scored higher than the other three groups on gregarious drinking.

The fallacy of the stereotypical views of Native Americans is most exposed in the fact of the high degree of variance found in the population. Native Americans differ across tribal groups, socioeconomic strata, age and living environments. Thus, it may not always be helpful to identify Native Americans as a target population because of this variance. For example, in a study comparing a sample of Native Americans in an urban treatment setting with a sample in a rural, reservation treatment setting, using the scales of the *AUI*, it was found that the rural Native Americans showed significantly less alcohol-related problems and disruption (Horn et al., 1987).

Outcome studies of alcoholism treatment have indicated low rates of success among Native Americans (Weibel-Orlando, 1987). In part, this is probably because clients in this population come to treatment at a late stage, having lost family support, being unemployed, with few job skills (Westermeyer, 1992). However, a conclusion that has been made about poor treatment outcome has been that the traditional European culture has not met the needs of the Native American client (Weibel-Orlando, 1987; Westermeyer, 1992). Such findings have led treatment and research experts to call for more *indigenous Native American healing methods* for alcoholism and drug abuse (Weibel-Orlando, 1987, 1989; Westermeyer, 1992).

Several treatment emphases are indicated from studies comparing Native Americans with other ethnic groups. High socializing and gregarious drinking would support the use of self-help and 12-step groups, peer mentoring and role modeling for this population. Because of the severity of drug abuse and social role disruption in socioeconomic functioning in this population, there is a high need for more structured programs, transitional living resources, high-impact job and vocational counseling and programs which address social role responsibility. Given these impressions and findings, the social-role learning and community reinforcement components of CBT should be strongly emphasized.

4 Substance Abuse Issues for Women

Demographics and Prevalence Rates

Over the past 20 years, the treatment of women with substance abuse problems has received priority status. This is in part due to the trend of an increased number of women with substance abuse problems and the equalization of the impact of AOD use on women as compared with men. For example, in the Horn & Wanberg studies in the late 1960s comparing men and women alcoholism patients, women scored lower on a factor measuring classical alcoholism-physiological symptoms, long binge drinking (Horn & Wanberg, 1973; Wanberg & Horn, 1970). Using samples from the same treatment center almost a decade later, this difference all but vanished (Horn et al., 1987). The proportion of women admitted to treatment in the 1960s was around 15 percent. Today, that percentage rate, in many treatment programs, is as high as 50 percent.

Williams, Grant, Harford and Noble (1989) estimated that in 1990 there were 1,811,000 adult women (age 18 and above) and 2,784,000 adult women who could be diagnosed as suffering from alcohol abuse and alcohol dependence respectively, in any 12-month period. The total of nearly 5 million women affected compares with more than 10 million males who suffer from alcohol abuse or dependence, showing a male:female ratio of about 2:1. Regarding drugs other than alcohol, 5.8 percent of American women admitted some illicit drug use during the past month (National Institute on Drug Abuse, 1987). Among women of child bearing age (18-34) the prevalence was higher: 14.1 percent for ages 18 to 25 and 9.6 percent for 26-to-34-year-olds. Regular use of marijuana, defined as once a week or more, was reported at 6 percent for women between the ages of 18 and 25. The 1987 Survey, by definition, excludes women not living in households (e.g. military, college dormitories, homeless); therefore, these prevalence rates must be considered as very conservative estimates (Blume, 1992).

Gender Differences

There are noticeable gender differences in the symptom pattern of addictive disorders. Today, although alcoholic women appear in treatment about the same age as male alcoholics, with about the same degree of alcohol dependence, they begin heavy drinking at a later age and their age of first drunk is significantly later than that of men (Gomberg, 1986; Schmidt, Klee & Ames, 1990; Wanberg & Horn, 1970; Wanberg & Knapp, 1969). This suggests a *telescoping* or more rapid development, of the course of the illness in women (Smith & Cloninger, 1981). While alcoholic women drink less than their male counterparts, they are more likely to use other sedative drugs (e.g. Valium or Xanax) in tandem with alcohol.

A number of studies point to three patterns that differentiate men from women. First, women tend to fit the *solo, isolative* pattern of use more than men (Gomberg, 1986; Horn & Wanberg, 1973; Horn, et al., 1987; Schmidt et al, 1990). However, this difference has clearly attenuated over the past 20 years, and the prevalence of gregarious, convivial drinking is a common pattern now found among women.

A second pattern that is gender-differentiative is that women tend to score higher on *emotional and psychological disruptions* resulting from AOD use. Women tend to use alcohol and other drugs, more than men, to manage moods and psychological distress (Blume, 1992; Horn & Wanberg, 1973; Horn et al., 1987). This same finding was found among adolescent females with AOD problems. Girls scored significantly higher on the psychological problems scale than boys (Wanberg, 1992).

Finally, a third pattern that is apparent is that women tend to indicate *less social role disruption* due to AOD use. For example, women score lower on the *Alcohol Use Inventory* social role maladaptation scale than do men (Horn et al., 1987). This is certainly congruent with fewer women in the criminal justice system.

Treatment Considerations

The above gender differences with respect to AOD use and abuse, as well as other psychosocial differences not discussed above call for sensitivity to women's special needs throughout the treatment process as shown in Table 8.3 (Blume, 1992, p. 801). The table provides some gender-specific treatment needs for women with AOD use problems.

Table 8.3

Gender-Specific Treatment Needs for Women

◆ attention should be given to a history of physical and sexual abuse with this topic gently approached because of the deep feelings of shame associated with physical and sexual abuse;

◆ assessment for concurrent mental health problems;

◆ assessment for medical problems—women develop late-stage physical damage more rapidly than men;

◆ involvement of family members is important partly due to the fact that women clients are more likely to have spouses with AOD problems, and children who suffer fetal alcohol or drug effects;

◆ parenting education and information about AOD addressing fetal AOD effects, AIDS prevention, and other STDs;

◆ availability of child care to enhance accessibility of treatment services;

◆ female role models, including women staff who have overcome AOD disorders, are helpful in treatment and utilization of women's self-help groups;

◆ assertiveness training may improve the characteristic low self esteem of chemically dependent women;

◆ issues of sexism (e.g., unequal social roles or undervaluation of women's contributions) should be explored in relationship to the client's personal experience;

◆ awareness that dependence on therapy may reinforce the social stereotyping and self-fulfilling prophecy that women can't make it on their own;

◆ special populations of women with AOD abuse need focused attention, such as lesbian women, who appear to have higher AOD dependency problems; they may profit from gay or lesbian self-help groups.

Blume (1992) finds that female AOD abusers in the criminal justice system are often overlooked, although their need for gender-specific treatment is high. Although there is no consensus regarding the treatment efficacy of individual versus group therapy for females, or all women versus mixed-sex groups, it is of fundamental importance that the woman client "have adequate opportunity to explore issues that she may find hard to discuss with male patients" (Blume, 1992, p. 802). Sensitive topics may be more thoroughly and appropriately discussed either in individual counseling or an all-female group. Vocational education opportunities for women in treatment should transcend traditional or stereotypic female job categories. Finally, staff training and ongoing supervision should be geared toward maintaining a non-sexist attitude in the treatment of women with AOD abuse problems.

5 The Culture of Poverty

There is a clear culture of poverty. Recessions in the late 1970s and early 1980s, reduction in government benefits paid to indigent people and welfare reform legislation of the 1990s have all contributed to the culture of poverty in the closing decade of the 20th century. By 1982 social services programs were funded at about $9 billion less than the funding allocation prior to 1981. During the 1980s poverty affected between 12 percent and 15 percent of the population. "By 1989 about 31.7 million Americans lived below the official poverty level of $12,675 per year for a family of four" (Joseph, 1992, p. 876). In addition, there was great imbalance in the racial distribution of poor people. From 1980 to 1989 the levels of poverty vacillated between 30 and 35 percent for African Americans, 25 and 30 percent for Hispanics and 10 and 20 percent for Anglos. About 19.6 percent of children under 18 years of age and 22.5 percent of those who were under 6 years were being reared in poverty, usually in one- parent families headed by the mother (Pear, 1990).

It was conservatively estimated that in 1987 there were roughly one-half million homeless persons living in the United States (Joseph, 1992). There is a significant correlation between substance abuse and the homeless, of which approximately 75 percent are male. Estimates of alcoholism range from 35 to 40 percent with hard-core substance abuse (heroin, cocaine, crack) estimated at about 10 percent to 20 percent. Approximately 10%-20 percent of the homeless have a concurrent psychiatric disorder (Interagency Council on the Homeless, 1989).

The combined effects of racism, poor education and unemployment have limited the opportunities for African Americans and Hispanics, leaving a large population entrenched in the dire conditions of inner-city squalor. Insufficient technical job skills in the current labor market, low wages in service industries, and unaffordable housing are reasons for poverty and homelessness in the inner cities. The social consequences of these conditions include crime and violence, substance abuse, homelessness, and the spread of HIV infection. Essential ingredients of effective treatment programs for the *culture of poverty*, therefore, include *vocational assessment, training, and, most critical, job placement*.

Summary

This chapter has discussed cultural influences on how we view the world, how we view ourselves, and how we view others. Stereotyping and racism are relatively common. They are based on ethnocentrism—valuing one's own cultural beliefs and identities above those of other cultures. Sometimes they are based on personal insecurities and the projection of those feelings onto others. The issue is not that we have cultural biases, but rather that they can automatically govern our behaviors, tainting our relationships with others. Effective *SSC* counselors assess their own cultural beliefs and appreciate how treatment outcomes are affected by cultural factors in the client, counselor, therapy group, social environment, treatment agency and community. We become effective when we help create for ourselves and for our clients a balance between preserving and strengthening our own unique cultural values and the cultural values of other people.

Competent treatment providers are conscious of the dynamics of cultural interactions, actively committed to self-assessment and developing skills for utilizing cultural strengths—in themselves and clients—to improve treatment outcomes. We also examined critical elements of cultural competence with general consideration of how valuing diversity can enhance treatment effects for minority populations.

We have seen that we develop cultural competence when we understand our own cultural biases and help clients to understand theirs. Cultural competence is developed when we see the specific treatment needs that emerge out of diversity and when we see the strengths in that diversity—diversity found in different communication patterns, different styles of learning, different socialization experiences, different verbal and non-verbal skills and different orientations to family and to community.

We become culturally competent in treatment when we capitalize on the commitment of the Hispanic Americans' honor and dignity for and commitment to family. We build competence when we capitalize on the African American's alliance to the power and strength of the group and shared sense of cultural identity and heritage (e.g., *Nguzo Saba, the Black Value System*). We grow in cultural competence when we not only capitalize on but integrate the Native American's *reverence for and spiritual bonding with nature, with rural values and with the artistic*. We capitalize on diversity when we strengthen the Asian American's dedication to *academic excellence* and to *learning*. We capitalize on the strengths of diversity when we can convey to the historically disenfranchised groups of our American society—African Americans, Hispanics, Native Americans—*that they have demonstrated an internal survival strength to succeed and maintain continuous change and growth in the face of the obstacles of prejudice and discrimination.*

We become culturally competent in treatment when we recognize the *different needs of gender* and of *people of poverty* and build on the strengths which helped these groups manage oppression, discrimination and adversity. Finally, we enhance cultural competence when we strengthen the concept of *renaissance-renewal*—rooted in European culture—and help that group share that cultural value of renewal with all cultural groups.

We build cultural competence and sensitivity in ourselves as providers and in our clients when we look for *common bonds across cultures*. One common bond is found in the area of alcohol and drug use. With respect to the impact of alcohol and other drugs on individuals, there are more similarities than differences across groups. The differences found across groups are also found within groups. Although women may be more apt to be solo drinkers, within the population of women with alcohol problems, there is a clear pattern of convivial and gregarious drinking. Alcohol and other drugs have a leveling effect on people of all cultures. Drugs are not biased. They do not discriminate. They can cause mental, emotional, social and physical impairment and dysfunction in all people. That is a commonality that binds together the diversity of cultures in AOD treatment and which unites us in one common treatment goal—to help the SAO to break out of the bonds of drug abuse and criminal conduct.

A sense of common purpose comes as we seek common values and search for what is important. Ultimately, we must heed the voice of Henry James. When asked by his nephew what he thought he ought to do in life, James replied: "three things in human life are important. The first is to be kind. The second is to be kind. The third is to be kind."

Commonality comes as we listen to the legends of other cultures and recognize that in those legends, all people want to touch the beauty of the natural world and the good of the world in which they live, that we all have longings, yearnings and strivings that we may not fully understand, but for which we grasp as we proceed on our path of self-improvement and change. This is what Longfellow (1898) was saying when he wrote of the Native American legend of the Song of Hiawatha:

> *Ye who love the haunts of Nature,*
> *Love the sunshine of the meadow,*
> *Love the shadow of the forest,*
> *Love the wind among the branches,*
> *And the rain-shower and the snow-storm,*
> *And the rushing of great rivers*
> *Through their palisades of pine-trees,*
> *And the thunder in the mountains,*

Whose innumerable echoes
Flap like eagles in their eyries;—
Listen to these traditions,
To the Song of Hiawatha!

Ye who love a nation's legends,
Love the ballads of a people,
That like voices from afar off
Call to us to pause and listen,
Speak in tones so plain and childlike,
Scarcely can the ear distinguish
Whether they are sung or spoken;—
Listen to this Indian Legend,
To this Song of Hiawatha!

THE TREATMENT PLATFORM

*I have found it enriching to open channels
whereby others can communicate their feelings,
their private perceptual worlds*

Carl Rogers

CHAPTER ⑨
CONCEPTUAL FRAMEWORK FOR
COGNITIVE-BEHAVIORAL TREATMENT
OF THE SUBSTANCE ABUSING OFFENDER

Introduction

The purpose of this chapter is to outline the structure and conceptual framework for *Strategies for Self-Improvement and Change* (SSC) for the SAO. A three-phase treatment and change model is utilized as the primary conceptual structure upon which the program rests. This three-phase structure is premised on theory regarding the process that individuals go through when experiencing self-improvement, personal growth and change. The conceptual framework of the program is defined by

- the provider skills required to facilitate growth and change within the program phases;
- the assessment components which provide the necessary data-base for treatment planning and client self-awareness;
- the treatment goals which guide the change process;
- the basic CBT treatment strategies used to bring about self-improvement and change which are the building stones for the treatment framework;
- the expected client experiences within the respective program phase; and
- the traditional stages of change which seem to be congruent with the three-phase program structure.

It is within this framework that the treatment experience modules are developed and delivered with the goal of effecting change and growth in the client.

As summarized in Chapter 6, the basic concepts and principles utilized in developing the program framework emerged out of the historical review and theoretical foundations presented in Section I of this manual. Again, these concepts and principles are

- motivational enhancement and building treatment responsiveness, trust and rapport;
- treatment readiness;
- clients go through identifiable stages when making change;
- importance of self-disclosure in developing self-awareness which opens the doors to self-improvement and change;
- cognitive-behavioral principles and methods provide a framework for understanding and facilitating change;
- relapse and recidivism prevention;
- utilization of community 12-step programs and self-help groups.

We first present a theoretical overview of the process of growth and change. Then, the program structure or phases of treatment is discussed along with the basic provider skills that facilitate change. A basic CBT model for change is presented including an adaptation of the Marlatt RP model for use with the substance abusing offender. Finally, the differences between therapeutic and correctional counseling is identified and principles of integration are reviewed. This discussion essentially covers the core elements of the program structure and conceptual framework as outlined in Figure 9.1.

Several resources for the development of the structure and conceptual framework of the SSC program were used. These include the work done by the authors in developing guidebooks and manuals for addictions counselors. These documents describe the treatment process and skill structures that are designed to facilitate the stages people go through when making changes in their cognitive, affective and behavioral patterns regarding criminal conduct (CC) and AOD (alcohol and other drug) abuse. Works by the following authors were also used: Prochaska et al., 1992), Miller and Rollnick (1991), the manuals utilized in Project MATCH (Kadden et al., 1992; Miller et al., 1994; Nowinski et al., 1992), Monti et al. (1989; 1995), Bush and Bilodeau (1993) and Marlatt and associates (Marlatt & Gordon, 1985; Dimeff & Marlatt, 1995).

The Process of Growth and Change

Most counseling theories identify the process of treatment and therapy as one of personal growth and change. Building on the concepts of learning and growth as presented by Kurt Lewin[1] and the Orthogenetic Principle developed by Werner (1957), a process structure for change in treatment was developed by Wanberg (1974, 1983, 1990).

1 This concept of growth and change was presented by Howard Ham, Ph.D. at the Iliff School of Theology in 1957 in his course on Theories of Personality. The Lewin material was taken from one of his unpublished lectures. See Lewin (1935, 1936, 1951) for more in-depth understanding of his Field Theory of psychology.

Figure 9.1 Conceptual Framework of the Cognitive-Behavioral Treatment of the Substance Abusing Offender

Treatment Phases	Challenge to Change	Commitment and Readiness to Change	Taking Ownership for Change
CHANGE PHASE	**UNDIFFERENTIATED**	**DIFFERENTIATED**	**INTEGRATIVE**
PURPOSE AND GOALS	Help client tell story. Unpack feelings, thoughts and problems.	Help client hear his or her story. Sorting, labeling, identifying feelings, thoughts.	Help client act on story. Putting together.
BASIC TREATMENT SKILL CATEGORIES AND SPECIFIC SKILLS	Responding attentiveness ⟹ Encouragers to share ⟹	⟹ ⟹	⟹ ⟹
		Paraphrasing ⟹ Clarification ⟹ Reflection of behavior feelings thoughts Therapeutic confrontation ⟹ Correctional confrontation ⟹	⟹ ⟹ ⟹
			Change Clarification, Confrontation: therapeutic correctional. Change Reinforcement: therapeutic correctional.
ASSESSMENT	**SCREENING**	**IN-DEPTH**	**CHANGE MONITORING**
TREATMENT GOALS	Build trust and rapport. Establish climate of caring. Open sharing and catharsis. Information to client on CC and AOD use. Decrease client resistance. Client thinks about change.	In-depth assessment in areas of CC and AOD. Formulate in-depth treatment plan. Get client to commit to change. Enhance self-reflection and self-evaluation. Client demonstrates change.	Establish measured pattern of change in AOD use and CC. Establish self-regulation self-direction self-determination Address individual client problems. Reinforce change. Address relapse and recidivism.
BASIC TREATMENT STRATEGIES	Self-evaluation: didactic. Motivational interviewing. Phase I Modules.	Self-evaluation: interactive. Develop therapeutic alliance. Phase II Modules.	Use multi-modal treatment methods. Relapse/recidivism prevention. Phase II Modules.
CLIENT EXPERIENCES	Openness Acceptance Release, catharsis.	Self-awareness Insight Awareness of change.	Consistent change in thought, feelings and behavior.
INTEGRATING STAGES OF CHANGE	Pre-contemplative Contemplative	Determination stage Action stage	Continued action Maintenance

Kurt Lewin conceptualized growth and change as being the same. He stated that the learning process involves three steps. The first is a global, *undifferentiated* response to a new situation or a new set of stimuli. This learning or growth stage can be observed in all living organisms. It occurs in a rapid, undifferentiated multiplication of cells in the first stages of a new organism; it can be observed in an infant child whose whole body responds to a stimulus such as when the hand reaches out for an object, the feet move up and out and the head lifts in motion with the arms. Resistance and tension are also identified in this stage of growth.

The second stage of growth occurs when the individual units of the organism begin to differentiate among one another. Different sizes and shapes of cells begin to emerge; now the infant can reach out with his arms without the rest of the body moving. Lewin describes this stage as the *differentiated* phase of growth and change. *Ambivalence* about existence is resolved and organism identity is defined.

The third and final stage of growth occurs when the various units begin to show purpose and *functional integration*. Now the elongated cells of the plant carry water and minerals to the flat cells in the leaf which are responsible for photosynthesis. The infant's reach now is for food which she successfully places in her mouth for nourishment. Lewin's theory of growth and change was probably a reaction to the stimulus-response learning theories being taught at the University of Iowa at the time that he was on the faculty there during the 1940s. He no doubt felt that learning was more complicated and involved more integration of the internal and external world of the organism than the simplistic theories of the stimulus-response models.

Werner, in his *Orthogenetic Principle,* conceptualizes growth and change taking place in a very similar manner. He states: "Wherever development occurs it proceeds from a state of relative globality and lack of differentiation to a state of increased differentiation, articulation, and hierarchic integration" (Werner, 1957, p. 126).

The constructivism school of philosophy views the *Orthogenetic Principle* (and thus, the concepts of growth and change developed by Lewin) as the manner in which the cognitive system develops and sustains itself (Delia, O'Keefe & O'Keefe, 1982). The constructivists view mental constructs as the most basic units of cognitive organization. The most general units of cognitive organization are called *interpretive schemes* (Delia et al., 1982), similar to Kelley's causal schemes constructs (Kelley, 1971) and Heider's balance schemes (1958). The *interpretive scheme* is simply a concept or classification method that people use to make sense of the world (for them).

In essence, the *interpretive scheme* or the interpretive construct becomes one of the main units of focus in cognitive therapy (Beck, 1995). The focus, as well, is on the emotional and behavior units that interact with the mental or cognitive units or interpretive schemes used to make sense of the world (Delia et al., 1982). These cognitive constructs are continually developing and become the basis through which the individual makes his or her adjustment to the world. Their development is in accord with the process of change and growth described above by Lewin and Werner. Thus, we can use the *Orthogenetic Principle* in understanding how individuals develop and change the specific units of cognitive responding. Or, we can use this principle in understanding how people respond in general to the treatment process.

Utilizing the concepts of the process of growth and change provided by Lewin and Werner's *Orthogenetic Principle,* Wanberg (1983, 1990) developed a *cyclical or spiral model* to explain the process of therapeutic change and a counseling skill structure to facilitate change. This is illustrated in Figure 9.2. The value of this model for *growth and change* is that it occurs over the course of treatment and it occurs within any one segment of treatment. It is not a linear model that describes change in a stepwise fashion. Rather, it describes change as spiral in nature, and the model is applied to each individual growth experience.

Thus, the phases of *unpacking* (client telling story), *sorting out* (client hearing story) and *integrating* (client acting on his story) may 1) occur around one topic or issue in a session; 2) occur several times in the course of one session; 3) occur over several sessions around one theme, problem or topic; or 4) be descriptive of the client's total treatment experience, that is, over the entire CBT (cognitive-behavioral treatment) program.

The spiral concept illustrates that the client never returns to the same place, but each cycle moves the client further away from the baseline conditions that brought him or her into treatment. Thus, the client may relapse, but if therapeutic intervention and change is effective, the relapse does not take the client back to the pre-treatment level of morbidity.

Utilizing this growth and change model, Wanberg (1983, 1990) has developed a process and skill structure to facilitate the change process through the three phases described above. The essential elements of this model were utilized in developing the structure of the treatment curriculum for this manual. This structure involves three phases of treatment to be described in detail below.

Figure 9.2   **The Cyclical Process of Growth and Change in Treatment**

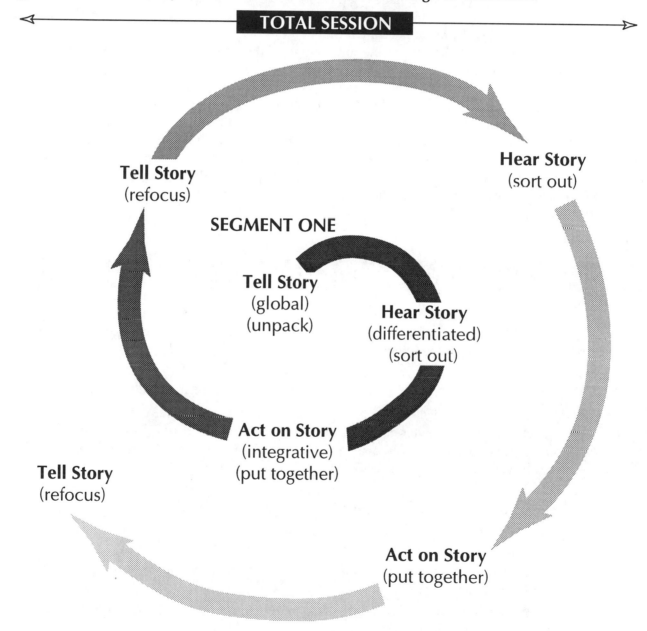

The Phases of Treatment

The three phases of the treatment structure are defined along with the skill structures required to facilitate the change process. As well, the expected client experiences are outlined along with how the stages of change as developed by Prochaska et al. (1992) integrate into this treatment framework. The specific assessment goals for each of these phases are briefly discussed.

1 Treatment Phase I: Challenge to Change—The Global and Undifferentiated Response

Basic to the development and implementation of Phase I of this program are the principles of client-centered counseling, motivational enhancement therapy, the concepts and ideas that define the pre-contemplative and contemplative stages of change, the CBT principles of client-counselor collaborative partnership, relapse prevention, and that change is mediated by cognitive processes. The primary objectives of Phase I are outlined in Table 9.1.

First, the initial phase of treatment or the initial stage of the presentation of a new treatment concept or experience finds the client in a *global* and *undifferentiated* response. At this stage, the client presents material at his or her own level of cognitive organization. Individuals in a highly defensive state or who are experiencing considerable anxiety or stress are often unable to get thoughts and feelings into organized mental, attitudinal or verbal components. This is often interpreted as *resistance* to change or ambivalence about changing. At this step in growth or change, there may be a strong reticence to talk or share or there may be a spurting forth of material that, at the most severe level of dysfunction, may be disconnected and uncontrolled. Clients differ with respect to the degree of global, undifferentiated states they are in when entering treatment, or when entering a new treatment experience or module.

Table 9.1

Objectives of Phase I: Challenge to Change

The overall goal of Phase I, Challenge to Change, is to help the client develop a basic trust in and rapport with the purpose of treatment and in the staff delivering the treatment program so as to effectively motivate the client to begin engaging in the change process. The objectives of this phase are

◆ Build rapport and trust so as to allow the client to openly share inner feelings and thoughts, and to unpack and tell his or her story;

◆ Clients develop a core knowledge base in the areas of criminal conduct, AOD abuse, the process of change, the cognitive-behavioral basis of change and the interaction of criminal conduct and AOD abuse. More specifically, it is expected that

- Clients develop an understanding of the key concepts and patterns of criminal conduct and how people develop and continue these patterns;
- Clients develop an understanding of the key concepts of the patterns of AOD abuse and how people develop and continue these patterns;
- Clients develop an understanding of the stages individuals go through when undergoing change;
- Clients develop an understanding of cognitive-behavioral processes and how these impact on the development, participation in and continuation of criminal conduct and AOD abuse behavior;
- Clients understand how criminal conduct and AOD abuse interact;

> - Clients develop initial self-awareness of their own cognitive sets and overt behaviors in the areas of CC and AOD abuse and then become motivated to commit to making changes and shifts in these cognitive sets and in CC and AOD behavior emerging from these sets;
> - Clients acquire the cognitive and behavioral concepts and tools of relapse and recidivism prevention.
>
> ◆ Clients, through a climate of trust and rapport, feel comfortable in disclosing critical information about self. More specifically the client will
>   - Disclose and reveal the realities of her/his criminal conduct:
>   - Disclose and reveal the realities of her/his AOD use and abuse patterns;
>   - Disclose and reveal how the realities of her/his criminal conduct and AOD use and abuse relate and interact to produce further criminal conduct or further AOD use and abuse.

An underlying premise of Phase I is that the first step in change is *self-awareness* and that self-awareness is enhanced through *self-disclosure*. Self-disclosure is enhanced through the use of *client-centered and motivational enhancement skills*.

The counseling skills that help to facilitate the goals and objectives of this phase of treatment are based on the skill categories of *responding attentiveness* and *invitations to share*. These skills are applied in order to facilitate change in the undifferentiated, global (pre-contemplative and contemplative) stage of growth. Utilization of these skills helps the client to effectively share and express concerns and problems, lower defenses and experience a release of cognitive and affective material. This provides the basis for differentiation of feelings, thoughts and behaviors. It is a necessary step to cognitive-behavioral change.

Assessment in this phase involves *screening* clients for problems in the area of AOD use and criminal conduct. Assessment of clients occurs in each session as clients explore and share their past AOD abuse and criminal conduct and their current thoughts, beliefs, attitudes and emotions in the area of AOD use and criminal behavior.

From the perspective of the stages that people go through when making changes as presented by Prochaska and associates (1992), the global, undifferentiated and *unpacking* phase of growth represents the pre-contemplative and contemplative stages of change.

2 Treatment Phase II: Readiness and Commitment to Change— The Differentiation Response

Important concepts that contributed to the development of Phase II of this program are:in-depth assessment, coping and social skills training, the feed back principles of client-centered counseling, motivational enhancement therapy, the concepts and ideas which define the determinative and action stages of change, the client-counselor collaborative partnership, enhanced self-awareness, and that change is mediated by cognitive processes.

Once the client has begun to "unpack" the thoughts and feelings related to the treatment focus, the *differentiation* process can unfold. This is a sorting out and labeling process. Thoughts and feelings are identified, and issues and concerns are prioritized and then explored in greater depth. The most critical experience for the client in this stage of treatment process is the *feedback loop*. This loop is the key process through which the client hears her story and hears her own dilemma. Through the feedback loop, the client also begins to *hear and see* her problems, dysfunctions and pathological responses to the world. Through this feedback loop, the defensive system begins to open up and allow increased self-awareness and self-understanding, critical to the growth and change process.

The awareness of needed growth and change occurs during this phase, but more than this, this phase is designed to motivate the client to commit to change and to begin to make specific and clear changes. In this phase, both *therapeutic* and *correctional* confrontation are used (see the discussion on integrating correctional and therapeutic confrontation).

Phase II: *Commitment to Change* represents a commitment to taking action in making cognitive and behavioral changes. In this phase, an *in-depth assessment* is completed to enhance the client's awareness of his or her own cognitive scheme and behavioral patterns associated with CC and AOD use and to identify the unique cognitive and behavioral patterns of the client. The client is then engaged in specific coping and skills training experiences (e.g., interpersonal and intrapersonal skill development training) to bring about shifts in the client's cognitive schemes and actual behaviors associated with criminal conduct (CC) and AOD (alcohol and other drug abuse). This phase is devoted to testing out and practicing behavioral changes. The principles and methods of *preventing relapse and recidivism* are continually practiced throughout this phase.

The overall goal of Phase II is to strengthen the client's commitment to change through strengthening and enhancing the basic skills essential for changing AOD abuse and criminal conduct patterns. Table 9.2 shows the specific objectives of Phase II: *Commitment to Change*.

Table 9.2

Objectives of Phase II: Commitment to Change

◆ As a result of engaging in self-disclosure and through more intensive feedback processes, the client will develop an awareness, understanding and clear recognition of his or her *own patterns of behavior* in the following areas:
  • Patterns of criminal conduct;
  • Patterns of AOD use and abuse;
  • How AOD abuse and criminal conduct interact and reinforce each other and feed into further involvement in both criminal conduct and AOD abuse;
  • How unique patterns of thinking, feeling and perceiving lead to involvement in criminal conduct and AOD abuse.
◆ As a result of developing an in-depth awareness of one's own CC and AOD abuse patterns and through coping and social skills training, the client will commit to engaging in specific patterns of change in cognitive schemes and changes in behaviors that strengthen prosocial and AOD abstinence:
  • The client commits to and demonstrates change in cognitive schemes underlying AOD abuse and CC;
  • The client demonstrates change in criminal conduct and AOD behavior;
  • The client becomes aware of the patterns of recidivism in criminal conduct and relapse in AOD use and abuse and prevents lapses into thinking patterns that lead to overt recidivistic and relapse behaviors.

The skill structure for this treatment phase is represented by the broad skill categories of *feedback skills* (reflection, paraphrasing, summarization, change clarification) and *confrontation skills* (therapeutic and correctional). Through the application of *feedback clarification skills,* the client begins to hear his own story, sorts out the feelings, thoughts and behaviors involved in dysfunctional and pathological responding and begins to develop a clear perspective of needed growth and change. This process increases self-awareness and self-understanding.

Therapeutic and correctional confrontational skills are used in this Phase II. Herein lies the difference between correctional and therapeutic treatment. This manual is designed to blend these two approaches in the treatment of the SAO client. The differences between these two skills and the blending process (an important component of SAO treatment) are discussed below.

Assessment in this phase of treatment is more *in-depth* and *differential*. The results of assessment are used in the feedback process to help clients sort out their own patterns of criminal behavior, AOD use, feelings, thoughts and emotions.

From the Prochaska et al. (1992) stage of change model, this phase represents the *determination* stage of change and the initiation of the *action* stage of change. Here the client is resolving the ambivalence to committing to change, some changes have been made, and there is continued involvement in cognitive and affective change.

3 Phase III: Taking Ownership of Change—The Integration Response

The integration and ownership phase of treatment represents the *strengthening* and *maintenance* of changes made in treatment. The client now puts together the meaning of the treatment experience and takes consistent action on his or her own story, goals and desired changes. The change goals, however, may also be those of some external system, such as the family, marriage or criminal justice system. What is important is that there is not only *consistent* demonstration of change, but the client also *internalizes* the change and *claims* it as his or her own.

In this phase, treatment builds on the client's increased self-awareness and the coping and change skills the client developed in Phase II. The counselor helps the client tie together various feelings, thoughts and behaviors that have emerged in the overall treatment experience. The counselor then reinforces and strengthens the client's improvement and change in specific areas. Relapse and recidivism prevention (RP) training is continued in Phase III. Clients are taught to utilize community resources and self-help groups in maintaining change. Objectives of Phase III are outlined in Table 9.3.

Table 9.3

Objectives of Phase III: Taking Ownership of Change

◆ As a result of experiencing change in thinking, feeling and behavior, the client will take ownership of these changes and will demonstrate maintenance of these changes over time. More specifically the client will

  • Be aware of and manage relapse and recidivism into AOD and criminal conduct thinking;

  • Prevent cognitive recidivism and relapse from manifesting into overt conduct and behavior;

  • Be able to utilize community support and reinforcement resources to maintain change.

◆ As a result of the client's commitment to and demonstration of change, the client will provide role modeling for other clients who are engaged in the process of change.

The counselor skill categories used to help the client to achieve *change ownership* are change clarification, change confrontation and change reinforcement. In this phase of treatment the client is confronted with the discrepancies between behaviors, feelings and thoughts (i.e., "you say you don't want to drink, but you keep spending time in the bars with your friends!"). Changes that can be made are clarified, and when change is noted, then this change is reinforced through the use of change reinforcement skills.

What is crucial in this phase of treatment is the concept of *attribution*. The ideal model for change is one that facilitates change from within the individual. The most effective changes occur when the client attributes the changes to himself, or when the changes are attributed to an inner motivation by the client himself (Kanfer, 1975, 1986). This represents the client taking ownership for the changes that do occur. The internalization of change is most likely to occur when the feedback reinforcement skills are utilized in such a manner that the client feels the changes are due to his or her efforts.

In this phase of treatment, the client experiences consistent *cognitive, affective* and *behavioral* changes and begins to feel the strength of the *maintenance* of these changes. Within the context of the Prochaska et al. (1992) model, this phase of treatment represents both the action and maintenance stages of change.

The Cognitive-Behavioral Model for Change: Underlying Assumptions and the Process of Change in Cognitive-Behavioral Treatment for the SAO

The *first assumption* underling the SSC curriculum is that the patterns of criminal conduct (CC) and the patterns of alcohol and other drug (AOD) use and abuse behavior are determined by the individual's *cognitive schemes:* 1) of thoughts, perceptions, feelings and beliefs about self and about the world, 2) which then are expressed in overt AOD abuse and criminal behavior. Thus, treatment is essentially directed at changing the thinking, feeling and perceiving of the individual, which will subsequently bring about change in behavior.

The **second assumption** is that external factors or events or inside memories and feelings lead to automatic thoughts which are based on *core beliefs* and *attitudes* about self and about the world. A primary focus of treatment is to help the client recognize those *automatic* thoughts and the errors and distortions in thinking associated with those thoughts, and to change the core beliefs and attitudes that underlie the automatic thoughts and thinking distortions. The treatment principle is: we can have control over our thoughts and feelings—we can *change and choose* our thoughts and our beliefs. Cognitive skills training is an important component of treatment at this point.

The **third assumption** is that the automatic thoughts and feelings, which are based on core beliefs and attitudes, lead to *overt behaviors*. The CBT model holds that the individual makes a *choice* in what behaviors he or she chooses to manage the external events and internal feelings and thoughts. Coping and social skills training provide the key interventions in helping the client learn to choose adaptive behaviors to manage outside events and feelings.

Finally, the coping actions we choose and the outcomes of those actions *reinforce* internal thoughts, feelings, beliefs and attitudes.

Recall our parolee in Chapter 6. He has been in treatment, not using drugs and "going straight." He and his wife are now separated, and he finds himself at home and alone. This precipitates a number of automatic thoughts—"no one cares," "I'm sober, going straight and what good did it get me. I just as well go down and join the guys (former criminal associates) and get drunk. I feel like going out and ripping someone off. They deserve it." He feels anger and resentment and some depression. He now reflects on some long-standing basic beliefs he has had since adolescence when he found himself alone—his father at the bar drinking and his mother working every evening and getting home late. "No one really cares. This has been my life. All my life I've had to struggle and look out for myself." He feels he has been the victim.

The CBT model holds that he has a choice at this point. He can be in charge of his thinking and actions. He can engage in positive thinking, change his thoughts, recall the work he had done in treatment on restructuring his basic belief system and begin thinking, "there are people who do care—I don't want to drink—to go back to doing crimes." He has the choice to call his sponsor, some friends in the program, his counselor or his parole office. If our parolee takes these routes, he will feel good about what he did and feel a sense of self-control and self-efficacy; this reinforces his choices and actions and the "new way of thinking."

If our parolee takes the other route, goes to the bar and gets drunk with friends, goes out and commits a crime, and gets caught, he will again feel he is a victim, and this will *reinforce* the old belief system and attitudes described above.

Figure 9.3 provides the basic CBT model for the process of learning and change. You can see how the illustration used above fits the model and how AOD use or engaging in criminal conduct become reinforced through this model of learning and change.

Figure 9.3   The Process of Cognitive and Behavioral Learning and Change

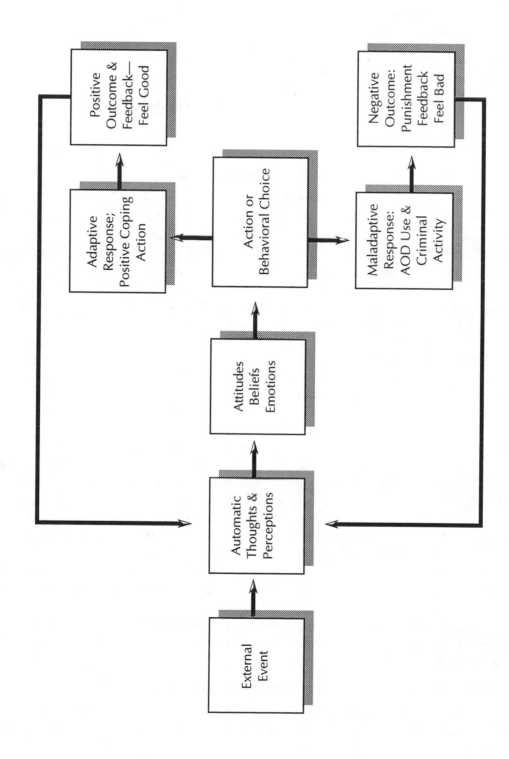

A number of specific CBT strategies will be used to implement treatment around this model. These strategies are part of the conceptual framework, as identified in Figure 9.1. These have been summarized in Chapters 2 through 6 and include

- motivational enhancement;
- coping and social skills training;
- problem solving;
- cognitive aversive training;
- stress management;
- community reinforcement and contingency management;
- self-efficacy training;
- challenging automatic thoughts and thought restructuring;
- managing drug cravings;
- relapse prevention.

The Integrated Model for Relapse and Recidivism

In Chapter 6, we looked closely at the Marlatt RP model and used the example of our parolee in terms of how that model works and how it can be applied to the treatment of the SAO. There are a number of elements of this model that we have enhanced and altered so that it can best fit our purposes in treating the SAO. These will be briefly reviewed and covered in more detail as we present the modules on Relapse-Recidivism (RR) and Relapse-Recidivism Prevention (RRP).

We want clients to see that the RR is a *gradual process of erosion* and that the first steps in the erosion process are to engage in high-risk (HR) thinking (I'll get drunk) and being exposed to high-risk situations (drinking soft drinks with friends at the bar). Thoughts about using drugs and thoughts about committing crimes represent initial steps of RR. Relapse begins with HR thinking which leads to use. Recidivism begins when the individual engages in HR thoughts that lead to criminal actions. Thus, RR refers to *lapsing back to thoughts, feelings and actions that lead to criminal conduct or that lead to drug use.* Thus, RR does not simply mean that the person has committed a crime or has started drinking.

As discussed in Chapter 6, an important modification of the Marlatt model has to do with the difference between the concept of lapses as it applies to drug use and to criminal conduct. A lapse in reference to drug use may be thinking about drinking, or actually returning to some drinking. In the SAO model, this is tolerable if we interpret the lapse in the light that recovery from drug abuse often does involve brief lapses into some drug use. With criminal conduct, we must interpret the lapse or the initial stages of recidivism as engaging in thoughts and actions that lead to criminal behavior. We do not need to apply *zero tolerance* criteria to substance use. We do need to apply the *zero tolerance* criteria to criminal behavior. This is not to say that if an offender does reoffend, we "write him or her off." Our professional stance in human services is that we continue to work with the client to service his cognitive and behavioral change needs as long as we have a professional relationship with that client.

Figure 9.4 represents the modification of the Marlatt Relapse Prevention Model for the treatment of the substance abusing offender. We will spell out in detail the essential elements of the RRP model in Module 5 of Section III.

Integrating Therapeutic and Correctional Treatment

We have seen how the two domains of substance use and criminal conduct differ with respect to an RRP model of intervention. There are other distinguishing features between the approach to the treatment of these two groups, as they have been treated independently in the past.

First, drug abuse by adults in and of itself does not have legal implications, only certain behaviors associated with AOD use. Driving while impaired is illegal. The possession of many drugs other

Figure 9.4   Cognitive-Behavioral Model for Relapse and Recidivism

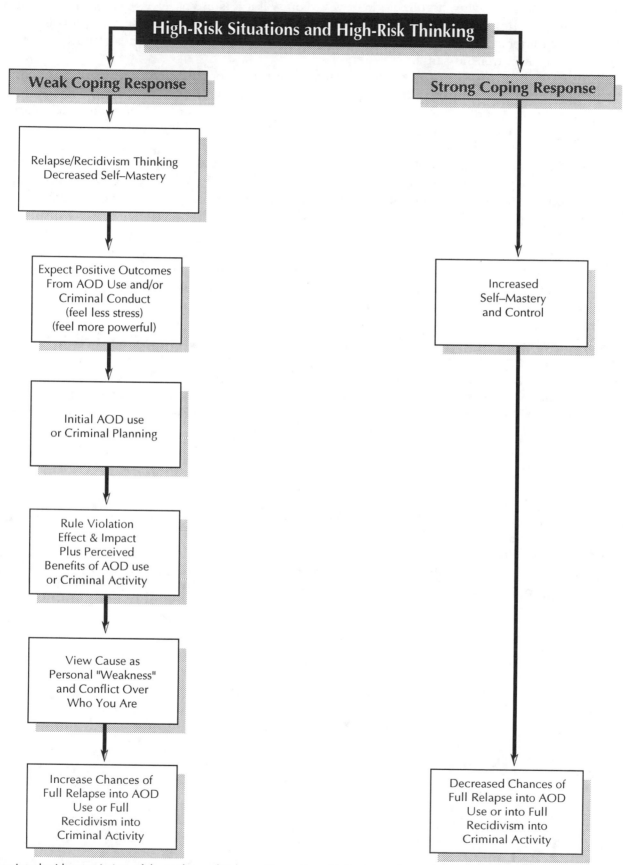

Reprinted with permission of the authors of Relapse Prevention: Maintenance Strategies in the Treatment of Addictive Behaviors (p.38) Edited by G.A. Marlatt and J.R. Gordon, The Guilford Press, 1985.

than alcohol is illegal, but the actual *use* itself may not be under legal sanctioning. You most likely will not get arrested for having heroin inside of you; you will if it is in your possession. There is legal sanctioning for the offender who is under the influence of a drug in that, in most cases, this is a violation of the conditions of parole or probation. However, for AOD abuse, treatment and legal sanctioning are most often not the same.

With the offender, this is not the case. Treatment and sanctioning for the offender are almost always integrally related. Primary intervention or treatment is usually part of the legal sanctioning process. Offender treatment is not based on the client's own goals and desires for change; it is based on the legal requirement to change. It is clearly directed at correcting the criminal behavior as society or the legal system requires.

This difference places a different light on treatment. The basic treatment of the AOD addicted person is, for the most part, psychotherapeutic. It is *client-oriented* in that counseling or therapy starts where the client is and with the client's self-perceived treatment needs (or in the case of collaterals, treatment needs as perceived by a significant other). With the offender, however, treatment needs are defined by *external* sources and systems outside of the treatment process. Treatment is, in part, society-centered and is directed at a behavioral pattern which is of threat to the society, which has violated the integrity and laws of society and thus is part of the sanctioning process. Thus, offender treatment is correctional and parenting whereas *AOD* treatment is much the same as mental health treatment—the healing expectations come from the client and it treats the client as an adult who is responsible only to himself.

This difference in focus between therapeutic and correctional treatment occurs mainly in the area of confrontation. Whereas *psychotherapeutically oriented* treatment for the AOD abuser confronts the client with his or her own self, *correctional* treatment confronts the client with the external expectations of the sanctioning system. That is, the therapist with the AOD client essentially states: "I confront you with you; I confront you with what you say you want and the contradictions in your thinking, emotions and behavior which violate your own needs and goals."

The correctional treatment specialist states: "I confront you with me; I represent the external world that you have violated and I confront you with the values and laws of society and I expect you to change."

Thus, in the treatment of the SAO client, the *therapeutic is blended with the correctional*. Treatment is both client-centered and society-centered. The treatment specialist works to help the client meet his or her needs as defined by the client, but, the SAO treatment specialist also works to help the client meet the needs and requirements of society in terms of compliance with the laws and rules of society. This is one of the most difficult treatment roles to be in: to relate to the client in an adult-to-adult manner while at the same time directing treatment in a correctional and parental manner.

C H A P T E R ⑩
CHARACTERISTICS OF THE EFFECTIVE COUNSELOR AND THE COUNSELING RELATIONSHIP

Do Psychosocial Therapies and Treatment Work?

Psychosocial-oriented therapies are now 100 years old. Research with respect to the effectiveness and outcome of psychotherapy and psychosocial-oriented therapies indicates that there is a general positive treatment effect. Summaries of meta-analyses of outcome studies conclude "Psychotherapy is effective at helping people achieve their goals and overcome their psychopathologies at a rate that is faster and more substantial than change that results from the client's natural healing process and supportive elements in the environment" (Lambert & Bergin, 1992). But what is responsible for this outcome? What components of psychosocial therapies work?

Common Factors of Change in Treatment

What is evident in the growing body of research literature regarding the outcome of psychosocial-oriented therapies is that no single clinical approach seems to be superior over another (Lambert & Bergin, 1992) and that different therapeutic approaches (behavioral, psychodynamic, client-centered) "appear to secure comparable outcomes" (Garfield, 1992, p. 349). Differences in outcome between various forms of treatment are simply not as pronounced as might be expected (Lambert & Bergin, 1992) and "other purportedly unique features of a system may be relatively inconsequential" (Strupp & Howard, 1992, p. 313).

This general finding of no difference in outcome across diverse therapies leads us to the following possible conclusions (Lambert & Bergin, 1992): 1) that different therapies can achieve similar goals through different processes, 2) different outcomes do occur but these are not detected by current research strategies, or 3) different therapies embody common factors that are curative but not emphasized by the theory of change central to a particular school.

The research literature today supports the third conclusion that the common features of psychosocial therapies may be the major contributor to the effectiveness of treatment (Frank, 1992, p. 393). This conclusion is supported by a long history of research on the efficacy and effectiveness of psychologically oriented therapies. The early work of Rogers and Dymond (1954) on the efficacy of client-centered therapy supports this conclusion. The research of Truax and Carkhuff (1967) on the effectiveness of the paraprofessional in effecting change in clients certainly supports the common factors theory. The Vanderbilt study (Strupp & Hadley, 1979), which found comparable outcomes among analytically oriented therapists, experientially oriented therapists and college professors is but another example of support for the common factors theory. Regardless of the theoretical orientation or even the type of disorder being treated, the common features or factors findings in psychosocial therapies is robust (Arkowitz, 1992; Elkin, 1986; Garfield, 1992; Glass & Arnkoff, 1988). But what are these common features?

1 Counselor Personal Characteristics

One common factor that contributes to the effectiveness of psychosocial therapies is a set of personal characteristics and features of the treatment provider. After some 50 years of studies, there has emerged what have been identified as the core dimensions and characteristics of the effective service delivery personnel of psychosocial therapies (e.g., Berenson & Carkhuff, 1967; Carkhuff, 1969; Carkhuff & Berenson, 1977; Rogers, Gendlin, Kiesler & Truax, 1967; Truax & Carkhuff, 1967; Truax & Mitchell, 1971). Much of this research and the description of these core dimensions are based on the work of Carl Rogers and his associates. Rogers (1957) concluded that the communication of genuine warmth and empathy by the therapist alone is sufficient in producing constructive changes within the client. He was the first to clearly identify in the literature the traits of *warmth, genuineness, respect and empathy* as essential in not only establishing a therapeutic relationship and alliance with the client, but also in producing the desired change in that client. The studies of Truax (1963) and Carkhuff and Truax (1965) support this conclusion. Through the therapist's warmth and empathy, even the most severely disturbed clients can be helped (Rogers et al., 1967).

Today, although interpreted in different ways, these core characteristics of empathic understanding, genuineness or congruence, positive regard and respect, warmth, and concreteness or specificity of expression are considered basic to the effective helping relationship and are consistently emphasized in textbooks on therapy and counseling (e.g., George & Cristiani, 1981; Wallace, 1986). More specific to our concern in this manual, George (1990) identifies the effective personal characteristics of the effective substance abuse counselor as *genuineness, ability to form warm and caring relationships, sensitivity and understanding, sense of humor, having realistic levels of aspirations for client change and self-awareness.* Lazarus (1971) found that the most desirable characteristics that clients found in counselors were sensitivity, honesty and gentleness. As Andrews and Bonta look at the effective counselor relationship with the offender, they emphasize the core characteristics of *caring, genuineness and empathy* (Andrews & Bonta, 1994).

2 The Counselor-Client Relationship

The core worker's characteristics of warmth, empathy and positive regard are also the core elements of an effective therapeutic relationship (Lambert & Bergin, 1992). What is most prominent among the common factors identified as being the primary basis for treatment effect across all forms of therapy is the client-counselor relationship. Strupp and Howard (1992) state poignantly: 'the growing research literature has strongly suggested, generic (or common) relationship factors in all forms of psychotherapy (e.g., empathic understanding, respect, caring, genuineness, warmth) carry most of the weight...' (p. 313). "Reviewers are virtually unanimous in their opinion that the therapist-patient relationship is central to therapeutic change" (Conners et al., 1997; Lambert & Bergin, 1992; Roue et al., 1997).

These are central to verbal therapies which are premised on acceptance, tolerance, therapeutic alliance, working alliance and support (Lambert, 1983). They are also seen as important elements in cognitive and behavioral therapies "as an essential means for establishing the rapport necessary to motivate clients to complete treatment" (Lambert & Bergin, 1992). These are also basic elements of developing motivation in the treatment of the substance abuser (Miller & Rollnick, 1991).

George and Cristiani (1981) contend that the essential elements that promote an effective treatment relationship are trust and acceptance of the client. They then outline the specific characteristics of the effective therapeutic and helping relationship as the following:

- The relationship is affective: it explores emotions and feelings;
- It is intense: the relationship promotes an open sharing of perceptions and reactions between client and worker;
- It involves growth and change: it is dynamic, continually changing;
- It is private and confidential;
- It is supportive: the treatment relationship offers a system of support;
- It is honest: it is based on honest and open and direct communication between the worker and client.

The more specific elements of the therapeutic change relationship have also been described. Marmor (1975) identified the following as important components of the treatment relationship:

- The relationship promotes a release of tension;
- It involves cognitive learning;
- It involves operant conditioning and reinforcement;
- The client identifies with the counselor;
- It involves reality testing.

Sloane, Staples, Cristol, Yorkston and Whipple (1975) indicate that successful clients in treatment identify a number of factors that were important to their change and improvement, several of which were specific relationship factors. These involve the therapist's helping them to understand their problems, receiving encouragement to practice facing the issues that bother them, being able to talk to an understanding person and developing greater understanding from the therapeutic relationship.

3 Other Common Factors: Cognitive-Behavioral Approaches

Other common factors have been identified across the various therapies (Lambert & Bergin, 1992). These are grounded in cognitive-behavioral approaches and include teaching intrapersonal and interpersonal skills, the development of self-efficacy through training in self-help skills and overall skill development. Cognitive and cognitive-behavioral therapy is often seen as a basis for psychotherapy integration (Alford & Norcross, 1991; Arkowitz, 1992; Beck, 1991; Goldfried, 1995).

Elements of the Effective Correctional Counseling Relationship

We will review some of the elements of effective correctional counseling and the counseling relationship which have been identified in the literature and which have emerged out of the clinical experience of the authors.

1 Essential Elements of the Effective Correctional Counseling Relationship

Andrews and Bonta (1994) have identified some essential elements of the effective correctional counseling relationship. "Effective workers: a) establish high quality relationships with the client; b) demonstrate anticriminal expressions (modeling); c) approve of the client's anticriminal expressions (reinforcement) and d) disapprove of the client's procriminal expressions (punishment) while at the same time demonstrating alternatives" (p. 203).

First, effective workers establish *high-quality relationships with clients*. Productive interactions between correctional counselors and their clients are predicated upon staff enthusiasm and openness to the free expression of attitudes, feelings and experiences. Mutual respect and caring facilitate the meaningful disapproval of procriminal expressions. Within the limits of mutually agreed upon boundaries for physical and emotional intimacy, counseling is offered in an atmosphere of genuineness, empathy and caring.

Second, effective correctional workers *demonstrate anticriminal expressions through modeling and serve as anticriminal models for their clients*. The offender is not only sharp in picking up deviancy and antisocial characteristics and behaviors of other people but also looks for these features in others. Finding them provides a justification for his or her own antisocial and deviant behaviors. The effective correctional counselor must be consistent and unerring in prosocial and high moral values.

Third, effective correctional workers *approve of and reinforce the client's anticriminal expressions* and disapprove of the client's procriminal expressions while at the same time *demonstrating alternatives*. This is a vigilant process. Missing opportunities to reinforce client changes and efforts to change may make significant differences in the overall change process. A continual reinforcement of abstinence from criminal and drug use behaviors should be an ongoing agenda for the correctional counselor.

2 Distinguishing Between Anticriminal Versus Procriminal Expressions

The first priority in developing correctional counseling acumen is learning how to distinguish between anticriminal and procriminal expressions. Staff members may unwittingly reinforce criminal conduct by not being attentive to their own expressions of antisocial attitudes. Some staff may adopt *con talk* to get closer to their clients and may express their own cynicism regarding the criminal justice system. Andrews (1980) found that the pro- or anticriminal expressions of officers during interviews with probationers are related to client recidivism. *Procriminal* expressions include specific attitudes, values and beliefs that imply criminal conduct is acceptable. Included in this category are negative attitudes toward the law, police and courts; acceptance of rule violations and disregard of the law; identifying with criminals; and endorsement of strategies for exoneration.

Anticriminal expressions include emphasizing the painful consequences of illegal activities for the offender, victim and community; rejecting rationalizations for criminal acts; highlighting the hazards of associating with criminals; and adopting their vocabulary, beliefs or styles of behavior. Specific criminal acts, such as sex or violent offenses, have characteristic language and thought patterns that may normalize and reinforce criminal conduct in criminal subcultures. Effective correctional counselors actively reinforce reduced association with criminal others and diminished interest in risk-taking activities and circumstances, such as the bar scene.

Offenders are encouraged to examine their own conduct while making self-evaluative judgments as to whether or not their behavior reflects anticriminal values and beliefs. They receive support for considering the consequences of their actions and weighing the benefits of alternative ways of acting in risky situations. Attending sessions and completing homework assignments are seen as exemplary anticriminal expressions. When both staff and clients jointly reinforce positive expression by offender participants, therapeutic effects are significantly enhanced. Crucial to increased counseling efficacy is staff selection and training that stresses the value of modeling and differential reinforcement of anticriminal expressions.

3 Reinforcing Positive Thoughts and Behaviors

Rewarding positive thoughts and behavior requires the availability of a wide variety of reinforcers in the repertoire of correctional counselors. Minimal visual cues such as eye contact or approving smiles may sometimes be effective while other anticriminal expressions may call forth explicit comments reflecting agreement and support. *The continuation of a positive and therapeutic counseling relationship may serve as the most powerful anticriminal reinforcer.*

Andrews and Bonta (1994, p. 205) offer specific suggestions regarding high-level reinforcement of offenders by their workers. These include

- Strong, emphatic and immediate statements of approval, support and agreement with regard to what the offender has said or done (nonverbal expression, eye contact, smiles, shared experiences);

- Elaboration of the reason why agreement and approval are being offered (i.e., exactly what it is you agree with or approve of);

- Expression of support should be sufficiently intense to distinguish it from the background levels of support, concern and interest that you normally offer;

- The worker's feedback should at least match the offender's statement in emotional intensity (i.e., be empathic) and his or her elaboration of the reason for support should involve some self-disclosure (i.e., openness).

4 Effective Punishment

Andrews and Bonta (1994) indicate that *effective punishment* occurs within the context of a *caring, genuine and empathic relationship*. Counselors may disagree with procriminal expressions with minimal fear of client retaliation or termination of services. Further, within the context of a positive counseling relationship, even reduced interest may be a successful punishing device. Expressed disapproval is more effective in an atmosphere of trust and mutual caring while supportive statements may outnumber disapproving ones in a ratio of 4:1. The following are some characteristics of effective disapproval in work with offenders (Andrews & Bonta, 1994, p. 205):

- Strong, emphatic and immediate statements of disapproval, nonsupport and disagreement with what the client has said or done (including the nonverbal: a frown, or even an increase in the physical distance between you and the client);

- Elaboration of the reason why you disagree and disapprove (this is an opportunity to model an anticriminal alternative);

- The expression of disapproval stands in stark contrast to the levels of interest, concern and warmth previously offered;
- The levels of disapproval should be immediately reduced and approval introduced when the client begins to express or display anticriminal behavior.

Effects of Specific Therapies

Although the common factors seem to account for a large percentage of favorable outcomes in treatment, specific therapies seem to have their impact in specific problem areas. When specific techniques are applied to specific problems, then the relationship factor may be less important (Morin & Azrin, 1988). Behavioral and cognitive approaches seem to "add a significant increment of efficacy with respect to a number of different problems" (Lambert & Bergin, 1992, p. 369). Some of these problems include phobias, anxiety and depression. Andrews and Bonta (1994) conclude that cognitive-behavioral approaches provide the greatest likelihood of success with offenders.

Client Characteristics as a Determinant of Treatment Efficacy

Limits and boundaries of the efficacy of the therapist-client relationship are often determined by the type and characteristics of the client being treated. Change in therapy is facilitated by optimal levels of anxiety and internal discomfort. It is commonly accepted that individuals with personality disorders, particularly those with antisocial features, are more resistant to change. Chronic and severe patterns of schizophrenia certainly limit the efficacy of the therapist-client relationship as described above. As well, treatment outcome is also bound by the client's readiness for treatment and the stage of change the client is in when entering treatment.

Three Broad Variables Involved in Treatment Change

Thus, considering the above common, specific and client type factors, there appear to be three broad variables involved in the treatment process which interact to bring about change in the client. These are *the counselor as person*, the *counselor-client relationship* and the *client as person*. These are depicted in Figure 10.1. Each of these broad variables is a source of variance that affects the outcome of treatment. Effective treatment providers utilize these variables in the change process.

Variables That Define the Profile of the Effective SAO Counselor

There are three broad dimensions that define the primary characteristics of the effective Substance Abusing Offender Specialist: *the counselor's personal characteristics and traits, technical development, and philosophical perspectives* (see Wanberg, 1983). Figure 10.2 provides an outline of these three dimensions.

1 The Personal Dimension

The personal dimension is defined by the core counselor traits of warmth, genuineness, empathy and respect. Whether these traits can be learned or whether they are natural to the individual is certainly debatable. However, each of these traits is observable, measurable, and thus trainable. Other personal characteristics that impact on effective SAO counseling are the counselor's values, beliefs, personal experiences, social role orientation and unresolved personal conflicts.

Biases with respect to orientation toward social and cultural roles, representative groups within the society and orientation toward job productivity can all influence the process of counseling. Each counselor has a set of unique personal experiences, personal values, attitudes and beliefs which can impact on treatment. Counselors with unresolved personal issues may find these issues getting in the way of being client-oriented and objective.

Figure 10.1
Interactive Components of the Treatment and Therapeutic Process

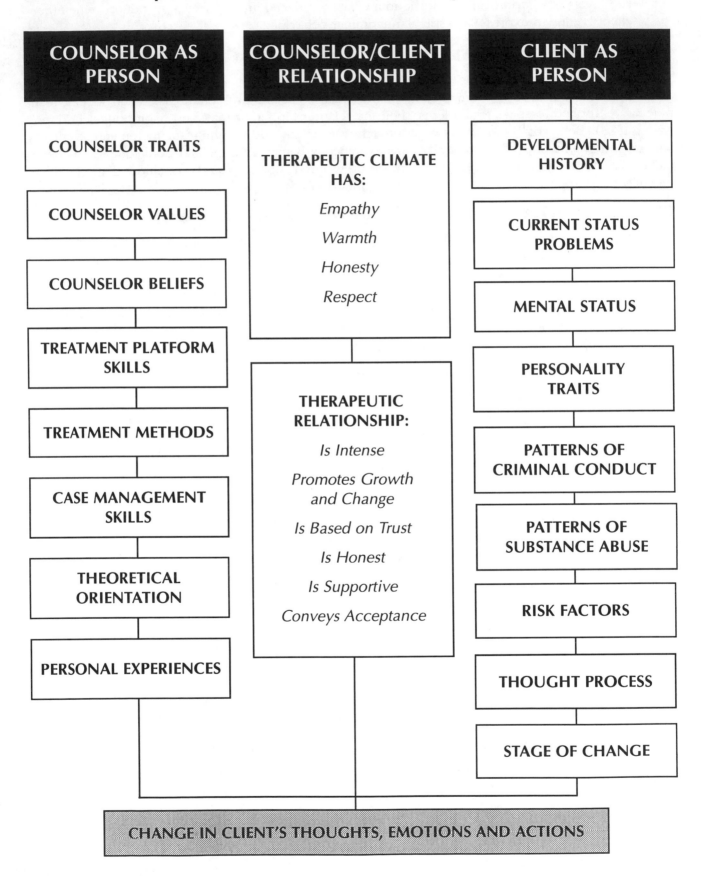

COUNSELOR AS PERSON	COUNSELOR/CLIENT RELATIONSHIP	CLIENT AS PERSON
COUNSELOR TRAITS	**THERAPEUTIC CLIMATE HAS:** *Empathy* *Warmth* *Honesty* *Respect*	DEVELOPMENTAL HISTORY
COUNSELOR VALUES		CURRENT STATUS PROBLEMS
COUNSELOR BELIEFS		MENTAL STATUS
TREATMENT PLATFORM SKILLS	**THERAPEUTIC RELATIONSHIP:** *Is Intense* *Promotes Growth and Change* *Is Based on Trust* *Is Honest* *Is Supportive* *Conveys Acceptance*	PERSONALITY TRAITS
TREATMENT METHODS		PATTERNS OF CRIMINAL CONDUCT
CASE MANAGEMENT SKILLS		PATTERNS OF SUBSTANCE ABUSE
THEORETICAL ORIENTATION		RISK FACTORS
PERSONAL EXPERIENCES		THOUGHT PROCESS
		STAGE OF CHANGE

CHANGE IN CLIENT'S THOUGHTS, EMOTIONS AND ACTIONS

Figure 10.2
Profile of the Cognitive-Behavioral Substance Abusing Offender Specialist

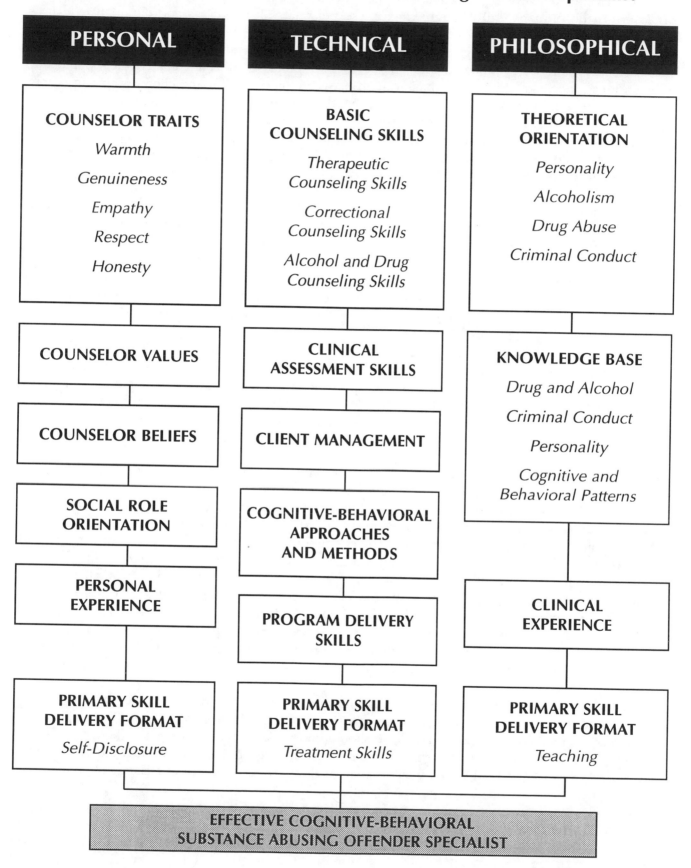

An effective counselor will have full awareness of his or her own values, beliefs, attitudes, personal experiences and biases and will understand how these personal characteristics can contribute to or hinder the delivery of effective counseling to the Substance Abusing Offender (SAO). *Self-disclosure* is the primary skill through which these personal values, beliefs and experiences can be effectively utilized in treatment (Wanberg, 1990).

Self-disclosure is the sharing of personal, emotional and experiential feelings and experiences. Self-disclosure material is personal and unique to the counselor. It can enhance the opening up process. It can increase treatment communication between the counselor and client or among clients. It can help the client feel more at ease knowing that the counselor has had very real and human feelings and experiences. Evidence that self-disclosure on the part of the counselor has worked can be noted in several ways: 1) *the client continues to share at a deeper and more personal level,* 2) *the client begins to utilize some of the personal approaches that the counselor has used in his or her own problem-solving and conflict resolutions,* and 3) *the client expresses greater acceptance of his own inner feelings and problems.*

Self-disclosure, however, can present major barriers in treatment (Wanberg, 1990). It can slow down or even stop the opening up and sharing process. If the counselor indicates having been through such and such an experience, the client may internally reflect that *there is no reason to go on; the counselor already knows what I've been through.* Self-disclosure may cause the client to lose confidence in the counselor, a finding that is born out in the self-disclosure research literature. As a consequence of self-disclosure, the client may move away from self-focus and focus more on the counselor's issues. Finally, self-disclosure may cause the counselor to lose concentration and attention on the content and affect flow of the client.

In summary, self-disclosure becomes effective when, following its use, the client truly feels better understood and more deeply supported and then continues to share personal material at a deeper level. It should be used with caution. It is a complex factor in the treatment process. It does not necessarily enhance, and may inhibit, the client seeing the counselor as empathic, trustworthy or competent. With the SAO client, it could *reinforce* procriminal and antisocial behavior.

2 The Technical Dimension

The second dimension that defines the effective SAO counselor is the area of technical training and development. This involves the development of the basic counseling skills, the skills of assessment and of client management. These skills form an important component of the conceptual framework of the treatment platform and were discussed in the last chapter.

A standard for the application of the technical dimension is found in the practice of surgery in medicine. During a surgical procedure, a physician's knowledge, skills and ethical behaviors are continually operating. At any given moment in the surgical process, the surgeon knows what skills he or she needs to use or is using. The surgeon knows the process for each surgical procedure. The skills, tools and instruments are precisely labeled and identified, and the surgeon knows under what conditions the application of the skills and the use of the instruments are needed. You would not only expect but also require that of a surgeon operating on you. Imagine being operated on, and you wake up and hear the surgeon say: "Gee, that's an interesting instrument. Don't know what it is, but I'll try it." Needless to say, you would be in shock.

Let us apply the same standard to counseling and psychosocial treatment. We should have an awareness of the process in therapy and therapeutic change (as defined in Chapter 9), we should be able to label our skills and tools, and then we should know when in the treatment and change process we apply those skills and tools. We should also have a fairly decent idea of the outcome of the application of the process and skills. We would expect no less of our surgeon; our clients should expect no less of us.

In psychosocial treatment, we may not always have the definitive knowledge of the process and the skills, as in medicine. Yet we should be grounded in a process that we feel works for us and we should be able to label the skills we use to implement that process of therapeutic and correctional change. One model for the process, skills and strategies is provided in Chapter 9. This model will provide a guideline for your own adaptation and use of psychosocial and correctional treatment.

3 Philosophical Perspectives

Finally, the dimension of philosophical perspective provides the counselor with a theoretical orientation and knowledge structure within which he or she practices the delivery of services to SAO clients. It is important that the counselor have some theory of human personality, a theoretical view of counseling and treatment, some theories or at least some ideas around drug abuse and alcoholism and some perspective on the nature, etiology and development of criminal conduct. Teaching and imparting knowledge is the primary skill through which the counselor brings to bear his or her knowledge and theoretical orientation on the treatment process. Sections I and II of this manual have been devoted to helping you become grounded in a theoretical and philosophical perspective in the treatment of the substance abusing offender.

C H A P T E R ⑪
ASSESSMENT OF THE SUBSTANCE ABUSING OFFENDER

Chapter 7 of this manual discussed the various concepts and approaches used in the assessment of clients with substance abuse and with a history of criminal conduct. This chapter presents a comprehensive assessment program for the SAO based on the assessment concepts and approaches discussed in Chapter 7. It is recognized that many programs utilizing this SSC program for the substance abusing offender will have their own client assessment program. It is recommended that those programs evaluate their own assessment approach in light of the assessment plan outlined in this chapter.

Based on our review in Chapter 7, it is recommended that five major areas be assessed in order to understand the needs, conditions and circumstances of the SAO client: 1) *AOD use and abuse,* 2) *history and extent of involvement in criminal conduct and antisocial behavior,* 3) *processing of thoughts and emotions,* 4) *the individual's background and current life problems and situations* and 5) *motivation and readiness for treatment.* Chapter 7 also identified two levels of assessment within these three areas: *1) screening and initial evaluation* and 2) *in-depth assessment.* These five areas and two levels of assessment are the basis upon which we gather information and develop a treatment plan for the SAO client.

Initial Screening and Assessment

The purpose of AOD screening is to determine whether a client is to be included into a category of having AOD problems. For individuals in the criminal justice system, being selected into such a category would initially identify that individual as being a Substance Abusing Offender (SAO). The goal of initial screening, then, is to make that determination.

It is recommended that the screening process involve three steps. The first two steps are considered to be pre-referral SAO screens and are done within the criminal justice system. The third step is done at the SSC program level and is the final program selection screening process done by the SSC treatment staff.

1 SSC/SAO Treatment Pre-Referral Steps

The substance abuse screening process currently used for adult offenders throughout the Colorado criminal justice system will be provided as a prototype for pre-referral screening for this SSC CBT program for the substance abusing offender.

Using the *Standardized Assessment Program* (Bogue & Timken, 1993), every adult felon, except first-class felons, undergoes an initial AOD assessment at probation, community corrections or within the *Department of Corrections.* This also includes persons convicted of drug misdemeanors or drug petty offenses. Steps One and Two of the screening process are done in the pre-sentencing investigation for individuals who are probation eligible, when offenders enter the community corrections system, or when they enter the *Department of Corrections.* This *Standardized Assessment Program* is explained in detail in the *Colorado Standardized Offender Assessment Manual* [1] (Bogue & Timken, 1993).

a. Step One Screening

Step One Screening includes the administration and scoring of the *Drug Abuse Screening Test 20* (DAST-20) (Skinner, 1982) and the Alcohol Dependence Scale (ADS) (Horn, Skinner, Wanberg & Foster, 1984). The purpose of *Step One Screening* is to make a quick assessment as to whether the individual may have AOD issues and problems that need to be addressed. Offenders who have a

---

[1]For information regarding the Colorado Offender Assessment and Treatment system manual, contact the Research and Assessment Coordinator, State Court Administrator's Office, Colorado Judicial Branch, 1301 Pennsylvania Street, Suite 300, Denver, CO 80203.

drug-related offense and a raw score of five or above on either the DAST or the ADS and all other non-drug offenders with a raw score of six or above meet the inclusion criteria for *Step Two Screening*.[2] An offender is also referred to *Step Two Screening* if he or she has a positive AOD urine test, or the offender requests help for AOD treatment or the corrections worker (e.g., probation officer) determines that the offender is in need of AOD service.

b. Step Two Screening

Once the offender is included into the AOD category, *Step Two Screening* is activated. This step involves administering and scoring the *Adult Substance Use Survey* (ASUS) (Wanberg, 1993a, 1993b) and the *Level of Service Inventory* (LSI) (Andrews, 1982). The *Substance Use History Matrix* (SUHM) (Bogue & Timken, 1993) may then be completed. It summarizes the scores from the DAST, ADS, ASUS and LSI. It also provides a structure to summarize the client's lifetime drug use pattern across nine drug categories. This part of the SUHM is completed during an interview with the client.[3]

From this second-level screening process, a client is given a score on the ASUS (based on the DISRUPT scale) and converted raw score on the LSI. The sum of these two scores is used to determine whether any education or treatment is necessary, and if treatment is necessary, what specific level of treatment is recommended.

The LSI converted raw scores ranges are as follows:

0-13 = 1.

14-20 = 2.

21-27 = 3.

28-54 = 4.

The ASUS DISRUPT converted raw score ranges are as follows:

0-20 = 0.

21-40 = 1.

41-60 = 2.

61 or above = 3.

These scores are added together to derive a total score and to determine level of services. The following levels of services have been designated with their corresponding score based on the sum of the total for the LSI and ASUS above.

1. No treatment = 1.

2. UA monitoring treatment and/or AOD education = 2.

3. Weekly outpatient = 3.

4. Intensive outpatient = 4.

5. Intensive residential treatment = 5.

6. Therapeutic community = 6.

7. Referral for in-depth evaluation for psychopathy and extreme antisocial condition = 7.

[2]The ADS and the DAST are copyrighted documents and are available through the Addiction Research Foundation, 33 Russell Street, Toronto, Ontario, Canada, M5S 2S1.

[3]Level of Service Inventory-Revised (LSI-R) is a copyrighted instrument. For information regarding its use, contact Multi-Health Systems, Inc., 908 Niagara Falls Blvd., North Tonawanda, NY 14120-2060; (800) 456-3003; FAX (888) 540-4484; E-Mail to Jerry Smith, Director of Marketing, [jerry_s@mhs.com]. The SUHM is a public domain instrument and may be used free of cost. The ASUS is a copyrighted instrument. For information regarding the use of the SUHM and the ASUS, contact the Center for Addictions Research and Evaluation, 5460 Ward Road, Suite 140, Arvada, CO 80002. The SUHM and ASUS are included in Appendix A.

c. Referral to Strategies for Self-Improvement and Change

Offenders recommended for the SAO Cognitive-Behavioral Strategies for Self-Improvement and Change program are those who fall in services categories 3 through 6 above. The adult criminal justice worker also uses other criteria and information to conclude that the offender will benefit from the program.

If the client is determined to be appropriate for the SSC program, the criminal justice worker completes the Referral Evaluation Summary (RES). The RES along with the DAST, ADS, LSI, ASUS, SUHM and a printout of the offender's official criminal history is placed in a referral packet and forwarded to the SSC provider or the individual doing the final selection process (the ASUS and SUHM are all included in Appendix A and the RES is in Appendix B).

2 Final Selection Screening for SSC

After the client has been referred to the SSC program, the provider completes a final screening as part of the intake process. The person conducting the final selection process will need to be familiar with the program and will need some basic training in the selection process and criteria. The final screening and intake process is outlined in detail in Chapter 12. Our purpose here is to discuss the elements of the final selection process itself.

The client is administered the *Adult Self Assessment Questionnaire* (AdSAQ), which is made up of several scales measuring readiness and motivation for treatment. (As part of the intake process, an interview is held with the client.) During this interview, the evaluator rates the client's willingness to be involved in the program. A *priority-eligibility* (PE) model is used as a guideline for selection. Candidates are given a *priority-eligibility score* based on general and specific criteria outlined below. All information, including the results from the AdSAQ, the PE score and interview impressions should be used in making final selection. The AdSAQ is provided in Appendix A.

a. General Selection Guidelines

Level of Risk: From the literature review provided in Section I of this manual, it was apparent that those most likely to benefit from the SSC program are those who are of higher risk with respect to both criminal history and conduct and AOD use and abuse. That is not to say that those who fall in the lower risk categories could not and would not benefit from the SCC program. However, lower risk individuals seem to be able to do well with less intervention and less treatment. Thus, to get the most out of the resources to be expended for this program, it is recommended that the target group should involve *higher* risk individuals in both areas of CC and AOD use. This level of risk is determined by specific scores on the ASUS and overall LSI score.

Minimal Symptom Criteria and Test Cutoff Values: Based on cutoff values on ASUS, the DAST and ADS, the client should meet at least minimal symptom criteria for selection into an AOD treatment program. Step One and Step Two Screenings (SSC pre-referral screening mentioned above) provide the preliminary basis of making sure that the client did reach a certain level of AOD disruption and symptoms to be selected for treatment. In the final selection process, the ASUS Disruption scale is used again to ensure that clients with a certain level of AOD symptoms are selected into treatment.

Specific Candidate Circumstances: The specific circumstances of the client will have bearing on the selection process. For example, since the program extends over a period of nine months to one year, the client will need to be in the criminal justice system long enough to complete the program. It is suggested that incarcerated offenders complete this program three to six months prior to release to the community.

Motivation and Self-Selection: Many clients enrolling in this program will be at the *pre-contemplative and contemplative* stages of change. Thus, the stage of change should not determine whether the client is enrolled in the program. However, motivation and interest in the program need to be considered. For example, an individual who states he or she simply will not put any effort into the program and will probably not attend would have a lower enrollment priority than say one who says "I think I would like to try it." A client who openly reports "I have a drug and alcohol problem and I want to be in treatment" is an individual who is selecting himself or herself into treatment and would have a higher priority rating.

Impaired Control Cycle: The client who clearly demonstrates a history of impaired AOD control and who has been caught up in the impaired control cycle, as described in Chapter 7, is a good candidate for treatment.

b. **Specific Criteria and Priority Value**

Scores from the ASUS, LSI and *Program Interest Questionnaire* (PIQ) will be used to determine a *priority-eligibility* (PE) score. The ASUS and LSI instruments will be in the client's referral file. The PIQ includes seven self-administered questions, four rater items and a table which is used to calculate the priority-eligibility score. The PIQ is provided in Appendix A. The scoring procedure for the PIQ self-administered questions is at the bottom of page 1. Scoring procedures for the four rater items on page 2 of the PIQ are found at the bottom of page 2.

Page 1 of the PIQ is completed by the candidate on a self-administered basis. The staff rating scale and the PE calculation table are on the reverse side of the PIQ. Before the candidate completes the PIQ, the staff member will interview the client and carefully describe the treatment program to the candidate. This interview should explore the client's alcohol and criminal conduct problems, client motivation and any unusual circumstances that may prevent full participation in the program. What the program expects of the client and the length of the program should be explained. From this interview, it can be determined whether the client fits the *impaired control cycle* and the *self-selection criteria*. Following this interview, the PIQ is completed and the PE score calculated.

Table 11.1 provides the scales and criteria to be used in determining the PE score. It is the same table that is in the PIQ. The raw scores and their respective weighted values are provided for the selected scales of the ASUS and the total LSI and PIQ scores. The evaluator finds the raw score for the ASUS INVOLVEMENT, DISRUPTION and SOCIAL scales and then puts the weighted score in column 3 corresponding to the client's raw score on these scales. The same is done for the total LSI score. The client PIQ score and the staff rating score are determined and the weighted value placed in column 3 corresponding to the respective raw score. Also provided in Table 11.1 is a rating of whether the client fits the impaired control cycle and whether the client sees himself or herself as a self-selected candidate into the treatment program. Each of these two factors is given a weight of one. Table 11.2 provides an example of scoring the PE table (Table 11.1) for a particular client.

The maximum possible raw score on the PE form is 19 and a minimum possible score is zero. No empirically based guidelines have been validated. However, the following rough guidelines can be used with respect to giving some description to numerical weights:

- PE scores of 0–4   low priority;
- PE scores of 5–8   low medium priority;
- PE scores of 9–12   medium priority;
- PE scores of 13–16   high medium priority;
- PE scores of 14–19   high priority.

The total PE score is a combination of a measurement of *drug use involvement and severity* (as measured by the ASUS and if the client fits the impaired control cycle), of *overall risk* as measured by the LSI, of *self-reported interest for the program, of staff rated client program interest* and whether the client is *self-selected,* using the criteria described above.

Table 11.1

Program Selection Criteria and Values

SCREENING INSTRUMENT SCALE	RAW SCORE	WEIGHTED VALUE	CLIENT SCORE
ASUS—INVOLVEMENT SCALE	0–3	0	
ASUS—INVOLVEMENT SCALE	4–10	1	
ASUS—INVOLVEMENT SCALE	11–19	2	
ASUS—INVOLVEMENT SCALE	>19	3	
ASUS—DISRUPTION	0–8	0	
ASUS—DISRUPTION	9–16	1	
ASUS—DISRUPTION	17–25	2	
ASUS—DISRUPTION	>25	3	
ASUS—SOCIAL	0–9	0	
ASUS—SOCIAL	10–14	1	
ASUS—SOCIAL	>14	2	
LSI—OVERALL SCORE	0–13	0	
LSI—OVERALL SCORE	14–20	1	
LSI—OVERALL SCORE	21–27	2	
LSI—OVERALL SCORE	>27	3	
PIQ—SELF REPORT	0–4	0	
PIQ—SELF REPORT	5–8	1	
PIQ—SELF REPORT	>8	2	
PIQ—RATER SCALE	0–3	0	
PIQ—RATER SCALE	4–6	1	
PIQ—RATER SCALE	>6	2	
FITS SELF-SELECTION CRITERIA	YES	1	
FITS IMPAIRED CONTROL CYCLE	YES	1	
REQUIRED TO TAKE TREATMENT	YES	1	
TOTAL WEIGHTED PRIORITY SCORE (SUM RIGHT COLUMN)			

Table 11.2

Example of Determining Weighted Score for a Particular Client

SCREENING INSTRUMENT SCALE	RAW SCORE	CLIENT SCORE
ASUS—INVOLVEMENT SCALE	13	2
ASUS—DISRUPTION	19	2
ASUS—SOCIAL	13	1
LSI—OVERALL SCORE	21	2
PIQ—SELF REPORT	8	1
PIQ—RATER SCALE	6	1
FITS SELF—SELECTION CRITERIA	YES	1
FITS IMPAIRED CONTROL CYCLE	YES	1
REQUIRED TO TAKE TREATMENT	YES	1
TOTAL WEIGHTED PRIORITY SCORE		12

In-Depth Differential Assessment

The screening process outlined above provides the data-base for the first phase of treatment: *Challenge to Change*. During this phase of treatment, clients are provided basic information around AOD use, criminal conduct and basic concepts regarding cognitive and behavioral change and reinforcement. In Phase I, Module 4, Sessions 12 and 13, clients are given the opportunity and challenged to disclose both current and past conditions related to AOD use and criminal conduct (CC) for the purpose of developing self-awareness as a step toward change. They evaluate their AOD and criminal history. They are retested on the DAST, ADS and ASUS and the criminal history part of the LSI to determine if they have shifted their perception of their AOD and CC problems as a result of treatment.

Building on the information and data already acquired about the client, Module 8 provides the structure for more in-depth assessment. Information from the in-depth assessment will be used for two purposes:

- to identify specific areas the client will work on in Module 9, which focuses on the development and strengthening of basic skills for self-improvement and change;
- to develop an individualized treatment plan for each client.

Throughout the in-depth assessment, the client's specific conditions and problem areas are identified and described. Individual treatment may then be developed in collaboration with the client. Up to the point of the in-depth assessment in Module 8, much information and data about the client's AOD use patterns, criminal conduct, thinking patterns and psychosocial problems will have already been gathered and assessed. This was done through the initial screening process outlined above, through testing completed at the intake session, and through the Phase I sessions designed to enhance the client's self-disclosure about his or her current condition and thinking patterns.

The individual in-depth, differential assessment may reveal a number of problems for many clients that simply cannot be addressed in the standard SSC program in this manual. Thus, it is important that treatment providers have resources to help clients address those special treatment needs. For example, as a result of the client's self-disclosure in Phase I and the in-depth assessment in Module 8, a severe marital problem might be revealed. The SSC program does provide basic intervention in this area; however, a more in-depth treatment for marital issues needs to be addressed outside of the SSC program.

The Basic Skills Module (9) focuses on developing skills to cope with both internal and external circumstances that lead to AOD use and abuse and criminal conduct. In this manner, this module will address many of the special treatment needs of clients.

The results of the in-depth assessment are described graphically and this description becomes the map for the client's commitment to change. It will identify the specific areas of change to be addressed in Module 9 and in individualized treatment with the client. It will provide a guide for developing resources beyond the SSC program itself in order to meet the individual treatment needs of the client.

1 Areas of Assessment

In the broadest sense, SSC assessment takes in all of the areas of the person's life that contribute to or represent maladaptive or problem thinking and behavior. In doing the SSC in-depth, differential assessment, five broad areas are covered: 1) *AOD use and abuse*, 2) *Criminal conduct and dynamic risk factors*, 3) *Cognitive processing*, 4) *Background and current life situation problems and conditions of the client* and 5) *Motivation and readiness for treatment*. Specific conditions within each of these four areas will be assessed. From this assessment, both the individual and generic treatment plans can be finalized for each client.

In the discussion below, certain instruments are recommended for use. There are many other instruments that might meet the needs of the provider utilizing this manual. Reviews of these instruments can be found in Allen and Columbus (1995), Cooney, Zweben & Fleming (1995), Inciardi (1994) and Miller, Westerberg and Waldron (1995).

a. Alcohol and Other Drug Use and Abuse

The following six AOD use and abuse areas should be assessed:

    1) Drugs of Choice:

- Alcohol involvement;
- Marijuana involvement;
- Cocaine involvement;
- Other drug involvement;
- Multiple drug use pattern.

    2) Styles of use:

- Convivial and gregarious;
- Sustained and continuous;
- Compulsive and obsessive.

    3) Benefits:

- Manage social discomfort;
- Manage psychological discomfort (anxiety and depression);
- Manage relationship problems and losses;
- Manage physical distress and pain.

4) Consequences from use:

- Loss of control over behavior when using (blackouts, getting verbally and physically abusive);

- Psychological disruption (feeling depressed, guilty, anxious due to drinking);

- Physical and mental disruption (withdrawal and hangover symptoms, hallucinations, etc.);

- Social role irresponsibility such as losing jobs due to AOD use, engaging in criminal conduct when using, etc.

5) Treatment Readiness:

- Awareness of AOD problems;

- Treatment receptiveness;

- Motivation to change and treatment readiness.

6) Degree of disruption.

A number of tests and instruments may be used to assist in completing this part of the assessment. The drug use portion of the *Addictions Severity Index* (McLellan, Kushner, Metzgter, Peters et al., 1992; 1985; McLellan et al., 1983) will provide a general overview of the client's drug use pattern.[4]

For an in-depth and differential assessment of alcohol use and abuse patterns, the *Alcohol Use Inventory* (Horn et al., 1987) is recommended. For clients who indicate a multiple-substance use history, the *Drug Use Self Report* (DUSR) is recommended along with the AUI (Wanberg & Horn, 1989a, 1989b). The AUI and DUSR profiles are included in Appendix A.[5]

The DUSR provides a multiple-substance use profile along with a brief mental health screen, a measurement of defensiveness, and a brief antisocial measurement. It is recommended that the AUI still be administered to the client in that most if not all AOD clients will have a noteworthy history of alcohol use and abuse.

These instruments will provide reliable and stable measures needed to do an in-depth, differential assessment of the client's alcohol and drug use patterns. Information from the LSI, DAST, ADS and ASUS will also be used in completing the differential assessment.

b. **Dynamic Risk Factors: Criminal and Antisocial Thinking and Conduct**

The assessment of antisocial and criminal thinking and conduct involves two areas: *Degree of involvement in criminal behavior* and *antisocial thinking and criminogenic needs*. These contribute to the risk of increased involvement in criminal conduct. The specific areas of assessment are recommended below:

1) Degree of involvement in criminal conduct:

- Property offenses I such as theft and burglary

- Person offenses I: direct physical harm to others such as physical assaults, violent acts, and sexual assaults

- Property offenses II: destruction of property, etc.

- Person offenses II: indirect harm such as harassments and threats

[4]Since the ASI is in the public domain, there is no cost for reproduction and use. Self-training tapes and manuals are available from ABT Associates (301) 913-0500. Hard copy materials may be purchased from Delta Metrics, 1-800-238-2433. The cost is for reproduction and postage. Cost is for reproduction and postage. A copy of the ASI is found in Appendix A.

[5]The Alcohol Use Inventory (AUI) may be purchased through the National Computer Systems, 1-800-627-7271. Profiles for the AUI and the DUSR are provided in Appendix A. Information regarding the use of the DUSR may be received from the Center for Addictions Research and Evaluation (CARE), 5460 Ward Road, Suite 140, Arvada, CO 80002. For providers who have purchased this manual, the only cost for the use of the DUSR will be for purchase of the DUSR starter kit which includes the manual, test booklet and answer sheet with profile.

- Motor vehicle—non AOD related
- Motor vehicle—AOD related

2) Antisocial attitudes and thinking and criminogenic needs:

- Association with antisocial, criminal peers, role models
- Impulsive thinking and behaving
- Self-centered thinking and behaving
- Criminal thinking, beliefs; lack of moral reasoning
- Need for family/social unit attachment
- Lack of social and interpersonal skills
- Lack of problem solving and self-management skills
- Angry, aggressive and resentful attitudes
- Rebellious and anti-authority attitude
- Sensation seeking and risk taking

The LSI provides measurement of many of these areas. The Social Scale on the ASUS and on the DUSR provides a short measure of the antisocial attitudes and behavior. The ASI (5th Edition) (McLellan et al., 1992) has a section on Legal Status which can assist in this assessment. The client's official criminal history and interview information should also be utilized for this assessment.

c. **Assessment of Thinking and Feeling Patterns**

A specific area of cognitive assessment is how a person thinks and feels, particularly in relation to thinking distortions or errors in thinking. Some of these areas overlap with the antisocial and criminal thinking patterns outlined above. The specific areas of thinking assessment are

- Victim Stance—Blame projection
- Narrow or restricted thinking
- Personalizing—feeling victimized
- Superior or grandiose thinking
- Self-centered, narcissistic thinking
- Self-defeating thinking (depressed, putting self down)
- Antisocial and irresponsible thinking

It is recommended that the provider rate the client across the seven categories listed above. The *Thinking Errors Rating Scale*–TERS (Wanberg & Milkman, 1996a) is found in Appendix A and may be used for this purpose. For a self-report instrument, the *Thinking Errors Check List-TECL* (Wanberg & Milkman, 1996b) may also be used. The TERS and TECL are found in Appendix A.

d. **Background and Current Life Situation Problems and Adjustment**

This focus will provide a differential assessment of the *client's background* and *current psychosocial problems and conditions*. The areas of assessment are

1) Background:

- Adolescent AOD use
- Delinquency
- Family problems
- School problems

2) Current status:

- Employment and job productivity
- Residential stability
- Social-interpersonal
- Marital-family relationship adjustment
- Health
- Psychological-emotional

Several instruments, in addition to interview data, can provide information concerning these background and current psychosocial conditions. Through the interview format, ASI provides measurement of medical status, employment and financial conditions, family and social relationship conditions and psychological and emotional status. The ASUS and DUSR provide a measurement of mood adjustment. The *Beck Depression Inventory* (Beck, 1978; Beck & Steer, 1987) and the *Mood Appraisal Questionnaire* (MAQ) (Wanberg, 1989) are short instruments that can provide reliable mood adjustment measures.[6]

e. Motivation and Readiness for Treatment

The client's motivation and readiness for treatment was initially assessed at the screening and admission level of assessment. The counselor continues to assess this area through observing the client's response to the treatment sessions. This area is again assessed in a more in-depth manner. It is suggested that the following areas be assessed:

- Client's awareness of problem
- Client's acknowledgment of need for help
- Client's willingness to accept help
- Client's perception of how others feel about his or her need for help
- Stage of change client is in; if client has taken action to change

Observations made of the client's response to the SSC sessions and interview data can be used to make this assessment. The primary scales of RECEPTIV and AWARENES and the general scale of REC-PAWAR within AUI provide reliable measures of awareness of alcohol problems and receptiveness for engaging in the treatment of an alcohol use problem (Horn, et al., 1987). Other instruments available to measure treatment readiness and motivation are the *Stages of Change Readiness and Eagerness Scale* (SOCRATES) (Miller & Tonigan, 1996) and the *Adult Self Assessment Questionnaire* (AdSAQ) (Wanberg & Milkman, 1993).[7]

[6]The Beck Depression Inventory may be ordered through National Computer Systems, 1-800-627-7271. The Mood Appraisal Questionnaire is provided in Appendix A and for purchasers of this manual, it may be used without cost. Scoring procedures and a brief manual may be ordered, at cost, from CARE, 5460 Ward Road, Suite 140, Arvada, CO 80002.

[7]SOCRATES is available through CASAA Research Division, Department of Psychology, University of New Mexico, Albuquerque, NM 8/131. The Adult Self Assessment Questionnaire is provided in Appendix A of this manual along with scoring procedures. For providers who have purchased this manual, it may be used without cost. Information on the AdSAQ may be received from CARE, 5460 Ward Road, Suite 140, Arvada, CO 80002.

Summary of Information Sources and the Master Profile

Table 11.3 provides a summary of the various sources of information that can be used to complete the in-depth assessment. After the testing has been completed and all of the information has been acquired, the client, in partnership with the counselor and the client's group, completes the *Master Profile* (MP), Figure 11.1.

The in-depth assessment and the *Master Profile* (MP) are completed in Module 8. The methods and procedures for completing this profile are outlined in that Module. The *Master Profile* (MP) is completed by using information from the sources listed in Table 11.3, which also provides information about when the particular test or instrument is administered. The MP is a rating scale for the provider to use to rate the client across all specific factors within the five broad areas of assessment discussed above.

What is important is that the in-depth assessment and the MP are completed in partnership with the counselor and with the client's treatment group. One approach is to have the provider and the client complete the MP independently and then to compare ratings. The group can provide feedback as to their perceptions of the client as well.

Developing the Master Assessment Plan (MAP)

The *Master Assessment Plan* (MAP) is developed from the *Master Profile*. The MAP becomes the guide for the work that the client will now do in the program. As additional information becomes available about the client through disclosure and feedback from others, both the MP and the MAP will be revised. Revisions may take the client into other territories of change. Figure 11.2 provides an example of a particular client on whom the MAP was completed.

Table 11.3

Sources of Assessment Information in Sequence of Recommended Administration

SOURCE OF INFORMATION	WHEN ADMINISTERED
DAST AND ADS	PRE-REFERRAL
ASUS AND LSI	PRE-REFERRAL
SUBSTANCE USE HX MATRIX	PRE-REFERRAL
FINAL SCREENING INTERVIEW	FINAL SCREENING
PROGRAM INTEREST QUESTIONNAIRE—PIQ	FINAL SCREENING
PRIORITY-ELIGIBILITY TABLE	FINAL SCREENING
INTAKE INTERVIEW	INTAKE
ADULT SELF ASSESSMENT QUESTIONNAIRE	INTAKE
ALCOHOL USE INVENTORY	INTAKE
DRUG USE SELF-REPORT	INTAKE
ADDICTION SEVERITY INDEX—ASI	INTAKE
THINKING ERRORS CHECK LIST—TECL	MODULE 3
THINKING ERRORS RATING SCALE—TERS	MODULE 3
INFORMATION FROM PHASE 1	MODULES 1–6
SELF-RATING ON STAGES OF CHANGE—AOD	MODULE 6
SELF-RATING ON STAGES OF CHANGE—CC	MODULE 6
SOCRATES	MODULE 8
BECK DEPRESSION INVENTORY	MODULE 8
MOOD APPRAISAL QUESTIONAIRE	MODULE 8
MASTER PROFILE	MODULE 8
SPECIAL PROGRAMS CHECK LIST	MODULE 8
INDIVIDUAL TREATMENT PLAN	MODULE 8

Figure 11.1
Master Profile

I. Alcohol and Other Drug Use Assessment

	Area of Assessment	Low				Moderate			High		
Drug Choice	Alcohol Involvement	1	2	3	4	5	6	7	8	9	10
	Marijuana Involvement	1	2	3	4	5	6	7	8	9	10
	Cocaine Involvement	1	2	3	4	5	6	7	8	9	10
	Amphetamine Involvement	1	2	3	4	5	6	7	8	9	10
	Other Drug Involvement	1	2	3	4	5	6	7	8	9	10
	Poly Drug User	1	2	3	4	5	6	7	8	9	10

	Area of Assessment	Low				Moderate			High		
Style	Convivial or Gregarious	1	2	3	4	5	6	7	8	9	10
	Sustained & Continuous	1	2	3	4	5	6	7	8	9	10
	Compulsive & Obsessive	1	2	3	4	5	6	7	8	9	10

	Area of Assessment	Low				Moderate			High		
Benefits	Cope with Social Discomfort	1	2	3	4	5	6	7	8	9	10
	Cope with Emotional Discomfort	1	2	3	4	5	6	7	8	9	10
	Cope with Relationships	1	2	3	4	5	6	7	8	9	10
	Cope with Physical Distress	1	2	3	4	5	6	7	8	9	10

	Area of Assessment	Low				Moderate			High		
Results	Behavioral Control Loss	1	2	3	4	5	6	7	8	9	10
	Emotional Disruption	1	2	3	4	5	6	7	8	9	10
	Physical Disruption	1	2	3	4	5	6	7	8	9	10
	Social Irresponsibility	1	2	3	4	5	6	7	8	9	10
	Overall Disruption	1	2	3	4	5	6	7	8	9	10

	Area of Assessment	Low				Moderate			High		
Ready	AOD Problem Awareness	1	2	3	4	5	6	7	8	9	10
	Treatment Receptiveness	1	2	3	4	5	6	7	8	9	10
	Motivation to Change	1	2	3	4	5	6	7	8	9	10

Figure 11.1 (continued)

II. Criminal & Antisocial Thinking & Conduct

	Area of Assessment	Low				Moderate			High		
Conduct	Property Offenses I	1	2	3	4	5	6	7	8	9	10
	Property Offenses II	1	2	3	4	5	6	7	8	9	10
	Person Offenses I	1	2	3	4	5	6	7	8	9	10
	Person Offenses II	1	2	3	4	5	6	7	8	9	10
	Motor Vehicle—Non AOD	1	2	3	4	5	6	7	8	9	10
	Motor Vehicle—AOD Involved	1	2	3	4	5	6	7	8	9	10

	Area of Assessment	Low				Moderate			High		
Criminal Thinking	Antisocial Peers & Models	1	2	3	4	5	6	7	8	9	10
	Impulsive Thinking/Acting	1	2	3	4	5	6	7	8	9	10
	Self-Centered Thinking	1	2	3	4	5	6	7	8	9	10
	Criminal Thinking/Thoughts	1	2	3	4	5	6	7	8	9	10
	Need for Family Attachment	1	2	3	4	5	6	7	8	9	10
	Social/Interpersonal Skills	1	2	3	4	5	6	7	8	9	10
	Problem Solving/Self-Management	1	2	3	4	5	6	7	8	9	10
	Angry/Aggressive Attitude	1	2	3	4	5	6	7	8	9	10
	Rebellious/Anti-Authority	1	2	3	4	5	6	7	8	9	10

III. Assessment of Thinking & Feeling Patterns

	Area of Assessment	Low				Moderate			High		
Thinking	Blame, Victim Stance	1	2	3	4	5	6	7	8	9	10
	Narrow-Restricted Thinking	1	2	3	4	5	6	7	8	9	10
	Personalizing Responses	1	2	3	4	5	6	7	8	9	10
	Superior/Grandiose Thinking	1	2	3	4	5	6	7	8	9	10
	Self-Defeating Thinking	1	2	3	4	5	6	7	8	9	10
	Irresponsible Thinking	1	2	3	4	5	6	7	8	9	10
	Self-Centered Thinking	1	2	3	4	5	6	7	8	9	10

Figure 11.1 (continued)

IV. Background: Problems of Childhood and Development

	Area of Assessment	Level of Problem Severity									
		Low				Moderate				High	
Background	AOD Use Adolescence	1	2	3	4	5	6	7	8	9	10
	Delinquency	1	2	3	4	5	6	7	8	9	10
	Family Problems	1	2	3	4	5	6	7	8	9	10
	Cope with Physical Distress	1	2	3	4	5	6	7	8	9	10

V. Current Life Situations Problems

	Area of Assessment	Low				Moderate				High	
Current Stage	Job and Employment Problems	1	2	3	4	5	6	7	8	9	10
	Residential Instability	1	2	3	4	5	6	7	8	9	10
	Social—Interpersonal Problems	1	2	3	4	5	6	7	8	9	10
	Marital—Family Problems	1	2	3	4	5	6	7	8	9	10
	Health and Physical Problems	1	2	3	4	5	6	7	8	9	10
	Emotional—Psychological	1	2	3	4	5	6	7	8	9	10

VI. Motivation and Readiness for Treatment

	Area of Assessment	Low				Moderate				High	
Readiness	Awareness of AOD/CC Problem	1	2	3	4	5	6	7	8	9	10
	Acknowledgment of Need for Help	1	2	3	4	5	6	7	8	9	10
	Willingness to Accept Help	1	2	3	4	5	6	7	8	9	10
	Others' Perception of Need	1	2	3	4	5	6	7	8	9	10
	Has Taken Action to Change	1	2	3	4	5	6	7	8	9	10

VII. Stage of Change

	Rate Each Stage Separately	Low				Moderate				High	
Stage	Challenged to Change	1	2	3	4	5	6	7	8	9	10
	Commitment to Change	1	2	3	4	5	6	7	8	9	10
	Ownership of Change	1	2	3	4	5	6	7	8	9	10

Figure 11.2

Master Assessment Plan Work Sheet

I. Alcohol and Other Drug Use Problem Areas

PROBLEM AREA AND DESCRIPTION	CHANGES NEEDED IN THOUGHT AND ACTION	PROGRAMS AND RESOURCES TO BE USED TO MAKE CHANGES	DATE WORKED ON
1. Have continual thoughts and desire to go out and drink with friends	Replace social drinking thoughts about going out with friends who do not drink	Specialized Program for Change (SPC): Social Skills Training	10/1/95 12/3/95
2. Drink to cope with marital relationship and stress	Use alternate action to deal with relationship stress	SPC: Problem Solving Skills Five marriage counseling sessions	10/1/95

II. Criminal and Antisocial Thinking and Conduct

PROBLEM AREA AND DESCRIPTION	CHANGES NEEDED IN THOUGHT AND ACTION	PROGRAMS AND RESOURCES TO BE USED TO MAKE CHANGES	DATE WORKED ON
1. Hanging around peers who are antisocial and involved in criminal conduct	Change who you think about being around and who you spend time with	SPC: Developing different lifestyle Attend AA and NA twice a week	

III. Thinking and Feeling Patterns

PROBLEM AREA AND DESCRIPTION	CHANGES NEEDED IN THOUGHT AND ACTION	PROGRAMS AND RESOURCES TO BE USED TO MAKE CHANGES	DATE WORKED ON
1. Always blaming others for my problems and difficulties	Change thoughts of blaming to thoughts of being responsible for my problems	SPC: AOD and CC errors in thinking Think report on event where I blame others	

IV. Current Life Situation Problems

PROBLEM AREA AND DESCRIPTION	CHANGES NEEDED IN THOUGHT AND ACTION	PROGRAMS AND RESOURCES TO BE USED TO MAKE CHANGES	DATE WORKED ON
1. Experiencing unusual depression and sadness	Focusing less on depressed thoughts	SPC: Handling feelings of anger and depression Three one-on-one sessions to talk about sadness	

C H A P T E R ⑫
PROGRAM OPERATIONAL
GUIDELINES AND PROCEDURES

Overview

The purpose of this chapter is to provide the guidelines and structure for the delivery of the CBT program of *Strategies for Self-Improvement and Change* (SSC). The program outline and time structure are defined. The admission and intake procedures are outlined and the respective forms for intake and admission are described. The program guidelines and ground rules are also summarized. Some guidelines regarding effective group facilitation and management are also provided. Finally, guidelines and instrumentation will be provided for evaluation of each session, the client's response to each session and post-program client outcome. It is recommended that programs evaluate their own admission procedures in light of the protocol presented in this chapter.

Program Structure

SSC as presented in this manual is a 9-month to one-year program. It comprises three phases. These phases have been discussed in Chapter 9 and are briefly reviewed here:

Phase I, *Challenge to Change,* is comprised of 18 two and one half hour sessions that include 30 minute breaks. Sessions during this phase are held two times a week and extend over a two-month period. A minimum of two hours is dedicated to delivering the lesson plan to clients.

Phase II, *Commitment to Change,* comprises 22 two and a half hour sessions to be held once a week over a six-month period.

Phase III, *Ownership for Change,* comprises 10 formal sessions to be held over a period of two months to be followed by a two-month continuing support and relapse prevention group.

Program Outline

Each of the three phases of the treatment program is defined by specific program modules and session plans. A detailed outline of the program is found in the *Introduction to Section III: The Treatment Curriculum.*

Individual Intake and Orientation Session

An individual intake and orientation session is completed with each client entering the program. The screening and pre-referral evaluation protocol being used by the *Colorado Division of Criminal Justice* were described in Chapter 11. The elements and instruments of the intake and admission process were also discussed in detail including the final screening selection process and the in-depth assessment. We will now outline the *intake, final screening and in-depth assessment process recommended for the SSC program.* Instrumentation resources were provided in Chapter 11. Those instruments included in Appendix A were also noted. Appendix B includes all of the forms recommended in this intake and admission protocol. The following protocol is recommended:

1. Review the *Referral Package* to be sure the referral file is complete. If any items are missing, they should be completed before proceeding with the admission process (e.g., if the ASUS is not in the file, then this should be administered *before* final selection is made so that data from the ASUS can be included in the selection protocol):

   ⮕ Referral Summary Evaluation (RES);

   ⮕ Copies of the DAST, ADS, ASUS, LSI and SUHM;

   ⮕ Client's criminal record and driving record;

   ⮕ Other documents including consent, releases, etc.

2. Determine appropriateness of the client for the SSC program by doing the following (the following instruments can be administered during the introductory interview or through client self-administration):

⟾ Conduct an introduction interview to brief the client on the program, and evaluate the client's willingness to enter the program. Included in that interview are the following:

- program outline and structure;

- program guidelines and expectations;

- program ground rules;

⟾ Complete the *Personal Data Questionnaire* (PDQ), preferably in an interview format, but it can be self-administered by the client;

⟾ Administer the *Adult Self Assessment Questionnaire* (AdSAQ) which measures treatment readiness and motivation;

⟾ Administer and score the PIQ (discussed in detail in Chapter 11);

⟾ Complete the *Priority-Eligibility Scale* using the scores of the PIQ, ASUS and LSI and information taken from the introduction interview;

⟾ Make a decision as to the client's motivation for and commitment to involvement in the program and as to overall appropriateness for the program, using the PE score, information from the intake interview and the AdSAQ.

3. If the client is admitted to the program, then the following should be done (all forms are in Appendix B):

⟾ Have the client complete Consent for Treatment;

⟾ Have the client read and sign the *Notice of Federal Requirements Regarding Confidentiality of Alcohol and Drug Abuse Patient Records* which will apply to staff and participants in the program;

⟾ Review confidentiality issues and discuss with the client any reports the client may want sent to particular components of the criminal justice system (e.g., probation, courts). Have the client read and sign the *Consent for Release of Confidential Information* form in order to make possible this release of information;

⟾ Present the *Full Disclosure Statement* to the client. This document is required by many states (e.g., required by Colorado state statutes and regulated by the Colorado Department of Regulatory Agencies, State Grievance Board, State of Colorado). This statement must include information about the counselor (provider), including education, training and certifications. The counselor must also provide the client with a card indicating name, certification, degree, address and phone number;

⟾ Review the *Client's Rights Statement and The Full Disclosure Statement* with the client. Address the following:

- treatment fees and cost;

- the length and nature of the treatment program;

- confidentiality laws and requirements;

- a disclosure that states "sexual contact between client and counselor is not a part of any recognized therapy, that such contact or intimacy between client and counselor is illegal and should be reported to the state grievance board" (this is required by Colorado state statutes);

⟾ *Administer the Drug Use Self Report* (DUSR);

➠ Administer *Optional Tests and Questionnaires:* These questionnaires will give an in-depth assessment of the psychosocial areas discussed in Chapter 11. Results from these tests are used in Module 8. The provider may want to wait until that Module to administer these tests. However, it is recommended that they be done at intake and then redone in Module 8 if the client displayed a high degree of defensiveness when taking the instruments at intake. These are the questionnaires:

- *Alcohol Use Inventory (AUI);*
- *Addictions Severity Index;*
- *Beck Depression Inventory;*
- *Mood Appraisal Questionnaire;*
- *SOCRATES*

➠ Introduce the client to the *Participant Workbook.* Take time to review the content and then ask the client to prepare for the first group session by reading over Part I of the Workbook.

4. A formal treatment file is now opened on the client and the client is assigned to an SSC group. The treatment file should include all of the intake forms, clinical assessment questionnaires, progress notes, releases and client evaluation forms completed following each session.

This entire intake process will take a little over two hours of the client's time and one hour of the counselor's time, depending on how many of the instruments are self-administered.

Outline of Program Guidelines and Ground Rules

The program guidelines, expectations and ground rules are discussed and established with the client at the client's individual orientation session. The following guidelines and ground rules are recommended. These have been taken from several sources including Monti et al. (1989). The provider may have other guidelines that address specific agency needs or requirements. These guidelines and ground rules should be reviewed with the client who continues on to the second and third phases of the CBT program.

1 Abstinence

The provider explicitly states the treatment goal of *complete abstinence* from any activity that may result in substance abuse or criminal conduct. It is common to have ambivalent feelings concerning accepting abstinence as a goal. If the group is to be successful, every member must be willing to work on remaining sober and crime-free. Members should discuss any difficulties with abstinence (e.g., fears of using, criminal associates, etc.). Members are encouraged to remain with the group even after a lapse as long as they renew their commitment to abstinence.

Members are asked not to come to a session if they are under the influence of alcohol or drugs because they will be unable to participate fully in the group and this would disrupt other group members' efforts to remain sober. Participants are informed that the group leader may require an alcohol or drug test at any time if there is a question of participants' sobriety. If the test is positive, then the client is not allowed to be in the group session. If the client is a threat to the safety of others because of intoxication, then appropriate measures must be made to protect the community (e.g., police called, client taken to detoxification treatment, etc.).

A positive breath alcohol reading or drug screen requires that the client be staffed to determine disposition. The client might be suspended from the program temporarily, be referred to a detoxification center, or be expelled from the program. These kinds of decisions need to be made on a case-by-case basis. If the appropriate releases are in the client's file, then notification of supervisory personnel (parole or probation worker) should be made.

2 Attendance

Explain meeting places and time; hand out schedules. Consistent attendance should be required for all clients. It is important to get the client to commit to completing Phase I of the program. If there are obstacles to attending, group members will discuss these issues with the group before withdrawing from treatment.

3 Promptness

If a client must be late or absent, s/he should call to notify the group leaders in advance. Otherwise, all clients are expected to be on time for each session.

4 Participation

Active participation in group exercises and role-playing demonstrations and timely completion of homework assignments are required aspects of the treatment process.

5 Confidentiality

Group leaders should explain that confidentiality is essential for the success of the group and should elicit a promise from the group members not to discuss group conversations with outsiders. The group leader should explain that confidentiality can be maintained to the extent that clients' behavior does not reflect imminent danger to themselves or the community.

Limits of Confidentiality: It is important that clients understand the limits of confidentiality. Leaders should not make a commitment to keep secrets about anything the sponsoring agency or supervisory personnel need to know. Assurance should be provided, however, that treatment details will be used appropriately and in context. Individual *Thinking Reports* or self-disclosing statements will not be shared with staff or become a part of the general correctional record. Summary progress reports will be part of the offender's permanent record.

Leaders should make an explicit point that information about specific crimes or planned crimes would be shared with appropriate authorities. However, this program neither requires nor asks for such information. While we require open channels of communication about styles of thinking, detailed information that constitutes legal evidence is not required.

6 Eating and Smoking in Group

Smoking is not allowed in group sessions. Some groups may decide to include coffee and/or cigarette breaks; however, two full hours should be allowed for each session.

7 Cravings and Slips

Clients may experience cravings or slips. It is important to encourage clients to discuss these experiences for 15-20 minutes at the onset of selected group sessions. Group leaders should reinforce self-disclosing problems while focusing on the pre-relapse high-risk situation and the cognitive-affective reactions to the incident. Leaders should avoid glorifying the high-risk behavior (e.g., successful evasion of social or legal consequences of substance abuse or criminal activity).

Principles of Effective Group Management and Leadership

Successful delivery of a cognitive-behavioral program of *Strategies for Self-Improvement and Change* will also depend on how the counselor manages his or her treatment group.

Individuals with various backgrounds have successfully facilitated cognitive-behavioral change programs. Educational backgrounds have varied from high school degree through various graduate degrees. Although formal training in teaching and counseling professions are both useful and relevant, such characteristics as *empathy, sensitivity, flexibility and a talent for logical self expression are considerably more important*.

The following are some basic guidelines and principles for effective group facilitation and management.

1 Treatment of the Group

There are many ways that a group counselor or leader can facilitate the activity of a group. One is to focus on individuals in the group. This is actually doing one-to-one facilitation or what we might call *individual counseling* within a group setting. Glassman (1983) calls this *treatment within the group*.

A second approach is to facilitate the *interaction among individuals* in the group. In this approach, the group counselor or facilitator tries to get people to interact and uses the interpersonal interactions to help individual clients to disclose themselves and work on their problems and issues. Glassman (1983) calls this *treatment or therapy with the group*.

A third approach involves seeing the *group as an individual*. The counselor or facilitator treats the client through the group itself. In this leadership approach, the group becomes the client. The counselor uses the *group as person* to facilitate the change and growth of the group as an individual. All of the skills that the counselor uses to facilitate the expression and change of the individual in individual counseling is now used on the group itself. The counselor invites the group to *share, disclose and tell its story*. The counselor reflects the group's feelings, thoughts and actions. The counselor gets the group to change and then reinforces that change. The development of *group cohesion* and *trust* become a primary focus. The group becomes a powerful initiator and reinforcer of the changes in its members. Glassman (1983) calls this *therapy or treatment of the group*.

In the third approach, the *group becomes the vehicle of change* and not just the counselor or the program content and process. Whereas individuals in the group will provide support for each other, only one individual—the group counselor or leader—will look after the group to nurture it, to help it grow, to protect it and to facilitate its growth. Eventually, individual members do become invested in this process. But it is the group leader who is charged with this primary responsibility.

2 Depersonalizing the Leadership Authority

Offender groups tend to see the authority for controlling and sanctioning behavior as centered in the group leader or counselor. In this case, an effective approach is to allow the structure, rules and guidelines of the program to manage the group and the individual behaviors of group members. In essence, this centers the authority on the *program rules and guidelines*.

Bush and Bilodeau (1993) identify this as *depersonalizing* the use of staff authority while maintaining control of the process and upholding the rules. The group leader needs to make it clear that the process will proceed as it has been defined, not because of an exercise of staff power, but rather because this is a change process that works, that is, "it's nothing personal." Disciplining behavior is part of the group leadership role with an offender population. The leader should communicate to the offender—always with courtesy and respect—that the behavior disrupts the task at hand. Communicate that the client has the choice whether or not to participate and be prepared to follow through with consequences. With regard to rules, leaders should communicate that our intent is not to force clients to comply, but rather to help them to succeed.

3 Center the Authority Within the Group

A more effective approach is to center the authority for managing and disciplining individual behavior with the group itself. This is congruent with the *leadership of the group* model described above. In this case, the group leader *facilitates group responsibility* in controlling and disciplining its own behavior. Sometimes this is not possible, and the center of authority tends to falls back on the group leader or counselor. However, in most cases, control and management of individual behavior in groups can be effectively done through the group itself. Often, this does not work because the group leader is unwilling to relinquish the power and control, or gets caught up in a power struggle with the group.

4 Center the Authority Within the Group Member

Another way to manage and control offender behavior within treatment programs is to place the authority and responsibility with the *individual offender* on questions of appropriate behavior. Group leaders need to draw out participants' own recognition of their patterns of thinking and behaving, rather than imposing their own views. Often the leader can describe the patterns that are observed in the offender, but the perception should be verified *in the offender's words*. It should be made clear that CBT empowers the SAO by teaching the skills to control his/her life. Part of the therapeutic and correctional confrontation strategy of CBT is that the counselor continually stresses that the *locus of control is always internal* and the decision to change or not to change is always within the power of the client.

5 Keep the Focus on the Basic Steps of Cognitive-Behavioral Self-Change

Each group session should focus on underlying cognitive-behavioral patterns. The group needs to remain aware that we are engaged in a process of finding and changing criminogenic (including AOD abuse) patterns of thinking and acting. Offenders should have a clear understanding of how the session content, exercises and homework assignments assist in the process of self-directed change. The two-step process of cognitive-behavioral change becomes the "theme song" of the program:

> Step 1: *Find your criminogenic and AOD abuse patterns of thinking and acting.*

> Step 2: *Find ways to change the criminogenic and AOD abuse thinking and acting patterns.*

6 Achieve Cooperation Between Group Members and Staff

Group management and facilitation is always directed at working to achieve cooperation between group members and staff (Bush & Bilodeau, 1993). The typical offender posture of "us or them" undermines group process. Ingrained patterns of hostility and social conflict need to be replaced with patterns of *prosocial cooperation* between participants and staff. When hostile offender attitudes block channels of communication, these attitudes may be exposed as disruptive and challenged according to the already established guidelines for program participation. If members appear to resent the leader's authority, this may indicate a need to allow offenders more freedom to express their views. At times, however, responsibility for resentment and undermining of the group effort may have to be placed squarely on the offender.

7 Maximize Individual Involvement in the Group Process

Effective group leadership will always be directed at maximizing the participation of group members. At the same time, the leader needs to be keenly aware that individuals differ with respect to group comfort, feeling at ease in a group and ability to be open and to share. As group cohesion and trust builds, even the most "threat sensitive" group member will begin to feel a greater degree of comfort in sharing with the group.

Within the guideline of respecting client differences around group comfort, leaders should develop skills to attend to all group members while at the same time attending to the group itself. This will involve helping each member to be actively involved in the discussions. Although the group leader may work with a single group member on a given exercise, all participants should be actively contemplating the lessons involved. Leaders may *check in* with the group to be sure that everyone is following what is going on. The group may be asked to assist the leader in actively engaging its members.

The Three Hats of the Group Leader and Counselor

Chapter 9 presented the three broad counselor variables involved in Treatment and Change. In essence, these are *three hats* that the counselor continues to wear when delivering the SSC program to the substance abusing offender. Let us look at these once again.

1 Personal

On the personal level, counselors who communicate *warmth, genuineness, empathy, respect and honesty* toward their clients have been shown to be most effective. Although we discussed the issue of self-disclosure in Chapter 9, issues regarding its use in the treatment of the SAO bears reviewing. We identified self-disclosure as a skill. Yet, it should be used cautiously and discreetly. Self-disclosure has the disadvantage of putting the focus on the counselor rather than the client. When the counselor's self-disclosure involves the sharing of life problems, the client may feel less confident in the counselor's ability to be an effective counselor. *Self-disclosure should be used only if it enhances rapport and trust, if it enhances the client's self-awareness, and if it provides a problem solving role model.* Often, self-disclosure is self-serving and ends up taking care of the counselor's needs and not the needs of the client.

2 Technical

On the technical level, counselors need to have a good command of counseling and therapeutic skills and a solid grounding in correctional as well as alcohol and drug counseling skills. The *therapeutic skills platform,* which was outlined in Chapter 9 of this manual, provides the basis of the technical aspect of the counselor's role.

3 Philosophical

It is important that the provider develops a philosophical or theoretical view of alcoholism and drug abuse, criminal conduct, and the treatment of these conditions. This gives the provider an orientation or framework when working with the substance abusing offender. For example, the counselor may hold a *medical model* view of alcoholism, a *cognitive* view of human behavior and a *moral* view of criminal conduct. The counselor may take a *client-centered* approach to treatment. Over time, the provider's philosophical and theoretical orientation will change as he or she builds knowledge and experience in the field.

Session Evaluation

Each session will be evaluated by both the client and counselor. The client will be asked to evaluate each session by completing the *Client Session Evaluation Summary* (CSES). The CSES, which will take about three to five minutes to complete, provides opportunity for the client to assess the value and effectiveness of each session and an evaluation of the counselor's performance. The CSES is found in Appendix B.

The counselor will evaluate each session through the use of the *Provider's Session Evaluation Summary* (PSES) which is found in Appendix B.

The CSES and PSES will be used to help the counselor improve program delivery effectiveness. Data from these instruments will be of value when program revisions and changes are made.

Client Session Response Evaluation

The staff presenting the program evaluate the client's participation in the program through the use of the *Behavior Rating Form* (BRF). The client is rated on classroom and homework completion, attendance, participation, attitude and promptness. The BRF is completed on a weekly basis for the first month of the program, then monthly for the rest of the program. A score is determined from these ratings. Low scores indicate poor motivation and high resistance. Although the BRF is not standardized, it provides the counselor with an idea of how the client is responding to the program. Clients are individually assessed as to their appropriateness for Phase II. A copy of the BRF is found in Appendix B. Clients with low scores may not be candidates for Phase II of the program.

At the discretion of the service provider, clients may be tested on program content. No protocol has been developed for this kind of assessment. It is suggested that the counselor follow through with some of this content testing to determine if the client is learning the concepts and ideas being taught.

Client Outcome Evaluation

An important part of any program assessment is evaluating the client's response to that program and changes in the client as a consequence of that program. Although different time frames may be used to structure outcome evaluation, one important evaluation point is at the time the client terminates the program, whether the client successfully completes the program or prematurely terminates.

Two instruments are included in this manual to assist the provider in outcome evaluation. The Provider Treatment Closure Questionnaire (PTCQ) is designed to evaluate the client at treatment closure. This is a rater instrument and is completed on the strength of what the provider knows about the client at the time the client terminates the program. This instrument, however, can be effectively used at the middle of the program or at a three- or six-month follow-up assessment. It is recommended that the PTCQ be completed on all the clients whether they complete the program or not. Data provided by the PTCQ completed on dropouts can give the provider valuable information with respect to evaluating program efficacy. The PTCQ is provided in Appendix A.

The follow-up Assessment Questionnaire (FAQ) is designed as a client *self-report* measure to assess the client's response to the program and the client's cognitive and behavioral adjustment at treatment closure. The FAQ may be administered through a structured interview or through self-administration. The FAQ can also be used at certain points during the program and at a three- or six-month follow-up assessment. The FAQ is also provided in Appendix A.

Summary

Chapters 1 through 12 have provided the essential concepts and knowledge in preparing for the delivery of the *Strategies for Self-Improvement and Change*. The next section of this manual provides the hands-on elements of program delivery. Good Luck.

THE TREATMENT CURRICULUM

What a man thinks of himself, that is what determines or rather indicates, his fate.

Henry David Thoreau

INTRODUCTION

Section I of this manual outlined the important principles of cognitive-behavioral treatment. It gave a historical review of how these principles have been applied to the treatment of the individual with substance abuse problems and to the treatment of criminal offenders. It provided a basis upon which to select the most relevant concepts, principles and approaches in the treatment of the substance abusing offender. First, it was clear that motivational enhancement and building treatment readiness were very important. Second, SAO treatment needed to be structured around the process and stages of change. Third, self-disclosure and building self-awareness were necessary to open doors for self-improvement and change. Fourth, substantive in the review was the finding that cognitive-behavioral principles and methods have been effective in bringing about change in the substance abuser and in the offender. The importance of programs directed at relapse prevention was made obvious. Finally, it was clear that changes that occurred in treatment could be strengthened and sustained through involvement in community programs that promote and reward prosocial activities. Such community reinforcement programs include self-help groups that emphasize the 12-step model.

In *Section II*, we provided the important components of the platform upon which this program is built. A conceptual frame for a cognitive-behavioral treatment program for the SAO was provided. We also identified the key characteristics of the provider and the relationship between the provider and the client. Specific operational guidelines were provided, and a format for client assessment and treatment planning was presented.

We took what we learned from our historical perspective and theoretical framework and constructed a treatment protocol with a specific course of treatment—the treatment curriculum. This section outlines this protocol and curriculum for the cognitive-behavioral treatment program, *Strategies for Self-Improvement and Change* (SSC), for Substance Abusing Offenders.

Structure of Treatment Program and Curriculum Manual (Section III)

The treatment protocol and curriculum is divided into three phases: *Challenge to Change, Commitment to Change* and *Taking Ownership of Change*. Each phase is introduced by an outline of the requirements for successful completion, including expectations for skill development as well as client participation.

The material for *Section III* is divided into 12 *modules* representing major themes that address the sequence of therapeutic activities. Modules are subdivided into *sessions* which represent discrete lessons to be covered during an individual group meeting. These are lessons to facilitate growth and change in the client. We will use the term *sessions* when referring to the specific program segments. However, we want the provider to keep in mind that the term *session* refers to lessons: lessons from which the client learns how to bring about self-improvement and change.

Each session is broken into six discrete parts:

1. Rationale of session;
2. Objectives of session;
3. Session content and process;
4. Classroom and homework assignments;
5. Outline of the presentation sequence;
6. Session and client evaluation.

The *Session Content and Process* part of the curriculum is written in such a manner that the material addresses the client in the second person. This helps to personalize the instructional material and also allows the provider to teach directly from the curriculum content in the provider's manual. Sometimes the content is presented in a factual manner without personalizing it in the second person ("you"). Exercises are also included in the content part of each session.

Participant Workbook

The *Provider's Manual* is accompanied by a *Participant Workbook*. Each session in the Workbook includes the objectives for the session, session content, written exercises, classroom and homework assignments and thought reports. Tables and figures are used liberally in order to illustrate the relevant content of each session. The content of each session in the Workbook is taken from portions of the Session Content and Process part of the *Provider's Manual*. Most often, the Workbook content is an extraction of the most relevant material from the curriculum manual and is often restated in more simplistic terms. The curriculum manual presents a more detailed and elaborate explanation of the session content. Many, but not all, of the figures and tables presented in the curriculum manual are presented in the Workbook. *Clients are required to bring their workbooks to each group meeting.*

The Themes of the Treatment Curriculum

Building on the findings of our historical and theoretical review, the treatment curriculum is built around key themes for self-improvement and change. These themes are not necessarily presented in sequence, but are embedded in the treatment curriculum content and process. These themes are

➠ Building trust within and rapport with the client;

➠ Enhancing motivation and readiness for treatment involvement;

➠ Developing knowledge about the process of change and about drug abuse, criminal conduct and the cycles of drug abuse and criminal conduct;

➠ Enhancing self-awareness through self-assessment and self-disclosure;

➠ Enhancing self-awareness through the assessment of others and feedback;

➠ Developing and strengthening the basic skills for coping with and managing intrapersonal and interpersonal relationships and problems, engaging in prosocial behavior and community responsibility, moral reasoning and values, preventing relapse and recidivism and developing a healthy lifestyle.

Resources for the Development of the Treatment Curriculum

A number of resources were utilized in developing the SSC treatment curriculum. First, a number of experts in the field were interviewed as to what they felt were important components for a CBT program for SAOs. About 20 experts working in substance abuse and correctional programs in Colorado reviewed the manual.

Second, a number of treatment manuals were reviewed. These include manuals developed by Bush & Bilodeau (1993), Kadden and associates (1992), King and associates (1994), Miller and associates (1994), Monti and associates (1989, 1995) and Ross and associates (Ross & Lightfoot, 1985; Ross & Ross, 1988; 1995; Ross et al., 1986). The program content, concepts and process described in these manuals were helpful in developing the SSC treatment curriculum.

The clinical, research and academic experience of the authors provided the most substantive basis for the development of the treatment curriculum. Kenneth Wanberg, Th.D., Ph.D., has 35 years experience in the evaluation, treatment and research of substance abuse problems and criminal conduct, both within public and private agencies and in private practice. Harvey Milkman, Ph.D., has 25 years of experience in developing multidisciplinary perspectives on the causes, consequences and solutions for addictive behaviors. The combined skills of the authors provided a substantial basis for the development of the content, skill practice and exercises of the treatment curriculum.

Finally, the reviews of the manual by Brad Bogue, M.A., Reid Hester, Ph.D., Alan Marlatt, Ph.D., Robert Ross, Ph.D., and David Timken, Ph.D., provided valuable input in review of the development of the program structure and process and curriculum content.

PROGRAM OUTLINE

PHASE I: CHALLENGE TO CHANGE

Screening Evaluation Session

Individual Intake and Orientation Session

MODULE 1: BUILDING TRUST AND RAPPORT

Session 1: Developing a Working Relationship

Session 2: Understanding and Engaging the Change Process

MODULE 2: BUILDING A DESIRE AND MOTIVATION TO CHANGE

Sessions 3 and 4: Building a Motivation to Change

MODULE 3: BUILDING THE KNOWLEDGE BASE TO CHANGE

Session 5: Understanding the Role of Thinking and Feeling in Learning and Change

Session 6: Understanding the Role of Behavior in Self-Improvement and Change

Session 7: Basic Knowledge About Drugs

Session 8: Understanding Alcohol and Other Drug (AOD) Addiction

Session 9: Understanding Criminal Conduct and the Influence of Drugs

MODULE 4: SELF-DISCLOSURE AND RECEIVING FEEDBACK: PATHWAYS TO SELF-AWARENESS AND CHANGE

Session 10: Learning Communication Tools and Skills

Session 11: Tools of Self-Disclosure: Autobiography, Thinking Reports, Journaling and Participating in the Reflection Group

Session 12: Deeper Sharing: Your Deep Emotions and Your AOD Use

Session 13: Deeper Sharing: Your History of Criminal Conduct

MODULE 5: PREVENTING RELAPSE AND RECIDIVISM: IDENTIFYING HIGH-RISK SITUATIONS

Session 14: Relapse and Recidivism Prevention I: Identifying High-Risk Situations and Understanding Relapse and Recidivism

Session 15: Relapse and Recidivism Prevention II: Learning the Cognitive-Behavioral Map for AOD Abuse and Criminal Conduct

MODULE 6: HOW DO PEOPLE CHANGE: UNDERSTANDING THE PROCESS OF SELF-IMPROVEMENT AND CHANGE

Session 16: Reviewing the Process and Stages of Change and Selecting Targets for Change

Session 17: Ways to Change and Barriers to Change

Session 18: Looking Forward: Making a Commitment to Change

PHASE II: COMMITMENT TO CHANGE

MODULE 7: INTRODUCTION TO PHASE II: DEVELOPING COMMITMENT TO CHANGE

Session 19: Recognizing Readiness to Change: Problem Solving and Doing Something Different— It's Your Choice

Session 20: Involving Significant Others

MODULE 8: IN-DEPTH ASSESSMENT: LOOKING AT THE AREAS OF NEED AND CHANGE

Session 21: In-Depth Assessment: Getting the Information to Plot the Master Profile

Session 22: Targets of Change and the Master Assessment Plan—(MAP)

MODULE 9: STRENGTHENING BASIC SKILLS FOR SELF-IMPROVEMENT AND CHANGE:

ACTING ON THE COMMITMENT TO CHANGE

PHASE III: TAKING OWNERSHIP OF CHANGE

MODULE 10: RELAPSE AND RECIDIVISM PREVENTION: REVIEW AND STRATEGIES FOR SELF-CONTROL AND LIFESTYLE BALANCE

MODULE 11: STRENGTHENING OUR OWNERSHIP OF CHANGE: DEVELOPING THE SKILLS OF CRITICAL REASONING AND SETTLING CONFLICTS

MODULE 12: MAINTAINING SELF-IMPROVEMENT AND CHANGE: DEVELOPING A HEALTHY LIFE STYLE OR MANNER OF LIVING

PHASE I
CHALLENGE TO CHANGE
INTRODUCTION AND OVERVIEW

PHASE I: CHALLENGE TO CHANGE

Introduction to Phase I

1 Overview

Phase I, the *Challenge to Change*, sets the stage for self-improvement and change. *Phase I* involves 18 two-hour sessions over a period of eight weeks.

One of the most important parts of this phase of treatment will be that of developing *rapport with and trust within the client* as to the intent and purpose of the program. To this end, *Module 1*, involving two sessions, is devoted to developing a working relationship with the client and helping the client understand the process of self-improvement and change. Yet, building and maintaining trust and rapport with the client are ongoing tasks in every module and every phase of treatment.

Developing client rapport and trust represents only a first step in the self-improvement and change process. Clients need to develop a readiness and motivation to change. *Module 2* involves two two-hour sessions for *building motivation* to change. Again, the development and maintenance of motivation for the client to change is an ongoing process in the treatment program.

Change is dependent on knowledge, knowledge that is generic and knowledge that is unique to the individual. Both sources of knowledge build self-awareness. *Module 3*, with five two-hour sessions, is designed to help the client build this knowledge base. This module includes sessions on *building a basic knowledge base* for achieving self-improvement and change, with a focus on the role of thinking, feeling and behavior in self-improvement and change. We also give the client a core knowledge base around drugs, drug use and the drug abuse patterns and cycles that are results of drug use. We also help the client gain a good understanding of the principles and cycles underlying criminal conduct and the relationship between criminal conduct (CC) and AOD use.

Self-awareness is dependent on self-disclosure. *Module 4* involves four two-hour sessions for enhancing *self-awareness through self-disclosure*. In preparing the client for self-disclosure, we help the client learn basic communication skills which are necessary for effective and meaningful self-disclosure. We focus on the identification of thinking errors and cognitive distortions, of emotions and feelings and of the client's background and history of involvement in AOD use and criminal conduct. In order to enhance the self-disclosure process, we assist the client in writing an autobiography and help the client to learn to use the self-disclosure tools of journaling and writing thinking reports. In *Module 5*, we introduce the client to the *concepts of relapse and recidivism* and to the prevention of these potential occurrences on the client's path to self-improvement and change. Although relapse prevention is often thought of as part of maintaining change and improvement, we feel that the potential for relapse and recidivism is always present and even portentous with the SAO throughout the treatment process. Thus, the SAO client needs to have knowledge about Relapse and Recidivism Prevention (RRP), needs to understand and identify the high-risk (HR) situations associated with RRP, and learn the skills to prevent relapse and recidivism.

Finally, we close *Phase I* of treatment, *Challenge to Change*, with *Module 6*, which focuses on *applying* the change process to the individual client. We assist the individual client to identify targets of change, apply the process of self-change and then *identify and overcome the barriers to change*. Most important, we now challenge the client to commit to change by engaging in *Phase II* of treatment.

2 Specific Goal and Objectives of Phase I

The overall goal of Phase I is to develop within the client a basic trust in and rapport with the treatment provider and with the purpose of the program so as to effectively motivate the client to engage in the change process. The specific objectives of Phase I are

⚏➡ develop rapport with and trust within the client to enhance the client's willingness to share and tell his or her story;

⟹ establish a climate of caring so as to facilitate sharing and catharsis;

⟹ enhance motivation for and resolve the ambivalence around commitment to treatment and to change;

⟹ help the client to feel comfortable in revealing her/himself and disclosing critical information about him/herself;

⟹ help the client to develop a core knowledge base in the areas of criminal conduct (CC), alcohol and other drug (AOD) abuse, the process of change and a cognitive-behavioral basis of change, and the interaction of criminal conduct and AOD use;

⟹ help the client to learn his or her own patterns of thinking that lead to criminal conduct (CC) and AOD abuse;

⟹ learn to recognize the warning signs of relapse and recidivism (RR) and learn the skills to prevent RR.

3 Basic Counselor Skills for Phase I

- Responding attentiveness;
- Encourages sharing between group members;
- Feedback clarification.

4 Basic Treatment Strategies

- Motivational enhancement skills and techniques;
- Enhancing self-disclosure and reflecting self-awareness;
- Self-evaluation;
- Relapse and recidivism prevention.

5 Client Experiences

- Openness;
- Acceptance;
- Release of feelings, thoughts and perceptions;
- Self-awareness.

6 Completion Requirements for Phase I

a. *Comprehension and Skill Development*—Clients will/should be able to:

1) Learn the basic principle of cognitive-behavioral *Strategies of Self- Improvement and Change* (SSC). Patterns of CC and AOD use and abuse are determined by an individual's style of thinking about oneself and the world and understanding that we improve the course of our lives by controlling how we think about ourselves and the world;

2) Learn basic facts about the patterns and cycles of CC and how people develop and continue these patterns;

3) Learn basic facts about the patterns and cycles of AOD abuse and how people develop and continue these patterns;

4) Learn about the stages that people go through when making changes;

5) Construct *Thinking Reports* and keep a personal journal of thoughts and attitudes about cravings and urges for both CC and AOD abuse;

6) Identify their own key patterns of thinking which led to CC and AOD abuse;

7) Identify their own personal characteristics that predispose them to CC and AOD abuse;

8) Develop alternatives to the pre-treatment patterns of thinking which have led to CC and AOD abuse;

9) Learn the high-risk (HR) situations in his or her own life that lead to RR and learn the skills to prevent RR.

b. *Participation Expectations*—Clients will/should

1) Attend at least 90% of all meetings, be punctual and complete all assignments;

2) Maintain a cooperative posture with respect to staff and other clients by

- functioning in a self-directed, businesslike manner while assisting others to complete the tasks of Phase I.

- self-disclosing by presenting *Thinking Reports* with the purpose of discovering alternative patterns of thinking and acting.

- Recognizing that satisfactory attendance does not automatically qualify participants for completion of Phase I. Participants who fail to meet minimal expectations regarding class participation and assignments may be asked to repeat *Phase I* or to take leave from the program until they feel that they are ready to fully experience all aspects of the program.

7 | Assignment of New Clients to Phase I

The SSC treatment program can be conducted on either an open or closed group basis. An *open group model* is one where clients can enter the program at any time. The *closed group model* involves the same clients starting and completing the program together with no new clients being enrolled during the program process. For most programs, adhering to the closed group model for the entire program may not be practical. Many programs may be able to begin the *Strategies for Self-Improvement and Change* (SSC) cycle only once or twice a year. Many of the modules have a "stand alone" quality in the sense that they are not based on the prerequisite of the presentation of another module.

There is a certain degree of continuity and sequentiality to the modules in all phases of the program. This is particularly true of the modules in *Phase I* and in subsets of modules in Phase II. Thus, it is recommended that *Phase I* be conducted using a *closed group* model. In this manner, clients will receive the benefits of the sequential nature of the sessions in *Phase I*. We have also provided *four logical break-points* for the sessions in *Phase II*. These break-points are clearly delineated in the text and allow the provider to bring in new clients at these break-points without disrupting the logical presentation of *Phase II* sessions. It is important for the client to be aware of the fact that he or she will be entering a program where clients have already been participating for as long as five or six weeks.

The particular delivery strategy will depend upon the circumstances of the particular agency or criminal justice unit offering the program.

Individual Intake and Orientation Session

An individual intake and orientation session is completed with each client entering the program. The specific protocol for intake and admission is provided in Chapter 12. All of the instruments, tests and intake and admission forms are found in Appendices A and B of this manual. The following is a review of the intake and admission process:

1. Review the Referral Package to be sure the referral file is complete. If any items are missing, they should be completed before proceeding with the admission process. These include

   ➡ Referral Summary Evaluation (RES)

   ➡ Copies of the DAST, ADS, ASUS, LSI and SUHM;

➠ Client's criminal record and driving record;

➠ Other documents including consent and releases.

2. Determine appropriateness of the client for the SSC program by doing the following:

➠ Complete the *Personal Data Questionnaire;*

➠ Administer the *Adult Self Assessment Questionnaire* (AdSAQ) which measures treatment readiness and motivation;

➠ Administer the PIQ;

➠ Score the PIQ;

➠ Conduct a brief interview regarding the client's willingness to enter the program and include in that interview the following:

• program outline and structure;

• program guidelines and expectations;

• program ground rules.

➠ Complete the *Priority-Eligibility Scale* using the scores of the PIQ, ASUS and LSI and information taken from the intake interview;

➠ Make a decision as to the client's motivation for and commitment to involvement in the program and as to overall appropriateness for the program.

3. If the client is admitted to the program, then the following should be done:

➠ Complete *Consent for Treatment;*

➠ Review *Notice of Federal Requirements Regarding Confidentiality of Alcohol and Drug Abuse Patient Records;*

➠ Complete *Consent for Release of Confidential Information;*

➠ Counselor presents *Full Disclosure Statement;*

➠ *Review Client's Rights Statement;*

➠ Review issues of confidentiality and discuss with the client any reports the client may want sent to particular components of the criminal justice system (e.g., probation, courts). Releases are then signed in order to make this possible.

➠ Administer the *Drug Use Self Report* (DUSR).

➠ Administer *Optional Tests and Questionnaires* (to be used in Module 8):

• *Alcohol Use Inventory (AUI);*

• *Addictions Severity Index;*

• *Beck Depression Inventory;*

• *Mood Appraisal Questionnaire;*

• *SOCRATES.*

➠ Introduce the client to the *Participant Workbook.* Take time to review the content and then ask the client to prepare for the first group session by reading over *Part I* of the Workbook.

4. A formal treatment file is now opened on the client and the client is assigned to an SSC group. The treatment file should include all of the intake forms, clinical assessment questionnaires, progress notes, releases and client evaluation forms completed following each session.

MODULE 1

Building Trust and Rapport

MODULE 1: BUILDING TRUST AND RAPPORT

Overview of Module 1

This is one of the most critical modules of the program. The attitude and response of the clients in this module will probably set the tone for their involvement throughout the program. The provider will have to work hard at dealing with the *ambivalence, resistance* and even *anger* of the clients at being in the program, particularly for those who feel that they are "forced" to attend. Some individual attention may have to be given to highly resistive clients. It is best if those issues can be resolved through the process of the group and group support. It may be that you have to ask some clients to leave the program because their attitudes and behaviors are disruptive to the flow of the group.

Building *trust* and *rapport* with clients in the SSC treatment program is an ongoing process and task throughout all of phases of the program. However, because these are such important components of treatment, and because treatment outcome is significantly dependent on the relationship of the client with the counselor and with the treatment group, during *Phase I* of the program, they are given special focus. The elements and principles of *motivational enhancement* and *motivational interviewing* are important applications in *Module 1* as in all of *Phase I*. It is important to remember the focal counselor skills to be used during Phase I:

- ⮕ *responding attentiveness;*

- ⮕ *encouragers to share;* and

- ⮕ *feedback clarification.*

Introducing the Participant's Workbook

The Participant's Workbook should be introduced in this module. It will be helpful to review the WELCOME section of the workbook, since this is presented in a positive and motivating manner. Some providers may want to review the *Participant's Workbook* in its entirety during the first session of this module. The workbook should be presented as representing the client's handbook for successful completion of the program.

Module 1 and Overall Program Sequence

Depending upon the specific program sequence strategy used by you or your agency, *Module 1* may be scheduled in several ways. All clients should start with *Module 1*. Thus, if the provider is using an open group model, with new clients introduced as the program progresses, it is recommended that *Module 1* be offered on a periodic basis so that all clients complete this module before proceeding to the other modules in *Phase I*. Upon completion of *Module 1*, clients then enter the group in which *Modules 2 through 6* are in progress. It is recommended, however, that the closed group model be used for *Phase I*. In this way, the *Phase I* session sequence as presented in the manual can be followed.

Session ❶: Developing a Working Relationship

1. Rationale of Session

Alcohol and other drug counselors often unwittingly become agents of substance control or *watch dogs.* This readily compromises the therapeutic effort. While overall goals may share certain measurable qualities, system and clinical concerns are not always one and the same. Group leaders are encouraged to differentiate system from clinical concerns. This approach begins the process of client responsibility while separating counselor from consequences. System limitations and expectations should be stated in a matter-of-fact manner while idealized treatment outcomes may be shared with encouragement and optimism.

Miller et al. (1994) point to the therapist characteristic of *accurate empathy* as a powerful predictor of therapeutic success with problem drinkers. Similarly, Andrews and Bonta (1994) find that offender recidivism is effectively reduced when rehabilitative programming is *ethical, decent and humane.* In contrast to some treatments that emphasize confrontation of denial regarding criminal or substance abuse motives, counselors are advised to explicitly avoid direct argumentation which may well evoke increased resistance and poor therapy outcomes. In fact, Miller and colleagues (1993) report that the degree to which therapists engage in direct confrontation has proportionately adverse effects on treatment outcome years post treatment.

The first sessions will be some of the most important, yet difficult, to lead. Clients will be anxious and even confused as to what is to happen in the program. The first sessions are therefore geared toward establishing group comfort and trust while explaining the rationale, goals and procedures of the group. After a brief introduction of the staff to present the program—including counseling and educational background—the counselor states that the introductory session will include an overview of the purpose of cognitive-behavioral therapy for SAOs, ground rules and some exercises for getting to know one another.

2. Objectives of Session:

➠ Provide participants with an overview of treatment philosophy and strategies for self-improvement.

➠ Introduce staff and group members through get-acquainted exercises.

➠ Establish the guidelines and ground rules for effective group management and program participation.

➠ Develop the foundation for trust and respect between staff and participants and among participants.

➠ Introduce and discuss the Participant Workbook. The Workbook was given to the client during the admission session.

3. Session Content and Process

During our first session together, we will give you an overview of what we are calling cognitive-behavioral *Strategies for Self-Improvement and Change.* We will get acquainted with each other and review the outline of the program. We will outline what you will need to do to complete Phase I of this program. We will discuss the program guidelines and ground rules.

a. **Overview of treatment philosophy and strategies for self-improvement and change.**

Substance abuse behavior and criminal conduct (CC) have much in common with each other. Both are acts that give us immediate rewards and a rush or high from taking part in the act itself. Both are usually followed by delayed negative or unpleasant results such as anxiety, guilt, social disapproval or criminal punishment. We can relapse into drinking or return to criminal conduct when we place ourselves in high-risk situations or when we allow ourselves to engage in certain patterns of thinking and feeling.

155

This program has two main goals: 1) *to help clients learn the basic skills and approaches for identifying patterns of thinking and behaving that lead to substance abuse and crime,* and 2) *to develop skills to change destructive patterns of thought and behavior.*

Each group session will focus on helping you to develop the necessary understanding, skills and attitudes for coping with high-risk situations that lead to substance abuse and crime. All group discussions, exercises and homework assignments are set up to explain and illustrate how the basic CBT principles and skills can be used to prevent relapse into AOD use and recidivism into criminal conduct.

You are encouraged to practice the skills taught in this program outside of the treatment setting, particularly in situations that are high risk for engaging in alcohol and other drug (AOD) use or criminal conduct (CC). As well, the CBT skill exercises practiced during group sessions are purposely designed to be intense, thereby helping members of the group to produce the desired skills when they are challenged during real-life situations.

b. **Introduction to program exercises.**

You will be asked to take part in many exercises in order to successfully complete this program. These exercises were set up for you to put into practice what you learn in the program. They are set up mainly for you to improve your life-management and coping skills.

The provider should rehearse the exercises suggested for each session prior to implementation. Providers are encouraged to use their discretion as to where they will implement the suggested exercises for this session. For example, some leaders may opt to involve the group in name recognition exercises early in the session whereas others may choose to establish the overall treatment perspective and guidelines before entering into the experiential domain. Group leaders should encourage participation in exercises by informing the group that many of the exercises are designed to exemplify how pleasurable feeling states may be derived from interpersonal encounters without the use of drugs or alcohol.

c. **Begin to build trust and rapport.**

One way to begin to build trust and rapport is to get to know each other. We will now take time to introduce ourselves and find out who we are and what we are about.

Warm-up—Self-Introduction Exercise: This process is done within the group using the structured round-robin technique of going around the circle and having each client structure their sharing around specific topics. In this case, the goal is to have each client share information around

1) biographical information including age, where they work, and who are the significant others in their lives;

2) their view of what brings them to the program;

3) what they want to get out of the program;

4) basic concerns or anxieties about being in the program.

Exercise: Get Acquainted Memory Game: Give clients one minute to meet another person and learn at least one thing about that person that wasn't revealed in the above interview exercise. Change partners every minute. With each new partner, a new piece of information must be shared. This continues until everyone in the room has met every person. Have each person then share what they remember about each person in the room.

d. **Present outline of SS program to participants.**

e. **Present and discuss program guidelines and ground rules.**

Our belief is that each individual has the ability to take part in this program in a responsible and adult manner. Even though this program will give you a lot of guidance and direction, what you get out of it and how you respond in the program is up to each individual. Yet, there are some common guidelines and ground rules that we feel are necessary for group members to follow if the program is to be successful for you and the group. Let us look at these ground rules and guidelines.

1) **Abstinence:** Our most basic ground rule is that we expect clients to commit themselves to the goal of remaining alcohol and other drug (AOD) free and to refrain from any activity that may result in substance abuse or crime. You may have mixed feelings about this commitment and accepting abstinence as a goal. If the group is to be successful, every member must be willing to work on remaining sober and crime free. You will want to discuss any difficulties with abstinence (e.g., fears of using, criminal associates, etc.). You are encouraged to remain with the group even after a lapse as long as you renew your commitment to abstinence. You are asked *not* to come to a session under the influence of alcohol or drugs because you will be unable to participate fully in the group and this disrupts other group members' efforts to remain sober. You may be required to take an alcohol/drug test at any time if there is a question of your sobriety. If the test is positive, you will be asked to leave. A positive breath alcohol reading or drug screen will require that you suspend your involvement in the program until you have worked out the problem with the staff or counselor working with you.

2) **Attendance:** You are expected to have consistent attendance in the program. We want you to commit yourself to completing the first phase of the program. If there are obstacles to attending, you will agree to discuss these issues with the group before withdrawing from treatment.

3) **Participation:** Active participation in group exercises and role-playing demonstrations, and timely completion of homework assignments are required aspects of the treatment process.

4) **Promptness:** If you are to be late or absent, you are asked to notify your group leader in advance. Otherwise, all clients are expected to be on time for each session.

5) **Confidentiality on the part of the participant:** This means that you are asked to *not* discuss any of the personal material that members share in the group with anyone outside of the program. This is essential for the success of the group. We need your commitment on this.

6) **Confidentiality on the part of counseling staff:** You need to know that by state and federal law, confidentiality can be broken by your group leader if he or she believes that you are of imminent (about to happen) danger to yourself or others. The group leader is bound by law in this respect.

There are other aspects of the limits of confidentiality. First, all of you signed a consent for involvement in the program at the time you had your individual orientation to the program. You must sign a consent for any information to be released as to your involvement in this program. Some of you did sign such a consent at the time you had your individual orientation. This was because for you to be involved in the program, it is necessary for us to send progress reports to your sponsoring agency, supervisory personnel or the court. You are fully aware of what you have consented to with respect to this. Assurance is provided, however, that treatment details will be used appropriately and in context. Individual *Thinking Reports* or self-disclosing statements will not be shared with staff or become a part of the general correctional record. Where you have given consent, summary progress reports will be part of the offender's permanent record. You also need to know that *information about specific planned crimes will be shared with appropriate authorities.* However, this program neither requires nor asks for such information. While we require open channels of communication about styles of thinking, detailed physical information that constitutes legal evidence is not required.

7) **Eating and smoking in group:** There will be no smoking during sessions. Some groups may decide to include coffee and/or cigarette breaks; however, two hours should be slotted for session contact.

8) **Cravings and slips:** You may experience cravings or slips, particularly if you have been out of treatment for a while. You are encouraged to discuss these experiences for 15-20 minutes at the onset of each group session.

9) **Honesty and self-disclosure:** You are where you are because you have had a hard time being honest about yourself and being truthful about what you have done in your life. You are challenged to make every effort to be honest when talking about your past criminal conduct and substance use and abuse.

10) **Other ground rules and guidelines** may be established by your group leader or by your group. At this time, you need to discuss your feelings about the above guidelines and ground rules and, with your group leader, discuss any additional guidelines and ground rules you want to establish.

Exercise: Discuss the above guidelines and have the group establish their own set of ground rules and guidelines.

f. **Reflecting on abstaining from alcohol and other drugs.**

It may be strange for you to make a commitment to this. Let's talk about it. Think of what will make this difficult for you. Are you afraid of this commitment? What are your thoughts and feelings about it?

Exercise: Developing Motivation & Rapport—"Getting Started": The purpose of this activity is to introduce members and help them begin to think about motivation and commitment to abstinence and living a crime-free life. Each client takes 5 minutes, with the leader acting as time keeper. Ask clients to tell who they live with, a typical day, and the benefits they receive from sobriety and crime-free lifestyles. After each member has talked, the provider then summarizes and highlights the material presented. For example, a benefit of crime free lifestyle might be "I don't have to be anxious about getting caught all the time."

g. **Reflection Group for 20 minutes.**

4. Classroom and Homework Assignments

a. Review the information presented for Session 1 in the Client Workbook. Be prepared to demonstrate that you understand the following information at the beginning of the next session:

1) *Strategies for Self-improvement* Course Sequence;

2) *Challenge to Change* Completion Requirements;

3) Guidelines and Ground Rules.

b. Reflect on what you want most in the program and bring that to your group for discussion at the next session.

5. Presentation Sequence

Although the program content and session experiences are presented in separate sections, they are to be presented in the following order:

a. present overview of treatment philosophy and strategies for self-improvement;

b. review objectives for this module;

c. present program as outlined in Session Content section;

d. reflection group session;

e. review classroom and homework assignments;

f. brief look at next session.

6. Session Evaluation

a. Have the client complete the Client Session Evaluation Summary (CSES).

b. Complete Provider's Session Evaluation Summary (PSES) and reflect on these questions:

1) *Did the provider communicate effective empathy, genuineness and respect toward the clients?*

2) *Did the provider model prosocial attitudes?*

3) *Did the group understand the program ground rules?*

4) *Did the group gain a basic overview of the three phases for Strategies for Self Improvement: Challenge to Change, Commitment to Change and Taking Ownership of Change?*

Session ❷: Understanding and Engaging the Change Process

1. Rationale of Session

In Sections I and II of this manual, we have outlined the basic assumptions and premises for an effective CBT program for substance abusing offenders (SAO). Effective SAO treatment is deliverable by a broad variety of counseling staff, all of whom have basic educational and counseling experience with criminals and substance abusers. Although we use the term *substance abusing offender* (SAO) for the sake of brevity, the treatment philosophy inherent to this approach regards the SAO as an *individual* with a history of criminal conduct and/or substance abuse behavior. Such a view allows us to focus on changing an individual's thinking or behavior, rather than having to change the person him- or herself.

Transformation involves first and foremost developing the *motivation to change.* It is recognized that individuals with more psychologically severe problems and more severe antisocial patterns will have more difficulty complying with this treatment program. For clients who can accept the interactive skill-building focus of this program, *self-regulating* skills may be learned through the basic principles of motivational counseling, therapeutic confrontation, and reinforcement of life-enhancing behavior. Sobriety and stability are maintained through effective relapse prevention strategies.

Cognitive-behavioral *Strategies for Self-Improvement and Change* (SSC) is assessment-driven, recognizing the multiple conditions contributing to substance abuse and crime. There are varied causes and patterns of criminal conduct and substance abuse disorders, fulfilling different needs at different times in an individual's life. The central elements for criminal conduct and addictions are multiple and additive. Contributing factors may be linked to the individual, family, peer group and community. Treatment strategies for achieving increased self-regulation for AOD abuse and criminal conduct must be tailored to the individual's level of awareness, cognitive development and determination to modify destructive patterns of thought and behavior. Implementing effective treatment strategies at particular stages of change is an integral part of successful treatment. Ideally, successful treatment engages not only the client, but also significant others in the client's life, such as parents and spouse.

In order to maintain responsible and comfortable living throughout the life span, the principles of relapse prevention must be utilized. In the case of the SAO, relapse and recidivism must be addressed within the context of both criminal conduct and AOD abuse. Finally, effective treatment is sensitive to the client's cultural values, competencies and strengths. Cultural identity and pride must be recognized and reinforced throughout treatment.

2. Objectives of Session

> ⵑ➡ Inform participants of the basic premises and assumptions of the treatment program.
>
> ⵑ➡ Differentiate the three phases of treatment.
>
> ⵑ➡ Outline the goals and objectives of *Phase I* treatment.
>
> ⵑ➡ Establish the foundations for effective group treatment.
>
> ⵑ➡ Create an ambience characterized by trust and respect between group members.

3. Session Content

a. **Review the SSC course sequence and the basic process and phases of treatment as found in the Introduction to Section III.**

b. **Review the *Challenge to Change* requirements as spelled out in the Introduction to Phase I.**

c. **Review the treatment guidelines and ground rules.**

d. **Discuss the two basic ideas of the SSC program.**

   1) patterns of criminal conduct (CC) and alcohol and other drug (AOD) use and abuse behavior are in part determined by how the SAO thinks and feels about herself or himself and the world; and

   2) the interaction between AOD abuse and criminal thinking promotes the development and continuation of both criminal conduct and AOD abuse.

e. **Present and discuss the following underlying assumptions of the change process.**

   1) change in criminal conduct (CC) and AOD abuse and the interaction of these two phenomena occur first through gaining control of and changing the cognitive schemes (thoughts, perceptions and emotions) associated with CC and AOD abuse;

   2) new cognitive schemes can be translated into new behaviors;

   3) changes in thinking and action get reinforced by positive feelings experienced by the client (self-reinforcement) and by others resulting in the maintenance of these changes.

f. **Some topics for guided group discussion.**

   1) The value of *trust* and *understanding* in achieving positive results from this program. Clients are asked to state and discuss their feelings of how things are going thus far in the treatment group. Is the information clear and sensible? Are there any trust problems thus far?

   2) What are the *basic ideas* held by clients about criminal conduct, drug abuse, and self-improvement? What previous courses or therapy groups have they attended? What did they learn about cognitive-behavioral treatments?

   3) Discuss how they relate to *Stages of Change*. Can they identify their own position on the *Stages of Change* continuum (e.g., challenge, commitment, ownership)?

   4) What are the clients' *understandings of how thoughts can influence behavior and feelings?* Leaders should promote early discussion of how thoughts may foster both criminal conduct and substance abuse. How do clients understand the interaction between substance abuse and crime?

   5) What *conditions* must be necessary for clients to feel comfortable in revealing heretofore private aspects of their experience? Will achieving higher levels of honesty and openness lead to desired increments in self-improvement?

   6) Discuss *how we know* who to trust and who not to trust. How do you develop trust in someone new? Discuss the importance of trust and honesty in developing a comfortable and responsible lifestyle. Discuss the lack of trust inherent in criminal and drug-abusing lifestyles. *Can you trust criminal friends? Did they come to see you in jail? Did they care what was happening to you?*

g. **Exercise:** *Blind walk:* After an explanation of the process of this exercise, divide into pairs. Have one partner blindfolded and the other lead the blindfolded partner by the hand around the room or building for about five minutes. Then have the blindfolded partner guided with words. Now, switch so the leader now wears the blindfold. Discuss the difference between leading and following. Discuss how the wrong people have caused problems in living. (Note: This exercise may be particularly frightening to some participants. Lack of participation should not be viewed as a sign of poor treatment motivation.)

h. **Structured Reflection Group at end of session for 20 minutes.**

4. Classroom and Homework Assignments

a. Review the information provided for Session 2 in the Client Workbook.

b. Write a paragraph on "The Importance of Trust in Living a Crime-Free, Drug-Free Life" (Workbook, p. 22).

c. Write a statement on how improving yourself and changing will keep you from further criminal conduct and AOD use and abuse (Workbook, p. 23).

d. Describe one situation in which a particular thought you had led you to committing a crime (Workbook, p. 23).

5. Presentation Sequence

a. Review last session and workbook assignments.

b. Present rationale of session and objectives.

c. Present session content as outlined in that section.

d. Review classroom and homework assignments outlined above.

6. Session and Client Evaluation

a. Have the client complete the CSES.

b. Provider completes the PSES and reflects on the following questions.

1) *Did participants grasp the two basic premises of this treatment program?*

2) *Did participants understand the underlying assumptions of the change process?*

3) *Can participants explain the basic expectations for successful completion of each treatment stage?*

c. Counselor completes the Behavioral Rating Form (BRF) and calculates the score. The BRF will be completed on a weekly basis during Phase I. Scores on the BRF will reflect possible changes (improvement or deterioration) in the client's response to the program over time.

MODULE 2

Building a Desire and Motivation to Change

MODULE 2: BUILDING A DESIRE AND MOTIVATION TO CHANGE

Sessions ❸ and ❹ : Building Motivation to Change

1. Rationale of Module

Miller (1995) as well as Bush and Bilodeau (1993) emphasize the need for *motivation to change* in the treatment of substance abusers and offenders. Antisocial behavior is frequently so deeply ingrained in SAO clients that they may be highly resistant or even hostile to changing what is comfortable for them. In fact, they are probably convinced that their attitude—that there is no reason to change—is correct. It is important to realize that we do not make the client change, but that they must become motivated to change *themselves*. It is important to elicit speech and actions that motivate them to change—their own words can convince them that they need to alter their lifestyle. They need to realize that their thoughts, beliefs and attitudes determine their criminal and addictive behaviors and they have the ability to control them. In the end *they decide* whether to change or maintain their way of life.

Miller and associates (Miller & Rollnick, 1991; Miller et al., 1994) discuss five principles basic to helping the client mobilize his/her *inner resources*. We will briefly review these principles.

a. **Express empathy.** Emphasize acceptance of the client *as they are,* simultaneously supporting them as they attempt to change.

b. **Develop discrepancy.** Help them realize the adverse consequences of their current lifestyle and the benefits of changing.

c. **Avoid argumentation.** Abstain from any attack on the client's lifestyle. It should be the client, not the therapist, who recognizes the need for change.

d. **Roll with resistance.** Ambivalence about making change is to be expected and needs to be explored. Do not oppose the resistance, but allow the client to find the solution.

e. **Support self-efficacy.** The client must believe that s/he can perform the task(s) to change the problem behavior and needs to be supported in this belief.

It is important for the counselor to remember in presenting this module that research has clearly shown that *treatment outcome is directly related to the degree of empathy* the counselor shows toward the client. These studies indicate that about two-thirds of the variance in six months drinking outcome is accounted for by the degree of empathy shown by counselors during treatment and that even after one year, empathy accounted for over half the variance predicting drinking outcome (Miller & Baca, 1983; Miller & Rollnick, 1991; Miller, et al., 1980).

Throughout this and all sessions, let the participants know you are really understanding their problems. Encourage this process using *reflective listening*—the process should result in self-motivating statements that encourage change.

Beginning in this session, the counselor may want to use a paradoxical evoking approach (Miller & Rollnick, 1991) when there is difficulty eliciting client concerns. "Maybe you would be happier if you made no change in your lifestyle" or, "You haven't convinced me you are really a candidate for this program...it requires more motivation than I'm hearing now." One must always be cautious in using any paradoxical intent technique in that there is a risk that you will reinforce the behavior which is the direct focus of the paradox. For example, to use the paradoxical intent "maybe you ought to continue drinking yourself to death" may in fact reinforce that very behavior.

2. Objectives of Sessions 3 and 4

> ➠ To focus in more depth on the concept of how attitudes, beliefs and thinking patterns control how we act and behave.
>
> ➠ To focus on the issues of resistance and perceptual defense as part of enhancing clients' motivation for change.
>
> ➠ To review the concept of ambivalence and resistance to changing antisocial and addictive behaviors in the SAO participant.
>
> ➠ To establish a sense of readiness and responsiveness to treatment and change.
>
> ➠ To establish a sense of appreciation and understanding of the power of individual choice in the process of change.

3. Session Content

Before delivering this module, it is recommended that the counselor review concepts of change and the motivation to change found in *Chapter 5* of this manual. This session is built around five key concepts. These concepts can be presented to the client in didactic form but are then experienced through the session experiences and exercises. They are basic concepts which the client will deal with throughout the treatment program.

a. **Concept I: Impact of attitudes, beliefs and thinking patterns. Our attitudes, beliefs and automatic thoughts control how we react to people and situations that are important in our everyday life.** Change comes when we change our attitudes, beliefs and thoughts.

1) An *attitude* is a thought, feeling or orientation for or against a situation, person, idea or object outside of ourselves. An attitude directs how we think, feel and act. An attitude will cause us to line up in a certain way to something or someone outside of you. We usually have feelings or emotions tied into our attitudes. Attitudes are described in terms of *good* or *bad*.

2) A *belief* is a value or idea we use to judge or evaluate outside events, situations, people or ourselves. A belief will bond us to some outside event. It is more powerful than an attitude, but will direct our attitudes toward things or people. "All people are created equal." "We believe in the team." It is a *"truth"* or a conviction. It is usually 100 percent. We hold on to beliefs.

3) An *automatic thought* is a *thinking pattern or thought habit*. It is a mental reaction already formed inside our head that happens automatically. It could be how we think about things or how we see or perceive things or what we think about things. They occur automatically when things happen to us or when we come up against things outside of us. It is a response to things outside of us or feelings and beliefs inside of us. A thought pattern may be made up of both our attitudes and our beliefs. Our response to someone who cuts in front of us when driving may be, "People are jerks." Or, when we perceive someone to ignore us, our automatic response might be, "she doesn't like me."

Attitudes represent a readiness to respond to a given situation in a certain way and are triggered by thoughts, feelings, or behaviors. We use our beliefs, our ideas and principles, to evaluate ideas and other people as well as ourselves. Give both positive and negative examples of how our attitudes and beliefs influence the way we act.

I voted in the last election and my candidate won. I have a good attitude about the political system and the way it works.

I never did my homework and sometimes slept in class. I have a bad attitude about school.

I believe people are basically good and try to do the right thing.

I believe people in authority have no respect for me.

Exercise: The *Belief Clutch* and a *do or die self-view* Round Robin Focus Group: Have each client identify one belief that they have *clutched* to over the years and one *do or die* view of self they have held on to over the years.

b. **Concept II: Reframing the concepts of resistance and denial into the concept of perceptual defense. When people are involved in what we conclude to be resistance and denial, what they are doing is defending their view of themselves.** Denial and resistance are not viewed as enduring personality traits or some ingrained personality pattern. Rather, denial and resistance is a *perceptual state* and thus can change. Therefore, we can view motivation as "a state of readiness or eagerness to change" (Miller & Rollnick, 1991, p. 14). It is a condition that changes and is not fixed. The condition of change is defined by both external conditions and internal states.

When we fight against changing ourselves, our attitudes, beliefs and thinking, what we are really doing is defending our view of ourselves. We hold on to beliefs. "I've never had a fair chance in life." We call this a *Belief Clutch*. It is a *do or die view of ourselves* that we have held for years. Sometimes we call this resistance or denial. It is our view of ourselves. This view can change. But in order to change, we have to want to change. We have to be motivated to change—to be eager to change.

c. **Concept III: Ambivalence. The key to change is resolving the individual's ambivalence to change.** This means that we have *mixed feelings* about change. We go back and forth about change or we are hesitant to change. Change means giving up a thought, feeling or action which has supported one's view of self and which has brought comfort and pleasure to the self. Giving them up is forgoing that pleasure or comfort. Sometimes they give us excuses for what we do. The ambivalence is resolved when we learn that the thoughts and actions lead to more pain and discomfort than comfort and pleasure. It is then that we stop wavering or stop being hesitant about change.

SAOs will continue on the same path they have been walking until they understand how their *faulty thinking has led to actions* that have caused pain to themselves and others. In the course of the discussion, they may have heard some alternatives to the way they have been thinking. Perhaps this has never happened before in their lives. The fact that they have alternatives must be reinforced, and they need to receive the message that they can change. It is important that they realize they are accountable for their behavior but that they will have personal support in their efforts to change. If they choose *not* to change, society has a right to protect itself from their antisocial and criminal behavior.

Exercise: Group exercise on ambivalence: Elicit statements from the group encouraging them to be open about the *benefits* and *costs* of their substance abuse and/or criminal activities. Have the group break up into pairs and spend the first 5 minutes of this exercise discussing the *pleasurable* aspects of drug or alcohol use. During the next 5 minutes, have them talk about the *negative* results of substance use. For the final 5 minutes, have an open discussion about how easy it is to feel that there are both good and bad aspects that make it hard to determine that they want to change.

d. **Concept IV: Stages of Change. Change takes place in stages.** In Sections I and II of this manual, we discussed the following three stage of change models:

1) Prochaska and DiClemente's (1992) five stages model of change which is discussed in Chapter 5.

2) The *Lewin and Orthogenetic Model* of change and growth: *Global* and massive responding (letting go of the defenses), the *differentiation* and sorting out (understanding why one held on to the old patterns and behaviors) and *integrating* new thoughts and behaviors (putting together effective skills and actions representing different and new patterns of behavior). This model is described in Chapter 9.

3) The stages of change upon which this program is built. The following will help our clients understand these three stages.

- A first step is we think about change. We may even get ready to change. We may even say or begin doing some changing. We even begin to let go of the defenses that have blocked making change. In our program of *Strategies for Self-improvement and Change* (SSC) we call this the *Challenge to Change*.

- Our next step is that we decide we want to change. We now have a better picture of what needs to be changed. We even put time and energy into it. We come to this program. We begin making changes. We even feel the power of change. We learn skills to change. We master change. In SSC, we call this *Commitment to Change*. We pledge to change.

- Our next step is that we learn ways to keep the change going. We learn what it means to really go back to the old ways. We find that the change we make and made are ours. The changes, the skills and the power of change belongs to ourselves. We learn: "It is mine. I own it." In SSC, we call this *Taking Ownership of Change*.

Exercise on Paradoxical Intent: The purpose of this exercise is to help participants understand *resistance to change* and *how change can take place*. Choose a person from the group who is willing to participate in role play with you. You will take the role of the SAO and the group member will take the role of therapist. You take the position that it is important *not* to change a long-held attitude about criminal and/or substance abusing behavior; s/he will take the opposite view and argue that it is important to change.

By hearing their own arguments for change, the participants may be motivated to act—but only *they* can change their thinking, we cannot do it for them. Review the arguments they have put forth in the discussion and point out the alternatives they have suggested as meaningful and possible choices. Inform them that they are responsible for their behavior and it is up to *them* to choose to change.

This is self-empowerment. Whatever their conscious and deliberate choice, they must realize that they are responsible for it (Bush & Bilodeau, 1993).

Using the Round Robin Group Focus technique, have clients identify where they are with respect to their stage of change as to

1) *Changing CC behavior;*

2) *Changing AOD use behavior.*

e. **Concept V: The Best Interest and Long-Term View Concepts.** Motivation is enhanced by helping clients take a long-term view of their own interests. It is in the best interest of the client to anticipate the long-term consequences of actions (Freeman et al., 1990). Address the concept of impulsivity as it relates to change. This Best-Interest, Long-term View model is designed to help the client control impulsivity long enough to see the consequences of antisocial or AOD use as not as rewarding as the long-term consequences of prosocial behavior and abstinence. Help clients think about the long-term consequences of their actions.

What is best for you in the long term: We take part in using drugs or crime many times on the spur of the moment. We don't think "what is in my best interest? What are my long-term interests?" We fail to think "I want a family but I can't if I'm in jail." Taking the "long-term look" will help us think about what are the results or consequence of what we think and then what we do.

The following are some points of focus for the Focus Group Discussions.

1) *What real problems has your behavior caused? What motivation exists to quit both CC and AOD use?*

2) Ask the group for their own examples of how *attitude affects behavior. How did the behavior get them into trouble or make life more enjoyable? If they changed their attitude about substance abuse or the criminal justice system, how would they feel about themselves?*

3) Discussion: *How do thinking patterns determine whether we behave positively or negatively toward people or in certain situations? The way we think determines the way we act.*

4. Classroom and Homework Assignments

a. Using the workbook, have clients identify one *Belief Clutch* they have held on to that has led to criminal conduct and one belief clutch they have held on to that has led to AOD use and abuse (Workbook, pp. 28-29). Check to see if clients have made changes in that belief. If so, how, what?

b. Using *Work Sheet 1* in the workbook (p. 30), complete the homework assignment on listing areas in which the client feels a need for change. Identify how the client resists change and then identify what change stage the client might be in using the three stages upon which this program is structured.

c. *Situational Assessment* as outlined in the Workbook (p. 29):

1) Describe a situation in your life that was important to you.

2) Identify the attitudes, beliefs and thinking patterns you used in that situation.

3) Identify the result or outcome of that situation.

4) If you changed your attitude or thinking pattern, could the situation have worked out differently?

5. Presentation Sequence for the 2 Two-Hour Sessions

a. First segment of module—two hours:

1) Review last session and homework completed.

2) Brief Reflection Group on clients' response to the program.

3) Present information on impact of attitudes, beliefs and thinking patterns as found in 3(a) above and do exercise.

4) Present material in sections 3(b) and 3(c) above and do exercises.

5) Review classroom and homework assignments.

b. Second segment of module—two hours:

1) Present material on stages of change and best interest and long-term view concepts, sections 3(d) and 3(e).

2) Do exercise on paradoxical intent.

3) Conduct Reflection Group around what has been done in these two sessions with use of focus topics.

4) Do the situational assessment assignment, preferably in the class.

5) Do Work Sheet 1, "Areas you feel you need to change."

6) Review homework for this module from workbook and give preview of Module 3.

6. Module and Client Evaluation

a. Have the client complete the Client Session Evaluation Summary (CSES) for this Module;

b. Provider completes Provider Session Evaluation Summary (PSES) using following questions as a guide:

1) *Did the group understand the issues of ambivalence and resistance and how these tendencies work against changing antisocial and addictive behaviors?*

2) *Is the group developing readiness and responsiveness to treatment and change?*

3) *Is there a sense of appreciation and understanding of the power of individual choice in the process of change?*

c. Counselor completes the BRF at the end of Session 4 of Module 2.

MODULE
3

**Building the
Knowledge Base
to Change**

MODULE 3: BUILDING THE KNOWLEDGE BASE TO CHANGE

Overview of Module 3

Change in thinking, feeling and action is premised on the individual having basic knowledge in the areas of proposed or desired change. Knowledge-based tools are the foundations of self-improvement and change. These tools also provide a platform for the client's involvement in the remainder of this SSC *(Strategies for Self-Improvement and Change)* treatment program. It is very important that the material for this module is presented in a concise and understandable manner to enhance the client's probability of remembering and utilizing the material in the process of self-improvement and change. This module is presented in five separate sessions. The following represent the five key components of this knowledge base:

- Understanding the role of thinking and emotions in self-improvement and change;
- Understanding the role of behavior and learning in self-improvement and change;
- Basic knowledge about AOD use and abuse;
- Understanding alcohol and other drug addiction;
- Understanding criminal conduct and the offender cycle and the interaction of AOD abuse and criminal conduct.

General Goals for Module 3

Although the overall goal of this module is to enhance the client's knowledge base around the five key components defined above, this process is part of achieving the overall goal of Phase I—of enhancing the client's willingness to share his or her history. Session experiences and exercises will help the client apply the knowledge base concepts to their own personal lives. The following are the general goals for Module 3:

- To help the client develop a core knowledge base around the cognitive-behavioral processes that contribute to the involvement in criminal conduct and AOD abuse;
- To help the client develop a core knowledge base in the areas of criminal conduct and AOD abuse;
- To help the client develop a working understanding of the relationship between criminal conduct and AOD abuse.

Time Structure for Module 3

Five two-hour sessions are used to deliver this component of the program. The structure follows the same pattern as in the previous modules.

Session ⑤ : Understanding the Role of Thinking and Feeling in Learning and Change

1. Rationale of Session

If we believe that cognitive-behavioral therapy (CBT) is an effective way to bring about self-improvement and change, then it is important that the client have an understanding of the *cognitive and behavioral* processes that lead to both maladaptive and adaptive thinking and acting. Further, an important component of self-improvement and change is enhancing a person's belief that he or she has the skills and confidence to make the desired improvement and change. The content and material of this session come from a variety of sources, including work by Bush and Bilodeau (1993), McMullin (1986), Ross & Ross (1995), Beck et al. (1993), Michaud and Bussard (1995), Freeman et al. (1989), Burns (1989) and the clinical experiences of the authors.

2. Objectives of Session

The primary objective of this session is to help the client learn the basic principles of cognitive self-improvement and change in order to lay the groundwork to help the client change his or her attitudes, beliefs or thinking patterns associated with CC or AOD abuse. More specifically, this session has two objectives.

> ➡ Learn how our mental (cognitive) events and thinking help us to learn and to change.
>
> ➡ Understand and learn five rules about thinking and acting.

3. Session Content

This session focuses on some very specific concepts and principles related to cognitive psychology. A *principle* is a rule or a law that tells us how things work. It is important that these principles or rules are taught in a very concrete and specific manner.

a. **Rule One: Cognitive self-improvement is based on the simple idea that your beliefs, attitudes and thoughts—not what happens outside of yourself—determine and control much of your actions, your emotions and your relationships with people.** Thus, it follows that your beliefs, attitudes and thoughts can lead to behavior problems and disturbed emotions and in turn, these disturbed or maladaptive actions and emotions can be changed or modified by changing your attitudes and beliefs, your thoughts and thinking patterns. It is through controlling what goes on inside our head in terms of attitudes, beliefs and thought patterns that we are able to control our actions toward the outside world. Now let us review the meaning of an attitude, belief and thought pattern.

1) *Attitude:* Remember, we said that an attitude represents a thought, feeling or orientation toward a situation, a person or an event outside of ourselves. An attitude may determine your posture or position toward something or someone. When applied to an airplane, attitude represents how the plane lines up with respect to some point such as the horizon.

Attitudes are usually described in terms of being good or bad, positive or negative; thus, an attitude has an underlying emotional quality that gets expressed when you express your attitude. It is when we are confronted with outside situations and events that our attitudes are formed, expressed or maintained. If that external situation or person represents a *threat* to us, then we will most likely have a *negative attitude* toward the external circumstance.

Exercise: Ask the group to identify an attitude toward something or someone. Then have the members place a value on that attitude, such as good or bad, positive or negative.

2) *Belief:* You will recall that a belief is an idea that we use to judge or evaluate external situations or persons or ourselves. It is a thought we have about an external event or situation or circumstances. It is an ideal that we hold within ourself and about people or events. Beliefs are powerful. They control our thinking and our behavior. The belief is embodied within the event or person. A belief bonds us more to the outside event. "We believe in God." We see it as the truth. It is usually 100 percent.

Exercise: After presenting the concept of *belief,* ask the group member to identify a belief and then have them place a value on the belief—such as "I believe 100 percent"; "I believe sometimes."

3) *Thought Pattern:* Recall that a thought pattern or thought habit is a mental response that is learned and occurs automatically when we experience certain events. We will now call these *automatic thoughts.* A thought pattern or automatic thought may combine both attitudes and beliefs. An important part of self-improvement and change is learning how to control our automatic thoughts and keep them from leading to actions or behaviors that get us into trouble.

Exercise: Have each of the participants identify an event and an automatic thought (thought pattern) that follows.

b. **Rule Two: That each person perceives (sees) the world and themselves differently. How we see the world, outside events and ourselves is set by our attitudes and beliefs (assumptions).** This means that our attitudes and assumptions shape our view and our interpretation of outside events. Two people can look at an event or a particular scene and see, feel and think different things. "Two men looked out from prison bars; one saw mud, the other saw stars." This leads to some very important considerations:

1) We bring to the *outside* world our own *inside* view—or our own attitudes, beliefs and thought patterns; we in fact create our own realities.

2) We make choices as to what our attitudes, beliefs and thoughts are about the world, and how we respond to the outside events. Again, our response will be determined by how we see things or our perceptions—which are based on our attitudes, beliefs and thought patterns.

3) If we have different perceptions of the world, then in most cases, no one view is right or wrong. However, we do form common ideas or opinions or beliefs *or laws*—which we call consensus—and we then, as a common group, say this is true, or this is right, or this is wrong. It is when our actions resulting from our beliefs, attitudes and thinking patterns about the world go against or violate these common beliefs or rules or laws that the thoughts and actions lead us into problems.

Exercise 1: Illustrate Rule Two by letting the group look at a picture of an individual who is expressing emotion. Then have each individual write down what they think is going on with that individual.

Exercise 2: Read a brief news report of an individual who committed a crime and was obviously guilty of the crime from the news report. Then have the group write down whether they feel that the individual was wrong or right. This will illustrate the common belief concept. Some SAO clients may have difficulty with this exercise because it may be similar to the crime that they may have committed.

176

c. **Rule Three: That our thought patterns or automatic thoughts which result from our experience of the outside world (and result from of our experiencing our inside attitudes and beliefs) can become twisted and distorted.** Beck (1976) calls these errors in logic or "cognitive (mental) distortions." These errors or twisted thoughts can lead to disturbed behaviors or emotions. We will study these errors in thinking in more detail in Session 9 of this module.

Exercise: Have the group practice identifying automatic thoughts that could represent errors in thinking. Have them put their own labels on these errors. This will prepare the group for Session 9 of this module.

d. **Rule Four: That thoughts, emotions and actions affect each other or they interact.** Emotions and moods can lead to certain thoughts, actions can influence how one thinks or feels and emotions can lead to certain behaviors. Figure 1 illustrates this interaction.[1]

Figure 1

Interaction of Thoughts, Feelings and Actions

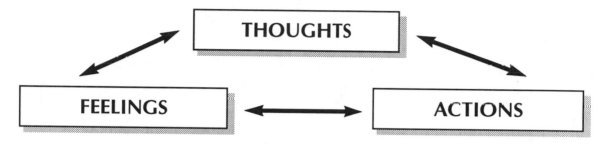

The primary assumption in cognitive-behavioral self-improvement and change is that your actions and feelings are not necessarily determined or controlled by events outside of you, but your beliefs, your attitudes and your thought patterns *(automatic thoughts)* play an important role in the development of your actions and feelings. In turn, your actions and feelings play an important role in shaping your thoughts.

e. **Rule Five: What happens outside of you will bring on certain thoughts based on your beliefs and attitudes. Those automatic thoughts can bring on certain feelings, possibly an overt behavior or action response.** An action response may be maladaptive or *negative.* It may violate the rights and privileges of others, or lead to criminal behavior or excessive drinking. Or, an action response may be a *positive* coping behavior. Thus, there are three responses a person can have to outside events or external events: the *thought response,* the *emotional response* and the overt *action response.* It is at the overt action response that criminal conduct and AOD use behavior occur. Yet, we have a choice before the overt response: the choice of how we think about the event and how we feel about the event, and thus a choice of what our actions will be in relationship to the event. Figure 2 illustrates this process for us.

---

[1]The figures and tables in Section III are numbered in sequence beginning with 1.

Figure 2
The Process of Cognitive Learning and Change

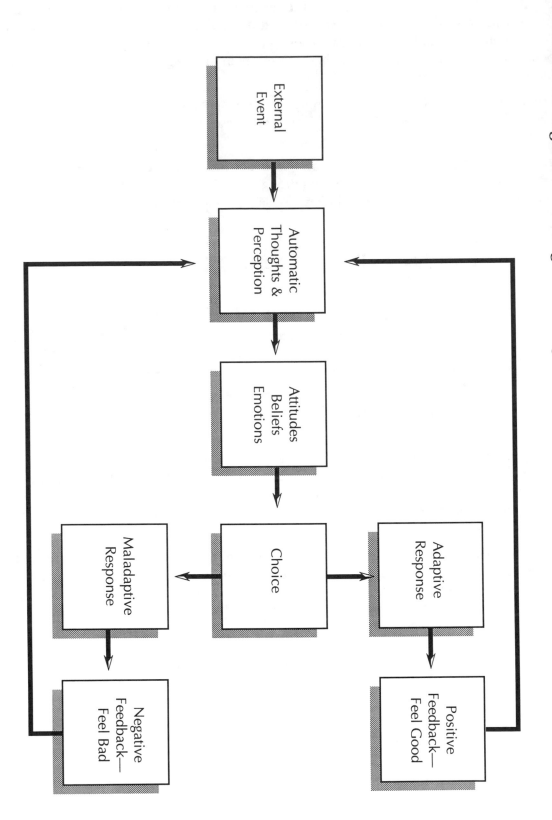

Example: Joe's girlfriend told him she's going out with another guy [external event]. Joe's automatic thought is "I'm getting screwed over again." He thinks "see, you can't trust women [belief]." He decides "I'm going to teach her a lesson." He breaks her car windows (choice and maladaptive behavior). He is arrested for destruction of property (negative consequences). Notice how positive or negative consequences ingrain or strengthen automatic thoughts.

Rule Five brings together all of the other four rules. However, what is most important is that the behavioral outcome, as illustrated in Figure 2, leads us now to understand how automatic thoughts and consequent behaviors are *reinforced*.

4. Classroom or Homework Assignment

a. Describe an event or situation you have experienced in the past and then identify your beliefs, attitudes and thinking patterns associated with that event or situation. Use the work sheet in Workbook (p. 36).

b. Identify an attitude or belief that has led to AOD use. Identify an attitude or belief that has led to criminal conduct (Workbook, p. 37).

c. During the week between sessions, identify a situation that has led to automatic thoughts. Using the work sheet in the Workbook, record the automatic thoughts and then give a cognitive distortion label to those thoughts. Then, write down a rational or adaptive thought in response to the automatic thought (p. 37).

d. Read material for Session 6 of Module 3.

5. Presentation Sequence

a. Review Homework from last session.

b. Follow the presentation sequence as provided in the Session Content section.

c. End the group with a 15-minute reflection group.

d. Review homework for the coming week.

e. Give preview of next week's session.

6. Evaluation

Evaluation for this session will be done following Session 6 in this module.

Session 6: Understanding the Role of Behavior in Self-Improvement and Change

1. Rationale and Overview of Session

Cognitive learning and change is only part of the overall picture of how people learn and change behavior. The other piece of the puzzle involves understanding how people learn behavior and how that behavior gets strengthened and reinforced. This piece must be in place in order for the client to fully understand how the cognitive-behavioral learning process applies to his or her own AOD use and criminal conduct.

2. Objectives of Session

> ➠ Have the client understand and apply the basic principles of behavioral learning and change.
>
> ➠ Help the client learn how the learning of behaviors fits into cognitive-behavioral change.

3. Session Content

a. Review: How our thoughts, beliefs and feelings get reinforced or strengthened.

Figure 2 shows us that thoughts, feelings and beliefs are reactions to outside events. These thoughts usually come from our attitudes, beliefs or feelings. Figure 2 also shows us the basis for how internal thoughts, beliefs and attitudes get strengthened. If our action or response resulting from our thoughts or beliefs is a *positive* (adaptive) response, this will result in positive feedback from the environment and a positive feeling about being successful. This strengthens or reinforces the internal positive thoughts and feelings (that led to the positive response). The thought might be "I handled that well," "I feel good about that," or "I feel successful." This might also reinforce a positive self-view or positive feelings about those who gave you positive feedback about the way you handled the issue, etc. Most important, it reinforces automatic thoughts such as "I can handle myself in tough situations."

On the other hand, if we choose to engage in *negative or maladaptive* thoughts, and this leads us to a negative (maladaptive) response, which in turn leads to negative or punitive responses from others, this can strengthen or reinforce our negative beliefs. For example, if our thoughts and beliefs lead us to criminal conduct, the outside world punishes us. This will probably reinforce or strengthen our belief that people are out to get us.

Often, an inside event can set off an *inside-the-mind response*. A memory may set off or stimulate an attitude, belief or emotion. When an action or behavior is reinforced, that behavior will most likely repeat itself under the same conditions. We then say that the behavior is learned. Figure 2 gives us a basis for how our thoughts, attitudes and beliefs are reinforced. But it does not explain how specific responses to the outside world get reinforced. How do our actions get reinforced?

b. The rules of how behaviors or actions are learned.

Once a behavior or response takes place, one of several things can occur. *First,* the behavior may never repeat itself. *Second,* the behavior may repeat itself, but not on any steady basis or in any consistent pattern. *Third,* the behavior may consistently repeat itself. It forms a behavioral pattern or what we call a *habit*. This is very much like a thought pattern, a thought habit or what we have called automatic thoughts.

Thus, in the last session, we learned the rules that decide how our thoughts, our feelings and beliefs get strengthened or reinforced. There are also rules that decide how our behaviors or actions get reinforced or strengthened and form habits or behavior patterns (Wanberg, 1990). In psychology, we call these learning principles. For our discussion, we call these *learning rules*. We look at three important ones. These three rules are important in understanding how we form drinking or drug use habits and how we form criminal habit patterns. These three rules are illustrated in Figure 3.

1) **Learning Rule I**—*Turning on positive events:* If a behavior turns on a positive event or a pleasant feeling or increases a sense of well-being, that behavior is reinforced and has a greater chance of repeating itself. We call this the *warm fuzzy* rule. When a behavior, action or response turns on a warm fuzzy, that response is reinforced. The "warm fuzzy" is the reinforcement. If drinking makes us feel good, or gives us warm fuzzies, then drinking is reinforced. We will do it again.

2) **Learning Rule II**—*Turning off negative events:* If a behavior turns off an unpleasant event, reduces stress, or shuts down negative feelings, memories or pain, that behavior is reinforced and has a greater probability of repeating itself. We call this the *Cold Prickly Rule Number One*. When a behavior turns off a cold prickly, that behavior gets reinforced. The *Cold Prickly Rule Number One* principle is very powerful with respect to reinforcing or strengthening behavior. When we feel stressed, we drink. The stress goes away. This reinforces the drinking.

Figure 3
Three Rules of Learning Behavior

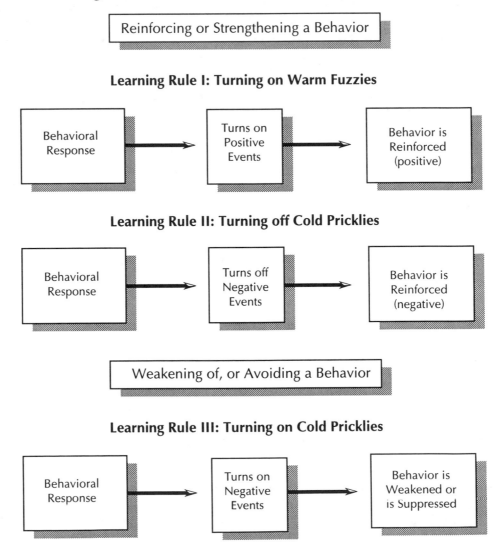

Reinforcing or Strengthening a Behavior

Learning Rule I: Turning on Warm Fuzzies

Behavioral Response → Turns on Positive Events → Behavior is Reinforced (positive)

Learning Rule II: Turning off Cold Pricklies

Behavioral Response → Turns off Negative Events → Behavior is Reinforced (negative)

Weakening of, or Avoiding a Behavior

Learning Rule III: Turning on Cold Pricklies

Behavioral Response → Turns on Negative Events → Behavior is Weakened or is Suppressed

3) **Learning Rule III**—*Turning on negative events:* If a behavior leads to an unpleasant event, pain, stress or something negative, that behavior is weakened, and has a lower possibility of occurring at some point in the future. We call this the *Cold Prickly Rule Number Two.* When a behavior turns on a cold prickly, that behavior gets weakened and may not occur again.

These principles help explain behavioral learning and the development of behavioral patterns. However, they do not apply to all behaviors and do not always work in the manner so indicated. For example, if the *Cold Prickly Rule Number Two* is valid, then why do some behaviors that clearly turn on strong negative events continue to occur? Why would one continue to drink to excess if one has had a seizure from drinking, or if one is told that drinking is producing liver problems? Why do people continue to smoke, even though they are told that continued smoking will probably lead to severe medical problems? Part of the answer has to do with the power of learning Rules I and II above. Even though a behavior turns on a negative event of great proportions, the more immediate *positive* reinforcement of the behavior is so powerful that this *overrides* the potential negative outcome. This is particularly true for behaviors that lead to immediate or quick rewards or pleasant events, or behaviors that eliminate strong negative or unpleasant experiences. The immediate positive results of getting rid of the immediate bad feelings (e.g., anxiety) are very powerful and even cloud rational cognitive processes which tell the individual the long-term outcome is bad.

For example, a person may drink to excess in an evening because the drinking *drowns* his or her sorrows, sorrows that are more immediately painful then the negative consequences that could result from excessive drinking (e.g., hangover, alcohol-related driving offense). An individual steals from a store for immediate gratification and reward, which overrides the potential long-term negative consequence of being placed in jail.

The negative results or consequences from a behavior also strengthen the internal attitudes, beliefs and automatic thoughts within the individual, as illustrated in Figure 2 (in Session 5). Thus, even though there may be long-term negative outcomes of a particular behavior, the immediate outcome is that it reinforces the already existing internal beliefs and attitudes, such as "I'm no good" or "you can't trust others," and help to maintain the consistency of one's view of him/herself.

c. **How thinking and acting leads to the process of learning.**

Now, let's put together the puzzle of how thinking and acting lead to the learning of thinking patterns or habits (automatic thoughts) and behavior or action habits. Figure 4 gives us a picture of this process. Figure 4 is the same as Figure 2 up to the point of where the behavior or actions take place. Now, we do not say whether the behavior is positive or negative, good or bad. The action or behavior can be any response such as drinking, talking to a friend, or committing a crime. It is what the behavior *does* for the person that counts. The behavior may *turn on* a warm fuzzy. It may *turn off* a cold prickly. It may turn *on* a cold prickly. The result of the first two is that the behavior is strengthened—or it is learned. It will become an action habit. But regardless of the *outcome* of the behavior—positive (adaptive) or negative (maladaptive), good or bad—the inside-the-mind stuff is reinforced or strengthened. There is feedback to the internal within-the-mind stuff that strengthens the already established beliefs, attitudes, thoughts and feelings. They are reinforced—they are *learned*. They become *thought habits* or *automatic thoughts*.

Figure 4
The Process of Cognitive and Behavioral Learning and Change

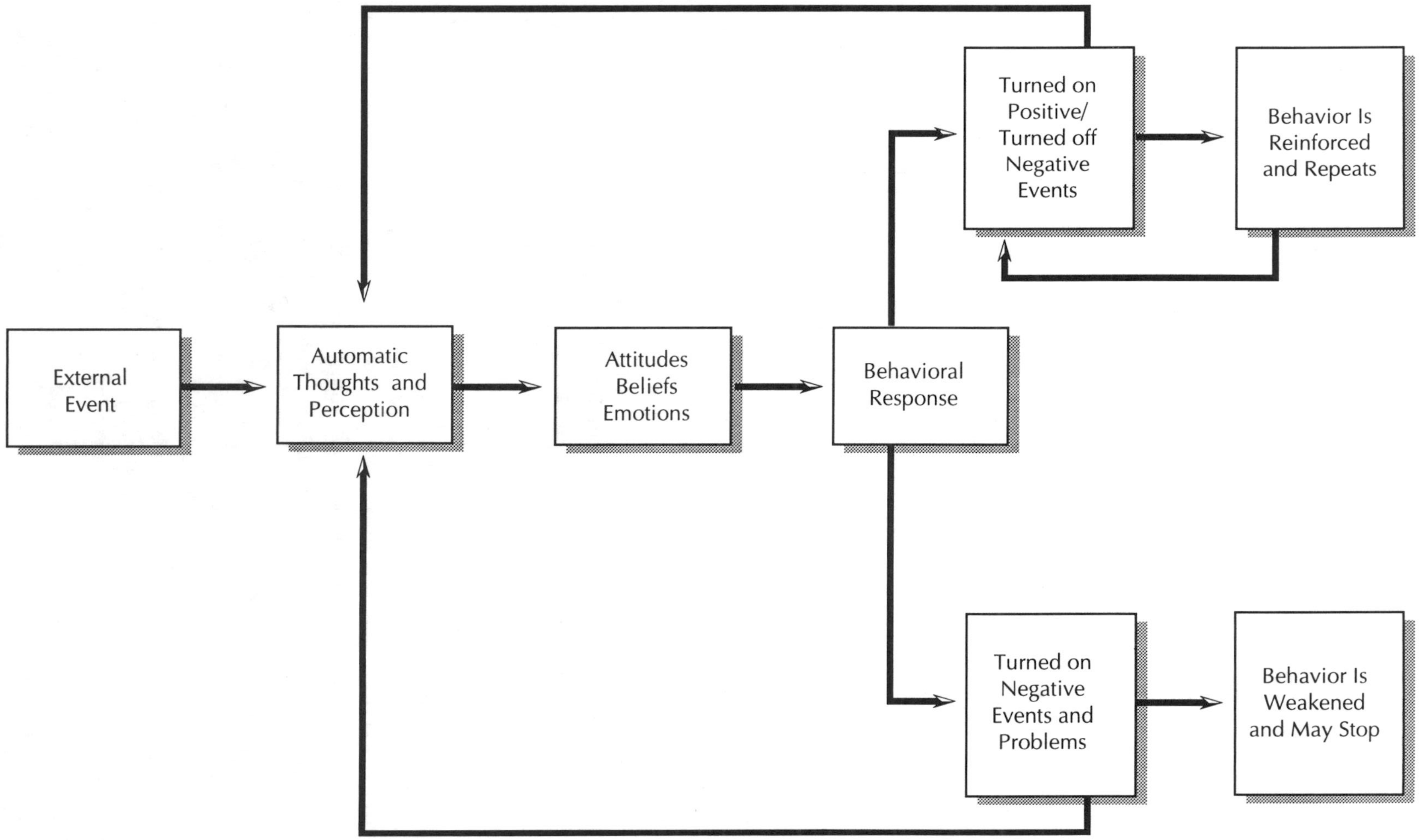

External
Event

Automatic
Thoughts and
Perception

Attitudes
Beliefs
Emotions

Behavioral
Response

Turned on
Negative
Events and
Problems

Turned on
Positive/
Turned off
Negative
Events

Behavior Is
Weakened
and May Stop

Behavior Is
Reinforced
and Repeats

In Summary, Figure 4 shows that the behavior that turns **on** positive events or turns **off** negative events gets reinforced and most likely repeats itself. The behavior that results in negative outcomes can still reinforce the internal beliefs, attitudes and feelings which can lead again to the behavior that causes negative outcomes. For example, being jailed for a criminal act is a negative outcome of the act or behavior. The negative outcome might strengthen or reinforce the internal belief that *nothing is fair, nothing good ever happens to me,* or *the world is out to get me.*

Exercise 1: Clients complete Work Sheet 2 in Workbook (p. 44). The client records events, thoughts and a behavior and subsequent results of turning on something positive, turning off something negative or turning on something negative and then indicates what was the result of that behavior. The counselor should model the completion of this task before having the group do it.

4. Classroom or Homework Assignment

a. Complete exercise (a) in Workbook (p. 43) based on something that happens to the individual during the week.

b. Describe an event or circumstances that led to an adaptive behavioral response and then record the feelings and emotions around the positive results of the adaptive response (Exercise (b), p. 43 of Workbook).

c. Read material for Session 7 in Workbook.

5. Presentation Sequence

a. Review last session and homework.

b. Present material in Session Content section above in a clear manner so that all participants understand the material. Take time for questions.

c. Complete exercises outlined above.

6. Session and Client Evaluation

a. Have the client complete the CSES for the last two sessions;

b. Provider completes PSES and reflects on these questions:
   1) *Did the client understand the five principles of cognitive change and reinforcement?*
   2) *Did the client understand the three behavioral learning principles?*

c. Counselor completes the BRF for the past two sessions.

Session 7 : Basic Knowledge About Drugs

1. Rationale and Overview of Session

In order for the client to meet our challenge to change behaviors and patterns in AOD use and abuse, it is important that the client has sufficient knowledge about alcohol and other drugs and about abuse and addiction. The purpose of this session is to provide the client with a *baseline knowledge about alcohol and other drugs.* Some clients may have been exposed to some information in this session in other treatment programs. The provider should assess the drug-awareness knowledge of the clients in the program and make adjustments in the material presented according to the group's knowledge level in this area.

2. Objectives of Session

> ➤ Have clients express their view of drug addiction.
>
> ➤ To provide the client with basic knowledge about drugs.
>
> ➤ To give the client some specific knowledge about alcohol and its effect on the human body.

3. Session Content

The content provided for this session is a description of some basic facts and knowledge about alcohol and other drugs. The provider is encouraged to adapt the information provided in this section to his or her own language and teaching style. This session is primarily didactic. However, the instructor is encouraged to have participants contribute their knowledge and experiences, to ask questions, and to facilitate discussion concerning the material presented, when appropriate. It is recommended that charts and overheads be developed to present these materials.

a. **About Drugs**

1) *Definition of Drug:* A drug is defined as "any substance, natural or artificial, that by its chemical or physical nature, changes physical, psychological or chemical functioning of a living organism" (Ray & Ksir, 1996). For our purpose in this program, we are referring to drugs that have a direct or indirect effect on the person in such a way that it changes or alters the persons's states of consciousness, emotions and moods, thinking and actions (Wanberg, 1990).

Even though the word *drug* comes from the French word *drogue,* which means dry substance, *drug* in this manual refers to any chemical that changes or alters the person's states of consciousness.

2) *Drugs work because they have an effect on the person's nervous system by changing the flow of electricity and the release of the body's natural nerve chemicals called neurochemicals or neurotransmitters.*

Our nervous system works through the flow of electricity and chemicals (what we call neurotransmitters) in the nerves and nerve endings (what we call dendrites). Drugs change how the person's nervous system works by changing the flow of electricity in the nerves and the release of the body's natural chemicals. They change the way that the body's natural chemicals (the nerve chemicals or neurochemicals) work in the body. They may slow down or speed up the action of the nerves. They may increase or decrease the release of nerve chemicals in the nerve endings. They can also directly affect the nerves. For example, alcohol not only affects the release of the nerve chemicals in the nerve endings but also can change the lining of the nerves to cause the nerves to *leak electricity* so as to slow down their action.

3) *There are two kinds of drugs: There are drugs that slow down the nervous system. There are drugs that speed up the working of the nervous system.*

We call those drugs that slow down the activity of the nervous system *suppressors* (they are often referred to as sedatives or downers). Such drugs are alcohol, barbiturates, tranquilizers and opioids such as heroin. These drugs sedate the body. They can slow down the body to the point of putting the body to sleep.

We call the drugs that speed up the nervous system *enhancers,* often referred to as stimulants. They pick up the system or excite the system. Sometimes they only excite or speed up our mental world, such as those drugs we call hallucinogens (acid). There are drugs that also excite or speed up the physical part of the body as well as the mental part. Speed (amphetamines) and cocaine are examples of these kinds of drugs. Table 1 provides you with this simple classification of drugs.

4) *Drugs have a direct and an indirect effect on people.*

When drugs are in the person's system, they have what we call a *direct effect* on people. This is due to the fact that the drug (chemical) is changing the person's nervous system by changing the flow of electricity and nerve chemicals in the nerves and nerve ending. For example, the direct effect of alcohol may be sleepiness, being confused, or slurring the speech. The direct effect is also due to the psychological changes the individual experiences when under the influence of the drug.

Drugs also have what we call an *indirect effect* on people. That is, when the drug is no longer in the body, the body reacts to its *absence*. We call this the *abstinence reaction* which will be discussed more below. For example, an indirect effect of alcohol may be insomnia, shakiness of the hands, being hyper or having a convulsion.

5) *Different kinds of drugs have different* **direct** *effects and different* **indirect** *(withdrawal) effects.*

The direct effect of a drug will be different and usually the opposite of an indirect effect of a drug. For example, alcohol slows down the nervous system to the point that you might go to sleep or go into a coma if enough alcohol is present. But when alcohol *leaves* the body after it has been in the system, the result is that *the nervous system speeds up* or becomes stimulated or agitated to the extreme point where the result might be an epileptic seizure. When cocaine is in the body, the nervous body nervous speeds up. But when cocaine *leaves* the body, *the nervous system slows down* and becomes depressed.

The direct and indirect effects are what impair the person, or are what cause the person problems from drug use. A direct or indirect effect from a drug may not always cause a problem. But, when a problem is caused from drug use, it is usually explained by either a direct or indirect effect. For example, one might get drowsy from using alcohol. This is not necessarily a problem. However, when it causes you to go to sleep when driving, it is a problem. Table 1 provides the direct and indirect effects from the two different classes of drugs.

6) *Mind- and mood-altering drugs make the body toxic.*

The drugs that are a focus of this program (drugs that change or alter the person's states of consciousness, moods, thoughts and actions) are *toxic agents*. When the body has been exposed to such drugs for a period of time, it is necessary for the body to detoxify when the drugs leave the body. That process can cause problems with the working of the chemical system of the body. The body can have a strong reaction from the loss of the drugs in the body. We call this the *abstinence syndrome or withdrawal*. This is the reaction of the body to no longer having the drugs upon which the body had become dependent. When the drugs are removed, the body has to get used to no longer having the drugs in the system. The electrical and chemical parts of the nervous system have to readjust. Sometimes this reaction is only psychological; often it is a physical response of the body. It can be dangerous. The reaction can be so strong that it can result in an epileptic seizure. Other less severe reactions can be shaking, vomiting, headaches, depression and symptoms that have been described in Table 1.

7) *Your tolerance for drugs can increase and you can become physically and psychologically dependent on drugs.*

As you use certain drugs, you may believe you need more and more of the drug to get the same reaction, or you may find that the same amount of drug will give you less of an effect. This is what we call tolerance. This will vary from drug to drug. For example, where two drinks may have brought on a *buzz* or a feeling of relaxation, after using alcohol for several years, you may find that you need four or five drinks to get the same *buzz* or to feel the same amount of relaxation. A daily quart of vodka may be required to get the same effect as once did a half pint of vodka. You may need as much as a ten- to twenty-fold increase with some narcotics to get the same effect. This is one of the reasons why some people get dependent on drugs.

8) *Mixing two drugs in the body at the same time may increase the strength of one or both drugs. We call this drug interaction.*

A drug interaction is any change in the effect or power of one drug because another drug is in the body. For example, the presence of alcohol and a barbiturate in the body at the same time may lower the lethal dose of the barbiturate by as much as 50 percent. Drug interactions may be very dangerous.

b. **About Alcohol**

Because alcohol is one of the most commonly used drugs, we will look at some specific facts about alcohol.

1) *Alcohol is a sedative-hypnotic drug.* Even though people say they use alcohol to *get high,* by its chemical nature, it is designed to put you to sleep. It is a system suppressor.

2) *Alcohol per drink:* One drink equals about one-half ounce (12 grams) of pure alcohol. One drink equals

　　a) A 12-ounce can of beer;

　　b) A four-ounce glass of wine;

　　c) One ounce of 80 proof (40 percent pure alcohol) or one-half ounce of pure alcohol.

3) *Alcohol in the body* is measured through the *Blood Alcohol Concentration* (BAC). This is the ratio of the weight of alcohol to the volume of blood. A BAC of .10 means that you have one tenth of 1 percent of alcohol in your blood. That doesn't sound like much, but look below.

4) *Our response to different BAC levels:*

　　a) .02-.03: Feel relaxed and decrease judgment;

　　b) .05: Do not walk normally; decrease judgment; perform poorly; in many states legally impaired.

　　c) .08: Definite driving impaired; legally drunk in some states.

　　d) .10: Clearly not able to function normally; lack of muscle control; poor coordination; poor judgment; decrease in emotional control.

Table 1

Two Classes of Drugs with Their Direct and Indirect Effects

SYSTEM SUPPRESSORS OR DEPRESSANTS	SYSTEM ENHANCERS (STIMULANTS)	
	MENTAL ENHANCERS	MENTAL–PHYSICAL

Alcohol	Cannabis	Amphetamines
Sedatives (Barbituates)	Hallucinogens (speed)	Cocaine
Inhalants (small amounts)	Phencyclidine (PCP)	Caffeine
Opioids (heroin)	MDMA (Ecstasy)	
Tranquilizers		

Direct Effects

- drowsiness
- slurred speech
- lack of motor coordination
- confusion
- aggressive actions
- poor work performance
- auto accident
- driving while intoxicated
- decrease of social & interpersonal involvement
- depression

Direct Effects

- insomnia
- weight loss
- tremors
- hyperactivity
- panic
- poor work performance
- hallucinations/delusions
- aggressive actions
- inappropriate social & interpersonal behavior
- stimulation

Indirect Effects

- hyper and excited
- stimulation
- agitation & irritability
- hallucinations/delusions
- anxiety, fear, panic
- shakes and tremors
- unable to sleep (insomnia)
- interpersonal impairment
- work impairment
- decreased responsibility to others

Indirect Effects

- sedated and slow
- depression
- fatigue
- guilt
- indifference, lethargy
- body slows down
- sleeping too much
- interpersonal impairment
- work impairment
- decreased responsibility to others

e) .15: More severe impairment as in d) above; 25 times more likely to have fatal accident.

f) .20: All of the above including amnesia, blackouts; 100 times more likely to have fatal accident.

g) .30: Lose consciousness;

h) .40: Almost all lose consciousness;

i) .45-.60: Fatal for most people.

5) *The level of BAC:* Depends on the weight of the person, the number of drinks and the time over which these drinks are taken. Table 2 provides the approximation information for number of drinks within three time periods which will result in either a .05 or .10 BAC. This table is generalized to men and women. Table 3 provides information regarding approximate number of hours from the first drink to a zero BAC based on varying number of drinks for both men and women.

6) *Absorption of alcohol:* Alcohol dissolves in water. About 98 percent is broken down in the digestive system; 2 percent leaves the body through the breath and urine.

7) An average drink of one half pure alcohol has about 80 to 90 calories. Four drinks make up 325 calories based on pure alcohol. One beer, one glass of wine or one mixed drink can give the body about 200 calories.

8) *The amount of alcohol used on one occasion can be classified as the following:*

a) Light drinker: one drink.

b) Moderate drinker: two to three drinks.

c) Heavy drinker: four to five drinks.

d) Excessive drinker: six or more.

9) *The frequency of drinking is classified as follows:*

a) Infrequent: Less than one time a month;

b) Occasional: Less than one time a week;

c) Frequent: One to three times a week;

d) Consistent: Four to five times a week;

e) Daily/sustained: six to seven times a week.

10) *What type of drinker have you been?* Find this out by putting together how often you drank with the amount you drank. For example, if you drank two to three drinks one to three times a week, you would be classified as a Frequent-Moderate drinker.

11) *Other variables that will have an effect on the impact of alcohol on the body and mind are* gender, amount of sleep, weight, amount of food in the system, degree of stress the person is under and length of time the person has been drinking. Tolerance will also make a difference as to how alcohol affects a person. A person who has used alcohol for many years and who has had six or seven drinks may not look drunk or intoxicated but may have a BAC of .10. This is due to the fact that the individual has developed what is called *behavioral tolerance*. Men can drink more with less effect. Alcohol will have greater effect when the person has not eaten, has had less sleep, is of light body weight and is psychologically relaxed.

12) *Impact on the body:*

Liver: The liver is the first to see alcohol and is most vulnerable to alcohol. The liver can become diseased when there is a buildup of fatty tissue in the liver. Then the fatty tissue separates the cells, resulting in decrease of liver function. It can become inflamed. When the

Table 2

Blood Alcohol Concentration (BAC) Levels by Body Weight, Hours over Which the Person Drinks and Number of Drinks (men and women will vary)

BAC based on number of drinks and body weight								
Number of hours of drinking	120 lbs		140 lbs		160 lbs		180 lbs	
	BAC .05	.09	BAC .05	.09	BAC .05	.09	BAC .05	.09
One hour	2*	4	2	4	3	5	3	5
Two hours	3	5	3	5	4	6	4	6
Three hours	4	6	4	6	5	7	5	7

*refers to number of drinks for time period

Table 3

Approximate Hours from First Drink to Zero BAC Levels—for men

Number of drinks	Your weight in pounds							
	120	140	160	180	200	220	240	260
1	2*	2	2	1.5	1	1	1	1
2	4	3.5	3	3	2.5	2	2	2
3	8	5	4.5	4	3.5	3.5	3	3
4	8	7	6	5.5	5	4.5	4	3.5
5	10	8.5	7.5	6.5	6	5.5	5	4.5

*refers to number of hours before reaching a BAC of zero

Approximate Hours from First Drink to Zero BAC Levels—for women

Number of drinks	Your weight in pounds							
	120	140	160	180	200	220	240	260
1	3*	2.5	2	2	2	1.5	1.5	1
2	6	5	4	4	3.5	3	3	2.5
3	9	7.5	6.5	5.5	5	4.5	4	4
4	12	9.5	8.5	7.5	6.5	6	5.5	5
5	15	12	10.5	9.5	8	7.5	7	6

*refers to number of hours before reaching a BAC of zero

fat separates the liver cells, less blood can get to the cells and the tissue can then die. This leads to what we call *cirrhosis* which is the replacing of dead liver cells with scar tissue. Greater than six drinks per day will increase the risk of liver disease and cirrhosis.

Fatty tissue builds up because as a result of the breakdown of alcohol. Hydrogen is produced and the liver uses the hydrogen for energy and does not need to burn the fat that builds up in the liver.

Digestive organs: Alcohol irritates the stomach lining and can lead to development of ulcers. This can occur in moderate to heavy drinkers, depending on how vulnerable the person is to stomach ulcers. This risk increases if alcohol is used with other stomach irritants such as aspirin.

Cardiovascular system: Alcohol increases the size of the body's blood vessels. A light amount of alcohol several times a week may decrease the risk of heart problems since this may increase high density lipid proteins that carry cholesterol to the liver and that break down the cholesterol. Heavy amounts of alcohol, particularly associated with smoking, can increase risk of heart problems and can increase blood pressure. One to two drinks a day will most likely not increase heart or blood pressure risks.

Nervous system: We have a blood brain barrier that attempts to keep the brain from getting alcohol. For men, five drinks or more over a period of several hours will break this barrier; for women, more than three drinks will break the barrier. When the blood-brain barrier is broken, it leaves the brain cells vulnerable to damage by alcohol. Excessive drinking can damage nerve cells in all parts of the body. Excessive drinkers are vulnerable to peripheral neuropathy, which is the damaging of the nerve cells in the hands, feet and other body extremities noted by the tingling of the fingers and feet.

13) *Metabolism of alcohol:* This is the breakdown of alcohol. When the body breaks down alcohol, it goes through the following chain:

$$\text{Alcohol} \longrightarrow \underset{\text{hydrogen}}{\text{acetaldehyde}} \longrightarrow \underset{\text{hydrogen}}{\text{acetic acid}} \longrightarrow \text{water} + CO_2$$

Notice that the element hydrogen is given off when alcohol is broken down. As we already talked about, the hydrogen becomes a source of energy for the liver. Thus, less fat is used for energy and fatty tissue starts to build up in the liver and may cause liver disease.

Breaking down alcohol: The body breaks down alcohol. We call this the metabolism of alcohol. The breakdown of alcohol depends on gender and body fat. A person with a lot of body fat will break down alcohol at a slower rate. That person may actually end up with a higher blood alcohol concentration (BAC). Table 3 shows that if a heavier person drinks the same as a lighter person, the heavier person may have a lower percentage of alcohol in his or her blood. But, if the heavier person has more body fat, the heavier person may end up with a higher BAC level. The person with high body fat may also have a greater risk of alcohol damaging or harming the body.

Because women have a higher percentage of body fat, they may be at *more* risk in developing physical problems from drinking. However, there are other reasons why women may be at higher risk for health problems due to alcohol use. For example, when weight and body fat are controlled (that is, taking men and women with the same body fat and weight), women still have higher blood alcohol counts for the same amount of alcohol over time. Thus, the difference between gender may be due to differences in hormones and levels of certain enzymes in the digestive tract. Women also metabolize alcohol more slowly and have higher levels of acetaldehyde than men. Thus, body fat may be only one of the contributing factors to putting women at higher risk with respect to health problems due to drinking.

14) *The frequent-heavy to frequent-excessive drinker increases his or her risk of the harmful effects of alcohol on the body.*

4. Homework Assignment

a. Have clients read the material in their Workbook for Session 8.

b. Have clients complete the *Drug Knowledge Test* in the Workbook (p. 51).

5. Presentation Sequence

a. Discuss last session and then review homework.

b. Before presenting the content of this session, have clients share their views of addiction.

c. Material presented in order as presented in the Content Section above. Again, the instructor is encouraged to add information to this knowledge base as s/he feels appropriate.

d. Review classroom and homework assignments for next session.

e. Reflection group: How did clients identify with material presented? Elicit participation during presentation of material.

6. Session Evaluation

a. Client completes the CSES for this session.

b. Counselor completes PSES.

Session ⑧: Understanding Alcohol and Other Drug (AOD) Addiction

1. Rationale and Overview of Session

If a client is to change patterns of AOD addiction and abuse, it is important that s/he have a clear understanding of the nature of these addiction patterns. The purpose of this session is to provide the client with the knowledge about how people become AOD addicted. The models for describing the pathways to AOD addiction will build on the concepts and principles presented in Sessions 5, 6 and 7.

2. Objectives of Session

> ⮕ To teach the client two pathways to AOD addiction that are based on the cognitive-behavioral learning and change principles taught in Sessions 5 and 6 of this module:
>
> 1) The psychological-addiction pathway;
>
> 2) The psychophysical-addiction pathway.
>
> ⮕ To have the client identify more clearly her or his own pattern of addiction as based on the two addiction models presented in this session.

3. Session Content

This session will help us understand the way we become addicted to alcohol and other drugs. We will learn two different pathways that explain how people become addicted to drugs. Figure 5 provides a view of these two pathways (or models). The first pathway, called the *psychological* addiction model, is based on how people develop mental and behavioral patterns as described in Sessions 5 and 6 of this module (note that in the Workbook, this addiction path is referred to as the *mental-behavioral addiction cycle*). The second path, the *psychophysical* basis of addiction (called the *mental-physical* addiction cycle), helps us understand how people get into an addiction cycle because of the physical and chemical changes in the nervous system.

We will also briefly look at the relationship between drugs and the neurochemical process, how this relationship helps explain the two addiction pathways and how the reward deficiency syndrome and cravings fit into this process. Finally, we will discuss the relationship of genetics to drug addiction.

a. The Psychological-Behavioral Addiction Pathway

We saw in Figure 3 of Session 6 of this Module two ways that people learn behavior. If we *expect* that something we do (behavior) will make us feel good, and it does, then we will do it again. If we *expect* that a behavior will take away something unpleasant (stress, tension), and it does, we will do it again. Figure 5 shows us how drug use fits this learning idea. With this idea of addiction we are saying that AOD use is learned and is based on the reinforcement principles described in Session 6.

First, if a person expects something positive to come from using a drug and this happens, then AOD use is strengthened and will repeat itself. It becomes a behavior habit. The positive things might be feeling relaxed, feeling euphoric or *on top of the world,* emotional and sexual pleasures, or improved thinking. Thus, individuals use drugs for these benefits, and these benefits in turn reinforce drug use behavior. There are a number of theories that have been used to explain this model including *Social Learning Theory* (Abrams & Niaura, 1987), *Expectancy Theory* (Goldman et al., 1987) and the *Opponent Process Theory* (Shipley, 1987).

Second, if a person expects a drug to shut down or turn off or decrease unpleasant or negative life experiences and this does happen, then the use of that drug is strengthened and will repeat itself. Again, AOD use becomes a *behavior habit.* Such unpleasant things might be stress, unpleasant memories, job or marital problems, or the bad results from the drug use itself. In this way, the person uses a drug to handle the stress of life.

Figure 5

The Psychological-Behavioral Pathway for Learning AOD Use Behavior: Reinforcing or Strengthening Drug Use Behavior

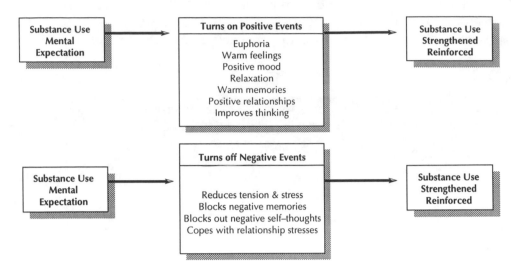

This is a coping model. Several theories have been offered to explain this aspect of the psychological addiction theory, including *Tension Reduction Theory* (Cappell & Greeley, 1987), the *Self-Awareness Model* (Hull, 1987), the *Opponent Process Theory* (Shipley, 1987) and the *Stress Reduction Dampening Theory* (Sher, 1987).

Figure 6 describes more completely this coping model and shows how the negative reinforcement of drug use takes place when drug use serves the purpose of coping with stressful or negative life situations or coping with stress and tension that come from life problems. Note that life situation problems may be either external problems (relationships, legal, social, etc.) or internal problems (such as unresolved losses and grief, negative self-view, etc.).

Figure 6

The Psychological Addiction Pathway—Coping with Stress and Life Problems: AOD Use Reinforcement Through Stress and Tension Reduction

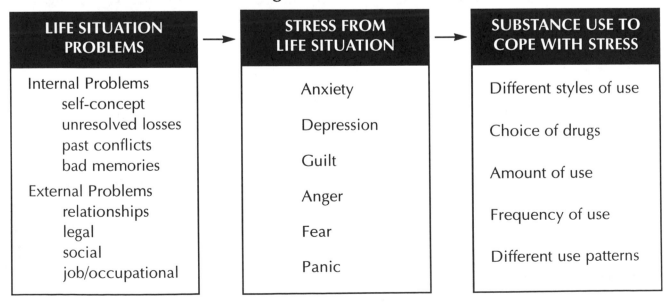

Psychological-behavioral addiction—The impaired control cycle: The pathways pictured in Figures 5 and 6 can lead to the *mental-behavior addiction* cycle pictured in Figure 7.

Our life situation (Point A in Figure 7) leads to a need or desire to increase pleasure or decrease discomfort. We expect that drug use will do this for us. So we use a drug (Point B). The outcome is as we expect: we find an increase in pleasure or decrease in discomfort (coping). The use of the drug is strengthened or reinforced (Point C). Most people never go beyond the Point A to C path. This path, however, can lead to the addiction cycle. Let us look at this cycle.

The addiction cycle begins: For some people, as a result of using a drug to feel good or to not feel bad, the use of the drug causes them problems (Point D). With many people, the painful consequences of AOD use leads to a change in AOD use patterns or a complete abandonment of the use of drugs. For others, there is a strong need to cope with the problems and stress that come from drug use itself. What's the best way to do this? Use more drugs (Point E of Figure 7).

The addiction cycle continues when further problems result from AOD use (Point F); further AOD use is engaged in (Point G) to handle the problems resulting from this further use. All along, however, the life situation problems not AOD related continue to occur, and the individual now needs to use drugs to deal with those problems, plus past problems resulting from AOD use plus the more immediate problems resulting from AOD use. AOD use at this point is based on the need of the individual to maintain psychological balance—or what we call *homeostasis* (balance at home). This *completes the addiction cycle.*

Some enter treatment at Point D when the first problems from AOD use start. Others wait until the problems begin to build up. Still others wait until they are so deep into the addiction and impaired control cycle that AOD use becomes their way of life. Now, the person uses drugs because he or she uses drugs. An old proverb sums it up: "A man takes the drink. The drink takes the drink. Then the drink takes the man."

Example: You stop off at the bar to have a few beers to handle your life problems. This works for you. One day, you get arrested for driving while intoxicated. You get convicted. Now, you find a great amount of stress from getting a DUI. You find that one way you can handle the stress is to drink. You have always drunk to handle your problems. So now you drink to handle the problem that came from drinking. This drinking leads to further problems. Now you drink to handle the additional problems that came from drinking. You also drink to handle your life problems. This is the *impaired control addiction cycle.*

Exercise and Discussion: Because much of the session will be taken up presenting the *psychological-behavioral* addiction cycle and the *psychological-physical* addiction cycle below, it is very important that the presenter engage the clients in discussion about how they identify with the cycle and to take time to deal with questions as they come up. At the end of the presentation, have each client share how they see themselves with respect to the cycle, and to what extent they have gotten into the *impaired control* process.

Figure 7
Mental-Behavioral Addiction: The Impaired Control Cycle

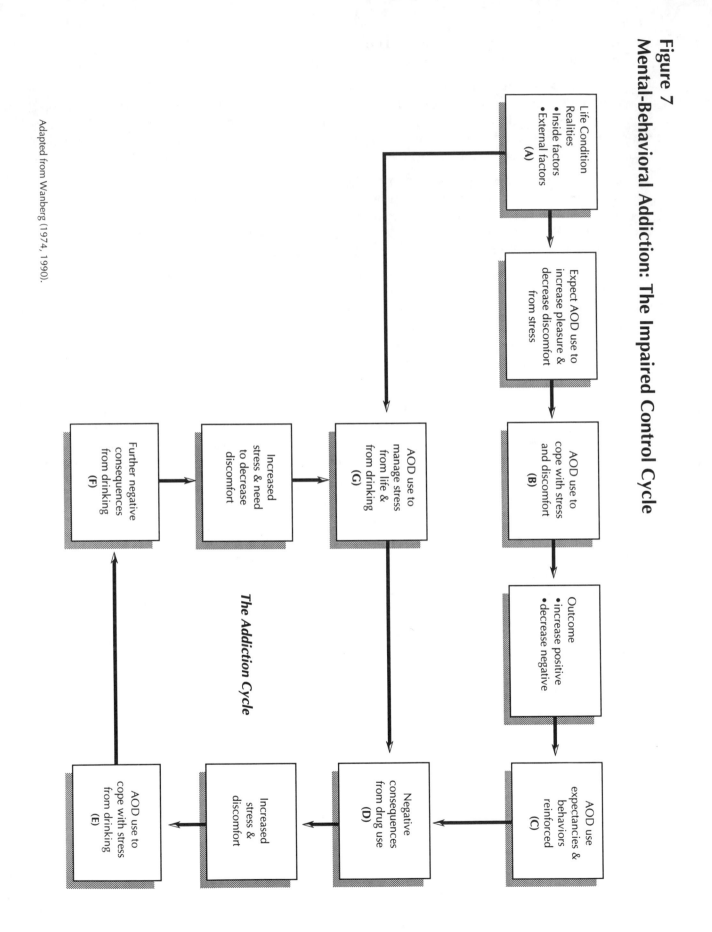

Adapted from Wanberg (1974, 1990).

b. **The Psychophysical Addiction Model**

The *psychophysical* addiction cycle is described in detail in this section. It is only summarized in the Participant Workbook. This pathway to addiction is based on the work of Gitlow (1970, 1982). It has been illustrated by Glenn and Hockman (1977), Glenn and Warner (1975), and Glenn, Warner and Hockman (1977), has been further discussed by Peyser (1988) and Grilly (1989) and has been illustrated in detail by Wanberg (1990). This pathway to addictions model is illustrated in Figure 8.

Simply stated, a person uses a drug for its direct effect. One drinks to feel relaxed, sedated and calm and to reduce mental and body stress. However, the indirect or withdrawal effects from the drug are just the opposite. For alcohol, the indirect effect would be stress, agitation, anxiety and mental and body tension. Thus, drinking produces the very condition for which the person drank. Thus, one must now drink to *cure* the symptoms coming from drinking. To maintain a balance in body tension, one must continue to drink or to abstain long enough to work through the distressful condition of withdrawal, and develop a drug-free state of balance. Let us now look at this addiction model in detail.

Figure 8
Psychological-Physical Addiction Model

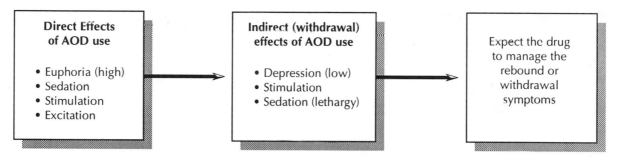

The physical addiction cycle: During the waking hours, we go through several cycles of high and low nervous and body activity. The number of these cycles we go though each day will differ from person to person and their nature is not clear. When we sleep, however, these cycles of activity have been studied and are quite clear. It appears that we go through about five of these cycles when we sleep. The dream or Rapid Eye Movement (REM) part of sleep is a period when our nervous system and brain is most active. When we are in deep sleep, or what we call level 4 sleep, we have very low brain and nervous system activity (see Cartwright, 1977, and Hartman, 1988, for a description of these cycles).

Figures 9 through 12 illustrate the *psychophysical addiction* model (Figures 9 through 12 are after Glenn and Warner, 1975).

Figure 9 provides a picture of what might be the increased and decreased levels of activity during our waking hours. The *average tension level* (ATL), or the nervous tension activity levels between lines A and B, would be a normal level of tension. When the level of nervous system activity goes above line A, we begin to feel some tension, irritation, agitation or even noticeable levels of anxiety. When the activity level falls below line B, we begin to feel relaxed, tired, weak and sleepy. Each cycle in Figure 9 is approximately two to three hours.

The high level of the cycle may be represented by both *positive* and *negative* types of stimulation. We could feel good and hyper and energetic; or we could feel agitated, anxious and tense. The nature of response at the high end will depend upon our mood, what is happening to us at the time and our psychological and physical needs.

Figure 9

Psychophysical Addiction Model:
Normal Daily Cycle of Average Tension Level (ATL)

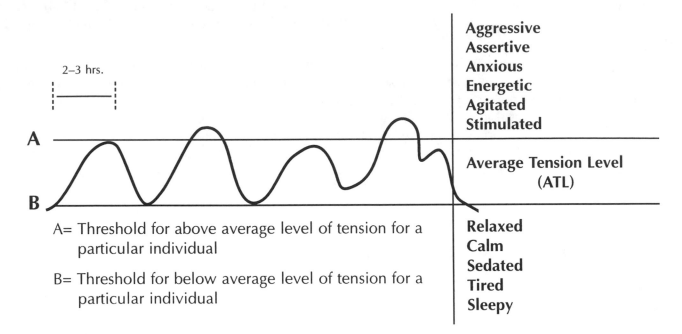

A= Threshold for above average level of tension for a
particular individual

B= Threshold for below average level of tension for a
particular individual

When we use drugs that slow down the nervous system, or what we earlier called nervous system *suppressor* drugs such as alcohol, sedatives or narcotics, these drugs will change the number of cycles and the level of activity in the nervous system activity cycle, as described in Figure 10 (Marijuana in low doses can meet the system suppressor criteria). The body's reactions that take place when we have the suppressor (sedative) drugs, such as alcohol, in us are noted in the lower right-hand corner of Figure 9.

When the suppressor or sedative type drug such as alcohol begins to wear off, we begin to experience the *rebound* or nerve-excitement effect. This is really the withdrawal reaction from the use of a sedative drug. This rebound effect is what Gitlow (1970, 1982) and Peyser (1988) call the asynchronous relationship between the short-term large-amplitude sedative effect of alcohol and its long-term agitating *(withdrawal)* effect.

If we take a drink at D1 (Figure 10), we begin to experience a period of sedation for up to one to two hours that is followed by a period of rebound into stimulation and agitation that can be for as long as three hours. A second drink taken about two to three hours later or at the peak of stimulation (D2) will have less of a sedative effect since it has to work against the body's rebound from the first drink. If we take a third drink at D3, or at the peak of the rebound from the first two drinks, then we will probably experience little sedative effect since that drink has to work against the body's rebound from the first two drinks. This is similar to what Ray and Ksir (1996) describe as the continuation of the body's response to compensate from the sedation of the body resulting from using a sedative or *suppressor* (alcohol) drug.

Figure 10

Psychological-Physical Addiction Model: The Countering Effect of Rebound or Withdrawal When Taking Several Doses of a Sedative Drug Such as Alcohol

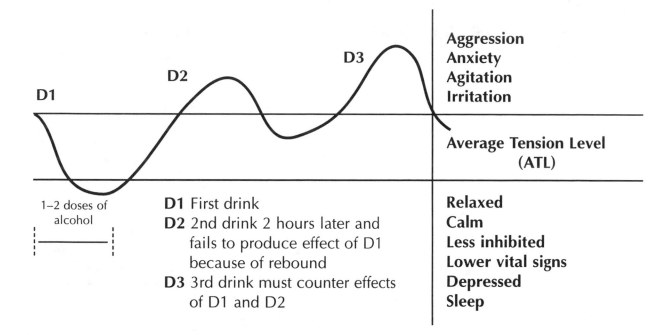

The rebound from sedation is the body's effort to keep from getting sedated. *Sedation* is the gradual slowing of the body's normal activity (heartbeat, breathing) that, if allowed to continue, would result in the stopping of all of these normal activities. This is why, during sleep, we stay in deep sleep for only a short time; the body automatically springs back from this deep sedation since it is close to all activity stopping—or death. Thus, the natural reaction of the body to a sedative drug such as alcohol is to work against that drug to keep the body's activity from stopping. It does this by producing its *own stimulant drug*. But, because the external sedative drug, such as alcohol, is so strong, it overpowers this natural process. If we take enough alcohol, we will stop all activity and go into a coma and die.

The body, then, must work against or compensate for this slowing down process. When the alcohol wears off, then the natural drugs that the body produced to work against the alcohol take over (these are stimulant-like drugs). This is the basis for going into *rebound*, or a state of stimulation and agitation.

If we extend our drinking period, the body may have stored up larger amounts of its natural stimulant drug. Thus, the rebound may be more intense and occur over a longer period of time—many times longer than the period that we were sedated or drugged by alcohol. This is illustrated in Figure 11. Just how strongly the rebound goes into the stress or agitation period will depend on how long we drink, how much we drink and the intensity of the drug's direct effect (Gitlow, 1982; Grilly, 1989, p. 95). This is drug *withdrawal*, or the *abstinence syndrome*. It is the body's reaction to the drug going out of the system.

The *rebound* or *withdrawal effect* may continue for several weeks or even months following a longer period of alcohol use. Although the stimulation and agitation effects will most likely not be very intense, or even noticeable, the very presence of this agitation creates an ongoing level of stress. When this low level of stress is added to normal daily tension, stressful events are more difficult to handle. This may be a factor that contributes to relapse. Thus, one may be more vulnerable to relapsing during the several weeks or months following quitting drinking.

Taking a drink is one way to avoid the rebound symptoms or to *"cure"* the stress and agitation from withdrawal from alcohol. If one takes a drink at D2 in Figure 11 this will *"take off the edge."* This is taking a *"hair of the dog that bit you."* It is one of the bases of addiction to sedative drugs (alcohol).

Figure 11

Psychophysical Addiction Model: Longer Periods of Rebound and Withdrawal from Longer Time of Heavy Drinking to Excessive Amounts of Alcohol Use

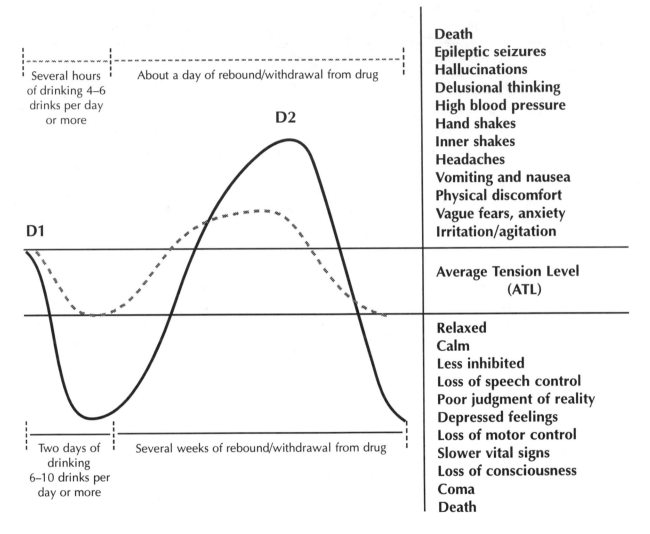

A person who has developed a pattern of daily, steady drinking may need to use the drug every one or two hours during non-sleep periods in order to avoid the agitation of withdrawal and *cure* the rebound effect. This describes the case of the *strung out* user that is pictured in Figure 12. In this situation, doses of alcohol spaced closely together must work against the rebound of prior doses. Thus, the rebound effect *reduces* the strength of each dose of alcohol.

This process, then, explains one reason why people become addicted to a drug. For many people, it will take the person into the addiction cycle or the impaired control cycle where the drug is needed to manage the withdrawal effects of the drug. Peyser (1988) calls this the "autonomous self-perpetuating" factor of addiction. The body demands more of the drug to maintain the body balance (homeostasis)—the very drug that set off the state of nervous system imbalance. It is related to what the drug does to the nerve chemistry at the nerve endings themselves.

Figure 12

Psychophysical Addiction Model: The *Strung Out User*

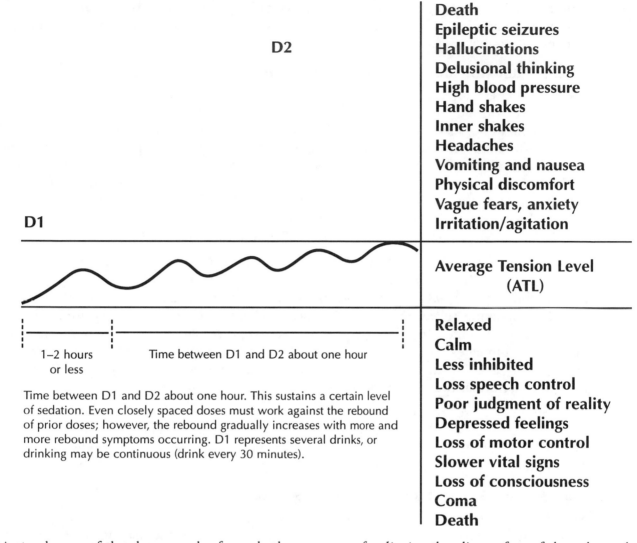

D2

D1

1–2 hours
or less

Time between D1 and D2 about one hour

Time between D1 and D2 about one hour. This sustains a certain level of sedation. Even closely spaced doses must work against the rebound of prior doses; however, the rebound gradually increases with more and more rebound symptoms occurring. D1 represents several drinks, or drinking may be continuous (drink every 30 minutes).

Death
Epileptic seizures
Hallucinations
Delusional thinking
High blood pressure
Hand shakes
Inner shakes
Headaches
Vomiting and nausea
Physical discomfort
Vague fears, anxiety
Irritation/agitation

Average Tension Level (ATL)

Relaxed
Calm
Less inhibited
Loss speech control
Poor judgment of reality
Depressed feelings
Loss of motor control
Slower vital signs
Loss of consciousness
Coma
Death

A steady use of the drug may be for only the purpose of *relieving* the discomfort of the rebound or withdrawal phase of use. If the drug is discontinued after a period of use, minor symptoms such as inability to sleep, shakes or being irritable may occur within 24 hours. For the person who has been drinking steady for several days to several weeks, more serious symptoms will begin to occur within 72 hours (Ciraulo & Ciraulo, 1988; Hodding, Jann & Ackerman, 1980). These symptoms may be very serious, depending on how strong and intense the rebound is. These symptoms are given in the upper right-hand column of Figure 12.

In almost every case, the effects of the rebound or withdrawal from a drug are the *opposite* of the direct or intoxicating effects of the drug (Grilly, 1989, p. 94). Thus, this psychophysical model can be applied to other drugs such as stimulants. The direct effects of a stimulant (amphetamines, cocaine) would be physical and mental excitability, stimulation or agitation. When the blood level of the stimulant drug drops, the rebound or withdrawal process begins and is the opposite of that for the sedative drugs or the supressors. This rebound causes depression and tiredness, and we get what is called the *crashing* effect. Some of these symptoms could also include a decrease in vital signs (blood pressure, heart rate). Again, the most effective short-term way to deal with these reactions is to re-engage in the use of the drug. Thus, the cocaine-addicted person begins to use cocaine to counteract the opposite or withdrawal effects of the cocaine.

In simple terms, psychophysical addiction is using the drug to "relieve" the rebound or withdrawal from the drug. A continuous AOD user is essentially trying to avoid the discomfort and pain of withdrawal. That pain is both mental and physical.

Note to Presenter: Again, because of the heavy didactic quality to this session, it is important that the presenter take time to have people ask questions and for clients to share where they identify with this physical addiction process.

c. **Cocaine Addiction and the Neurochemical Process**

Because stimulants, particularly cocaine, are drugs often used by the SAO, it is important that clients have some understanding of the neurochemical explanation of cocaine addiction. We have seen in the psychophysical addiction pathway that when the presence of cocaine (or other stimulants) in the system declines, an opposite effect of euphoria, pleasure and stimulation occurs—neurological slowing and depression. This depression is also experienced at the psychological level. The "best" way to treat the depressive effects (both physically and psychologically) is to use more cocaine. There is extensive scientific data in the literature on the relationship between cocaine and brain chemistry (Blum et al., 1996; Milkman & Sunderwirth, 1987; Ray & Ksir, 1996; Roehrich, Dackis & Gold, 1987; Volkow et al., 1993).

The principal place where cocaine takes effect is the dopamine D2 receptor. Neuronal excitement can induce the flow of dopamine, a neurotransmitter that activates the brain pleasure centers (Roehrich et al., 1987). Under normal conditions of dopamine flow, the excess is recycled into the dopamine releasing nerve cells and deactivated. When cocaine is used, the excess dopamine is prevented from being recycled and excessive pleasure or euphoria results. More dopamine stimulates other neurons to produce still more dopamine leading to increased euphoria or pleasure. In essence, cocaine prevents the dopamine releasing neurons from performing the normal reuptake process.

After prolonged use, cocaine leaves the system, there is a depletion of the D2 receptors, and an opposite effects of pleasure and euphoria are felt. Chronic administration of cocaine results in a decrease of D2 receptors, resulting in a *craving* for cocaine to achieve effects of pleasure and euphoria (Volkow et al., 1993).

d. **Genetic Factors: The Reward Deficiency Syndrome**

We summarized some of the biological factors that increase risk for substance abuse. One of the most common concerns that substance abuse clients have is whether alcoholism or drug abuse is inherited. This issue has been thoroughly examined during the past 30 years. The outcome is certainly mixed. However, two facts seem apparent. First, as Blum et al. (1996) indicate, there appears to be no specific gene for alcoholism (p. 132) and for other types of drug addiction. Second, what is apparent is that there is an association between genes and various behavior disorders and addictions (alcohol abuse, cocaine abuse, etc.). As noted in Chapter 2, Blum and associates conclude that there is a strong link between substance abuse and what they call the *reward deficiency syndrome* (RDS).

Blum and associates conclude that the RDS is based on what they call the *reward cascade*. This *cascade* is a chain of neurons within the limbic system that interact through various neurotransmitters. If there is a deficiency in one or more of these neurotransmitters (e.g., dopamine), an individual's feelings of well-being can be replaced by feelings of anxiety, or a craving for the substance that can relieve the person of the anxiety.

Blum and associates provide evidence to indicate that a large percentage of persons with addictive problems have a reduction in the dopamine D2 receptors which activate the brain's pleasure centers. Further, they found that this depletion of the D2 receptors is related to the *dopamine D2 receptor gene* called the *A1 allele*. They found that a larger percentage of persons with alcohol and cocaine addiction had this A1 allele variation.

The presence of this genetic variation associated with the RDS has been linked with other risk factors. For example, in one study, 87 percent of cocaine addicted individuals had the A1 allele variation if they had the following three risk factors: *parental alcoholism and drug abuse, early-childhood deviancy and a history of a more potent method of cocaine use* (smoking crack) (Noble et al., 1993). The studies of Blum and associates and other studies indicate that there are biogenetic variations of a significant percentage of individuals with AOD addiction problems. Yet, most studies concur with Blum and associates (Blum & Payne, 1991) that biological risk factors are interactive with psychological and social risk factors. Most conclude that the psychological and social risk factors are very potent factors in the development of AOD abuse problems.

Although biogenetic factors are important in helping us understand AOD addiction problems, we should be cautioned in overstating their influences (see Fingarette, 1988, for a discussion of this issue). For example, the Goodwin, Schulsinger, Hermansen, Guze and Winokur (1973) study is classic in terms of being quoted as providing evidence of a genetic basis for alcoholism (other studies found similar results). That study took children whose fathers were alcoholic but who were adopted shortly after birth and not raised by their biological parents. The rate of alcoholism among the adopted children with alcoholic biological parent (85 percent had fathers considered alcoholic) was about 3.6 times as large as that among adoptees whose biological parents were not alcoholic.

As Fingarette (1988) notes, the full picture of these findings must be elucidated. In Goodwin's study, 18 percent of the sons who had alcoholic parents developed alcoholic problems versus 5 percent of the sons with nonalcoholic parents. This means that 82 percent of the sons with alcoholic parents did not become alcoholics (or four out of five). As Fingarette concludes: "Either the relevant genes are usually not transmitted or the genes arc transmitted but are usually outweighed by other factors" (p. 53). Thus, the genetic factor must be one of many that determine alcohol addiction—but one which apparently adds to the risk.

e. **Exercise: Cocaine and the Brain**[2]

This demonstration shows how a multisensory approach to "hard" science can capture the attention of the participant and creates the desired learning effect.

Ask for seven volunteers. One person is dressed in white to represent cocaine and will be called *cocaine*. The other six are placed in two lines of three with a three-foot space between them. *Cocaine* stands to the side. The sensation is a beautiful sunset.

Beautiful sunset   Cocaine

Pre	**1**	**2**	**3**	**synapse**	**post**	**4**	**5**	**6**

At one end (presynaptic terminal)—triggered by sensations from sunset—person #1 makes a motion (taps #2 on the shoulder), and #2 taps #3—who is standing at the synapse—on the shoulder. Then #3 reaches into the synaptic vesicle (a tennis ball container holding three balls).

The tennis ball, which represents the neurotransmitter dopamine, is right at the top so #3 gives it across synapse to #4. As soon as #4 has the dopamine (ball) he then touches #5 and #5 touches #6 who says "Whoa!" and waves his hand in ecstatic delight (representing the perception of joy that may result from the sunset).

[2]The authors wish to thank Stanley Sunderwirth, Ph.D., Professor of Chemistry, Purdue University, for developing this exercise.

When #4 sends the message on, s/he hands the neurotransmitter (ball) back to #3 who replaces it in the synaptic vesicle. Then #1 at the presynaptic neuron starts the process again. Let the group practice this for five to ten times until it runs smoothly.

Now in comes *cocaine* dressed in white. The message comes in normal fashion, that is, #1 taps #2, and so on. The dopamine (ball) crosses the synapse and when #4 attempts to give it back to #3, *cocaine* grabs the ball and hands it back to #4 (blocks the re-uptake of the dopamine), and #4 sends the message in the usual fashion by tapping #5. As soon as #4 taps #5, #4 attempts to return the ball to #3 but cocaine takes it and hands it straight back.

#6 is saying, "whoa!" real fast (excessive dopamine).

Then you see #3 just sitting there with the remaining balls in the synaptic vesicle (the cylinder), and he doesn't need them anymore. So #3 empties the cylinder and dumps the balls on the floor. The policeman comes and grabs the *cocaine* and then the neurotransmitter (balls) can no longer be accessed from the cylinder.

Withdrawal comes, then, when the cocaine is no longer available, and the pleasure derived from the neurotransmitter is no longer there because the nerve cells felt they were no longer necessary. This leads to a cocaine withdrawal effect.

Exercise: At the end of the presentation of the *psychological-physical addiction model,* ask participants to identify where they fit with respect to Figures 9 through 12.

4. Classroom and Homework Assignments

a. Have clients read the material in the Workbook for Session 9 to prepare for the next session.

b. Have clients complete classroom or homework (a) in the Workbook.

5. Presentation Sequence

a. Review the last session and homework for the past week.

b. Present *Psychological Addiction Cycle*.

c. Have each client identify how they fit the *Psychological Addiction Pathway* (Figure 6).

d. Present the *Psychological-Physical Addiction Cycle*.

e. Have each client identify how they fit the *Psychophysical Addiction Cycle* as presented in Figures 9 through 12.

6. Session and Client Evaluation

a. Give clients Figure 7 with blank blocks and have them complete the blocks.

b. Have client complete the CSES for Sessions 7 and 8 of this module based on whether the client understood the two addiction models.

c. Provider completes PSES.

d. Counselor completes the Behavioral Rating Form (BRF) for this session and calculates the score.

Session ⑨: Understanding Criminal Conduct and the Influence of Drugs

1. Rationale and Overview of Session

Just as it is important for the AOD abuser to understand the AOD addiction cycles he or she engages in, it is important for the offender to also understand the criminal conduct cycles that he or she engages in. The purpose of this session is to help the SAO client to understand these criminal conduct (CC) cycles.

2. Objectives of Session

> ⇒ To help the client understand the cognitive styles and thinking patterns that lead to or determine criminal conduct;
>
> ⇒ To help the client understand the criminal conduct and offender cycles;
>
> ⇒ To help the client understand the relationship between criminal conduct and AOD use and abuse.

3. Session Content

a. Review of the AOD addiction cycles

We have concluded that AOD use and abuse are *learned behaviors*. These behaviors are responses to the individual's reaction to the external world and to what goes on inside of the individual. Alcohol and other drugs are used to cope with life problems and situations and the stress and discomfort resulting from these problems and situations. AOD use behavior gets strengthened and reinforced when it becomes an effective tool in dealing with the problems and stresses of living. However, at some point in the individual AOD user's life, AOD use produces negative consequences—problems in living. It is when the individual begins to engage in AOD use to cope with the problems that come from use that the AOD addiction cycle makes full circle. The cycle continues as the individual continues AOD use, leading to further negative consequences that are then subsequently managed by further AOD use.

b. Understanding criminal conduct and the offender cycle

Patterns of criminal conduct are also *learned behaviors*. These behavior patterns are also responses to the individual's external and internal world and are ways of coping with that world and with the inside reaction (e.g., stress, anger) to that world. Just as with AOD use, criminal conduct gets reinforced because it can turn *on* positive feelings and events for the individual or it can *turn off* stress and unpleasant events. However, just as irresponsible AOD use will lead to negative consequences, irresponsible behavior in the community such as criminal conduct will lead to negative consequences. Although the negative results from CC (punishment, criminal sanctioning) can contribute to the weakening of this behavior, it also strengthens this behavior because it reinforces the internal automatic thoughts, perceptions, attitudes and beliefs of the individual. These pathways are illustrated in Figure 13. Just as with AOD use, the individual will engage in CC to cope with the negative consequences that come from criminal conduct itself.

1) What is criminal conduct?

A working definition of criminal behavior has been provided by Andrews and Bonta (1994): "Criminal behavior refers to antisocial acts that place the actor at risk of becoming a focus of the attention of criminal and juvenile justice professionals" (p.24). There are four ways to look at the definition of criminal conduct (Andrews & Bonta, 1994):

- From a **legal view,** it is an act prohibited by the state and punishable by law;

- From a **moral view**, it is an act that goes against the norms of a religion and morality and thus is punishable by a supreme power;

- From a **social view**, it is an act that goes against the custom and tradition of a community and thus is punishable by the community;

- From a **psychological view**, criminal conduct is antisocial; it is an act that brings pain and loss to others but is rewarding to the criminal.

Exercise: Have clients share their own definitions of criminal conduct. Do a round robin and have each client identity which of the above definitions fits them.

2) **What are the factors of people's pasts that tend to bring people to be involved in criminal conduct?**

- A history of early involvement in deviant or antisocial and criminal conduct;

- Having grown up in a disruptive, abusive and neglectful family where there was lack of parental attention and supervision;

- Failure in school, work and leisure time;

- AOD use and abuse at an early age.

We cannot change these factors. We can, through treatment, understand how these events have changed our lives and we can work through the feelings resulting from these life situations. We can also learn to accept them as realities and *not* make them a part of our irrational thoughts and errors in thinking process.

3) **What are the present risk factors that lead to criminal conduct and that can be changed?**

These have been called dynamic risk factors or what Andrews and Bonta call *criminogenic needs*. These are needs that people have who become involved in criminal conduct. A list of these *criminogenic needs* is provided in Table 4. This list is based on several sources including Andrews and Bonta (1994), Hollin (1990), Ross and Ross (1995) and Bush and Bilodeau (1993). Table 4 provides the criminogenic needs and the related cognitive and behavioral responses that lead to self-correction and change.

Exercise: Have clients see how they identify with the factors listed in Table 4 by using *Work Sheet 3* in the *Workbook*. The risk factors in *Work Sheet 3* are listed somewhat differently from in Table 4.

4) **Cognitive distortions: Errors in thinking or thinking distortions**

A *cognitive distortion* is a way of thinking that is automatic to the point that we continue to engage in the errors of thinking even though our experiences and the facts do not support the thinking error.

Yochelson and Samenow (1976) define *thinking errors* as the mental process required by the criminal to live his kind of life. They feel that thinking errors are habitual and *are clearly obvious in the daily transactions of the criminal.* Correcting or eliminating criminal thinking patterns is an essential part of the treatment of the SAO client.

Table 5 provides a list of errors in thinking. These were compiled from a variety of sources (Beck, 1976; Burns, 1980, 1989; Yochelson and Samenow, 1976, 1977). The purpose of this part of the session is to introduce the client to the concept of *cognitive distortions* and to review the list in Table 5. This area becomes a focus of one complete session in Module 9, Session 28.

Exercise: The thinking errors in Table 5 have been placed in *Work Sheet 4*. Have clients use this work sheet to rate themselves on thinking errors. Then have the group discuss their ratings, comparing their ratings with those of others. Have the clients then look at how these errors in thinking have led to past AOD use and criminal conduct.

Table 4

Criminogenic Needs Which Bring People to Criminal Conduct and the Cognitive-Behavioral Responses for Self-Correction and Change

Criminogenic Needs	Related Self-Corrections
Involvement with antisocial peers, friends and associates	Develop associations with prosocial associates
Poor problem solving and self-management skills	Develop problem solving and life-management skills
Procriminal and antisocial thinking, beliefs and attitudes	Changing procriminal beliefs, thinking and attitudes
Procriminal and antisocial feelings and emotions	Managing and changing antisocial feelings and emotions
Identifying with procriminal role models	Develop relationships with prosocial role models
Impulsive responding and acting out behavior	Develop self-control: thought between impulse and action
Self-centered thinking—not able to see view of others	Learning role-taking or seeing through the eyes of others
Self-oriented communication patterns	Learning other-directed communication patterns
Need for family closeness and communication	Develop ties with family or family-like relationships
Need for primary social unit structures such as family	Develop positive social unit and family structures
Involvement in antisocial and deviant behaviors	Replace antisocial with prosocial behaviors
Need to manipulate and to control others	Develop self-control and self-confidence
Receive rewards through criminal conduct	Shift reward potential to non-criminal conduct
Participate in environments of high-risk for criminal conduct	Develop skills to avoid or cope with high-risk settings
Blame others for own action and behaviors	Develop responsibility for own behavior and actions
Impaired moral reasoning; hold self-serving/antisocial moral codes	Develop prosocial and more other-reflective moral codes
Overall impaired social and interpersonal skills	Develop social and coping skills through social skills training
Overt acting out of feelings of anger and resentment	Learn self-regulation of angry feelings and other emotions
Thinking in a "black and white" concrete manner	Develop skills to increase abstract reasoning and thinking
Need to use substances to support criminal and antisocial conduct	Develop recreational, vocational and interpersonal alternatives to AOD use and criminal conduct

Table 5

Selected Thinking Errors and Distortions Often Held by Individuals Who Engage in Criminal Conduct

1. **Power thrust:** *Putting someone down* so you can be in control.

2. **Closed channel:** *Seeing your way as the only way.*

3. **Victim stance:** *Blaming others* for what's happening to you.

4. **Pride and superiority:** You really *feel superior to others* and know it all; you feel the world owes you a living.

5. **Lack of empathy and concern for how others are affected:** Not thinking how your actions affect others or the emotional/physical pain you cause others.

6. **Seeing trust as a one way street—can't trust anybody:** You demand people trust you but you do not trust others.

7. **I can't:** You *refuse to do something you don't want to do.*

8. **Irresponsible commitment:** *You want what you want right now* and will spend little time getting it; don't follow through with commitments or complete the task, particularly if it doesn't give you immediate reward.

9. **Take what you want from others:** I deserve it.

10. **Rejection dependency:** You *refuse to lean on someone,* to depend on someone, to ask others for help because this is a sign of weakness. Yet you take from others which makes you dependent on others.

11. **Put off doing what should be done:** You put off things; you put off changing. You say "tomorrow I'll quit" or someday you will stop taking part in actions that make other people victims.

12. **Rejecting obligations—I don't have to do that:** You may have enough money to get drunk but you delay paying your rent.

13. **Concrete and rigid thinking:** *You have your ideas and will not change.*

14. **Either or, black or white thinking:** One is either successful or not successful, pretty or ugly. *There is no in-between, no shades of grey.*

15. **Mountains out of molehills:** This is *catastrophizing.* It is blowing up something out of proportion; treating something common as a catastrophe.

16. **Feeling singled out:** Feeling that what is happening to you is unique; *feeling picked on.*

17. **They deserve it:** *If they hadn't been so stupid* and locked their doors, they wouldn't have been robbed.

18. **I feel screwed.**

19. **Selected attention:** *Tuning out what one should hear;* focus on one statement, one result. Hear the negative but tune out the positive.

20. **Antisocial thinking:** You spend a long time *thinking about criminal things* and are busy planning doing unlawful things.

21. **Lying or exaggerating the truth:** You may lie so often that it becomes automatic; you exaggerate the truth to *look important or big.*

5) The criminal conduct cycle:

Just as with AOD use and abuse, criminal conduct occurs in a cyclical manner and the cycle gets reinforced. Figure 13 provides a description of this cycle. Individuals will differ as to the precipitating events, the unique cognitive processes (different automatic thoughts, different attitudes and beliefs), the specific cognitive reactions and responses and the fact that an action choice can be made in response to the internal cognitive reactions and responses. As well, individuals differ as to the kind of criminal conduct they choose to engage in and the kind of victim targeted.

Even though individuals will differ as to particular thinking and behavioral responses, we hold that this cycle applies to most individuals who engage in criminal conduct. The following are the important parts of this cycle:

- Preceding criminal conduct are *cognitive reactions* that are responses to external and internal events in the person's life.

- Most persons who become involved in CC choose to do so; they make a *conscious choice* as to the type of criminal conduct and who they will victimize.

- Once criminal conduct is engaged in, it sets off *new cognitive reactions* that reinforce the underlying criminal thinking.

- Finally, the cognitive responses and reactions to the criminal conduct are *reinforced* which strengthens the criminal behavior itself.

Correction and change in this cycle can occur at three points.

- *First,* correction and *change* takes place in *your mental reactions* to what happens outside of you. These are your mental choices. You can replace your criminal thinking with what we call *prosocial thinking.* This is thinking that says "I want to follow the laws of society. I want to be a positive part of my community."

- *Second,* you can *change or correct your actions.* You can do something different. You can use actions that are not criminal.

- *Third,* you can *change the events* or things outside of you that set off the criminal actions. For example, you can avoid situations that are high risk for being involved in criminal conduct. We would call these preventive measures. However, we are not able to shelter ourselves from all outside and inside events which lead to mental reactions that lead to criminal conduct.

Remember: What is most important is that true change and self-correction comes when you handle the mental reactions. Change comes when you change your thinking and beliefs. Change comes when you learn the skills that help you to choose positive social actions.

Exercise: General discussion around the CC cycle. Does it make sense? Does it apply to the participants?

6) Relationship between AOD use and criminal conduct cycle:

Alcohol and other drug (AOD) use interact, feed into and reinforce criminal behavior and the criminal conduct cycle in several ways.

- Alcohol and other drugs may be part of the events that set off criminal thinking. AOD intoxication lowers self-control, stops good judgment and gets us into irrational beliefs and errors of thinking;

- Drugs are often part of situations of high risk for criminal activity;

Figure 13
The Criminal Conduct and Corrective Behavior Cycles

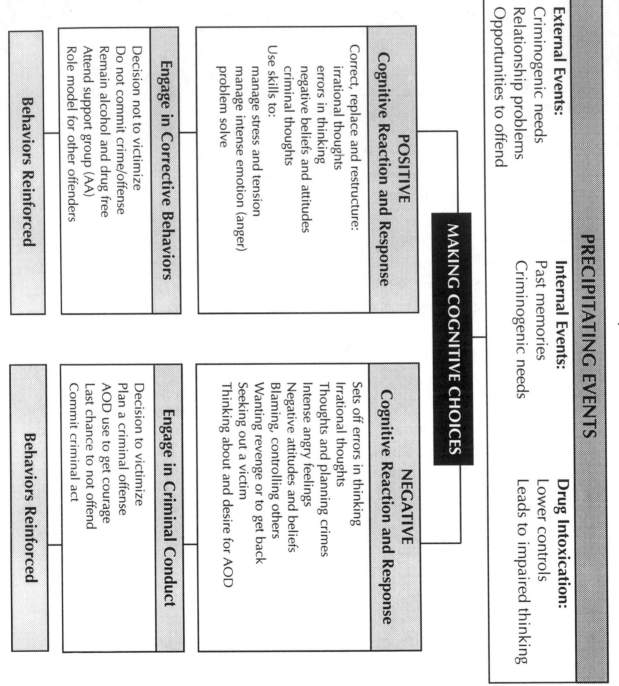

PRECIPITATING EVENTS

External Events:
Criminogenic needs
Relationship problems
Opportunities to offend

Internal Events:
Past memories
Criminogenic needs

Drug Intoxication:
Lower controls
Leads to impaired thinking

MAKING COGNITIVE CHOICES

POSITIVE
Cognitive Reaction and Response

Correct, replace and restructure:
irrational thoughts
errors in thinking
negative beliefs and attitudes
criminal thoughts
Use skills to:
manage stress and tension
manage intense emotion (anger)
problem solve

NEGATIVE
Cognitive Reaction and Response

Sets off errors in thinking
Irrational thoughts
Thoughts and planning crimes
Intense angry feelings
Negative attitudes and beliefs
Blaming, controlling others
Wanting revenge or to get back
Seeking out a victim
Thinking about and desire for AOD

Engage in Corrective Behaviors

Decision not to victimize
Do not commit crime/offense
Remain alcohol and drug free
Attend support group (AA)
Role model for other offenders

Engage in Criminal Conduct

Decision to victimize
Plan a criminal offense
AOD use to get courage
Last chance to not offend
Commit criminal act

Behaviors Reinforced

Behaviors Reinforced

212

- AOD use and influence can stop you from using positive and corrective mental activities. It can block the use of skills to stop relapse and recidivism. It can cause the person to pass up self-correction;

- AOD use and intoxication can strengthen errors in thinking which excuse criminal conduct. It can prevent the person from feeling fear and guilt before committing the criminal act. It can block fear and guilt which should follow a criminal act.

Exercise: Group discussion following the presentation of material in this section. Focus question: *How do each of the participants see AOD use relating to their criminal conduct and how does their CC relate to their AOD use?*

4. Classroom and Homework Assignments

a. Complete *Work Sheets 3 and 4 in Workbook*.

b. Read Introduction to *Module 4* and material for *Session 10*.

5. Presentation Sequence

a. Review Homework from *Session 8*

b. Exercise: Group discussion of definitions of CC and which ones do each client fit.

c. Presentation of the risk factors of the past and present (sections 2 and 3 under b), p. 208. Then have group discuss these factors and have clients share how these might fit them.

d. Briefly present the idea of *cognitive distortions and errors in thinking*. Review the list in Table 5. Indicate that these will be dealt with in more depth in a later module.

e. Present the *Criminal Conduct Cycle*. Make sure they understand this cycle. Have group members discuss whether it fits them.

f. Present material on relationship of AOD to CC. Do a structured group discussion around how AOD use fits into their own CC.

6. Session and Client Evaluation

a. Have client complete the CSES for session.

b. Provider completes PSES and BRF, calculates and records score.

MODULE 4

**Self-Disclosure and
Receiving Feedback:**

**Pathways to Self-Awareness
and Change**

MODULE 4: SELF-DISCLOSURE AND FEEDBACK: PATHWAYS TO SELF-AWARENESS AND CHANGE

Overview of Module 4

Self-awareness is a key element to the process of correcting and changing one's thinking, feelings and actions. The primary pathway to self-awareness is to fully explore and disclose the personal experiences and problems one has had in the areas of desired change and to receive feedback from others as to what they think and feel about your disclosure.

Self-disclosure is not an easy thing to do since much of our lives we have been told to *not* express our feelings, to *not* talk about ourselves, or if we did express our feelings and thoughts, we often experienced disapproval and even punishment from others. This is particularly true with negative feelings and thoughts, particularly feelings and thoughts of anger and sadness. Often during our years of childhood and youth, we were told not to get angry or to be happy when we were sad. Or, if we did show our feelings, it was because we stored up those feelings and then they came out by *blowing up* or throwing a tantrum or we would just pout and get sullen. Many people when growing up did not have a chance to talk about their feelings and thoughts with parents and adults. If feelings and thoughts were shown, they were often not received and accepted by parents and adults.

Not only did we lack opportunity to express our feelings and thoughts during our developing years, we most likely did not learn or were not taught the important skills and tools to express ourselves in healthy ways. We were often taught to blame others, since that is the way most adults solve their frustrations and problems. Or, we learned that you solved problems between people by someone being right and someone being wrong. As we mature, we try to move away from the *childish* ways of expressing thoughts and feelings. Yet we tend to hold on to the old ways of showing our feelings and thoughts by losing our temper when upset or of pouting and being sullen when we don't get our way.

Receiving feedback—or having other people tell us how they see us—is also difficult. For one reason, the feedback we get from others is usually done in *reaction* to what we say or do and not by *interacting* with what we disclose. As well, the feedback often comes in a blaming manner, or as if we were wrong, and not in a way which says that the other person understands that this is his or her view (perception) of us. They give us feedback as if *this is the way we are*. When another person tells us that this is his or her opinion of us, but that s/he may be wrong, it is much easier to accept that feedback.

When you enter a treatment program of self-improvement and change, the opposite is expected of you. Now we want and encourage you to talk about yourself, expressing feelings and thoughts, to explore your past and present feelings, thoughts and actions, to tell your story.

As well, when you enter a treatment program, you say to staff and those in the program with you that it is OK to have feedback about yourself. This is an unwritten contract. But the feedback will be given to you in a non-blaming manner. You will not be told you're right or wrong. The feedback will not be to make the person giving the feedback feel he or she is right. Rather, the feedback is given to you to help you become more aware of yourself. Yet, when that feedback does come, it is often difficult to handle because it may not fit into how you see yourself.

The challenge for clients in this module is to help them *engage in an honest and open sharing* about themselves and help them to *take the risk of receiving feedback* as to how people see and experience them.

Goals and Objectives for Module 4

The overall goal of this module will be to help the clients to explore who and what they are and to openly disclose and share what they discover about themselves. To achieve this goal, we will

➠ Help clients learn communication skills which are basic to self-disclosure.

➠ Help clients learn some tools on how to record thoughts and life experiences.

➠ Give clients the opportunity to explore themselves in greater depth in the areas of AOD use and involvement in criminal conduct.

➠ Help clients be open to receiving feedback on how staff and other persons in the program see them and then for clients to evaluate whether that feedback fits with how they see themselves.

Many of the exercises in the past sessions encouraged clients to disclose personal material through the various exercises in those sessions. This module represents the first step in challenging the client to make specific disclosure around their *past criminal behavior and drug and alcohol use* within the context of the treatment program. A more in-depth disclosure will take place in *Module 8*, where we will help the client through a differential assessment to identify the various life conditions which may need to be addressed in more depth.

Time Structure for Module

This module will involve 4 two-hour sessions. The presenter is encouraged to use his or her own illustrations, ideas and exercises in accomplishing the goals of the module.

Session ⑩ : Learning Communication Tools and Skills

1. Rationale and Overview of Session

Many substance abusing offenders have never developed an awareness of their own and others' communication patterns and skills. Because of this, they are often unable to effectively communicate to others how they feel or what they think. Or, they are unable to allow others to openly and effectively express their feelings and thoughts. They may also engage in faulty automatic thinking that further allows them to ignore the problems in their personal lives and relationships. Thus, sharing the wide variety of emotions, thoughts and experiences has become difficult for substance abusing offenders.

Another problem is that people use AOD to overcome fear or anxiety that they experience when communicating with others. They may only share feelings and thoughts when AOD-intoxicated. Thus, talking about the self and sharing feelings and thoughts will have to be learned under a new condition—that of being free of alcohol and other drugs.

Learning to share feelings and to listen attentively can be learned and the benefits of doing so are considerable. The shy person may be better understood if he or she overcomes the barriers to communication; relationships can be strengthened, strangers can become friends (Monti et al., 1989). Self-disclosure is a way to build trust, to let others know they are not alone in their emotions. Listening lets the other person know we are interested and helps us learn about others, the world, and sometimes about ourselves.

2. Session Time Frame and Objectives

This session requires three hours of classroom time. The overall goal of this session is to help the client to learn communication skills which are basic to self-disclosure. We will do this by helping the client to

> ➠ Understand and explore the meaning of verbal and nonverbal communication.
>
> ➠ Learn the process and tools of self-oriented communication or talking about the self and receiving feedback from others so as to encourage and increase self-disclosure and then self-awareness.
>
> ➠ Explore the basic tools of other-oriented communication in order to help the client to get others to talk and to get others to be receptive to feedback so as to develop effective interpersonal interactions.

3. Session Content and Client Experiences

Telling your story and receiving feedback is basic to *self-disclosure* and thus to self-correction and the change process. In this session, we look at how people communicate both verbally and nonverbally. We also learn some basic tools of how to talk about yourself and how to receive feedback from others. This is only part of the communication puzzle. Communication that leads to meaningful and positive relationships also involves other-oriented communication or how to listen to others and how to give feedback to others in such a way that it keeps the communication and the relationship open. We look at these various parts of communication.

a. Two kinds of communication that we use in relating to others—nonverbal and verbal

1) **Nonverbal communication** is "talking" without words. We show it through our face, how we move our body and our hands, and in the tone of our voice. In this way we tell people what we think and feel. What we show by our "talking" *without* words (nonverbal communication) often is not the same as our talking *with* words (verbal communication). If we are to have people understand us, we must say the same thing with words that we say without words.

219

Exercise: Take the following situations and make your choice after each one. Take about 5 minutes for this. Then discuss the results. Give the participants 5 minutes to make their choices. When the time is up, discuss the results for another 5 minutes. Then give the information following the three scenes below. Take time to discuss how the additional information influences judgment (exercise adapted from Ross et al., 1986):

a) *When a judge asks a young man whether he stole the money, the man holds his head down and claims to be innocent. In your opinion, he is:*

  • *innocent or*

  • *guilty.*

b) *After a funeral, you see a woman dressed in black speaking quietly and seriously to another woman. She is probably:*

  • *expressing her sorrow or*

  • *discussing business.*

c) *You have just been interviewed for a job. The personnel officer has looked at you without smiling throughout the interview. When he finishes, he smiles briefly. He is smiling because:*

  • *he thinks you can do the job or*

  • *he is polite.*

Additional information about the three scenes:

a) *The man is from a country in which it is considered rude to look a judge in the eye.*

b) *The woman in black is holding a calculator.*

c) *You learn the personnel officer has not shown any feelings at all when he interviewed some of your friends. You are the only one he has smiled at.*

These examples show how we tend to interpret what is going on around us—even if we can't hear what people are saying. Infants learn quickly to read their parents' attitudes and feelings by how they are handled when fed or diapered and by how long they are allowed to cry before someone checks to see what the problem is. No matter how we try, we cannot NOT communicate.

Exercise: Find a partner and then take turns telling your partner something emotional that happened to you in the recent past. Look for the nonverbal expressions and body language which also help tell that story. Look for facial expressions, change in voice tone, body posture and eye expressions. Then, when your partner completes the story, give him or her what you saw nonverbally.

Body language can give us important clues to what others are thinking and feeling. By learning to be aware of these clues, we can improve our understanding of others, learn to communicate more effectively and increase our problem solving abilities.

Exercise: Now, have people in the group express the following emotions without words. Then discuss your feelings and thoughts you had during the exercise.

ANGER   BOREDOM   FEAR   EMBARRASSMENT   JOY

SHAME   LOVE   DISGUST   CONFUSION   SURPRISE

Ross and colleagues (1986, p. 58) give three reasons why we might misinterpret nonverbal communications:

- Not observing carefully enough;
- Jumping to conclusions too quickly;
- Simply interpreting incorrectly.

These first three reasons are mistakes we might make observing another person. Another reason is the other person *may not be communicating feelings clearly*. This can result in not understanding the other person and not knowing what the situation or problem may be. Sometimes people say one thing and mean another. For instance, how many times have we seen someone red-faced and furious insist that s/he is not angry? Ask the group for other examples of people saying one thing, but their body language indicating something else.

By being more observant and careful when watching and communicating with others, we can improve our ability to communicate accurately and to solve problems with other people.

2) **Verbal communication** is talking with words. When using words to communicate, we need to check out if the other person is understanding us. Keep in mind that people have different opinions. Those opinions are based on how each of us sees the world. Most often, these opinions are not right or wrong. They are opinions. Clear and honest verbal communication helps other people understand us. Clear and honest verbal communication will help us better understand our own thoughts, feelings and behaviors. Then we can change those thoughts and behaviors that are hurting us and others.

Verbal communication is not as natural a skill as most of us believe it to be. One problem with communication skills is that we are inclined to believe that everyone else is thinking what we are thinking; therefore, there is no need to check that we are being understood. Ross et al. (1986) indicate that when the offender notices a difference in the way he or she is understood, they simply believe the other person is wrong because he or she doesn't view things in the same way the offender does.

OPINIONS are different from FACTS. We can solve problems if we stick to the facts and hear the opinion of others. Sometimes the same words have different meanings, like *music or food*. Sometimes different words have the same meaning, like *young man, boy and lad*. Opinions, facts, different meanings—that's why it is sometimes hard to communicate clearly.

We said that OPINIONS are different from FACTS. What is the difference? Why, if we are attempting to settle a disagreement or solve a problem, should we stick to the facts? In situations where you are trying to problem solve, it is helpful for at least one person to be able to tackle the problem ONE STEP AT A TIME. What if neither of you knows the difference between facts and opinions—what do you think will happen?

Exercise: In the group, each person identifies their favorite music, food and sport. Look at how many different opinions there are.

Each of us likes different things—is there anything wrong with that? We all have different likes and dislikes—it is not wrong to be different. One does not have to come from another culture, country, or religion to be different from us and have different opinions. Almost everyone we know is different from us and has different opinions than ours—and that's OK! To believe that our way is the only way is to invite problems and hassles with those around us. Remember—that is one of the *thinking errors* we talked about in the last session. Try instead to understand their point of view and, if you can't accept it, know that it is alright to think differently. In fact, wouldn't it be boring if each of us thought the same way, dressed the same way, liked the same things and never had a different opinion? Discuss this briefly.

Different words have different meanings—you know this now about food, TV, music, and many other things. Different words sometimes mean the same—*young man, boy, and lad*.

Exercise: The same words may have different meanings. WHAT DOES THE WORD *FLY* MEAN TO YOU? You will get different responses if depending on whether the person in the group thinks of the zipper or the insect or an airplane (Ross et al., 1986), pp. 67–69). The same word can be associated with different feelings. What feelings about the word *fly* would you have if you were a pilot? If you had been in a crash? If a person you love had just flown away to live in another city?

Just as your opinions are determined by your experiences, so are the meanings of words. And if words can mean so many different things, what about the meanings of sentences and conversations? It is important to know that people may not do a good job of communicating what they really want to say. It is important to try to discover what the person is feeling by watching body language, asking questions and asking him/her what it is he or she is feeling.

b. **Developing self-awareness through self-oriented communication and other-oriented communication**

There are two ways that we direct ourselves in communicating with others: self-oriented communication and other-oriented communication. Both are important if you want to understand and be understood. You need skills to do both.

1) **Self-oriented communication** is made up of two kinds of communication: *self-disclosure* and *receiving feedback*.

Self-disclosure involves talking about yourself and not the other person. It is sharing with someone—your counselor, your group—how you see your past and your current feelings, thoughts and actions. It is using the "I" message in communication. Your message is: "This is how I see myself," "this is what has happened to me," "I feel," "I think." Self-disclosure does three things. These are keys to change.

- First, it tells you about yourself. It is *you talking to yourself*. You are disclosing to yourself. Thus, you are *making yourself more aware*. This is how you see the truth about yourself and how you break through defenses which prevent you from seeing the reality of who you are. It is a basic step in breaking through denial.

- Second, honest self-disclosure *allows others to see who you are* and allows others to give you honest feedback on how they see you. This is also a key to change and self-correction.

- Third, honest self-disclosure *helps others to self-disclose to you*. Thus, self-disclosure breeds self-disclosure.

Use the word *I* and not *you* in this kind of communication. When we start with the word *you* we are talking about the other person, and not about our own feelings and thoughts. When we are mad at someone, or in conflict, we use the word *you*. We want to blame, tell the other person what he or she should do or did. Practice talking with others using only the word *I* and not the word *you*.

When we do talk about the other person, it is important that we talk about ourselves in relationship to that person. This means that we may use the word *you* but we use it after we have used the word *I*. For example, let's say we want to tell someone that what they did really bothered us. If we say "you did this," the focus is on the other person. But our goal is to tell the other person how we felt about what they did—that it hurts, that it didn't feel good, that you felt sad. The purpose of this kind of communication is to get across what is happening to you and not what you see happening to the other person.

Exercise: Have group members share with the group a conflict they have had recently with another person. Have them describe that situation. Then, give them feedback as to how well they stuck with the self-oriented communication. Did they talk mostly about themselves or about the other person?

Receiving feedback involves listening to someone as to how they see you. Feedback is less threatening if the other person makes you feel that this is only his or her opinion and is not necessarily true. What you really say is "Tell me about me." We will look at what makes up good feedback statements as we look at other-oriented communication below.

When we receive feedback from others, it is important that we want them to tell us how they see us. As well, we want to *not be defensive*, for when we get defensive, we stop the other person from sharing views and thoughts about us. When feelings and emotions are high between two people, this is not always possible. The feedback becomes blaming and people get defensive. If you want feedback, you will want to try not to get defensive.

Look at Figure 14. This provides a picture of *self-oriented communication*. When we self-disclose, we increase self-awareness and we allow others to give us feedback about ourselves which also makes us more self-aware. Talk to a person close to you about this picture. How does it fit you?

Exercise: Have each group member receive feedback from one other member about how they see the other person responding to the treatment program. Only listen.

Figure 14
The Self-Disclosure Model

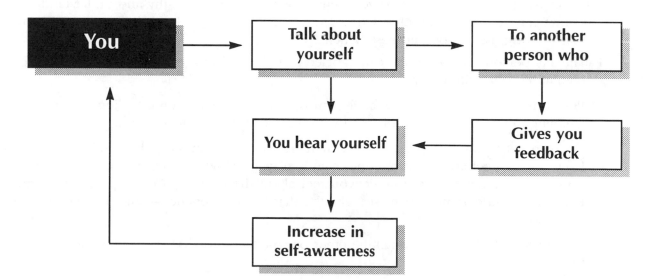

2) ***Other-oriented communication*** is getting people to talk to you and you share how you see them. This communication involves the use of two important skills: Using the *open statement or question* to encourage people to tell you about them and using the *feedback or reflective statement*.

- The **open statement** or open question skill: This encourages people to tell you about them. The open statement or question gets the other person to expand their response rather than give just a yes or no answer. "How are you feeling today?" is an open question. "Tell me how you feel" is an open statement. A person has a hard time giving just a yes or no answer to these kinds of statements. "Are you upset?" is a closed question and elicits either a yes or no response. Other-oriented communication will capitalize on the power of the encouragers to share or open statements or questions.

- The **feedback** or reflective listening skill: We call these reflective listening or active listening skills. The reflective or feedback skill restates and paraphrases what the other person is saying. This skill category essentially states "this is how I see you," or "this is what I hear you saying." "You seem upset" and "it sounds like you are tired" are examples of the reflective or feedback statements.

We will focus more on this kind of communication in *Module 8*.

Here are some important guidelines for effective communication through the feedback process (Johnson, 1972).

- Focus on the person's behavior—what s/he does, not what you imagine that person to be;

- Avoid making conclusions;

- Describe the person rather than judge;

- Share ideas and information rather than give advice;

- Feedback what the person *might do* rather than giving answers or solutions;

- Let the person know it is your view and not necessarily the truth.

c. **What are the benefits of self-disclosure and active listening?**

Self-disclosing and sharing and active listening of others with empathy and understanding are skills that can be improved with practice. Monti et al. (1989, pp. 41-42) discuss several benefits of such sharing. Let us look at these benefits.

1) The shy person can avoid being mislabeled as *cold or aloof* and improve his/her chances of communication with others.

2) Relationships with friends and family can be improved. By sharing feelings, deeper, more meaningful conversations can be had with important people in one's life.

3) You can get to know a person better by merely asking them how they feel about a topic: How do you feel about the way the team is playing? How do you feel about having "boot camps" for young SAOs? How do you feel about the chance to participate in the group? Friendship and closeness increases with the sharing of experiences—and it works with families, too!

4) When you self-disclose, you tell the other person it's ok to share with you and permissible to talk about feelings.

5) Sharing your own feelings can provide comfort and support to other people. They may feel less alone in the world or with their problems when they find other people have the same feelings or similar emotions.

It is essential that, as skill improves, the client is aware that we have all experienced a range of feelings and had important experiences; that it is alright to share both the good and the bad. Also, we don't share with just anyone—friendships grow gradually, and only when you know someone well do you generally feel comfortable sharing your deepest feelings.

Learning to *listen* well is also a skill to be learned and practiced. Active listening skills can be enhanced by the listener's nonverbal behavior such as eye contact, leaning forward slightly, and perhaps touching in a sympathetic manner. As we learned earlier, the good listener is aware of the nonverbal behavior of the speaker; facial expressions, tone of voice, and posture can indicate much about what someone is feeling. Verbal feedback that you understand can be helpful and well-timed sharing of similar experiences and can indicate that you understand what they are going through (don't interrupt your friend's thought to tell your story).

Exercise: Have the group break up into pairs. Then practice self-disclosing with partners by talking about feelings and thoughts. Have each partner practice the skills of active listening— open questions and reflections. Monitor the activity. After 5 minutes, ask the partners to reverse roles for the next 5 minutes. Spend another 5 minutes discussing the experience in the group. *When self-disclosing, did the person use "I" statements? Did he or she talk about him/herself or the other person? When in the active listening role, did that person remain non-judgmental and not give his or her opinion? How did it feel to be the listener? Can anyone in the group identify how his or her thinking patterns influenced the feeling or mood s/he was talking about?*

4. Classroom and Homework Assignments

a. The first assignment is to start talking with someone (p. 69 of the Workbook). Share a *feeling* about something during the conversation. Pay attention to the *verbal and nonverbal responses* to what you say (adapted from Monti et al., 1989).

1. Who was the person?

2. What was the *feeling* you shared?

3. What did the other person say or do?

4. What *nonverbal behavior* did the other person display?

b. Use only *I* messages for the coming week. Have them record the times they found themselves talking about the other person, and not about their feelings and thoughts about the other person. Did their communication use the *you* message more than the *I* message?

c. Have clients watch (monitor) themselves as to how often they get defensive or defend themselves when someone talks about them. Record responses in the Workbook.

5. Presentation Sequence

Since this session requires three hours, if the treatment sessions are two hours long, it will be necessary to use the first hour of the subsequent session to complete the material for this lesson.

a. Review homework and last session in Reflection Group.

b. Give an overview of Module 3.

c. Present the session content and exercises as outlined above.

d. Review homework assignments for the week.

e. Spend 30 minutes in Reflection Group to talk about the session.

6. Evaluation of Session and Client

a. Have client complete CSES.

b. Complete the PSES and evaluate the following:

1) *Did the group demonstrate a growing awareness of the different kinds of communication: non-verbal and verbal; self-oriented and other-oriented?*

2) *Were there indications that the group was grasping the techniques involved in communicating feelings and listening to others?*

c. Complete BRF.

Session ⑪ : Tools of Self-Disclosure: Autobiography, Thinking Reports, Journaling and Participating in the Reflection Group

1. Rationale of Session

Building communication skills does not come easily. For people to communicate what they think, feel and do, it is often helpful to record their thoughts, feelings and actions, or just to write down (journal) what is happening to them. To assist the participant in achieving this, we will teach clients how to do an *autobiography, journaling* and *thinking reports.*

2. Objective of Session

> ⮕ Review thought distortions or thinking errors.
>
> ⮕ Train the client to use the autobiography, journals and thinking reports as tools to promote awareness of thoughts, attitudes and beliefs as these relate to AOD use and criminal conduct which contribute to the self-correction and change process.

3. Session Content

Communicating our past and present experiences, thoughts and feelings is not always easy. Sometimes it is difficult to just talk about our past and what is happening to us in the present. One way to help us *tell our story* is to write down our experiences, thoughts, feelings and action. There are three ways that we will do this in our program: through our autobiography and through journaling; through what we call thinking reports. But before we look at these tools, let us again revisit our understanding of *thinking errors* or what we call *cognitive distortions.*

a. **Errors in thinking:**

When we use errors in thinking or twisted thinking, our thinking is automatic. These are thoughts that we have in similar situations, like when you see your boss coming toward you and wonder if you are in trouble—again. Sometimes we use these thoughts, even though they are not based on fact. This may help us get through a hard time. This kind of thinking helps us deal with stress and problems. But sometimes our thinking errors cause us big problems. Once again, go back over *Work Sheet 4 in Session 9 of Module 3.*

Here are some examples of how this happens.

1) You see a man you know with someone else's wife at lunch two days in a row. You assume they are having an affair—but they are planning a surprise birthday party for the man's wife.

2) You decide to use the rent money to bet on the races—after all, you are going to win, aren't you?

The provider, at this point, could model how a thinking distortion caused a significant problem in his or her life. For example: "I thought it was positive to blow off steam and yell at my wife until I realized otherwise."

Exercise and Discussion: Have group members give their own examples of cognitive distortions or thinking errors. Discuss each example briefly.

It is important that everyone understand the meaning of thinking errors. It is difficult to look at the distortions we use in our own lives since this is really being critical and hard on ourselves. Yet, this is important for our work at self-correction and change and it should be easier in this program knowing that we are in a non-threatening and supportive environment.

b. **Our tools for directing change**

We now look at three tools that will help direct our self-improvement and change. They are 1) *autobiography;* 2) *journaling,* and 3) *thinking reports.* But what is the mental basis upon which these tools can be used?

There are three important parts to our mental life: *memories, mental responding* to the here-and-now, and our *dreams.*

Memories: It is through our *memories* that we construct our history—our autobiography. Without memory, much of the meaning of life would be lost. As we grow older, memories—particularly the positive and good memories—become even more important. But memories come from the fabric of everyday experiences. So our memories will be set or determined by how we choose to live each day. So we control our memories by how we choose to live. Yet, things happen to us beyond our control. But we always have a choice of how we handle what happens to us. So *how* we choose to handle what happens to us also will determine our memories.

Current mental responding: Our journaling and thinking reports will capture our mental responding to the here-and-now. Three most important parts of our mental responding to the here-and-now are *thinking, feeling* and *speaking* (spoken language). What sets us apart from the animal world is our ability to use spoken language. Lower animals probably *think* and *feel.* Using spoken language is the way we communicate our thoughts and feelings. But what really makes thinking, feeling and speaking work are *learning and reasoning.* Learning and reasoning organize our thinking and feeling. They are the glue that holds our mental life together. If we take reasoning and learning away, we lose two of the most important pieces of our mental life which allow us to respond to and manage everyday experiences. Learning and reasoning take place in the here and now. They determine what we experience; they are our responses to what we experience. They make it possible to do our journals and construct our thinking reports.

Dreaming: Dreaming, setting goals, planning and hoping are the maps of living. They tell us where we want to go. But we make that map possible if we know where we have been (memory) and where we are now (mental responding to the here-and-now). Our *journal* and *thinking reports* help us keep track of our dreams.

Here are the three tools that will help us record our memories, our current responding and our dreams (goals).

1) **Recording our History—Our Autobiography**

We will write our autobiography over the next four weeks. This represents our history. It describes our roots and our past experiences. A tree stands on its roots and trunk. That is its history. We cannot stand in the present in any meaningful way without memory—without our history.

Not all of our history and our roots are pleasant. But it is important that we look at both the unpleasant and the pleasant, the negative parts as well as the positive parts of our history. This is why it is not easy to write your autobiography. But it is important in your effort for self-correction and change.

If you have already written your autobiography, you do not have to do it over. Read it again. But, as a result of our program thus far, you may have remembered some parts of your history that you did not recall when you first wrote your autobiography. You may find that parts of the autobiography we now want you to write were not part of the one you have already written. Then you are asked to add that part to your own autobiography.

Here is the outline that we want you to follow:

a) Describe the family you grew up in;

b) Describe your childhood from first memories through your teen years;

c) Describe your adult years including your education, jobs, marriages(s) and interests;

d) Then, write a history of your criminal conduct, beginning with your first offense;

e) Write a history of your AOD use beginning with your first use of alcohol or other drugs;

f) Describe what brought you into this program.

Each participant can determine the length and extent of his or her autobiography. The provider will want to review this work on a weekly basis. Clients are asked to take a piece at a time and take three to four weeks to complete it. It should be completed before entering *Phase II* of this treatment program.

Exercise: Have each member share an episode he or she would write in the autobiography.

2) **Your Journal**

You will use your journal to write down your thoughts, feelings and actions on a *daily* or *weekly* basis. It is a way for you to pay attention to your thoughts, feelings and actions. You might write on a particular day: "I had a good day at work." This will help us look at how we think and feel over time. It is helpful to include the following in each journal entry you make: the situation, your feelings and your thoughts and what you did in that situation. Did you handle it well? How would you have done it differently? It is important that you use your journal as a friend, *someone to talk to.*

From time to time, you may be asked to write on specific topics in your journal. These might include

- relapse and recidivism thinking;
- craving for a drug;
- everyday experiences with family, friends;
- what you are getting out of the program;
- homework exercises;
- your daily thoughts, moods and feelings.
- patterns and cycles of your feeling and thinking;
- changes you are making in your life.

3) **Thinking Reports**

Several resources were used in developing the guidelines for using thinking reports, including the experiences of the authors and the work of Bush and Bilodeau (1993), which provided a guide for the thinking report structure used in this curriculum.

A thinking report will help you to pay attention to your thoughts and actions. The first step in making changes in our lives is learning to pay attention to our own thinking. What are the things we say to ourselves? What is it that we feel moment to moment?

A thinking report involves writing down a brief description of a situation you have experienced, followed by a list of all the thoughts and feelings you had at the time. This is followed by a report of your attitudes and beliefs about the situation (Bush & Bilodeau, 1993). This is not an easy task but with practice you will become good at sorting out your thoughts and emotions and the beliefs and attitudes that cause them. Then, you will be able to understand how your automatic thoughts and errors of thinking get you into trouble. Hopefully, the thinking report will help you correct your distorted thought patterns and your errors in thinking.

Here are the basic parts of the thinking report.

a) **Event:** Describe in a few words the situation; do not write thoughts and feelings now. Be factual and describe what you see (or be objective):"I'm in the mall on the way to my car and can't find the keys. They're not in my pocket."

b) **Thoughts:** What thoughts do you remember. You do not have to explain or blame or condemn or make excuses: "Could I have locked them in the car? I hope I haven't lost them. I've got so much stuff to do. What will I do if they're locked in there. They're probably under the stuff on the seat. Yeah, that's where they are. Oh, damn! What do I do now? Do I feel stupid. I was in such a rush to get home. Didn't want her (wife) to get mad. She's always pressuring me. I'll call AAA. No, that'll take too much time. Then I'll really be late. I could break the window."

c) **Feelings:** Make a list of all the feelings you had: Nervous, angry, irritated. "I feel dumb. But I'm mad. She's always suspicious if I'm late. Damn her."

d) **Attitudes and beliefs:** What attitudes and beliefs are related to this event? "What a stupid thing to do. Why don't I ever learn? I'm so spaced out but I can't let anyone know. I'm just a failure. But if she trusted me. Its not fair. Life ain't fair. Just can't please them (women)."

e) **Outcome:** What was your action and behavior that came from this event and the thoughts, feelings, beliefs and attitudes that went into the whole event? "I'll bust the window. (After breaking the window, he sees the keys under the car where he had dropped them.) Hell, there they are. I give up."

At this point, the provider may share a thinking report of his/her own verbally. What were your thoughts and feelings? What were your attitudes and beliefs about the situation?

Make it clear that you are writing what happened as the thoughts come to you—you are not criticizing or purposely omitting any thoughts. Describing the outcome is very important since it gives you an idea as to how you are handling the particular situation. But, do not condemn yourself if the outcome was not what you wanted.

Exercise: Now, have each group member talk through a thinking report. Have them describe an *event,* identify their *thoughts,* then their *feelings, attitudes* and *beliefs* and then identify the *outcome* that took place. Time may not allow for all clients to do this. Have the group discuss their reactions and feelings as to how they did.

4. Classroom and Homework Activities

To reward the hard work during the week on homework, plan a social event, taking time prior to the next session for a potluck meal or ordering pizza and socialize.
Here are the classroom and homework assignments for this week (p. 73 of the Workbook).

a. Start your autobiography.

b. Write each evening in your journal one sentence as to how the day went for you. Record two thoughts and two feelings.

c. Journal project assignment: Describe past drinking patterns that have led to a drinking problem.

d. Do one thinking report about an event that happened during the week. Use the outline in the workbook on page 72.

5. Presentation Sequence

a. Review the homework for the week and last session.

b. Present material as outlined in the Session Content section above.

c. Introduce journals.

d. Introduce thinking reports and do exercise on talking through a journal project topic.

e. Review homework for this week. Plan the pizza or potluck meal.

f. If time permits, do a 20-minute reflection group.

6. Session and Client Evaluation

a. Have the client complete the brief CSES for this session.

b. Provider completes PSES and BRF.

Session ⑫: Deeper Sharing: Your Deep Emotions and Your AOD use

1. Rationale of Session

As clients move closer to the *Commitment to Change* phase of treatment, it will be important that they have a firm grip on the nature of the past problems with AOD use and criminal behavior. As well, it is important that they have moved to a deeper level of sharing thoughts, feelings and actions. This session is designed to encourage the group to share more of their thoughts, feelings and history than any previous group. Well-timed self-disclosure on their part can be a helpful tool. This area should be approached with caution, and the guidelines provided around counselor self-disclosure should be reviewed (see *Chapter 10 in Section II*).

This session focuses on two areas: Helping the client get in touch with some *deeper emotions* and more *in-depth self-disclosure* around AOD use and abuse. This involves retaking three tests that they originally took when screened into this program. Thus, at least 30 minutes are needed to complete this task.

2. Objectives of Session

The overall goal of this session is for clients to develop a full awareness of their past AOD use and their past criminal conduct and see how their perceptions of these areas have changed from the time they were first screened for this program to the present time. The following are the specific objectives of this session.

> ➡ Structure the sharing of a deep emotion that they have been holding on to for some time.
>
> ➡ Share the thinking report around their past drinking pattern.
>
> ➡ Complete the following instruments:
> - The DAST.
> - ADS.
> - ASUS.
>
> ➡ Compare the client's scores on these instruments now with those taken when being screened for the program.
>
> ➡ Explore how honest the client felt he or she was. Take time in the reflection group to talk about this.

3. Session Content and Process

a. Introduction to session

We have come to the point in our program where we need to take an honest look at who we are and what has happened to us as to our emotional life and as to our AOD history and our history of criminal conduct. In this session we will focus on two areas: 1) *Looking at an underlying and deeper emotions and feelings we have carried with us for some time* and 2) *disclosing fully about our past AOD use.* This will not be easy, because as we have said before, we hold on dearly to a certain view of ourselves. This often causes us to use thinking errors and it often causes us not to clearly address our past behaviors. But now you have prepared yourself for this moment. Now you have met the challenge to improve and change. You would not be in this program now had you not met that challenge in a mature and adult manner.

b. Our deeper emotions

You are going to be asked to look at a deeper emotion that you have carried with you for some time. That might be a hurt, a disappointment, a feeling of being betrayed, or a deep resentment toward someone who has hurt you. One counselor reported having seen a client who was a substance abusing offender for over four years. During one session, the client broke down and sobbed for 15 minutes. He finally disclosed that he had a son in his first marriage. Because of his drinking, he and his first wife were divorced when his son was age four. He deeply loved his son, loved coming home to play with him. He had dreams of his son being a great baseball player, of then going on to become a lawyer. Now, it was 14 years later. He had not seen his son since the day he left the marriage. He remembered saying goodbye. That was it. He identified his feelings: they were many. The strongest was a deep sadness inside about what his son had missed. This was empathy. He hurt for his son. After sharing this story in therapy, he proceeded to get in touch with his son. The story is still unfolding as both move on into the years.

Exercise: Have the clients write a few lines about the feeling or emotion they have carried with them (p. 75 of Workbook). Briefly describe the episode or several episodes which you feel is the basis of this deep emotion. Then, have them answer the question on page 76 of the Workbook: *How does the deep emotion you shared relate to your alcohol or other drug use?*

c. **A look at your alcohol and other drug use history and problems**

Now you are asked to look more honestly than ever at your past AOD use and problems. You will now retake the tests you took when being selected for this program. Your counselor will help you score the tests and plot the profile on the ASUS. Then you will review the test results now and compare them with your previous scores. After you score your tests, write down the scores on *Work Sheet 5*. Then, write down in *Work Sheet 6*, as many as you can remember, the specific negative or problem episodes that resulted from your drinking. Then, when you complete those tasks, we will use the rest of the time in group to talk about the results of these exercises.

Exercise: Complete the following:

1) Complete the DAST, ADS and ASUS and record your first and second scores on these tests on Work Sheet 5.

2) Complete the *AOD Negative or Problem Episodes* list on Work Sheet 6.

Share the test results from this exercise. Have each client talk about the comparison of scores and their list of negative consequences from AOD use. Take as much time in this exercise as needed.

4. Classroom or Homework Assignments

a. Have the client write in his or her journal the following: On three different occasions this coming week, write one word to describe a situation or event you experienced this week. Then, write one thought and one feeling related to that situation.

b. Have the client do a thinking report to identify the event, thoughts, beliefs, feelings and results of one criminal offense he/she was involved in. The counselor will review the basic parts of the thinking report. Ask the client to share this with the group next session.

c. Have the client continue the autobiography.

5. Presentation Sequence

a. Hold the pizza or potluck social prior to session.

b. Review the homework or classroom assignments from last session. This will take about 45 minutes. Reinforce the client's efforts in this homework.

c. Introduce the session to the group.

d. Do the *Deepest Emotion Exercise*. Take time to discuss this in group.

e. Have clients retake the tests and score them. Also, have clients complete the work sheet on past AOD problems. Give the clients their original scores on their tests and compare them with the current results. Also take time to discuss the results of the AOD problems work sheet.

f. Review homework for next session.

g. Conduct a reflections group if there is time.

h. Take time to review each client's progress on his or her autobiography. This should be done before and after sessions.

6. Session and Client Evaluation

a. Have the client complete the CSES for this session.

b. Post session test: Have clients list the five parts to the thinking report. Make this an open book test.

c. Provider completes the PSES and BRF.

Session 13 : Deeper Sharing: Your History of Criminal Conduct

1. Rationale and Overview of Session

Again, as clients move closer to the *Commitment to Change* phase of treatment, it will be important that they have a firm grip on the nature of the past criminal conduct and offenses. This will also be a difficult session for the client. Even the hard core criminal does not like to look at his or her criminal history. Even though most individuals with a criminal history have seen their *rap* sheet and are aware of their past criminal offenses and convictions, most offenders have not carefully processed that history. As well, with many offenders, there is a strong defense system which prevents a full awareness, let alone the emotional processing, of this history. This session is designed to help the client thoroughly review and process his or her offense history. Clients will be asked to record their past criminal events and then indicate whether they were arrested or convicted of the offense.

2. Objectives of Session

The goal of this session will be for clients to develop a full awareness of the past criminal conduct and offenses they have been involved in and to then evaluate whether and how substance use was involved in the offense. The specific objectives are to help the client to:

> ⟹ Increase awareness of past criminal conduct and offenses by logging all past arrests and convictions;
>
> ⟹ Relate this logging of offenses with their court recorded legal history;
>
> ⟹ Review the thinking report assignment which dealt with one past offense;
>
> ⟹ Develop an understanding of how AOD use was related to their past criminal offenses.

3. Session Content and Process

a. Introduction to session

We all want to feel that we are good people with intent to do good. Even persons with a long history of offenses have a hard time accepting the extent of their involvement in criminal conduct. Most offenders are aware of their past criminal history, but many offenders have not taken a clear and honest look at that history. Many offenders have not related that history to their use of alcohol and other drugs. Be as honest as you can in doing this session's work.

b. A look at your Level of Supervision Inventory

Exercise: Now complete the ten items in the *Level of Service Inventory, Work Sheet 7*, in your *Workbook* (p. 80). Compare your score now with the one you received when you were screened for this program.

c. A summary of your criminal history using the History of Criminal Conduct Log

Exercise: Recording of all past arrests using the *Criminal Conduct Log Work Chart* on *Work Sheet 8* in your *Workbook* (p. 81). Start with any criminal arrests or convictions during your teenage years. Complete only the first five columns:

1) The arrest date;

2) Type of charge;

3) Date convicted;

4) Put dates of probation if this applies;

5) Put dates of time served if this applies.

d. **Comparing your recorded legal history with your Log**

Exercise: Now compare your recorded legal history with your list of offenses in the *Criminal Conduct Log, Work Sheet 8.*

e. **How is your AOD history related to your criminal history?**

Now, have the client complete the last column in the *Criminal Conduct Log Work Chart* which has to do with whether drugs were involved in the specific offense. Have the client write yes if AOD were involved; no if AOD were not involved. Then have them briefly note if they drank or used other drugs *before the offense* (B), *during the offense* (D) or *after the offense* (A). If all three apply, then put *BDA* after the offense. Then have the client note with a (C) if they felt that the AOD use caused the criminal offense.

f. **Focus group discussion**

Have clients share their facts, findings and feelings in group.

4. Review Homework for the Coming Week

a. Do a *thinking report* on one event or time when the use of alcohol or other drugs led to a criminal offense. Remember, you record the situation, thoughts, feelings, attitudes and beliefs and the outcome. The outcome is important.

b. Using only a few words, record in your *journal* a time in the past when you were not honest about your substance abuse and your criminal behavior. In one sentence, now write an honest response.

c. Continue your *autobiography*.

5. Presentation Sequence

a. Review homework and assignments from last session.

b. Follow the sequence of presentation and exercises in the Session Content and Process Section above.

c. Take time in the reflection group to share thoughts and feelings from the session.

d. Review homework for this week.

e. Continue to review clients' autobiographies.

6. Session and Client Response Evaluation

a. Have the client complete the CSES for this session.

b. Provider completes the PSES.

c. Complete a BRF for this session. Then sum all of the scores for this module. Compare each client's average score for this module with his or her scores for Modules 1 through 3. Is there improvement? Plot the scores on a graph. What does it look like?

MODULE 5

Preventing Relapse and Recidivism:
Identifying High-Risk Situations

MODULE 5: PREVENTING RELAPSE AND RECIDIVISM: IDENTIFYING HIGH-RISK SITUATIONS

Overview of Module 5

The goal of *Module 5* is to learn to *identify high risk situations* or *high risk thinking* related to relapse and recidivism (RR). We look at the process, cycles and warning signs of relapse and recidivism. *Module 5* is presented in two sessions. The principles of these sessions are fundamental to RR prevention.

We often think of relapse as going back to drinking or to the use of other drugs. Likewise, we often think of recidivism as going back to committing criminal acts. The purpose of *Module 5* is to give SAO clients a different view of relapse and recidivism so as to help them avoid going back to AOD use and abuse and to criminal behavior.

Relapse into AOD use and abuse is a *gradual process of erosion*. The first steps in that erosion process occur when the individual is involved in situations that have involved AOD use and abuse in the past. These are called *high-risk situations*. Often, either before or while clients are in those situations, they let themselves become involved in thoughts about AOD use. This is called *high risk thinking*. This manual makes the distinction between these two high-risk circumstances. Different cognitive and behavioral skills may be needed to handle these two high-risk circumstances.

This manual makes the distinction between the *process of relapse, a lapse* and *a full relapse*. **Relapse** is a process that begins when clients place themselves in high-risk situations or become involved in high-risk thinking. A **lapse** in the relapse process is defined as an episode of AOD use. A **full relapse** is when the person once again becomes involved in a pattern of substance use that leads to abuse.

Clients learn to prevent lapses into actual drinking or a full relapse into a prior AOD abuse pattern through the use of cognitive and behavioral skills to handle high-risk thinking or learn to avoid (or manage the unavoidable) high-risk situations. This is what much of this program is about—learning those skills. But the high-risk situation or high-risk thinking may result in a lapse.

An example of a high-risk situation in the relapse process is when the client spends time at the bar with friends and drinking soft drinks. Reacting to stressful situations by thinking "just one drink would calm me" is an example of high-risk thinking.

Recidivism into criminal conduct is also a gradual erosion process. It begins long before a crime is committed or before the person reoffends. This process is much the same as that of relapse into AOD use patterns. The process begins when clients place themselves in situations that lead to criminal behavior or when clients become involved in criminal and deviant thinking.

An example of a high-risk situation for recidivism is when the individual begins to spend time with peers who are actively involved in criminal behavior. Thinking about robbing or stealing with the thought "I can get away with it just this time" is high-risk thinking.

Full recidivism, or the actual involvement in a criminal act—reoffending—is always preceded by involvement in high-risk situations or high-risk thinking. Again, the purpose of this program is to learn the mental and action skills to *prevent* full recidivism.

It is important to help the client understand the difference between relapse and recidivism. A lapse or even a full relapse may not necessarily result in legal sanctioning or punishment. If a client does relapse into a pattern of *AOD abuse*, the client has *a chance* to recover from the full relapse and get back on track without necessarily experiencing legal sanctioning or punishment. The provider does not have to apply a zero-tolerance standard to lapses or even a full relapse.

With *recidivism*, a zero tolerance standard must be applied. Recidivism must be checked at the points when the client becomes involved in high-risk situations or high-risk (criminal) thinking. Full recidivism leads to legal results which will be followed by legal punishment.

An important assumption underlying the RR model is that the client makes conscious choices to become involved in high-risk situations or high-risk thinking. The model of cognitive-behavioral change presented in the previous modules clearly stresses this *assumption of choice*.

One purpose of this module is to help clients recognize high-risk situations or high-risk thinking that represent the first steps to relapse or recidivism. With the SAO client, high-risk situations for both relapse and recidivism are often one and the same, only too often, the SAO client does not recognize that the high-risk situation for relapse is also a high-risk situation for recidivism. The provider should continually stress that there is an integral and close relationship between drug use and criminal behavior for the SAO client.

Recognition of high-risk thinking and high-risk situations is only the first step in the RR prevention process. The second step is to learn and put to work the mental and action skills that prevent full relapse or that prevent reoffending. Although we look at some of these skills in this module, the skills to be learned and practiced in *Module 9* are also directed at RR prevention.

For this module and the remainder of the manual, we use RR to refer to *relapse and recidivism,* HR to refer to *high-risk* (situations or thinking) and RP to refer to *relapse and recidivism prevention.*

Session ⑭ : Relapse and Recidivism Prevention I: Identifying High-Risk Situations and Understanding Relapse and Recidivism

1. Rationale and Overview of Session

It is self-evident that when the SAO becomes reinvested in thoughts and behaviors associated with substance abuse, criminal conduct is more likely to occur. The two sessions in this module are designed to help clients learn the basic concepts of *Relapse and Recidivism Prevention* (RP). These sessions are also designed to help clients understand the purpose of each of the interpersonal and intrapersonal basic skills sessions in *Module 9.*

Daley and Marlatt (1992) identify two common elements across the range of RP strategies:
- the use of *experiential learning* (e.g., role playing, homework);
- the use of a *daily inventory* (e.g., thought reports) aimed to get patients to continuously monitor their lives so as to identify high-risk factors (including subjective warning signs and situational cues) that would contribute to a relapse.

High-risk (HR) factors for SAO clients are usually those situations in which clients used AOD prior to arrest or substance abuse treatment. Annis (1986) suggests that intrapersonal and interpersonal situations in which the client used substances during the year preceding treatment represent HR situations. Gorski (1993, 1994) has developed exercises for analyzing the relapse warning signs in both chemical dependency and criminal behavior.

Many relapse prevention programs focus only on high-risk situations. Our RP program will focus on helping the client to identify and manage both high-risk situations and high-risk thinking.

2. Objectives of Session

> ⮞ Clients will develop the skills to identify interpersonal and intrapersonal warning signs for criminal behavior.
>
> ⮞ Clients will develop the skills to identify the interpersonal and intrapersonal warning signs for substance abuse.
>
> ⮞ Clients will increase their understanding of the relationships between AOD abuse and crime.

3. Session Content and Process

a. Defining high-risk (HR) situations for Relapse (AOD use) and Recidivism (criminal conduct)

High-risk (HR) situations for AOD use are usually those situations that have led to AOD use and abuse in the past. They are situations in which you think or feel that you need to use alcohol or other drugs. For example, conflict with your significant partner which produces undue stress may lead to the feeling of needing to drink. A high-risk situation is also one that increases the urge, craving and desire for alcohol. Having a romantic evening with your significant partner may lead to the desire or urge to drink. A high-risk situation may be defined as *any circumstance or situation that is a threat to your sense that you cannot cope without the use of drugs.* You begin relapse when you expose yourself to these high-risk situations, even though you have not yet used substances. Episodes of relapse often occur after you are in a stressful situation which you are unprepared to deal with. Remember, **RELAPSE OCCURS WHEN WE BEGIN TO THINK ABOUT ALCOHOL OR OTHER DRUG USE AS AN OPTION TO DEAL WITH THESE SITUATIONS. OR, RELAPSE OCCURS WHEN WE EXPOSE OURSELVES TO SITUATIONS THAT HAVE LED TO AOD USE IN THE PAST.**

High-risk situations for recidivism are *any situations that lead up to being involved in criminal behavior.* They are situations in which you think or feel you need to be involved in criminal actions. A high-risk situation is one that increases your impulse or desire to commit a crime.

It is any situation that threatens your sense that you cannot go on without engaging in criminal conduct. One clear high-risk situation is hanging out with peers actively involved in criminal behavior. Another is allowing yourself to be in a situation which, in the past, has involved violence or assaultive acting out.

Discussion: One way to think about a relapse is when we feel powerless or incompetent to deal with a feeling or problem that we encounter. **Again, remind the client that relapse occurs when we begin to think about alcohol and other drug use as an option to cope with the situation.** If drinking or taking drugs changes the way you act, think and feel, we need to find out what the situations are in which you are most likely to use, and what you are thinking and feeling at the time. By understanding everything we can about these high-risk situations, we can determine what kinds of things trigger or maintain your abuse of alcohol or other drugs. Then we can explore other ways that you can deal with these high-risk situations without becoming vulnerable once again to the many problems associated with AOD abuse. Kadden et al. (1992) present guidelines for participant discussion:

- *In what kinds of situations do you use substances? What are your triggers for AOD abuse?*

- *Can you give a specific example (e.g., a relapse story)?*

- *Can you remember your thoughts and feelings at the time?*

- *What were the positive consequences of AOD involvement?*

- *What were the negative consequences?*

b. **Defining high-risk thinking for AOD abuse and criminal conduct**

High-risk thinking for AOD use and abuse are those thought habits or automatic thinking patterns that lead to the use of substances. These thought habits could be set off by involvement in HR situations or HR thinking and can lead you into high-risk circumstances. Such thoughts as "I need a drink, I've had a tough day," or "I might just as well get high, no one gives a damn" are examples of automatic high-risk thinking habits. Such thinking often takes place when you feel threatened, cheated, or not treated fairly. High-risk thinking also may be hooked in with cravings and desire for using substances.

HR thinking for engaging in criminal conduct involves those thought habits and automatic thoughts that lead to committing criminal acts. Again, these high-risk thought habits usually take place before you engage in criminal activities. They could be set off by involvement in HR situations or could lead you into high-risk situations. Intense thoughts of being *treated badly, deserving more than what I'm getting,* getting something *fast and easy,* or thinking about committing a crime are examples of high-risk criminal conduct thinking.

c. **Defining relapse and recidivism**

Relapse begins to occur when you put yourself in situations that have led to AOD use and abuse in the past. Relapse is also defined as engaging in thought habits or automatic thoughts about using substances as an option to dealing with high-risk situations. The early stage of relapse is when you engage in AOD use but have not gone back to a pattern of AOD abuse. A full relapse is when you return to a prior pattern of use which has led to AOD problems and abuse.

Recidivism begins to occur when you start to engage in high-risk thought habits that lead to criminal conduct. It also occurs when you start to engage in actions or put yourself in situations that, in the past, have led to criminal activities. Thus, recidivism does not necessarily mean you have committed another crime. *Full* recidivism means just that.

d. A look at triggers for Relapse/Recidivism (RR)

One way to think about a relapse is when you feel you do not have the power or strength to deal with a feeling or problem that you face. If drinking or taking drugs changes the way you act, think and feel, you need to find out what the situations are in which you are most likely to use, and what you are thinking and feeling at the time. By understanding everything you can about these high-risk situations and high-risk thinking, you can figure out what kinds of things trigger involvement in AOD use and abuse or involvement in criminal conduct. Then you can test other ways that you can deal with these high-risk situations without becoming weakened once again by the many problems associated with AOD abuse and criminal conduct. What are your triggers for relapse/recidivism (RR)? Here are some that may fit you (Emrick & Aarons, 1990):

1) **Conflict with another person:** You feel frustration and anger resulting from your interactions with another person. You don't feel competent to handle the conflict without alcohol or drugs.

2) **Social or peer pressure or hanging out with criminal peers:** You witness others enjoying themselves or having a good time during a party or other festive occasion. You may be offered a drink or drug or challenged to explain why you are not joining in the fun.

3) **An unpleasant feeling (stress, depression, intense anger):** You feel depressed, anxious, bored or lonely. The prospect of getting away from the uncomfortable feelings state by taking a drug or drinking is too much to resist.

4) **A change in self-image:** This involves change in seeing the self as an abstainer to again being a user; change from the image of living a straight, crime-free life to one who does criminal acts. When we take a drink or use a drug after a period of abstinence, we may continue to drink because of a change in how we view ourselves—we now see ourselves not as abstainers, but as users.

Exercise: Have participants give their personal examples of the above situations which have triggered their involvement in AOD use and abuse.

Role-Play: Group members role-play their personal experiences, drawing upon material from the prior discussion.

The Relapse/Recidivism (RR) Log (adapted from Kadden et al., 1992): Using *Work Sheet 9* (p. 87) in the *Workbook*, have the group take each of the four high-risk situations described above and write down a specific situation that applies to them. Then have them write their thoughts and feelings and either their positive (coping) or negative (relapse/recidivism) thinking and behavior. Then they will use *Work Sheet 10* to write down how they coped with each of those specific situations that applied to them.

Discussion: What were your *expectations* about alcohol or other drugs? What did you think they were going to do for you? Did you believe that by having alcohol or a drug you could relax or have fun or deal with very uncomfortable feelings? If participants believe they need alcohol or drugs to carry out any of these routine activities of daily living, then they are challenged with the assertion that they are psychologically dependent on substances "You believe you need alcohol to cope with life."

Role-Play: Each role-play of an ineffective coping response is followed by the group member role-playing what an effective coping response would be to the same situation.

e. Relapse and recidivism (RR) calendar (adapted from Gorski, 1993)

What has been your RR history? Relapse prevention begins to take place when you fully understand your own RR history. You can understand this pattern by using the *RR Calendar in Work Sheet 11*. This will help you understand your AOD and criminal RR pattern. You will gain insight into how your AOD use and legal problems are related. Write in the dates of your first serious attempts to stop AOD abuse and criminal behaviors. Use a straight line to indicate periods of sober and non-criminal behavior. Use a wavy line to indicate periods of relapse or recidivism. When you come to the next session, describe the series of events that led to AOD relapse and crime.

f. Closure discussion

Close the session with a discussion of the *benefits of a life without AOD*. One of the most harmful consequences of dependence on alcohol or drugs is that you do not have a clear picture of who you are or what you are capable of. You believe that you can't cope with life without introducing a chemical into your system. You do not see yourself as competent to manage the natural crises or low spots that are inevitable, and your self-esteem is damaged. By changing your relationship with AOD, so that you no longer depend on the *quick fix,* you will feel better about yourself. In addition, you will most probably get along better with the people who are important to you. They will hold you in higher regard and you will feel more positive about yourself in relationship to them. Also, you will be relieved of the enormous legal burdens associated with an AOD lifestyle. Nor will you have the physical and mental problems that alcohol and drugs bring when you are constantly responding to *rebound effects* as discussed in the session on knowledge about AOD. Finally, you will experience life more positively, with a sense of optimism and pride that may have been lost when you became dependent on alcohol or other drugs.

4. Classroom or Homework Activities

a. Start the Relapse/Recidivism Log in *Work Sheet 9* in class and then have clients continue this for their homework during the week.

b. Have clients begin *Work Sheet 10,* and then have clients continue this as homework. This involves having the clients write a short description of how they have coped or now cope with the situations described below:

1) *Conflict with another person*

2) *Social or peer pressure*

3) *An unpleasant feeling*

4) *A change in self-image*

c. Have clients start *The Relapse/Recidivism Calendar* (adapted from Gorski, 1993) during class and then continue this as homework. This will help clients examine their AOD and criminal relapses. This should help them gain insight into how their AOD and legal problems are related. Have them write in the dates of their first serious attempts to stop AOD abuse and criminal behaviors. Use a straight line to indicate periods of sober and responsible behavior. Use a wavy line to indicate periods of relapse or recidivism. At the next session, have clients describe the series of events that led to AOD relapse and crime.

5. Presentation Sequence

a. Review homework and major points from the previous session.

b. Present the Rationale and Objectives for the session on Relapse Prevention.

c. Discuss and define high-risk situations, high-risk thinking and relapse and recidivism.

d. Delineate the four major triggers for relapse and discuss participant vulnerabilities to each situation.

e. Participants role-play specific circumstances that triggered relapse.

f. Discuss expectations that have led participants to relapse and confront the issue of psychological dependence.

g. Participants role-play effective coping responses.

h. Discuss benefits of a life without AOD abuse.

i. Reflection on group session.

j. Begin exercises and outline homework assignment.

k. Brief look at next session.

6. Session and Client Response Evaluation

a. Have client complete the CSES.

b. Provider completes the PSES and reflects on these questions:

1) *Did participants demonstrate an appreciation for different types of high-risk situations and high-risk thinking?*

2) *Did participants develop the skills to recognize the specific ineffective coping responses (e.g., negative feeling states, automatic thoughts ad positive expectations about AOD use) that triggered their relapse episodes?*

3) *Did clients increase their understanding of the relationships between AOD abuse and crime?*

Session ⑮ : Relapse and Recidivism Prevention II: Learning the Cognitive-Behavioral Map

1. Rationale and Overview of Session

Clients are better prepared for dealing with the challenges of high-risk situations if they are aware of the fact that relapse occurs within a context of *biological, psychological* and *social* events in their lives. There are clues or *warning signs* that indicate a client is into a relapse process. These precede lapses or full relapse into substance use and criminal conduct. Even though a full relapse may appear to be the result of an impulsive act on the part of the recovering person, there are almost always *attitudinal, emotional, behavioral and cognitive shifts* that precede the actual ingestion of substances. Clients can learn to identify these shifts as links in a relapse chain (Marlatt, 1985c). SAOs who experience full relapse or return to criminal conduct report that their warning signs appeared days, weeks or even longer before they ingested substances or committed a crime. It is helpful to have clients review their experiences in detail so they can learn the connections among thoughts, feelings, events or situations and relapse to substance abuse. (Daley & Marlatt, 1992).

2. Objectives of Session

> ⫸ Clients will understand the idea of progression of relapse—the RR erosion;
>
> ⫸ Clients will develop an understanding of the external and internal events that lead to relapse;
>
> ⫸ Clients will identify the cognitive and behavioral skills to avoid relapse by recognizing the thoughts, feelings and attitudes that trigger AOD relapse and CC (criminal conduct) recidivism.

3. Session Content and Process

a. The RR erosion

RR is a process of erosion. Soil erosion is a gradual wearing away of the topsoil that contains the power to produce rich and healthy crops. Soil erosion is often hidden and difficult to see. It takes place over a long period of time. The same is true in the process of relapse and recidivism. There is a gradual wearing away of the rich resources of the mind. It is gradual and may take place over long periods of time. Sometimes, it takes a year or two before this gradual wearing away leads to a full relapse (relapse into the full behavior of AOD use or crime) even though the RR episode may appear to be the result of an impulsive act (spur of the moment). Figure 15 gives us a picture of this erosion process.

Figure 15: The Relapse Process
(adapted from Daley and Marlatt, 1992, with permission)

b. Understanding the RR process: The RR and road signs Steps

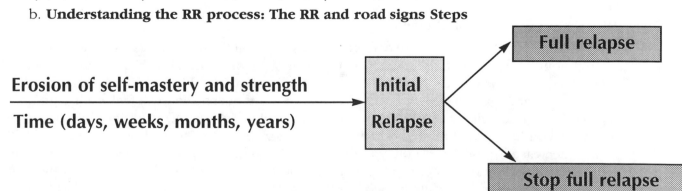

Relapse and recidivism (RR) occur in steps. These steps represent the map of the RR erosion process. There are clear signs of this erosion process—*critical road signs*—that indicate where we are in this journey. These signs show that the erosion process has reached a critical step— an initial lapse or involvement in high-risk situations or thinking that lead to criminal conduct. One fork can lead to full relapse or recidivism; another fork in this journey can lead to recovery. Figure 16 describes these RR steps or road signs: Any situation that threatens your sense of control thereby increases the risk for RR. Review some of the essential points covered by the classroom and homework assignments in the last session.

Self-Efficacy or Self-Mastery

This is your judgment about how well you cope with stressful or difficult situations. This is based on whether or not you have succeeded or failed in similar situations, how others judge or influence you, and your emotional state.

Expected Outcome

These are what you expect the outcome to be. You may expect a drug to have a particular desired effect (e.g. makes you feel good). However, *expected effects* may be quite different from *real effects*. When the prospect of AOD use is hooked in with a positive outcome of AOD use, the probability of relapse skyrockets. Or, you feel that the crime you are thinking you are going to do will make you feel more powerful.

Rule Violation Effect

This is your reaction resulting from a fall from complete abstinence or some deviation from an absolute rule (e.g., *never go into a bar*). You have been seeing yourself as *clean and sober*. Then you use (drugs) or plan a crime. That view of yourself as *clean and sober* must change. You are now getting in touch with a part of your old self. So what are you? *Clean and sober* or *user and offender?* You now are experiencing a lot of inner conflict. To solve this conflict, you are likely to return to your old view of yourself—substance abusing offender. The strength of this rule violation will depend on 1) *cognitive dissonance*—how much conflict and guilt you feel due to your RR; and 2) *personal attribution*—how much you blame your personal weaknesses for the cause of the RR behavior.

Self-Attribution or Self-Credit

This type of thinking is most important when you find yourself taking part in an out-of-bounds or relapse behavior. If you believe that the initial relapse is due to your personal *weakness,* then you may be setting yourself up for continuing the relapse. This is because you believe you have lost total control or it is beyond your control. If you credit strength to yourself by stopping at the point of initial relapse (engaging in thinking or action that leads to drinking or actual drinking) or stopping at initial recidivism (engaging in obsessive CC thinking) then it is unlikely that you will go into a full relapse/recidivism.

c. **RR erosion warnings and signs**

You become weakened to relapse or to going back into thinking and beliefs which lead to criminal conduct when you find yourself in high-risk situations or high-risk thinking. But more important, it is how you deal with the HR situation or thinking. When you engage in thinking and acting that *helps* you cope with the HR situations or thoughts, you will feel a sense of inner power (increased self-mastery) and you will avoid full relapse (AOD use) and full recidivism (criminal conduct). If your thinking and actions are *weak,* you will feel a loss of power and feel weak (decreased self-efficacy) but you might feel the initial expected positive outcome of the effect of the substance or committing a crime. You have thus relapsed, you will feel the *rule violation effect,* plus the positive effects of the substance.

Figure 16
Cognitive-Behavioral Model for Relapse and Recidivism

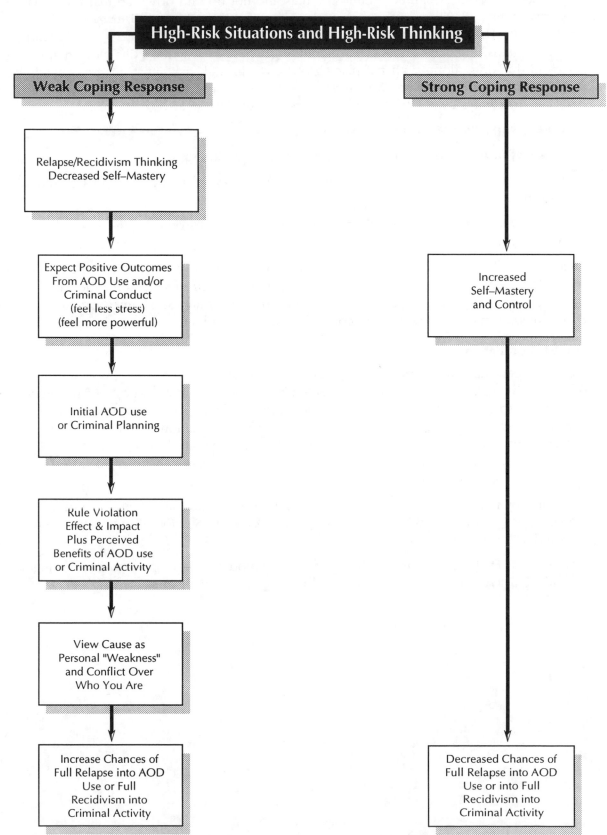

Reprinted with permission of the authors of Relapse Prevention: Maintenance Strategies in the Treatment of Addictive Behaviors (p.38) Edited by G.A. Marlatt and J.R. Gordon, The Guilford Press, 1985.

This increases the possibility of *full relapse* and *recidivism*. Let us now return to our example of soil erosion. The farmer has learned to prevent erosion with proper care of the land. He uses his skills to build up terraces or rows of soil which are barriers to the water wearing away the topsoil. Crops are planted around the hills and not up and down so that the rains do not wash away the soil. There is the continual adding of soil food or fertilizer to refresh and build up the soil. The same is true with our lives. We need to build good mental and action *defenses* against high-risk situations and thinking. These are mental skills we can apply to our errors in thinking, along with not placing ourselves in high-risk situations or becoming overcome with high-risk thinking. We refresh ourselves with healthy friends and positive activities. And we are always aware of the RR warnings. Some of these are:

1) *Changes in attitudes:* from positive to negative;

2) *Changes in thoughts:* from self-confidence to self weakness;

3) *Changes in emotions and moods:* from an up and hopeful mood to depressed mood, from a calm to an anxious mood;

4) *Changes in actions:* from activities not involving alcohol or other drugs to activities that are AOD involved.

Discussion: Ask participants if they have ever found it useful to travel with the aid of a road map. How does the road map assist travelers in finding their destination? Whereas we can all become hopelessly lost, especially in foreign territory (which sometimes can become quite dangerous), a map can keep us on course and easily lead us to where we want to go.

d. **The RP Road Map**

We have seen that RR is a process of gradual wearing away of the strengths of abstinence and prosocial living. This erosion process eventually leads us to a critical point of recovery where we can fail to use the skills to prevent erosion and which leads to collapse; or where we build and use good mental and action skills to manage high-risk situations and thinking. Even though we *lapse* into an episode of AOD use or into serious criminal thinking and feelings, we can resist those situations and thoughts and take the prolapse road to recovery. Figure 17 provides a picture of this map (Parks & Marlatt, 1997).

The counselor (provider) will want to introduce the RP Road Map (figure 17) in this session. However, it is also dealt with in more detail in Module 10, Session 42 when RR prevention is revisited and reviewed.

Discussion: Have clients discuss how they fit the models and maps presented in Figures 15, 16 and 17. Have them share their personal relapse and recidivism stories.

Forks in the Road to Recovery

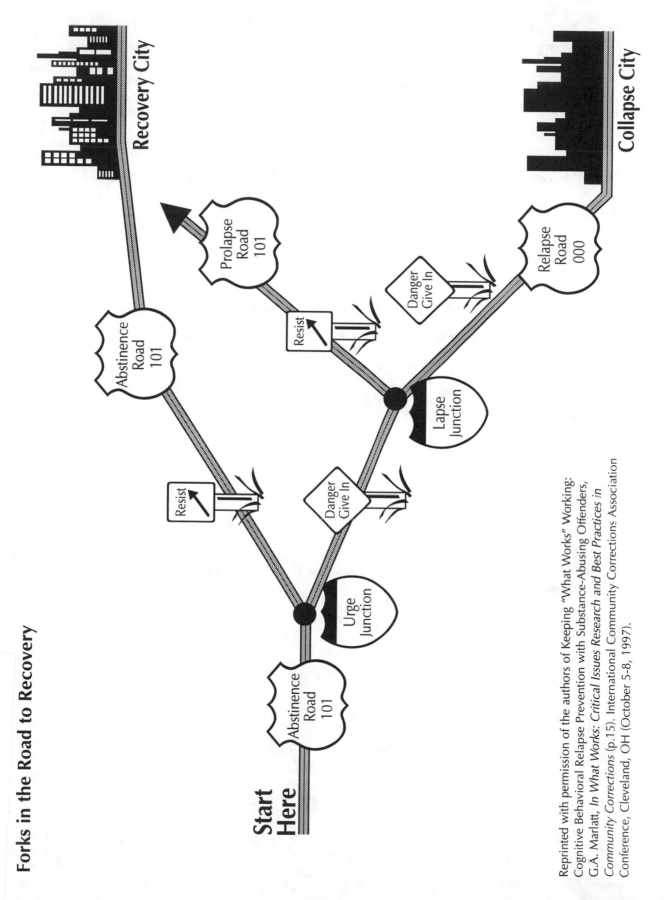

Reprinted with permission of the authors of Keeping "What Works" Working: Cognitive Behavioral Relapse Prevention with Substance-Abusing Offenders, G.A. Marlatt, *In What Works: Critical Issues Research and Best Practices in Community Corrections* (p.15). International Community Corrections Association Conference, Cleveland, OH (October 5-8, 1997).

4. Classroom and Homework Activities

a. **Exercise:** The group leader describes a typical high-risk situation for the SAO. Participants are encouraged to describe two oppositional chains of events: 1) *an effective coping response* and 2) *an ineffective coping response.* The high-risk situation, for example, may be running into an old girlfriend or boyfriend with whom you used to do a lot of drugs. You still have feelings for the person and he or she offers you the drug that you did a lot of together. After eliciting comments about what might constitute a coping response, participants are asked to elaborate on the likely chain of events that may occur in the case of an ineffective coping response.

b. Have clients write in their journal what high-risk situations they have put themselves in and high-risk thoughts they have during the coming week.

5. Presentation Sequence

a. Review previous session and homework.

b. Discuss rationale and objectives for learning the *Cognitive-Behavioral Map* for substance abuse, crime and violence.

c. Present material as outlined in Content Section above.

d. Demonstrate *Marlatt's Cognitive-Behavioral Model* of the Relapse Process.

e. Participant exercise: Ineffective coping responses for example provided.

f. Reflection on group session.

g. Outline homework assignment.

h. Brief look at next session.

6. Session and Client Response Evaluation

a. Have client complete CSES.

b. Counselor completes PSES using guide below:

1) *Did clients demonstrate an understanding of how decreased self-efficacy and positive outcome expectancies can lead to RR?*

2) *Did participants gain the skill to monitor their own internal processes as protective factors against relapse and recidivism?*

c. Counselor completes the BRF for past four sessions.

MODULE 6

How Do People Change:
Understanding the Process
of Self-Improvement and Change

MODULE 6: HOW DO PEOPLE CHANGE: UNDERSTANDING THE PROCESS OF SELF-IMPROVEMENT AND CHANGE

Overview of Module 6

In Module 4, we learned that the first step to making improvement and change was to develop an awareness of those areas which have caused us problems in the past, and which need changing. We also learned that the primary pathway to self-awareness is to fully explore and disclose the personal experiences and problems one has had in the areas of desired change and to receive feedback from others.

We now are at the point of deciding whether we want to change. We have spent a lot of time and energy looking at patterns and cycles around how we get into and continue our thoughts and actions which have caused problems for us and for people around us. We are now at the point of deciding *do we want to change?* Or, if we have made that decision, we now are at the point of deciding *what* do we want to change? Once we have made this decision, we then make our commitment to change and enter Phase II of treatment. Phase II is set up to help us learn "the what and the how" of change and then to more fully put that change into practice.

Objectives for Module 6

Module 6 represents the final step in our challenge to get clients to *commit to change*. The following five objectives of this Module are designed to help clients meet this challenge and move on to the commitment stage of change. The objectives of this Module are to help clients

- Understand the stages people go through when making change. This means we will review the thinking and behavioral cycles we learned in Module 3: Building the Knowledge Base;
- Identify thinking and behavioral targets of change;
- Learn some specific techniques and skills in addressing these targets of change;
- Understand the barriers to making change;
- Make a decision to commit to the full process of change and a commitment to Phase II of treatment.

Time Requirements for Module 6:

Three two-hour sessions are devoted to this module. It is important that one full two-hour session be used to allow the group members to make a decision as to whether they continue on into Phase II of the program. A review of the requirements, outline and expectations of Phase II needs to be carefully spelled out in the final session of this module.

Session 16 : Reviewing the Process and Stages of Change and Selecting Targets for Change

1. Rationale and Overview of Session

Information has been presented in previous modules to describe how people change. We have looked at the stages of change and the specific process of how cognitive and behavioral learning and change takes place. We have set the stage for change by helping clients develop *self-awareness,* through self-disclosure of past and current problems in thinking and behavior. This self-awareness should provide the basis on which clients decide to change and identify areas in which change is needed. *First,* it is important to review the concepts of cognitive change. *Second,* we want clients to assess what stage of change they might be in. *Finally,* clients learn how to select targets for change, since this is important for the skill development and enhancement to be done in Phase II.

In preparing for the presentation of this session, it is important that we recall the stages that people go through when making change. We have, in this program, identified three stages: 1) *Challenge to Change,* 2) *Commitment to Change* and 2) *Taking Ownership of Change.* The challenge to change phase in this program is represented by Prochaska and colleagues' (1992) pre-contemplative and contemplative stages of change. The *Commitment to Change Phase* is represented by the Prochaska et al. (1992) determination and action phases of change. The *Ownership Phase* of this program represents the Prochaska et al. (1992) maintenance stage of change.

Using these stages of change, where do group members see themselves? Some remain resistive to change, avoiding self-evaluation and still struggling with the challenge to change. Hopefully, the majority of clients have experienced the challenge to change in which they are open to receiving information about criminal conduct and AOD use and open to feedback about their own AOD use and their CC. They have probably not taken any real firm action to change and have not fully committed themselves to change. They are beginning to consider the existence of problems and have some awareness that they have the potential that they can overcome them. Others are fully committed to change and have clearly made changes, and these changes have persisted.

It is wise at this point to remember that THE CLIENT HAS TO MAKE THE CHANGES. We cannot force someone to change. We may be able to enhance the process by recalling the acronym *FRAMES* (Miller, 1995, p. 93) as used in work with alcoholics and substance abusers:

a. **FEEDBACK** of personal risk or impairment

b. Emphasis on personal **RESPONSIBILITY** for change

c. Clear **ADVICE** to change

d. A **MENU** of alternative change options

e. Counselor **EMPATHY**

f. Facilitation of client **SELF-EFFICACY** or optimism

In a similar way, Freeman and colleagues (1990) emphasize that criminal conduct must also be recognized as counterproductive; that, in the long run, prosocial behavior is in the offender's best interest. The goal is to develop a collaborative relationship that is trust-based and directed toward recognizing and changing problem behavior. This will be accomplished by continuing to help clients learn to control their thoughts, perceptions and emotions (cognitive sets or schemes) and translating *cognitive* changes into *behavioral* changes.

As we approach the end of Phase I of the program, clients should have learned a great deal about their AOD use and criminal conduct and the interaction between the two. They should have gained initial self-awareness of their cognitive sets and overt behaviors. The participants should also be more motivated to commit to making changes in those cognitive sets and their self-defeating CC and AOD behavior. Ambivalence may be high at this time and the task of the provider is to encourage the decision in favor of change.

2. Objectives of Session

3. Session Content and Process

a. Introduction to session

You have worked hard to get to this point in your program. You have learned many different ideas and approaches to help you understand how people change and the stages that people go through when changing. We have set the stage for self-correction and change by helping you become more aware of your past and current problems in thinking and action. You have done this by taking great risks in sharing your personal feelings, thoughts and past actions. This sharing has brought you to a better understanding of the problems you have had with AOD use and your criminal and deviant conduct. These learnings were all important to prepare you for really committing yourself to change. Now we are ready to see where you are in making changes in your life.

b. Review of the process of change

Figure 18 again provides a picture of this change process. This is similar to the diagram we saw in Session 5 of Module 3, *"The Process of Cognitive Learning and Change."* This picture, however, now identifies the specific behaviors we engage in—AOD abuse and criminal conduct. We can see that external and outside events, or memories and feelings inside of us, lead to our automatic thinking. Automatic thinking then sets loose certain attitudes, beliefs and emotions. These *inside workings* often lead to behavior or action. Remember: *We can choose what behaviors and actions to take part in*. Now, through self-awareness we know the outcomes. Review the picture in Figure 18 and then go to the following exercise.

Exercise: Have each member of the group complete Work Sheets 12 and 13 in the Workbook.

1) *Work Sheet 12:* Choose a past event that led to an AOD use episode. Fill in the bottom part of the cycle first. How would you change things? Fill in the coping behaviors to show how you would do it.

2) *Work Sheet 13:* Choose an event in the recent past that could have led to criminal conduct. Again, fill in both the top and bottom part of the chart.

c. The stages of change—where are you?

Studies of people who have developed an addiction to drugs indicate that when they change, they go through some specific steps or stages (Prochaska et al., 1992). Although there are different ways to describe this process of change, we identified three important stages of change around which our program has been developed. These are *Challenge to Change, Commitment to Change* and Taking *Ownership of Change*. These phases are built around what we know to be stages that people go through when making changes. It is important for you to know where you are at this time. Have you been challenged to give serious thought to change? Have you begun to do some changing? What is your commitment to making change? Are you determined yet you have not really taken action? Let us look again at these phases of change, so that you can see where you are.

1) **Challenge to Change:** If you are in this stage, you have begun to meet the challenge to give thought to change and to look seriously at yourself to see where and what changes need to be made. You are open to getting information about yourself and your problems. If you are in the early phase of this stage, you are building self-awareness. If you are in the latter part of this stage, then you are taking greater risks in disclosing your problems and talking about yourself. You have met the challenge when you are willing to commit to continued and even more intense treatment and a desire to learn the skills to be free of AOD use problems and avoid criminal conduct. The key words here are *thinking* or being thoughtful, being *self-aware,* being aware of *areas needing change, self-disclosing and being willing* to commit to further help.

2) **Commitment to Change:** If you have made a commitment to change, you are now open to *disclosing* or talking about your problems, to talking openly about what changes need to be made. You are making efforts to change your thoughts, attitudes and beliefs. You have been able to go a definite period of time AOD free. You feel less desire to drink or use other drugs. You find yourself changing your thinking when you start thinking about getting involved in criminal conduct. You replace drug use activities with alternative activities. You catch yourself thinking about using drugs but replace those thoughts. You have made a promise and pledge to change. You are now more involved in learning the skills of thinking and acting which keep you away from criminal activity and AOD use. You practice those skills. If you are in the early part of this phase, you have been able to *correct* your thinking and actions which lead to criminal behavior and AOD use. If you are in the latter part of this stage, you have been able to demonstrate *control* over involvement in criminal conduct (CC) and AOD use problems.

3) **Taking Ownership of change:** When you reach this stage, you are making changes because *you* want to and not because others—the court, family, probation officer, counselor—want you to. You have been able to go a long time free of AOD problems and free from criminal conduct thinking. You have clearly replaced your criminogenic needs and the need to use alcohol or other drugs. You feel strong in your abstinence from drugs and criminal involvement. You are not nagged and bugged by thoughts of doing crimes. You may relapse into AOD use thinking or CC thinking but you prevent relapse back into the action part of the relapse cycle. You are in the program because you *want* to be, not because you *have* to be.

Exercise: Have each client identify where they think they are in terms of each of these stages for AOD use and Criminal Conduct (CC) by completing *Work Sheet 14* for AOD use and *Work Sheet 15* for criminal conduct. Have clients rate themselves on each of the key elements that identify each stage of change. Figures 19 and 20 can be used by the provider to rate each client. Compare your ratings with the client's profile. Are they different? Explain to clients that they may be in different stages for different areas of change. For example, a person may be in the high range of *Challenge to Change* as to quitting smoking, but in the medium range of *Commitment to Change* with respect to AOD use.

Figure 18
Pathways to Changing AOD and Criminal Conduct

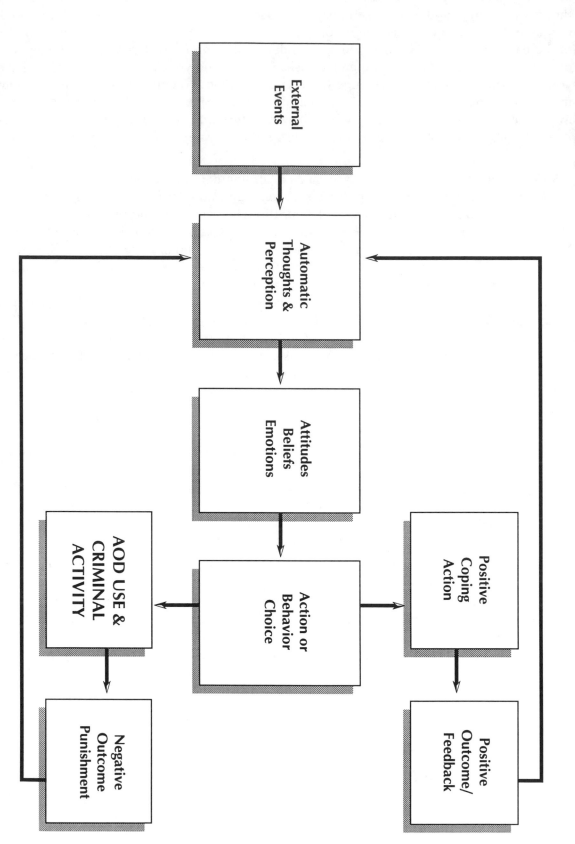

d. **Picking target thoughts and behaviors for change:**

We have learned that our first step in change is to increase self-awareness through self-disclosure. We also learned that one of the most important persons we disclose to is ourself. It is ourself that we want to be most honest with. It is through this disclosure that you see what you need to change. Therefore, the next step to change is to *select target thoughts* and *target behaviors or actions* that you want to change. *Target behaviors* (Bush & Bilodeau, 1993) are actions you have done in the past that you want to change. They are behaviors that are causing problems in your life and you have decided you want to change. *Target thoughts* are specific thoughts or thought patterns (e.g., errors in thinking) that lead to problem behavior. What is important is that you can change these without having to change a behavior. You don't have to wait for a behavior to come along. The thoughts are there.

You can identify the target thoughts and behaviors for change. Others may help you spot them. But only *you* can make the choice as to what changes you make and whether to in fact make those changes. No one else can do it. Although many people may have told you about what you should be doing, only you can say "I'm going to make my life different."

e. **Here are the steps to change a target behavior**

The following are steps to be used as a classroom exercise with clients. First go through the steps. Then ask for a volunteer to provide an example of a target behavior he or she wants to change. Take that client through these steps of change.

1) **IDENTIFY A TARGET BEHAVIOR.** Is there any target behavior that you would like to change? Look at the thinking report you did for your homework. (Ask for volunteer(s) to respond to this question. REINFORCE SELF-DISCLOSURE.)

2) **RECOGNIZE THE ATTITUDES AND BELIEFS BEHIND THE THOUGHT OR THE THINKING BEHIND THE TARGET BEHAVIOR.** Can you tell us the thinking behind the behavior?

3) **THINK HOW YOU WOULD LIKE TO ACT AND BEHAVE—SET GOALS.** This is new. Stop and think—if we are going to think differently, what would the new thought be? If we are going to behave differently from how we did, what would we want the new behavior to be? Make sure these are goals that can be realized—things you can do. Be very clear about what the goals are. What were your old ways of behaving in a similar situation? What did you do that would cause you problems? Think how it would be to behave in a different way. You may feel uncomfortable about changing and that's ok. New goals require a gradual change—give yourself time to make the change. Once you have set a goal, you have challenged yourself to live up to it. Whether you do it or not will be determined by whether you really want to change. Has anyone identified a goal they would be willing to share? Can you think of things that will keep you from changing?

4) **IDENTIFY A THINKING OR ACTION METHOD (CALLED INTERVENTION).** This is a method you will use to change your thoughts or behaviors. We will begin to learn these in the next session, but we will really focus on these methods in Phase II. Ask the clients to discuss how they might make some of these changes now.

5) **CHANGE THE TARGET BEHAVIOR.** This, too, is a project of phase II where you will learn the skills to reach goals you have set for yourself. If you really want to change, you will. Practice the method to replace or eliminate the old thought or behavior.

4. Homework Assignments

a. Have clients write another segment in their *autobiography*.

b. Have clients do a *thinking report* on a situation involving either substance use and abuse or criminal conduct. An example might be: Your wife/husband or another loved one was angry with you. Have clients identify their situation, how they responded and what they did. Have them bring this report to the next session.

c. Have clients write one sentence each night in their *journal* as to a thought that bugged them or that they carried around all day.

d. Have them pick one target behavior they want to change. Ask them not to do anything but pick the behavior. Challenge them to think about it all week, but not try to change it. Examples: Getting irritated at a spouse, swearing, or a nervous habit. But just have them pick one.

5. Presentation Sequence

a. Review this past week's homework and share results in the rehash group.

b. Present introduction to the session.

c. Review the change process and Figure 18. Do the exercise.

d. Present the three stages of change upon which this program is built. Have each client draw the profile in *Work Sheets 14 and 15*. Have them discuss where they see themselves. Then, compare the provider's rating profiles with the clients' ratings.

e. Present the material on picking target thoughts and behaviors for change. Do the exercise.

f. Review homework for next week.

g. Hold a reflection group to reflect on this session.

6. Session and Client Evaluation

a. Client completes the CSES for this session.

b. Counselor completes the PSES using the following questions as guidelines:

1) *Did the group demonstrate an increased tendency to self-disclose during the discussion of the homework and thinking reports?*

2) *Were responses generally positive to identifying targets of change? Were there obviously some members more ready to participate than others?*

c. Provider completes the BRF for this session.

Figure 19

Provider's Rating of Client on Stages of Change for AOD Use Only

CHALLENGE TO CHANGE									
KEY ELEMENTS IN STAGE	LOW			MODERATE			HIGH		
Given thought to changing	0	1	2	3	4	5	6	7	8
Want information about self	0	1	2	3	4	5	6	7	8
Level of self-awareness	0	1	2	3	4	5	6	7	8
Commitment to more treatment	0	1	2	3	4	5	6	7	8

COMMITMENT TO CHANGE									
KEY ELEMENTS IN STAGE	LOW			MODERATE			HIGH		
Pledge to change	0	1	2	3	4	5	6	7	8
Open to self-disclosure	0	1	2	3	4	5	6	7	8
Efforts to change attitudes	0	1	2	3	4	5	6	7	8
Efforts to change thoughts	0	1	2	3	4	5	6	7	8
Use relapse prevention skills	0	1	2	3	4	5	6	7	8
AOD thought-free for long period	0	1	2	3	4	5	6	7	8
Corrected relapse thinking	0	1	2	3	4	5	6	7	8
Learned skills to avoid AOD thought	0	1	2	3	4	5	6	7	8

TAKING OWNERSHIP OF CHANGE									
KEY ELEMENTS IN STAGE	LOW			MODERATE			HIGH		
In program because want to be	0	1	2	3	4	5	6	7	8
No desire for AOD involvement	0	1	2	3	4	5	6	7	8
Long time free of AOD thinking	0	1	2	3	4	5	6	7	8
Replace need for AOD use	0	1	2	3	4	5	6	7	8

Figure 20

Provider's Rating of Client on Stages of Change for Criminal Thinking and Conduct Only

CHALLENGE TO CHANGE

KEY ELEMENTS IN STAGE	LOW			MODERATE			HIGH		
Given thought to changing	0	1	2	3	4	5	6	7	8
Want information about self	0	1	2	3	4	5	6	7	8
Level of self-awareness	0	1	2	3	4	5	6	7	8
Commitment to more treatment	0	1	2	3	4	5	6	7	8

COMMITMENT TO CHANGE

KEY ELEMENTS IN STAGE	LOW			MODERATE			HIGH		
Pledge to change	0	1	2	3	4	5	6	7	8
Open to self-disclosure	0	1	2	3	4	5	6	7	8
Efforts to change attitudes	0	1	2	3	4	5	6	7	8
Efforts to change thoughts	0	1	2	3	4	5	6	7	8
Use recidivism prevention skills	0	1	2	3	4	5	6	7	8
CC thought-free for long period	0	1	2	3	4	5	6	7	8
Corrected recidivism thinking	0	1	2	3	4	5	6	7	8
Learned skills to avoid CC thought	0	1	2	3	4	5	6	7	8

TAKING OWNERSHIP OF CHANGE

KEY ELEMENTS IN STAGE	LOW			MODERATE			HIGH		
In program because want to be	0	1	2	3	4	5	6	7	8
No desire for CC involvement	0	1	2	3	4	5	6	7	8
Long time free of CC thinking	0	1	2	3	4	5	6	7	8
Replace need for CC	0	1	2	3	4	5	6	7	8

Session ⑰ : Ways to Change and Barriers to Change

1. Rationale and Overview of Session

Before clients are ready to make the decision to move to a more intense level of treatment, it is important that they have a feeling for the power of change and an awareness of the barriers that people present to making changes.

Selecting cognitive and behavioral targets is the first step for making concrete changes. The next step is to develop specific *interventions* or techniques to make change. This is where the client will begin to experience the power of the cognitive process in making change. It is an introduction to the more intensive process of change to be experienced in Phase II of this program.

Resistance to and ambivalence about change is experienced by most people, regardless of the nature of their problems or degree of disturbance. Resistance and ambivalence, characteristic of the SAO client, are manifested in cognitive and behavioral barriers to change. If clients are to resolve the resistance and ambivalence to change, it is important that they understand the barriers they put in the way of the change process.

2. Objectives of Session

> ➠ To help clients learn several specific methods and techniques for changing target thoughts and behaviors.
>
> ➠ To help clients identify and understand the barriers they put in the way of change.

3. Session Content and Process

a. Some thoughts for this session:

In the last session we learned to identify change targets. These change targets can be beliefs, thoughts, attitudes or actions. We don't have to engage in a behavior to change. We change our thoughts.

Example: We find ourselves thinking about something that makes us angry—such as paying for something that we felt was not worth it—or the thought of being cheated. We can let that thought *eat us up* and eventually lead to *cheating someone else to get back* or we can change that thought.

Example: We find ourself thinking about getting together with friends and *getting high*. We can change that thought before we actually engage in the behavior. This is the power of the mind. But even more powerful is the discovery of certain techniques or methods to change target thoughts or behavior.

We have worked hard at understanding how people change. We have been open to sharing information about ourselves in order to have better awareness of our past and present problems. We have learned and have been willing to identify specific thinking and behavioral targets to change. With all of that, it would seem that we would have no problem making the changes we and others feel need to be made. Yet, it is not that easy. As we have already discussed, we are very invested in protecting how we see ourselves, in defending our self-honor, and in avoiding receiving information that may run counter to the view we have of ourselves. This defensiveness causes us to resist change or at least to have mixed feelings about change. This resistance and defensiveness causes us to put up *barriers* to the way of change. We look at these barriers in this session.

Exercise: Have clients write down three thoughts that they have put up as roadblocks or barriers to change.

b. **Learning some specific techniques and strategies for intervention and change**

What do we do after we choose a target behavior for change? What methods do we use? We look at some methods that you can learn to intervene in and change the target thought or behavior.

1) **Methods of "self-talk."** Many of the techniques for changing thought and behavior are called *"self-talk"* methods. One part of self-talk is to instruct yourself on the use of certain cognitive techniques to change a target thought or behavior. This is also called *self-instructional training* (e.g., Kendall & Bemis, 1983; Meichenbaum, 1977). These techniques are commonly used by many therapists, and some of these below have been illustrated by Bush & Bilodeau (1993). Let us look at some *self-talk methods* (interventions) to change thinking and behavior.

   a) **Thought Stopping** (Beck, 1995; Burns, 1980; Bush & Bilodeau, 1993; Leahy. 1996): I want to stop my target behavior of being distrustful. If I find myself thinking, "I can't trust this stranger," I can stop this automatic thinking by saying, "I'm feeling distrustful, I'm not going to think this way." I may still feel slightly distrustful, but I have interrupted my automatic thinking and am making myself think new thoughts. I may need to remind myself of *why* I want to stop thinking this way, of how much more positive it is to think *well* of people.

   b) **Thinking *Responsibility* and *Their Position*** (Bush & Bilodeau, 1993): What if I were in THEIR POSITION?—What are they thinking? RESPECT the other person as a human being. Think of your PAST EXPERIENCE in similar situations. How did you feel? Think of THE PERSON YOU WANT TO BE. Remember that in most situations more than one person is involved and that they may share blame for problems. Learn to look at the part of the problem for which you are to blame. Try to imagine how you would feel if you were the other person. Learn to respect the other person as a human being. *Responsibility* and *Their Position* are remedies for antisocial behavior and criminal conduct. *Responsibility* makes us take ownership of our own behavior; *Their Position* makes us place ourselves in the other's position.

   c) **Planting Positive Thoughts:** When you find yourself thinking negatively, *replace* a negative thought with a positive thought. Do it every time it happens. Sometimes negative thoughts can be helpful if they are used to problem solve, but not if you dwell on them. They will soon lead to negative behavior or acting out the negative thoughts. Train yourself to have POSITIVE THOUGHTS toward others. Take time to think. If there is a real problem, slow down and think of alternatives. It is important to think of as many solutions as possible when solving a problem. If you are resorting to old thinking patterns, think of something negative that has resulted from thinking that way in the past. Remind yourself of the fact that you want to change your negative behavior and the kind of person you want to be. As you change your thinking patterns, you are training yourself to have different and more positive thoughts toward people with whom you normally have problems.

   d) **Countering** (McMullin, 1986): When you argue against an error in thinking or a thought that is not rational or doesn't make sense, and you do it every time, that thought becomes weaker. A counter can be one statement: 'That's stupid." "Not true." Sometimes the counter is a coping statement: "I can do it." Or it can be a joking statement: "It's terrible to make mistakes. Babe Ruth hit 714 home runs but struck out 1,330 times."

2) **Shifting the View (Perceptual Shifting)** (McMullin, 1986): Whereas the above techniques are *self-talk* or *self-language* methods, this method of changing our mental sets is based on how we see things inside and outside ourself. Getting caught up in destructive (to ourselves and others) ideas, beliefs and thoughts will often lead us to AOD use and abuse or criminal conduct. These often are errors of how we see the world—our beliefs. But if we can change or shift our view, we can often see the *other* side of the belief or thought.

Studies of the brain by Hobson and McCarley (1977) tell us that not only does our brain take in and store information and not only does it try to understand the information it takes in, but it also changes how we see that information. The brain changes (or transforms) the information and turns it into ideas, beliefs, patterns or story themes. A good example of how the brain can change what it brings in is in Figure 21, which is Boring's (1930) famous old woman-young woman visual shift picture. Depending how the brain *views* the picture, you see an old woman or a young woman.

Over a long period of time, you may have held on to the belief "I deserve more than what I'm getting, I've been cheated." This view of yourself and the world will lead eventually to you going out and getting what you feel you have coming. This, for many, results in criminal behavior. To change this view, one must shift how you see yourself or the world. "There have been a lot of people who have done things for me." There are many different kinds of *view shifting* you can do.

3) **Exaggerate or overstate the thought (paradoxical intent):** This technique has been used for many years. It was developed by the famous psychiatrist Victor Frankl (1963) when he was in the German concentration camps. When he found people wanting to give up, he would say "Go ahead and give up. See if I care. Do it right now. Give up." He found that in almost every case, this forced the person back to reality and doing just the opposite. You can do this to yourself. When you find yourself worrying about something in an irrational way (a way that doesn't make sense), you can say, "OK, I'm going to worry about this for the next ten hours. I'll show you how much I can worry about this." When we do this, it forces us to look at the error in thinking or the irrational belief. It is like *typing the error* to realize you make the error and then you correct it.

Figure 21

What we perceive is often due to our expectations. When looking at this famous ambiguous figure, do you see a young woman or an old woman?

Figure 21 was drawn by cartoonist W.E. Hill and was originally published in *Puck* November 6, 1915, later published by E.G. Boring, 1930.

Example of Shifting the View: Old Woman-Young Woman

4) **Conditioning: Making our thoughts weaker or stronger** (McMullin, 1986): You can *reward* the positive thoughts. You can make your destructive or negative thoughts weaker. For example, if you think about drinking, then think about all of the bad things that happened when you drank in the past. When you think about replacing drinking with a positive activity, think about the rewards that come from the positive activity. When you do not drink but want to, reward yourself. Buy yourself something.

5) **Logical (sensible) study—going to court with your thought** (McMullin, 1986): This technique involves fighting your errors in thinking or your nonsense or irrational thoughts with logic or sensible thinking. You want to go out to drink. You have a thought about stealing something. Think: How much sense does this make? In the long run, is it logical? Three simple steps to this technique of going to court with your thought: *State your thought; get your evidence; make your verdict.* This gives you time to think it through.

6) **Learning relaxation skills:** When we are under stress and tense, we are more likely to let our automatic thoughts or thought habits take over. We get tired or fatigued. The fatigue and stress reduces our mental control. We are more likely to let our thought habits and our behavior habits take over. Learning to *relax* will help us regain control; it will give us control. There are several relaxation skills that can help you deal with stress and tension as well as anger and depression. It is recommended that the provider go through a training session on the use of these relaxation skills before teaching them to clients.

   a) **Progressive muscle relaxation** (see Benson, 1975; Bernstein & Carlson, 1993; Jacobson, 1938;1970; Norris & Fahrion, 1993): First, you actively tense each muscle group for a few seconds, after which you release the muscles and relax and then concentrate on the muscles as they relax. The sequence of tension, relax and attention may be sequentially applied beginning with the hands and moving through the forearms, upper arms, forehead, facial muscles, neck, throat, shoulders, stomach, upper legs, calves, and feet. The major emphasis is on somatic or *physical* relaxation.

   b) **Calm scenes:** With eyes closed, imagine being in a very calm and relaxing scene such as the oceanside, by a stream in the mountains, or sitting in front of the fire place. Each person can pick the scene that works best for him/her.

   c) **Passive body focus or what we call autogenic training:** (Benson, 1975; Linden, 1993): This is mentally relaxing parts of your body. Here one focuses on parts of the body and gives relaxing verbal commands such as: "My hands are heavy; my arms are relaxed; my forehead is cool; my hands are warm." One can progress through parts of the body, relaxing the body in a passive manner through verbal commands. It is best to sit in a soft chair with your eyes closed.

   d) **Deep breathing** (Benson, 1975; Fried, 1993): This is very powerful and you can do this at any time in most situations. You come to a stop sign and you can take a deep breath. You can do this in many ways. You can take ten deep breaths, with each breath getting deeper and then ten more going from the deep breathing to normal breathing. Close your eyes or keep them open, but concentrate on your breathing. Feel yourself relax.

Now, you can start to use these techniques. Feel their power to help you change your thinking and doing.

Exercises: Have volunteers role-play the following examples and then have another person use one of the interventions described above. If it is a *situation* (labeled "situation"), have two people role-play with one giving the intervention response. Repeat the scenario. Let several members give responses. If it is a *thought* (labeled "thought"), have one person think out loud and the other person be his "conscience" and talk out loud for the person. We call this *doubling*. Have the double stand by the person to be his or her conscience. Each time, have the double label the intervention.

For each of the various scenes or thoughts, determine which method or intervention works best. Discuss the intervention after each scene or thought.

Situation: Your boss has just caught you arriving late to work. He tells you this is the last time he will tolerate tardiness. What do you do? Example intervention: RESPONSIBILITY—What are you doing to contribute to the situation?

Situation: You are the boss and you have just caught your employee arriving late to work. What do you do? Intervention: What if I were in THEIR POSITION?—What are they thinking?

Situation: You are approached by a dealer who offers to sell you drugs. How do you respond? Intervention: Think of THE PERSON YOU WANT TO BE—what behavior is important?

Situation: You and your mother-in-law have never gotten along. She is at your house for dinner and finds something wrong with everything. Intervention: Train yourself to have POSITIVE THOUGHTS toward her and others.

Thought: "Taking a few drinks is about the only way a person can really let down and relax." Have the double use an intervention or method to change the thought.

Thought: "Every boss is usually going to end up screwing you over and taking advantage of you."

Thought: "I'm worried about whether I'm going to get fired."

Thought: "I feel depressed about my job. It's getting me down."

Exercise: Guide the group through progressive muscle relaxation. Teach them some autogenic or passive body focus. Take them through one calm scene and then help them practice deep breathing.

c. **Barriers to involvement in change**

We can put up many barriers to change. We put these barriers up because it is too uncomfortable to change or just too much of a burden. Sometimes it involves just not coming to the session. Sometimes it involves just *getting tired of pleasing people and throwing in the towel.* Sometimes we see other things as more important than involving ourselves in the change process. Most often, however, it involves thinking barriers—which are often automatic thoughts or just errors in our thinking.

Many substance abusing offenders find it difficult to believe that their thinking is not like everybody else's. "Everyone tries to take advantage of a situation if they can get away with it." If you believe you are right, why should you change? No one is comfortable changing what they think is the way they should be.

We are asking you to change thoughts, behaviors, attitudes, beliefs—most of them deeply ingrained—the things that make you "me." Most of us are comfortable with our beliefs, no matter how many people may disagree with us about whether they are true or not. It makes us very uncomfortable to make major changes in our belief system. This is what you are being challenged to do. Can you convince yourself:

• that you need to change?;

• that you can change without a lot of distress?;

• that you can learn new ways of thinking that will have more rewards than your old ways of thinking?

Here are some thinking and behaving roadblocks we put up as barriers to change. How do these fit you? (adapted from King et al., 1994).

1) "EVERYONE THINKS THE WAY I DO";

2) "I'VE GOT TO BE HONEST, THIS IS WHAT I REALLY BELIEVE";

3) "THERE ARE NO ALTERNATIVES";

4) "MY THOUGHTS AND FEELINGS DON'T NEED CHANGING IN THIS SITUATION BECAUSE I'M RIGHT";

5) BUILDING YOURSELF UP TO PUT DOWN THE IDEAS OF CHANGE;

6) BEING SILENT IN GROUP;

7) NOT LISTENING OR ATTENDING;

8) STATING "I'VE TRIED THAT AND IT DIDN'T WORK";

9) THINKING "I'VE ALWAYS DONE IT THAT WAY";

10) ATTACKING OTHERS.

Exercise: Take number 4 above and work on that as a group. Use the following suggestions as a guideline for discussion.

If you feel that you are absolutely entitled to feel the way you are feeling, you are probably wrong. Sticking to our own way of thinking without considering alternatives may lead to trouble. Even if you are doing a good job of practicing change, you may run into this barrier. Don't forget, even if what is happening seems unfair, there are many ways to think about the situation.

Open the door to other ways of thinking that people may have identified as barriers to change in their lives. Are there any patterns or evidence of resistance? Do people in the group recognize any patterns or barriers that they use to resist change?

If we don't find things that make changing worthwhile, we will not find rewards in changing. With no rewards, we will not make the effort.

d. **Make the effort—it's worth it:**

What happens if we change one thing in our thinking and behavior that keeps us out of trouble? We find that this makes life better. Then we look for another thing to change to make it better. When you do this, you are *practicing change* and, with practice, we overcome one of the greatest roadblocks to change: NOT MAKING THE EFFORT TO CHANGE (Bush & Bilodeau, 1993, p. 3-64). To avoid this barrier, be honest with yourself. If you are *not really trying* to change, admit it.

We may find that feeling good about what we are doing and doing what most of the world finds *right* pays off. It is better than any payoff we found when we were abusing drugs and doing criminal activities.

4. Classroom or Homework Activities

a. Have clients finish their *autobiography* and bring it to the next session.

b. Encourage clients to practice all of the above interventions this week. Have them record in their journal the date and the event or circumstance when they did put them to work. Have them ponder on the power of these techniques. They put them in control.

c. Have clients write in their *journal* each day the strongest feeling or emotion they felt during the day. Have them only write the feeling down; nothing else.

d. *Thinking Report:* Have clients recall a situation when their friends and associates "led" them to stray from changing one of their target behaviors. Maybe the target behavior was to not be around people who use drugs. But they spend time with their friends who are using. Remember the parts of your thinking report:

SITUATION

THOUGHTS

FEELINGS

ATTITUDES AND BELIEFS ABOUT THE SITUATION

THE OUTCOME OF THE SITUATION AND EVENT

e. Encourage clients to think seriously this week about the program they have been in. Have them be prepared to evaluate and share their commitment to change.

5. Presentation Sequence

a. Review homework from last week. Review the autobiography. Do this individually with each client. Remind the client that the autobiography is to be finished by next week.

b. Present the introduction material for this session.

c. Present the intervention techniques and methods and do the exercises. Clients are not going to learn these overnight, and they will need ongoing practice.

d. Present the material on barriers to change and do exercises.

e. Do a reflection group to prepare the group for the next and last session in Phase I. Have them ready to discuss their commitment to change and entering Phase II.

f. Plan a social event for next session, either a pizza meal or potluck. Also, plan on giving clients the Phase I certificate of completion.

6. Session and Client Evaluation

a. Client completes the CSES.

b. Counselor completes the PSES using the following questions as guides:

1) *Does the group appear ready to change and have they been able to identify some of the barriers that may stand in their way?*

2) *Was there general recognition of the fact that, in spite of the discomfort involved in change, the rewards can outweigh the distress?*

3) *Did the group demonstrate an understanding of the various interventions introduced in this*

section and apply them to the various exercises presented in this session?

c. Provider completes the BRF and score. At this point, the provider may calculate a summary score on the BRF. Then review the client's progress and write a summary statement of the client's progress. Provider needs to determine whether the client is motivated and ready for Phase II.

Session ⑱: Looking Forward: Making a Commitment to Change

1. Rationale and Overview of Session

This session will be devoted only to the review of homework, the review of the autobiographies and the client making a commitment to change—which means a commitment to entering Phase II of the program. Most of the two hours will be needed to process this decision. The provider may elect to meet with each client *individually* to review his or her progress and make the decision whether the client will continue into Phase II. If the group has bonded well, then it will be important that these decisions are made by the group. The provider may choose to have the group deal openly and honestly about these decisions and choices and about the Provider's own recommendation. Using the *group process* is recommended. In this way, we can maximize the value of the reinforcing power of the group. If you have conducted open group sessions, it may be that every three or four weeks, you will have some clients making this decision to move on to Phase II.

2. Objectives of Session

> ⮕ Have each client honestly review and evaluate their involvement in the program and the progress made toward change;
>
> ⮕ Have clients identify the specific changes they have made;
>
> ⮕ Have clients receive feedback from other members of the group as to their perception of each client's change and progress;
>
> ⮕ Have the provider give feedback to group members;
>
> ⮕ Have clients make a decision around commitment to change and involvement in Phase II.

3. Session Content and Process

You have now come to a fork in the road in your treatment journey. You have experienced a lot, you have learned a lot, you have worked hard and you have grown and matured immensely. Now you will need to address the question of whether you want to continue in this program. For some of you, this may be a requirement. Even if this is the case, we want you to express your feelings and opinions honestly and openly. We will do the following activities in this session

a. First you will be asked to complete the *Adult Self-Assessment Questionnaire* again. We will then score that and compare your profile now with the one you had when you first started the program.

b. Review your homework and your *autobiography*. You will be asked to share one important piece of that autobiography.

c. The group discussion now will focus around the following:

1) How are you feeling now about the program?

2) What have you gotten out of the program?

3) Where do you see yourself now as to your stage of change?

4) Have each person in the group give you feedback as to where they see you, how you have responded to the program and how they see you as to your stage of change. The provider will also give you this feedback. The provider may have already met with you around his or her recommendations. If this is the case, you are asked to share what he or she told you.

5) Do you now want to commit yourself to change? Do you want to continue in this program?

Discuss your feelings and thoughts.

4. Presentation Sequence

    a. Review homework and *autobiography*. Be sure all autobiographies are completed.

    b. Introduce client to the session and spend rest of session in the reflection group dealing with the issues outlined above.

    c. Schedule next session.

    d. Have the social event.

5. Complete the client's Phase I evaluation and client's response to the program. Complete all required reports. Be sure and get releases from the client before any report is sent.

PHASE II
COMMITMENT TO CHANGE
INTRODUCTION AND OVERVIEW

PHASE II: COMMITMENT TO CHANGE

Introduction and Overview of Phase II

The primary goal of **Phase I** was to prepare the client for *Commitment to Change*. This preparation process involved developing rapport with and trust within the client as to the intent and purpose of the program. We made an effort to help the client develop a readiness and motivation for change. Change is based on self-awareness. Thus, we helped the client develop both a core knowledge base that was generic and knowledge that was unique to the individual. This knowledge base focused on the role of thinking and behavior in self-improvement and change and knowledge around drugs, drug use, and the drug abuse patterns and cycles that are results of drug use. We also helped the client develop an understanding of the principles and cycles underlying criminal conduct and the relationship between criminal conduct and AOD use.

Self-awareness is dependent on *self-disclosure*. Thus, Phase I helped the client to enhance self-awareness through self-disclosure. We taught and practiced basic communication skills necessary for effective and meaningful self-disclosure. We focused on the identification of thinking errors and cognitive distortions, of emotions and feelings, and of the client's background and history of involvement in AOD use and criminal conduct. In order to enhance the self-disclosure process, the client wrote an autobiography and learned to use the self-disclosure tools of journaling and writing thinking reports. This "unpacking" or "telling the story" part of Phase I was crucial not only in developing self-awareness but also in setting the stage for Phase II—having the client hear his or her own story and then beginning to take action on that story.

An important part of Phase I was learning about relapse and recidivism and beginning to practice the skills to prevent full relapse and full recidivism. Finally, we brought Phase I to a close by beginning to apply the change process to the individual client, by helping the client to begin to look at the idea of targets of change, and then identifying and overcoming the barriers to change.

Phase II involves a sorting out and labeling process. Thoughts and feelings were identified; issues and concerns were prioritized and then explored in greater depth. The most critical experience for the client in this stage of treatment process is the *feedback loop*. This loop is the key process through which the client hears his/her story and dilemma, problems and dysfunctions and pathological responses to the world. Then, the client can begin to take action on that story. Through this feedback loop, the defensive system begins to open up and allows increased self-awareness and understanding, critical to the growth and change process. The awareness of needed growth and change occurs during this phase; but more than this, this phase is designed to *get the client to commit to change*. In this phase, both therapeutic and correctional confrontation begin to occur through the feedback loop process.

Phase II, then represents a commitment to taking action in making cognitive and behavioral changes. In this phase, an in-depth assessment is completed to enhance the client's awareness of his or her own cognitive set and behavioral patterns associated with CC and AOD use and to identify the unique cognitive and behavioral patterns of the client. From this assessment, a Master Profile and Master Assessment Plan is developed. The client is then engaged in programs designed to develop and strengthen *basic skills for self-improvement and change* (e.g., interpersonal and intrapersonal skill development training). The purpose of these skills is to bring about shifts in the client's cognitive sets and actual behaviors associated with CC and AOD abuse and to prevent relapse and recidivism. Thinking and behavioral changes will be practiced and reinforced.

From the perspective of the Prochaska et al. (1992) stages of change model, this phase represents both the *determination* and *action* stages of change. Here the client is resolving the ambivalence to committing to change and applies the interpersonal and intrapersonal skills to effect change.

Specific Goals and Objectives of Phase II

The following are the more specific goals and objectives of this phase:

⟹ As a result of engaging in more intensive self-disclosure and through the feedback process, the client will develop a deeper awareness, understanding and clear recognition of thinking and behavioral patterns in the following areas:

- Criminal conduct;

- AOD use and abuse;

- How AOD abuse and criminal conduct interact and reinforce each other and feed into further involvement both in criminal thinking and conduct and in AOD abuse;

- How unique patterns of thinking, feeling and perceiving lead to involvement in criminal conduct and AOD abuse;

- The individual's own unique life problems, to aid in understanding how these problems interact with AOD abuse and CC and in taking action in solving these problems.

⟹ As a result of developing an in-depth awareness of CC and AOD abuse patterns and through developing and enhancing the basis skills for self-improvement and change, the client commits to and begins to make substantial changes in cognitive sets and in behaviors that strengthen prosocial actions and AOD abstinence.

- The client commits to and demonstrates change in cognitive sets underlying AOD abuse and CC;

- The client demonstrates change in criminal conduct and AOD behavior;

- The client is aware of the patterns of recidivism in criminal conduct and AOD cognitive sets and prevents recidivism and relapse of cognitive sets from leading into full recidivistic and relapse behaviors.

Basic Provider Skill Structure for Phase II

a. **Feedback Skills:** The skill structure for Phase II is represented by the broad categories of feedback skills (e.g., reflection paraphrasing, summarization, change clarification, change confrontation). Through the application of feedback clarification skills, the client begins to hear her or his own story. This helps the client to sort out the feelings, thoughts and behaviors involved in dysfunctional and pathological responding. The client begins to develop a clear perspective of needed growth and change. This process increases self-awareness and self-understanding. Both therapeutic and correctional confrontational skills are used in this Phase.

b. **Reinforcement Skills**: When changes occur, the provider utilizes reinforcement skills to strengthen changes in thinking and behavior.

c. **Assessment Skills:** Assessment in this phase of treatment is more in-depth and differential. The results of assessment are used in the feedback process to help clients sort out their own patterns of criminal behavior, AOD use, and feelings, thoughts and emotions.

d. **Skill Learning Facilitation:** One of the primary skills that the provider will use in this phase is that of facilitating the learning of life-coping and life-adjustment skills in the sessions that focus on the basic skills for self-improvement and change.

e. **Group Facilitation Skills:** Phase II represents an increase in the use of group interaction and process to achieve program objectives. The utilization of group facilitation skills as outlined in Chapter 13 of this manual will help the provider achieve this purpose.

f. **Change Confrontation and Reinforcement Skills.** These are key skills in change. Both therapeutic and correctional confrontation skills will be needed. The difference between these two skills is discussed in Chapter 11.

Basic Treatment Strategies

a. In-depth self-evaluation.

b. Getting the client to respond to feedback.

c. Facilitate learning the basic skills for self-improvement and change.

d. Client practices change.

The Client Will Experience

a. In-depth self-awareness.

b. Therapeutic and correctional confrontation.

c. Insight.

d. Change in cognitive and behavioral patterns.

Completion Requirements for Phase II

a. Comprehension and skill development:

1) Complete the in-depth differential assessment.

2) Complete all Basic Skills sessions.

3) Demonstrate specific changes in AOD and Criminal Conduct thinking and behavioral patterns.

b. Participation expectations:

1) Required to attend at least 90 percent of all meetings. Punctuality and completion of homework assignments (as determined by group leaders) are required for all sessions.

2) Maintain a cooperative posture with respect to staff and other clients.

3) Function in a self-directed manner while assisting others to complete the tasks of Phase II.

4) Complete *thinking reports* and work in *journals*.

5) Participate fully in the basic skills for self-improvement and change sessions.

Presentation Structure and Time Requirements for Phase II

Phase II involves 22 two-hour sessions over a period of six months. Client evaluations are done on a monthly basis to determine progress in the program and whether the client is meeting program expectations.

The logistics of presenting Phase II may depend upon the unique system of the service provider and the staffing pattern available to deliver the program. Below are some recommendations for the delivery of Phase II.

Modules 7 and 8 represent the introduction to Phase II and will take one month to deliver. Module 9 is made up of a series of skill building sessions over a period of 18 weeks. It is recommended that Modules 7 and 8 be offered several times to small closed groups who have completed Phase I. Because of the length of Module 9, it is recommended that it be delivered in an open group manner. Then the clients completing Modules 7 and 8 can be positioned to enter Module 9 at appropriate times. There are segments in Module 9 within which sessions are logically connected and need to be presented in sequence. These segments run in a three- to four-week series. It would be appropriate that clients enter Module 9 at the beginning of these logically connected segments. These break-points for introducing new group members are indicated in the manual as the sessions of Module 9 are presented.

MODULE 7

Introduction to Phase II:

Developing Commitment to Change

MODULE 7: INTRODUCTION TO PHASE II: DEVELOPING COMMITMENT TO CHANGE

Overview of Module 7

Modules 7 and 8 are introductions to Phase II. In some ways, this represents a new enrollment period in that clients made a conscious decision to continue into this Phase of treatment. It will be important to take time to have people become acquainted with each other.

Goals and Objectives for Module 7

The overall goal for this module is to introduce the client to Phase II, Commitment to Change. Whereas Phase I challenged the client to change by offering opportunity to change, there was no clear expectation or test of change. We are now stepping up a second level of challenge—that of expectation and testing. This test will be achieved through the following goals:

- Clients review and recall their accomplishments in Phase I and look at the major issues addressed in that Phase.

- Clients recognize their own readiness to change.

- Clients learn the basic steps of problem solving and alternatives to current thinking and behaving.

- Clients understand that real change is based on a freedom of choice.

- Clients put into practice problem solving and alternative responding.

- Clients bring their most significant other(s) into program involvement.

Time Structure for Module 7

This introduction module for Phase II takes two sessions. Session 19 needs three hours and Session 20 will need two hours. Clients will need time to process their commitment to Phase II in group. As noted earlier, it is recommended that a closed group method be used for Modules 7 and 8. Then, clients can be started at the designated break-points in Module 9.

Session ⑲ : Recognizing Readiness to Change: Problem Solving and Doing Something Different—It's Your Choice

1. Rationale and Overview of Session

The client at this point has made a commitment to continue into Phase II. This is a major commitment, and time is needed to process this commitment. A portion of this session should be devoted to this processing. The client should be increasingly aware of how thinking and thought processes lead to certain behavioral consequences. The client now should be more able to recognize when change is needed and to choose alternatives to engaging in criminal and substance abusive behavior. Finally, personal responsibility for change comes when the individual is aware that he or she has free choice to change.

Recognizing the client's readiness to change: If a client is to recognize a readiness to change, it is important that the provider be able to recognize that readiness, and communicate this to the client. How does one recognize readiness to change in the client? Miller (1995) stresses the importance of timing in recognizing that the client has reached the point of determination. Though there are no *universal* signs, he identifies the following changes that might be observed in the client who is ready to commit to action (p. 27):

a. The client stops resisting and raising objections;

b. The client asks fewer questions and shares more personal material;

c. The client appears more settled, resolved, unburdened, or peaceful;

d. The client makes self-motivational statements indicating a decision (or openness) to change ("I guess I need to do something about my drug use." "If I wanted to kick this, what could I do?").

Allowing setbacks by everyday problems: In order to maintain motivation and make the decisions necessary to change, the client needs to understand that problems are going to arise and are part of everyday life. Although this is only too obvious, what tends to occur is that clients may abandon their efforts to change when common, everyday problems arise. They see these problems as making change "not worth it. If I'm going to have problems anyway, why change?" SAO clients are particularly vulnerable to allowing everyday problems to set them back because they have not learned effective coping skills for dealing with problems, problems that tend to lead them back into old habits of substance abuse and criminal thinking. They fail to do anything about the problem, or act impulsively rather than analyzing the situation and finding an effective solution that does not cause relapse into old behavior (Monti et al., 1989).

Ambivalence, resistance and free choice: The decision to change may be gradual rather than clear-cut. Even after such a decision is made, ambivalence and resistance may exist and Phase I strategies should not be completely abandoned as we move into Phase II. The client needs a growing understanding that the decision to change is of his or her own free choice.

Criminal conduct and substance abuse are associated with a pattern of attitudes and beliefs that are difficult to let go. Most offenders have lived with the notion that in order for them to receive the satisfaction of *winning,* someone else has to lose. The reward has been incarceration, probation or parole. It is time to learn other ways of attaining gratification. Many clients will be at a critical point at this stage of the program—to make the decision to change or continue their self-destructive behavior. The choice at all times belongs to the individual. In this session, we discuss problem solving and the alternatives to impulsive acting. These concepts are presented within the framework that change comes from within and is based on free choice.

During this session, it is important for the presenter to spend time discussing the concept of *free choice and resistance.* We need to remember that the client has invested a lifetime being the way he or she is. The habits, attitudes and beliefs of a lifetime are not easily changed. The therapist must listen to the ambivalent statements and even arguments against change with empathy. The wavering decision maker may be helped by questions regarding the consequences of not changing.

Reinforcement of any move toward change is imperative, coupled with statements that essentially say, "It's up to you to make the choice." "You are free to make that choice."

The importance of breaking old patterns of thinking and developing alternative ways of thinking cannot be emphasized enough. If the group member has too much invested in his/her old ways of behaving, we cannot force the change that is so important at this point. A conscious decision, acceptance of responsibility, and true commitment to new behavior can belong only to the client. There will be no coercion to change.

Resistance may take one of two forms. It may be open and direct and the person refuses to get with the program and make any move toward change. This person, if openly obstinate and/or uncooperative, should be encouraged to not continue into Phase II until there is a change in attitude toward treatment.

Resistance may also be expressed in the form of ambivalence, as discussed above. In this case every effort should be made to be empathetic and supportive, encouraging the person to admit that s/he has a problem and needs to take steps to solve that problem and change his/her life. Miller and his colleagues (1994) stress that this cannot be done by arguing with the client and suggests several alternative tactics. For instance, they encourage the provider to use *simple reflection,* or restatement of the patient's own words, or, as an alternative, *reflection with amplification* in which the provider exaggerates what the client says to the point that s/he cannot agree with the statement. *Reframing* is another method to help motivate change in the participant. The purpose is to use the client's own words and comprehension of the problem to place it in a more optimistic and positive frame as being solvable (Miller et al., 1994, pp. 23-25).

For the person wavering on the brink of change, the skills of problem solving and alternative replacement will help. SAO clients know what their life has been; what are the consequences of continuing in the same manner? Once they start seeing the consequences of their decisions, it is up to the providers to assist them to see the situation as clearly as possible. The *thinking report* is our primary tool in achieving this goal.

2. Objectives of Session

What we want to achieve in this session is to recognize that change is not just *knuckling under.* It is empowering the self to make things different and better in the long run. There are four specific objectives of this session:

> ⮕ Review the progress and change clients have made in Phase I and review the commitment made to Phase II.
>
> ⮕ Help clients recognize their readiness to change by attending to an increase in their statements and behavior that indicate movement toward change.
>
> ⮕ Enhance motivation to change by teaching clients problem solving skills and introducing the concept of finding alternatives to current behavior.
>
> ⮕ Help clients become aware that change comes from within and that change is of free choice.

3. Session Content

Real change comes from within. It is just not *knuckling under.* It is giving yourself the power to make things different and better in the long run. We look at recognizing *when* you are ready to change. Then we look at learning the skill of problem solving and the skill of using alternative thinking and actions.

a. **How do you know you are ready to change?**

How do you really recognize that you are ready to change? Here are some points that may help you to be aware of your readiness to make change (Miller, 1995):

1) You are open to people talking to you about your drug use and your past criminal actions;

2) You see that you have a problem with AOD use;

3) You talk about wanting to make things different and to change;

4) You hear yourself saying that you can change.

Even more important, if you have made some change, then you are saying *"I'm ready to change."* Here are some changes you may have made to tell you that you commit to or promise to change.

1) You ask fewer questions;

2) You don't raise objections;

3) You talk more about yourself;

4) You are more settled and at peace;

5) You hear your self-talk saying you need to do something about your AOD use. You hear yourself talk about change, wanting to change and having made certain changes.

How do you keep up the change? You need to know that you will get discouraged. Every day problems come up and you may feel "Is it worth it?" This is part of everyday life. If you have not learned the skills of dealing with everyday problems—which will be what we will be learning in this Phase of the program—problems may lead you to fall into old habits of drug use or criminal thinking. Learning these skills is important. That is why we will spend some time to learn the skill of problem solving and begin to learn to replace old thoughts and actions with new thoughts and actions. If you are willing to problem solve, you are saying that you do want to change.

b. **Learning problem solving**

Introduce problem solving with this situation: John's driver's license is suspended. He is driving a friend's car, well within the speed limit, and he hears the whine of a siren. In his rearview mirror he sees a police car behind him, red lights flashing. John has a problem—does he pull over or run? What should John do? What might be happening other than John being in trouble?

A *problem* is a behavior, situation, or circumstance that causes you difficulty. The difficulty might boil down to not getting your way in a situation, not being sure what is expected of us, conflict with another person over how things should be done, a difference between our own goal and the goal of someone close to us or trying to find someone or something. Usually, there is a goal attached to our problem.

John has a GOAL to get to where he is going and to stay out of jail. The appearance of the police car presents an OBSTACLE to achieving his goal. Goals and obstacles are characteristics of problems. Common problems may include (King et al., 1994, p. 15)

• wanting to get our way in a situation;

• difficulties caused by not being sure what is expected of us;

• a difference between our own goal and the goal of someone close to us; or

• a search for someone or something.

(P.S. The policeman had just received an emergency call and only wanted to clear traffic).

When we are faced with problems, we may have physical symptoms: Our heart beats fast, we sweat, we cry and get angry. Most problems involve other people. Some problems are serious, others are easy to solve. Sometimes we identify that we have a problem but are not able to clearly figure out what the problem is. This often leads us to be anxious and uneasy until we can clearly identify the problem or the situation causing the problem. To become good problem solvers, we need to be able to identify situations that are going to cause us a problem (Ross, et al., 1986).

A problem may only be in our thinking. That is the best place where we can solve our problem. We solve it in our head before it takes place in our actions.

Here are the simple steps of problem solving:

1) *Identify the problem* situation.

2) *What is my goal?* What would I like to see as the solution to the problem? What do I want the outcome to be?

3) *What are the various solutions* to the problem? What is in my power to do? What action should I take or can I take? Are there different solutions? Get information you need to make the best choice.

4) *What gets in the way of solving the problem—what are the obstacles?*

5) *Make a choice and start the action.*

6) *Study the outcome* of your choice. What was the result? Was it in my best interest? Could I have done something different? What will I do next time?

Exercise: Use this as an example of a thinking problem. John would like to go out with his friend Cliff tonight, but Cliff always drinks. That means he will drink if they go out together. When he goes out and drinks with Cliff, he usually puts himself at risk of getting into trouble. Apply the steps above to this example.

This can be solved at the thinking level. Get several examples from the group. What is a problem you have had lately? Have group members apply the above steps to solving a problem you have. What was your goal? What was the obstacle? How did you resolve it?

A problem may only be in our thinking. That is the best place where we can solve our problem. We solve it in our head before it takes place in our actions.

Problem Solving Exercise: Have clients do *Work Sheet 16* in the Workbook.

c. **Learning to apply different choices or alternatives**

An alternative or *different choice* method allows you to think in many different directions. You have learned to do one kind of thing in a certain situation. Change that choice. It is in your power. Think of a problem situation where you can replace the old choice with a new one. Sometimes we know we have a problem, but we need more information to make a good decision and find a way to solve it.

FIRST, stop and think—don't rush headlong into a solution. We may have a lot of OPINIONS from other people, but very few FACTS.

A fact is something that is known to be true. An OPINION may be true, but we do not know for sure that it is.

SECOND, slow down—get more information. Details are important. Brainstorm, thinking of all the possible answers to the problem you can come up with.

FINALLY, choose what appears to be the *best* approach to the problem.

Here are the simple steps of applying choice alternatives:

1) LEARN TO BE AWARE YOU ARE MAKING A DECISION—A CHOICE: STOP AND THINK. Don't rush into a solution. When you can make a decision, you have a choice. Practice this. Even in the simple things. "I can decide to go to the grocery store first or the hardware store." This leaves you with a choice. It is your freedom. You look at the alternatives.

2) GET INFORMATION. TAKE YOUR TIME. Details are important. Brainstorm, thinking of all the possible answers. Ask yourself: "What do I still need to know?" "What else might be contributing to the situation?" "What is another way I can think of this?" "How can I figure out what might happen? What are the possible outcomes?"

3) MAKE YOUR DECISION—your choice.

4) LOOK AT THE OUTCOME—THE RESULTS: Did it save time to go to the grocery store first? Replay the tape. What would be different had you gone to the hardware store first?

Thus—always think—I have a decision to make. Make your choice. Process the outcome.

d. Are you blocking change? Are you resisting?

You have a lifetime of habits, attitudes and beliefs. You may even argue inside yourself against making change. Will you continue to do things as you always have? You have a choice. You can problem solve. You can find alternatives. If you have too much of yourself invested in these old patterns of thinking and acting, you may fight changing. No one can force you. But if you don't change, what will be the results? If you do, what will be the long-term result?

If you find yourself fighting being in the program, you are blocking—resisting. You can do several things inside your head. Hold a debate with yourself. Go ahead and argue. But after you do that, then just echo or reflect back what you heard inside. "I don't want to be in this program." "But I don't want to go back to breaking the law and ending up in jail." "No, I want to be free. I have a choice."

e. Review of Thinking Reports

These will be important tools in problem solving, looking at different choices and in seeing the outcome of our actions. Now we see the *Thinking Report* and *Journals* in a new light. When we look at an outcome now, we know we had a choice—we made a decision in that event.

Remember the basic parts of the *Thinking Report:*

1) Event: Describe the situation.

2) What were your thoughts about and during the event? What were the automatic thoughts?

3) What were your feelings before, during and after the event?

4) What were your attitudes and beliefs? Were these long-held beliefs?

5) What was the outcome of the event? Did your decision or choice make a difference?

4. Classroom and Homework Assignments

a. Apply the problem solving step to a problem that you had this week.

b. Do a thinking report around the problem: Events, thoughts, feelings, beliefs and outcome.

5. Presentation Sequence

a. Hold a reflection group to discuss feelings and thoughts about completing Phase I. Do a focused discussion around what was most helpful about Phase I.

b. Continue the reflection group to focus on participant commitment to change and their commitment to entering Phase II. Encourage members to be honest about their commitment or decision to go into Phase II.

c. Present the material in the Rationale and Session Content sections above and do exercises in the order outlined above.

d. Review the thinking report and homework.

e. REMIND CLIENTS THAT THEY ARE TO HAVE THEIR FAMILY MEMBERS OR SIGNIFICANT OTHERS ATTEND THE NEXT SESSION. Spend about 20 minutes in the closure group to talk about their feelings and thoughts about family members and significant others coming to the session. What will it mean and feel like?

6. Session and Client Evaluation

a. Have client complete the CSES for this session.

b. When doing the Provider Session Evaluation Summary (PSES) address these questions:

1) *Was there evidence of understanding of the techniques and benefits of problem solving and thinking of alternatives and consequences?*

2) *Is there an indication (at least in some of the members) that they are enthusiastic about learning new ways to cope with life...that they are ready to change?*

Session ⑳ : Involving Significant Others

1. Rationale

The role of social support in maintaining physical and mental health is well documented in psychological and behavioral medicine literature. The AOD client's circle of support may have lessened because of the disruptive nature of the drug use or criminal conduct pattern. The client may feel let down by lack of support, even though the client's behavior is directly related to this decrease of support. However, the support of family and significant others (SOs) is one of the most valuable resources the client may have (Kadden et al., 1992).

Monti and his colleagues (1989) encourage the participation of significant others but warn that there is frequently a great deal of *distrust and miscommunication* in families where substance abuse and antisocial behavior have been a problem. They suggest limiting skills training to safe areas of communication such as "giving and receiving compliments, criticism, assertiveness and nonverbal behavior" at least early in treatment (p. 139). Obviously, in a single session with the SOs, the goals should be modest, hoping to encourage the beginning of honest, caring communication about the behavior problems and how they impact the lives of the families and/or friends.

Miller and associates (1994) feel that there are significant advantages to involving SOs in treatment, especially when there will be an opportunity for them to work together in resolving issues that might impair the attainment of treatment goals. They enumerate several goals for involving the SO in treatment, including among others:

- raising awareness of the severity of the problem;
- strengthening the SO's commitment to helping the abuser;
- understanding the importance of the SO's role in helping to change the behavior;
- promoting increased satisfaction and solidarity of the partner's relationship.

The feedback of the SO regarding the damage the SAO's behavior may have caused to the relationship and the family may be sufficient to push the client into a final decision to change. It may emphasize to the group member the danger of losing family if the choice is to continue to behave as in the past. It is important however, that the client not become overwhelmed and ganged up on. One technique to achieve this is to allow the client to respond to a comment before eliciting any additional statements from the SO. If comments have been especially harsh, one may ask for encouraging and affirming statements from the SO.

It is important that the goals of the SO be consistent with those of the client in order for them to work together to solidify the commitment to change. The focus of the session should be the SAO, not the SO. The goal is always to *encourage and motivate* the client, not to intimidate.

2. Session Objectives

> ⇒ Provide an opportunity for the SOs to get acquainted with the program and begin to feel comfortable about being involved in the future.
>
> ⇒ Provide a supportive environment for communication between the SAO and SO to communicate about what the client's progress has been in the program.
>
> ⇒ Give the client's significant other(s) opportunity to discuss the effects that the offender's behavior has had on SO(s) and/or the family. This knowledge may increase the likelihood of commitment to change.
>
> ⇒ Allow the SO to express his/her expectations for the relationship in light of the current goals of the SAO and assess the compatibility of those goals.

3. Session Content

a. Our need for closeness and our need for separateness

A famous psychologist by the name of Abraham Maslow concluded that people have five basic needs (Maslow, 1954). These are:

1) *Physiological Needs:* Needs for that which sustains life such as food, air, sleep, elimination and water;

2) *Safety Needs:* Need for protection from danger and threat;

3) *Social Needs:* Need for friendship, acceptance, love;

4) *Esteem Needs:* Need for self-esteem or to have self confidence and self-respect; need for esteem from others, to be recognized, be important and be appreciated;

5) *Self-Actualization Needs:* Need to fulfill your talents; to bring out from within you your best.

What is important here is that we have two important needs in relationship to people around us. We have a need to be loved, to be in a relationship, to be close to people. But we have a need to be ourselves, to be individual, to be separate and to fulfill the best within us. How do we balance these two needs? We do this by respecting both of these needs in ourselves and in others. We need to put energy and effort into keeping healthy and meaningful relationships. We need to keep and maintain our self as a separate human being. We need to give to relationships; we need to give to ourselves.

The three diagrams below in Figure 22 indicate how we might see the relationship between the need for closeness and the need for separateness. **Circles Set One** shows a situation where there is no individuality in the relationship; it is all relationship. The person cannot go fishing, read the paper, or do anything separate without the relationship trying to control the person. **Circles Set Two** shows no relationship, and the individual's energy is directed only at the self. **Circles Set Three** shows a good balance; there is separateness of the individual, and there is closeness and relationship.

As we involve our SOs in our program, it is important that we keep this balance in mind. What we think about and do in our relationships will have a very important influence on how meaningful these relationships become to us. We now know that our AOD behavior and our behavior that got us into trouble with the law affected our relationships with our family and people close to us.

b. Involvement of your significant other(s) in this program

You were asked to bring a person or people who are close to you to this session. Up to now, you have been in the program without having them involved. Now we would like to have them feel a part of this program. There are four ways that your family members and people close to you may be involved in the program beyond this session:

1) Join a *Significant Others Support Group;*

2) Depending on the outcome of our in-depth assessment to be done in our next Module, you and your spouse, significant other, or close adult family member are asked to join a *Multi-Family Problem Solving Reflection Group.* This group will be directed at solving problems. It is not set up to be a therapy group. You can be in that group as long as you want with your significant others until you feel you have addressed and solved the problems you may have between and among you;

3) Depending upon the results of the in-depth assessment to be done in Module 7, you and your significant partner or family members may be referred to more in-depth marital or family counseling;

4) Your SOs will be asked to join you in two of our *Special Programs for Change* sessions.

c. **Multi-Family Problem Solving Reflection Group**

Most of this session will be spent in a reflection group with your significant other(s) and family members. We will do the following in this group tonight:

1) Make introductions;

2) Have clients talk about what has been the most meaningful parts of Phase I;

3) What have the SOs in your life noticed as to your being involved in this program? What changes have they noticed? What has this change meant to them?

4) You will present your thinking report homework in the group so that your SOs will have a feeling for some of the kinds of homework you do and how you present that in the group;

5) Ask selected clients to share the *thinking report* they did last week in the Multi-Family Problem Solving reflection group, if time allows. This should be voluntary, and client confidentiality should not be compromised.

d. **On-going Multi-Family Problem Solving and Reflection Group**

1) It is recommended that the Provider start an open-ended Multi-Family Problem Solving reflection group which meets at least twice monthly and is on-going;

2) Although the group should be led by a staff member of the Provider's agency, it is recommended that the group be as self-directed as possible, and that leadership within the group should be encouraged.

4. Classroom and Homework Activities

a. Social Support: (Adapted from Monti et al., 1989, pp. 209-210). Describe a problem that you would like help with now. Who might help you with this problem? What would you want this person to do that would be helpful? How can you ask this person for help? What do you think you should say to get help with your problem? Pick a good time to ask this person for help and do it. What was the outcome? Describe what happened in your *journal*.

b. Preparing for Module 8, the In-Depth Self-Assessment: To prepare for next session, have each client complete *Work Sheet 17* in the Workbook. THIS IS EXTREMELY IMPORTANT. It lays the groundwork for the in-depth assessment.

5. Presentation Sequence

a. Have SOs and clients introduce each other in the group. Have each person share in the group something important or unique about themselves.

b. Present the Relationship Circles concept and other session content information outlined above as seen appropriate.

c. Proceed with the reflection group and follow the discussion outline above. Don't forget to have the client share the homework thinking report in group. If it is too sensitive, have the client share another thinking report.

d. Discuss homework for next session.

Figure 22

Description of Relationship Balance Between Closeness and Separateness

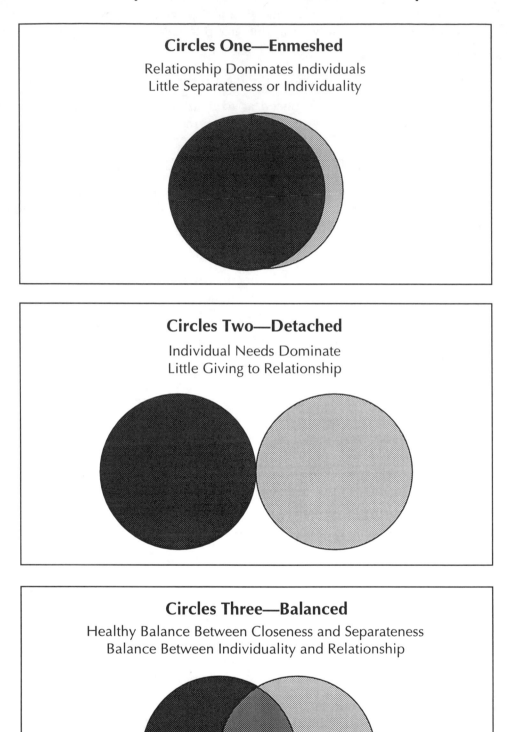

Circles One—Enmeshed

Relationship Dominates Individuals
Little Separateness or Individuality

Circles Two—Detached

Individual Needs Dominate
Little Giving to Relationship

Circles Three—Balanced

Healthy Balance Between Closeness and Separateness
Balance Between Individuality and Relationship

6. Session Evaluation

a. Have the client complete the CSES for the session.

b. Provider: Keep the following in mind when completing the PSES:

1) *Was communication in the session generally positive, especially in regard to increasing commitment to change and support from the SO? Has rapport increased between the couples?*

2) *Was there discord that was disruptive between the couples? If so, should the involved parties be referred for further counseling?*

MODULE 8

In-Depth Assessment:

Looking at the Areas
of Need and Change

MODULE 8: IN-DEPTH ASSESSMENT
LOOKING AT THE AREAS OF NEED AND CHANGE

Overview of Module 8

During the Challenge to Change phase of this program, clients were provided basic information around AOD use, criminal conduct and basic concepts regarding cognitive and behavioral change and reinforcement. Individualized assessment and treatment planning were not a primary focus. Clients were given opportunity and challenged to disclose both current and past conditions mainly for the purpose of developing self-awareness as a step toward change.

One of the goals of Phase II is to complete an in-depth, *differential assessment* of the client. This Module devotes two sessions of three hours each to this task. The Module is set up so as to represent a workshop type of process. The purpose of this assessment is to identify the client's specific conditions and problem areas that need to be addressed in the treatment program. This assessment will build on information about the client's AOD use patterns, criminal conduct and thinking patterns already acquired in Phase I. This information was gathered through the initial screening process, through testing done at the intake session, and through the Phase I sessions designed to enhance the client's self-disclosure about his or her current condition and thinking patterns.

The results of the in-depth program will be described graphically that will become the *map* for the client's commitment to change. It will identify the specific areas of change to be addressed in Module 9: *Strengthening Basic Skills for Self-Improvement and Change*. It will provide a guide for developing resources beyond the SSC program itself in order to meet the individual treatment needs of the client.

Goals and Objectives for Module 8

The overall goal of this module is to help clients take a closer look at their past and present problems and situation. The more specific objectives are

- Do a differential assessment in the following areas:
  - Patterns of AOD use and abuse;
  - Criminal conduct and dynamic risk factors;
  - Cognitive processing (patterns of thinking and feeling);
  - Background and current life situation problems and conditions of the client.

Specific conditions within each of these four areas will be assessed. From this assessment, both the *individual* and *generic* treatment plan can be finalized for each client.

- From these areas of assessment, identify specific areas to address and specific targets of change.
- Develop the Commitment to Change Program and individualized treatment plan.

Time and Presentation Structure for Module 8

Two three-hour sessions will be used for this Module. Some of the testing for the differential assessment was done at Intake and Admission to the program. Additional testing will be done during the sessions. Thus, three hours per session will be needed. Clients will score their own test, draw their profiles and complete the program and individual treatment plan.

Most work will be done within the session. Much of the work will be done by the individual alone with staff providing assistance when needed. Each client will share the results of the assessment with the group. Clients will have the discretion to share what they feel is appropriate and comfortable for them.

The homework for this session was done following Session 20, using *Work Sheet 17, "List of Problems to Work On."* The client will utilize all information gathered in order to complete the Master Profile and the Master Assessment Plan in the Workbook. A more detailed description of the assessment process is provided in Chapter 12 of Section II.

The Self-Disclosure and Feedback Communication Channels as the Framework for Assessment

One of the basic assumptions of this CBT SSC program is that change occurs through a *partnership* between the client and the provider and the client and the group. Assessment becomes meaningful only when self-disclosure is facilitated and when there is a strong feedback process that allows the client to receive back what the client has shared.

Self-disclosure and *feedback,* then, are the two key communication channels that have been the basis of much of what we have done with clients in this program. Effective assessment is able to tap more deeply into the self-disclosure channel of communication. The differential and in-depth assessment will use self-report instruments to enhance the *self-disclosure* channel. The *feedback* channel is used when both the program staff and clients give feedback to each individual in the program. The client was introduced to these two channels in Module 4.

What are the sources of information that go into assessment? One source is information the client knows about him/herself that others do not know. There is also information that others can see and that is obvious that the client may not be aware of. Then there is information about the person that the person knows and other people know. Finally, there is information about the person that is unknown. Sometimes we call this the *unconscious*.

The *Johari Window* (Luft, 1969), Figure 23, can provide a framework for structuring the assessment communication channels and the sources of information. The Johari Window is named after Joe Luft and Harrington Ingram and represents a way of looking at the self. It also provides us with a framework for assessment. The goal in assessment is to expand the *Free Area* and shrink the *Blind and Hidden Areas*. Self-report instruments are self-disclosing methods to allow the client to disclose the hidden parts of self. Instrument profiles and the observations of staff and peers provides the basis for feedback and thus shrinking the *Blind Areas*.

As the client discloses and receives feedback, the *Free Area,* or what is known by the client and the provider, is expanded. Yet, that information needs to be organized and structured. This is the purpose of standardized questionnaires and tests. Such instruments allow the information that the client discloses to be organized into ideas, expressions, concepts or constructs. The instrument profile provides a picture of that information organized into a construct.

In this assessment process, the client will take the specific ideas or constructs from each of the tests and build what we will call the Master Profile. The provider will help the client interpret the individual test profiles and help the client to build the Master Profile. This will become the basis for developing the Master Assessment Plan (MAP). This master plan will become the MAP for the work that the client will do in the rest of the program. As additional information becomes available about clients through their disclosure and feedback from others, both the MP and the MAP will be revised. Such revisions may take the client into other areas or territories of change.

Figure 23

The Assessment Framework: The Johari Window

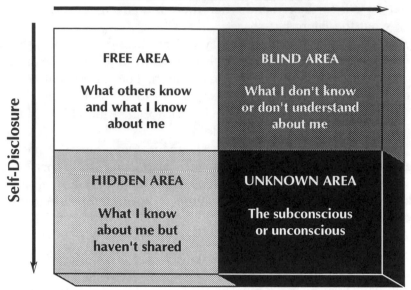

Solicits or Receives Feedback

Self-Disclosure

FREE AREA	BLIND AREA
What others know and what I know about me	What I don't know or don't understand about me
HIDDEN AREA	UNKNOWN AREA
What I know about me but haven't shared	The subconscious or unconscious

Adapted from Luft (1969). Reprinted by permission of Mayfield Publishing Co., formerly National Press.

Session ㉑ : In-Depth Assessment: Getting the Information to Plot the Master Profile

1. Rationale for Session

Change occurs when the individual is self-aware. Often many areas of change are not seen clearly by the SAO client. *Self-disclosing* through sharing in individual interviews or group sessions provides one basis for understanding these areas of change. We can organize these kinds of disclosure into what we call *ratings,* or how the provider sees the client in a certain area of problems. For example, the provider may rate the client high on marriage problems. We call this *other-report* data.

The other basis for developing information so as to increase self-awareness is through *self-report information*. This occurs through self-administered tests and questionnaires. Information from this source gets structured and organized into ideas that can be understood. We display these constructs or ideas into profiles. This profile then becomes the basis for developing the Master Assessment Plan.

This session will intensify our gathering of information about the client and will help construct the Master Profile. This profile will provide the guideline for developing our overall treatment plan (MAP).

The methods and procedures for this assessment, including the specific areas of assessment and the tools and tests to be used, are presented in Chapter 12.

2. Objectives of Session

The overall goal of this session is facilitate the client's disclosure of information and data pertaining to the assessment of several important areas of life adjustment risk factors. This information will be used to construct the client's Master Profile that will graphically describe the client across these major risk factor areas. More specifically, the objectives of this session are

> ➠ Clients will complete and score the self-administered tests that will provide an in-depth look at problems associated with AOD use, criminal conduct and other life adjustment risk factors;
>
> ➠ Clients will complete the List of Problems to Work On, *Work Sheet 17,* which was the client's homework for this past week.

3. Session Content

a. Introduction to session

At this point in our program, it is important for you to develop a Master Assessment Plan or MAP for change. Up to this time, you have shared a lot about yourself. Much of this information has been about the general areas of your AOD use and your involvement in criminal conduct. Now, we will look more in depth at these two areas. We will give you a chance to tell us more about how you see yourself doing in a number of other areas. We will want to see if there are specific problem areas and conditions that you need to address and change. This information will help you get the most out of the *Basic Skills for Self-Improvement and Change* sessions and your individual treatment plan.

An important part of Cognitive-Behavioral Treatment is that change occurs through a *partnership* between you and your provider and your peers in the program. Thus, this in-depth look at yourself will be done together with your provider, and in some ways, with the peers in your group. But this in-depth evaluation is for you—it is to benefit *you.*

b. The Assessment Window

We now know that we learn about ourselves through sharing and disclosing and through the feedback we get from others. *Self-disclosure* and *feedback* are two very important ways that we communicate with others. There are several areas of information about ourselves that are communicated. There are things we know about ourselves that others do not know. This is the

Hidden Area. There are things that others see about us that we don't see. That is the *Blind Area*. There are things about ourselves we do not know and others do not know. This is the *Unknown Area*. Then there are things about ourselves that we see and know and that other people see and know. This is called the *Free Area* or the *Open Area*. Our goal of assessment is to *increase* that *Open Area*.

The *Johari Window* in Figure 23 gives us a picture of these areas of information. This is a way of looking at and understanding the self. The goal of this module is to make the Free Area larger and to shrink the Blind and Hidden areas. This will be done through tests and surveys that allow you to report more about yourself. You will also do this through getting feedback from others. From all of this, you will put together what we will call a *Master Profile* (MP). This MP will become the guide for making up a *Master Assessment Plan* (MAP). The Master Profile will help you to organize and put together all of this information about yourself. From the Master Profile, you will develop the Master Assessment Plan.

c. **The areas of in-depth study and self-assessment**

Our in-depth study of ourselves involves looking at several important areas of our life in order to understand our thoughts and behavior habits, and to identify problems that have developed from these habits and patterns. We began to prepare for this self-study through our work on the Problem Focus Work Sheet *(Work Sheet 17)* that was part of this week's homework. We will now complete that work sheet in class. Here is an outline of the important areas of our life that we will address:

1) Alcohol and Other Drug use and abuse:

- Drugs of choice;

- Styles of use;

- Benefits of using alcohol and other drugs;

- Type of problems from use;

- Readiness for help;

- Degree of problems from use.

2) Criminal and Antisocial Thinking and Conduct:

- Degree of involvement in criminal conduct;

- Type of involvement (property offenses, person offenses, etc.);

- Antisocial attitudes and thinking and criminogenic needs.

3) Thinking and Feeling Patterns:

- Victim Stance: Blame projection;

- Narrow or restricted thinking;

- Personalizing-feeling victimized;

- Superior or grandiose thinking;

- Self-centered (narcissistic) thinking;

- Self-defeating thinking (depressed, put self down);

- Antisocial and irresponsible thinking.

4) Background Problems and Adjustment:

- Adolescent AOD use;

- Delinquency;

- Family problems;

- School problems.

5) Current life-situation problems:

- Employment and job productivity;

- Residential stability;

- Social-interpersonal;

- Marital-family relationship adjustment;

- Health;

- Psychological-emotional;

- Legal and criminal.

6) Interest and readiness for treatment.

- Awareness of AOD/CC problems:

- Acknowledge need for help;

- Willingness to accept help;

- Other perception of my need for help;

- Taken action to change.

7) Stage of change:

- Challenged to change;

- Commitment to change;

- Taking ownership of change.

d. **Exercises for session**

1) Complete the following instruments:

- Life Situation Questionnaire (LSQ);

- Mood Appraisal Questionnaire;

- Addictions Severity Index (do as a group).

2) Clients will score the following instruments taken at admissions and construct profiles:

- Alcohol Use Inventory (or equivalent instrument);

- Drug Use Self Report (or equivalent instrument).

3) Construct the Profile on the other instruments.

4) Use the *Johari Window* as a basis for discussing what clients learned from the various tests and profiles. Have clients discuss their alcohol and drug use patterns in group. Share what they learned from completing *Work Sheet 17*.

5) For the next session, use all of the following tests and information in developing your Master Profile and your Master Assessment Plan:

- The tests that you took before you entered this program and that you took again in Sessions 12 and 13. These are
  - Level of Service Inventory;
  - Alcohol Use Questionnaire (measures the Alcohol Dependence Syndrome—ADS);
  - Drug Use Questionnaire (DAST-20);
  - Adult Substance Use Survey (ASUS);
  - Simple Screening Inventory (SSI).
- The tests you took at admission to program:
  - Alcohol Use Inventory (AUI);
  - Drug Use Self Report (DUSR).
- The tests you took in this session:
  - Mood Appraisal Questionnaire (MAQ);
  - Life Situation Questionnaire (LSQ);
  - Addictions Severity Index (ASI).
  - The Problem Focus Work Sheet *(Work Sheet 17)*.

4. Homework Assignment

Providers may opt to assign the LSQ as homework.

5. Presentation Sequence

a. Rehash last week's session.

b. Present the material in the Introduction section of Module 8 and in the Rationale and Session Content sections for this session. Take about 20 minutes for this.

c. Have the client complete the following tests:
- Addiction Severity Index (done as a group);
- Life Situation Questionnaire (may do as homework);
- Mood Appraisal Questionnaire.

d. Score all tests including the AUI and DUSR and all other instruments and construct profiles for various instruments. This will take considerable time, and each client will need assistance. It is recommended that mentors or staff assistants help with this process.

e. Close session with reflection group and have clients use the *Johari Window* as a basis for sharing and receiving feedback regarding their testing.

6. No formal evaluation for this session.

Session ㉒ : Targets of Change and the Master Assessment Plan (MAP)

1. Rationale for Session

This is a continuation of Session 21 of this Module. The purpose of this session is to organize the information gathered in Session 21 into a *Master Profile*. From this profile, we will put together a *Master Assessment Plan* or the client's MAP for change. This will help the client identify target areas of change and the resources to be used in making change. The MP and MAP provide the differential assessment basis upon which to build both the programmatic focus and the individualized treatment plan.

2. Objectives of Session

> ⫸ Have clients complete their *Master Profile* (MP) from the self-report and other-report database;
>
> ⫸ Have each client develop a *Master Assessment Plan* (MAP).

3. Session Content and Exercises

a. **Introduction**

You have given information about yourself in the tests and questionnaires you completed and in the information you gave through the homework you did on the *Life Problems Work Sheet 17* (p. 124 in Workbook). You have looked at the results of these tests. Now we will make a Master Profile (Figure 24 below and *Work Sheet 18*, p. 134 in Workbook). From this, we will help you make a Master Assessment Plan (Figure 25 below and *Work Sheet 19*, p. 137 in Workbook). This plan or MAP will be a guide for you during the next five months of this program. Your MAP will change as you add new problems.

b. **Exercise 1:** Have clients develop the Master Profile (MP), *Work Sheet 18*. Use Figure 24 as a guide. First complete Part I of the MP, the Alcohol and Other Drug Use Assessment. Use the results from the AUI, the DUSR and the ASI (or comparable instruments). Then, have clients complete the other parts of the MP, using the relevant questionnaire data and information and profiles.

c. **Exercise 2:** Using *Work Sheet 19*, have clients complete the MAP from the MP. Use Figure 25 as a guide. Have them identify a specific problem area, what changes in thinking and action need to be made and the specific treatment activities needed to correct and change the problem. Identify as many problems as you want for each of the four main areas.

4. Classroom or Homework Assignments

a. **Complete exercises 1 and 2 above.**

b. **Reflect on the Master Profile.**

Have client give some thought to his/her Master Profile this week. Is it accurate? Did the client feel he or she was honest in completing the questionnaires and test upon which the MAP was developed?

c. **Assessing a problem area in the MAP.**

Have clients take one problem in the MAP and have them evaluate changes they have made in that area or changes they need to make. For a homework assignment, have clients discuss this one problem area with someone they trust or feel close to. Have clients record in their *Journal* the feedback they received from the other person.

5. Presentation Sequence

a. Give overview of the MP and the MAP.

b. Help each client complete the profile. There may be other areas or problems not in the profile. Add these to the appropriate part of the profile. If one pertains to AOD use, add it to the AOD section of the MP.

c. Construct the MAP.

d. Have clients discuss their MAP in the reflection group.

e. **IMPORTANT: INTRODUCE CLIENTS TO MODULE 9. This is particularly important for programs that are using an *open-ended* model for Module 9. Clients need to be told that they will be entering a Module 9 group which is already in progress. The provider needs to allow for 30 minutes to introduce Module 9.**

6. Evaluation

a. Have client complete the CSES.

b. Provider completes the PSES.

c. Complete the Behavioral Rating Form (BRF) and score the form.

Figure 24: MASTER PROFILE (MP)

I. Alcohol and Other Drug Use Assessment

	Area of Assessment	Low				Moderate				High	
Drug Choice	Alcohol Involvement	1	2	3	4	5	6	7	8	9	10
	Marijuana Involvement	1	2	3	4	5	6	7	8	9	10
	Cocaine Involvement	1	2	3	4	5	6	7	8	9	10
	Amphetamine Involvement	1	2	3	4	5	6	7	8	9	10
	Other Drug Involvement	1	2	3	4	5	6	7	8	9	10
	Poly Drug User	1	2	3	4	5	6	7	8	9	10

	Area of Assessment	Low				Moderate				High	
Style	Convivial or Gregarious	1	2	3	4	5	6	7	8	9	10
	Sustained & Continuous	1	2	3	4	5	6	7	8	9	10
	Compulsive & Obsessive	1	2	3	4	5	6	7	8	9	10

	Area of Assessment	Low				Moderate				High	
Benefits	Cope with Social Discomfort	1	2	3	4	5	6	7	8	9	10
	Cope with Emotional Discomfort	1	2	3	4	5	6	7	8	9	10
	Cope with Relationships	1	2	3	4	5	6	7	8	9	10
	Cope with Physical Distress	1	2	3	4	5	6	7	8	9	10

	Area of Assessment	Low				Moderate				High	
Results	Behavioral Control Loss	1	2	3	4	5	6	7	8	9	10
	Emotional Disruption	1	2	3	4	5	6	7	8	9	10
	Physical Disruption	1	2	3	4	5	6	7	8	9	10
	Social Irresponsibility	1	2	3	4	5	6	7	8	9	10
	Overall Disruption	1	2	3	4	5	6	7	8	9	10

	Area of Assessment	Low				Moderate				High	
Ready	AOD Problem Awareness	1	2	3	4	5	6	7	8	9	10
	Treatment Receptiveness	1	2	3	4	5	6	7	8	9	10
	Motivation to Change	1	2	3	4	5	6	7	8	9	10

Figure 24: MASTER PROFILE (continued)

II. Criminal and Antisocial Thinking and Conduct

	Level of Problem Severity									
Area of Assessment	**Low**				**Moderate**				**High**	
Conduct Property Offenses I	1	2	3	4	5	6	7	8	9	10
Property Offenses II	1	2	3	4	5	6	7	8	9	10
Person Offenses I	1	2	3	4	5	6	7	8	9	10
Person Offenses II	1	2	3	4	5	6	7	8	9	10
Motor Vehicle—Non AOD	1	2	3	4	5	6	7	8	9	10
Motor Vehicle—AOD Involved	1	2	3	4	5	6	7	8	9	10

	Level of Problem Severity									
Area of Assessment	**Low**				**Moderate**				**High**	
Criminal Thinking Antisocial Peers & Models	1	2	3	4	5	6	7	8	9	10
Impulsive Thinking/Acting	1	2	3	4	5	6	7	8	9	10
Self-Centered Thinking	1	2	3	4	5	6	7	8	9	10
Criminal Thinking/Thoughts	1	2	3	4	5	6	7	8	9	10
Need for Family Attachment	1	2	3	4	5	6	7	8	9	10
Social/Interpersonal Skills	1	2	3	4	5	6	7	8	9	10
Problem Solving/Self-Management	1	2	3	4	5	6	7	8	9	10
Angry/Aggressive Attitude	1	2	3	4	5	6	7	8	9	10
Rebellious/Anti-Authority	1	2	3	4	5	6	7	8	9	10

III. Assessment of Thinking and Feeling Patterns

	Level of Problem Severity									
Area of Assessment	**Low**				**Moderate**				**High**	
Thinking Blame, Victim Stance	1	2	3	4	5	6	7	8	9	10
Narrow-Restricted Thinking	1	2	3	4	5	6	7	8	9	10
Personalizing Responses	1	2	3	4	5	6	7	8	9	10
Superior/Grandiose Thinking	1	2	3	4	5	6	7	8	9	10
Self-Defeating Thinking	1	2	3	4	5	6	7	8	9	10
Irresponsible Thinking	1	2	3	4	5	6	7	8	9	10
Self-Centered Thinking	1	2	3	4	5	6	7	8	9	10

Figure 24: MASTER PROFILE (continued)

IV. Background: Problems of Childhood and Development

	Area of Assessment	Low				Moderate				High	
Ready	AOD Use Adolescence	1	2	3	4	5	6	7	8	9	10
	Delinquency	1	2	3	4	5	6	7	8	9	10
	Family Problems	1	2	3	4	5	6	7	8	9	10
	Cope with Physical Distress	1	2	3	4	5	6	7	8	9	10

V. Current Life Situations Problems

	Area of Assessment	Low				Moderate				High	
Current Stage	Job and Employment Problems	1	2	3	4	5	6	7	8	9	10
	Residential Instability	1	2	3	4	5	6	7	8	9	10
	Social/Interpersonal Problems	1	2	3	4	5	6	7	8	9	10
	Marital/Family Problems	1	2	3	4	5	6	7	8	9	10
	Health and Physical Problems	1	2	3	4	5	6	7	8	9	10
	Emotional/Psychological	1	2	3	4	5	6	7	8	9	10

VI. Motivation and Readiness for Treatment

	Rate Each Stage Separately	Low				Moderate				High	
Readiness	Awareness of AOD/CC Problem	1	2	3	4	5	6	7	8	9	10
	Acknowledgement of Need for Help	1	2	3	4	5	6	7	8	9	10
	Willingness to Accept Help	1	2	3	4	5	6	7	8	9	10
	Other's Perception of Need	1	2	3	4	5	6	7	8	9	10
	Has Taken Action to Change	1	2	3	4	5	6	7	8	9	10

VII. Stage of Change

	Rate Each Stage Separately	Low				Moderate				High	
Stage	Challenged to Change	1	2	3	4	5	6	7	8	9	10
	Commitment to Change	1	2	3	4	5	6	7	8	9	10
	Ownership of Change	1	2	3	4	5	6	7	8	9	10

Figure 25: Master Assessment Plan (MAP) Work Sheet

I. Alcohol and Other Drug Use Problem Areas

Problem Area & Description	Changes Needed in Thought & Action	Programs & Resources to Be Used to Make Changes	Date Worked On

II. Criminal and Antisocial Thinking and Conduct

Problem Area & Description	Changes Needed in Thought & Action	Programs & Resources to Be Used to Make Changes	Date Worked On

III. Thinking and Feeling Patterns

Problem Area & Description	Changes Needed in Thought & Action	Programs & Resources to Be Used to Make Changes	Date Worked On

IV. Current Life Situation Problems

Problem Area & Description	Changes Needed in Thought & Action	Programs & Resources to Be Used to Make Changes	Date Worked On

MODULE
9

Strengthening Basic Skills for Self-Improvement and Change:

Acting on the Commitment to Change

MODULE 9: STRENGTHENING BASIC SKILLS FOR SELF-IMPROVEMENT AND CHANGE: ACTING ON THE COMMITMENT TO CHANGE

Overview of Module 9

Module 9 is made up of a series of skill building sessions over a period of 18 weeks. All of the previous modules and their respective sessions were in preparation for this component of Phase II. It is a final test of the client's commitment to action. This is not to say that the client has *not* demonstrated commitment up to this point. Without commitment to change, the client would not have progressed this far in treatment.

The specific programs of change that make up this Module are directed at skill building—building interpersonal and intrapersonal skills to make change in the thoughts, feelings and behavior that lead to AOD use and abuse and criminal conduct.

Goals and Objectives of Module 9

The overall goal of Module 9 is to have the client demonstrate, through the learning and use of basic intrapersonal and interpersonal skills, substantial changes in cognitive and behavioral sets that will strengthen *prosocial lifestyles* and *AOD abstinence*. These skills will provide clients with the self-confidence and mastery to bring about changes in their lives and to strengthen positive thoughts about themselves and how they relate to others and their community. The specific aims of Module 9 follow.

- In order to help clients manage their *social and interpersonal* world, they will learn the following coping and communication skills:
  - Communicate and express feelings, thoughts and beliefs to others and to help others do the same;
  - Initiate and reinforce effective interpersonal interactions;
  - Effectively handle social and intimate interpersonal relationships and expectations (e.g., marriage, intimate partner relationships; social involvement);
  - Effective assertiveness in relationship to others;
  - Prevent aggression and violence;
  - Practice empathy.

- In order to help clients manage and cope with their *cognitive and intrapersonal* world, they will learn to
  - Recognize and manage negative thoughts and negative thinking;
  - Manage and respond effectively to the emotional and intrapersonal needs and problems in the areas of stress, anger, guilt and depression;
  - Effectively manage attitudes, beliefs and errors in logic and thinking which lead to AOD abuse and CC;
  - Solve problems with problem solving skills.

- In order to help clients manage and cope with the *cravings, urges and need to engage* in AOD use and criminal activities, the client will learn to
  - Identify high-risk situations and thinking for AOD use and criminal conduct;
  - Manage AOD cravings and urges;
  - Utilize AOD refusal skills;
  - Utilize CC refusal skills.

- In order to help clients to *develop positive responses and social responsibility,* the client will
  - Understand the meaning of values and moral development and apply the skills of moral responsibility to community living;

- Enhance positive and responsible driving attitudes;
- Review the MP and MAP from time to time to see how the *Basic Skills for Change* help clients to achieve the goals of their MAP.

The Structure for Module 9

Module 9 will run for approximately 18 weeks. Sessions will be two and one-half hours in length to include breaks. This module will be conducted in an open-ended group manner; new participants will enter at appropriate *break-points*. These *break-points* for introducing new group members are indicated in the manual as the sessions of Module 9 are presented. Some sessions are sequential, and the integrity of the sequence needs to be maintained. As new participants are enrolled in this module, session time needs to be devoted to getting acquainted.

Session 23: Coping and Social Skills Training: Basic Communication Skills—Active Sharing and Active Listening

Break-Point: Sessions 1 through 3 are delivered in sequence. New participants may be brought into the program at this point.

1. Rationale and Overview of the Session

Both offenders and substance abusers suffer from a deficit in *social skills,* both interpersonal and intrapersonal; however, it has been shown that the necessary skills can be taught. Without adequate social skill, an individual's ability to communicate is restricted, leaving him/her without control or alternatives in certain situations. Frequently such deficits restrict the ability of the person to obtain social and emotional support from others and contribute to criminal behavior or substance abuse. Intrapersonal factors, such as reduced coping ability, negative thinking, stress and anxiety, may also contribute to undesirable behavior. The purpose of the training in this module is to give the SAO new skills with which to solve personal problems and to avoid the problems before they start (Monti et al., 1989; Ross et al., 1986).

We will start out our coping, interpersonal and intrapersonal skills training program by building the foundation for good communication. All communication is based on the two sets of skills we will learn in this session:

- active sharing;
- active listening.

Active sharing is *self-directed communication.* Active listening is called *other-directed* communication. Active sharing is the only way you can tell others about your feelings, thoughts and needs. Active listening is the only way you can learn about others. This involves listening skills which are important in getting people to talk and relate to you. Listening gives you insight into the perspective others have of a situation and allows them to re-examine their own perspective. When one listens attentively, it encourages self-disclosure and gives an opportunity to learn things about the other person.

There is overwhelming evidence of the efficacy of reciprocity in self-disclosure. Based on Jourard's early hypothesis (Jourard, 1959) and continued research by him and his colleagues (e.g., Jourard & Friedman, 1970; Jourard & Resnick, 1970) and many other studies (see Cappella, 1985, p.409), self-disclosing to another person will facilitate self-disclosure in the other person. Further, partners tend to match the level of self-disclosure.

We will also look again at the two types of communication of verbal and non-verbal. Both of these are basic to the use and practice of the skills of active sharing and active listening.

2. Objectives of Session

> ➡ To learn and practice the basic skills of self-oriented communication—**Active Sharing—** and how one uses these skills in everyday conversations;
>
> ➡ To learn and practice the basic skills of other-oriented communication—**Active Listening—** and how one uses these skills in everyday conversations.

3. Session Content and Process

a. **THERE IS POWER IN WHAT WE ARE ABOUT TO LEARN AND PRACTICE. IT IS THE POWER OF COMMUNICATION. IT IS THE POWER OF TALKING AND THE POWER OF LISTENING.**

b. **Communication is a two-way street.**

As we have learned, there are two key parts to communication:

1) Active sharing;

2) Active listening.

Self-disclosure is accomplished through the use of active sharing skills. Active sharing (self-directed or self-oriented communication) is important in sharing both positive and negative feelings, and sharing our thoughts and feelings is a key to good communication process. But communication is a *two-way street*. Other-directed communication is just as important. We accomplish this through active listening. Listening requires more than just sitting quietly while the other person talks or speaks. BUT REMEMBER, WHEN WE SELF-DISCLOSE, OTHERS ARE MORE APT TO SELF-DISCLOSE. SO ACTIVE SHARING PRODUCES THE MATERIAL FOR ACTIVE LISTENING. We'll look at these two ways to communicate.

c. **Active Sharing.**

There are two key skills in active sharing or self-directed communication. To be successful in this, these must be used:

1) The first skill is telling the other person about you; using the "I" message. This is talk about you. There are four basic parts to this communication:

  - I feel;

  - I need;

  - I think;

  - I do or I act.

  The most unselfish thing you can do is to start a sentence off with "I." Why? Because when you use the word "I" you share yourself. That is not selfish. Active sharing is about you, not about the other person. It's not bragging. It's just being honest about you. Most important, you hear yourself through you.

2) The second key skill to active sharing is being open and listening *to feedback from others about you*. You hear yourself through others. This is hard to do. But you give people permission to do this. When people talk about you—it should be on the basis that you give them permission. The key to receiving feedback is to *not get defensive*. When we get defensive—or push away and ward off—with someone who gives us feedback, then we stop that person from giving us feedback. If the feedback is critical or negative, we often get openly defensive. But even when the feedback is a compliment or positive, we still tend to push that feedback away. We will look at the skill of receiving compliments in a later session.

Exercise: Do a round-robin in *group* by having everyone share a personal experience. Have them practice "I" feel, "I" think, "I" see statements. Then have each person request feedback from several people in the group about themselves.

Exercise: Break up into triads. One person shares, one listens, one observes. Have clients share a real experience. Have them keep the focus on themselves.

d. **Active Listening.**

1) There are two key skills in other-directed or other-oriented communication or active listening communication:

  - The first is to invite the other person to share by using OPEN STATEMENTS OR QUESTIONS: "How are you today?" "Tell me more about your accident." Avoid "Do you?"

questions. Those are closed questions. Closed statements get a *yes* or *no* answer. This is hard to do because we usually are looking for the other person to confirm our beliefs. We often have an *agenda*. If we have an *agenda,* then we will ask closed questions to get the answer we want. But if we are truly interested in what the other person has to say, we will not try to get the answer we want; we will try to get the other person to tell us about themselves.

- Reflect back what you hear the other person saying. "I hear you saying you are upset." "You seem to feel happy today." *When our invitation is more open ("tell me about you")* rather than closed (*"did you do that?"),* then we will get more from the other person to reflect back to them. When we reflect back what we hear the other person saying, we tell them *we are listening,* and we also better understand what they are saying. This helps us in understanding the other person.

2) We have to really work to listen to other people's talk. It requires working to really grasp what the other person is saying. This is what we pay attention to:

- THEIR WORDS

- THE TONE OF THEIR VOICE

- THEIR BODY TALK.

3) What helps us to practice other-directed communication and to actively listen? First, we must learn to bypass our thinking filters: This means we choose an *open channel* to listen:

Our *thinking filters* are the screens through which we run what other people say. These thinking filters are our beliefs, our attitudes and our values. We don't have to give up these beliefs and attitudes to listen. We can have an open *listening channel.* We can then make our response come from that channel and not our *thinking filters.*

When we run what we see and hear through our *thinking filter*, we may twist and distort what we are hearing. It is easy to run it through our own "filters"—which are our beliefs and our attitudes and our values.

4) What helps us to practice other-directed communication and to actively listen? We *listen* to body talk. Here is some body talk that we can listen to and learn from:

- POSTURE;

- FACIAL EXPRESSION;

- TONE OF VOICE;

- PERSONAL SPACE;

- HAND, FACE AND FEET GESTURES.

5) What helps us to practice other-directed communication and to actively listen? We respect the other person's personal space:

Maintain a space of about *two feet* between you and the other person when engaged in a conversation, which is normally the *personal space* with which people feel comfortable. Different people and different cultures vary in this requirement, but this is probably a safe distance to start with.

6) Here are some points for good active listening:

- Look at the person you are talking with; establish eye contact;

- Watch the person's body language: facial expression, gestures, tone of voice;

- Pay attention to what is being said, try to understand. If you don't understand, ask open questions;

- When you do understand, nod your head to encourage the speaker;

- Round off the process by then using ACTIVE SHARING skills. Share who you are and what you feel and think with the other person—*self-disclose*. Then, *reflect back* what you hear; mirror back what you hear; this tells the other person you hear them.

Exercise: MODELING: Role-play a situation in which one party has just been busted for selling drugs. Demonstrate the two key skills of other-directed communication: *Inviting others* to share and *reflecting back* what you hear them say.

Exercise: ROLE-PLAY: Situation: One party doesn't show up for his/her appointment with a probation officer. Role-play the conversation in which s/he tries to explain what happened. Practice the two skills of other-directed communication: *Invitation* to talk; *reflecting*.

Exercise: Break up into groups of three. Again, have one share, one be the active listener and one observe. Have the observer give feedback on what he or she saw. PRACTICE...PRACTICE...PRACTICE...

- Inviting others to share with open questions and statements;
- Reflecting back what you heard them saying. It is parroting back; it is being a mirror.

4. Classroom and Homework Activities

a. For the first few days of this coming week, have clients practice only ACTIVE SHARING. Use *I messages* not *you messages*. Talk about you. Don't talk about the other person.

b. For the rest of the week, have clients focus on using invitations to talk and reflection. Have them reflect at the end of the day how successful they were.

c. Have clients do the ACTIVE SHARING *Work Sheet 20* in the classroom: Homework for Active Sharing.

d. Have clients do the ACTIVE LISTENING *Work Sheet 21* either in the classroom if time allows, or as homework, having them choose one of the following options and then addressing the statements in the Work Sheet (adapted from King et al., 1994):

Option 1. Start and continue a conversation with someone you know. Pay attention to the skills that have been discussed during this session;

Option 2. Watch a conversation between two other people, paying attention to the skills that have been discussed during this session.

5. Presentation Sequence

a. Review previous session and homework.

b. Discuss the rationale and objectives for Session 23.

c. Present content of session. Do exercise as outlined above.

d. Conduct modeling and role-playing exercises.

e. Discussion of exercises and role-play of influence of intoxicants.

f. Do *Work Sheets 20* and *21* either in class or for homework.

g. Discuss other homework activities.

h. Hold a reflection group and look at next session.

6. Session and Client Response Evaluation

   a. Have clients complete the CSES.

   b. Complete PSES. Attend to these issues:

   1) *Are the participants more able to role-play and interpret conversations and communication styles?*

   2) *Have they demonstrated an expanded knowledge of the skills that they need for effective communication?*

   3) *In role-playing and group, have they demonstrated active listening skills?*

Session 24 : Coping and Social Skills Training: Basic Communication Skills—Starting Conversations

1. Rationale and Overview of Session

We now start to build on the key foundation skills of active listening and active sharing. We use these foundation skills to learn and practice social and interpersonal coping skills. One important skill to build is that of starting a conversation. This is a basic communication skill—it is our door to communicating with those we know, to meeting new people, to buying a car, to getting a job. Sometimes people find themselves lonely and isolated because they do not feel confident around developing meaningful interactions and relationships. Often, this is due to a reticence in initiating talk and interactions with others. For many people, this becomes one of the reasons for becoming involved in a substance abuse pattern. Often, people who are highly anxious or who have negative feelings about themselves feel they cannot function in a social situation without a drink or a fix. Finally, to avoid the negative influence of former companions and accomplices, the SAO may be forced (and wise) to develop another social network—this cannot be done without conversational skills.

2. Objectives of Session

The following are the objectives for this session.

> ➡ Clients review the skills of active sharing and active listening;
>
> ➡ Clients understand the basic techniques involved in starting a conversation and improve communication skills;
>
> ➡ Clients develop the ability to communicate in unfamiliar situations.

3. Session Content and Process

In Session 10 of Module 4, we learned about verbal and non-verbal communication. In our last session, we also learned about *self-oriented* communication skills and *other-oriented* communication skills. Now we will take what we have learned from that session and look at one important area of communicating: Starting conversations.

a. **Remember two important parts of self-oriented communication:**

   1) *Self-disclosure:* talk about yourself; use the I message;

   2) *Receiving feedback:* be open to have people tell you about how they see you.

b. **Remember the two important parts of other-oriented communication:**

   1) Using *open statements* or questions to get people to tell you about themselves: "How are you feeling?" "Tell me about your fishing trip."

   2) Use *feedback* or reflective statements—act as a mirror for others—to have the other person feel that you are listening to them. We call this *reflective listening*.

   3) Conversations can be long or short—they should be fun for both parties.

   REMEMBER, THERE IS POWER IN COMMUNICATION. THERE IS POWER IN TALK. YOU WILL FEEL THIS POWER WHEN YOU PUT THESE COMMUNICATION SKILLS TO WORK.

c. **Suggestions for making or starting conversation more simple** (Monti et al., 1989, pp. 29-30):

   1) *You don't have to have an important topic.* What is important is to have fun in your conversations. Start with easy topics the other person is likely to be familiar with, like the weather.

2) *Conversation is a two-way process:* You don't have to do all the talking. Give the other person an opportunity to respond.

3) *It's ok to talk about yourself:* Although some people are uncomfortable doing this, how else are others going to learn if you like the same things, have similar values and beliefs? You don't have to tell your deepest secrets, but let them know simple things, like where you went to school or what kind of car you drive (or would like to drive). The level of self-disclosure that is appropriate varies with the circumstances. *REMEMBER, OTHER PEOPLE WILL BE MORE OPEN TO YOU IF YOU ARE OPEN WITH THEM.*

4) *Watch and listen to what is going on around you:* Watch body language. Listen to what is being said. What topics are interesting to others? Who looks bored with the conversation? When you start a conversation, don't interrupt—wait until there is a quiet time to make your comments.

5) *Speak up:* Don't wait for the person to talk to you. Make eye contact and say something. Remember that *small talk is ok.*

6) *Use open statements and open-ended questions:* Tell other people you want them to talk with you. Don't ask questions that can be answered with a simple "yes" or "no," but those that prompt a response. Don't ask, "Did you watch the game last night?" Do ask, "What did you think of that game last night?

7) *Conversations can be long or short, but they should be fun for both parties:* Watch the person you are talking with. Are they still interested and engaged in what is being said, or are they showing signs of being bored with what is going on? End the conversation diplomatically or change the topic if you see that your partner is losing interest.

8) *End the conversation gracefully:* When it is time to end the conversation, do it gracefully by saying "goodbye" in a pleasant way. "It has been very nice meeting you, I hope we see each other again." Most important is that you leave the other person with the impression that you enjoyed your talk with them. If you both feel the experience was pleasant, you are likely to want to talk with each other again.

d. **Exercises on starting conversations:**

Exercise: Have each member of the group contribute an idea of where to meet people or a place you might have to start a conversation with someone you don't know. As participants name the situation, have them talk about how hard—or easy—it would be to start a conversation in that situation. Is this something that would ordinarily give them problems, or does starting conversations come easily to them?

Exercise: Have the group take turns role-playing initiating an interaction or starting a conversation in these scenarios between two people:

• Two strangers at a party;

• Between two workers at coffee break, one of whom just came to work for the company;

• Two people who see each other for the first time since high school.

After scenarios are role-played, have the group discuss to what extent they demonstrated the skills introduced above and what could have been done to enhance the conversation. Have clients practice

• Self-disclosure through using "I" messages. Avoid using "you" messages;

• Receiving feedback from others;

- Using open-ended statements and questions;
- Using statements to reflect back what others are saying.

4. Review of Classroom or Homework Activities

a. Practice starting a conversation. Use skills learned above. Remember who, where, what you shared, how the other person responded, verbal and non-verbal communications used.

b. Do a thinking report on starting conversations. Use your *journal* to do this. Use one of these options:

Option 1. Describe a situation in which you were meeting someone that you were nervous about meeting. Do a *thinking report*.

Option 2. Do a *thinking report* on the conversation you had for homework.

Review the parts of the thinking report:

SITUATION;

THOUGHTS;

FEELINGS;

ATTITUDES AND BELIEFS ABOUT THE SITUATION;

OUTCOME OR WHAT HAPPENED.

5. Presentation Sequence

a. Review previous session and homework.

b. Review the rationale for Module 9.

c. Warm-up exercise-starting conversations.

d. Present session content and discuss each element of Workbook outline.

e. Role-play and group discussion of effective conversations.

f. Conduct a 20-minute reflection group.

g. Outline homework assignment.

h. Brief look at next session.

6. Session and Client Response Evaluation

a. Have clients complete CSES.

b. Staff completes PSES using these as guideline evaluation points:

1) *Did the group understand the techniques involved in starting a conversation and demonstrate improved communication skills?*

2) *Was there some self-disclosure about their ability or inability to communicate in unfamiliar situations?*

Session 25 : Coping and Social Skills Training: Basic Communication Skills—Compliments

1. Rationale and Overview of Session

Building on our communication skills platform, we will now learn and practice the social skill of *reinforcing* (strengthening) and *receiving reinforcement* of the positive thoughts, feelings, behaviors and characteristics of others and ourselves. One specific way that we reinforce (strengthen) the positive features of other people is through giving and receiving compliments. Successful relationships depend on this reinforcement process—and more specifically, an atmosphere of give and take where positive experiences are shared and strengthened. Our chances of receiving in a relationship are increased when we give in that relationship. Likewise, our chances of giving in a relationship are increased when we receive something from that relationship. We call this the *quid pro quo*–something for something–of relationships. It is, therefore, important that people learn both to give and accept compliments, the nice things that people say to and about one another.

Frequently, people fail to share the good things they think about their friends, acquaintances and family, especially in long-term relationships. They may assume that it isn't necessary to let the other person know how they feel, assuming that it is obvious that they hold the person in high esteem. On the other hand, a person may have no problem telling other people how much they appreciate them but may not be able to graciously accept compliments.

In a relationship that may have been damaged by criminal conduct and substance abuse, the *good* things in the friendship or union may have been all but forgotten. Learning to express appreciation for the good times, the kind responses, the positive moments, is one way to heal ruptures in an important relationship. On the other hand, negative self-feelings may make it hard for SAOs to accept anything kind that might be said to or about them. It is important that they realize it is painful to other people when they reject compliments that are offered and they may feel that they can't say positive things in the future. When a person hears *nothing* positive about themselves, it is hard to believe that they are worthwhile.

2. Objectives of Session

> Ⅲ➡ Clients learn the skills involved in giving sincere compliments;
>
> Ⅲ➡ Clients learn to accept compliments in a gracious and appropriate manner.

3. Session Content and Process

Feeling good about yourself and about how others feel about you are important as we learn to develop thoughts that lead away from substance abuse and criminal behavior. We show we feel good about ourselves and about other people when we receive and give positive reinforcement around specific things that we or others do. We look at two specific ways that we can give and receive positive reinforcement (Monti et al., 1989, and Ross et al., 1986, were used as guides for developing material for this session):

- Learning to accept praise and compliments from others;

- Giving sincere compliments and praise to others.

a. Receiving compliments:

1) Receiving compliments is based on the second key skill of *self-directed communication*—being open and listening to feedback from others about you. Remember that we shut down the feedback we get from others when we get defensive or push away the feedback. We sometimes do this when we receive compliments. Maybe the compliment is embarrassing. Maybe receiving a compliment means that we take ownership for our positive behaviors. Maybe we don't want to be that responsible since this will mean that we have to take responsibility for our negative behaviors. To own a compliment will also mean that we may have

323

to take ownership of a criticism or of a correction of our behavior. Or, we may push away a compliment because we don't think a lot of ourselves. If we have poor self-esteem, we will push away compliments.

HERE ARE SOME TIPS ON *RECEIVING* COMPLIMENTS:

- Take time to *listen* to the praise.

- Do not deny the praise that other people give you. Be gracious. Let them know it makes you feel good. When someone is saying something nice about you, don't turn the compliment down. You may not be used to hearing nice things about yourself, but be gracious. If you say they are wrong about you, you are saying that they don't have good judgment. Learn to say a simple, "thank you."

- Use clear words to respond back to the praise.

- Even though you may not agree, let them know you like what they said and that you appreciate their kind thoughts and positive feedback. This is not a dishonest response, only an appreciative response.

b. **Giving compliments:**

Giving compliments is based on other-directed communication or *active listening*. Compliments are effective when you know about the other person. We get to know the other person when we use *open statements* and *open questions*. The actual giving of a compliment involves using the *reflection* skill. A compliment is reflecting back what you see as positive about the other person.

HERE ARE SOME TIPS ON *GIVING* COMPLIMENTS:

- Make the compliment sincere and real: It should be around something the person has done that is good and positive.

- What is the point you want to recognize? Find something nice to say about someone; What would that person like to hear?

- Be brief with your praise.

- Be specific. What is the action you want to compliment? Rather than saying "You're a good guy," it is better to be specific as to why you think the person is a *good guy.* "It was good of you to give me a ride home."

- State the compliment in terms of your feelings and not just the facts as you see them. Not only "it was good of you to take me home," but also "I felt good to know you offered to give me a ride home." This helps the other person feel that the compliment is sincere and really comes from you and not from them. People don't like to compliment themselves;

- Be sensitive to the other person's personality when you give compliments. Some people get embarrassed if they are complimented with others around. If the person is shy, he or she might feel better if you gave them praise when no one is around.

- Listen to the person's response to your praise.

c. **Guided Focus Group Discussion:**

Do a guided focus discussion group around the above guidelines on receiving and giving compliments.

d. **Modeling:**

The provider role plays an *effective* and *ineffective* manner of giving compliments. Use your own scenario. Discuss the results of the different examples that were just given.

e. **Exercise:**

Make groups of threes. Have a pair practice giving and receiving compliments and praise while the third person observes. Situations can include a conversation between friends, with family, or with a companion at work. Have the observer give feedback. Have observer practice compliments if the pair did well. Rotate roles. Have them share how it felt receiving and giving compliments. Was it unnatural or easy? Did their responses agree with their reported feelings? Were the compliments sincere or insincere? What were the consequences?

f. **Relating the Basic Skills for Self-Improvement and Change to the Client's Master Profile and Master Assessment Plan:**

1) How did these three sessions address the client's problem areas and risk factors as identified in the client's MP? For example, if a client scored high on the *Coping with Social Discomfort* scale on the MP, did the basic communication concepts and skills help that client to more effectively deal with social discomfort without using drugs?

2) What specific problem areas on the MAP did these sessions address for each client? Have clients share their observations around this question in group.

4. Other Classroom or Homework Activities

a. Homework on COMPLIMENTS. Use this example: Think of a close friend or family member that may not know how much you appreciate her/him. Before the next group meeting, make a point of complimenting that person. Use *Work Sheet 22* for this exercise or homework.

b. Do a *thinking report* on RECEIVING COMPLIMENTS.

Think about the last time someone complimented you. How did you respond? Remember these are the parts of your thinking report:

SITUATION

THOUGHTS

FEELINGS

ATTITUDES AND BELIEFS ABOUT THE SITUATION

OUTCOME

5. Presentation Sequence

a. Review previous session and homework.

b. Discuss the rationale for giving and receiving compliments.

c. Review workbook outline "Giving and Receiving Compliments."

d. Guide focus group discussion (this replaces reflection group for this session).

e. Model effective and ineffective strategies for giving compliments.

f. Outline homework assignment and look at next session.

6. Session and Client Response Evaluation

a. Have clients complete the CSES.

b. Provider completes the PSES. Keep these in mind:

   1) *Did the group demonstrate an understanding of the skills involved in giving and receiving compliments?*

   2) *Did they appreciate the importance of talking feelings, instead of facts; of accepting a compliment graciously?*

c. Do a Behavior Rating Form (BRF) on clients. Score the form and evaluate how the client is doing at this point. The BRFs will be done at the end of each of the break-point segments for Module 9. Provide client with feedback on how he or she is doing in the program.

Session 26 : Recognizing and Being Aware of Negative Thoughts and Negative Thinking

Break Point: The next four sessions will focus on learning and practicing skills to change mental sets. At this break-point, new participants may be brought into the program.

1. Rationale and Overview of Session

The next four sessions represent a series of lessons on managing and changing thoughts and feelings which lead to life problems in general and more specifically, to AOD abuse and CC. We will begin with negative and distorted thinking. It is important to review Figure 18 in Module 6, Session 16; it is repeated below in Figure 24.

It is important that we continue to review with clients that **THE WAY WE THINK INFLUENCES HOW WE FEEL AND BEHAVE.** *Negative* thinking will influence feelings and trigger behavior.

When negative thinking becomes a way of life, it is as comfortable as the other distorted thoughts to which people may cling. Learning *not* to think negatively may produce as much ambivalence and distress as giving up other patterns of thinking. Negative thoughts lead to negative emotions that are generally accompanied by tension from which the SAO wants to escape. The escape may take the form of using and/or criminal conduct. This behavior, in turn, may lead to negative feelings about oneself including reduced self-respect, anger and depression.

2. Objectives of Session

> ➡ Review Figure 26 which describes the pathways to changing AOD and CC;
>
> ➡ Recognize negative thought patterns;
>
> ➡ Recognize how negative thought patterns contribute to problem behaviors.

3. Session Content and Process

a. Introduction to session:

Remember: THE WAY WE THINK INFLUENCES HOW WE FEEL AND ACT. *Negative* thinking can become a way of life. It leads to negative and angry behavior. It may be difficult not to think negatively.

Negative thoughts lead to negative emotions which then lead to tension. The escape may be to use drugs or to engage in criminal conduct. Sometimes we can have an overall negative feeling about the world. "The world sucks!" When we believe that long enough, we then believe that the world doesn't deserve anything positive. It makes it easier to *take what you want*, regardless of how it might hurt people.

Negative thinking can led to negative feelings about oneself including reduced self-respect, anger and depression.

When we change our negative thoughts, we experience POWER. The power comes in using certain techniques to manage and control negative thinking. There is *power in positive thinking*. The power is in becoming self-competent and self-confident. We learned that this gives us greater self-mastery or what we call *self-efficacy*.

b. Understanding negative thoughts and negative thinking:

A *negative* thought denies or works against an outcome that is positive. It works against your goals and what you want to accomplish. It dashes hopes and dreams. Negative thinking is a pattern of negative thoughts. People get into a pattern of negative thoughts. When some event happens, this pattern automatically happens. It throws a damper on having fun, on feeling good about yourself. The pattern can lead to depression.

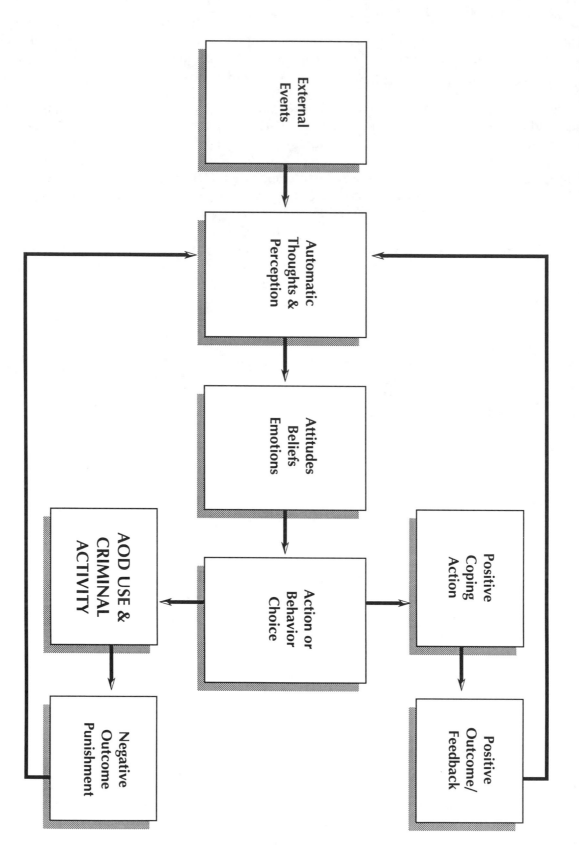

Figure 26
Pathways to Changing AOD and Criminal Conduct

External
Events

Automatic
Thoughts &
Perception

Attitudes
Beliefs
Emotions

AOD USE &
CRIMINAL
ACTIVITY

Action or
Behavior
Choice

Positive
Coping
Action

Negative
Outcome
Punishment

Positive
Outcome/
Feedback

It is easy to get into negative thinking. We see so many things in this world that discourage us, that get us down, and about which we automatically think in negative terms. But the negative thoughts also can lead to negative feelings and to AOD use and criminal behavior.

c. **Recognizing negative thoughts and thinking:**

Before we can change negative thoughts and the pattern of negative thoughts—negative thinking—we have to learn to recognize them. Sometimes they are so automatic, we don't recognize them. They just lead right to a negative or destructive behavior.

Negative thoughts can be errors in thinking. We looked at some errors in thinking in Phase I. These can be found in Session 9 of Module 3 (Table 5 in Providers Manual and *Work Sheet 4* of Participant's Workbook). Here are some of these errors in thinking which represent negative thoughts (Kadden et al., 1992; Monti et al., 1989):

1) EXPECTING THE WORST: The worst always happens—you can count on bad results: *"I know it won't work out."*

2) SELF-PUTDOWNS: *"I'm no good."*

3) JUMPING TO CONCLUSIONS: *"I'm going to get fired."*

4) CATASTROPHIZING: *"I know something terrible happened."*

6) SELF-BLAME *"I deserve it."*

7) MAGNIFYING: *"No matter what may happen, it couldn't be worse."*

Exercise: Using *Work Sheet 24* in the Workbook, list 10 negative thoughts that you get into in column 1. Then, in column 2, label these thoughts using the list above or the list of errors in thinking in Sessions 1 and 5 of Module 3.

d. **Two essential steps in changing negative thinking:**

1) *Notice the negative thinking:* What kind of automatic thinking patterns have you developed over the years? Learn to pay attention when they occur and what moods might accompany them.

2) *Replace the negative thoughts:* When it occurs, stop the automatic negative thinking pattern, think of a more positive or realistic thought and act on that positive thought.

e. **The ABC method for understanding rational or wise thinking:**

Albert Ellis (1962, 1975; Ellis & Harper, 1961), in his work on developing *Rational Emotive Therapy,* has given us what he calls the *ABC method of rational (wise or logical) thinking* which also helps us understand how negative thoughts lead to negative feelings and behavior. This ABC method is much like the model we presented in Figure 26 to help us understand the pathways to changing AOD use and criminal conduct. **A** stands for the *antecedent* or the event (the forerunner) which precedes and leads to **B** or our *beliefs and thoughts.* The beliefs or thoughts then lead to **C** or what Dr. Ellis calls the *consequences* which are our feelings and actions.

As we have learned in our other sessions, the **A,** or events, can lead to *automatic thoughts* or beliefs. Often, these thoughts are not wise; they are irrational or crazy and unsound. Such thoughts or beliefs can lead to automatic behavior or action habits. Dr. Ellis makes it clear that we can make choices to either use an *irrational* (crazy, unsound, silly) thought or a *rational* thought. By choosing a rational or sensible thought, we will then be on the path to take rational or sensible action. It is our choice. We have the **POWER** to change the automatic thoughts that are irrational or that are errors in thinking to rational thoughts. We may not be in control of the **A**, but we are in control of the **B** and the **C**. Here is the ABC method as suggested by Dr. Ellis:

$$A \text{-------} \blacktriangleright B \text{-------} \blacktriangleright C$$

ANTECEDENT -------▶ **BELIEFS** -------▶ **CONSEQUENCES**

EVENTS --▶ **THOUGHTS** --▶ **FEELINGS/BEHAVIOR**

Exercise: Apply the ABC method. Have group pick an event or **A** which leads to negative thoughts or **B** and then to feelings and behavior or **C**. Discuss how we bypass the thoughts or the automatic thoughts lead to feelings and behaviors that are negative (AOD use or antisocial).

Exercise: Have each member discuss at least one incident in which negative thoughts or negative thinking led to a strong emotional response and led to substance abuse or criminal conduct. How did they feel after they had behaved as they did? Do they feel their behavior was justified by the event or have they reached the point that they recognize the decision and responsibility for their actions is theirs alone? Do they think they would have behaved differently if they had stopped long enough to consider alternatives and consequences?

f. **Relating the Basic Skills for Self-Improvement and Change to the Client's Master Profile and Master Assessment Plan:**

Have clients review their MP and MAP in the areas of Criminal and Antisocial Thinking and Conduct. Have them identify the specific areas of their *Master Profile* that they need to change and the specific problems in their *Master Assessment Plan* that they need to work on. Have clients identify how this session helped them work on their MAP. Have them particularly look at the elements of the profile and MAP that relate negative thinking and errors in thinking to their criminal conduct.

4. Classroom or Homework Activities

a. Using *Work Sheet 24,* have clients list their negative thoughts and then list what errors in thinking (from *Work Sheet 4* or from those listed in this session) each of the negative thoughts might represent.

b. Have clients compare Ellis's ABC method with the model outlined in Figure 26 or in the Participant's Workbook Figure 12. How are these the same? How are they different?

c. Have clients apply the ABC method using *Work Sheet 25* in the Workbook.

Sometimes it seems the behaviors triggered by an event happen so fast that we don't have time to *THINK ABOUT THE CONSEQUENCES.* It may be easier to describe your reaction to the event before you describe the thoughts you had. Even if you don't remember your exact thoughts, you should be able to think of the things you probably said to yourself.

1) Describe an EVENT that made you want to drink or use.

2) List as many of the things that you might have been thinking that would help explain why the event upset you so much.

3) Describe your feelings or behaviors in response to the event.

d. **Thinking Report: Negative Thought Patterns**

Have clients do a *thinking report* of a situation around an event where negative thoughts led to an emotional outburst and/or substance abuse/criminal conduct. Remember the parts of the thinking report:

SITUATION

THOUGHTS

FEELINGS

ATTITUDES AND BELIEFS ABOUT THE SITUATION

OUTCOME OR RESULTS

c. Review Session 27 in Workbook.

5. Presentation Sequence

a. Review previous session and homework on compliments. Keep in mind that if you are using an open-ended model, new clients entering Module 9 at this break-point will not have done the homework on compliments. They can learn from other participants as they discuss their homework.

b. Discuss the rationale and objectives for session.

c. Present the content portion of session and do exercises in sequence outlined.

d. Review the ABC rational thinking model.

e. Have clients discuss how these sessions related to their MP and their MAP.

f. Review homework.

g. Hold a 20-minute reflection group at end of session.

h. Outline homework assignment.

i. Brief look at next session.

6. Session and Client Response Evaluation

a. Client completes the CSES.

b. Provider completes the PSES using these two questions as guidelines:

1) *Are individuals becoming more aware of their negative thought patterns and willing to discuss them?*

2) *Did members demonstrate an awareness of the relationship between events, thoughts and behavior and realize that it is possible to stop negative thought processes?*

Session 27 : Managing and Changing Negative Thoughts

1. Rationale and Overview of Session

Our emphasis up to this point has been on recognizing and becoming aware of negative thought patterns. Now we will focus on how to *manage or stop* the negative thoughts and replace them with more positive ones. Some of the specific techniques for managing and changing cognitions (thinking, feeling, perceiving) which were presented in Module 6, Session 17 will be used to change negative thinking. These techniques will be used repeatedly in handling maladaptive cognitions and behaviors in this module. It will only be with repetition and practice that these techniques are learned. It will take participants time to notice a change, probably reflected in a more positive outlook on life. Impetuous behavior and *one-track thinking* are tendencies that need to be overcome in order to stop negative thinking (Ross et al., 1986, p. 76). Finally, it is important to *act* on the more positive thoughts and turn them into positive behaviors and feelings.

2. Objectives of Session

> ➤ Identify the specific negative thoughts that lead to AOD use and abuse;
>
> ➤ Put into practice the various techniques learned in Phase I that are used to handle cognitive processes which lead AOD use and abuse and CC;
>
> ➤ Understand and own the notion that each person is in control of his or her own behavior, and can choose to respond in a positive or negative manner.

3. Session Content and Process

a. **You are in control:**

People and events in your life can lead to bad results if you allow them to do so. You are in control of everything you think or say to yourself. "People don't upset you; you allow them to upset you" (Monti et al., 1989, p. 112). As Cassius said to Caesar: "Caesar, my dear friend, your fate lies not in the stars, but within you."

In all circumstances, you have a choice of responses, as we have seen in Figure 12 of your Workbook and also *Work Sheet 24* from last session. You may say you are justified in your actions that hurt others, that you had no choice, they made you do it. This is not so. No one made you do it. It was *your* choice.

There is power in acting *prosocial*. When you are prosocial, you gain self-respect. Self-respect leads to further prosocial action which in turn leads to further self-respect. And...you get the respect of others.

b. **What are the negative thoughts that have led you to AOD use and/or criminal conduct?**

1) Review the classroom or homework in *Work Sheets 24* and *25* for last session;

2) Then, have clients use *Work Sheet 26* to list negative thoughts that may have led them to AOD use or criminal conduct.

c. **Practice changing negative thinking:**

1) Use two methods to change negative thoughts: These two methods were given in Module 6, Session 17, page 105 of the workbook (McMullin, 1986; Monti et al., 1989):

a) *Thought Stopping:* Allow yourself to think a negative thought. Then STOP the thought right away. Be aware of your negative thought first. Note that it is *automatic* for some events. Then tell yourself to STOP the thought. Choose one target negative thought. (e.g., "nothing works out.") Every time that happens, STOP the thought.

BE AWARE! STOP THE THOUGHT!

b) *Planting Positive Thought:* Pick a target negative thought. Every time you have that thought, immediately replace it with a positive thought.

NEGATIVE THOUGHT! REPLACE WITH POSITIVE THOUGHT! THOUGHT STOPPING IS MORE POWERFUL IF YOU USE THE PLANTING POSITIVE THOUGHT METHOD.

2) Use the ABC method to handle negative thoughts. Pick a situation (A). Identify the irrational or negative thought or belief (B). What were the feelings that came from the thought (C)? Now, replace the negative thought or belief (B) with a positive thought or belief B (replacement). What are the new feelings or behaviors that come from the thought replacement?

A -------► B (replacement) -------► C (new feelings)

EVENT -------► NEW THOUGHT -------► NEW FEELING

Exercise: Pick a situation that leads to negative thought (A). Then identify the irrational or negative thought (B). What were the feelings—the emotional response (C)? Then what was the positive thought you used to replace the negative?

Exercise: Have group pick a situation (A) that can lead directly to certain feelings and behaviors that are negative. For example, a wife is late getting home from work (A). Her husband accuses her of being out with another man (C). This may be preceded by automatic thought "she's running around." But the accusation comes almost before the person thinks. Now, take the same situation and let the thought occur. Then intervene with THOUGHT STOPPING or PLANTING POSITIVE THOUGHTS.

d. **Positive Thought Arming:**

This is arming yourself with positive thoughts. It's having the thought and action there ready to use. It's like knowing where the light switch is before entering a dark room. You don't stumble around. You go right to the switch. The same with *thought arming*. Those thoughts are ready. You don't stumble around. But, the thoughts should be based on real positive thoughts, experiences and outcomes you have had. Have clients use *Work Sheet 27* to make a list of positive thoughts that they can arm themselves with. Here are some examples:

1) REMEMBERING GOOD THINGS: What are the good things in life, the things you do well, the people that you care about?

2) STATEMENTS OF HOPE: Make positive self statements, such as "I can manage this situation"; or "This may be hard, but I am strong enough to do this."

3) SELF-REWARDS: When you have done something well, reward yourself with positive self-talk. "I came close to using, but I found another way to cope. I did a really good job controlling myself." This is a key to change. Reward yourself when you have made the change. The idea of self-reward will come up again. This is *self-reinforcement*. This is how we make sure the changes we have made will stick. We reinforce those changes ourselves.

e. **Remember, Self-Talk? That's what it is about:**

A lot of what we are doing is self-talk. It is talking to yourself. When you replace a negative thought with a positive thought, you are telling yourself to do this. This is *self-talk*. Self-talk is powerful. But it can also be negative and irrational. Our goal is to replace *negative* self-talk with *positive* self-talk. We will continue to use self-talk as a tool for change.

f. **Reflection group:**

Have group focus on *positive arming*. What are other ways they can develop good feelings and positive thoughts? What kind of positive things might happen when we act on the positive thoughts? Did the group mood improve as they talked about positive things?

4. Classroom or Homework Activities

a. Practice Thought Stopping and Planting Positive Thoughts. Have client do *Work Sheet 28.*

b. *Thinking Report:* FREEDOM OF CHOICE.

Think of a time when you thought "I have no choice" but to do something you shouldn't. Do a *thinking report* on the situation.

5. Presentation Sequence

a. Review previous session and homework.

b. Discuss the rationale and present session content.

c. Review the stages of changing negative thoughts.

d. Have group give personal examples of how they were able to avoid a negative outcome by developing positive thoughts.

e. Hold 20-minute reflection of group at end of session.

f. Outline homework assignment.

g. Brief look at next session.

6. Session and Client Response Evaluation

a. Have clients complete CSES.

b. Provider completes PSES using the following as guidelines:

1) *Was there evidence that some members were becoming enthusiastic about the positive effects of thought stopping and positive thinking?*

2) *Did they understand thought stopping?*

Session 28 : Errors in Logic and Thinking

1. Rationale and Overview of Session

In Module 3, Sessions 5 and 9, we introduced the idea of distorted thinking or errors in thinking. Errors in thinking most often do not represent what is either real or accurate but a distortion of reality. We have discussed that *distorted thinking* is sometimes used as a coping device. We also saw how thoughts or thinking habits, or what we called *automatic thoughts,* can lead to action-habits that get us into trouble. In this session, we will look further at the role that distorted or erroneous thinking plays in perpetuating criminal or AOD behavior.

2. Objectives of Session

> ⮕ Understand how certain thinking patterns (thought habits) and the attitudes and beliefs that accompany them can underlie behavior or action-habits that get them into trouble;
>
> ⮕ Recognize distorted thinking patterns (thought habits) in themselves and begin to rectify that thinking.

3. Session Content and Process

a. **Introduction to session:**

Our attitudes, beliefs and thinking patterns have not always served us well in the past; they have gotten us into trouble with the law. They have been *barriers* to change. However, we know they are very difficult to change. Our goal is to change the ways we have been thinking incorrectly and *replace* those thoughts with correct and more rewarding ideas. In fact, we want to replace them with beliefs that can lead us to the most satisfying lifestyle possible.

Exercise: Have group practice Thought Stopping during the opening group discussion when reviewing last session and homework.

Review: Review the definitions of attitudes, beliefs and thinking patterns from Module 2 ("Building a Desire and Motivation to Change" in Workbook):

1) Our attitudes, beliefs and thinking patterns control how we react to people and situations that are important in our everyday life;

2) Our attitudes are our basic thoughts for or against persons, ideas and objects in our life; attitudes affect how we think, how we feel, and how we act;

3) Our beliefs are values, ideas and principles we use to evaluate other people and ourselves;

4) Thinking patterns or thought habits are automatic thoughts we have in similar situations.

b. **Common thought patterns or thought habits that lead us to errors in thinking and become barriers to change:**

Present these common thought patterns and then discuss them in group (adapted from King et al., 1994):

1) *I had no choice:* After having reviewed our *thinking reports* we should be convinced that "I had no choice" is rarely a true statement, but it is one of the most commonly used excuses to do something wrong. We must take the initiative to find alternatives that are responsible choices for our lives.

2) *Everyone thinks the way I do:* The fact is, there is no subject on which everyone agrees. It is a great comfort to the person who steals to believe that everyone would steal if they weren't afraid of getting caught. But it is not a fact. The fact is, everyone controls their own thinking and you can too.

3) *I'm right in this situation and my thoughts don't need changing:* Sometimes we have done a pretty good job of trying to change in other situations but fall into old habits when we feel strongly about an issue. Sometimes being right or wrong is not the issue, but stubborn refusal to think differently may mean getting into trouble. Again, there is no issue in the world where there isn't another way of thinking about it. Don't let *stubbornness* be a barrier to change.

c. **Beliefs and errors in thinking that get us into trouble:**

1) Errors in thinking are distortions or misrepresentations that we make as a matter of habit. They become so automatic that we accept them even if we have no facts to support what we think (Bush & Bilodeau, 1993).

2) Table 4 in your Workbook (which is Table 6 below) gives you a list of common *distortions* that get people in trouble with the law. These are the same as those you worked on in Session 9 of Module 3 (page 62). In *Work Sheet 4,* you checked how those errors of thinking applied to you. Now Table 4 puts a name on them. Go back to your Work Sheet 4 in Session 9 and look at the errors in thinking you checked that you use a lot or use all of the time. Now find that error in thinking in Table 4. Try to remember the name that is now given to that error in thinking. Use *self-talk* in reviewing this. For example, take the error *can't trust anybody.* We are calling that CAN'T TRUST. Now think of a situation where you thought that way. Now use self-talk. "Can't trust anybody. CAN'T TRUST." Now counter that. "That's not true. I can trust some people. I trust I'm going to get paid for each day I work at my job." Think of someone you do trust. Use self-talk. "I do trust..."

Exercise: Identify the thinking patterns that can still get you into trouble. How are you trying to stop them? Do people learn negative thinking patterns in jail? What are they and how can they be changed?

Exercise: Use the Thought Change skill "Shifting the View" that was presented in Module 6, Session 17 (page 106). Take the error in thinking "I feel I've been screwed." You may have had this view a long time. This may be the basis of your anger. Shift the view. Use some statements that change that view of people. Try this one: "I've had some things go my way." "I know of several people who have helped me and not 'screwed' me."

d. **Discussion: Select several items from Table 6 (Workbook Table 4) and discuss the following questions (this exercise will take the rest of the session):**

1) HAVE YOU EVER USED THIS DISTORTION IN YOUR OWN THINKING? WHAT IS AN EXAMPLE?

2) CAN YOU IMAGINE HOW USING THIS DISTORTION COULD GET A PERSON IN TROUBLE WITH THE LAW?

e. **Relating the Errors in Logic and Thinking to the client's Master Profile and Master Assessment Plan:**

Have clients relate the errors in logic and thinking discussed in this session to their criminal and antisocial thinking and conduct profile. Have them reevaluate themselves across the various scales in this section of the profile. Did they change their self-ratings? What were the problem areas of criminal thinking and conduct that they identified in their MAP?

4. Classroom and Homework Activities

a. Have clients work on thinking distortions or errors in thinking by doing *Work Sheet 29* in Workbook (Work Sheet 29 was adapted from Bush & Bilodeau, 1993).

b. Have clients work on recognizing errors in thinking this week and then use "Shifting the View" changing these beliefs and thoughts.

5. Presentation Sequence

a. Review previous session and homework.

b. Discuss the Rationale and Objectives for Session.

c. Present session content in order as outlined above.

d. It is important to review definitions of attitudes, beliefs and thinking patterns (group leaders should review previous definitions from Module 2, "Building a Desire and Motivation to Change").

e. Do exercises as outlined above.

f. Review Workbook Outline of Thinking Distortions.

g. Hold a reflection group at end of session.

h. Review homework assignment and look at next session.

6. Session and Client Response Evaluation

a. Have clients complete the CSES.

b. Staff completes the PSES and reflects on these evaluation issues:

1) *Was the group receptive to the idea that they have developed thinking patterns that can get them into trouble?*

2) *Was there evidence of willingness to see their own use of distortions and the role this may play in the lives of the SAO?*

Table 6

Common Thinking Distortions or Errors in Thinking

(Adapted from Beck, 1976; Burns, 1980, 1989; King et al., 1994; Yochelson & Samenow, 1976, 1977)

LIST OF ERRORS IN THINKING IN SESSION 9, WORK SHEET 4

1) POWER THRUST—put people down; dominate over others;
2) CLOSED CHANNEL—Seeing things only your way;
3) VICTIM STANCE—Blaming others;
4) PRIDE—feeling superior to others;
5) DON'T CARE—Lack concern as to how others are affected;
6) CAN'T TRUST—Can't trust anybody;
7) WON'T MEET OBLIGATIONS—Refuse something you don't want to do;
8) WANT IT NOW—Want what you want now and won't settle for less;
9) STEALING—Take what you want from others;
10) DON'T NEED ANYBODY—Refuse to lean on anyone;
11) PROCRASTINATE—Put off things until tomorrow;
12) DON'T HAVE TO—I don't have to do that;
13) STUBBORN—Won't change your ideas;
14) RIGID THINKING—Think in black or white terms; has to be one way or the other;
15) CATASTROPHIZING—Mountains out of molehills; blowing things out of proportion;
16) FEEL PICKED ON—feel singled out and picked on;
17) THEY DESERVE IT—People have it coming; people deserve to get ripped off;
18) SCREWED—Feeling that you are being screwed over; mistreated;
19) SELECTIVE HEARING—Tune out what you hear people say if it doesn't fit your thinking;
20) WON'T GIVE—Demand from others but won't give;
21) CRIMINAL THINKING—Think about criminal things; doing crimes;
22) LYING—lying is almost automatic for you;

ADDITIONAL LIST OF ERRORS AND THEIR NAMES:

1) ANGER—rage that makes you illogical and irrational;
2) LONER—feeling separated, isolated and different from others;
3) REFUSAL—Feeling that you don't have to do that;
4) FAIR DESSERTS—I deserve more than what I'm getting; I've been cheated;
5) THEY DESERVE IT—People have it coming;
6) NO EMPATHY—Can't put yourself in another person's position;
7) FAILURE TO CONSIDER HARM TO OTHERS—lack of concern how others are affected by you;
8) SEE SELF AS GOOD—In spite of having harmed others;
9) NO EFFORT—Won't exert energy to achieve a goal; do what comes easy;
10) CONCRETE THOUGHTS—Won't change your ideas;
11) FICKLE—Change your mind or goals all the time;
12) SEXUAL POWER—using sex as a way to increase your self-image;
13) ZERO STATE—Feeling of no value; worthy of nothing.

Session ㉙ : Errors in Thinking and the Entitlement Trap

1. Rationale and Overview of Session

The rationale of the last session is incorporated into this session. The concept of *the entitlement trap,* however, is added. The entitlement trap for the SAO is this: By some quirk of fate, the SAO has earned the right to commit crimes and to abuse substances! "I have spent my life being abused by my parents, or living in the ghetto, or enduring some other difficult experience. I am entitled to whatever I can get from the world." The SAO might begin feeling this way because of having been "clean" for 6 or 8 or 20 weeks, and consequently feeling he or she has *earned* the right to shoot up. Whatever the behavior, SAOs often feel they are entitled to experience what they want to experience because they have earned it in some manner. This feeling of *entitlement* is included, in part, in the cognitive distortions of *the victim stance, failure to put yourself in another's position,"* and *ownership and possessiveness."*

2. Objectives of Session:

a. Review and reinforce the objectives of the last session:

> ⇒ Understand how thinking distortion patterns (thought habits) underlie problem behaviors;
>
> ⇒ Identify personal thinking distortions and begin to rectify them.

b. Understand and change the concept of entitlement as a distortion in SAO thinking and replace the attitude with a more prosocial stance.

3. Session Content and Process

a. **Review homework assignment and work clients did last session on the two most often used errors in thinking that each client identified for themselves:**

What are your two most often used thinking errors? How do these errors or distortions get you into trouble? What do these errors in thinking do for you? Does the group seem to agree on the way you see each distortion?

- **Now, what thoughts did you replace those errors with?**

- **How did the mental change skill "Shifting the View" work for you?**

Discussion: Have clients report in some detail their homework assignment on the two cognitive distortions or thinking errors they most often use *(Work Sheet 29)*. Have them look closely at the question of how these distortions can get them into trouble. Encourage *honesty*. Have them share their findings with the group. The provider is encouraged to reward critical self-reports. What were the most frequent distortions reported by the group? Does the group seem to agree on the way they interpret each distortion, or are there some important differences? Point out the variety of ways people use each distortion and how differently they can be interpreted.

If clients had not gotten into trouble, would the act have been rewarding? What were the alternatives to getting themselves in trouble? If they had taken time to slow down and think of the alternatives, would they have done something different? Why?

b. **The "Entitlement trap"**

Many substance abusing offenders use this as a way to excuse or explain their criminal and substance abusing behavior. Because of past problems and hurts—which you feel were *beyond* your control— you may feel you were the victim. You may feel you were punished, deprived, or badly treated. This makes you feel you have something coming. You may feel *entitled* to

341

whatever you can get. Here is a story told by a SAO who committed crimes because he felt he had something coming:

"I had a rough childhood. I was abused by my alcoholic dad. We didn't have money. He sometimes told us to steal if we needed something. He beat up my mom. But she really had a hard time caring for us. She'd always protect him. I got high when I was nine. It was a way out of hell. Then stealing became fun. Then it became the way I 'earned' my living. I needed some big cash. I got drunk. Stuck up the liquor store. Got away with it. I told myself 'I deserved it.' The second time went easy. Got caught the third time. Guess I was relieved. No more running. But I still feel I got something coming."

1) Use the self-talk cognitive change skills you learned in Module 6, Session 17 (page 105 of the Workbook) to change the *entitlement trap* thinking:

   - THOUGHT STOPPING;

   - THINKING "RESPONSIBILITY" AND "THEIR POSITION";

   - PLANTING POSITIVE THOUGHT (IF YOU HAVE WATERED AND FERTILIZED THESE THOUGHTS, THEY SHOULD BE GROWING WELL);

   - STRONG COUNTERING.

   Exercise: Think of a thought that falls into the *entitlement trap* class. Now, counter that thought. Argue against it hard. Now, share with the group how that felt.

   Exercise: Take another thought that falls into the *entitlement trap* class. Now, apply the skills of *thought stopping, planting a positive thought,* and *their position.*

2) Have clients identify which errors in thinking in Table 6 (Table 4 of Workbook) illustrate the *entitlement trap.* Discuss this in the group.

3) **Exercise:** Play out this scenario in the group using role-playing:

   Have volunteers from the group role-play a scenario in which one person assumes s/he is entitled to take whatever they want from the other person. How does the victim respond? Have the group discuss the issues and their own feelings if they were victimized in this manner. (REPEAT THE SCENARIO WITH DIFFERENT ACTORS IF TIME ALLOWS.)

c. **Review the use of the mental change skill "Shifting the View" (page 106 in Workbook):**

   - Apply this cognitive skill on the two thinking distortions you identified in Work Sheet 29 which you did for last session.

   - How did this skill work for you?

   - Also, look at whether the skills *thought stopping* and *planting a positive thought* could have worked with these cognitive distortions.

4. Classroom and Homework Activities

a. Do *Work Sheet 30* in the Workbook on the Entitlement Trap.

b. Have clients identify entitlement traps all week, then record at least three of these in their journals.

c. Have client continually use the cognitive change skill *Countering* all week. Work at it hard.

d. *Thinking report* called ALTERNATIVES:

   Have clients think of a situation in which they were tempted to perform a crime, but decided against it. Have them do a thinking report on the situation. Remember the parts to the thinking report:

SITUATION;

THOUGHTS;

FEELINGS;

ATTITUDES AND BELIEFS ABOUT THE SITUATION;

WHAT WAS THE OUTCOME.

5. Presentation Sequence

a. Review the objectives for last session.

b. Review last week's homework—identifying two thinking distortions that each client tends to use most often.

c. Discuss the rationale and objective for errors in thinking and the Entitlement Trap.

d. Present program as outlined in session content above and do identified exercises. Time may not allow for all of these exercises.

e. Close session with a reflection group.

f. Outline homework assignment.

g. Brief look at next session.

6. Session and Client Response Evaluation

a. Have clients complete the CSES.

b. Provider completes the PSES and reflects on these questions:

   1) *Was there evidence that the group appreciated the lessons contained in the thinking distortions?*

   2) *Was the idea of "entitlement" understood and appreciated as being a thinking distortion?*

c. This segment brings work on changing cognitive sets to a close. Do a BRF on the client, calculate his or her score and provide feedback on their progress.

Session ③⓪ : Recognizing High-Risk Situations for AOD Use and CC and Refusal Training

Session Break: The next four sessions will focus on AOD and CC cravings and learning; learning and practicing assertiveness skills and behavior and learning more in-depth problem solving skills. At this break-point, new participants may be brought into the program.

1. Rationale and Overview of Session

For the SAO, association with criminals who use drugs and/or alcohol is an exceedingly high-risk situation. It should be avoided if at all possible. Clients must guard against *victim stance* thinking that will encourage them to abandon efforts to change. It will take effort, including control of their anti-social thinking to prevent relapse. Nothing short of a wholehearted effort on the part of the SAO will be adequate to correct antisocial behavior and substance abuse (Bush & Bilodeau, 1993).

Learning to *just say no* to the offer of drugs and/or alcohol is frequently not enough, especially in the early stages of recovery. Along with a commitment to not using, the client must be assertive enough to act on that decision. Awareness of previous patterns of behavior that were successful or unsuccessful in keeping the client out of trouble is important. Difficult situations will still come up, even if the client has been successful in avoiding old companions and the peer pressure they exert. People who are unaware of a person's problem may casually offer a drink. Some who are aware could be thoughtless and even try to force the issue. Different situations will present different difficulties. Practice in how to refuse invitations to relapse will be part of this session in *refusal skills* (Hester, 1995, Kadden et al., 1992; Monti et al., 1989, 1995; Smith & Meyers, 1995).

It is important that the Provider is sensitive to cultural differences in *saying no*. Be cautious that eye contact and body language as well as type and degree of assertiveness may vary between cultural groups. It is suggested that the Provider re-read Chapter 8, "Understanding and Enhancing Cultural Competence".

2. Objectives of Session

> ⫸ Review the important points in Module 5, Preventing Relapse and Recidivism;
>
> ⫸ Learn and practice refusal skills to cope with high-risk situations and high-risk thinking;
>
> ⫸ Identify those high-risk situations that are most resistant to refusal of AOD and CC involvement.

3. Session Content and Process

a. **Relating refusal skill development to clients' Master Profile and Master Assessment Plan:**

What are the features in the clients' MP that should be attended to with respect to developing AOD and criminal involvement refusal skills? For example, clients who rate themselves high on Antisocial Peers and Models (Part II of the MP) may have more difficulty in practicing criminal involvement refusal skills with past criminal associates. Clients with convivial or gregarious drinking patterns may have more difficulty in putting to practice drink-refusal skills (Part I of the MP). Do clients need to add to their MAP based on this study?

b. **Review of work done in relapse and recidivism prevention:**

In Module 5, Session 14, we spent a lot of time learning to spot the high-risk (HR) situations that lead to relapse and recidivism. **Recall these ideas:**

1) *High-risk situations* are those situations that have led you to AOD use and abuse in the past or that have led up to your being involved in criminal behavior in the past. They are situations in which you think or feel you need to use alcohol or other drugs. They are situations in which you think or feel you need to be involved in criminal conduct;

345

2) *High-risk thinking* involves thought habits that lead to use of substances or involvement in criminal behavior or that place you in high-risk situations that lead to the use of substances or involvement in criminal behavior;

3) *Relapse* begins with high-risk thinking or high-risk situations that have led to AOD use and abuse in the past. It starts when you take part in thought habits or automatic thoughts about using substances as another way to deal with high-risk situations;

4) *Recidivism* begins with high-risk thinking or high-risk thought habits that lead to criminal conduct. It also starts when you take part in actions or put yourself in high-risk situations that, in the past, have led to criminal activities.

c. **Learning and practicing the Refusal Skills:**

Refusing to take part in the opportunity to use drugs or to engage in criminal behavior will require that you are not only committed to *refusing* but that you have learned and practiced the skills of refusal. It will also require that you are very aware of the high-risk thinking and situations you can get involved in.

Here are some keys to REFUSAL SKILLS (adapted from Monti et al., 1989):

1) *Saying "no" without hesitation and in a firm, clear voice:* This not only gives a message to the person asking you to get involved in use or CC; it also doesn't give you time to think and maybe convince yourself that it might be all right or fun *just this once;*

2) *Looking at the person directly:* This makes it clear that you do not want to relapse; it emphasizes your determination;

3) *Don't feel guilty about refusing:* You should not feel guilty about refusing. You won't hurt anyone by saying "no," but you could hurt yourself by saying "yes;"

4) *Choose another action:* Do something else. Go to a movie, or to dinner, or have coffee and talk;

5) *Ask the person to change:* If the person toward whom your refusal message is directed is insistent or often asks you to do something you shouldn't, ask that person to change. If they want to remain your friend, they will hear your message;

6) *Make it clear what you have to lose:* This will be an important message for others—"This is what I have to lose";

7) *Make your "no" statement and change the subject:* After you say "no," change the subject to something else. Don't get into a debate about whether or not you should do what they want;

8) *Don't make excuses:* Making an excuse implies that, while you don't want to do the behavior now, you may do it at another time. Under certain circumstances, however, it may be acceptable to make an excuse. Think of some circumstances in which this would be true.

Exercise: Practice these skills in class by having group members role-play the various skills. Give feedback to the person role-playing as to his or her effectiveness.

d. **Identifying high-risk situations for AOD use and criminal conduct in which refusal will be difficult:**

Learning the skills of refusal will also mean that you know the situations in which refusal will be most difficult.

Exercise: Let's try to identify situations that you think will place you at high-risk for AOD use problems or becoming involved in criminal conduct. These should also be situations that will make it difficult for you to say "NO" to AOD use or criminal behavior. Make your list, using *Work Sheet 31*. Check whether it applies to AOD use, CC, or both. If you know what to expect, it may be easier to hold your own. Share your list with the group.

Exercise: Use *Work Sheet 32* and recall three occasions in the past where different people have offered you drinks and you accepted. Imagine that you can repeat the scene and say no. How would you do this?

e. **Further practice of refusal skills:**

1) Modeling by counselor: Counselor role-plays person being pressured to drink or engage in CC with the client being the pressure person;

2) Have group pick several scenarios and role-play. Reverse roles. Have each client play role of the person who refuses and the person who puts on pressure. Mix scenarios between AOD and CC circumstances.

f. **Group Discussion:**

Have group discuss the difference between AOD refusal and CC refusal. Is there a difference? Do they require different skills? Are the situations different?

1) Relapse into active AOD use may not land you in jail. Full CC recidivism will.

2) Is there more or less pressure from the outside for AOD use than to relapse into criminal behavior?

4. Classroom or Homework Activities

a. Complete *Work Sheet 31* in Workbook, listing high-risk situations in which it is difficult to refuse AOD use and CC.

b. Use *Work Sheet 32* and recall 3 occasions in the past where different people have offered you drinks and you accepted. Imagine that you can repeat the scene and say no. How would you do this?

c. Do *thinking report* on REFUSAL SKILLS:

Think of a time when someone wanted you to commit a crime and you didn't do what they asked. Do a thinking report on the situation. Again, review structure of thinking report with clients:

SITUATION,

THOUGHTS,

FEELINGS,

ATTITUDES,

OUTCOME.

5. Presentation Sequence

a. Review previous sessions and homework. For providers using the open-ended model for Module 9, new clients entering this module will not have done the *Entitlement Trap* homework assignment.

b. Discuss the Rationale and Objectives for CC and AOD Refusal Training.

c. Present content in order of outline above.

d. Do reflection group at end of session.

e. Outline homework assignment.

f. Brief look at next session.

6. Session and Client Response Evaluation

a. Have clients complete the CSES.

b. Counselor completes the PSES using these questions as guidelines:

1) *Did the participants identify situations in which they might have trouble when confronted with decisions to use alcohol or other drugs or commit a crime?*

2) *Were the group members able to demonstrate refusal skills in role-play?*

Session ㉛: Managing Cravings and Urges About CC and AOD Use

1. Rationale and Overview of Session

The SAO should expect to experience *cravings and urges* to drink or use other drugs. Or, the SAO may experience a desire or eventually an urge to successfully commit a criminal act. A craving is the wanting of relief. The *urge* is feeling like doing something about the craving. A *craving* is uncomfortable but does not mean something is going wrong. Actually, it should only last a short while, at most, a few hours. Clients should be prepared to cope with the discomfort. These cravings may be triggered by things in the environment. Being around friends who use, going to a party where there is liquor, or high-stress situations will often trigger cravings. An urge is the actual movement toward relieving the craving. Urges may cause physical symptoms such as a feeling of nervousness or tightness in the stomach. Urges may cause psychological symptoms such as bringing on positive memories of being high or socializing over a drink. Urges, which follow cravings, also will tend to peak quickly and then subside. As the client learns ways of coping with cravings and urges, impulses to use or do something unlawful will become less frequent (Kadden et al., 1992).

What is important here is that there is a period of time between the craving and the urge. It is helpful for the client to know the difference between these two. To catch the craving before it moves to a strong urge (the actual movement to relieve the craving) is the most effective way to prevent relapse or recidivism.

2. Objectives of Session

> ⬤➡ Learn and practice how to insulate or avoid things around them that are high-risk for setting off cravings for drugs or the desire to take part in criminal activities;
>
> ⬤➡ Develop the skills to cope with cravings and urges when high-risk situations that trigger these internal states cannot be avoided.

3. Session Content and Process

a. Introduction to session:

You will have *cravings*—or the wanting or desire to use drugs. Expect this. You may have a desire to commit a criminal act and get by with it. Cravings are not comfortable, but they do not necessarily mean something is going wrong. Actually, they will last only a short time. But the problem is, they will begin to move into urges. A craving is a desire or wanting to use drugs or commit a crime. An *urge* is moving toward fulfilling the craving. An urge may mean that you have even started to use drugs or commit a crime. Cravings may be triggered by some event that happens to you; such as being around friends who use, going to a party where there is liquor; a high-stress situation, talking with an old partner in crime. The craving may trigger an urge. Urges may cause physical symptoms such as a feeling of nervousness or tightness in the stomach. Urges may cause psychological symptoms such as bringing on positive memories of being high or socializing over a drink. Urges also tend to peak quickly and then subside. The best way to stop an urge is to stop the craving. If you have an urge, you have to stop the action and response that goes with the urge. Craving is *mental;* urge becomes more *action.*

b. Relating AOD and CC cravings and urges to clients' Master Profile and Master Assessment Plan:

Have clients again study their MP and MAP to determine if there are specific areas they need to focus on with respect to AOD and CC cravings and urges. For example, clients with high scores on the *Sustained-Continuous and Compulsive-Obsessive* patterns (Part I of the MP) may have more difficulty in controlling urges and cravings to use drugs. Clients with high scores on the *Impulsive Thinking and Acting* criminal thinking pattern may be more prone to following urges to commit criminal acts. Have clients study all of the features of the MP. Do clients need to augment their MAP based on this study?

c. Common situations that trigger cravings and urges:

Some common situations that trigger cravings for substances or for criminal conduct and should be avoided include (Kadden et al., 1992; Monti et al., 1989)

1) Exposure to substances;

2) Seeing other people using;

3) Being with people who are using or who are involved in criminal conduct;

4) Certain emotions, including fatigue, stress, self-doubt, nostalgia, anger, frustration, excitement or accomplishment.

Exercise: Have the group identify what makes them want to use drugs or perform criminal acts. Which ones can be avoided? When they can't be avoided, what can they do to keep from getting themselves into trouble?

d. Here are some ways to cope with cravings and urges (Kadden et al., 1992; Monti et al., 1989):

1) *Finding another activity:* This will distract you from the craving or urge. Doing something active may help (e.g., taking a shower); sometimes eating will suffice. With time, other behaviors will feel more natural and you will need to use fewer replacements;

2) *Talking to family or friends about the cravings or urges:* This may help identify what triggered the craving; it may also help restore some honor in the relationship with that person that may have been damaged;

3) *"Toughing it out"* or *"urge surfing"* (Kadden et al., 1992): Gain control of the craving by simply bearing the discomfort; it will go away with time. Here is how you do it:

- Pay attention to how you experience the craving. What are your thoughts and feelings about the craving? Is it in your stomach?

- Is it still a craving? Or is it now an urge? If you feel it in your body and you are now taking action to fulfill the craving—like going to the liquor store, or calling an old buddy you used to do crimes with—it is an urge. *Remember.* Cravings are mental; urges have body senses and move you to action.

- When you feel the craving go to an urge, focus on your body where you feel the urge. *Talk down* the urge with self-talk. *Turn the corner* and go to talk to a non-using friend instead of continuing to the liquor store. The urge will go away faster than you think. But you have to TURN THE CORNER.

4) *Remember the bad things that can happen:* What are the negative outcomes that result from using drugs or committing a crime? What are the rewards of being drug-free, or of engaging in positive or prosocial behavior in the community? With the help of your counselor and group, make two lists:

- Make a list of *bad things* that have happened to you because of your AOD use—pain, ending up in jail, losing money—and because of your criminal conduct;

- Make a list of the *positive things* that come with sobriety (non-using) and prosocial or positive community acting. This may include better physical health and improved family life;

- Talk to yourself about your goals. What is it you are trying to accomplish? Remind yourself of your accomplishments so far, such as staying in the treatment program;

- What statements make you more uncomfortable? When you find one, challenge the thought. Convince yourself that you will get better and you can survive the discomfort.

   5) *Stop and Think:*

   - What are the joys and pleasures you have to lose by giving in to the urge to use?

   - What are the joys and pleasures you have to lose by doing a crime?

   Exercise: Do *Work Sheet 33,* Loss of Joys and Pleasures

e. **Practice managing a craving or urge using the cognitive change skills:**

   1) Choose an episode of craving. What are the thoughts behind the craving?

   2) Use thought stopping and countering. Try *shifting the view.* How do these work?

   3) What was the self-talk you used in managing the craving?

   4) Were you managing a craving or an urge? It is much harder to deal with the urge. Try to stop the craving before it moves to an urge.

f. **Discussion:**

   What methods of coping have group members used to get through difficult periods? Have clients describe the experience and how long it took to get through a bad time.

g. **Practice managing a craving or urge using the cognitive change skill:**

   1) Have each client choose an episode of craving. What are the thoughts behind the craving?

   2) Use thought stopping and countering. Try *shifting the view.* How do these work?

4. Classroom or Homework Activities

a. Use *Work Sheet 33* to have the client identify his or her pleasures and joys. Is there a risk of losing these if the client uses or reoffends?

b. Use *Work Sheet 34*—Dealing with Cravings:

Have each client make up a plan to deal with an episode of craving. Have them pick two or three of the strategies suggested in class and show how they would use them when they feel a relapse coming on. What activities would they choose to distract themselves? Who might they call for help? (Adapted from Kadden et al., 1992.)

c. *Thinking Report*—Dealing with cravings:

Have clients recall the last time they had an urge to use or drink and were able to keep from doing it. Have clients write a thinking report on what happened.

5. Presentation Sequence

a. Review previous session and homework;

b. Discuss the Rationale and Objectives;

c. Present the session as presented in the content outline;

d. Hold a reflection group at end of session;

e. Outline homework assignment;

f. Briefly review next session.

6. Session and Client Response Evaluation

    a. Have clients complete the CSES;

    b. Counselor completes the PSES. Address these questions:

        1) *Were clients able to identify high-risk situations for cravings and urges that they need to avoid?*

        2) *Was there general understanding of ways to cope with the urge to drink, use drugs, or engage in criminal conduct?*

Session ③ : Assertiveness Skills Development

1. Rationale and Overview of Session

There are three ways that people try to solve problems and deal with conflicts that often lead to undesirable outcomes: 1) *avoidance* (flight); 2) *aggression* (fight); and 3) *being passive-aggressive.* When the SAO uses these methods to resolve conflict or solve problems they often result in negative outcomes involving relationship problems, substance abuse or criminal conduct. Change and self-improvement for the SAO involves finding different methods, other than the three approaches, to solving interpersonal conflict and relationship problems. It becomes a matter of learning a different style of getting needs met and responding to outside situations. The development of assertiveness skills provides the solution. (A variety of resources was used to develop this module, including Alberti & Emmons, 1995; Monti et al., 1989; and Ross et al., 1986.)

At the beginning of the session, have clients look at their *Master Profile* (MP) to see what areas might need special attention with respect to being assertive. For example, clients who score high on the drug use benefits scales, such as *Coping with Social Comfort or Coping with Relationships,* may be dependent on alcohol or other drugs to express themselves and to be assertive.

2. Objectives of Session

> ⮕ Clients learn about the four ways people handle conflict and get their needs met: being aggressive, being passive, being passive-aggressive and being assertive;
>
> ⮕ Clients learn and practice assertiveness skills.

3. Session Content and Process

a. Review work done in last session:

The work that clients did last session on managing cravings and urges is crucial to change in the substance abusing offender. Review the ideals and concepts presented in that session and the work done on developing a plan to deal with a craving episode *(Work Sheet 34)*. Hold a reflection group at the beginning of the session to discuss how clients have improved in their skills on managing cravings and urges. Review the *thinking report* clients did for last session on a time when the client was successful in avoiding cravings or the urge to drink or use other drugs. Hold a reflection group and discuss the elements of that thinking report, including:

- In the situation clients reported on, were there other people trying to encourage them to use?

- Who were those people, and what did the clients say to refuse?

In this session, we look at ways to be more assertive that will help us in those high-risk situations involving pressures from others to relapse into full AOD use.

b. Three old ways to deal with conflict or solve problems that, in the long run, don't work at getting your needs met:

1) Avoid the problem or be passive: *FLIGHT.* The person who avoids problems:

- Gives up his or her rights when there is any conflict with what someone else wants;

- Doesn't get what he or she wants at her or his own expense;

2) To attack others or get aggressive: *FIGHT.*

- The aggressive person protects her/his own rights but gets what he or she wants at the *expense* of others;

- With the aggressive person, others pay.

3) To be passive-aggressive: *FAKE.*

- FAKE falls between avoiding and being aggressive;

- Person is not direct in approaching problems;

- Fails to express needs in a way that other people can respond to them;

- Passive-aggressive people don't get what they want at the expense of themselves and others;

- Both others and the person pays.

None of these gives a positive result. None of these get your needs met in healthy ways. All three methods drive people away. When this happens, we will often use drugs or engage in criminal behavior to get our needs met. Engaging in criminal behavior is both passive-aggressive and aggressive behavior.

c. **What is the healthy choice? Being Assertive—FAIR:**

Many of our problems come from trying to get our needs met. Learning to be assertive attempts to get your needs met but *not* by making others pay for it.

- The healthy choice is to learn and practice the skills of being assertive;

- The assertive person does not compromise his or her rights;

- The assertive person does not get something at the expense of others.

d. **The art of being assertive—Here are 10 key ways to be assertive:**

1) Recognize your rights in a situation without trespassing on the rights of others;

2) Know how to clearly state your opinions and what it is you want from others: Assertive people know how to clearly state their opinions and what it is they want from others. By being assertive, we gain more control over our lives. While it doesn't guarantee that we will get our own way every time, it does improve the chances that our needs will be met without hurting others (Monti et al., 1989; Ross et al., 1986).

3) Consider the needs of others as you get your own needs met: Assertive people keep the needs of others in mind as they work at getting their own needs met;

4) Be flexible and give, yet at the same time continue to make your position clear;

5) Avoid blaming; avoid using *"you";*

6) State how you feel and think; use "I" messages;

7) Have your goals clearly in mind; know what you want;

8) Confront the issues head on. Attack the problem and not the person.

9) Become part of the solution and not part of the problem;

10) Once you make a decision, stick with what you have decided. Don't relive or continually rehash *what might have been.*

e. **Applying the skills of assertiveness:**

Exercise: You want to take a Friday afternoon off so that you can attend your son's football game. It is very important to you. You are out of vacation time. You have two days of sick time. The football game is two weeks away. Work is busy and the boss is not giving time away easily.

1) Give a statement to illustrate each of these four ways to handle the problem:

- Avoiding—FLIGHT;

- Aggressive—FIGHT;

- Passive-aggressive—FAKE.

- Assertiveness—FAIR.

2) Now, apply the 10 keys to being assertive to this situation. Come up with several assertive statements you can use with the boss.

Exercise: Role-play the following scenario. An employee's boss promised her a bonus for working on the weekend. The extra money does not appear on her/his paycheck. Role-play various styles of handling this situation: avoidant and passive, aggressive, passive-aggressive and assertive. The goal is to get the bonus without offending the boss. After each situation, have the observers identify the personality type that was depicted and tell whether the employee's goals were met.

Exercise: Have clients choose a real situation to role-play. Keep the focus on the assertive style.

Have the group give feedback and suggestions regarding how the assertive character could have achieved the desired outcome. Here are some examples that can be used:

- You have paid all your bills, but a department store says your bill is delinquent.

- You buy an appliance for full price and a day later see it advertised for one-third off.

- A friend wants to borrow money so he can purchase some drugs that he can sell at a very high profit.

- A friend wants to borrow money for drugs. You know he has been trying to stay clean.

4. Classroom or Homework Activities

a. Either during class or during the following week, have clients choose three situations in which they have an opportunity to be assertive and report on them. These may be simple instances in everyday life. Use *Work Sheet 35* in the Workbook.

b. **Homework:** Have clients choose a recent time when they were frustrated with a situation and needed it to be resolved. Have them do a *thinking report* on what happened and record the elements in their journal. Review the elements of the thinking report with clients:

SITUATION,

THOUGHTS,

FEELINGS,

ATTITUDES AND BELIEFS ABOUT THE SITUATION,

OUTCOME.

5. Presentation Sequence

a. Review previous session and homework;

b. Discuss the Rationale and Objectives for Assertiveness Skills Development;

c. Present content as outlined;

d. Model avoidant, aggressive and assertive styles. Discuss outcomes of each presentation;

e. Outline homework assignment and briefly look at next session.

6. Session and Client Response Evaluation

   a. Have clients complete CSES;

   b. Counselor completes PSES using following guideline questions:

      1) *Do participants understand the difference between being aggressive and being assertive?*

      2) *Are clients able to use the assertiveness skills?*

Session ③③ : Deeper Problem Solving

1. Rationale and Overview of Session

Many substance abusers and offenders have poor problem solving skills. We began to look at problem solving in Module 7, Session 19. We will take a closer look at problem solving and alternative solutions in this session. Problems are part of life, they happen every day. They can originate in social situations and in our own thoughts, attitudes and beliefs. The SAO tends to problem solve by being impulsive, by thinking rigidly, by reacting from old habits and patterns. We will focus on helping the SAO change these old problem solving thinking and action patterns. It is important that the client learn problem solving since the frustration and hopelessness presented by unsolved problems can lead to relapse.

Hopefully, the group has already grasped the importance of *stop and think,* and knows to gather more information (facts, rather than opinions) about the problem before they try to solve it. The lesson of this session is not to choose the first solution that comes to mind, but to look at as many *alternatives* as possible and then choose the best of those alternatives.

2. Objectives of Session

> ⇒ Review the basic steps of problem solving learned in Module 7;
>
> ⇒ Clients will expand their skills in identifying and solving problems and analyzing their needs in different situations;
>
> ⇒ Clients will learn to consider alternative solutions and select the most promising way to solve the problem;
>
> ⇒ Clients learn cooperation or compromise when neither party can agree completely with the other's solution to a problem.

3. Session Content and Process

a. We haven't been good problem solvers:

Substance abusers and people with a history of criminal conduct have not been good problem solvers. Problems are part of life. They happen every day. They can come up in social situations and in our own thoughts, attitudes and beliefs. Often, we problem solve on the spur of the moment (impulsively). We often fail to see different solutions. We often don't get the facts. We tend to keep our attention on the person we are problem solving with rather than the problem. One way we have learned to solve problems is to use drugs or commit a crime. Good problem solving skills will keep us from going back to drugs (relapsing) or criminal conduct (recidivism).

b. Remember the simple steps of problem solving we learned in Module 7, Session 19 (page 118 of Workbook)?

1) *What is the problem?*

2) *What is my goal?* What would I like to see as the solution to the problem? What do I want the outcome to be?

3) *What are the various solutions?* What is in my power to do? What action should I take or can I take? Are there different solutions? Get information you need to make the best choice;

4) *What are the obstacles to a solution?*

5) *Choose a solution—take action.*

6) *Study the outcome.* What was the result? Was it in my best interest? Could I have done something different? What will I do next time?

c. **Here are some deeper steps to good problem solving. These steps are essentially rooted in John Dewey's (1910) classic description of how people solve problems and modified by the authors and other sources, (e.g., King et al., 1994, Monti et al., 1989, Smith Meyer, 1995):**

1) *Study the problem:* Slow down—stop and think! Identify the problem! What is it you don't like? What is it you want? Can you say what your goal is? What is keeping you from reaching your goal? What do you need to change?

2) *Do we have all the facts?* What other information would be good to have? Get more facts.

3) *Have you been here before?* If so, what did you do that time? The solution may have to be changed a little, but if it was successful in the past, it may be a good place to begin.

4) *Consider alternatives*—different solutions: It helps to try to get another perspective on the problem. Can you think of how the problem might look to the other person involved? If it were not another person's problem, would that person be able to give someone else advise about it?

5) *Brainstorm:* Come up with all of the alternatives you can think of—they don't have to be good solutions, just ideas.

6) *Consider the consequences:* REMIND THE GROUP THAT WE LEARNED EARLIER THAT THERE IS A REACTION TO EVERYTHING WE DO. Choose several of the suggested alternatives and consider what the positive and negative outcomes would be if each were used. Be sure to consider both long- and short-term results to everyone involved. What do you think the outcome will be—short-term and long-term?

7) *Choose the best solution:* Consider the best solutions that have been suggested and order them in terms of desirability and consequences. Select the best one to be implemented first.

8) *Work the solution:* Try it. Be open minded. Make it work. If it doesn't, start over.

9) *Study the results* or the outcome.

10) *Try the solution again* with another problem.

Until you have tried a solution, it cannot be assessed. Remember that some things take time, so you may have to work at the situation to change it. Can you do something more to improve the outcome? If it is not effective in a reasonable amount of time, then review the solutions you came up with before and see if the second-best one will do the trick.

d. **How do we know we have a problem?**

Where can we get a clue to what is going on? Monti and his colleagues (1989) suggest that you can pay attention to your *body and behavior.* Do you feel signs of indigestion, anxiety, or depression? Are you not doing your work as well as usual, or not acting as you would like with your family? Are you not getting along with other people or do they seem to avoid you? If you are feeling uncomfortable about a situation, you probably have a problem.

e. **Make your problem solving solution focused. Here are the keys to this (from Fisher & Ury, 1981):**

* Keep your attention on the problem and not the person;

* Keep your attention on the needs and interests of people involved and not on the positions they take;

* Don't argue the positions people take;

* Pick solutions for the gain of all, and not just for yourself.

f. **Reflection group and exercises:**

Discussion: Let's start by talking about problems you are already aware of. Could someone tell us about a personal problem that is bothering you now and tell us how it makes you feel? Does it influence how you act with other people or make you feel uncomfortable inside? (Get several examples from the group, but only IDENTIFY THE PROBLEMS AND THE FEELINGS ASSOCIATED WITH THEM AT THIS TIME, DON'T TRY TO SOLVE THEM.)

Exercise: Use *Work Sheet 36*. Choose a problem identified earlier by the group for analysis. Follow the outline above in helping the group work through the problem.

4. Review of Homework for the Coming Week

a. Use *Work Sheet 36*. Have clients identify a problem they are having difficulty solving. Describe the problem, go through the problem solving process, and choose a possible solution. Use these simple steps reviewed above for studying and coming up with solutions to this problem. Then, apply the more in-depth steps outlined above.

b. *Thinking Report*—PROBLEM-SOLVING:

Have clients think back on a problem they have had in the past. What were the consequences of the solutions to the problem? Do a thinking report on what happened.

SITUATION,

THOUGHTS,

FEELINGS,

ATTITUDES AND BELIEFS ABOUT THE SITUATION,

OUTCOME.

5. Presentation Sequence

a. Start out with a Reflection Group. How are people doing? Review previous session and homework.

b. Discuss the rationale and objectives for *Deeper Problem Solving*.

c. Present session as in content outline above;

d. Choose a problem cited by a group member for analysis by the group. Repeat exercise with another problem.

e. Outline homework assignment.

f. Brief look at next session.

6. Session and Client Response Evaluation

a. Clients complete CSES;

b. Counselor completes PSES using the following questions as guides:

1) *Did the group successfully identify some real problems in their lives and analyze their needs in the problem situation?*

2) *Was the group helpful in developing alternative solutions and helping to select the best solution?*

c. This segment brings to a close work on AOD and CC cravings and urges, learning and practicing assertiveness skills and behavior and learning more in-depth problem solving skills. Do a BRF on each client, calculate the score and provide feedback on progress.

Session ㉞ : Handling Feelings—Anger Management

Session Break: Sessions 34 through 36 are to be delivered in sequence. New participants may be brought into the program at this point.

1. Overview of Sessions 34 Through 36 and Rationale for This Session

The next three sessions will focus on the management of anger, aggression, guilt and depression and the prevention of violence. These are major problems for the SAO. At the beginning of this session, the provider should have clients review their *Master Profile* (MP). A number of the scales in the MP address issues of anger, guilt, depression and violence. In Part I, *AOD Use Assessment,* these include *Coping with Relationships* and *Behavioral Control Loss*. In Part II, *Criminal and Antisocial Thinking and Conduct,* these include *Impulsive Thinking and Acting, Criminal Thinking and Thoughts, Angry and Aggressive Attitudes* and *Rebellious Anti-Authority*. There are other scales which are also relevant. It is helpful for the clients to re-rate themselves across these scales. Have clients share in group whether they changed their ratings. Do they need to revise their *Master Assessment Profile* (MAP) based on new findings?

Criminal conduct is *anger* conduct. Anger drives much of the behavior of the substance abusing offender. The SAO is an angry person. This anger comes from errors in thinking. The beliefs and thoughts of being "shortchanged," of not being treated fairly, of being a victim of unfair situations all lead to an angry attitude. But many substance abusing offenders are not aware of their anger. Therefore, managing angry feelings, controlling angry behavior, and changing angry thoughts and beliefs are important parts of self-improvement and change for the SAO. This module will concentrate on the management of anger, but the skills involved should be helpful in handling other emotions as well.

Emotions are closely related to thinking; seldom do we experience one without the other. When the emotion is stronger than the thought, the SAO may be ruled by the emotion rather than logic. It is important to teach the offender the cognitive techniques that allow the control of emotions rather than being controlled by emotions. Ross and his co-workers (1986) propose that offenders' successful social adaptation requires that they are able to

a. Respond to interpersonal conflict in a manner that effectively prevents them from becoming emotionally aroused;

b. Maintain or reduce their level of arousal to a moderate level in emotionally provoking situations;

c. Recognize the psychological and physiological indications of arousal so that they may be able to acquire control of their emotions.

2. Objectives of Session

> ➠ Clients recognize angry thoughts and feelings;
>
> ➠ Clients understand that anger is usually caused by, or part of, some problem, and that we need alternatives for successful problem solving;
>
> ➠ Clients become aware of the events that normally trigger anger in them as individuals and of the physiological and psychological signals they experience when angry;
>
> ➠ Clients learn and practice the social skills and self-control techniques that will help them manage anger and avoid the destructive effects of anger.

3. Session Content and Process

a. **Anger is a big part of substance abuse and criminal conduct:**

Anger has been the basis of much of your substance abuse and criminal behavior. A criminal act is an angry act. Often, getting high or drunk is an angry act, since you know that the results will hurt others. Hurting others is an angry act. This is not an easy thing to be aware of. You may reject these statements. But give them some thoughts. Substance abuse behavior and criminal conduct are angry things to do. These behaviors strike out at others. Managing your angry thoughts and feelings is very important in your effort to change.

b. **What is behind our anger?**

There are many things behind our anger. See if these fit:

1) The beliefs and thoughts of being "shortchanged";

2) Feelings of not being treated fairly;

3) Feeling that you are a victim;

4) Feeling that your personal space or territory (something or someone that is yours) has been taken away, tread upon or violated;

5) Feeling that you are being humiliated.

All of these can lead to an angry attitude. But you are often not aware of your anger. So, before you can *manage* your anger, you have to know you are angry. Then, you need skills to manage your angry thoughts and your angry actions. *Remember:* It's our thoughts that produce our emotions. Angry thoughts lead to angry feelings and actions. Anger is not caused by events, but by our thoughts in response to that event.

c. **Anger is set off by some problem:**

A big part of handling your anger is through problem solving. But remember: It's your *thoughts* that produce your emotions. Angry thoughts lead to angry feelings and actions. Anger is *not caused* by events, but by your thoughts in response to events.

d. **Basic steps to manage and control anger and other emotions:**

1) Be aware of your anger:

- Be aware of your anger when you feel it. Use *self-talk*. Say to yourself "I'm angry."

- Be aware of what you are angry about and what are your angry thoughts. They're different. Use *Work Sheet 37* to list what you are angry about and to list your angry thoughts. Are they different for you?

- Pay attention to what goes on inside you when you get angry. You may feel your stomach churn, increased sweating, clenched fists, tight muscles, or any number of other sensations. Pay attention to these internal cues. Not everyone responds in the same way.

2) Know the difference between *feeling angry* and the results of *being angry*. Being angry might include aggression and violence. Anger is a powerful feeling. It is not good or bad. It is how we show or *act out* our anger that makes the difference. It can be destructive or constructive.

3) Recognize *destructive* anger. Destructive anger confuses people and leads to bad decision making. It makes us aggressive. This blocks communication. It gets people mad at you. It leaves you feeling helpless. It destroys your feelings of self-worth.

4) Recognize *constructive* anger. Constructive anger expresses the emotions in such a way that you feel better afterward. It builds communication. People know you are angry and they listen. Constructive anger can trigger problem solving. It helps you to be assertive. It allows people to listen. It gives you power (Monti et al., 1989).

5) When the anger builds, use some basic techniques to get self-control. Without self-control, you can't express your anger in constructive ways. You just get angry. These skills will help:

- Use self-talk: "CALM DOWN AND TRY TO STAY COOL."

- Include some techniques that work for other people such as taking 5 deep breaths and exhaling slowly, *chilling out,* relaxing, counting to ten or counting backwards from 20, or just leaving the situation.

6) Now, *express* your anger. Tell people you are angry. Don't just get angry. Don't act it out. Use the "I" message. "I'm feeling angry. I'm mad." You act out your anger when you blame others, when you use the "you message," when you yell, and when you turn against someone physically. There are two healthy reasons for expressing anger:

- To get it off your chest;

- To communicate the thoughts that bring on the anger. If you yell, you don't communicate thoughts. *They can't hear what you think.*

7) After you express your anger:

- Again ask yourself "What am I angry about?" Was it rational? Did it make sense?

- Let the other person respond.

8) Study your anger and your angry thoughts after you have expressed your anger and you're over it. What am I really angry about? Did the person really attack or insult me? Are they trying to get me angry? What are the positive things about this situation? Think about the situation piece by piece so that you understand exactly what happened.

9) Move your anger into problem solving. Apply the problem solving skills learned in Sessions 19 (p. 118) and 33 (p. 185):

- Think about your options (alternatives) in the situation.

- What can you do that would be in your best interest? I need to do some problem solving. Which alternative is the best one?

- Try to resolve the problem, remembering that the other person is also upset. Try to "COMMUNICATE THE MESSAGE" and "HEAR AND BE HEARD" (King et al., 1994, p. 56);

- It is possible you will not be able to resolve the conflict. Do not argue. You can't fix everything. Try not to think about the situation over and over, it will only upset you more.

10) If you are successful, be proud and congratulate yourself. Reward yourself.

REMEMBER: YOU GET ANGRY SO THAT YOU CAN EXPRESS YOUR ANGRY THOUGHTS, NOT JUST YOUR ANGRY FEELINGS.

"You're so angry I can't hear your thoughts."

e. **Practice exercise in managing anger:**

Exercise: Use this scenario to practice how we manage our anger. Your parole officer has denied you privileges for two weeks. How are you going to react to this? Do you have any choices in this situation? What can you do to resolve the problem? (adapted from King et al., 1994). HAVE THE GROUP DEMONSTRATE THAT THEY UNDERSTAND THAT NORMAL PROBLEM SOLVING SKILLS SHOULD BE EMPLOYED, EVEN IN A SITUATION WHERE THEY HAVE LITTLE POWER.

Exercise: Have the members of the group tell what things make them angry most often and how they feel at the time. Think about situations when you were driving, at home, at work, or with friends. Make a list of those feelings. What are the *physical* reactions (e.g., pounding heart, tension in the muscles) and the *psychological* reactions (feeling blamed, guilty, tired or depressed)?

Exercise: What kind of things do you say to yourself when you are getting angry? What do you do to try and control your anger? Does it work? Make a list of the things people do that help themselves.

Exercise: Have the group divide into dyads. Using examples of anger cited in the class discussion. Each group member should roleplay a situation in which he or she demonstrates a constructive response to conflict.

f. **Focused reflection group around the following topics:**

- Have the group share examples of when they were so angry that they wouldn't talk to the other person;

- When the other person was so angry they wouldn't listen to what s/he had to say;

- When they were so angry they couldn't express their position and then reacted with violence;

- In each condition, have group members reflect on what they should have done.

g. **Group leader modeling:**

The group leader selects one of the examples presented by group members. The client who became angry plays the part of the person who triggered his or her angry response. The group leader models an appropriate response to the situation by demonstrating how he or she manages to

- stay cool;

- use soothing self-talk;

- think about options;

- communicate clearly;

- listen to the other person's perspective; and

- accept the conflict gracefully if it cannot be resolved.

4. Classroom and Homework Activities

a. Have clients complete *Work Sheet 37:* List what makes you angry and list your angry thoughts.

b. Using *Work Sheet 38,* have clients identify triggers and symptoms of anger.

c. *Thinking Report*—Self-Control: Think of a recent event in which you became angry but managed to control the emotion. Write a thinking report on that incident.

5. Presentation Sequence

a. Review previous session and homework. If the provider is using an open-ended model, then this is a break-point session, and new clients may not have had Session 33.

b. Discuss the rationale and objectives for Handling Feelings—Anger Management.

c. Present content as outlined above.

d. Review classroom and homework activities.

e. Close with a 20-minute reflection group if time allows.

f. Take a brief look at the next session.

6. Session and Client Response Evaluation

a. Clients complete CSES.

b. Do PSES. Use these questions:

1) *Did the group understand the relationship between management of emotions, specifically anger, and problem solving?*

2) *Were the participants aware that there are psychological and physiological responses to emotion?*

3) *Did the group members demonstrate that they were appreciating the importance of self-control in handling anger?*

Session ③⑤ : Preventing Aggression and Violence

1. Rationale and Overview of Session

For the SAO, failure to control anger and avoid aggressive and violent behavior is a threat to continued or eventual freedom from incarceration. Furthermore, for many of the offenders, anger and aggression may be typical responses to frustration. Thus, self-control in anger-producing situations is an important skill to master.

It is important to make clear to the clients that physical aggression is violence. They are the same. We can be verbally aggressive. This might be called *verbal violence or abuse*. We reserve the word violence for aggression which is of a physical nature.

We have introduced the basic approach to controlling anger. The offender's success will depend largely on her/his ability to control emotions and practice self-control. Recognizing that all conflict cannot be avoided, it is important that, when aroused, the substance abusing offender can maintain a moderate level of arousal in an emotionally charged situation. It is only with practice that sufficient skill in self-control will be learned. This session is devoted to understanding aggression and violence, understanding and recognizing high-arousal situations, and then to practicing the skills for maintaining self-control skills in these situations. Self-control and coping skills are among the most important components of cognitive behavioral therapy in general and specifically in the rehabilitation of the substance abusing offender (e.g., Curry & Marlatt, 1987; Dimeff & Marlatt, 1995; Freeman et al., 1990; Goldfried, 1995; Hester, 1995; Monti et al., 1989; Monti et al., 1995). These are essential in preventing full relapse and/or recidivism.

2. Objectives of Session

> ➠ Clients understand the different types of aggression and which type of aggression each client may be more prone to become involved in;
>
> ➠ Clients become aware of the situations in which they are most likely to respond to arousal in an aggressive manner;
>
> ➠ Clients gain the necessary skills to maintain their self-control in circumstances that could lead to aggressive behavior and violence.

3. Session Content and Process

a. **This session is about self-control and keeping your freedom:**

Failure to control your anger will lead to aggressive behavior. That is a threat to your freedom. It's all about *self-control*. This is one of the most important skills for you to learn. Your success will depend on self-control.

b. **Anger is an emotion or feeling—aggression is a behavior:**

We dealt with handling your anger last session. This is a powerful emotion that often results in impulsive acts and/or aggression. Experts considered aggression a behavior rather than an emotion, attitude, or motive. Aggression is "any form of behavior directed toward the goal of harming or injuring another living being who is motivated to avoid such treatment" (Baron, 1977, p. 12). Aggression may be non-physical or physical.

1) *Non-physical aggression* is verbal and non-verbal behavior that abuses, injures or hurts someone emotionally or psychologically:

- It can damage another person's sense of dignity and self;

- It can lower another person's self-esteem;

367

- It can be directed at someone's sexual well-being;

- It can damage a person emotionally creating lasting emotional injury (e.g., fear, anxiety, depression, hostility and anger);

- It can cause another person to withdraw from others and feel threatened by any expression of anger;

- It can be calculated or impulsive;

- It can be controlled or uncontrolled rage.

2) *Physical aggression:* When aggression becomes physical, it is *VIOLENCE*. Violence does everything that non-physical aggression does, but it involves the person being physical. It causes physical harm and damage to things and people:

- Violence can be directed toward objects, involving smashing and breaking things, but this violence is always person oriented; it is always about someone you know;

- Violence can be directed at a person and can focus on the person's

  - Position of strength or power: this is when the victim has the strength or power to get in the way of the violent person's needs or goals and the violent person is initially weak;

  - Position of weakness: this is when the victim is weak and the violent person has to maintain a position of strength;

  - Position of sex: this is when the victim is a target of the violent person's distorted sexual needs and drives.

3) Sooner or later, non-physical aggression will end up in violence unless the aggression is controlled and dealt with in a positive manner.

4) Look at your own history of aggression and violence and be prepared to share how you see yourself in this arena.

c. **High-charged situations:**

Remember: events do not cause anger. It is our *thoughts* that come from the events that cause our anger. These thoughts that lead to anger are usually caused by some problem. There are *high-charged* situations. These are situations that bring angry thoughts. This is part of self-control. Self-control comes when we see alternatives to solve a problem. We can control much of our anger by controlling these thoughts and by seeing the alternatives. But we can also deal with much of our anger by not being involved in these high-charged situations. Use *Work Sheet 39* in your Workbook to list situations for you that could lead to aggression. Then check the right column if these situations could lead to physical aggression or violence.

d. **Remember the clues that tell you are getting angry:**

1) Feeling your body change—your physical reaction to anger. These are inside clues that will tell you that you are becoming angry.

   Exercise: Have each group member talk about their own physical cues—their own inside reactions that tell them they are getting angry.

2) Feeling irritable, agitated, on edge, tense.

3) Losing your temper: **Discussion:** Have the group members talk about a time that they lost their temper to the point that they became aggressive. What was the situation? How did they feel? Why couldn't they control themselves? Was this situation similar to other times that they lost control? Are there common themes to help them avoid similar situations in the future?

4) Feeling impatient; feeling things are not going your way; feeling not in control.

5) Feeling provoked or pushed by someone; maybe in a bar; maybe by your spouse; maybe by the boss.

    Exercise: Have two group members roleplay a situation in which one insults the other and they respond to the point that one becomes angry. Try deep breathing to control the anger. Have the players discuss how they felt.

6) Thinking and feeling you are not being treated fairly.

e. **Self-control is the key: How to manage anger and aggressive impulses (review the skills to change thinking and doing and self-control in Session 17, p. 105):**

1) When feeling the anger: Use the *relaxation techniques* you learned in Session 17. *Deep breathe*. Close your eyes and think of a calm scene. Feel your hands get heavy.

2) Use *self-talk*. Hear your own voice calm yourself. Hear the angry thought. Use *thought stopping*. Think of the long-term consequences of getting aggressive and violent.

3) *Thought replacement:* Replace the angry thoughts with positive thoughts. Remember in Session 27 (p. 159) how you armed yourself with positive thoughts. Use one of those methods.

4) When you begin to feel the anger, problem solve:

- What are my angry thoughts?

- What is the problem that is bringing the thoughts?

- What is my goal?

- Choose an action. This action should replace the angry thoughts.

5) The other person may also be angry and not reasoning well.

f. **Let's practice self-control with these exercises:**

Exercise: Have clients in the group imagine a scene that arouses anger. Now lead them in practicing relaxation techniques. Have the group take slow, deep breaths. Use these words: "Take a deep breath. Hold your breath. Hold it, hold it, hold it. Now, let it go slowly through your mouth. Slowly blow out the air in your lungs. Clear your mind of your thoughts as you let go of the air." Now, tell yourself, "I am relaxed, I feel calm, I feel relaxed." Repeat this three times with the group. Then, have clients do it on their own.

Exercise: (adapted from Ross et al., 1986). Use this scenario with clients and use these words: "Imagine you are in a line for tickets that you really want. There are only so many tickets for sale and you have been in line for 30 minutes. The line is moving very slowly."

Wait for 30 seconds

"Picture the people ahead of you and behind you."

Wait for 30 seconds

"Your feet hurt, you are hungry, it is hot, and you are tired. Imagine this feeling."

Wait for 15 seconds

"All of a sudden a guy in a 3-piece suit barges up and gets into the line ahead of you. Can you picture it clearly?"

"You tell him politely but firmly that 'there is a line here.' He turns around and says, 'go to hell.' Think about this. Focus your thoughts on this. What are your thoughts? Now, write them down as you think them."

Allow 1 minute

"What you just wrote are the things you were saying to yourself, your 'self-talk.' Our thoughts are what we say to ourselves. It's natural to talk to yourself. Our self-talk can be things that make us more angry and aroused, or things that will allow us to calm down and consider the alternatives in the situation. Now share your thoughts."

Use a flip-chart or chalkboard and list the thoughts reported by the group.

Most of the thoughts can be expected to be angry comments. Point out that these are called "destructive self-talk" and will probably increase the client's own anger (Ross et al., 1986, p. 170). They are to be expected but will not help defuse the situation.

Are there any comments that will work to reduce anger and help them calm down? Underline them if there are any. If not, suggest some that would be constructive in the situation. Can the group think of any others? These positive thoughts are called *control self-talk*.

Remember that it is not productive to try to solve the problem with someone who is angry and aggressive. Try to get them to calm down and then you can work it out instead of fighting it out.

Exercise: Have clients pick a scene that arouses anger in the client. Have them imagine the scene. Now have them practice these relaxation techniques:

- Relax by taking slow, deep breaths;

- Inhale slowly, hold your breath, count to five, and then release your breath;

- Repeat your deep breathing exercise, releasing your breath slowly;

- Now clear your mind of all thoughts, and if a thought interrupts, tell yourself, "I AM RELAXED." REPEAT THIS EXERCISE.

Exercise: Now, have clients take another scene that brings up anger inside of them. This time, have them use self-talk to address the feelings of anger and to develop control over the anger. Use thought stopping to do this. Use the other tools you have learned to manage your anger.

4. Classroom or Homework Activities

a. Classroom task: Have clients do *Work Sheet 39* on high-charged situations.

b. Have clients do *Work Sheet 40,* Managing Aggression.

c. Review next week's session in Workbook.

d. No thinking report this week. Hooray!

5. Presentation Sequence

a. Go over the major points of the last session. Continue to emphasize the fact that, regardless of the emotion or nature of the problem being experienced, the skills of the previous sessions can be utilized to deal with the situation.

b. Review the *Thinking Report* homework on self-control. Have some clients share their particular event in which they became angry and that they were able to control. Were participants able to generate alternative explanations of the events that triggered the anger? Was there any pattern to the thoughts reported?

c. Discuss the rationale and objectives for managing aggression.

d. Present the session as outlined in Section 3 above.

e. Close with reflection group.

6. Session and Client Response Evaluation

a. Clients complete CSES;

b. Counselor does PSES: Address these issues:

1) *Was the group aware of their patterns of arousal or the triggers that make them likely to respond to arousal in an aggressive manner?*

2) *Did most of the clients appear to understand what skills are necessary to respond to circumstances that lead to aggressive behavior?*

Session 36 : Managing Guilt, Anger and Depression: The Emotional Cycles of Rehabilitation

1. Rationale and Overview of Session

Emotional or psychological disturbances found among substance abusing offenders can be viewed as either *primary* or *secondary*. A **primary** psychological disturbance or disorder exists relatively *independently* from yet interacts with substance abuse or criminal conduct. Depression, anxiety or psychotic symptoms are underlying and primary. The primary disturbance categories are often expressed in various typology systems. For example, the *Neurotic-Anxious* type of offender in the Quay (1984) classification most likely represents an expression of primary emotional disturbance. Studies attempting to determine the prevalence of primary mental disturbances among offenders vary as to results. When all categories of mental disturbances are considered, including personality disorders, from 75 to 100 percent of offenders receive some kind mental disorder diagnosis (Andrews & Bonta, 1994). Most studies (e.g., Cloninger & Guze, 1970; Daniel et al., 1988; Guy et al., 1985; Hodgins & Cote, 1990; Teplin & Swartz, 1989) indicate that the prevalence of severe mental disorders, such as schizophrenia or other psychotic expressions, ranges from 1 to 10 percent. These same studies indicate that the prevalence rates of primary depression or other affective disorders range from 1 to 17 percent. A study by Wanberg (1992) suggests that up to 20 percent of committed juvenile offenders are experiencing primary psychological problems.

Most likely, SAOs with primary emotional or psychological disturbances have been identified before being referred to the SSC program. The testing done at admission and in the in-depth assessment done in Module 8 will provide further assessment for these conditions. For example, the *Beck Depression Inventory* will provide further assessment for primary depressions. Our focus in this session, however, is on secondary emotional or psychological problems or disturbances.

Secondary emotional or psychological problems are found in many substance abusing offenders. These are problems that are *interactive with* or *consequences* of involvement in substance abuse and criminal behavior. For example, lapses in the SAO can lead to feelings of depression, guilt, anger and self-blame. Addicted people often catastrophize, thinking they'll never be successful in their quest to remain clean. Guilt, anger and depressive moods are common during the recovery and rehabilitation process. They can be related to the actual toxic effects of the substance being used. (Recall Module 3, Session 8, the "psychological and physical addictions model.") There may, however, be actual losses experienced by the recovering SAO such as divorce and other circumstances estranging the SAO from significant others. Feelings of *guilt* and *depression* should be considered high-risk situations, for they may lead to relapses and a vicious cycle of repeated failures. These thoughts and related feelings need to be challenged since they are often part of recidivism and relapse.

As in other obstacles we have discussed, guilt and depression can be addressed as problems that need to be solved. The client needs to change the way s/he thinks and behaves and increase the pleasant activities in her/his life. Each symptom of depression should be treated as a separate problem, but since the symptoms of depression are related to each other, improvement in one will lead to improvement in another symptom (Kadden et al., 1992).

2. Objectives of Session

> ➠ Clients will become aware of the signs of depressed, angry or guilty automatic negative thoughts and take action to change their thinking patterns.
>
> ➠ Clients will learn to more effectively manage negative feeling states of anger, guilt and depression by changing the thoughts and behaviors that promote them.
>
> ➠ Clients will learn and identify with the guilt-anger cycle.

3. Session Content and Process

a. Review the client's Master Profile and Master Assessment Plan:

Have the client review his or her MP and MAP. Attend particularly to the scales of emotional disruption in Part I of the profile, the *Angry/Aggressive Attitude* scale in Part II and *Emotional-Psychological* scale in Part II. Are there clients who have special needs in these areas?

b. The big three emotions: Anger, guilt and depression:

In the two previous sessions, we spent a lot of time looking at how we can manage angry thoughts and feelings and how we can prevent these thoughts and feelings from manifesting into aggression and violence. Anger, however, has many faces. One dimension of anger is how it is related to guilt and depression. Thus, as we look at the emotions and moods of guilt and depression, we also look at how anger interacts with these two companion emotions.

c. How lapses and relapse are related to the three mood states:

Lapses or initial relapse (either going back to patterns that lead to using drugs or actually using drugs) can lead to feelings of depression, guilt, anger and self-blame. But these emotions and thoughts around them can lead to lapses. It becomes a vicious circle. All of these emotions get mixed together. People with AOD and CC problems often see the worst of things. They catastrophize; *it will never work out*. These thoughts, if not corrected, will lead to further failure.

Guilt, anger and depressive moods will be common during your recovery and rehabilitation process. They can be due to the lasting toxic effects of the drugs you used or to the losses you had during your drug using and criminal period of life. Feelings of guilt, anger and depression are very high-risk states. They can lead to relapses and a vicious cycle of repeated failures.

d. The guilt-anger cycle:

Guilt, anger and depression are common with all folks. You are not special in having these feelings and thoughts. You are special in that your guilty, angry and depressive thoughts and feelings lead to drug use and criminal conduct. This is special. You must get a handle on these feelings if you want to keep your status of free choice.

As we have talked about before, during our growing up period, we were often not allowed to be angry, feel guilty or get depressed. If we showed anger, we were told to cool it and so we did not learn to express it. If we felt overly guilty, someone would say, *it's OK, you don't have to feel bad about what you did.* If we got depressed, we were told cheer up. It is no wonder that we never developed skills to deal with these moods and thoughts. But we expressed these emotions through using drugs. It was easier to get angry with a few drinks and feel guilty after drinking. We used drugs to express these feelings, but when using drugs, we often did not control them. Thus, we began to experience the *guilt-anger cycle*. Here is how it works.

Because we did not learn healthy outlets for anger and hostility, we built them up inside. When we got high, we could let them go, but in destructive ways. We blew up, were irrational, or hurt others emotionally and even physically. After we sobered up, we would often have strong thoughts and feelings of guilt. This again keeps us from dealing with our anger. We feel too guilty. We again build up these feelings. They reach a peak, and when using drugs, we again let them out in hurtful ways. We start the cycle over. Figure 27 (Figure 16 in Workbook) describes this cycle. How do we break the cycle? Let's look at some ways.

Exercise: Have clients describe in group how they see themselves fitting the guilt-anger cycle.

e. Breaking the cycle: Managing the moods of guilt, anger and depression:

Here are some ways that we can manage our moods of guilt, anger and depression and break the guilt-anger cycle:

1) Learn to become aware of having guilty, angry and depressed thoughts and feelings. Here is what we look for:

- First, *recognize the thoughts* of guilt, anger, depression. "I'm no good." "I let her down." "They deserve that." "What's the use?"

- *Notice when your mood changes.* Pay attention to your body. What are your posture and facial expressions?

- Are you *avoiding people and activities* that you used to enjoy? Do you have trouble concentrating or making decisions?

- Are you sitting around a lot, *doing nothing?*

- *Thinking and feeling hopeless.*

- *Not eating or overeating.*

Exercise: Have clients use *Work Sheet 41* in their Workbook and make a list of their thoughts of guilt, anger and depression.

Exercise: Have clients retake the *Beck Depression Inventory* and the *Mood Appraisal Questionnaire.* Look over their answers. These instruments measure guilt, anger and depression. Discuss their results in group.

2) Deal directly with your angry, guilty and depressive thoughts and feelings;

3) Change guilt, anger and depression by doing these things (Kadden et al., 1992):

- Be aware of your negative thoughts;

- Replace these thoughts with positive ones; and

- Make these new positive thoughts part of your everyday life.

4) Use skills you have learned. Review Module 6, Session 17:

- Self-talk skills;

- Shifting your views;

- Relaxation skills.

5) Increase your involvement in positive activities:

This helps you change your thinking and lift your feelings of depression. When active, depressed people feel better, experience less fatigue, feel more motivated, and feel more capable mentally.

f. **Be aware of your thoughts of guilt, anger and depression:**

Discussion: When do you feel guilty or depressed? What is going on around you? How do you respond? (Not everyone in the group will own these feelings, but those who do can provide valuable clues to the rest of the group.)

Remember, the first step in handling your anger, guilt and depression is to be aware of your *thoughts* of anger, guilt or depression. They often are *automatic thoughts.* They lead us to negative thinking and uncontrolled feelings of anger, thoughts and depression. Here are some examples of these automatic thoughts that can lead us to depression, guilt or anger (examples adapted from Kadden et al., 1992, pp. 69-70):

Magnifying—Blowing negative events out of proportion. *This is the worst thing that could happen to me.*

Jumping to conclusions—*I have a swollen gland. This must be cancer.*

Overgeneralizing—*I always fail—I fail at everything I ever try.*

Self-blame—*I'm no good.* Blaming total self rather than specific behaviors that can be changed.

Discussion: Ask the group to discuss what angry, guilty or depressive thoughts they have about themselves or their lives. Are they realistic thoughts? How do these thoughts affect their lives and behavior? What relationships, if any, do feelings of guilt, anger or depression have to the use of substances or the commission of crimes? Can there be another explanation for what causes the negative thoughts?

Exercise: Have clients role-play substituting positive but realistic thoughts for negative (guilt, anger, depression) automatic thoughts that may lead to substance abuse or crime.

4. Recommended Classroom and Homework Activities

a. Do *Work Sheet 41* in the Workbook. Discuss it in group.

b. *Thinking report*—depression and guilt:

Think of a situation in which you felt depressed and/or guilty. Do a thinking report.

SITUATION,

THOUGHTS,

FEELINGS,

ATTITUDES AND BELIEFS ABOUT THE SITUATION,

OUTCOME.

5. Presentation Sequence

a. Review previous session and homework.

b. Discuss the rationale and objectives for managing guilt and depression.

c. Present session as outlined in content section. Have clients retake the *Mood Appraisal Questionnaire* and the *Beck Depression Inventory*.

d. Reflection of group session.

e. Review homework assignments.

f. Brief look at next session.

6. Session and Client Response Evaluation

a. Clients complete CSES.

b. Provider does PSES using these questions as a guide:

1) *Did depressed participants receive information that would help them feel differently about themselves and the world?*

2) *Are participants more adept at handling feelings of guilt?*

c. This session brings to a close the work on recognizing and managing anger, aggression, violence, guilt and depression. Complete a BRF on each client. Calculate the raw score. How is each client doing? The provider may want to give clients feedback as to how they are doing.

Figure 27

The Guilt-Anger Cycle

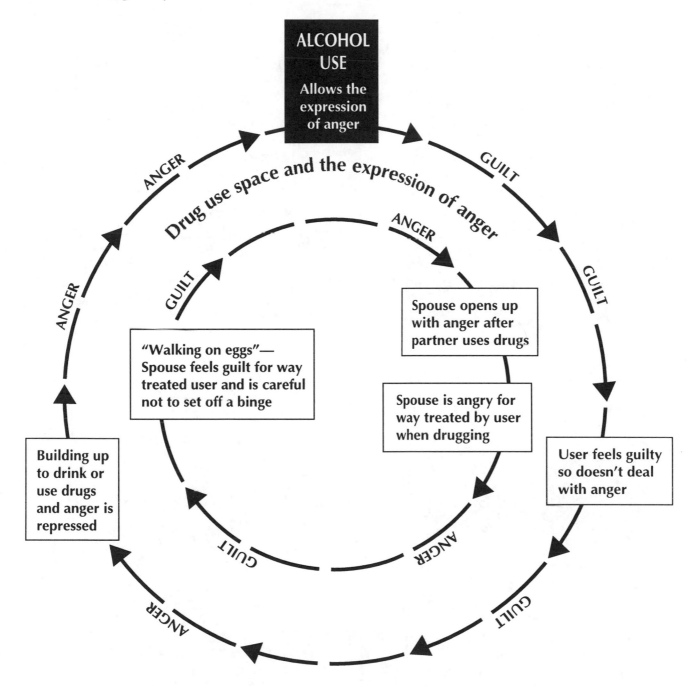

Session ㊲ : Developing and Keeping Intimate and Close Relationships

Session Break: Sessions 37 through 40 are to be delivered in sequence. These sessions will focus on intimate and close relationships, understanding values and moral development in relationship to others, empathy and responsible action in the community.

1. Rationale and Overview of Session

Most substance abusing offenders have a long history of problems in relationships and intimacy. Often, this is because the SAO lacks the skills and maturity necessary to develop and maintain close relationships over time. The purpose of this session is to help the client to build on the previously learned communication skills to enhance his or her ability to develop and maintain healthy close and intimate relationships. A key idea in this session is that using *good communication skills* with our intimate partners or people close to us is different from using them in the rest of our world. The difference lies in the fact that emotions and feelings are factored into the equation.

2. Objectives of Session

> ▶ Clients improve awareness regarding the importance of good communication in intimate and close relationships.
>
> ▶ Clients develop improved communication skills that will enhance intimacy and satisfaction from close relationships.

3. Session Content and Process

a. Review the client's Master Profile and Master Assessment Plan:

Have the client find the particular scales in the *Master Profile* that relate to developing and maintaining close and intimate relationships. Here are some of the scales to look at:

1) *Alcohol and Drug Use:*

- Coping with Social Discomfort;
- Coping with Relationships;
- Behavioral Control Loss;
- Social Responsibility.

2) *Criminal and Antisocial Thinking and Conduct:*

- Social and Interpersonal Skills;
- Angry and Aggressive Attitude.

3) *Current Life-Situation Problems:*

- Social and Interpersonal Problems;
- Marital and Family Problems.

Did the client address these when defining the problem areas in the MAP? Should the client make additions in these areas to the MAP?

b. Background for this session:

Many of our sessions have been given to working on developing *good communication skills*. These skills can improve our relationships and strengthen bonds with everyone from strangers and casual acquaintances to our closest friends and relatives. Frequently it is more difficult to solve problems with those with whom we are most intimate than with strangers. Sometimes this is true simply because of the emotional ties. We want to avoid anger, or tend to become angry too easily with them. We may fear failing in our relationship, or our inability to communicate may be influenced by our rigid expectations of the other person. We may have relied on alcohol or other drugs to deal with difficult feelings associated with people we love, work with or are responsible to. In this session, we will attempt to improve the specific skills necessary to improve intimate and close relationships.

Monti and his colleagues (1989) remind counselors that communication between people in intimate relationships should include problems or concerns about sexual issues. Since this may be an uncomfortable group topic, we suggest that the counselors be prepared with hypothetical examples as well as instructional material on discussing sexual topics. This will make the participants aware of how important good communication is in intimate relationships and also make it easier for them to discuss the topic in a direct manner.

REMEMBER, THERE IS POWER IN COMMUNICATION. IT IS THE POWER OF TALKING AND THE POWER OF LISTENING.

c. **Let's recall the two basic communication skills that we learned about in Sessions 23 through 25 of Module 9.**

1) *Active Sharing.* This is self-directed communication and is based on using the skills of

- Sharing about yourself—using "I" messages;

- Receiving feedback from others about you.

2) *Active Listening.* This is other-directed communication and is based on using the skills of

- Inviting the other person to share by using open statements or open questions;

- Reflecting back what you hear the other person saying so they know that you have heard them and are interested in what they have said to you.

Developing and keeping up good communication with people depends on your using these two skills. Also remember the two important parts of active sharing and active listening that we learned in Sessions 24 and 25:

1) Starting conversations;

2) Giving compliments.

These are also very important in keeping up good communication with people close to you.

d. **Good communication with a person close to you will:**

1) Help you feel closer to that person.

2) Help both understand each other better and know the other person's point of view.

3) Help you to solve problems and arguments that you have with each other and in life.

4) Result in more positive feelings and fewer negative feelings toward each other. For example, if you are nagging at each other about money all the time, you may feel negatively about each other in other ways and stop expressing affection to each other.

5) Result in you being less likely to start using substances or engaging in criminal conduct if you have an effective way to solve your problems in your personal relationships.

Discussion: Discuss the following questions: What are the things that keep you from being really close in a relationship? Why do you feel you may have trouble if people close to you know how you are feeling?

e. **Getting closer to your intimate partner:**

Here are some guidelines for good communicative skills in close relationships and for getting closer to your intimate partner or significant other(s) (adapted from authors' experience and from Monti et al., 1989, and Kadden et al., 1992).

TAKE TIME TO DISCUSS EACH ONE AFTER IT IS PRESENTED:

1) *Don't expect your partner to read your mind.* It is not fair to expect her/him to automatically know what it is you want or feel, or think. This is especially true in sexual matters where we may have been taught that there is something bad about the topic. Not being willing to discuss sex with your partner may increase your anxiety and the problems in your relationship, as well as depriving both of you of a great deal of pleasure.

2) *Don't let things build up.* It is easy to let things build up between you. To keep from being bothered about these things and to keep them from building up, tell your partner what bothers you. Do this as soon as you can. Stop and think before you say anything. Avoid blaming. Avoid *you statements.* If you let things build up, you will probably blow up and this just damages the closeness.

3) *Express your positive feelings.* Remember the skill *Giving Compliments?* (Briefly review the skills from Module 9, Session 25 on giving compliments.) It is important in any relationship to express things you appreciate about the other person. If you let your partner know that there are things you dislike, back that up with something you do like. The positive must always outweigh the negative. Otherwise, it will be a negative relationship. If the positive parts are not there, intimacy will not be there. All parts of the relationship are made better if the positive expressions are there. That is particularly true for sexual and physical intimacy. Sexual intimacy can't take place without positive feelings between the couple.

4) *Be an active sharer.* Take part in story telling. Share your day. This brings you closer.

5) *Be an active listener.* When you practice the active listening skills you are communicating with your partner. This behavior will make your relationship more close, supportive and satisfying. Even in a situation where you are simply discussing the events of the day, it is important to be an active listener.

f. **Very important: Keep the balance between closeness and separateness:**

1) Look back at Module 7, Session 20 and review the overlapping circles. A healthy relationship allows each person to have their separateness while at the same time maintaining closeness. Sometimes, relationships get so close, we feel swallowed up. When we feel we are losing our separateness and our uniqueness, we will fight closeness. Yet, you need to give part of yourself to the relationship. You can't have it all your way. The overlapping circles represent the relationship. That part needs to be fed, watered and nurtured through all of the above ideas that make for good communication.

2) **Exercise:** Draw two circles to show how you see your relationships. Are you feeling swallowed up? Are you feeling too separate and there is too much distance? Use *Work Sheet 42* for this.

3) **Exercise:** Use *Work Sheet 43*. In one column, list those things that represent intimacy and closeness (going to movies together). Then list those things that you do separate from the relationship that keeps your own sense of self and identity.

g. **Putting to practice what we have learned:**

Exercise: Role-play strong versus weak communication patterns between intimate associates. (If couples are present at this session, have them role-play together.) Practice active sharing and active listening. Remember the two key elements of each. Review Session 23 of Module 9.

Exercise: Role-play around giving and receiving compliments and criticism. Then, with your significant other, just take time to talk and share about whatever comes to your mind. If the client doesn't have a significant other at the session, have group members play the part of the spouse. Reverse roles.

4. Classroom and Homework Activities

a. Do *Work Sheet 42*. Draw your relationship with your intimate partner or spouse using the two circles like we did in Module 7, Session 20. Write down how you feel about what you see.

b. Do *Work Sheet 43*. Share your findings with the group and with your spouse or significant other.

c. Have clients do a *Thinking Report* on Close Relationships. Have them pick an event that is positive, such as a time they spent together that was pleasant and positive. Have the couple do the thinking report together. Review the elements of the thinking report.

5. Presentation Sequence

a. Review the major points made in the last session. Review and discuss homework. Discuss the thinking reports.

b. Have clients review their MP and MAP. Have them focus on those problem areas having to do with relationships.

c. Discuss the rationale and objectives for managing intimate and close relationships.

d. Review communication skills from Module 9, Session 23.

e. Present session as outlined in content section.

f. Have client do exercises in workbook.

g. Hold reflection group involving intimate partners. If the Provider is conducting a support group with couples, encourage clients and partners to attend.

h. Brief look at next session.

6. Session and Client Response Evaluation

a. Clients complete CSES.

b. Counselor completes the PSES using the following questions as guidelines:

1) *Did participants demonstrate a growing awareness of the importance of communication with significant others?*

2) *Did participants demonstrate an understanding of the skills that were discussed in the session?*

Session **38** : Understanding Values and Moral Development

1. Rationale and Overview of Session

Throughout the program we have focused indirectly on values and moral development. One very clear value has been stated: *concern for other people*. This has been an unstated goal of the program. The skills taught have been designed not only to help the client improve and change, but also to instill a sense of values—the values underlying living a positive life in the community. These are prosocial values. Our *values* influence and determine our actions and thoughts. The role of the Provider has been to both model and strengthen the prosocial thinking, talking and acting. This is a gradual process of helping offenders change their values. This cannot be accomplished by preaching morality, or even stating directly what correct values are. Instead, change can be accomplished by encouraging the SAOs to look at their belief systems, questioning them in ways so that they will examine their views and, if they cannot see alternatives, to suggest other ways that they can consider the situations and problems presented. The purpose of this session is to deal directly with the issues of values and how these affect our thinking and our actions.

2. Objectives of Session

> ➡ Clients understand prosocial values;
>
> ➡ Clients understand their own set of values and morals and look at their own ideas of morality;
>
> ➡ Clients understand the morals and rules of their own community and of society and compare their view of their own morals and values with those of the community in which they live.

3. Session Content and Process

a. **Review MP and MAP:**

Have clients review Part II of their *Master Profile*. This will provide some guidelines with respect to what areas they need to address with respect to values and moral development. Did they identify any particular problems in their MAP that relate to this area of moral development and values?

b. **Introduction to session:**

We have learned that thoughts cause feelings and actions. We have also learned that our attitudes and beliefs are the basis of our thinking. Our *values* and our *morals* are two of the most important pieces of our beliefs and attitudes. You might say that we have not focused on any particular morals or values in this program. Yet, throughout our program, we have continued to leave you with some very important ideas that have to do with values and morals:

1) *The value of change:* We have taught the value of change. The skills you have been learning support that value;

2) *The value of freedom:* Many of the skills that you have learned will help you keep your freedom;

3) *Positive relationships with others and your community:* We have held up the value of developing positive social relationships or what we call prosocial (in opposition to procriminal values);

4) *Being concerned about others:* We have held up the value of being concerned about people. This has been a clear but unstated goal of this program.

c. **Understanding the meaning of values and morals:**

Before we go on in this session, it is important that we learn the meaning of the key words we are using in this session. Here they are:

1) *Values:* Something that we see as worthwhile, that means a lot to us, that is important to us; guiding principles of our life;

2) *Personal Morals:* Has to do with what you see as right and wrong in relation to human behavior or action; it is the good or correctness of our behavior or actions; it comes from our sense of what is right and what is wrong;

3) *Community Norms or Standards of Conduct:* These are the rules or guidelines that we live by and that have to do with what is right and what is wrong in relation to our actions or behaviors in the community and society in which we live;

4) *Prosocial:* Thinking and acting in such a way that we take part in and build positive family, community and social relationships.

d. **What are your values? Your morals? Do you live up to them?**

The following exercises are designed to help clients first identify their own set of values and morals, to compare their own values with their own morals, and then to compare them with what they see as the important standards and rules of their community and society. Participants may have difficulty being honest in these exercises. Encourage honesty about their own feelings. They will not be punished if they list values that are deviant from their society's. The goal is to identify which values and morals they adhere to, that deviate from those of their community, and of those that do deviate which might underlie their criminal conduct and AOD use and abuse.

Exercise: Using *Work Sheet 44,* have clients list in the first column what they value most, and then check if they feel that they live up to those values.

Exercise: Using *Work Sheet 45,* have clients list ten morals important to them and that they live by. Then, as to whether you live up to each of these morals, check no, sometimes or always. See the definition of values and morals above.

e. **What are some basic norms or standards of conduct of your community and society?**

Exercise: Using *Work Sheet 46,* have clients list 10 basic norms or standards of conduct that society lives by. Now, how these clients see themselves with respect to living up to those standards of conduct can be indicated by checking no, sometimes or always.

f. **The value dilemma:**

This takes place when your values *go against or conflict* with your basic morals or the norms of your community and society. Think of some value dilemmas you have had in the past. Here are some examples:

1) The value of being loyal to a friend who wants you to go against your moral principle of upholding the law;

2) The value of having a lot of money yet living up to the moral of not stealing.

What are ways your values *go against or conflict* with your own set of morals? What are some ways that your values go against or conflict with the set of norms or standards of conduct you listed as most important to the society or community you live in?

Exercise: See which of the values you listed in Work Sheet 44 go against the morals you listed in *Work Sheet 45* and the basic norms or standards of conduct of society you listed in *Work Sheet 46*. If a value in *Work Sheet 45* goes against a moral or norm (community standard of conduct) listed in *Work Sheet 45* and *46*, then put the number of the value next to the norms you listed in *Work Sheets 45* and *46*.

4. Classroom and Homework Activities

a. Complete *Work Sheets 44* and *45*.

b. Complete for homework, *Work Sheet 46*, Norms or the Standards of Conduct.

5. Presentation Sequence

a. Summarize the major points made in the last session, emphasizing that concern for a partner or friend is paramount in what was discussed in the previous session on Developing and Keeping Intimate and Close Relationships.

b. Review clients MP and MAP and see what areas they need to address for this session.

c. Discuss the homework.

d. Review the thinking report from last session. As the group discusses the situations presented, are they able to verbalize how they would handle the situation differently now?

e. Present session as outlined in content section.

f. Reflection on group session.

g. Outline homework assignments.

h. Brief look at next session.

6. Session and Client Response Evaluation

a. Clients complete the CSES;

b. Counselor completes the PSES reflecting on these questions:

1) *Has the group been able to examine the questions posed in the value dilemmas from the perspective of prosocial values and morals and their group norms?*

2) *Were they able to define and understand conflicts between their values, morals and standards of conduct?*

Session (39) : Understanding and Practicing Empathy

1. Rationale of Session

One of the most important underlying goals of the skill building sessions in this Module is that of helping the SAO build self-control. Gottfredson and Hirschi (1990) suggest that low self-control is a single construct that accounts for a significant amount of variance in explaining criminal behavior. An important component of their low self-control construct is *lack of empathy,* self-centeredness, indifference and insensitivity to the suffering and plight of others, and not identifying with or putting oneself in the place of others. The SSC program sees *self-control* as underlying the values of change, freedom, positive relationship with others and community, and concern about others. The latter two values have to do with empathy.

Most workers in the field of criminal justice would agree that individuals with a history of criminal conduct have serious problems in identifying with the suffering of others, in placing themselves in the *shoes of another person,* particularly their victims, and in being sensitive to and concerned about others. Although some research would indicate that low empathy may not be a good predictor of recidivism (Andrews et al., 1985) there is a strong agreement in the field that empathy training should be an important component of offender treatment (e.g., Agee, 1979, 1986; Feshbach, 1984; Ross & Lightfoot, 1985). Ross and associates (1986) see *empathy* as one of the most important values the offender can learn as the offender makes efforts to change from a procriminal to a prosocial lifestyle.

Any discussion of empathy must include a discussion of the concept of sympathy. *Sympathy* is an emotional response that is aroused by a stimulus outside of ourselves. It is feeling sorry for someone and having a sense of or feeling the pain of others. The James-Lange theory of emotions (James, 1890) concludes that our subjective emotional experience is merely the awareness of our own bodily changes in the presence of outside emotionally arousing stimuli. Cannon (1927), however, felt that this purely autonomic (sympathetic nervous system) arousal explanation was not enough. He felt that the emotional arousal is more than just an awareness of our visceral responses or sympathetic nervous system's discharge since we are able to differentiate different kinds of emotions.

Schachter and Singer (1962) took a step further and emphasized the role of cognitive factors or processes in the emotional response. We attribute meaning to our emotional responses, or we interpret our emotional responses based on our prior experiences and what we experience going on around us. This cognitive interpretation of emotion lays some groundwork for the understanding of empathy. Sympathy is an emotional response that certainly involves a cognitive attribution process. Feeling sorry for someone must involve more than just a visceral response; it involves understanding. Allport (1937), however, states neither "an 'instinct of sympathy' nor a theory of 'emotional contagion' will account for our understanding of others" (p. 529). The author of empathy (as cited by Allport, 1937), Theodore Lipps (1907), saw empathy based on our capacity to imitate others. He saw knowledge as having three spheres: *sensory perception, inner perception* and *empathy* (Lipps, 1907, as cited in Allport, 1937).

Empathy is not only the understanding of another person but also involves being able to put oneself in the place of the other person. Allport (1937) states "empathic knowledge achieves a unity through a welding of the objective and the subjective" (p. 533). Empathy is a deeper experience. It goes beyond the egocentric point of view. It assumes "that the knowledge of others has complete priority over self-knowledge" (p. 533). Identification is emotional *and requires no specific mimicry*. Empathy does not require identification, although it can be part of empathy. We can develop empathy for someone who has no particular emotional significance to us (Allport, 1937).

The important factor is that empathy involves *imitation* and *mimicry*. The techniques of role reversal and doubling, used in psychodrama (Bischof, 1970), are powerful methods for enhancing the individual's understanding of the other person's position. It brings one beyond the ego (self). During *role reversal,* the individual plays the role of the other person. With the *doubling technique,* the double repeats back the words of the other person with the inferred emotional intonation and expression. But more than this, there is the kinetic mimicking of the other person. The best example of this is when the observer of another person makes actual bodily movements similar to those of the person being observed. Allport uses the example of observers of a high jumper actually lifting their legs as they watch the person clearing the high jump bar.

Both sympathy and empathy are important in developing prosocial attitudes and self-control. This session will focus on understanding and practicing empathy.

2. Objectives of Session

➠ Continue to look at idea of morality;

➠ Understand the difference between sympathy and empathy;

➠ Learn to consider the position of other people—learn empathy;

➠ Through the moral dilemma exercise, experience how difficult it is to make moral decisions.

3. Session Content

a. **An important value and moral for all:**

Values and morals differ across all peoples and nations. Yet, there are laws across all nations that have one thing in common: the safety and welfare of people. This is basic to most communities and cultures. Basic to this concern for others is what we call *empathy*. Robert Ross, a person who has taught us a lot about how to help offenders change, feels that empathy is one of the most important values we can learn as we change our life from substance abuse and criminal conduct to prosocial living and responsible attitudes toward our community (Ross et al., 1986). Ross and associates teach that the person will have a greater chance to change his or her offender beliefs and thinking when he or she learns to consider the attitudes, feelings, and views of others—or to become more understanding toward and caring of others. In our classroom, we can learn empathy by changing our thinking. We can do this by looking at what Ross calls situations that present us with a *moral dilemma*—or situations in which our ideas clash with those of other people. We will spend time in this session doing just this.

b. **What is sympathy?**

Sympathy is different from empathy. When we have sympathy for another person, we

- May feel sorry for that person;
- Have an understanding of the other person;
- Have compassion for the other person;
- Sense or feel another person's hurt or pain.

c. **What is empathy?**

Empathy goes one step beyond sympathy. It is not only understanding the other person, or feeling the other person's pain, but is actually being able to put yourself in the place of the other person. That is a deeper experience, a deeper emotion. We can feel sorry for someone but not really put ourselves in the place of another person. When we have empathy for another person, we are able to

- Relate to or know another person's feelings, motives, ideals or situation,
- Feel concern for another person,
- Feel another person's pain and suffering

BECAUSE WE ARE ABLE TO PUT OURSELVES IN THE PLACE OF THE OTHER PERSON— WE ARE TRULY ABLE TO *WALK IN THE SHOES* OF THE OTHER PERSON.

d. **Practice having empathy or feeling empathic:**

Work Sheet 47 gives four stories telling about something that happened to another person. Have clients read each story and then have them put themselves in the place of that person. Have them close their eyes when they do this and really feel what the person in that story went through. Then have them note in the second column what their feelings and thoughts were after they put themselves in the place of the person in the story.

e. **The moral dilemma:**

We can learn empathy by changing our thinking. We can do this by looking at what Ross calls situations that present us with a *moral dilemma*—or situations in which our ideas clash with those of other people. A moral dilemma may put you in conflict with a value or moral that you hold and a rule that is placed on you by someone other than yourself. It could be two moral beliefs you hold that are in conflict with each other. We will do an exercise in class to help us experience the moral dilemma.

1) Procedures for conducting the sessions presenting moral dilemmas (adapted from Ross et al., 1986, p. 194):

- *Present the moral dilemma:* The dilemma may be presented orally or on an overhead. Discuss the event, the characters and the circumstances, ensuring that the group understands the facts, the relationships between characters, and what is happening. Have someone in the group accurately describe the problem of the central character.

- *Take a position in the situation:* Each member should state what he thinks the central character should do and why s/he should do it and give their reasons for their position.

- *What is the group view?* If there is general agreement in the group, use the additional information contained in *Alternative Dilemmas* to increase the possibility that there will be considerable disagreement among the participants.

- Discuss the reasoning leading to the decision.

2) The group should divide into smaller groups to talk about the reasons for their various positions. Ross and associates (1986) present several alternatives for different configurations for the discussion phase. After the small group discussion, the whole group should talk about the dilemma in terms of the issues (discuss the morality of the positions). What would be the consequences of the various solutions presented? Has the group knowledge of or experience in similar situations?

3) Evaluating the client's response:

- Have the group members reflect on their earlier position, considering the arguments that have been presented. Have their positions changed? If so, why or why not? Have group members justify their positions.

- List every reason for and against the positions presented and have the group make a decision as to what is the best alternative of all the solutions presented.

4) The purpose of these exercises is to get clients to think beyond their own egocentric point of view and consider the point of view of both the central character in the dilemma and that of the other group members. If they fail to do this, encourage them to think in terms of others. Reinforce all *prosocial* thinking. This is also an opportunity to practice *problem solving and critical reasoning,* and to *avoid impulsive thinking.* Whenever you can do so without interfering with the primary purpose of the exercise, reinforce any behavior that demonstrates the skills of earlier sessions.

5) Dilemma: (Adapted from Ross et al., 1986, pp. 202-203):

A security guard patrolling the grounds of General Hospital came across a man lying on the ground. He had a wound in his chest, was bleeding heavily, and was writhing in pain. He had to have immediate medical attention.

The guard ran into the hospital emergency room, where the only people he saw were a hysterical mother and her child who appeared to have a broken arm. He was able to find a nurse on emergency room duty and tried to get her to go out to help the wounded man. The nurse said she could not leave the emergency room and all of the doctors were out. "This man will die if you don't help him," the guard insisted. The nurse pointed to a sign on the wall that declared that *"HOSPITAL EMPLOYEES MAY NOT LEAVE THE BUILDING WHEN ON DUTY."* She wanted to help but couldn't because of the rules.

Should she stay on duty or go help the wounded man?

a) **Alternative dilemmas:**

- If the group decides the nurse should help the man, give the group the following information:

Two weeks earlier a nurse was fired for leaving the emergency room to help the victims of a traffic accident.

- If the group feels the nurse should not leave but should obey hospital rules, tell them the following:

Based on the symptoms the guard described to her, the nurse knew the man would die if she didn't help him.

6) Questions to be considered:

1. Is there an obligation for the nurse to save the man's life?

2. Is she bound to follow the hospital rules?

3. What is her obligation to the mother and child in the waiting room?

4. What would the mother in the emergency room think the nurse should do?

5. When should a rule be broken?

6. Should the nurse be responsible if she doesn't go to the man and he dies?

7. Should the nurse be punished by the hospital if she goes to help the man?

4. Classroom and Homework Activities

a. Complete *Work Sheet 47:* Practicing Feeling Empathy for Another Person.

b. Complete the moral dilemma exercise.

c. For homework have clients complete *Work Sheet 48,* which is to find a newspaper article that presents a moral dilemma. The clients are asked to put themselves in the place of that person who is experiencing the dilemma and to see what they feel and what they should do.

d. Read next week's session.

5. Presentation Sequence

a. Review last session and homework using *Work Sheet 46,* Norms or the Standards of Conduct.

b. Present session as outlined in Session Content above.

c. Have clients identify how this session relates to their MP and MAP.

d. Hold reflection group at end of session and focus on the Moral Dilemma exercise.

e. Review next session with clients.

6. Session and Client Response Evaluation

a. Clients complete the CSES;

b. Counselor completes the PSES reflecting on these questions:

1) *Did client understand the difference between sympathy and empathy?*

2) *Were clients able to relate the session content to their own criminal conduct?*

3) *Were clients able to be empathetic to the positions of all of the characters, especially the central character (the nurse)?*

Session ④ : Responsibility Toward the Community: Reflection and Review and Driving Attitudes and Patterns

1. Rationale of Session

The last four sessions have focused on responsibility and values in close relationships and in one's community. Fulfillment of responsibility toward others and toward community is based on the set of values and moral beliefs one holds. Beyond morals and values, however, is developing and practicing *empathy*. Through empathy for others, we demonstrate our values and moral beliefs and our caring for others. Moving from antisocial and procriminal beliefs and actions toward a prosocial lifestyle involves a set of values and morals based on a willingness to change, valuing our freedom, building positive relationships with others and showing concern towards others. The practice of empathy is the vehicle through which we put those values to work in our lives.

This is the last session of this series. The provider is encouraged to spend about 45 minutes having clients reflect on the changes they feel they have made in the areas of values, moral development and the practice of empathy. During this period, clients will review their *Master Profile* and *Master Assessment* Plan and look at important areas they are yet to work on and to see if they need to change their self-ratings across the *Master Profile* scales. The second hour will be spent looking at group members' driving patterns and attitudes. Driving a motor vehicle is one of the most dangerous activities in our society. It is a high-impact responsibility. This provides a good metaphor for clients with respect to responsibility toward others and toward the community.

2. Objectives of Session

> ➠ Clients review their Master Profile and Master Assessment Plan;
>
> ➠ Clients reflect on their progress in the program;
>
> ➠ Clients reflect on issues around community responsibility;
>
> ➠ Clients focus on one area of responsibility—driving a motor vehicle.

3. Session Content and Process

a. Review and reflection:

1) Have clients review their MP and MAP. Have them re-rate their MP and look at what changes they made. Pay particular attention to Parts II and III of the MP to assess where they now see themselves with respect to their criminal conduct, criminal thinking and overall thinking patterns.

2) Review and discuss their homework from last session: *Work Sheet 48, Moral Dilemma.*

b. Introduction to session:

We spent last session looking at our values and moral attitudes. We looked at the idea that an important value to hold, and one that will help us in our change process, is to have concern for others. We will take about 45 minutes to reflect on our values, our moral attitudes and just where we are in the program at this time. Then, we will look in some depth at one of the greatest privileges we have in our society: driving a motor vehicle.

c. The Responsibility metaphor: Driving a motor vehicle:

The most dangerous activity we take part in is driving a car. More people are killed in car accidents every four years than in all of the four wars (World War I, World War II, Korean War and Vietnam War) this country has fought. Between 60,000 and 70,000 are killed every year on the highway. Over 60 percent of the deaths are related to the use of drugs and alcohol.

There is no one single behavior we engage in that requires more responsibility toward the community and toward others than that of driving a car. When we are driving a car, we

- continually have to be alert;

- are at risk and danger;

- have opportunity to be concerned and considerate toward others;

- have opportunity to test our good will and patience;

- feel emotions and stress.

It is a challenge. All of the lessons we have learned in this program can come to bear on our driving on the streets and highways.

d. **Driving attitudes and behaviors:**

Research has shown that people are really different as to their attitudes around driving and their driving behaviors. What are your attitudes? What kind of driving patterns do you show?

Discussion: Take time to talk about driving habits, the stress of driving and feelings that people have when driving.

e. **The Driving Assessment Survey (DAS) (Wanberg & Timken, 1991):**

Exercise: Have clients complete the DAS and score it in class. Encourage clients to be as honest as they can. They should know that the results will be used only for this session and for their own self-awareness. Have the client plot the profile. The profile is provided in *Work Sheet 49*. Then discuss the results in class. Have each person talk about what driving attitudes, thoughts and behaviors they can change. The DAS, answer sheet and profile are found in Appendix A of this manual.

Exercise: Use *Work Sheet 50* to make a list of the driving habits and attitudes the client can change.

4. Classroom Activities

a. Use *Work Sheet 49* to plot client's driving profile.

b. Use *Work Sheet 50* to describe their overall driving pattern and have clients list those driving habits and attitudes that they can change.

c. Do a *Thinking Report* in class:

Think of a situation when you clearly found yourself not acting responsible toward the community. Remember the parts of the *thinking report:*

SITUATION,

THOUGHTS,

FEELINGS,

ATTITUDES AND BELIEFS ABOUT THE SITUATION,

OUTCOME.

5. Presentation in Sequence

a. Review last session and homework, *Work Sheet 48*. Review their self-ratings on all of the MP scales. Have them revise and add to their MAP.

b. Present session conduct as outlined above.

c. Complete the DAS and profile and complete *Work Sheet 50*.

d. This is the last session of this segment. For programs that are open-ended, prepare the group for any new clients who will begin sessions next week. For providers using a closed-ended model, this represents the last session of Phase II. Thus, some time should be taken to discuss that transition. Have clients read the introduction to Phase III before the next session.

6. Session and Client Response Evaluation

a. Clients complete CSES.

b. Counselor completes PSES. Reflect on these questions:

1) *How do clients see themselves now with respect to the issues of moral development, values and responsibility toward others and the community?*

2) *Do clients reflect more of a commitment to live a prosocial life?*

3) *How did clients handle the DAS? Were they honest?*

c. This session brings this segment to a close. Complete the BRF on clients and calculate their score. Evaluate the progress of each client. How are they doing? For some clients, this will be the last session of Phase II. Assess each client as to whether he or she is motivated to enter Phase III. It is recommended that the Provider hold a one-to-one interview with each client to review the client's overall progress and response to the program.

PHASE III
TAKING OWNERSHIP OF CHANGE

Phase III: Taking Ownership of Change

The *Taking Ownership of Change* phase of the *Strategies for Self-Improvement and Change* (SSC) program represents the strengthening and maintenance of changes made in treatment. It is the integration phase of SSC. Clients now put together the meaning of the treatment experience and take consistent action on their own story, goals and desired changes. The change goals, however, may also be those of some external system, such as the family, marriage or the criminal justice system. What is important is that there is consistent demonstration and ownership of change over time.

In this *Taking Ownership of Change* phase, treatment builds on the client's increased self-awareness and the coping and change skills learned and practiced in Phase II. The Provider helps the client tie together various feelings, thoughts and behaviors that have emerged in the overall treatment experience. Treatment experiences are designed to reinforce and strengthen this commitment and established changes. To this end, Phase III of SSC will help clients strengthen their skills to prevent relapse and recidivism. Ownership of change will be further strengthened by helping clients develop the skills of critical reasoning and settling conflicts. These might be considered as advanced skills in the recovery and rehabilitation process for the substance abusing offender.

Taking Ownership of Change will also be strengthened by helping clients learn how to develop a lifestyle balance through involvement in healthy play and leisure time and improving productivity in work and occupation. The ownership and maintenance of change is further reinforced when clients *reach out* to receive help and support from peers and other community resources and when they provide support and reinforcement to others who are also in the process of rehabilitation and change. These are the enduring elements of change and rehabilitation. The substance abusing offender who reaches out for support from peers and self-help groups and who in turn provides modeling and mentoring for others in their process of change may have the greatest probability for full recovery and to live a drug-free and prosocial life.

Review of the Strategies for Self-Improvement and Change

It is important to congratulate clients on completing Phases I and II of the program and entering Phase III. To have come this far, clients have shown a commitment to responsible living through changes in thoughts, attitudes and behavior. Clients have given a lot of energy and time to learning the skills and attitudes necessary to relax, create and enjoy. Working on building close and caring relationships has allowed them to greet life's challenges with joy and grace.

Acquiring and practicing the skills to develop a positive lifestyle has been part of the challenge and commitment to change. Making the decision to continue a drug- and crime-free lifestyle is also part of that commitment. Continuing to build and maintain personal harmony and a sense of purpose throughout the life span is another matter. This involves internalizing and taking ownership of these changes—our focus for Phase III.

As clients enter this phase of *Strategies for Self-Improvement and Change,* it would be helpful to summarize what they have experienced in Phase I and II of SSC. A summary of Phase III, with its goals and specific objectives should be provided.

Phase I, **Challenge to Change,** focused on enhancing the clients' knowledge and facts about alcohol and drug abuse and the cycles of abuse. They learned about criminal conduct and the cycles of criminal behavior; about the part that thoughts, beliefs and attitudes play in controlling behavior and action and about the rules of how thoughts and behavior are strengthened and reinforced.

We stressed that change begins with self-awareness. But self-awareness depends on self-disclosure and getting feedback from others about yourself. In Phase I clients took many risks to talk about themselves and their problems. They opened themselves up to feedback from their peers. They learned and practiced basic communication skills to help in self-disclosure and to receive and give feedback. We focused on spotting thinking errors and cognitive distortions. In order to help clients to become more aware of themselves, they wrote an autobiography, wrote in a journal and wrote thinking reports.

Toward the end of Phase I, there was a strong focus on relapse and recidivism. Clients learned about high-risk thinking, high-risk actions and high-risk situations that lead to relapse and recidivism. They discovered that recidivism and relapse start long before one actually uses drugs or takes part in criminal acts.

Finally, we brought Phase I to a close by helping clients make the methods of change work. They learned to spot thinking and behavioral targets that they could work on to change. They learned to identify and overcome the barriers to change.

Phase II, **Commitment to Change,** focused on helping clients to sort out and label their thoughts, feelings and actions. They explored these in great depth. They received feedback from staff and peers as to their AOD problems and their criminal history. They took action on their story. They completed 18 sessions to learn and enhance the basic skills for self-improvement and change. The goal was to help clients become competent and self-sufficient in handling their problems. More than that, Phase II helped them to feel better about their life, to make life better for themselves and those close to them and for their community.

Now we enter the last phase of the SCC program: **Taking Ownership of Change.** This phase of the program provides time to reflect and think back. We want clients to think back on the changes they have made and how these changes have helped them to develop the skills to live free of problems related to AOD use. We want clients to look at and think about the changes that have helped them to become better citizens, to be prosocial in their beliefs and actions and to live in harmony with their community.

Introducing Clients to the Content of Phase III

Each day that you remain free from drugs and criminal acts, you will feel power and strength. Your self-confidence will grow. This power and self-confidence will give you ownership of the changes you have made. But you will always need to keep in mind the high-risk thoughts, actions and situations that lead to relapse and recidivism. Taking ownership of change means that you take *responsibility* for the high-risk thinking, high-risk actions and high-risk situations that lead to relapse and recidivism. You learned how to handle these high-risk situations in Module 5. During this program you have put to work the skills that prevented relapse and recidivism. We will again visit and review those important ideas about relapse and recidivism in Module 10.

Taking ownership of the changes you have made means you do your *own* thinking and that you allow your own values and morals to be the guide for your behavior. The skills of critical reasoning and decision making will help you to do this.

Often, our values and morals are put to test when we find ourselves in conflict with other people. Learning to manage and resolve conflicts helps you maintain those values and morals when you are challenged with conflict. Module 11 helps you learn the skills of critical reasoning and to manage and resolve conflicts.

An important part of maintaining and keeping ownership of the changes you have made is to make changes in your lifestyle activities. It may also mean that you need to improve your ability to manage your work and job situation. We cover these two topics in Module 12.

We know we take ownership of our self-improvements and change when we want to share the joy and power of the changes we have made with other people. There are two ways to do this. One is to *become an example* or model for other people who are starting to make changes in their lives so that they can live free of AOD problems and free of problems of criminal conduct. We will help you look at ways that you can become a mentor—a guide, or teacher or tutor—for others.

Another way we *share the joy and power of the changes* we have made is to be part of a group whose members support each other in the changes they have made. Being part of a *support group* is an important part of this phase of the program. Module 12 will give us a chance to look at how we can be an example for others who are making changes and how we can be part of a support group to help us keep the changes that we have made.

Specific Objectives of Phase III

The main goal of this phase is to help clients take ownership of the changes they have made and to keep those changes over time. Our more specific objectives are to:

- Strengthen awareness of and reinforce skills to manage the high-risk thinking, actions and situations that lead to relapse into AOD use and criminal conduct thinking;

- Prevent mental recidivism and relapse from leading into alcohol and other drug use and criminal behavior;

- Strengthen the changes that clients have made by learning the skills of critical reasoning, decision making and managing conflict;

- Explore how to be a mentor or example for others who are making self-improvement and change;

- Learn to use a support group in strengthening the changes.

Time Structure for Phase III

The first 10 weeks of Phase III are spent in formal sessions. The last session of Module 10 looks back at the accomplishments clients have made and looks forward to continued change and self-improvement. Following the completion of the 10 weeks of formal sessions, clients are placed in a weekly two-hour reflection and support group. This group provides opportunity for clients to reflect on what they have learned in the program, the changes they have made, and their ongoing efforts to put into practice the skills and tools they learned. The decision as to the length of time clients spend in this reflection and support group depends on the unique needs of each client and is made in a partnership decision-making process between the client and the provider. During this period, clients are also encouraged to become involved in community self-help groups and to seek support from other community resources.

Clients have worked hard in this program and have accomplished a lot. These accomplishments need continual reinforcement. It is recommended that the provider hold a graduation ceremony for clients who have successfully completed the program. A certificate of completion should be issued.

MODULE
10

Relapse and Recidivsm Prevention: Review and Strategies for Self-Control and Lifestyle Balance

MODULE 10: RELAPSE AND RECIDIVISM PREVENTION: REVIEW AND STRATEGIES FOR SELF-CONTROL AND LIFESTYLE BALANCE

Overview of Module 10

Clients at this point will have met many relapse and recidivism (RR) challenges and many opportunities to practice their RP skills. In this module, we focus on high-risk situations and high-risk thinking patterns that clients have encountered during the past six months and on the RP skills clients have used that have been effective in managing and avoiding RR. Finally, we look at strategies for self-control and lifestyle balance. Module 10 involves 2 two-hour sessions.

Objectives for Module 10

- Review the basic concepts of relapse and recidivism (RR) and relapse prevention (RP);

- Strengthen clients' ownership of RP skills and action.

Content for Introduction to Module 10

Each day that we live alcohol- and drug-free, we become stronger. Each day we prevent ourselves from taking part in thinking that leads to criminal conduct, we become stronger. Taking ownership of the power and strength in keeping away from AOD use and from criminal thinking is a way we prevent relapse and recidivism (RP).

In Module 5 we learned that RR (relapse and recidivism) takes place long before a person starts to use drugs or takes part in criminal conduct. We also learned that RR into AOD use and abuse and into criminal conduct and behavior is a gradual process of erosion. This erosion process begins when you do *high-risk thinking* or *place yourself in high-risk situations*. These are thoughts or situations that have led to AOD use and abuse and to criminal conduct in the past. We learned that engaging in high-risk thinking or situations can be prevented through the use of cognitive and behavioral skills. We also learned that a full relapse is when you once again become involved in a pattern of substance use that leads to abuse, and that full recidivism is actual involvement in a criminal act.

The ideas that we learned in Module 5 are so important that we want to spend two sessions reviewing them and strengthening our ownership of RP skills and actions. We will review the process and cycles of relapse and recidivism and again look at the warning signs of relapse and recidivism. We will also have you look at how you have handled your high-risk thinking and situations in the past six months.

Session ④1 : Strengthening Relapse and Recidivism Prevention Skills

1. Overview

What have been the RR challenges that clients have faced in the past six to nine months? What have been the RP skills that have worked best for the client? We will explore these questions in this module.

2. Objectives of Session

> ➠ Review the basic definitions and ideas related to high-risk thinking and high-risk situations;
>
> ➠ Review the triggers for relapse/recidivism.
>
> ➠ Review the RR process and steps (from Module 5, Session 15);
>
> ➠ Evaluate the high-risk situations and thinking that clients have faced in the past six months and have clients identify those thinking and acting skills that they used to manage RR.

3. Session Content and Process

a. **Review of RP concepts and ideas:**

1) A *high-risk situation* for relapse (AOD) and recidivism (criminal conduct) is any situation that has led to AOD abuse and criminal conduct in the past;

2) *High-risk thinking* for relapse (AOD) and recidivism (criminal conduct) is any thinking process or pattern that has led up to being involved in criminal behavior and AOD abuse in the past;

3) *Relapse and recidivism (RR) begins* when you engage in high-risk thinking or place yourself in high-risk situations;

4) *Relapse and recidivism prevention (RP)* is using the thinking and acting skills that replace high-risk thinking or that avoid high-risk situations.

b. **High-Risk situations that can trigger RR:**

Remember these high-risk situations you need to look for that can trigger relapse and recidivism:

1) conflict with another person;

2) social or peer pressure;

3) an unpleasant feeling of anger, depression or guilt;

4) a change in self-image.

c. **Here are the steps in the RR process (have clients review Figure 11, Module 5 in Workbook):**

1) Involvement in high-risk situations and high-risk thinking;

2) Lack of mastery of skills and loss of self-confidence or failure to use those skills that provide self-control and self-confidence;

3) Expectation of a positive outcome from AOD use or involvement in criminal conduct;

4) Reaction to the violation of the rule to not use drugs or to not engage in criminal thinking or criminal conduct:

403

- *I couldn't handle my thinking or situation;*

- *I relapsed because of my personal weakness;*

- *Conflict over who I am and what I am: Clean and sober or a user? A straight person or a criminal?*

6) Increased chance of full relapse or full recidivism.

REMEMBER: YOU ARE INTO RELAPSE/RECIDIVISM WHEN YOU PLACE YOURSELF IN HIGH-RISK SITUATIONS OR BEGIN TO ENGAGE IN HIGH-RISK THINKING.

d. **Here are the steps for the RP process (have client review Figure 11, Module 5 in Workbook):**

1) Involvement in high-risk situations and high-risk thinking:

2) Demonstrate a mastery of coping skills that *prevent* RR;

3) Increase in self-mastery and self-control;

4) Decrease chances of full relapse into AOD use and full recidivism into criminal activity.

e. **Review the following techniques and skills that clients have learned in SSC and have used to avoid RR:**

1) Basic knowledge about alcohol and drugs;

2) Knowledge of criminal conduct and the influence of drugs;

3) Tools for self-disclosure (*Autobiography, Thinking Reports, Journaling, Group discussions*);

4) Understanding stages of change;

5) Applying relaxation techniques;

6) Utilizing strategies for changing target thoughts or behaviors (i.e., methods of *self-talk, shifting the view, exaggerating, overstating the thought*);

7) Refusal skills;

8) Improved communication skills (e.g. maintaining drug-free *conversation*, giving and receiving *compliments*);

9) Managing negative beliefs and attitudes;

10) Understanding and correcting errors in logic;

11) Dealing with cravings and urges;

12) Using assertiveness skills;

13) Using problem solving skills;

14) Managing anger, guilt and depression;

15) Improving intimacy;

16) Understanding others;

17) Decision-making and negotiating skills.

f. **Evaluating your high-risk situations and high-risk thinking and your RP skills:**

Exercise: Using *Work Sheet 51* in the Workbook, have clients make a list of the *thinking skills* they have learned and that have worked for them in avoiding relapse/recidivism (RR) or in managing high-risk situations that might have led to relapse or recidivism in the past six months.

Exercise: Using *Work Sheet 51,* have clients make a list of the *action or behavioral skills* they have learned and which have worked for them in avoiding relapse/recidivism (RR) or in managing high-risk situations which might have led to relapse or recidivism in the past six months.

Exercise: Using *Work Sheet 52,* have clients list five high-risk AOD use patterns of thinking they were involved in over the past six months. Then have them note the thinking skills or behaviors that they used to deal with these thoughts.

Exercise: Using *Work Sheet 53,* have clients list five high-risk CC situations they placed themselves in over the past six months and note the thinking or behavioral skills they used to deal with these situations.

Exercise: If time permits, have several clients volunteer to share a brief relapse/recidivism story, explaining the progression from high-risk situation to high-risk thinking through decreased self-efficacy, positive outcome expectancies, initial use of drugs (if any), rule violation effects and RR outcome.

Exercise: If time permits, have all clients share a personal story of how they successfully used any of the techniques learned in this program to avoid relapse and/or criminal activity. They are asked to draw upon their experiences with one or more of the above skills and techniques they learned for RP (section "e" above).

g. **Provider's expression of respect and appreciation for clients:**

This session ends with the provider expressing respect and appreciation of group members' success at learning and putting to work the skills and attitudes that they gained through open-mindedness, commitment to themselves and the people they care about, attentiveness and their hard work through Phases I and II of *Strategies for Self-Improvement and Change.*

4. Classroom and Homework Activities

a. Have clients complete *Work Sheets 51* through *53* in Workbook.

b. Have clients make a note each day in their *Journals* that describes confidence they have in themselves.

c. Briefly review Module 11 with clients.

5. Presentation Sequence

a. Present the Rationale and Objectives for Module 10 and for this session.

b. Review high-risk situations that trigger relapse.

c. Follow content section for rest of session presentation. Do exercises involving *Work Sheets 51* through *53* in class. Take time for this. These are very important exercises. If time permits, do the relapse sharing and successful RR management exercises.

d. Outline homework assignment.

e. Brief look at next session.

6. Session and Client Response Evaluation

a. Clients complete CSES.

b. Provider completes PSES using following questions as guides:

1) *Were clients able to identify RP high-risk situations and thinking that they may have encountered during the past six months?*

2) *Were clients able to identify specific skills that they have used in RP over the past six months?*

Session 42 : Relapse Prevention: Strategies for Self-Control and Lifestyle Balance

1. Overview and Rationale

We have seen that high-risk thinking and high-risk situations are often triggers that set into motion the RR process. Often these thought-events or external situations create an internal desire to indulge in a behavior that *I deserve*. With relapse or recidivism, often, the payoff is quick. Both can give immediate gratification. Individuals who are most vulnerable to what Marlatt (1985c) calls the *relapse setup* are those whose lifestyles are out of balance. But the setup is internal. At close look, as Marlatt and Gordon describe, the individual has made conscious choices that lead closer and closer (or choices that increase the erosion process) to a lapse or a full relapse or recidivism. The individual would probably *deny* responsibility in the setup process, but responsibility is clearly there. Choices are clearly made.

The choices, however, do not completely rest in the relapse steps themselves. It is also found in the vulnerability of *lifestyle imbalance*—based on choices that the individual also makes. Marlat (1985c) suggest "that the degree of balance in a person's daily life style has a significant impact on the desire for indulgence or immediate gratification. Here, balance is defined as the degree of equilibrium that exists in one's daily life between those activities perceived as external 'hassles' or demands (the 'shoulds'), and those perceived as pleasures or self-fulfillment (the 'wants')" (p. 47).

When the person is operating out of the imbalance of the *shoulds,* that person begins to feel deprived. There is a corresponding desire for gratification that can come only through indulgence—using drugs or committing a crime. The inside messages are

- "I deserve more than this";
- "I work hard and don't get nowhere";
- "They have more than I do. I deserve as much as they do";
- "I deserve a good time—a few drinks."

As the desire for indulgence increases, so does the need to *"restore balance and equilibrium"* (p. 48). This can lead to cravings and urges. This sequence can subsequently lead to what Marlatt calls the *cognitive antecedents of relapse:* rationalizing or making an excuse to engage in a certain behavior, denial of any intent to use drugs or commit a crime, and decisions or choices associated with the RR process. The decision or choice process can present in a benign or unsuspecting manner and certain actions the individual chooses may seem even irrelevant to the possibility of relapse. Marlatt and Gordon call these choices *Seemingly Irrelevant Decisions* (SIDs). The individual becomes even more vulnerable if he or she engages in high-risk thinking ("I'll go down to the bar and chat with a couple of buddies") or a high-risk situation (friend drops by with some dope). This process is illustrated in the boxed components of Figure 28. This part of Figure 28 is what essentially precedes the RP map provided in Figure 11 in the Workbook.

Clients in this program have learned a set of skills and cognitive strategies to manage high-risk thinking and high-risk situations. However, we must go beyond merely teaching clients these coping skills. For long-term maintenance and ownership of change, we must help clients to create a *stable* and *on-going life style balance.* As Marlatt has noted, "simply teaching the client to respond mechanically to one high-risk situation after another is not enough" (p. 59). Broader or more global strategies are needed. Providers cannot deal with each and every high-risk situation their clients encounter. Thus, the Provider needs to make a global effort to intervene in the client's lifestyle so as to help the client develop a generalized ability to deal with stress and cope with high-risk situations. In this manner, the client develops and exercises "self-control strategies to reduce the risk level of any situation that might otherwise trigger a slip" (Marlatt, 1985c, p. 60).

Figure 28 provides a picture of these global or broad self-control strategies (Marlatt, 1985c, p. 61). As noted, the boxed components of Figure 28 (Figure 17, in Workbook) provide the process and antecedent conditions leading up to relapse (recidivism). The circled components provide the various intervention strategies that mitigate the boxed RR antecedents. Although these circled intervention components are relatively obvious, they will be briefly discussed.

Creating a balanced lifestyle and engaging in positive *addictions* are counters to the *shoulds* message of imbalance that will lead to feeling self-deprivation. The lifestyle daily balance is a process that is ongoing and stable. It involves built-in activities that are part of daily living and that give positive and meaningful gratification to the individual. Substituting indulgences are similar; however, they are directed at countering the desire to indulge. The substitute clearly is different from the normal indulging behavior of using drugs or committing a crime. These are activities that provide immediate self-gratification (such as eating a nice meal, sexual activity, etc.).

Intervening in the cravings and urges antecedents involves countering the external cues that precipitate the cravings and urges (e.g., smell of alcohol, seeing people drink, noticing a gang of friends on the street, seeing oneself commit a crime, etc.). As Marlatt notes, simply *removing oneself* from the external cues will do the job. Detaching from and labeling the cravings or urges are ways to *ride out* the urge. The client needs to know that the urge or craving will not last forever. It does go away. Labeling and detaching will often speed up the process of *going away*.

A powerful component of the relapse process is rationalization and denial and *Seemingly Irrelevant Decisions* (SIDs). Clients can use several strategies to manage this antecedent component of relapse and recidivism. First, being able to label SIDs will make them more relevant and increase awareness of the dangers of the SIDS and the warning signs. The labeling process increases clients' awareness of the danger signs of relapse and recidivism.

Another strategy to deal with the rationalization and denial process is to have clients develop what Marlatt (1985c) calls the *Decision Matrix* (p. 58). Figure 29 (*Worksheet* 54 in the Workbook) provides a sample of this matrix with criminal conduct as the behavioral reference. It is helpful for each client to develop their own matrix around both substance use and criminal conduct. This matrix can change over time. Whereas, at one point, the client might have included only minimal immediate and delayed positive consequences of not engaging in criminal behavior, as treatment progresses, the positive cells can be added to and the negative cells may be reduced.

We have already dealt with a number of strategies that clients can use in dealing with the high-risk situations component of Figure 28. Figure 28 provides two global strategies that clients can utilize. The first is developing powerful techniques to *avoid* high-risk situations or thinking. These can be *cognitive, behavioral or geographic*. For example, a geographic strategy would be to never go in the area of the city where the client's old drug dealer operates, or to never go into a bar again.

A final strategy that Parks & Marlatt (1997) used in dealing with the high-risk events has been to help clients conceptualize and develop their own relapse and recidivism road map. Marlatt and Gordon use the *highway metaphor* as a way of illustrating the choices that the client has at the point leading to high-risk situations. This RP map was presented and discussed in Module 5, Session 15, Figure 17, of the Providers Manual. We now present it for the participants in this Module (Figure 18 of the Workbook). It is of particular relevance now in that the client can get a feel for the choices of routes that can be taken when being confronted with urges and cravings. If the client has given in to the cravings and has lapsed, or has engaged in behaviors that will clearly lead to recidivism into crime (now spending time with criminal associates), the RR Map of Figure 18 indicates that choices can still be made.

2. Objectives of Session

> ➠ Learn how life imbalances can increase the client's vulnerability to high-risk situations and RR;
>
> ➠ Learn broad or global self-control plans or strategies that can prevent relapse and recidivism.

3. Session Content

a. **How lifestyle imbalance leads to relapse and recidivism:**

Living a drug- and crime-free life requires that you live a balanced lifestyle. Life can quickly get out of balance. You begin to feel pressured, hassled and controlled. You feel the pressure of the *shoulds* or the *oughts*. You begin to feel deprived and even cheated. You have no time for yourself. The demands of work, of family, of *everyone* become overwhelming.

How do we get our needs met under these circumstances? A balanced lifestyle involves keeping a healthy balance between those activities that we see as causing us pressure and hassles and those activities that bring us meaning, pleasure and self-fulfillment.

When life gets out of balance because of the imbalance of the *shoulds,* we begin to feel a strong desire to meet our needs right away, to indulge in what satisfies us. We want to gratify our needs *now.* As the desire to indulge increases, so does the need to get back the balance. This can lead to cravings and urges for drugs or to commit a crime. When this happens, particularly after we have made a commitment to live a drug- and crime-free life, we have to make excuses for what we want to do. So, we say:

- "I deserve more than this";

- "I work hard and don't get nowhere";

- "they have more than I do—I deserve as much as they do";

- "I deserve a good time—a few drinks";

- "I have something coming."

This all can lead to relapse and recidivism. With relapse or recidivism, the payoff is quick. Both give immediate gratification. But our choice to indulge may be hidden. The choice may sneak up on us. We call this *Seemingly Irrelevant Decisions* (SIDs). We become even more vulnerable for relapse or recidivism when we engage in high-risk thinking ("I'll go down to the bar and chat with a couple of buddies") or high-risk situations (a friend drops by with some dope). This process is illustrated in the boxed parts of Figure 17 in the Workbook.

b. **Develop a balanced lifestyle—Arming ourselves with a broad relapse and recidivism prevention (RP) plan:**

1) *Arming ourselves with a self-control plan:*

Remember, we make conscious choices to relapse or to reoffend. We are most apt to make this choice when our lifestyle gets out of balance. We have learned many skills to prevent relapse and recidivism. But, we are always faced with high-risk thinking and situations that can lead to RR. It would be important that we have a plan for self-control—that we don't have to come up with a plan every time we face a high-risk situation or every time we take part in high-risk thinking. We should have a plan ready to go. This is like arming ourselves with positive thoughts and having them ready to go when we need them. Remember, we did this in Session 27, *Managing and Changing Negative Thoughts.* Figure 17 in our Workbook gives us such a plan.

2) *Filling in the spaces for a balanced daily lifestyle:*

The circled parts of Figure 17 in our Workbook give us general ways or strategies that help us handle the boxed parts of Figure 17. As can be seen in Figure 17, we can build a balanced lifestyle by building in daily activities that give us positive feelings and gratifications. We should try to put those activities in each day of our life. When we do feel a desire to indulge in AOD use or criminal behavior, we can put something else in their place. We call this substituting or replacing indulgences. We should be ready with those when we need them. These are activities that provide immediate self-gratification (such as eating a nice meal, sexual activity, getting a massage, etc.).

3) *Detaching and labeling:*

Cravings and urges are another thing. We may get urges when we smell alcohol, see people drink, notice a gang of friends on the street, or imagine committing a crime. The best strategy or way to handle these is to just detach or remove yourself from those situations. You can also put a label on the urge and craving, and then tell yourself, *ride it out.* The urge does go away.

4) *Don't make excuses and watch those decisions that don't seem important:*

A powerful part of RR is making excuses, or dening you have the feelings or urge. Or, you think that the small choices you are making that move you toward relapse or recidivism do not seem to amount to anything—or SIDs *(Seemingly Irrelevant Decisions)*. You can do a number of things at this point. First, you can put a label on these as warning signs. For example, you can label: "I deserve it" and call it *poor excuse (PE).* When you think this, it should warn you that you are close to relapse—very close. You can also look at the short-term and long-term good and bad parts of a decision to not use drugs or offend or a decision to use drugs or to commit a crime. We call this your *decision window.* Or, you can just avoid those high-risk situations that are steps to relapse and recidivism.

Exercise: Figure 29 provides the decision window with examples of short-term and long-term positive and negative outcomes for decisions to use or not to use drugs or to live a crime-free life or to be involved in crime. *Work Sheet 54* in the Workbook provides this decision window for the clients to complete. Clients will need help in completing this work sheet. Discuss it once it is completed.

c. **Your highway map to recovery or collapse:**

A final plan that you can use to build a balanced lifestyle is to look at relapse and recidivism as a highway map. We talked about this map in Module 5, Session 15. A picture of this map is found in Figure 18 in the Workbook. During this program, you have found yourself on this highway several times. You have faced urges and cravings. You have resisted and stayed straight or abstinent. You may have lapsed (used drugs) once or twice. You may have done things or thought things that brought you close to committing a crime (what we call recidivism, but not full recidivism). But you have been set on staying on Road 101—to recovery city. Always keep this map in your mind. It is one of the best ways to remind you of where you want to go. But whichever direction you take—collapse city or recovery city—remember: **IT IS YOUR CHOICE. YOU ARE IN THE DRIVER'S SEAT.**

4. Classroom Activities

a. Have clients fill in the circles in Figure 17. Do this in class. Help them see that these represent their general strategies in developing self-control in RP.

b. Have clients complete the blank decision window under Worksheet 54. Have them discuss their window with the group.

5. Presentation Sequence

a. Briefly review last session and have clients share with the group the notes they made this past week in their journals that describe confidence they have in themselves.

b. Present session content. Take time to go over the Global Self-Control Strategies, Figure 17.

c. Have clients complete the circles in Figure 17 and the decision window in *Worksheet* 54. Have them share their results.

d. Have clients study the RR map.

e. Hold a 20-minute reflection group at the end of the session.

6. Session and Client Response Evaluation

a. Clients complete the CSES.

b. Provider completes the PSES.

Figure 28

Relapse Prevention: Global Self-Control Strategies

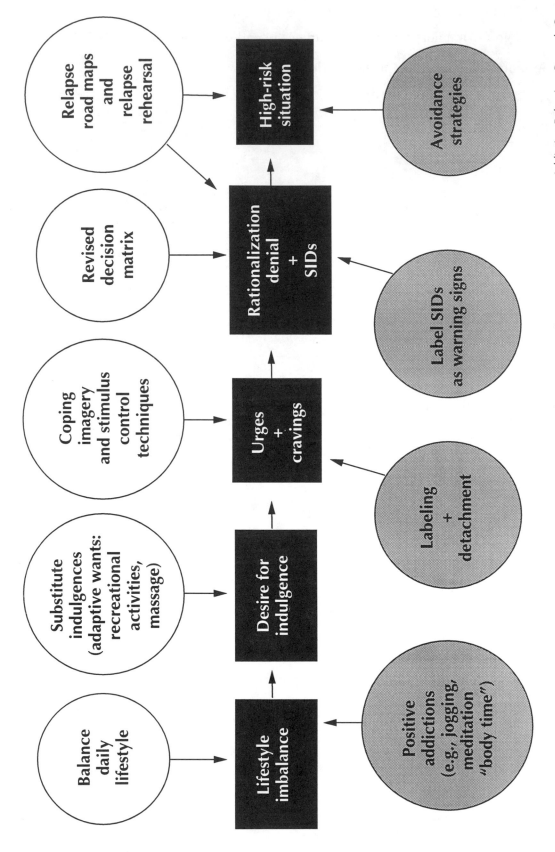

Reprint with permission of the authors of Relapse Prevention: Maintenance Strategies in the Treatment of Addictive Behaviors (p.61) .Edited by G.A. Marlatt and J.R. Gordon, The Guilford Press, 1985.

Addictive Behaviors Resarch Center
University of Washington

Figure 29

The Decision Window for Criminal Conduct

Decision Window: Example of Decision Window for AOD Use and Abuse

	IMMEDIATE OUTCOME		DELAYED OUTCOME	
	POSITIVE	NEGATIVE	POSITIVE	NEGATIVE
Live an alcohol- and drug-free life	Family and friends not upset with my use No hangovers	Miss getting high and having fun drinking Miss old drinking buddies	Save money Feel better More time doing non-drinking activities	Lose old friends Have to replace the many hours spent in bar
Continue to use and abuse alcohol and other drugs	Spend time with drinking friends Good way to relax	Morning hangovers Don't feel like going to work on Mondays	Be able to keep old drinking buddies Forget problems on weekends	May lose marriage Won't worry about getting DUI

Decision Window for Criminal Conduct

	IMMEDIATE OUTCOME		DELAYED OUTCOME	
	POSITIVE	NEGATIVE	POSITIVE	NEGATIVE
Live a crime-free life	Don't have to deal with police Increase in self-confidence	May not have money needs met Look like a chicken to old buddies	No fear of being arrested Looked up to by family and friends	Lose all of old associates and friends
Continue to commit crimes and offend	Meet money needs right now Big man with old buddies	Let family and children down Loss of self-control	Always have old buddies and criminal friends Quick money	Lose freedom—locked up Lose self-respect and respect of others

Adapted with permission of the authors of <u>Relapse Prevention: Maintenance Strategies in the Treatment of Addictive Behaviors</u> (p.58). Edited by G.A. Marlatt and J.R. Gordon, The Guilford Press, 1985.

MODULE 11

Strengthening Our Ownership of Change:

Developing the Skills of Critical Reasoning and Settling Conflicts

MODULE 11: STRENGTHENING OUR OWNERSHIP OF CHANGE: DEVELOPING THE SKILLS OF CRITICAL REASONING AND SETTLING CONFLICTS

The sessions in Module 9 focused on a number of coping and social skills that were designed to help clients more effectively manage their interpersonal and intrapersonal world. These included basic communication skills, problem solving, increasing self-confidence through assertiveness, dealing with irrational thinking, managing the internal feelings of guilt, depression and anger, skills in coping with cravings and urges, developing prosocial values and behaviors, and building skills that help develop and maintain close and meaningful relationships. We saw these as basic skills, essential in the process of self-improvement and change.

There are three additional skills that the literature indicates to be important in the rehabilitation of individuals with substance abuse problems and a history of criminal conduct. These involve *critical reasoning, creative thinking* and *resolving conflicts* through negotiation. We see these as advanced problem solving and cognitive-change skills.

To effectively use the skills of critical reasoning, creative thinking and negotiation, the individual must have a certain level of self-awareness. As we saw in previous sessions, self-awareness occurs through self-disclosure and the willingness to receive feedback from others. Both self-disclosure and openness to feedback from others build self-confidence. A certain level of self-confidence is thus necessary to effectively use these advanced skills.

We typically see offenders as *tough* and *bullying* and people who *con* others. However, often, offenders are the ones who are easily persuaded and "conned" by associates or peers to commit a crime or to use drugs. They get sold "a bill of goods" by one or more people to engage in crime. When we look at the many reasons for excessive drinking or criminal behavior, logically and critically, none stands up to the simple scrutiny of *making sense*. One of the goals of this module is to help the SAO develop a logical and critical *eye* for any effort to be persuaded by others to take part in activities that "do not make sense" from the standpoint of being responsible, of being free and of being healthy.

Being critical and creative often leads to independent action and wanting things our way. This in turn leads to conflicts with others. However, resolving conflict through the skills of negotiation provides opportunity to engage in critical and creative thinking and problem solving, usually resulting in a win-win solution that empowers us with self-confidence.

Session ㊸ : Critical Reasoning: Decision Making and Creativity (I)

1. Rationale and Overview of Session

We have spent a number of sessions on problem solving. Alternative thinking and action have been a primary emphasis throughout the program. In this session we will attempt to expand the clients' abilities by introducing some techniques to encourage critical and creative thinking. Many SAOs suffer from "cognitive rigidity" or inflexibility in their thinking (Ross et al., 1986, p. 175). They tend to think about new situations or problems in the same way they have previously handled things, failing to consider the adequacy or applicability of the old solution in the new circumstances. They frequently have difficulty considering alternatives, understanding complex situations or adjusting to change. Repetitive behavior is a possible result. This inability to adapt may result in unacceptable, anti-social behavior when the inability to cope is accompanied by a low tolerance for stress. It may be that offenders are unable, cognitively, to adapt to the demands of the world and to conceive of alternative ways to solve problems. This lack of perspective puts them at risk to respond poorly to counseling. Because they often cannot conceive new ideas, they are particularly resistant to the ideas of others.

Critical thinking is the art of thinking logically, rationally and carefully. The goal is to come to conclusions that are based on adequate and correct information. The logic behind the conclusion is accurate and not based on distorted or biased thinking and incorrect assumptions. As the group learns these skills, they will become better able to use the skills they have learned earlier, to think less emotionally and more logically (Ross et al., 1986).

2. Objectives of Session

> ⮕ Clients learn the skills of critical reasoning.
>
> ⮕ Clients learn the importance of listening to what is being said and what is being implied, especially in a persuasive situation.
>
> ⮕ Clients learn to adequately assess the validity of what is being said and, rather than assuming they have accurate information, learn to distinguish fact from opinion.

3. Session Content and Process

a. **Looking at all sides:**

Studies have shown that many substance abusing offenders have problems in being flexible. They have what we call *mental rigidity*. They have problems of looking at all sides of a situation. They think about new situations or problems in the same old way. They don't change their way of thinking about how they solve problems or the way they think about things in general. This may not apply to you, but what we will do in this session may help you look at things differently. We are going to work on what we call critical thinking and being creative. To be creative is to think of new ways to do things that give a good outcome, a good experience.

b. **Critical and creative thinking:**

Critical thinking is the art of thinking clearly about something, making sense out of something and getting the facts before you make a decision. We call this logical thinking. We also call it rational thinking. To think sensibly or critically we

1) *Always get the facts:* We need the correct information. The goal is to come to conclusions that are based on the most correct information we can get.

2) *Do not let our emotions make the decision:* We make a lot of decisions because we are angry. "I'm not going to shop there again because the *clerk was a jerk."* That shoots you in the foot if the store has what you want. Counter the thought: "It is just a clerk. He doesn't own the store. He couldn't care less."

3) *Make sense of the facts:* See how the facts fit together; what do the facts tell us.

4) *See if we are being conned?* When you come to a conclusion by being convinced by the needs or wishes of other people, you are being *conned* (fooled). You are conned when you let others persuade you to do something or believe something before you get the facts or before you can reason critically. Your friends might persuade you to use drugs. But what are the facts? *Every time I use drugs, I get into trouble with the law. Where will I end up?* Critical thinking will prevent us from being conned or conning ourselves. When people try to convince you to agree with their way of thinking they are using what we call *propaganda.* Propaganda is a statement someone makes to persuade us that something they want us to believe is true. It may or not be true. When we buy into propaganda, we fail to reason critically.

c. **Here are some ways people try to talk us into things. These are methods of propaganda:**

1) **ONE-SIDED ARGUMENTS:**

EXAMPLE: Job placement worker to a recent high school graduate: "This is a great job, it pays well, and you are likely to get promoted to a management position within a year."

EXAMPLE: Friend who is concerned about the high school graduate taking a job out of town: "This would be an awful job. You are going to be living in a one-horse town with nothing to do with all the money you are going to be making. Besides that, they aren't really going to give a green kid a job as a manager."

In both situations, the high school graduate is hearing propaganda because each person is giving a ONE-SIDED argument. The job placement worker is giving only the good points of the job; the friend who wants to keep his buddy in town is giving only the bad points. Propaganda often features a one-sided argument.

2) **THE BANDWAGON APPROACH:**

Another propaganda technique used frequently is the BANDWAGON approach, designed to make you believe that you are not well-informed or part of the in-group if you don't buy the product (Ross et al., 1986):

EXAMPLE: Mark:"Let's get some speed and shoot-up."

Betty: "I would never do that. I don't believe using drugs is smart."

Mark: "Everybody does it. Why are you so uncreative and boring?"

EXAMPLE: Advertisement: "Women everywhere are discovering that Insta-Youth improves the texture of their skin within 10 days."

3) **REPETITION IS ANOTHER WAY TO CON YOU:**

Advertisers use REPETITION to get their propaganda across.

EXAMPLE: A new product's name is mentioned time and time again, or ads are repeatedly shown in the same hour of television.

4) **TRANSFER:**

EXAMPLE: Associating a young and attractive person with a particular product.

5) **TESTIMONIAL:**

Sometimes the propaganda is presented by a famous person who presents a TESTIMONIAL for or against a proposal, hoping that the name of the famous person will result in transfer of loyalty to the product or issue that is being promoted.

6) **EXIGENCY:**

A popular sales tool is to tell the buyer that there is only a limited time in which they can buy the product or get it at a reduced price. This technique is EXIGENCY.

7) **BARGAIN:**

Sometimes the advertiser or salesperson will encourage you to buy because you will get something FREE or at a BARGAIN rate.

d. **How do your past AOD use and criminal conduct relate to these methods of propaganda?**

1) First, learn more about the methods of propaganda discussed above by doing *Work Sheet 55;*

2) Take each of the methods of propaganda listed above. How have they led you into AOD use and criminal conduct? Take the statement: "They all stop by for a few beers after work!" Does this sound like the BANDWAGON APPROACH? Now, do *Work Sheet 56* to see how these various methods of propaganda are related to your past use of drugs or your past involvement in criminal behavior.

EXERCISE: Ask the group to identify the nature of the propaganda in each of the following examples:

1) A handsome macho man in a magazine advertisement is shown holding a pack of cigarettes. [Transfer]

2) Your son comes to you begging to use the car. "All the kids are going to be driving." [Bandwagon]

3) Television ad showing a famous politician stating that "Taxes will not be raised. Taxes cannot be raised. Raising taxes will place the economy of our country in jeopardy. Join your fellow Americans in supporting Proposition 9 on the ballot." [Bandwagon, repetition and testimonial]

4) Newspaper advertisement: "Crazy Ed's entire stock of used cars will be available at 5% down only through Saturday noon." [Exigency]

5) Drug dealer: "I only have ten more hits of acid left in this batch. Next week they'll all be gone. Tomorrow the price will double." [Exigency and Bargain]

Have group come up with some examples.

Discussion: Have the group discuss the techniques described in the examples above. What other kinds of schemes have they seen used to get people to do what the speaker wants? What should they be able to do now to avoid being *conned* by someone else? How might they *con* themselves into doing something that is not wise?

Have the group discuss their own examples of how they were conned by different propaganda techniques.

4. Classroom and Homework Activities

a. Propaganda advertisement:

Describe 5 different advertisements that you have seen either in newspapers and magazines or on TV. What propaganda technique did each one use? Use *Work Sheet 55.*

b. *Thinking Report*—Propaganda:

Option 1: Think of a time you have *conned* someone else in order to get what you wanted. Do a thinking report on the incident.

Option 2: Think of a time when a friend has *conned* you. Do a thinking report on the situation.

Review the parts of the thinking report with clients.

5. Presentation Sequence

a. Start session by reviewing the key ideas and concept of RR. Then, have clients share the statements they wrote in their journal that describes confidence they had in themselves.

b. Present rationale of session and objectives.

c. Present session as outlined in Content section.

d. Reflection group at end of session.

e. Outline Homework assignments.

f. Brief look at next session.

6. Session and Client Response Evaluation

a. Clients complete CSES.

b. Provider completes PSES. Use these questions as guidelines in evaluating the session:

1) *Were clients able to see ways in which they have been victims of propaganda?*

2) *Were clients able to identify how the various propaganda methods led them to drink or to engage in criminal behavior?*

Session ④④ : Critical Reasoning: Decision Making and Creativity II

1. Rationale and Overview of Session

In previous sessions, we looked at the importance of putting our thoughts and feelings into words or talk—when we express our differences, our desire for information, our opinion, our stand that we will not use drugs. Often, the words are said inside of ourselves—*self-talk*. Whether it's self-talk or talk to others, putting our reasoning and critical thinking into words allows us and others to hear where we are. In this session, we look a little deeper into critical reasoning and take time to review what was covered during last session.

2. Objectives of Session

> ⮕ To augment and expand the goals of the last session concerning persuasive and clear communication;
>
> ⮕ To continue to work on the skill of critical reasoning.

3. Session Content and Process

a. Reflection and review:

1) Review last week's session in a reflection group. Particularly review the work done in *Work Sheets 55* and *56*.

2) Have clients share their thinking report. Some clients may not have done the homework. Have them talk about why they did not. For those who did, take time to review their work.

b. Introduction to session:

We continue on our journey of understanding critical reasoning. This is a difficult skill to learn. Our old beliefs, our old attitudes and our old ways get in the way. Every day we have to deal with issues that challenge our commitment to sobriety and to living a crime-free life. We are often persuaded by friends to *have a few,* to *commit one more crime so we'll get rich,* to put ourselves in high-risk situations. Critical reasoning helps us in making good decisions. In the last session, we learned some of the ways we can practice the skill of critical reasoning. The most important was to get the facts and be aware that there are always other people who try to get you to make decisions based on their needs and not on your needs.

c. Let us look a little deeper into critical reasoning. Here are some more pieces of the puzzle:

1) *Words are important:*

We live our lives using talk and words. Words are important. "Sticks and stones may break my bones, but words 'can really hurt me.'" Words can hurt if we don't understand what they mean. The same word may mean one thing to you and something different to the person with whom you are speaking. If you use words that don't mean the same to each of you, you will not communicate with each other. If other people use words that do not have the same meaning to each person, they risk not communicating. They may end up in an argument. Learn to ask yourself what it is that others are saying. Do this with people on TV or radio. *What are they saying?*

Discussion: Have the group discuss what the word *hot* means to them. Is it different when they think about food than when they think about weather? What about sex? How about the word *snow?* Would it mean something different if you lived in the south or in Canada? Would it be different if you were a child or a skier? What about drugs? What if you had to drive 20 miles to work? Are there other words you can think of that might mean different things to different people?

2) *People often don't say what they really mean:*

Learn to recognize what people imply by what they say. People don't always tell what they mean in a clear manner. Don't always assume. As you know, assuming without getting the facts or without having good communication often ends up making an ASS out of U and ME. Ask questions if you don't understand. There is no dumb question, only dumb answers. Figure out what the other person is assuming. Pay attention. Remember, few people are able to say what they mean in a CLEAR way. We often have to figure out what is being said. FIGURE OUT.

EXAMPLE:

Joe: "You heard that Gina is pregnant."

Maria: "Gina is going to have a baby? I don't believe it!"

Is Maria saying that Joe has the wrong information?

Is Maria calling Joe a liar?

Is Maria indicating the news is a great surprise to her?

Is Maria saying that she thought Gina would never have a baby?

Discussion: What would be the worst of these guesses, and what might it mean to the relationship? Don't rush to make a judgment, since there are three alternative choices. If Maria didn't mean to imply that Joe was lying, how should she have worded her response?

3) *Listen to what people are assuming:*

Recognize assumptions. You know a good deal about good communications skills and critical reasoning. Remember to listen carefully to the feeling that people communicate when they use a particular word. Pay attention to body language and facial expression.

Now, learn to read between the lines. Even though the person may not tell you, figure out what the person is assuming.

EXAMPLE: (adapted from Ross et al., 1986):

Robert is an 18-year old senior in high school. Last year his grades were good, but he has done poorly this semester. He spends almost every night with his friends drinking and sleeps during the day, missing most of his classes. His teacher assumes that Robert is not interested in an education. He says, "I don't believe that Robert will graduate from here. Perhaps he should drop out of school and maybe try to get a G.E.D."

Robert's father assumes that this is just part of growing up and becoming a man. He says, "Robert is just like I was at his age. School is doing a lot of good for him."

His mother assumes there is something serious bothering him. She says, "What a terrible attitude you have. Our son needs our help."

His brother assumes he is being immature and is very angry with him for upsetting the family this way. He says, "Make him go to work." " Throw him out of the house."

None of the people involved have actually stated their assumptions but each one has stated a different opinion of what is happening to Robert based on those assumptions. They disagree with one another but will not be able to settle the matter unless they recognize the fact that they are starting with different assumptions.

When we are discussing a matter with other people, it is important that we verify that we are starting with the same assumptions. Remember that it is easier to figure out what people are inferring than to learn their assumptions, but it is just as important if you are to understand what is being communicated.

4) *Fact Versus Opinion:*

Once you have understood what the other person's assumptions are, it is important to determine whether they are based on fact or on opinion. This is not always easy to do but some clues might be

- Phrases that give you some indication that they are stating their opinion, such as "in my opinion," "I think," or "it seems to me."

- Emotional statements indicate that people are expressing an opinion rather than fact. "Big business don't care anything about their employees. All they want to do is make a buck!"

- Very general or extreme statements are generally an opinion rather than fact (e.g., "everyone smokes bud").

If you cannot tell whether the person is expressing a fact or opinion, ask enough questions to make a judgment.

Exercise: Have the group determine whether the following statements are likely to be fact or opinion:

"All cops can be bought." [opinion];

"To me, football is the most exciting game on earth." [opinion];

"My birthday is March 23rd." [fact];

"It's a harder world for kids to grow up in today than it was 25 years ago." [Fact or opinion].

4. Classroom or Homework Activity

Have clients do a *Thinking Report* on Critical Reasoning. You may want to do this in class, or at least start the exercise in class.

Have clients think of a recent event in which they had a misunderstanding with someone they were talking with. Have them do a thinking report on what happened. Review the elements of the *Thinking Report* again:

SITUATION

THOUGHTS

FEELINGS

ATTITUDES AND BELIEFS ABOUT THE SITUATION

OUTCOME

5. Presentation Sequence

a. Summarize the last session, reminding the group of the various propaganda techniques that were used.

b. Hold a reflection group and discuss the homework. Did the members demonstrate a grasp of the different types of persuasion techniques that can be used?

c. Review their *thinking reports*. How did people feel about being *conned?*—About *conning* someone else?

d. Present material as outlined in Content section.

e. Close with another reflection group. You may want to have clients start their Thinking Report in group.

f. Outline homework assignment.

g. Brief look at next session.

6. Session and Client Response Evaluation

a. Clients complete CSES.

b. Provider completes PSES using the following as guides:

1) *Did the group demonstrate increased ability to listen and interpret what was being implied and assumed?*

2) *Was a heightened awareness of how to distinguish fact from opinion obvious in the session?*

Session 45 : Resolving Conflicts: Negotiation and Social Skills Development

1. Overview of Conflict Resolution and Rationale of Session

We could define *conflict* in terms of its synonyms: Contention, controversy, rivalry, active opposition, friction, clash, competition, struggle, tussle, strife, and so on. It is more helpful, however to define conflict as an interpersonal and intrapersonal process (Kelley, 1987). A good process definition of conflict has been offered by Peterson (1983): "conflict is an interpersonal process that occurs whenever the actions of one person interfere with the actions of another" (p. 365). This definition presents the interpersonal dimension of conflict. However, the interference with the *action of the other person* involves an intrapersonal process. The following example illustrates how the interpersonal interferences also creates an intrapersonal interference:

A couple begins to argue following the wife's request that her husband help vacuum the house in preparation for the guests coming over for dinner that evening. The husband is in his study presuming reading a book, but really mulling over a problem he had with his boss on Friday. She begins to vacuum, which annoys him and interferes with his musing over the problem. He jumps up, grabs the vacuum cleaner and starts to vacuum. She responds in anger and hurt, tells him that he can entertain the guests himself and leaves the house slamming the door behind her.

The conflict between the couple is defined not only by what Kelley (1987) calls the *interchain* (sequence of transactions between the couple) causing interference but also by the interference in *intrachain* organization of events (the thinking and pondering going on inside the husband). What is also important about Peterson's definition and the above illustration is that feeling, thought and action (the three components of CBT focus) interact in producing the intra- and interpersonal interference. This provides the basis for the focus of conflict resolution: the interchain of feeling, thought and action in the interference process.

Kelley (1987) indicates that *conflict* has three aspects: structure, content and process. *Structure* refers to the situation and persons involved. These are the relatively stable factors that give rise to the conflict and represent the context of the conflict process—husband, wife, guests coming, vacuuming the house. *Content* refers to what the conflict is about—wife requesting husband to help vacuum, and husband resisting. The *process* is the conflictual interaction or the interpersonal and intrapersonal interference process—wife asks husband to help with house cleaning and vacuuming, husband resists because he is busy musing about a work situation, wife gets irritated and intentionally vacuums in his presence, husband gets angry and starts vacuuming, wife gets angry and leaves.

Although conflict resolution must include dealing with content, structure and process, we will focus mainly on *process* as we provide clients with a basis for resolving conflicts and engaging in negotiating as a method of conflict resolution.

Most conflicts can be defined by the following process (Patton & Griffin, 1981):

- Antecedent condition and circumstances are the structures or characteristics of a situation that lead to conflict.

- Conflict—interference in the action of another person:

  Perceived conflict;

  Felt conflict.

- The resulting action or overt behaviors—aggression, debate, argument.

- Conflict ends: either through resolution by agreement, or through suppression of one party by the other, or of both parties—win-win, win-lose, lose-lose.

- Aftermath or results of conflict: parties are alienated, brought closer together, neutralized.

Substance abusing offenders often respond to potential conflict or actual conflict by engaging in

AOD use or even abuse or by engaging in antisocial and criminal conduct (Ross et al., 1986). The consequences of these responses are often escalation of the conflict, damage to the relationship or alienation of others.

An alternative response that will serve the client more effectively is *negotiation*. Negotiation is working toward compromise and agreement between the parties that allow both to satisfy their needs. What is important to recognize is that "the act of engaging in communication is a process of negotiating our meanings with those of others" (Ruben, 1988, p. 105). When we communicate, what we really do is to negotiate meanings and understandings with other people. Thus, we practice the art of negotiation—because we engage in communication every day. When our meanings match well, we can say we are communicating—and we are in fact *negotiating*. It is important that the offender understand this.

It is also important that the offender understand that compromise and negotiation is not defeat, but a way of achieving "no-lose" solutions to problems. As Ross and associates (1986) note, negotiating is not a show of weakness, but requires social skill and courage to face the conflict in a constructive manner. The social skills related to negotiation and effective problem solving include being able to convince people to agree with a point made and being able to make a legitimate complaint (King et al., 1994).

2. Objectives of Session

> ⏩ Clients learn that it is possible that two people can both be partly right in a discussion, that an open-minded approach to problems can be the most fruitful way to reach a solution;
>
> ⏩ Clients learn that an open-minded approach to conflict and problem solving can be the most fruitful way to reach a solution or to resolve the conflict;
>
> ⏩ Clients strengthen their ability to identify problems and their consequences, and to find alternative ways to solve those problems.

3. Session Content and Process

a. What this session is about:

We have already learned many problem solving skills and to understand the outcome of our own actions. One of the most important skills is having the self-control and ability to calm ourselves down while disagreeing with someone else. In addition, it is helpful to know that everyone experiences and views the world from a different point of view and their attitudes, values and beliefs should be respected. These differences don't always require that one person is wrong and the other right, but both individuals can have a sound point of view and both can be partly correct. Let's look at ways that you can approach a situation or conflict and how you can find what we call *win-win* outcomes. But first, we briefly review the ways that people try to solve conflict that do not lead to positive or good outcomes. We looked at these ways in depth in Session 32, *Assertiveness Skills Development*.

b. Remember the three old ways you have used to deal with conflict or friction:

1) FIGHT: become aggressive and forceful to get your way which only increases the conflict or friction;

2) FLIGHT: withdraw or remove yourself from the conflict or friction and nothing is resolved;

3) FAKE: you go along with the other person but then do what you want anyway and things are left up in the air.

c. Working for a win-win outcome:

When you feel there is a conflict with someone else you can back down, become angry, or do what they want you do to. Each of these responses can put you in a bad position, and none of them is likely to achieve the result you really want. Alternatives to these responses are the skills of negotiation and bargaining. In *negotiation and bargaining,* you try to work out an agreement with the other person. Each of you changes your demands just enough so that each of you gets part of what you want. You find alternatives or options that allow both of you to be satisfied with the outcome. When both people succeed we may refer to the situation as *win-win.* Everyone gains; no one loses completely.

Here are some skills that you can use to get a good outcome and reach an agreement or a win-win solution around a conflict or problem (adapted from several sources, including King et al., 1994 and authors' experience):

- First, you state your own thoughts and feelings;

- Second, you ask others involved what their idea is about the matter;

- You then explain why you think your idea is better;

- If you are a good communicator, you give the other persons a chance to consider what you have said before you expect them to make up their minds.

Exercise: Ask the group for examples of situations in which they have wanted to convince someone else to do things their way. Have them role-play at least one situation that they have reported.

d. **The skill and steps of negotiation (adapted from authors' experiences and from King et al., 1994; Ross et al., 1986):**

1) DECIDE: Are you having a difference of opinion with someone else? Tell the other person your position. Describe what you think the other person's opinion is.

2) LISTEN: Did you understand the other person? Be open-minded.

3) THINK: Think about the other person's position; What are the options that might work?

4) SUGGEST A COMPROMISE: Can you suggest a compromise?

5) DISCUSS: Discuss the options and decide what is best.

Scenario: You have been on the job for only a week and your new boss calls you over. He tells you that you are not dressing in a manner that is appropriate for your job and that you need to get some new clothes. You don't have enough money to buy clothes right now.

Discussion: Have the group discuss the problem and consider both the alternatives and consequences of each solution. (A suggested alternative is to ask/agree with the employer that you will buy some new clothing with your next paycheck.)

Exercise: Have the participants suggest other situations in which they might have trouble coming to a good solution. Have them pair with another member and role-play negotiating a solution. Have the rest of the group determine if the pair has followed each of the steps involved in negotiation and leading to a win-win settlement. This should include consideration of active listening, body language and using assertive communication skills. (Let all clients role-play.)

e. **Steps in dealing with a complaint:**

Sometimes problems cannot be solved by negotiation or convincing the other person that your point of view is correct. You have to resort to making a formal complaint. This is not as easy to do as one might think. There are several steps that might help you in being successful in making a formal complaint (adapted from King et al., 1994):

- Find a way to express your complaint clearly.

- Who is the best person to complain to?

- Where and when should you make the complaint?

- How would you like to have the complaint resolved? (TELL THE PERSON WHAT YOU WANT.)

- Listen to the person's response.

- Try to offer helpful suggestions to resolve the problem.

Exercise: Have the group suggest some situations in which you might have no alternative other than to make a complaint. Role-play the situation and discuss the outcome.

f. **A guide for diagnosing how you approach a conflict:**

A prayer has become known as the serenity prayer of Alcoholics Anonymous (1976):

God, grant me the strength to change the things I can, the patience to accept the things I cannot change, and the wisdom to know the difference.

Diagnose each potential or actual conflict that you may be a part of. Ask yourself the question: Is the circumstance of such a nature that you can in fact change the situation or negotiate a settlement? Or, is it simply impossible to change what exists? If you decide that change and settlement is possible, then negotiate with strength and courage (courage is the word that AA has substituted for strength in the serenity prayer). If you truly see that change is not possible and there is no hope for negotiation, then accept what is with patience. But most important—use your best wisdom and intelligence to know the difference.

4. Classroom and Homework Activities

a. Do *Work Sheet 57:* Describe a conflict situation in which you had the opportunity to practice your negotiation skills. Address each question in the Work Sheet.

b. Do a *Thinking Report* on the situation described in *Work Sheet 57.*

5. Presentation Sequence

a. Review the main points covered in the last session on critical reasoning.

b. Review the *Thinking Report* on PROPAGANDA done this past week.

c. Discuss the Rationale and Objectives for Negotiation and Social Skills Training. Provider may want to use additional material presented in the Overview and Rationale section in the session presentation.

d. Present content as outlined in above text.

e. Hold reflection group at end of session.

f. Outline homework assignments.

g. Brief look at next session.

6. Session and Client Response Evaluation

a. Clients complete the CSES.

b. Provider completes the PSES using these questions as guides:

1) *Has the group accepted the premise that an open-minded approach to problems is generally the best way to solve arguments?*

2) *Have the members demonstrated a growing ability to find alternative ways to solve problems?*

c. Complete a Behavioral Rating Form on each client. This may be a good time to review where the client is in Phase III. This is the last BRF to be done on the client. It is important to review with all clients the progress they have made in the program. Look at the changes across the past BRFs completed. Provide feedback to the client.

MODULE 12

Maintaining Self-Improvement and Change:

Developing a Healthy Lifestyle or Manner of Living

MODULE 12: MAINTAINING SELF-IMPROVEMENT AND CHANGE: DEVELOPING A HEALTHY LIFESTYLE OR MANNER OF LIVING

The challenge of the *Ownership of Change* phase of treatment is for clients to maintain the changes they have made over the past nine months. The challenge for the provider is to provide the necessary support and reinforcement to make these changes stick. Of particular importance is for the client to complete the program. Program completion will give the client a heightening sense of accomplishment and will strengthen change and self-improvement.

One important way to maintain changes that clients have made is to help them integrate or unite these changes into a healthy lifestyle. From the very start of the program, as clients have learned to make changes in their thinking, beliefs, feelings and actions, this integration process has been taking place. But now, the goal is to help the client become fully aware of the need to integrate these changes into an overall healthy lifestyle.

There was a time when the use of drugs and involvement in criminal behavior were a central part of the clients' lifestyle. Through the various SSC sessions, and particularly our basic skills development program, clients learned to change their thoughts, feelings and actions in order to live a drug-free and crime-free life. Now, we are pointing clients in the direction of lifestyle patterns as alternatives to a lifestyle of drug use and crime. Whereas before clients had ownership of a lifestyle of drug use and criminal conduct, now we are challenging them to take ownership of an alternative lifestyle.

In this module, we look at four alternatives to AOD use and criminal behavior that build a healthy lifestyle: *Alternatives of play;* of work or being *productive;* of *sharing* our strengths; and of *finding support* from others in our efforts to grow and change. We first look at play or finding pleasure in our lives. We then look at ways to manage our work and job issues in a healthy and productive way. Third, we look at how we can share our strengths through being a mentor or role model for others who are searching for and making change. Finally, we look at how we can find support in others to strengthen our healthy lifestyle and the changes we have made in our manner of living.

The specific objectives of this module are:

- Clients learn to identify and begin to practice lifestyle changes that will strengthen their drug-free and crime-free living;

- Clients learn to develop a balance among work, play, supporting others and getting support from others.

432

Session ④ : The Alternatives of Healthy Play and Leisure Time

1. Rationale and Overview of Session

AOD use and criminal conduct have been part of the SAO's lifestyle. If clients are to be successful in making change, they have to develop alternatives to this lifestyle. Healthy play and leisure time are among these alternatives.

Most SAO clients have spent a considerable amount of time in AOD use or spending time with criminal associates or in criminal activities. Once these elements are removed, clients are likely to experience a sense of loss and emptiness. They most likely derived a considerable degree of pleasure from these activities. If they have not replaced that *empty time* with other healthy pleasurable activities, they may feel that life is an endless cycle of eating, sleeping, and working. Unless the void is replaced with some pleasant activities, there is an increased probability that group members will experience loneliness, boredom and depression.

Monti and his colleagues report "that the number of pleasant activities a person engages in is directly related to the occurrence of positive feelings" (1989, p. 87). People who spend all their time doing required activities, the things we consider *shoulds* and *have tos,* will experience little reward in life. We addressed this issue in Session 42 with respect to developing lifestyle balance. We saw that creating a balanced lifestyle and engaging in positive *addictions* are counters to the *shoulds* message of imbalance that will lead to feeling self-deprivation. The lifestyle *daily balance* is a process that is ongoing and stable. It involves built-in activities that are part of daily living and that give positive and meaningful gratification to the individual. Unless this happens, clients become vulnerable to relapse and recidivism. Unless an alternative lifestyle is developed which includes a balance of work and play, clients are likely to feel they deserve to reward themselves with a drink, a hit, a night out with friends who may be criminal associates, or even committing a crime. It is important that clients develop a balance in life by devising a schedule of pleasant things that they want to do.

2. Objectives of Session

> ➠ Clients understand the meaning of healthy play and about activities that can bring healthy pleasure;
>
> ➠ Clients discover that they have replaced AOD involvement with healthy activities not involving AOD use;
>
> ➠ Clients learn to plan and fulfill healthy pleasures through leisure time activities that become a regular part of their lifestyle.

3. Session Content and Process

a. Introduction to session:

Your involvement in drugs and criminal behavior has been a central part of your lifestyle. At times, you probably have strong feelings of emptiness because of the time you did spend in your AOD use. Unless you replace that void with some pleasant activities, there is a greater chance that you will experience loneliness, boredom and depression. In maintaining a drug-free and crime-free lifestyle, the alternative of healthy play is vital.

Discussion: Discuss the dangers of not experiencing enough time in which they are doing pleasant things for themselves. Explain the idea that it is possible to have pleasant and *healthy pleasures*. These are activities that have some mental, physical, or spiritual value for the individual and that do not necessarily depend on having someone else to do them with.

b. What is healthy play?

There are many definitions of play. Most important among these many definitions is the idea that to play is to take part in fun, to have pleasure, to be amused, to enjoy an activity or to take

433

part in a recreation. An important part of the meaning of play is to *move freely within a space*. The lifestyle alternative we are referring to is more than just play. It is healthy play. This means that play is wholesome, it is of benefit to us, and most important, when we have finished our play, we feel good about ourselves. We feel fulfilled.

c. **Play through fulfilling our pleasures:**

We know that the number of pleasant activities you engage in is directly related to how positive you feel about yourself. People who spend all their time doing required activities, the things we consider *shoulds* and *oughts,* will experience little reward in life and are likely to feel they deserve to reward themselves with a drink, a hit, or a night out with friends with whom they should not associate. One way to learn healthy play is to know what pleases you—or to know your pleasures.

If you know what pleases you or what activities that give you pleasure, then you will know how to play and your play will be more fulfilling. You can find out what pleases you by completing the *Personal Pleasure Inventory* (PPI) and the PPI profile (Milkman & Sunderwirth, 1993; Wanberg, Milkman & Harrison, 1992).

Exercise: Have clients complete the *Personal Pleasure Inventory* (PPI) found in *Work Sheet 58* of the Workbook. Scoring instructions are in the Work Sheet. Assist clients in scoring the PPI and constructing the PPI Profile on *Work Sheet 59.* There are four broad areas of pleasure that are measured by the PPI. These are:

• Physical expression;

• Focus on the self;

• Artistic or aesthetic activities;

• Cooperative harmony or working together.

Use time for clients to examine their findings. Have them look at their high scores. Discuss their findings in group.

d. **Identifying specific leisure time activities:**

Have clients identify leisure time activities that bring them pleasure and allow them to play in a healthy way. Can these activities replace the time they spent in AOD use in the past?

Exercise: Using your PPI profile and *Work Sheet 60,* clients make a list of specific activities that will bring them pleasure and joy. How often do they do these? Are these part of their lifestyle? Are they now replacements or alternatives to AOD use or criminal activities?

Exercise: Using *Work Sheet 61,* have clients make a list of play activities that they will take part in this week. Then, using the bottom part of *Work Sheet 61,* have clients make a personal time schedule, and then plan what their activity will be in that schedule. This will help them to begin to develop a balance in life between work and healthy play. Have clients address these questions in group:

• What kind of problems are you experiencing in finding alternative ways to fill your time?

• Have you been successful in finding new friends and acquaintances with whom to share leisure time?

Discussion: Encourage the group to frankly discuss the changes that are necessary in their lives to stay out of trouble. What kind of problems are they experiencing in finding alternative ways to fill their time? Have they been successful in finding new friends and acquaintances with whom to share leisure time?

4. Classroom and Homework Activities

a. Have clients complete the PPI in *Work Sheet 58* and construct the Profile in *Work Sheet 59*. Assist them in scoring the instrument. Then, using the PPI profile, have them complete the Leisure Time Activities Work Sheet, *Work Sheet 60*.

b. Have clients complete *Work Sheet 61* by writing down several pleasant activities that they believe they would enjoy doing in the next week. Then, using the chart, have clients plan 30 to 60 minutes each day that they set aside as their own personal time. Encourage clients to make time for this in advance and to select things from the list and take the time to do them. Have them write down their feelings about what they did.

c. Have clients write in their journal one thing they did that they felt good about during the week. Was that related to their pleasant activities homework?

5. Presentation Sequence

a. Review previous session and homework they did using *Work Sheet 56*—Negotiation Skills. Also, have them review their Thinking Report on using negotiation skills in handling a conflict.

b. Discuss the rationale and objectives for Developing Alternative Lifestyle Activities.

c. Discuss the problems associated with too little pleasure in one's life; discuss the concept of *healthy pleasures*.

d. Do all exercises.

e. Hold a reflection group at end of session.

f. Discuss the homework and look briefly at the next session.

6. Session and Client Response Evaluation

a. Clients complete CSES.

b. Provider completes PSES using these questions as guides:

1) *Was the group able to identify ways in which their lifestyles need to be adjusted to maintain a sober and responsible life?*

2) *Did they appear open and cooperative to finding ways that they can make their lives more pleasant and rewarding?*

Session ❹⑦ : The Alternative of Productive Work: Managing Work and Job Issues

1. Rationale and Overview of Session

Productive and meaningful work is an element essential in maintaining a drug-free and crime-free life and a balanced lifestyle. It represents another primary alternative to drug use and a criminal lifestyle. Research has shown that those individuals who are gainfully employed and who enjoy their job have a much higher probability of recovering from substance abuse. For those SAO clients who are on disability, are retired, or for other reasons are unable to be gainfully employed, it is still important that they find outlets for being productive in their living. This productivity might be in doing volunteer work or in maintaining the upkeep of their personal property or home. It is also important that people feel that they have some kind of vocation or avocation with which to identify. This identity goes beyond just having a job. Thus, we focus on helping clients see the difference between one's *work* and one's *job*. We also explore the issues of being gainfully employed and the skills of finding employment. Clients who are employed may become role models for other group members, or help those who are not employed in finding work. They will also benefit from the program of learning the skills of finding a new job or improved employment.

2. Objectives of Session

> ⮞ Clients learn what their work is or what is their area of work;
>
> ⮞ Clients learn skills necessary to take part in and achieve rewarding employment.

3. Session Content and Process

a. Productive Work: Our first alternative to AOD use:

We see productive and meaningful work as our first main alternative to AOD use and engaging in criminal conduct. Although you have most likely worked all of your adult life, you may not have seen your work and your job as a way to express yourself in healthy ways and as a way of replacing AOD use and involvement in criminal conduct.

There is a difference between your work and your job. Your work is a physical or mental activity and effort that is directed toward accomplishing something. Your work is the means through which you practice your skills, fulfill your talents and earn your livelihood. Your job is what you go to in order to fulfill your work. You take your work to your job. You own your work. It is yours. You don't own your job; it is loaned to you in order for you to do your work. Work is one way you define your lifestyle.

b. Being effective in your work:

Dr. Steven R. Covey (1989) has identified what he calls *Seven Habits of Highly Effective People*®. These "Habits" can help clients be more effective in their work, in the job where they apply their work and in their daily lives. The Provider may want to read Covey's book and become more intimately acquainted with the Seven Habits®. They are:

1) *Habit 1: Be proactive*® —*when doing your work:* Or to take responsibility for your life by having a *personal vision* of what you want to do and accomplish. This involves taking the initiative that you choose, that you respond and not just react.

2) *Habit 2: Begin with the End in Mind*® —*when Doing your work:* This means you think about what you want to do, and then you do it. You take *personal leadership* of yourself. You lead yourself in the direction you want to go. To begin with the end in mind means knowing where you want to go. You need to have a map of your journey. Your map is made up of your personal goals.

3) *Habit 3: Put First Things First®* —*when doing your work:* This means that you manage our own time, your energies and your goals. It is *personal management* of what you do. To achieve your vision and achieve your goals, you have to manage your life. How do you manage your money? You may have the goal of buying a car or taking a vacation. But, if you spend every cent you have on things you really don't need and if you don't save some money, you won't achieve that goal of buying a car or taking a vacation.

4) *Habit 4: Think Win-Win®* —*when doing your work:* Win-win is the key to your *personal relationships* and a key to how you solve problems and settle conflicts. When people around you come out ahead *along with you,* everyone wins. It means sharing responsibility and victory. It means supporting people you work with. If only *you* do a good job where you work, then eventually, who you work for will fail. Then you end up failing. Think how you can help others do a good job where you work. When you help others achieve in their work, you have a lot of influence. That may be better than being the boss.

5) *Habit 5: Seek First to Understand, Then to Be Understood®* . This is putting yourself in the other person's shoes; this has to do with empathy, with *empathetic communication.* We worked hard on empathy in Session 39. Remember, you put empathy to work when you take part in active listening. You are effective in your work when you use empathy with people with whom you work. When you try to understand the other person, you are putting empathy to work. Put empathy into your work. You will win and no one loses.

6) *Habit 6: Synergize®* . *When doing your work, work together in a cooperative way for the common good:* Dr. Covey calls this *Synergy. Work for the common good.* This means that the whole of things is more than the sum of its parts. By working together, we cause things to happen that go beyond the sum of each person's efforts. Again, this is win-win. But more than just you and those around you win. The whole that you are a part of wins.

7) *Habit 7: Sharpen the Saw®.* This is *renewing your personal self.* It is to refresh yourself across your physical, emotional, mental and spiritual being. You can do your work in productive ways when you keep yourself renewed and refreshed in these four areas. This is not something you do just at work; it is your lifestyle to keep a balance between your physical, emotional, mental and spiritual worlds. A part of sharpening our saw is taking part in healthy play and healthy leisure.

c. **Defining YOUR work:**

Exercise: Use *Work Sheet 62* to identify what your work is. First, give a name to the work you do. Then write down as many things as you can that define your work. For example, a person may write down: Truck Driver. Then, what is involved in that work? Being safe? Listening to the sounds of the truck as it is running? Driving the speed limit? Being on time for a delivery? Maintaining the vehicle? Now, feel a sense of pride in your work. Think about approaching your work using the Seven Habits discussed above. How can you improve your work by applying these Seven Habits? Discuss this with your group and with a close friend. Again, feel the pride in your work. You may not like your job, but you can love your work. Feel power in that.

Clients will have difficulty doing the task of relating the Seven Habits to their work. The provider should take a job example and then go through the process of relating that job to the Seven Habits. Table 7 provides an example of relating a particular job to the Seven Habits.

d. **Skills in finding a job that matches your work:**

THINK ABOUT THIS: You may not have a job, but you have work. To prove this, just read what you did in *Work Sheet 62.* If you have a job, your job may not match your work. By working on the following skills and doing the exercises, you may begin to see that your job matches your work. If you don't have a job, you can apply these skills in helping you find a job that matches your work—your work as you defined it above. Having or finding a job that matches your work is achieving an important lifestyle alternative to AOD involvement. It is important to remember that a job search is a full-time job. Here are the skills needed to find a job:

1) *Developing a Resume:* A resume describes your work history and desire for work. Make it look neat. It might be a simple letter or a more detailed document. The resume is the first step in finding a job that matches your work. Try not to leave large periods of time that you can't account for on the resume. Explain such periods by saying: "I was looking for a job that matched my work." It is important that the document be carefully typed and accompanied by a good cover letter. Your counselor and group will help you with your resume.

   Exercise: Have clients look over sample resumes.

2) *The Job Application:* The job applicant needs to be able to emphasize personal strengths and strong job skills. Attend to every question when filling out an application. This is not always an easy task. Sometimes it is hard to answer certain questions. If you don't understand certain parts of the application, ask the prospective employer—or a friend. Remember, the first job you do for the job you are seeking is to complete the job application. Did you do a good job?

   Exercise: Provide the group with sample job applications. Have them practice filling one out. Hold a discussion around what was most frustrating about filling out the application.

3) *Job Leads:* Remember, job seeking is a full-time job in itself. Go after each one until you succeed. Talk about your disappointment with friends, family and group. Develop a way to make a list of all available jobs. Use every resource possible: Yellow pages, newspaper, friends, walk the shopping malls and look for "help needed" signs.

   Exercise: Using *Work Sheet 63*, have clients make a list of 10 possible jobs and employers. The client may need some structure and careful monitoring in this chore. Have clients fill in every space in *Work Sheet 63*.

4) *Developing Telephone Skills:* Rehearsal of proper skills is an important step in finding a job. When making phone calls, *introduce yourself properly, and ask to speak to the person in charge* of hiring for the company. When you speak with that person, introduce yourself again. You may say that you have heard that the company is a good employer and that you would like an opportunity to discuss a possible job. *Set up an appointment.* If you are unable to speak with the appropriate person the first time you call, ask for his/her name so that you may ask for the appropriate person when you call back. Practice your phone skills with a friend or in your group.

   Exercise: Have clients rehearse several scenarios and discuss them in the group until clients have the skills necessary to complete the initial phone call.

5) *The Interview:* Rehearse the job interview. Be prepared for success and failure. Remember: you have work to sell. You own that work; you can sell it. You can't buy the job; you sell your work.

   Exercise: Role-play a job interview. Make some role-play situations result in a failure to get hired. How did the person not hired feel? The SAO is often sensitive to failure and gets discouraged after being refused a job. Have clients talk about the fact that most people who find a job have many interviews before they are finally hired.

6) *Set Goals:* Where are you going? What are your short-term goals? What are your long-term goals? Look at your plan for school and/or work for the next three years.

   Exercise: Use *Work Sheet 64: School and Work Plan for Next Three Years.*

4. Review of Classroom and Homework Activities

   a. Complete all Work Sheets for this session.

   b. Have clients prepare an up-to-date resume or letter of introduction including present employment (if the client is currently employed). Provider should provide sample resumes.

5. Presentation Sequence

   a. Review the major points from the previous session. Have clients relate the ideas in that session to the current session. Have them see that both sessions are dealing with two very important lifestyle alternatives.

   b. Discuss the rationale and objectives for the session.

   c. Present session as outlined in the Session Content section.

   d. Hold a reflection group at end of session. Have clients focus on anxieties related to work and their job or looking for a job.

   e. Spend time on the homework for this week—preparing an up-to-date resume or letter of introduction.

   f. Brief look at next session.

6. Session and Client Response Evaluation

   a. Clients complete CSES.

   b. Provider completes PSES. *Reflect on whether the group demonstrated an understanding of the skills and perseverance necessary to get employment.*

Table 7

Relating a Specific Job Description to the Seven Habits™

PARTS STORE SERVICE WORKER	
1. *Habit 1: Be Proactive®*— in doing your work: Look ahead, have a personal vision.	Have a "map" of the parts store in mind to know where everything is; arrive at work ahead of time and have your work area ready to go; look ahead to supervising a parts store or department of a large parts store.
2. *Habit 2: Begin with the End In Mind®.* Know what you want to achieve; take personal leadership.	Know how many customers you expect to serve in one day; set a goal of satisfying every customer. When you don't, study what you did and correct it.
3. *Habit 3: Put First Things First®.* Take personal management of what you do; organize yourself.	Keep a log of the mistakes you made and of the problems in the job. Don't get ahead of yourself; one customer at a time.
4. *Habit 4:Think Win-Win®*— when doing your work: A key to good work relationships.	Listen to other workers and if they are having a problem finding a part, help them; you have a "map" of the store in your mind.
5. *Habit 5: Seek First to Understand, Then to Be Understood®.* Have empathy.	Understand a customer's frustration about his car not working; identify with other workers that some customers are a pain.
6. *Habit 6: Synergize®.* Work for the common good.	Be willing to help another worker who is having a problem with a customer; be part of organizing your work area. Remember: the more satisfied customers you have, the more customers you have and you might get a raise.
7. *Habit 7: Sharpen the Saw®.* Remember to renew your personal self.	Take your morning and afternoon break; disconnect yourself from the job for a few minutes; talk about fishing to a co-worker.

Session 48 : Role Modeling Change

1. Rationale and Overview of Session

It is only when we own something that we can share it. When we truly own the changes we have made, it is then that we can share those changes. But the reverse is true. It is when we share what we own that we feel we truly own it. The same is true with knowledge. When we truly know something, we can then teach it. But when we teach it, we truly know it. Again, research has shown that recovering substance abuse clients have a greater probability of maintaining recovery when they help other people in the recovery process. We see this in the 12-step work with Alcoholics Anonymous.

This is the exciting part of being a provider of *Strategies for Self-Improvement and Change*. We have brought our clients to the point that they can share what they now own—the changes they have made. Some may do it in a formal way and actually become involved as a counselor or in a provider's vocation. Most will not do this. But all who are owning the changes they have made, all who are in the ownership stage of change, can model their changes and can become an inspiration to others to change their lives. This session will focus on that very issue. It is important that clients are not made to feel that they must place themselves in a formal role-model role. Yet, for those who do want to explore this, we need to open doors for that opportunity.

2. Objectives of Session

> ➠ Clients review the homework they did using *Work Sheet 64* and their resume or letter of introduction.
>
> ➠ Clients understand the power of being a role model or mentor for others who are working to change.
>
> ➠ Clients look at being in a partnership with someone who is trying to make changes in AOD use and criminal conduct.

3. Session Content

a. **Maintaining change through being a role model or mentor:**

It is well known that the changes people make in their lives become more stable and permanent when they become teachers and mentors of that change. But it is only when we own something that we can share it with someone else. When we have full ownership of our self-improvements and change, we feel secure enough to share with other people the joy and power of the changes we have made. One way to do this is to become an example, a model or sponsor for other people who are starting to make changes in their lives so that they can live free of AOD problems and free of criminal conduct. This is the wisdom of the *12-Step program*. The 12th step is to become sponsors or mentors of others in their effort to change. In this session, we look at ways that you can become a mentor—a guide, or teacher or tutor—for others.

b. **Two ways to be a sponsor or mentor:**

1) *Informal mentoring or role modeling:* This means that you do not formally mentor or sponsor another person. It is informal. You present yourself as someone who has changed, who has control of your life with respect to AOD use and criminal conduct. Other people will see this, will identify with you and want to be *like you*.

2) *Formal mentoring or sponsorship:* This is when you formally sponsor someone who is being challenged to change. You make yourself available for supportive contacts and involvement. But you must be ready for this. You must be secure in your own changes first.

c. **The steps of formal mentorship:**

Here are six very simple steps in becoming a mentor or sponsor for others who are making changes in their lives.

1) *First, feel secure* in your own change and in your ownership of that change;

2) *Identify what are your strengths* at this time in your life as to the changes you have made;

3) *Identify the areas you are most vulnerable* or the weakest in and keep track of these as you mentor others. For example, if you see yourself as vulnerable when you are in a bar, then you need to keep that in mind when you are sponsoring or mentoring another person;

4) *Find someone who is in need of support* in the changes they are making. Be available to them in their struggle to change. Use all of the skills you have learned in this program in developing a supportive and healthy relationship with that person;

5) *Find your own sponsor,* mentor or counselor who you can get support from as you mentor or sponsor another person;

6) *Go slow* and lend yourself to *support only one person to begin with*.

Exercise: Have clients use *Work Sheet 65* to identify the strengths of their change that they can bring into a mentorship or sponsorship with another person who is being challenged to change.

Exercise: Have clients use *Work Sheet 66* to identify the areas that they are most vulnerable in or their weakest areas. These are areas that clients need to monitor closely when they are mentoring or sponsoring someone else.

4. Classroom and Homework Activities

a. Complete *Work Sheets 65* and *66*.

b. Have clients write in their *Journal* this week about their strengths and weaknesses.

c. Have clients look for opportunities for both informal and formal mentorship and modeling. Have them make notes in their journal about these opportunities and then discuss them in the next session.

5. Presentation Sequence

a. Review homework from last session on preparing an up-to-date resume or letter of introduction. Have group members share this in an opening reflections group.

b. Discuss the rationale and objectives for session.

c. Present session as outlined in the Session Content section.

d. Hold a reflections group at end of session. Have clients identify someone who they might sponsor or mentor.

e. Brief look at next session.

6. Session and Client Response Evaluation

a. Clients complete CSES.

b. Provider completes PSES. *Reflect on whether the group demonstrated an understanding of the skills and perseverance necessary to get employment.*

Session ㊾ : Preparing for Maintaining Your Changes: Exploring Self-Help Groups and Other Community Support Programs

1. Overview and Rationale of Session

The effectiveness of self-help groups in bringing out and maintaining changes in the lives of people is well documented. The efficacy of the 12-step program has been demonstrated in Project MATCH, which we discussed in Chapter 2 of this manual. There are many self-help groups that the SAO can utilize to strengthen and reinforce the changes that clients have made in this program. These include Alcoholics Anonymous, Narcotics Anonymous and Cocaine Anonymous. For the SAO whose spouse has an alcohol or drug problem, Al Anon can be very helpful.

Many of the clients in the program already will have sought support and help from the various self-help groups in the community. Many Providers already will have encouraged clients to have explored these self-help groups as a source of support. This session is designed to have clients engage in a formal review and exploration of these groups.

2. Objective of Session

> ➠ Review clients' homework from last session as to their looking for opportunities for mentoring and sponsoring another person;
>
> ➠ Clients learn to find support in community self-help programs and other community resources.

3. Session Content

a. Learning to seek outward for help: Exploring self-help groups and other community support programs:

A large part of this program has been focused on *seeking inward* to find help in our efforts to change and improve ourselves. But we have also learned that we gain help in our efforts to change by *seeking support* and help from *outside of ourselves*. This is often difficult to do. During our growing up years, we were often taught to solve our own problems, to do it on our own, to not take our problems outside of ourselves or to *not hang our dirty linen in public*. But when we are committed to making change, or when we feel true ownership of that change, we feel secure enough to reach out and seek help and support from other people, from groups that are set up to help people and from our community. We have done this within our program group and with our program's provider. There are, however, many outside resources to help you keep up the changes you have made. One of the most important sources of such support is in the self-help groups in the community. We have found that when people seek the help of others who have problems similar to ours, we find the kind of support which helps us to continue our change and maintain the changes we have made.

b. Finding a self-help group that meets your needs:

Each person has different needs and different problems. There is probably a self-help group in the community that will meet your needs to keep up the changes you have made. For some, Alcoholics Anonymous may be the kind of group which will best meet your needs. It may be that you will find the support you need in a group that focuses more on a specific drug pattern such as cocaine. In that case, Cocaine Anonymous may be the best choice. There are many other groups that may be good choices for you. These may include Narcotics Anonymous, Overeaters Anonymous, Al Anon, or one of many others. One of the objects of this session is for you to explore those groups.

Exercise: Have clients use *Work Sheet 67* to explore the different self-help groups that are in their community. Have clients make a list, and then call some of these groups and talk with one of their members. Have them make notes as to how the conversation feels. Have clients attend a meeting before the next session.

4. Classroom and Homework Activities

a. Clients complete *Work Sheet 67,* Preparing a List of Self-Help Groups.

b. Clients write in their journal this week about their feelings around reaching out for help from others.

5. Presentation Sequence

a. Begin session with reflections group. Have clients review what they wrote in their journal about their strengths and weaknesses. Have clients share their experience around looking for another person for whom they can be an informal mentor or a formal sponsor.

b. Discuss the rationale and objectives for session.

c. Present session as outlined in the Session Content section.

d. Hold a reflection group at end of session. Use these points for a focus of discussion:

- Have clients share their experiences around being involved in self-help groups.

- What are their feelings now around attending or being involved in a self-help group?

- How are clients feeling about this being the next to last of the formal sessions? This should be an important part of this reflections group session.

e. Brief look at the next session.

6. Session and Client Response Evaluation

a. Clients complete CSES.

b. Provider completes PSES. Reflect on *whether the group demonstrated an understanding of the skills and perseverance necessary to identify worthwhile self-help groups for themselves in the community.*

Session ⑤⓪ : Preparing for Your Program Change Support Group

1. Rationale and Overview of Session

After this session, for the next two months, clients will attend a weekly group to reinforce and strengthen their changes and living a drug-free and crime-free life. This group will be spent reviewing many of the skills and concepts learned in the past nine months. Much of the session will be devoted to having the clients share where they are in their lives at this time. The Provider may want to review some of the most important concepts of the program.

This is in essence a termination group for the formal program. Time needs to be spent in group talking about feelings and thoughts around bringing the formal part of the program to a close.

2. Objectives of Session

> ➤ Have clients look back at their changes and self-improvement;
>
> ➤ Prepare clients for their change support group.

3. Session Content and Process

a. **Overview of session:**

For the next two months, you will attend a weekly group to reinforce and strengthen your changes and living a drug-free and crime-free life. You may also want to attend a self-help group. This is your last formal program session. We will spend time during this session talking about what you have learned from the program and reviewing many of the skills and concepts you have learned in the past nine months. Much of the session will be devoted to your sharing where you are in your life at this time and what is different now compared to where you were nine months ago. We will then do these things in this group session:

b. **Specific areas the provider may want to focus on in this closure group:**

1) Review the important skills learned in the last nine months.

2) Review the *Johari Window* as a model for ongoing group involvement.

3) Review the active sharing and active listening skills.

4) Review the changes that clients have made in the past nine months.

5) Review what clients think has been most helpful in the program.

4. Review of Homework for the Coming Week

a. Have clients write in their *Journal* the most important things they have learned in the program. Encourage them to have their thoughts and feelings come freely.

b. Do a *thinking report* on what was the most difficult thing you did in the program. Remember the parts:

SITUATION,

THOUGHTS,

FEELINGS,

BELIEFS AND ATTITUDES,

OUTCOME.

5. Presentation Sequence

a. Review the major points from the previous session.

b. Spend time reviewing homework done on job search, finding an individual to mentor and finding a self-help group.

c. Devote most of the session to a reflections closure group. Have members talk about how it feels to bring sessions to a close.

6. Session and Client Response Evaluation

a. Clients complete CSES.

b. Provider completes PSES. Reflect on whether the group demonstrated an understanding of the skills and perseverance necessary to maintain the changes that they have made while in the program.

c. Give clients time to reflect on value of the program.

d. Do a final BRF on each client and write a formal closure note on the formal part of the program.

EPILOGUE

*And when you have
reached the mountain top,
then you shall begin to climb.*

Kahlil Gibran—*The Prophet*

EPILOGUE

The comprehensive differential assessment done in this program provided a sound basis upon which to build an individualized treatment plan for clients. The *Master Profile* (MP) provides a summary of the assessment data and the *Master Assessment Plan* (MAP) gives the treatment provider the necessary information upon which to build the individualized treatment plan. However, the authors recognize that a manual-based, group-delivered program such as *Strategies for Self-Improvement and Change* (SSC) is limited in addressing the individual needs of clients.

The individualized treatment services go beyond the scope of this program. As the client proceeds through the program, various treatment needs will arise that can be met only through individualized treatment services. These services may include individual therapy, marital therapy, family conjoint therapy or other individualized treatment services as are seen necessary. The service provider for this program should be constantly alert for these specialized needs.

Because of the nature of some of the sessions in this program, various psychological problems may emerge. The provider should not hesitate to request a special evaluation around these problems. The provider will want to be particularly attuned to affective disorders that might become obvious in clients. It is not at all uncommon to find AOD clients manifest clinical depression once they have committed themselves to AOD abstinence.

It is recommended that service providers have at their disposal resources for mental health evaluation and treatment. As well, a few clients will have periods of psychosocial crises. These should be dealt with by the service provider using routine crisis management procedures. However, occasions will arise when crisis intervention will need more structure. Again, service providers need to have the resources available, either directly or on a referral basis, for these kinds of needs.

Finally, our work is not conclusive. There is still much to learn and much to develop with respect to our work with the substance abusing offender. Providers are encouraged to use their own experience, skills and knowledge in going beyond what we have provided in this SSC manual. Drawing upon one of the strengths of cognitive-behavioral treatment—that therapist and client become partners in developing the most effective approach to treatment—we see you as our partner in offering the most effective treatment for your clients. We encourage you to take this manual—what we have offered to you—as your partner in the work you do with individuals with substance abuse problems and a history of criminal conduct.

REFERENCES

Abrams, D. B., & Niaura, R. S. (1987). Social learning theory. In H. T. Blane & K. W. Leonard (Eds.), *Psychological theories of drinking and alcoholism* (131-178). New York: Guilford.

Agee, V. L. (1979). *Treatment of the violent incorrigible adolescent.* Lexington, MA: Lexington Books.

Agee, V. L. (1986). Institutional treatment programs for the violent juvenile. In S. Apter & A. Goldstein (Eds.), *Youth violence: Programs and prospects.* New York: Pergamon.

Alberti, R. E., & Emmons, M. L. (1995). *Your perfect right: A guide to assertive living* (7th ed.). San Luis Obispo, CA: Impact Publishers.

Alcoholics Anonymous. (1976). *Alcoholics Anonymous: The story of how many thousands of men and women have recovered from alcoholism* (3rd ed.). New York: Alcoholics Anonymous World Series.

Alford, B., & Norcross, J. C. (1991). Cognitive therapy as an integrated therapy. *Journal of Psychotherapy Integration, 1,* 175-190.

Allen, J. P., & Columbus, M. (1995). *Assessing alcohol problems: A guide for clinicians and researchers.* Bethesda, MD: National Institute on Alcohol Abuse and Alcoholism, U.S. Department of Health and Human Services, Public Health Services, National Institutes of Health.

Allen, J. P., Eckardt, M. J., & Wallen, J. (1988). Screening for alcoholism: Techniques and issues. *Public Health Reports, 103,* 586-592.

Allen, J. P., & Kadden, R. M. (1995). Matching clients to alcohol treatment. In R. K. Hester & W. R. Miller (Eds.), *Handbook of alcoholism treatment approaches: Effective alternatives* (pp. 278-291). Boston: Allyn & Bacon.

Allport, G. W. (1937). *Personality: A psychological interpretation.* New York: Henry Holt and Company.

American Psychiatric Association. (1994). *Diagnostic and statistical manual of mental disorders* (4th ed.). Washington, DC: Author.

Andrews, D. A. (1980). Some experimental investigations of the principles of differential association through deliberate manipulations of the structure of service systems. *American Sociological Review, 45,* 448-462.

Andrews, D. A. (1982). *The Level of Supervision Inventory (LSI): The first follow-up.* Toronto: Ontario Ministry of Correctional Services.

Andrews, D. A. (1994). *Social learning and cognitive approach to crime and corrections: Core elements of evidence-based correctional intervention.* Ottawa, Canada: Department of Psychology, Carleton University.

Andrews, D. A. (1995). The psychology of criminal conduct and effective correctional treatment. In J. McGuire (Ed.), *What works: Reducing reoffending* (pp. 35-61). New York: Wiley.

Andrews, D. A., & Bonta, J. (1994). *The psychology of criminal conduct.* Cincinnati, OH: Anderson.

Andrews, D. A., Bonta, J., & Hoge, R. D. (1990). Classification for effective rehabilitation: Rediscovering psychology. *Criminal Justice and Behavior, 17,* 19-52.

Andrews, D. A., Wormith, J. S., & Kiessling, J. J. (1985). *Self-reported criminal propensity and criminal behavior: Threats to the validity of assessment of personality* (Programs Branch User Report). Ottawa: Solicitor General Canada.

Andrews, D. A., Zinger, K. I., Hoge, R. D., Gendreau, P., & Cullen, F. T. (1990). Does correctional treatment work? A clinically-relevant and psychologically-informed meta-analysis. *Criminology, 28,* 369-404.

Anglin, M. D., Hser, Y. (1990). Treatment of drug abuse. In M. Tonry & J. Q. Wilson (Eds.), *Drugs and Crime* (pp. 393-460). Chicago: University of Chicago Press.

Annis, H. M. (1986). A relapse prevention model for treatment of alcoholics. In W. R. Miller & N. Heather (Eds.), *Treating addictive behaviors: Process of change* (pp. 407-433). New York: Plenum.

Annis, H. M. (1988). Effective treatment for drug and alcohol problems: What do we know? *Forum on Corrections Research, 2,* 18-23.

Annis, H. M., & Davis, C. S. (1989). Relapse prevention. In R. K. Hester & W. R. Miller (Eds.), *Handbook of alcoholism treatment approaches: Effective alternatives* (pp. 170-182). New York: Pergamon.

Arkowitz, H. (1992). Integrative theories of therapy. In D. K. Freedheim (Ed.), *History of psychotherapy: A century of change* (pp. 261-304). Washington, DC: American Psychological Association.

Armor, D. J., Polich, J. M., & Stambul, H. B. (1978). *Alcoholism treatment.* New York: Wiley.

Arnkoff, D. B., & Glass, C. R. (1982). Clinical cognitive constructs: Examination, evaluation, and elaboration. In P. Kendall (Ed.), *Advances in cognitive-behavioral research and therapy* (Vol. 1). New York: Academic Press.

Arnkoff, D. B., & Glass, C. R. (1992). Cognitive therapy and psychotherapy integration. In D. K. Freedheim (Ed.), *History of psychotherapy: A century of change* (pp. 657-694). Washington, DC: American Psychological Association.

Atkinson, D. R., Morten, G., & Sue, D. W. (1993). *Counseling American minorities: A cross-cultural perspective* (4th ed.). Dubuque, IA: Brown & Benchmark.

Bachelor, A. (1991). Comparison and relationship to outcome of diverse dimensions of the helping alliance as seen by client and therapist. *Psychotherapy, 28,* 234-249.

Baird, S. C., Heinz, R. C., & Bemus, B. J. (1979). *Project report No. 14: A two-year follow-up.* Madison, WI: Department of Health and Social Services, Case Classification/Staff Deployment Project, Bureau of Community Corrections.

Baker, L. H., Cooney, N. L., & Pomerleau, O. F. (1987). Craving for alcohol: Theoretical processes and treatment procedures. In W. M. Cox (Ed.), *Treatment and prevention of alcohol problems: A resource manual* (pp. 184-204). New York: Academic Press.

Bandura, A. (1969). *Principles of behavior modification.* New York: Holt, Rinehart & Winston.

Bandura, A. (1977). *Social learning theory.* Englewood Cliffs, NJ: Prentice-Hall.

Bandura, A. (1978). The self-system in reciprocal determination. *American Psychologist, 33,* 344-358.

Bandura, A. (1986). *Social foundations of thought and action: A social cognitive theory.* Englewood Cliffs, NJ: Prentice-Hall.

Bandura, A., & Adams, N. E. (1977). Analysis of self-efficacy theory of behavioral change. *Cognitive Therapy and Research, 1,* 287-310.

Baron, R. A. (1977). *Human aggression.* New York: Plenum.

Beck, A. T. (1963). Thinking and depression. *Archives of General Psychiatry, 9,* 324-333.

Beck, A. T. (1964). Thinking and depression: II. Theory and therapy. *Archives of General Psychiatry,* 10, 561-571.

Beck, A. T. (1970). The role of fantasies in psychotherapy and psychopathology. *Journal of Nervous and Mental Disease,* 150, 3-17.

Beck, A. T. (1976). *Cognitive therapy and the emotional disorders.* New York: International Universities Press.

Beck, A. T. (1978). *Depression Inventory.* Philadelphia: Center for Cognitive Therapy.

Beck, A. T. (1991). Cognitive as the integrative therapy. *Journal of Psychotherapy Integration,* 1, 191-198.

Beck, A. T. (1996). Beyond belief: A theory of modes, personality, and psychopathology. In P. M. Salkovskis (Ed.), *Frontiers of cognitive therapy* (pp. 1-25). New York: Guilford.

Beck, A. T., & Steer, R. A. (1987). *Manual for the revised Beck Depression Inventory.* San Antonio, TX: The Psychological Corporation.

Beck, A. T., Wright, F. D., Newman, C. F., & Liese, B. S. (1993). *Cognitive therapy of substance abuse.* New York: Guilford.

Beck, J. S. (1995). *Cognitive therapy: Basics and beyond.* New York: Guilford.

Bell, P., & Evans, J. (1981). *Counseling the black client: Alcohol use and abuse in black America.* Minneapolis, MN: Hazelden Foundation.

Bennion, L., & Li, T. K. (1976). Alcohol metabolism in American Indians and whites. *New England Journal of Medicine,* 284, 9-13.

Benson, H. (1975). *The relaxation response.* New York: Morrow.

Berenson, B. G., & Carkhuff, R. R. (1967). *Sources of gain in counseling and psychotherapy.* New York: Holt, Rinehart & Winston.

Berglas, S. (1987). Self-handicapping model. In H. T. Blane & K. W. Leonard (Eds.), *Psychological theories of drinking and alcoholism* (pp. 305-345). New York: Guilford.

Bernal, M., & Knight, G. P. (Eds.). (1995). *Ethnic identification.* Newbury Park, CA: Sage.

Bernstein, D. A., & Carlson, C. R. (1993). Progressive relaxation: Abbreviated methods. In P. M. Lehrer & R. L. Woolfolk (Eds.), *Principles and practice of stress management* (2nd ed., pp. 53-88). New York: Guilford.

Bischof, L. J. (1970). *Interpreting personality theories.* New York: Harper & Row.

Blane, H. T., & Leonard, K. W. (1987). *Psychological theories of drinking and alcoholism.* New York: Guilford.

Blum, K., Cull, J. G., Braverman, E. R., & Comings, D. E. (1996). Reward deficiency syndrome. *American Scientist,* 84, 132-145.

Blum, K., & Payne, J. E. (1991). *Alcohol and the addictive brain: New hope for alcoholics from bio-genetic research.* New York: Free Press.

Blume, S. B. (1992). Alcohol and other drug problems in women. In J. H. Lowinson, P. Ruiz, R. B. Millman, & J. G. Langrod (Eds.), *Substance abuse: A comprehensive textbook* (pp. 794-807). Baltimore, MD: Williams & Wilkins.

Bogue, B., & Timken, D. (1993). *Standardized assessment of the adult offender*. Denver: Judicial Branch, State of Colorado, State Court Administrator's Office.

Bordin, E. (1979). The generalizability of the psychoanalytic concept of the working alliance. *Psychotherapy: Theory, Research and Practice,* 16, 252-250.

Boring, E. (1930). A new ambiguous figure. *American Journal of Psychology,* 42, 444.

Botvin, G. J. (1986). Prevention of adolescent substance abuse through the development of personal and social competence. *In Preventing adolescent drug abuse: Intervention strategies* (NIDA Research Monograph 47, pp. 115-140). Rockville, MD: Department of Health and Human Services, National Institute on Drug Abuse.

Botvin, G. J., & Botvin, E. M. (1992). School-based and community-based prevention approaches. In J. H. Lowinson, P. Ruiz, R. B. Millman, & J. G. Langrod (Eds.), *Substance abuse: A comprehensive textbook* (pp. 910-927). Baltimore, MD: Williams & Wilkins.

Brickman, P., Rabinowitz, V. C., Karuza, J., Coates, D., Cohn, E., & Kidder, L. (1982). Models of helping and coping. *American Psychologist,* 37, 368-384.

Brown, S. A., Goldman, M. S., Inn, A., & Anderson, L. R. (1980). Expectations of reinforcement from alcohol: Their domain and relation to drinking patterns. *Journal of Consulting and Clinical Psychology,* 48, 419-426.

Bukstein, O. G. (1995). *Adolescent substance abuse: Assessment, prevention and treatment*. New York: Wiley.

Burgess, E. W. (1928). Factors determining success or failure on parole. In A. A. Bruce, A. J. Hjarno, E. W. Burgess, & J. Landesco (Eds.), *The workings of the indeterminate-sentence law and the parole system in Illinois*. Springfield, IL: State Board of Parole.

Burns, D. D. (1980). *Feeling good: The new mood therapy*. New York: William Morrow.

Burns, D. D. (1989). *The feeling good handbook*. New York: William Morrow.

Bush, J. M., & Bilodeau, B. C. (1993). *Options: A cognitive change program* (Prepared by J. M. Bush and B. C. Bilodeau for the National Institute of Corrections and the U.S. Department of the Navy). Washington, DC: National Institute of Corrections.

Butcher, J. H. N., Dahlstrom, W. G., Graham, J. R., Tellegan, A. M., & Kaemmer, B. (1989). *MMPI-2: Manual for administration and scoring*. Minneapolis: University of Minnesota Press.

Butler, J. P. (1992). Of kindred minds: The ties that bind. In M. A. Orlandi, R. Weston, & L. G. Epstein (Eds.), *Cultural competence for evaluators: A guide for alcohol and other drug abuse prevention practitioners working with ethnic/racial communities* (pp. 23-54). Rockville, MD: U.S. Department of Health and Human Services.

Caddy, G. R. (1978). Towards a multivariate analysis of alcohol abuse. In P. E. Nathan, G. A. Marlatt, & T. Loberet (Eds.), *Alcoholism: New directions in behavioral research and treatment*. New York: Plenum.

Cannon, W. B. (1927). The James-Lang theory of emotions: A critical examination and an alternative theory. *American Journal of Psychology,* 39, 106-124.

Cappell, H., & Greeley, J. (1987). Alcohol and tension reduction: An update on research and theory. In H. T. Blane & K. W. Leonard (Eds.), *Psychological theories of drinking and alcoholism* (pp. 15-54). New York: Guilford.

Cappella, J. N. (1985). The management of conversations. In M. L. Knapp & G. R. Miller (Eds.), *Handbook of interpersonal communication* (pp. 393-438). Beverly Hills, CA: Sage.

Carkhuff, R. (1969). *Helping in human relations* (Vols. 1 and 2). New York: Holt, Rinehart & Winston.

Carkhuff, R. (1971). *The development of human resources: Education, psychology and social change.* New York: Holt, Rinehart & Winston.

Carkhuff, R. R., & Berenson, B. G. (1977). *Beyond counseling and therapy* (2nd ed.). New York: Holt, Rinehart & Winston.

Carkhuff, R. R., & Truax, C. (1965). Training in counseling and psychotherapy: An evaluation of an integrated didactic and experimental approach. *Journal of Consulting Psychology, 29,* 333-336.

Carter, D. J., & Wilson R. (1992). *Minorities in higher education: American Council on Education eleventh annual status report on minorities in higher education.* Washington, DC: American Council on Education, Office of Minority Concerns.

Cartwright, R. D. (1977). *Night life: Explorations in dreaming.* Englewood Cliffs, NJ: Prentice-Hall.

Catalano, R., Howard, M., Hawkins, J., & Wells, E. (1988). Relapse in the addictions: Rates, determinants, and promising prevention strategies. In *1988 Surgeon General's report on health consequences of smoking.* Washington, DC: Office of Smoking and Health, Government Printing Office.

Cautela, J. (1966). Treatment of compulsive behavior by covert sensitization. *Psychological Record, 16,* 33-41.

Cautela, J. (1990). The shaping of behavior therapy: An historical perspective. *The Behavior Therapist, 13,* 211-212.

Center for Substance Abuse Treatment. (1994). *Screening and assessment for alcohol and other drug abuse among adults in the criminal justice system.* Rockville, MD: U.S. Department of Health and Human Services, Public Health Service.

Centers for Disease Control. (1986). Acquired immunodeficiency syndrome (AIDS) among Blacks and HispanicsUnited States. *MMWR, 35,* 655-665.

Chaney, E. F. (1989). Social skills training. In R. K. Hester & W. R. Miller (Eds.), Handbook of alcoholism treatment approaches: *Effective alternatives.* New York: Pergamon.

Chick, J., Ritson, B., Connaughton, J., Stewart, A., & Chick, J. (1988). Advice versus extended treatment for alcoholism: A controlled study. *British Journal of Addiction, 83,* 159-170.

Cicourel, A. V. (1974). *Cognitive sociology.* New York: Free Press.

Ciraulo, D. A., & Ciraulo, A. M. (1988). Substance abuse. In J. P. Tupin, R. I. Shader, & D. S. Harnett (Eds.), *Handbook of clinical psychopharmacology* (pp. 121-158). Northvale, NJ: Jason Aronson.

Clark, D. A., & Steer, R. A. (1996). Empirical status of the cognitive model of anxiety and depression. In P. M. Salkovskis (Ed.), *Frontiers of cognitive therapy* (pp. 75-96). New York: Guilford.

Cloninger, C. R., & Guze, S. B. (1970). Psychiatric illness and female criminality: The role of sociopathy and hysteria in the antisocial woman. *American Journal of Psychiatry, 127,* 79-87.

Collingwood, R. G. (1945). *The idea of nature.* London: Oxford University Press.

Collins, J. J., & Allison, M. (1983). Legal coercion and retention in drug abuse treatment. *Hospital and Community Psychiatry, 34,* 1145-1149.

Collins, J. J., Hubbard, R. L., Rachal, J. V., & Cavanaugh, E. (1988). Effects of legal coercion on drug abuse treatment. In M. D. Anglin (Ed.), *Compulsory treatment of opiate dependence*. New York: Haworth.

Colorado Department of Public Safety. (1991). *Colorado offender assessment and treatment system manual*. Denver: Division of Criminal Justice, Colorado Department of Public Safety.

Conners, G. J., Carroll, K. M., DiClemente, C. C., Longabaugh, R., & Donovan, D. M. (1997). The therapeutic alliance and its relationship to alcoholism treatment participation and outcome. *Journal of Consulting and Clinical Psychology, 65,* 582-598.

Cooney, N. L., Kadden, R. M., Litt, M. D., & Gerter, H. (1991). Matching alcoholics to coping skills or interactional therapies: Two-year follow-up results. *Journal of Consulting and Clinical Psychology, 59,* 598-601.

Cooney, N. L., Zweben, A., & Fleming, M. F. (1995). Screening for alcohol problems and at-risk drinking in health-care settings. In R. K. Hester & W. R. Miller (Eds.), *Handbook of alcoholism treatment approaches: Effective alternatives* (pp. 45-60). Boston: Allyn & Bacon.

Cose, E. (1997, January 13). Why Ebonics is irrelevant. *Newsweek,* pp. 78-80.

Covey, S. R. (1989). *The seven habits of highly effective people: Restoring the character ethic*. New York: Simon & Schuster.

Cox, W. M. (1987). *Treatment and prevention of alcohol problems: A resource manual*. New York: Academic Press.

Crime in America. (1996, June 8-14). *The Economist,* pp. 23-25.

Cross, T. L., Bazron, B. J., Dennis, K. W., & Isaacs, M. R. (1989, March). *Towards a culturally competent system of care* (Monograph Vol. 1). Washington, DC: National Institutes of Mental Health.

Cummings, N. A., Gordon, J., & Marlatt, G. A. (1980). Relapse strategies of prevention and prediction. In W. R. Miller (Ed.), *The addictive behaviors*. Oxford, UK: Pergamon.

Curry, S. G., & Marlatt, G. A. (1987). Building self-confidence, self-efficacy and self control. In W. M. Cox (Ed.), *Treatment and prevention of alcohol problems: A resource manual* (pp. 117-138). New York: Academic Press.

Daley, D. C., & Marlatt, G. A. (1992). Relapse prevention: Cognitive and behavioral interventions. In J. H. Lowinson, P. Ruiz, R. B. Millman, & J. G. Langrod (Eds.), *Substance abuse: A comprehensive textbook* (pp. 533-542). Baltimore, MD: Williams & Wilkins.

Dana, R. H. (1993). *Multicultural assessment perspectives for professional psychology*. Boston: Longwood.

Daniel, A. E., Robins, A. J., Reid, J. C., & Wifley, D. E. (1988). Lifetime and six month prevalence of psychiatric disorders among sentenced female offenders. *Bulletin of the American Academy of Psychiatry and the Law, 16,* 333-342.

Darkes, J., & Goldman, M. (1993). Expectancy challenge and drinking reduction: Experimental evidence for a mediational process. *Journal of Consulting and Clinical Psychology, 61*(2), 344-353.

DeLeon, G. (1984). *The therapeutic community: Study of effectiveness* (DHHS Publication No. ADM 84-1286). Rockville, MD: National Institute on Drug Abuse.

Delia, J. G., O'Keefe, B. J., & O'Keefe, D. J. (1982). The constructivist approach to communication. In F. E. X. Dance (Ed.), *Human communication theory*. New York: Harper & Row.

Derogatis, L. R. (1977). *SCL-90 administration: Scoring and procedures manual*. Baltimore, MD: Johns Hopkins University Press.

Dewey, J. (1910). *How we think*. Washington, DC: Heath & Co.

DiClemente, C. C. (1991). Motivational interviewing and the stages of change. In W. R. Miller & S. Rollnick (Eds.), *Motivational interviewing: Preparing people to change addictive behavior* (pp. 191-202). New York: Guilford.

Dimeff, L. A., & Marlatt, G. A. (1995). Relapse prevention. In R. K. Hester & W. R. Miller (Eds.), *Handbook of alcoholism treatment approaches: Effective alternatives* (pp. 176-194). Boston: Allyn & Bacon.

Dobson, K. S., & Block, L. (1988). Historical and philosophical basis of the cognitive-behavioral therapies. In K. S. Dobson (Ed.), *Handbook of cognitive-behavioral therapies* (pp. 3-38). New York: Guilford.

Donovan, D. M., & Mattson, M. E. (1994). Alcoholism treatment matching research: Methodological and clinical issues. *Journal of Studies on Alcohol,* Suppl. 12, 5-14.

Dunlap, K. (1932). *Habits: Their making and unmaking*. New York: Liveright.

Dunn, W. (1991, April 11). Survey shows Hispanic diversity: Minority grows at rapid rate. *USA Today,* p. 3A. Arlington, VA: Gannett Publications.

D'Zurilla, T. J., & Goldfried, M. R. (1971). Problem solving and behavior modification. *Journal of Abnormal Psychology,* 78, 107-126.

Edwards, G., Gross, M. M., Keller, M., & Moser, J. (1976). Alcohol-related problems in disability perspective: A summary of the consensus of the WHO group of investigators on criteria for identifying and classifying disabilities related to alcohol consumption. *Journal of Studies on Alcohol,* 37, 1360-1382.

Edwards, G., Gross, M. M., Keller, M., Moser, J., & Room, R. (1977). *Alcohol-related disabilities*. Geneva: World Health Organization.

Elkin, I. (1986). *NIMH treatment of depression collaborative research program*. Paper presented at the annual meeting of the Society for Psychotherapy Research, Wellesley, MA.

Elliot, D. S., Ageton, S. S., Huizinga, D., Knowles, B. A., & Canter, R. (1983). *The prevalence and incidence of delinquent behavior:* 1976-1980 (National Youth Survey Report 26). Boulder, CO: Behavioral Research Institute.

Ellis, A. (1962). *Reason and emotion in psychotherapy*. New York: Stuart.

Ellis, A. (1975). *A new guide to rational living*. Englewood Cliffs, NJ: Prentice-Hall.

Ellis, A. (1990). Live demonstration of rational-emotive therapy (Audio tape from *The Evolution of Psychotherapy: A conference*). Phoenix, AZ: The Milton H. Erickson Foundation.

Ellis, A., & Harper, R. A. (1961). *A guide to rational living*. Englewood Cliffs, NJ: Prentice-Hall.

Emrick, C. D. (1975). A review of psychologically oriented treatment of alcoholism: II. The relative effectiveness of different treatment approaches and the effectiveness of treatment versus no treatment. *Quarterly Journal of Studies on Alcohol,* 36, 88-108.

Emrick, C. D., & Aarons, G. A. (1990). Cognitive-behavioral treatment of problem drinking. In H. B. Milkman & L. I. Sederer (Eds.), *Treatment choices for alcoholism and substance abuse* (pp. 265-286). New York: Lexington Books.

Eysenck, H. J. (1960). *Behavior therapy and the neuroses.* London: Pergamon.

Farris, J. J., & Jones, B. M. (1978). Ethanol metabolism in male American Indians and whites. *Alcohol and Clinical Experimental Research, 2,* 77-81.

Feshbach, N. D. (1984). Empathy, empathy training and the regulation of aggression in elementary school children. In R. M. Kaplan, V. J. Konecni, & R. W. Novaco (Eds.), *Aggression in children and youth.* The Hague: Martinus Nijhoff.

Festinger, L. (1957). *A theory of cognitive dissonance.* Evanston, IL: Row, Peterson & Company.

Field, G. (1989). A study of the effects of intensive treatment on reducing the criminal recidivism of addicted offenders. *Federal Probation, 53,* 51-56.

Fingarette, H. (1988). *Heavy drinking: The myth of alcoholism as a disease.* Los Angeles: University of California Press.

Fisher, R., & Ury, W. (1981). *Getting to YES: Negotiating agreement without giving in.* Boston: Houghton Mifflin.

Frances, R. J., & Miller, S. I. (1991). *Clinical textbook of addictive disorders.* New York: Guilford.

Frank, J. D. (1992). Historical development in research centers: The Johns Hopkins Psychotherapy Research Project. In D. K. Freedheim (Ed.), *History of psychotherapy: A century of change* (pp. 392-395). Washington, DC: American Psychological Association.

Frankl, V. E. (1963). *Man's search for meaning.* New York: Washington Square Press.

Franks, C. M., & Barbrack, C. R. (1983). Behavior therapy with adults: An integrative perspective. In M. Hersen, A. E. Kazdin, & A. S. Bellack (Eds.), *Clinical psychology handbook* (pp. 507-524). New York: Pergamon.

Franks, C. M., & Wilson, G. T. (1973-1975). *Annual review of behavior therapy: Theory and practice* (Vols. 1-7). New York: Brunner/Mazel.

Freeman, A., Pretzer, J., Fleming, B., & Simon, K. M. (1990). *Clinical applications of cognitive therapy.* New York: Plenum.

Fried, R.0 (1993). The role of respiration in stress and stress control: Toward a theory of stress as a hypoxic phenomenon. In P. M. Lehrer & R. L. Woolfolk (Eds.), *Principles and practice of stress management* (2nd ed., pp. 301-332). New York: Guilford.

Fuller, R. K., Branchey, L., & Brightwell, D. R. (1986). Disulfiram treatment of alcoholism. *Journal of the American Medical Association, 256,* 1449-1455.

Garfield, S. L. (1992). Major issues in psychotherapy research. In D. K. Freedheim (Ed.), *History of psychotherapy: A century of change* (pp. 335-359). Washington, DC: American Psychological Association.

Gaston, L. (1990). The concept of the alliance and its role in psychotherapy: Theoretical and empirical considerations. *Psychotherapy, 27,* 143-153.

Gendreau, P. (1993, February). *Does "punishing smarter" work? An assessment of the new generation of alternative sanctions.* Paper prepared for Corrections Research, Ministry Secretariat, Solicitor General.

Gendreau, P., Little, T., & Groggin, C. (1996). A meta-analysis of the predictors of adult offender recidivism: What works. *Criminology, 34,* 575-607.

George, R. L. (1990). *Counseling the chemically dependent: Theory and practice*. Englewood Cliffs, NJ: Prentice-Hall.

George, R. L., & Cristiani, T. S. (1981). *Theory, methods and processes of counseling and psychotherapy*. Englewood Cliffs, NJ: Prentice-Hall.

George, W. H., & Marlatt, G. A. (1983). Alcoholism: The evolution of a behavioral perspective. In M. Galantere (Ed.), *Recent developments in alcoholism: Vol. 1. Genetics, behavioral treatment, social mediators and prevention, current concepts in diagnosis* (pp. 105-138). New York: Plenum.

Gerstein, D. R., & Harwood, H. J. (1990). *Treating drug problems*. Washington, DC: National Academy Press.

Gitlow, S. F. (1970). The pharmacological approach to alcohol. *Maryland State Medical Journal, 19,* 93-96.

Gitlow, S. F. (1982). The clinical pharmacology and drug interaction of ethanol. In E. M. Pattison & F. Kaufman (Eds.), *Encyclopedic handbook of alcoholism* (pp. 1-18). New York: Gardner.

Gitlow, S. F. (1988). An overview. In S. E. Gitlow & H. S. Peyser (Eds.), *Alcoholism: A practical treatment guide* (2nd ed., pp. 1-18). Philadelphia: W. B. Saunders.

Glass, C. R., & Arnkoff, D. B. (1988). Common and specific factors in client descriptions of and explanations for change. *Journal of Integrative and Eclectic Psychotherapy, 7,* 427-440.

Glass, C. R., & Arnkoff, D. B. (1992). Behavior therapy. In D. K. Freedheim (Ed.), *History of psychotherapy: A century of change* (pp. 587-628). Washington, DC: American Psychological Association.

Glassman, S. (1983). In, with, and of the group: A perspective on group psychotherapy. *Small Group Behavior, 14,* 96-106.

Glenn, H. S., & Hockman, R. H. (1977). *Substance abuse*. Unpublished manuscript, NDAC.

Glenn, H. S., & Warner, J. W. (1975). *Understanding substance dependence*. Unpublished manuscript, Social Systems, Inc.

Glenn, H. S., Warner, J. W., & Hockman, R. H. (1977). *Substance dependence*. Unpublished manuscript, NDAC.

Gold, M., & Mann, D. W. (1984). *Expelled to a friendlier place*. Ann Arbor: University of Michigan Press.

Goldfried, M. R. (1995). *From cognitive-behavioral therapy to psychotherapy integration: An evolving view*. New York: Springer.

Goldfried, M. R., Decenteceo, E. T., & Weinberg, L. (1974). Systematic rational restructuring as a self-control technique. *Behavior Therapy, 5,* 247-254.

Goldfried, M. R., & Kent, R. N. (1972). Traditional versus behavioral personality assessment: A comparison of methodological and theoretical assumptions. *Psychological Bulletin, 77,* 409-420.

Goldiamond, I. (1965). Self-control procedures in personal behavior problems. *Psychological Reports, 17,* 851-868.

Goldman, M. S., Brown, S. A., & Christiansen, B. A. (1987). Expectancy theory: Thinking about drinking. In H. T. Blane & K. E. Leonard (Eds.), *Psychological theories of drinking and alcoholism* (pp. 181-226). New York: Guilford.

Gomberg, E. S. L. (1986). Women: Alcohol and other drugs. In B. Segal (Ed.), *Perspectives on drug use in the United States*. New York: Haworth.

Gomez, A. G., & Vega, D. M. (1981). The Hispanic addict. In J. H. Lowinson & P. Ruiz (Eds.), *Substance abuse: Clinical problems and perspectives* (pp. 717-728). Baltimore, MD: Williams & Wilkins.

Goodwin, D. W., Schulsinger, F., Hermansen, L., Guze, S. B., & Winokur, G. (1973). Alcohol problems in adoptees raised apart from alcoholic biological parents. *Archives of General Psychiatry, 28*, 238-243.

Gorski, T. T. (1993). *Relapse prevention therapy with chemically dependent criminal offenders: The relapse prevention workbook for the criminal offender*. Independence, MO: Herald House/Independence Press.

Gorski, T. T. (1994). *Relapse prevention therapy with chemically dependent criminal offenders: A guide for counselors, therapists, and criminal justice professionals*. Independence, MO: Herald House/Independence Press.

Gottfredson, M. R., & Hirschi, T. (1990). *A general theory of crime*. Stanford, CA: Stanford University Press.

Gough, H. G. (1965). Cross-cultural validation of a measure of asocial behavior. *Psychological Reports, 17*, 379-387.

Grilly, D. M. (1989). *Drugs and human behavior*. Boston: Allyn & Bacon.

Guidano, V. F. (1987). *Complexity of the self: A developmental approach to psychopathology and therapy*. New York: Guilford.

Guidano, V. F., & Liotti, G. (1983). *Cognitive processes and emotional disorders: A structural approach to psychotherapy*. New York: Guilford.

Guthrie, E. R. (1935). *The psychology of learning*. New York: Harper.

Guy, E., Platt, J. J., Zwerling, I., & Bullock, S. (1985). Mental health status of prisoners in an urban jail. *Criminal Justice and Behavior, 12*, 29-53.

Hanson, N. R. (1958). *Patterns of discovery*. Cambridge, UK: Cambridge University Press.

Hare, R. D. (1980). A research scale for the assessment of psychopathy in criminal populations. *Personality and Individual Differences, 1*, 111-119.

Hare, R. D. (1986). Twenty years experience with the Cleckley psychopath. In W. H. Reid, D. Door, J. I. Walker, & J. W. Bonner (Eds.), *Unmasking the psychopath*. New York: W. W. Norton.

Harris, G. T., Rice, M. E., & Quinsey, V. L. (1992). *Psychopathy as ataxon: Evidence that psychopaths are a discrete class* (Research report 11(2), May). Penetanguishene, Ontario: Penetanguishene Mental Health Center.

Harris, K. B., & Miller, W.R. (1990). Behavioral self-control training for problem drinkers: Components of efficacy. *Psychology of Addictive Behaviors, 4*, 82-90.

Hart, L. S., & Stueland, D. S. (1979). An application of the multidimensional model of alcoholism: Differentiation of alcoholics by mode analysis. *Journal of Studies on Alcohol, 40*, 283-290.

Hart, S. D., Kropp, P. R., & Hare, R. D. (1988). Performance of male psychopaths following conditional release from prison. *Journal of Consulting and Clinical Psychology, 56*, 237-242.

Hatsukami, D. K., & Fischman, M. W. (1996). Crack cocaine and cocaine hydrochloride: Are the differences myth or reality? *The Journal of the American Medical Association, 276,* 1580-1588.

Hawkins, J. D., Lishner, D. M., & Catalano, R. F. (1985). Childhood predictors and the prevention of adolescent substance abuse. In C. L. Jones & R. J. Battjes (Eds.), *Etiology of drug abuse: Implications for prevention* (NIDA Research Monograph 56). Rockville, MD: National Institute on Drug Abuse.

Heather, N., Wodak, A., Nadelmann, E., & O'Hare, P. (1993). *Psychoactive drugs and harm reduction: From faith to science.* London: Whurr.

Hedlund, J. L., & Vieweg, M. S. (1984). The Michigan Alcoholism Screen Test (MAST): A comprehensive review. *The Journal of Operational Psychiatry,* 15, 55-65.

Heider, F. (1958). *The psychology of interpersonal relations.* New York: Wiley.

Henry, W. A. III (1990, April 9). Beyond the melting pot. *Time,* pp. 28-31.

Hester, R. K. (1995). Behavioral self-control training. In R. K. Hester & W. R. Miller (Eds.), *Handbook of alcoholism treatment approaches: Effective alternatives* (pp. 148-159). Boston, MA: Allyn and Bacon.

Hester, R. K., & Miller, W. R. (1989). *Handbook of alcoholism treatment approaches.* New York: Pergamon.

Hester, R. K., & Miller, W. R. (1995). *Handbook of alcoholism treatment approaches: Effective alternatives* (2nd ed.). Boston: Allyn & Bacon.

Hobson, A., & McCarley, R. (1977). The brain as a dream state generator: An activation-synthesis hypothesis of the dream process. *American Journal of Psychiatry,* 134(12), 1335-1348.

Hodding, G. C., Jann, M., & Ackerman, I. P. (1980). Drug withdrawal syndromes: A literature review. *The Western Journal of Medicine,* 133, 383-391.

Hodgins, S., & Cote, G. (1990). Prevalence of mental disorders among penitentiary inmates in Quebec. *Canada's Mental Health,* 38, 1-4.

Hoffman, P. B. (1983). Screening for risk: A revised salient factor score (SFS 81). *Journal of Criminal Justice,* 11, 539-547.

Holder, H. D., Longabaugh, R., Miller, W. R., & Rubonis, A. V. (1991). The cost effectiveness of treatment for alcohol problems: A first approximation. *Journal of Studies on Alcohol,* 52, 517-540.

Holland, S. (1982). *Residential drug-free programs for substance abusers: The effect of planned duration on treatment.* Chicago: Gateway Houses.

Hollen, S., & Beck, A. T. (1986). Research on cognitive therapies. In S. L. Garfield & A. E. Bergin (Eds.), *Handbook of psychotherapy and behavior change.* (3rd ed., pp. 443-482). New York: Wiley.

Hollin, C. R. (1990). *Cognitive-behavioral interventions with young offenders.* New York: Pergamon.

Horn, J. L., Skinner, H. A., Wanberg, K. W., & Foster, F. M. (1984). *Alcohol Use Questionnaire* (AUQ). Toronto, Canada: Addiction Research Foundation.

Horn, J. L., & Wanberg, K. W. (1969). Symptom patterns related to excessive use of alcohol. *Quarterly Journal of Studies on Alcohol,* 30, 35-58.

Horn, J. L., & Wanberg, K. W. (June, 1973). Females are different: On the diagnosis of alcoholism in women. In *Proceedings of the First Annual Alcoholism Conference of the National Institute on Alcohol Abuse and Alcoholism* (pp. 332-354). Washington, DC: U.S. Department of Health, Education, and Welfare.

Horn, J. L., Wanberg, K. W., & Foster, F. M. (1987). *Guide to the Alcohol Use Inventory (AUI).* Minneapolis, MN: National Computer Systems.

Horvath, A. O., & Symonds, B. B. (1991). Relation between working alliance and outcome in psychotherapy: A meta-analysis. *Journal of Counseling Psychology, 38,* 139-149.

Hubbard, R. L. (1992). Evaluation and treatment outcome. In J. H. Lowinson, P. Ruiz, R. B. Millman, & J. G. Langrod (Eds.), *Substance abuse: A comprehensive textbook* (pp. 596-611). Baltimore, MD: Williams & Wilkins.

Hubbard, R. L., Collins, J. J., Rachal, J. V., & Cavanaugh, E. R. (1988). The criminal justice client in drug abuse treatment. In C. G. Leukefeld & F. M. Tims (Eds.), *Compulsory treatment of drug abuse: Research and clinical practice* (DHHS Publication No. ADM 88-1578, pp. 57-80). Rockville, MD: National Institute on Drug Abuse.

Hubbard, R. L., Marsden, M. E., Rachal, J. V., Harwood, H. J., Cavanaugh, E. R., & Ginzburg, H. M. (1989). Drug abuse treatment: *A national study of effectiveness.* Chapel Hill, NC: University of North Carolina Press.

Hubbard, R. L., Rachal, J. V., Craddock, S. G., & Cavanaugh, E. R. (1984). Outcome prospective study (TOPS): Client characteristics and behaviors before, during and after treatment. In F. M. Tims & J. P. Ludford (Eds.), *Drug abuse treatment evaluation: Strategies, progress, and prospects* (DHHS Publication No. ADM 88-1329, pp. 42-68). Rockville, MD: National Institute on Drug Abuse.

Hull, C. L. (1943). *Principles of behavior.* New York: Appleton-Century-Crofts.

Hull, J. G. (1987). Self-awareness model. In H. T. Blane & K. W. Leonard (Eds.), *Psychological theories of drinking and alcoholism* (pp. 272-304). New York: Guilford.

Hunt, W. A., Barnett, L. W., & Branch, L. G. (1971). Relapse rates in addiction programs. *Journal of Clinical Psychology, 27,* 455-456.

Hunt, W. A., & Matarazzo, J. K. (1973). Three years later: Recent developments in the experimental modification of smoking behavior. *Journal of Abnormal Psychology, 81,* 107-114.

Hyman, M. M. (1976). Alcoholics 15 years later. *Annals of the New York Academy of Sciences, 273,* 613-623.

Inciardi, J. A. (1994). *Drug treatment and criminal justice.* Newbury Park, CA: Sage.

Inciardi, J. A. (1995). The therapeutic community: An effective model for corrections-based drug abuse treatment. In K. C. Hass & G. P. Alpert (Eds.), *The dilemmas of punishment* (pp. 406-417). Prospect Heights, IL: Waveland Press.

Ingram, R. E., & Kendall, P. C. (1987). The cognitive side of anxiety. *Cognitive Therapy and Research, 11*(5), 523-536.

Institute of Medicine. (1989). *Broadening the base of treatment for alcohol problems.* Washington, DC: National Academy Press.

Institute of Medicine, Committee to Identify Research Effectiveness in the Prevention and Treatment of Alcohol Related Problems. (1989). *Prevention and treatment of alcohol problems.* Washington, DC: National Academy Press.

Interagency Council on the Homeless. (1989). *The 1989 annual report of the Interagency Council on the Homeless*. Washington, DC: Author.

Isaacs, M. R., & Benjamin, M. P. (1991). *Towards a culturally competent system of care* (Monograph Volume 2). Washington, DC: National Institutes of Mental Health.

Izzo, R. L., & Ross, R. R. (1990). Meta-analysis of rehabilitation programs for juvenile delinquents. *Criminal Justice and Behavior*, 17, 134-142.

Jacobson, E. (1938). *Progressive relaxation* (2nd ed.). Chicago: University of Chicago Press.

Jacobson, E. (1970). *Modern treatment of tense patients*. Springfield, IL: Charles C Thomas.

Jacobson, G. R. (1989). A comprehensive approach to pretreatment evaluation: I. Detection, assessment and diagnosis of alcoholism. In R. K. Hester & W. R. Miller (Eds.), *Handbook of alcoholism treatment approaches: Effective alternatives* (pp. 54-66). New York: Pergamon.

James, W. (1890). *Principles of psychology*. New York: Henry Holt.

Johnson, D. (1972). Reaching out: *Interpersonal effectiveness and self-actualization*. Englewood Cliffs, NJ: Prentice-Hall.

Johnson, G., & Hunter, R. M. (1992). *Evaluation of the specialized drug offender program* (Report for the Colorado Judicial Department). Boulder: University of Colorado, Center for Action Research.

Joseph, H. (1992). Substance abuse and homelessness within the inner cities. In J. H. Lowinson, P. Ruiz, R. B. Millman, & J. G. Langrod (Eds.), *Substance abuse: A comprehensive textbook* (pp. 875-889). Baltimore, MD: Williams & Wilkins.

Jourard, S. M. (1959). Self-disclosure and other cathexis. *Journal of Abnormal and Social Psychology*, 59, 428-431.

Jourard, S. M., & Friedman, R. (1970). Experimenter-subject "distance" and self-disclosure. Journal of Personality and Social Psychology, 15, 278-282.

Jourard, S. M., & Resnick, J. L. (1970). The effect of high revealing subjects on self-disclosure of low revealing subjects. *Journal of Humanistic Psychology*, 10, 84-93.

Kadden, R., Carroll, K., Donovan, D., Cooney, N., Monti, P., Abrams, D., Litt, M., & Hester, R. (1992). *Cognitive-behavioral coping skills therapy manual: A clinical research guide for therapists treating individuals with alcohol abuse and dependence* (Project MATCH Monograph Series, Vol. 3). Rockville, MD: National Institutes on Alcohol Abuse and Alcoholism, U.S. Department of Health and Human Services, National Institutes of Health.

Kadden, R. M., Cooney, N. L., Getter, H., & Litt, M. D. (1989). Matching alcoholics to coping skills or interactional therapies: Posttreatment results. *Journal of Consulting and Clinical Psychology*, 57, 698-704.

Kandel, D. B., Simcha-Fagan, O., & Davies, M. (1986). Risk factors for delinquency and illicit drug use from adolescence to young adulthood. *Journal of Drug Issues*, 15, 67-90.

Kanfer, F. H. (1970). Self-regulation: Research, issues and speculations. In C. Neuringer & J. L. Michael (Eds.), *Behavior modification in clinical psychology* (pp. 178-220). New York: Appleton-Century-Crofts.

Kanfer, F. H. (1975). Self-management methods: In F. H. Kanfer & A. P. Goldstein (Eds.), *Helping people change*. New York: Pergamon.

Kanfer, F. H. (1986). Implications of a self-regulation model of therapy for treatment of addictive behaviors. In W. R. Miller & N. Heather (Eds.), *Treating addictive behaviors: Processes of change*. New York: Plenum.

Karenga, M. (1980). *Kawaida theory: An introduction*. Inglewood, CA: Kawaida Publications.

Kazdin, A. E. (1978). Behavior therapy: Evolution and expansion. *The Counseling Psychologist, 7,* 34-37.

Kazdin, A. E. (1983). Treatment research: The investigation and evaluation of psychotherapy. In M. Hersen, A. E. Kazdin, & A. S. Bellack (Eds.), *The clinical psychology handbook* (pp. 265-284). New York: Pergamon.

Kelley, H. H. (1971). Causal schemata and the attribution process. In E. E. Jones, D. E. Kanouse, H. H. Kelley, R. E. Nisbett, S. Valins, & B. Weiner (Eds.), Attribution: *Perceiving the causes of behavior.* Morristown, NJ: General Learning Press.

Kelley, H. H. (1987). Toward a taxonomy of interpersonal conflict process. In S. Oskamp & S. Spacapan (Eds.), *Interpersonal processes* (pp. 122-147). Beverly Hills, CA: Sage.

Kelly, G. A. (1955). *The psychology of personal constructs* (2 vols.). New York: Norton.

Kendall, P. C., & Bemis, K. M. (1983). Thought and action in psychotherapy: The cognitive-behavioral approaches. In M. Hersen, A. E. Kazdin, & A. S. Bellack (Eds.), *The clinical psychology handbook* (pp. 565-592). New York: Pergamon.

Kendall, P. C., & Hollon, S. D. (1979). Cognitive-behavioral interventions: Overview and current status. In P. C. Kendall & S. D. Hollon (Eds.), *Cognitive-behavioral interventions: Theory, research and procedures.* New York: Academic Press.

King, K., Rene, S., Schmidt, J., Stipetich, E., & Woldsweth, N. (1994). *Cognitive intervention program.* Madison, WI: Department of Corrections.

Klinger, E. (1987). Imagery and logotherapeutic techniques in psychotherapy: Clinical experiences and promise for application to alcohol problems. In W. M. Cox (Ed.), *Treatment and prevention of alcohol problems: A resource manual* (pp. 139-156). New York: Academic Press.

Kosten, T., Rounsavalle, B. J., & Kleber H. D. (1985). Ethnic and gender differences among opiate addicts. *International Journal of Addiction, 20,* 1143-1163.

Krupnick, J. L., Sotsky, S. M., Simmens, S., Moyer, J., Elkin, I., Watkins, J., & Pilkonis, P. A. (1996). The role of therapeutic alliance in psychotherapy and pharmacotherapy outcome: Findings in the National Institute of Mental Health Treatment of Depression Collaborative Research Program. *Journal of Consulting and Clinical Psychology, 64,* 532-539.

Kuhn, T. S. (1970). *The structure of scientific revolutions* (2nd ed.). Chicago: University of Chicago Press.

Lambert, M. J. (1983). Introduction to assessment of psychotherapy outcome: Historical perspective and current issues. In M. J. Lambert, E. R. Christensen, & S. S. DeJulio (Eds.), *The assessment of psychotherapy outcome.* New York: Wiley.

Lambert, M. J., & Bergin, A. E. (1992). Achievements and limitations of psychotherapy research. In D. K. Freedheim (Ed.), *History of psychotherapy: A century of change* (pp. 360-390). Washington, DC: American Psychological Association.

Lange, A. J., & Jakubowski, P. (1976). *Responsible assertive behavior.* Champaign, IL: Research Press.

Lazarus, A. A. (1971). *Behavior therapy and beyond.* New York: McGraw-Hill.

Leahy, R. L., (1996). *Cognitive therapy: Basic principles and applications.* Northvale, NJ: Jason Aronson, Inc.

Leahy, R. L. (1997). Cognitive therapy interventions. In R. L. Leahy (Ed.), *Practicing cognitive therapy: A guide to Interventions* (pp. 3-20). Northvale, NJ: Jason Aronson Inc.

Lecky, P. (1961). *Self-consistency: A theory of personality*. New York: Shoe String Press.

Lehrer, P. M., Carr, R., Sargunaraj, D., & Woolfolk, R. L. (1993). Differential effects of stress management therapies on emotional and behavioral disorders. In P. M. Lehrer & R. L. Woolfolk (Eds.), *Principles and practice of stress management* (2nd ed., pp. 339-369). New York: Guilford.

Leland, J., & Joseph, N. (1997, January 13). Hooked on Ebonics. *Newsweek,* pp. 78-80.

Leukefeld, C. G., & Tims, F. M. (1992). Directions for practice and research. In C. G. Leukefeld & F. M. Tims (Eds.), *Drug abuse treatment services in prisons and jails* (NIDA Monograph No. 118). Rockville, MD: National Institute on Drug Abuse.

Levinson, R. B. (1988). Developments in the classification process: Quay's AIMS approach. *Criminal Justice and Behavior,* 15, 24-38.

Lewin, K. (1935). *A dynamic theory of personality*. New York: McGraw-Hill.

Lewin, K. (1936). *Principles of topological psychology*. New York: McGraw-Hill.

Lewin, K. (1951). *Field theory in social science: Selected theoretical papers* (D. Cartwright, Ed.). New York: Harper.

Liese, B. S., & Franz, R. A. (1996). Treating substance use disorders with cognitive therapy: Lessons learned and implications for the future. In P. M. Salkovskis (Ed.), *Frontiers of cognitive therapy* (pp. 48-74). New York: Guilford.

Lillyquist, M. J. (1980). *Understanding and changing criminal behavior*. Englewood Cliffs, NJ: Prentice-Hall.

Linden, W. (1993). The autogenic training method of J. H. Schultz. In P. M. Lehrer & R. L. Woolfolk (Eds.), *Principles and practice of stress management* (2nd ed., pp. 205-230). New York: Guilford.

Lipps, T. (1907). Das wissen von fremden ichen. *Psychol. Untersuchungen,* 1, 694-722.

Lipsey, M. W. (1989, November). *The efficacy of intervention for juvenile delinquency: Results from 400 studies*. Paper presented at the 41st annual meeting of the American Society of Criminology, Reno, NV.

Lipsey, M. W. (1992). Juvenile delinquency treatment: A meta-analytic inquiry into the variability of effects. In T. D. Cook, H. Cooper, D. S. Cordray, H. Hartmann, L. V. Hedges, R. J. Light, T. A. Louis, & F. Mosteller (Eds.), *Meta-analysis for explanation* (pp. 83-127). New York: Russell Sage Foundation.

Lipsey, M. W., & Wilson, D. B. (1993). The efficacy of psychological, educational and behavioral treatment: Confirmation from meta-analysis. *American Psychologist,* 48, 1181-1209.

Lipton, D. S. (1994). The correctional opportunity: Pathways to drug treatment for offenders. *Journal of Drug Issues,* 24, 331-348.

Litt, M. D., Babor, T. F., DelBoca, F. K., Kadden, R. M., & Cooney, N. L. (1992). Application of an empirically-derived typology to treatment matching. *Archives of General Psychiatry,* 49, 609-614.

Longfellow, H. W. (1898). *Song of Hiawatha*. New York: Hurst and Company.

Lowinson, J. H., Ruiz, P., Millman, R. B., & Langrod, J. G. (1992). Substance abuse: *A comprehensive textbook*. Baltimore, MD: Williams & Wilkins.

Luborsky, L., McLellan, A. T., Woody, G. E., O'Brien, C. P., & Auerbach, A. (1985). Therapist success and its determinants. *Archives of General Psychiatry,* 42, 602-611.

Luft, J. (1969). *Of human interaction*. Palo Alto, CA: National Press.

Lurie, N. O. (1971). The world's oldest on-going protest demonstration. *Pacific Historical Review,* 40, 311-332.

MacKay, P. W., Donovan, D. M., & Marlatt, G. A. (1991). Cognitive and behavioral approaches to alcohol abuse. In R. J. Frances & S. I. Miller (Eds.), *Clinical textbook of addictive disorders* (pp. 452-484). New York: Guilford.

Mahoney, J. J. (1990). *Human change processes: Theoretical bases for psychotherapy*. New York: Basic Books.

Mahoney, M. J., & Arnkoff, D. B. (1978). Cognitive and self-control therapies. In S. L. Garfield & A. E. Bergin (Eds.), *Handbook of psychotherapy and behavior change* (2nd ed.). New York: Wiley.

Marlatt, G. A. (1978). Craving for alcohol, loss of control, and relapse: A cognitive-behavioral analysis. In P. E. Nathan, G. A. Marlatt, & T. Loberg (Eds.), *Alcoholism: New directions in behavioral research and treatment*. New York: Plenum.

Marlatt, G. A. (1985a). Cognitive factors in the relapse process. In G. A. Marlatt & J. R. Gordon (Eds.), *Relapse prevention: Maintenance strategies in the treatment of addictive behaviors* (pp. 128-200). New York: Guilford.

Marlatt, G. A. (1985b). Cognitive a assessment and intervention procedures for relapse prevention. In G. A. Marlatt & J. R. Gordon (Eds.), Relapse prevention: *Maintenance strategies in the treatment of addictive behaviors* (pp. 201-279). New York: Guilford.

Marlatt, G. A. (1985c). Relapse prevention: Theoretical rationale and overview of the model. In G. A. Marlatt & J. R. Gordon (Eds.), Relapse prevention: *Maintenance strategies in the treatment of addictive behaviors* (pp. 3-70). New York: Guilford.

Marlatt, G. A., Baer, J. S., & Larimer, M. E. (1995). Preventing alcohol abuse in college students: A harm-reduction approach. In G. M. Boyd, J. Howard, & R. A. Zucker (Eds.), *Alcohol problems among adolescents: Current directions in prevention research* (pp. 147-172). Hillsdale, NJ: Lawrence Erlbaum.

Marlatt, G. A., & Barrett, K. B. (1994). *Relapse prevention. In M. Galentern & H. Kleber (Eds.), The textbook of substance abuse treatment*. New York: American Psychiatric Press.

Marlatt, G. A., & Gordon, J. R. (1980). Determinants of relapse: Implications for the maintenance of behavior change. In P. O. Davidson & S. M. Davidson (Eds.), *Behavioral medicine: Changing health lifestyles*. New York: Brunner/Mazel.

Marlatt, G. A., & Gordon, J. R. (1985). *Relapse prevention: Maintenance strategies in the treatment of addictive behaviors*. New York: Guilford.

Marlatt, G. A., & Gordon, J. R. (1996). Reducing the harmful effects of weight control. The *Weight Control Digest,* 6(6), 569-574.

Marlatt, G. A., Larimer, M. E., Baer, J. S., & Quigley, L. A. (1993). Harm reduction for alcohol problems: Moving beyond the controlled drinking controversy. *Behavior Therapy,* 24, 461-504.

Marlatt, G. A., & Tapert, S. F. (1993). Harm reduction: Reducing the risks of addictive behaviors. In J. S. Baer, G. A. Marlatt, & R. McMahon (Eds.), *Addictive behaviors across the lifespan* (pp. 243-273). Newbury Park, CA: Sage.

Marmor, J. (1975). Foreword. In B. Sloane, F. Staples, A. Cristol, N. J. Yorkston, & K. Whipple (Eds.), *Psychotherapy versus behavior therapy*. Cambridge, MA: Harvard University Press.

Maslow, A. H. (1954). *Motivation and personality.* New York: Harper.

Massey, R. F., & Goldman, M. S. (1988, August). *Manipulating expectancies as a means of altering alcohol consumption.* Paper presented at the 96th Annual Convention of the American Psychological Association, Atlanta, GA.

May, P. A. (1977). Alcohol beverage control: A survey of tribal alcohol statutes. *American Indian Law Review,* 5, 217-228.

May, P. A. (1989). Alcohol abuse and alcoholism among American Indians: An overview. In T. D. Watts & R. Wright (Eds.), *Alcoholism in minority populations* (pp. 95-119). Springfield, IL: Charles C Thomas.

McDermott, S. P., & Wright, F. D. (1992). Cognitive therapy: Long-term outlook for a short-term psychotherapy. In J. S. Ruttan (Ed.), *Psychotherapy for the 1990s* (pp. 61-99). New York: Guilford.

McGuire, J., & Priestley, P. (1995). Reviewing "What works": Past, present and future. In J. McGuire (Ed.), *What works: Reducing reoffending* (pp. 3-34), New York: Wiley.

McLellan, A. T., Kushner, H., Metzger, D., & Peters, F. (1992). Fifth edition of the Addictions Severity Index. *Journal of Substance Abuse Treatment,* 9, 199-213.

McLellan, A. T., Luborsky, L., Cacciola, J., Griffith, J., Evans, F., Barr, H. L., & O'Brien, C. P. (1985). New data from the Addiction Severity Index: Reliability and validity in three centers. *Journal of Mental and Nervous Disease,* 173, 412-423.

McLellan, A. T., Luborsky, L., O'Brien, C. P., & Woody, G. E. (1980). An improved evaluation instrument for substance abuse patients: The Addiction Severity Index. *Journal of Nervous and Mental Disease,* 168, 26-33.

McLellan, A. T., Luborsky, L., Woody, G. E., O'Brien, C. P., & Druley, K. A. (1983). Predicting response to alcohol and drug abuse treatments: Role of psychiatric severity. *Archives of General Psychiatry,* 40, 620-625.

McMullin, R. E. (1986). *Handbook of cognitive therapy techniques.* New York: W. W. Norton.

Megargee, E. I., & Bohn, M. J. (1979). *Classifying criminal offenders: A new system based on the MMPI.* Beverly Hills, CA: Sage.

Meichenbaum, D. (1975). A self-instructional approach to stress management: A proposal for stress inoculation training. In I. Sarason & C. D. Spielberger (Eds.), *Stress and anxiety* (Vol. 2). New York: Wiley.

Meichenbaum, D. (1977). *Cognitive-behavior modification: An integrative approach.* New York: Plenum.

Meichenbaum, D. (1985). *Stress inoculation training.* New York: Pergamon.

Michaud, J., & Bussard, R. (1995). *Substance involvement criminal addiction program.* Canon City: Colorado Territorial Correctional Facility.

Milkman, H. B., & Sunderwirth, S. G. (1987). *Craving for ecstasy: The consciousness and chemistry of escape.* Lexington, MA: D. C. Heath.

Milkman, H. B., & Sunderwirth, S. G. (1993). *Pathways to pleasure: The consciousness and chemistry of optimal experience.* Lexington, MA: Lexington Books.

Milkman, H. B., Weiner, S., & Sunderwirth, S. (1984). Addiction relapse. In H. Shaffer (Ed.), *Addictive behaviors* (pp. 119-133). New York: Haworth.

Miller, W. R. (1989). Matching individuals with interventions. In R. K. Hester & W. R. Miller (Eds.), *Handbook of alcoholism treatment approaches: Effective alternatives* (pp. 261-271). New York: Pergamon.

Miller, W. R. (1994). *SOCRATES: The stages of change readiness and treatment eagerness scale.* Albuquerque, NM: Department of Psychology, University of New Mexico.

Miller, W. R. (1995). Increasing motivation to change. In R. K. Hester & W. R. Miller (Eds.), *Handbook of alcoholism treatment approaches: Effective alternatives* (pp. 89-104). Boston, MA: Allyn and Bacon.

Miller, W. R., & Baca, L. M. (1983). Two-year follow-up of bibliotherapy and therapist-directed controlled drinking training for problem drinkers. *Behavior Therapy, 14*, 441-448.

Miller, W. R., Benefield, R. G., & Tonigan, J. S. (1993). Enhancing motivation for change in problem drinking: A controlled comparison of two therapist styles. *Journal of Consulting and Clinical Psychology, 61*, 455-461.

Miller, W. R., Brown, J. M., Simpson, T. L., Handmaker, N. H. S., Bien, T. H., Luckie, L. F., Montgomery, H. A., Hester, R. K., & Tonigan, J. S. (1995). What works? A methodological analysis of the alcohol treatment outcome literature. In R. K. Hester & W. R. Miller (Eds.), *Handbook of alcoholism treatment approaches: Effective alternatives* (12-44). Boston: Allyn & Bacon.

Miller, W. R., & Cooney, N. L. (1994). Designing studies to investigate client-treatment matching. *Journal of Studies on Alcohol, Suppl.* 12, 38-45.

Miller, W. R., & Hester, R. K. (1980). Treating the problem drinker: Modern approaches. In W. R. Miller (Ed.), *Addictive behaviors: Treatment of alcoholism, drug abuse, smoking and obesity.* New York: Pergamon.

Miller, W. R., & Hester, R. K. (1986a). The effectiveness of alcoholism treatment: What research reveals. In W. R. Miller & N. Heather (Eds.), *Treating addictive behaviors: Processes of change.* New York: Plenum.

Miller, W. R., & Hester, R. K. (1986b). Inpatient alcoholism treatment: Who benefits? *American Psychologist, 41*, 794-805.

Miller, W. R., & Hester, R. K. (1989). Treating alcohol problems: Toward an informed eclecticism. In R. K. Hester & W. R. Miller (Eds.), *Handbook of alcoholism treatment approaches: Effective alternatives* (pp. 3-14). Boston: Allyn & Bacon.

Miller, W. R., & Hester, R. K. (1995). Treating alcohol problems: Towards an informed eclecticism. In R. K. Hester & W. R. Miller (Eds.), *Handbook of alcoholism treatment approaches: Effective alternatives* (pp. 1-11). Boston: Allyn and Bacon.

Miller, W. R., & Marlatt, G. A. (1984). *Manual for the Comprehensive Drinker Profile.* Odessa, FL: Psychological Assessment Resources.

Miller, W. R., & Rollnick, S. (1991). *Motivational interviewing: Preparing people to change addictive behavior.* New York: Guilford.

Miller, W. R., Taylor, C. A., & West, J. C. (1980). Focused versus broad-spectrum behavior therapy for problem drinkers. *Journal of Consulting and Clinical Psychology, 48*, 590-601.

Miller, W. R., & Tonigan, J. S. (1996). Assessing drinker's motivation for change: The Stages of Change Readiness and Treatment Eagerness Scale (SOCRATES). *Psychology of Addictive Behaviors, 10*, 81-89.

Miller, W. R., Westerberg, V. S., & Waldron, H. B. (1995). Evaluating alcohol problems in adults and adolescents. In R. K. Hester & W. R. Miller (Eds.), *Handbook of alcoholism treatment approaches: Effective alternatives* (pp. 61-88). Boston: Allyn & Bacon.

Miller, W. R., Zweben, A. D., DiClemente, C. C., & Rychtarik, R. G. (1994). *Motivational enhancement therapy manual: A clinical research guide for therapists treating individuals with alcohol abuse and dependence* (Project MATCH Monograph Series, Vol. 2). Rockville, MD: National Institute on Alcohol Abuse and Alcoholism, U.S. Department of Health and Human Services, National Institutes of Health.

Monti, P. M., Abrams, D. B., Kadden, R. M., & Cooney, N. L. (1989). *Treating alcohol dependence: A coping skills training guide.* New York: Guilford.

Monti, P. M., Rohsenow, D. J., Colby, S. M., & Abrams, D. B. (1995). Coping and social skills training. In R. K. Hester & W. R. Miller (Eds.), *Handbook of alcoholism treatment approaches: Effective alternatives* (pp. 221-241). Boston: Allyn & Bacon.

Moos, R. H., & Moos, B. S. (1981). *Family Environment Scale.* Palo Alto, CA: Consulting Psychologist Press.

Morin, C. M., & Azrin, N. H. (1988). Behavioral and cognitive treatments of geriatric insomnia. *Journal of Consulting and Clinical Psychology, 56,* 748-753.

Mowrer, O. H. (1947). On the dual nature of learning-a reinterpretation of "conditioning" and "problem-solving." *Harvard Educational Review, 17,* 102-148.

Mowrer, O. H., & Mowrer, W. M. (1938). Enuresis: A method for its study and treatment. *American Journal of Orthopsychiatry, 8,* 436-459.

Nash, G. (1976). An analysis of twelve studies of the impact of drug abuse treatment upon criminality. *In Drug use and crime: Report of the panel on use and criminal behavior.* Research Triangle Park, NC: Research Triangle Institute.

National Institute on Drug Abuse. (1983). *Data from the national drug and alcoholism treatment utilization survey (NDATUS), main finding for drug abuse treatment units* (Statistical series, Report F:10, DHHS Publication No. ADM 83-1284). Washington, DC: Government Printing Office.

National Institute on Drug Abuse. (1987). *National household survey on drug abuse: Population estimates 1985* (DHHS Publication No. ADM 87-1539). Washington, DC: Government Printing Office.

National Council on Alcoholism, Criteria Committee. (1972). Criteria for the diagnosis of alcoholism. *Journal of Psychiatry, 129,* 127-135.

Newcomb, M. D., & Bentler, P. M. (1989). Substance use and abuse among children and teenagers. *American Psychologist, 44,* 242-248.

Newcomb, M. D., Maddahian, E., & Bentler, P. M. (1986). Risk factors for drug use among adolescents: Concurrent and longitudinal analyses. *American Journal of Public Health, 76,* 525-531.

Newman, C. E. (1997). Substance abuse. In R. L. Leahy (Ed.), *Practicing cognitive therapy: A guide to Interventions* (pp. 229-245). Northvale, NJ: Jason Aronson.

Nezu, A. M., Nezu, C. M., & Perri, M. G. (1989). *Problem-solving therapy for depression: Theory, research and clinical guidelines.* New York: Wiley.

Noble, E. P., Blum, K., Khalsa, M. E., Ritchie, T., Montgomery, A., Wood, R. C., Fitch, R. J., Ozkaragoz, T., Sheridan, P. J., Anglin, M. D., Paredes, A., Treiman, L. J., & Sparks, R. S. (1993).

Allelic association of the D2 dopamine receptor gene with cocaine dependence. *Drug and Alcohol Dependence, 83,* 271-285.

Norris, P. A., & Fahrion, S. L. (1993). Autogenic biofeedback in psychophysiological therapy and stress management. In P. M. Lehrer & R. L. Woolfolk (Eds.), *Principles and practice of stress management* (2nd ed., pp. 231-262). New York: Guilford.

Nowinski, J., Baker, S., & Carroll, K. (1992). *Twelve step facilitation therapy manual: A clinical research guide for therapists treating individuals with alcohol abuse and dependence.* Rockville, MD: National Institutes on Alcohol Abuse and Alcoholism.

Nuffield, J. (1982). *Parole decision-making in Canada.* Ottawa: Solicitor General of Canada.

Orford, J., Oppenheimer, E., & Edwards, G. (1976). Abstinence or control: The outcome for excessive drinkers two years after consultation. *Behavior Research and Therapy, 14,* 409-418.

Orlandi, M. A., Weston, R., & Epstein, L. G. (Eds.). (1992). *Cultural competence for evaluators: A guide for alcohol and other drug abuse prevention practitioners working with ethnic/racial communities.* Rockville, MD: U.S. Department of Health and Human Services.

Padilla, A. M., Lindholm, K. J., Chen, A., Duran, R., Hakuta, K., Lambert, W., & Tucker, G. R. (1991). The English-only movement: Myths, reality, and implications for psychology. *American Psychologist, 46,* 120-130.

Palmer, T. B. (1971). California's community treatment program for delinquent adolescents. *Journal of Research in Crime and Delinquency, 8,* 74-92.

Palmer, T. B. (1984). Treatment and the role of classification: A review of basics. *Crime and Delinquency, 30,* 245-267.

Parks, G. A., & Marlatt, G. A. (1997). Keeping "What Works" Working: Cognitive Behavioral Relapse Prevention with Substances-Abusing Offenders. In *What Works: Critical Issues Research and Best Practices in Community Corrections.* International Community Corrections Association Conference, Cleveland, OH (October 5-8, 1997).

Patterson, G. R., DeBarsyshe, B. D., & Ramsey, E. (1989). A developmental perspective on antisocial behavior. *American Psychologist, 44,* 229-335.

Pattison, E. M., & Kaufman, E. (1982). The alcoholism syndrome: Definitions and models. In E. M. Pattison & E. Kaufman (Eds.), *Encyclopedic handbook of alcoholism* (3-30). New York: Gardner.

Pattison, E. M., Sobell, M. B., & Sobell, L. C. (1977). *Emerging concepts of alcohol dependence.* New York: Springer.

Patton, B. R., & Griffin, K. (1981). *Interpersonal communication in action: Basic text and readings.* New York: Harper & Row.

Pavlov, I. P. (1927). *Conditioned reflexes: An investigation of the physiological activity of the cerebral cortex* (G. V. Anrep, Trans.). London: Oxford University Press.

Pear, R. (1990, September 26). *United States reports poverty is down but inequality is up: Report of the census bureau.* New York Times, p. A14.

Peterson, D. R. (1983). Conflict. In H. H. Kelley, E. Berscheid, A. Christensen, J. H. Harvey, T. L. Huston, G. Levinger, E. McClintock, L. A. Peplau, & D. R. Peterson (Eds.), *Close relationships.* New York: W. H. Freeman.

Peyser, H. S. (1988). Implications of the disease model for psychotherapy and counseling. In S. E. Gitlow & H. S. Peyser (Eds.), *Alcoholism: A practical treatment guide* (pp. 142-155). Philadelphia: W. B. Saunders.

Piaget, J. (1954). *The construction of reality in the child*. New York: Basic Books.

Price, J. A. (1975). Applied analysis of North American Indian drinking patterns. *Human Organization, 34,* 17-26.

Prochaska, J. O., & DiClemente, C. C. (1986). Toward a comprehensive model of change. In W. R. Miller & N. Heather (Eds.), *Treating addictive behaviors: Processes of change* (pp. 3-27). New York: Plenum.

Prochaska, J. O., & DiClemente, C. C. (1992). Stages of change in the modification of problem behavior. In M. Hersen, R. Eisler, & P. M. Miller (Eds.), *Progress in behavior modification* (pp. 184-214). Sycamore, IL: Sycamore Publishing.

Prochaska, J. O., DiClemente, C. C., & Norcross, J. C. (1992). In search of how people change: Applications to addictive behaviors. *American Psychologist, 47,* 1102-1114.

Project MATCH Research Group (1993). Project MATCH: Rationale and methods for a multisite clinical trial matching patients to alcoholism treatment. *Alcoholism: Clinical and Experimental Research, 17,* 1130-1145.

Project MATCH Research Group. (1997). Matching alcoholism treatments to client heterogeneity: Project MATCH posttreatment drinking outcomes. *Journal of Studies on Alcohol, 58,* 7-29.

Quay, H. C. (1965). Psychopathic personality as pathological stimulus-seeking. *American Journal of Psychiatry, 122,* 180-183.

Quay, H. C. (1984). *Managing adult inmates: Classification for housing and program assignments.* College Park, MD: American Correctional Association.

Quay, H. C. (1987). Patterns of juvenile delinquency. In H. C. Quay (Ed.), *Handbook of juvenile delinquency.* New York: Wiley.

Raue, P. J., & Goldfried, M. R. (1994). The therapeutic alliance in cognitive-behavior therapy. In A. O. Horvath & L. S. Greenberg (Eds.), *The working alliance: Theory, research and practice* (pp. 131-152). New York: Wiley.

Raue, P. J., Goldfried, M. R., & Barkham, M. (1997). The therapeutic alliance in psychodynamic-interpersonal and cognitive-behavioral therapy. *Journal of Consulting and Clinical Psychology, 65,* 582-587.

Ray, O. S., & Ksir, C. (1996). *Drugs, society, and human behavior*. St. Louis, MO: C. V. Mosby.

Riley, D. M., Sobell, L. C., Leo, G. I., Sobell, M. B., & Klajner, F. (1987). Behavioral treatment of alcohol problems: A review and a comparison of behavioral and nonbehavioral studies. In W. Cox (Ed.), *Treatment and prevention of alcohol problems: A resource manual* (pp. 73-116). New York: Academic Press.

Roehrich, H., Dackis, C. A., & Gold, M. S. (1987). Bromocriptine. *Medical Research Review, 7,* 243-269.

Rogers, C. R. (1951). *Client-centered therapy*. Boston: Houghton Mifflin.

Rogers, C. R. (1957). The necessary and sufficient conditions of therapeutic personality change. *Journal of Consulting Psychology, 22,* 95-103.

Rogers, C. R. (1961). *On becoming a person: A therapist's view of psychotherapy*. Boston: Houghton Mifflin.

Rogers, C. R., & Dymond, R. (1954). *Psychotherapy and personality change*. Chicago: University of Chicago Press.

Rogers, C. R., Gendlin, E. T., Kiesler, D., & Truax, C. B. (1967). *The therapeutic relationship and its impact: A study of psychotherapy with schizophrenics.* Madison: University of Wisconsin Press.

Rogers, S. (1981). *Factors related to recidivism among adult probationers in Ontario.* Toronto: Ontario Ministry of Correctional Services.

Rohsenow, D. R., Monti, P. M., Binkoff, J. A., Liepman, M. R., Nirenberg, T. D., & Abrams, D. B. (1991). Patient-treatment matching for alcoholic men in communication skills versus cognitive-behavioral mood management training. *Addictive Behaviors, 16,* 63-69.

Rosenhan, D. L., & Seligman, M. E. P. (1995). *Abnormal psychology* (3rd ed.). New York: W. W. Norton.

Ross, R. R., Antonowicz, D. H., & Dhaliwal, G. K. (1995). *Going straight: Effective delinquency prevention & offender rehabilitation.* Ottawa, Ontario, Canada: Air Training & Publications.

Ross, R. R., Fabiano, E. A., & Ross, R. D. (1986). *Reasoning and rehabilitation: A handbook for teaching cognitive skills.* Ottawa, Ontario: University of Ottawa.

Ross, R. R., & Lightfoot, L. O. (1985). *Treatment of the alcohol abusing offender.* Springfield, IL: Charles C Thomas.

Ross, R. R., & Ross, R. D. (1988). *Cognitive skills: A training manual for living skills-Phase 1.* Ottawa, Ontario: Correctional Service of Canada.

Ross, R. R., & Ross, R. D. (1995). *Thinking straight: The reasoning and rehabilitation program for delinquency prevention and offender rehabilitation.* Ottawa, Ontario: Department of Criminology.

Rotter, J. (1966). Generalized expectancies for internal versus external control of reinforcement. *Psychological Monographs, 80*(1), 1-28.

Ruben, B. D. (1988). *Communication and human behavior.* New York: Macmillan.

Ruiz, P., & Langrod, J. G. (1992). Substance abuse among Hispanic Americans: Current issues and future perspectives. In J. H. Lowinson, P. Ruiz, R. B. Millman, & J. G. Langrod (Eds.), *Substance abuse: A comprehensive textbook* (pp. 868-874). Baltimore, MD: Williams & Wilkins.

Russo, N. R., Olmedo, E. L., Stapp, J., & Fulcher, R. (1981). Women and minorities in psychology, *American Psychologist, 36,* 1315-1363.

Salkovskis, P. M. (1996a). The cognitive approach to anxiety: Threat beliefs, safety-seeking behavior, and the special case of health anxiety and obsessions. In P. M. Salkovskis (Ed.), *Frontiers of cognitive therapy* (pp. 48-74). New York: Guilford.

Salkovskis, P. M. (1996b). *Frontiers of cognitive therapy.* New York: Guilford.

Salter, A. (1949). *Conditioned reflex therapy.* New York: Farrar, Straus.

Sanchez-Craig, M., Wilkinson, D. A., & Walker, K. (1987). Theory and methods for secondary prevention of alcohol problems: A cognitively-based approach. In W. M. Cox (Ed.), *Treatment and prevention of alcohol problems: A resource manual.* (pp. 287-332) New York: Academic Press.

Sarason, I. G., & Sarason, B. R. (1995). *Abnormal psychology: The problem of maladaptive behavior.* Englewood Cliffs, NJ: Prentice-Hall.

Saxe, L., Dougherty, D., Esty, K., & Fine, M. (1983). *Health technology case study 22: The effectiveness and costs of alcoholism treatment.* Washington, DC: Office of Technology Assessment.

Schachter, S., & Singer, J. (1962). Cognitive, social and physiological determinants of emotional state. *Psychological Review,* 69, 379-399.

Schmidt, G., Klee, L., & Ames, G. (1990). Review and analysis of literature on indicators of women's drinking problems. *British Journal of Addiction,* 85, 179-192.

Schultz, A. (1967). *The phenomenology of the social world* (G. Walsh & F. Lehnert, Trans.). Evanston, IL: Northwestern University Press. (Original work published 1932).

Scott, N. E., & Bordovsky, L. G. (1990). Effective use of cultural role taking. *Professional Psychology: Research and Practice,* 21, 167-170.

Seligman, M. E. P. (1974). Depression and learned helplessness. In R. J. Friedman & M. M. Katz (Eds.), *The psychology of depression: Contemporary theory and research.* Washington, DC: V. H. Winston.

Seligman, M. E. P. (1975). *Helplessness: On depression, development, and death.* San Francisco: W. H. Freeman.

Sells, S. B. (1979). Treatment effectiveness. In R. L. DuPont, A. Goldstein, & J. O'Donnell (Eds.), *Handbook on drug use.* Washington, DC: Government Printing Office.

Selzer, M. L. (1971). The Michigan Alcoholism Screening Test: The quest for a new diagnostic instrument. *American Journal of Psychiatry,* 127(2), 1653-1658.

Shaffer, H. J. (1992). The psychology of stage change: The transition from addiction to recovery. In J. H. Lowinson, P. Ruiz, R. B. Millman, & J. G. Langrod (Eds.), *Substance abuse: A comprehensive textbook* (pp. 100-105). Baltimore, MD: Williams & Wilkins.

Shaffer, H. J., & Gambino, B. (1990). Epilogue: Integrating treatment choices. In H. B. Milkman & L. I. Sederer (Eds.), *Treatment choices for alcoholism and substance abuse* (pp. 351-375). Lexington, MA: Lexington Books.

Sher, K. J. (1987). Stress response dampening. In H. T. Blane & K. W. Leonard (Eds.), *Psychological theories of drinking and alcoholism* (pp. 227-271). New York: Guilford.

Shipley, T. E. (1987). Opponent process theory. In H. T. Blane & K. W. Leonard (Eds.), *Psychological theories of drinking and alcoholism* (pp. 346-387). New York: Guilford.

Shure, M., & Spivack, G. (1978). *Problem solving techniques in childrearing.* San Francisco: Jossey-Bass.

Sisk, J. E., Hatziandren, E. J., & Hughes, R. (1990). *The effectiveness of drug abuse treatment: Implications for controlling AIDS/HIV infection.* Washington, DC: Office of Technology Assessment.

Sisson, R., & Azrin, N. (1989). The community reinforcement approach. In R. K. Hester & W. R. Miller (Eds.), *Handbook of alcoholism treatment approaches* (pp. 242-258). New York: Pergamon.

Skinner, B. F. (1938). *The behavior of organisms: An experimental analysis.* New York: Appleton-Century-Crofts.

Skinner, B. F. (1953). *Science and human behavior.* New York: Macmillan.

Skinner, H. A. (1982). The Drug Abuse Screening Test. *Addictive Behaviors,* 7, 363-371.

Sloane, B., Staples, F., Cristol, A., Yorkston, N. J., & Whipple, K. (1975). *Psychotherapy versus behavior therapy.* Cambridge, MA: Harvard University Press.

Smart, R. G. (1976). Outcome studies of therapeutic community and halfway house treatment for addicts. *International Journal of the Addictions,* 11, 143-159.

Smith, E. M., & Cloninger, C. R. (1981). Alcoholic females: mortality at 12-year follow-up. *Focus on women,* 2, 1-13.

Smith, J. E., & Meyers, R. J. (1995). The community reinforcement approach. In R. K. Hester & W. R. Miller (Eds.), *Handbook of alcoholism treatment approaches: Effective alternatives* (pp. 251-266). Boston: Allyn & Bacon.

Snake, R., Hawkins, G., & La Boueff, S. (1977). *Report on alcohol and drug abuse Task Force Eleven: Alcohol and drug abuse* (Final report to the American Indian Policy Review Commission). Washington, DC: American Indian Policy Review Commission.

Southwick, L. C., Steele, C., Marlatt, A., & Lindell, M. (1981). Alcohol-related expectancies: Defined by phase of intoxication and drinking experience. *Journal of Consulting and Clinical Psychology,* 49, 713-721.

Sovereign, R. G., & Miller, W. R. (1987). *Effects of therapist style on resilience and outcome among problem drinkers.* Paper presented at the Fourth International Conference on Treatment of Addictive Behaviors, Os/bergen, Norway.

Spivack, G., Platt, J., & Shure, M. B. (1976). *The problem solving approach to adjustment.* San Francisco: Jossey-Bass.

Spivack, G., & Shure, M. B. (1974). *Social adjustment of young children: A cognitive approach to solving real-life problems.* San Francisco: Jossey-Bass.

Stockwell, T. (1995). Anxiety and stress management. In R. K. Hester & W. R. Miller (Eds.), *Handbook of alcoholism treatment approaches: Effective alternatives* (pp. 278-291). Boston: Allyn & Bacon.

Strupp, H. H., & Hadley, S. W. (1979). Specific versus nonspecific factors in psychotherapy. *Archives of General Psychiatry,* 36, 1125-1136.

Strupp, H. H., & Howard, K. I. (1992). A brief history of psychotherapy research. In D. K. Freedheim (Ed.), *History of psychotherapy: A century of change* (309-334). Washington, DC: American Psychological Association.

Sue, D. W. (1990). Culture-specific strategies in counseling: A conceptual framework. *Professional Psychology: Research and practice,* 21, 424-433.

Sue, D. W., & Sue, D. (1990). *Counseling the culturally different* (2nd ed.). New York: Wiley.

Sue, S., & Zane, N. (1987). The role of culture and cultural techniques in psychotherapy: A critique and reformation. *American Psychologist,* 42, 37-45.

Teplin, L. A., & Swartz, J. (1989). Screening for severe mental disorders in jails. *Law and Human Behavior,* 13, 1-18.

Thorndike, E. L. (1931). *Human learning.* New York: Century.

Tims, F. M., & Ludford, J. P. (1984). *Drug abuse treatment evaluation: Strategies, progress and prospects* (DHHS Publication No. ADM 84-1143). Rockville, MD: National Institute on Drug Abuse.

Tinklenberg, J. R., Murphy, P., Murphy, P. L., & Pfefferbaum, A. (1981). *Drugs and criminal assaults by adolescents: A replication study. Journal of Psychoactive Drugs,* 13, 277-286.

Toulmin, S. (1972). *Human understanding: Vol. 1. The collective use and evolution of concepts*. Princeton, NJ: Princeton University Press.

Troester, R., & Kelley, C. (1991). *Peacemaking through communication*. Annandale, VA: Speech Communication Association.

Truax, C. B. (1963). Effective ingredients in psychotherapy. *Journal of Consulting Psychology, 10*, 256-263.

Truax, C. B., & Carkhuff, R. R. (1967). *Toward effective counseling and psychotherapy*. Chicago: Aldine.

Truax, C. B., & Mitchell, K. M. (1971). Research on certain therapist interpersonal skills in relation to process and outcome. In A. E. Bergin & S. L. Garfield (Eds.), *Handbook of psychotherapy and behavioral change: An empirical analysis*. New York: John Wiley.

U.S. Bureau of the Census. (1990a). *Statistical abstract of the United States*. Washington, DC: Government Printing Office.

U.S. Bureau of the Census. (1990b). *Social and economic characteristics*. Washington, DC: Government Printing Office.

U.S. Bureau of the Census. (1990c). *Persons of Hispanic origin in the United States*. Washington, DC: Government Printing Office.

U.S. Bureau of Justice Statistics (1983a). *Prisoners and alcohol*. Washington, DC: U.S. Department of Justice.

U.S. Bureau of Justice Statistics (1983b). *Prisoners and drugs*. Washington, DC: U.S. Department of Justice.

U.S. Bureau of Justice Statistics. (1987, December). *Probation and parole, 1986* (Bureau of Justice Statistics Bulletin). Washington, DC: Author.

U.S. Bureau of Justice Statistics. (1988). *Profile of state prison inmates, 1986*. Washington, DC: U.S. Department of Justice.

U.S. Bureau of Justice Statistics. (1991). *Drugs and jail inmates, 1989* (Special Report). Washington, DC: U.S. Department of Justice.

U.S. Bureau of Justice Statistics. (1992). *Compendium of federal justice statistics, 1989*. Washington, DC: U.S. Department of Justice.

Vaillant, G. E. (1983). *The natural history of alcoholism: Causes, patterns, and paths to recovery*. Cambridge, MA: Harvard University Press.

Van Voorhis, P. (1987). *Correctional effectiveness: The cost of ignoring success*. Federal Probation, 51, 56-62.

Vigdal, G. L., & Stadler, D. W. (1992). Comprehensive system development in corrections for drug abusing offender: The Wisconsin Department of Corrections. In C. G. Leukefield & F. M. Times (Eds.), *Drug abuse treatment in prisons and jails* (pp. 126-141). Washington, DC: U.S. Government Printing Office.

Volkow, N. D., Fowler, J. S., Wang, G., Hitzemann, R., Logan, J., Schlyer, D., Dewey, S., & Wolf, A. P. (1993). Decreased dopamine D2 receptor availability is associated with reduced frontal metabolism in cocaine abusers. Synapse, 14, 169-177.

Wackwitz, J. H., Diesenhaus, H., & Foster, F. M. (1977). *A model for defining substance abuse*. Paper presented at the National Drug Abuse Conference, San Francisco, CA.

Wallace, B. C. (1991). *Crack cocaine: A practical treatment approach for the chemically dependent.* New York: Brunner/Mazel.

Wallace, W. A. (1986). *Theories of counseling and psychotherapy.* Boston: Allyn & Bacon.

Wanberg, K. W. (1974). *Basic counseling skills manual.* Denver: Alcohol and Drug Abuse Division, Colorado Department of Health.

Wanberg, K. W. (1983). *Advanced counseling skills: The process and structure of therapeutic counseling, a client-oriented, therapist-directed model.* Denver: Alcohol and Drug Abuse Division, Colorado Department of Health.

Wanberg, K. W. (1989). *Mood Appraisal Questionnaire.* Arvada, CO: Center for Addictions Research and Evaluation.

Wanberg, K. W. (1990). *Basic counseling skills manual.* Denver: Alcohol and Drug Abuse Division, Colorado Department of Health.

Wanberg, K. W. (1991a). *A descriptive study of clients in Colorado adolescent outpatient intervention and treatment programs.* Denver, CO: Colorado Department of Health, Alcohol and Drug Abuse Division.

Wanberg, K. W. (1991b). *The Adolescent Self Assessment Profile (ASAP).* Arvada, CO: Center for Addictions Research and Evaluation.

Wanberg, K. W. (1992). *A user's guide for the Adolescent Self Assessment Profile.* Arvada, CO: Center for Addictions Research and Evaluation.

Wanberg, K. W. (1993a). *The Adult Substance Use Survey (ASUS).* Arvada, CO: Center for Addictions Research and Evaluation.

Wanberg, K. W. (1993b). *A user's guide for the Adult Substance Use Survey (ASUS).* Arvada, CO: Center for Addictions Research and Evaluation.

Wanberg, K. W. (1994). *Classification of juvenile offenders using the scales of the Adolescent Self-Assessment Profile.* Arvada, CO: Center for Addictions Research and Evaluation.

Wanberg, K. W. (1995). *The Life Situation Questionnaire (LSQ).* Arvada, CO: Center for Addictions Research and Evaluation.

Wanberg, K. W., Befus, J., & Embree, J. (1990). *The use of multiple concepts and measures in assessing drug use in the committed juvenile offender.* Paper presented at the annual meeting of the Academy of Criminal Justice Sciences, Denver, CO.

Wanberg, K. W., Fairchild, D. M., & Bonn, E. (1977). *Treatment of the chronic alcoholic.* Denver, CO: Fort Logan Mental Health Center.

Wanberg, K. W., & Horn, J. L. (1970). Alcoholism symptom patterns of men and women: A comparative study. *Quarterly Journal of Studies on Alcohol,* 31, 40-61.

Wanberg, K. W., & Horn, J. L. (1983). Assessment of alcohol use with multidimensional concepts and measures. *American Psychologist,* 38, 1055-1069.

Wanberg, K. W., & Horn, J. L. (1987). The assessment of multiple conditions in persons with alcohol problems. In W. M. Cox (Ed.), *Treatment and prevention of alcohol problems* (27-56). New York: Academic Press.

Wanberg, K. W., & Horn, J. L. (1989a). *The Drug Use Self Report.* Arvada, CO: Center for Addictions Research and Evaluation.

Wanberg, K. W., & Horn, J. L. (1989b). *The Drug Use Self Report: User's guide*. Arvada, CO: Center for Addictions Research and Evaluation.

Wanberg, K. W., Horn, J. L., & Foster, F. M. (1977). A differential assessment model for alcoholism: The scales of the Alcohol Use Inventory. *Journal of Studies on Alcohol, 38*, 512-543.

Wanberg, K. W., & Knapp, J. (1969). Differences in drinking symptoms and behavior of men and women. *British Journal of the Addictions, 64*, 1-9.

Wanberg, K. W., Lewis, R., & Foster, F. M. (1978). Alcoholism and ethnicity: A comparative study of alcohol use patterns across ethnic groups. *International Journal of the Addictions, 13*, 1245-1262.

Wanberg, K. W., & Milkman, H. B. (1993). *The Adult Self Assessment Questionnaire (AdSAQ)*. Arvada, CO: Center for Addictions Research and Evaluation.

Wanberg, K. W., & Milkman, H. B. (1996a). *The Thinking Errors Rating Scale (TERS)*. Arvada, CO: Center for Addictions Research and Evaluation.

Wanberg, K. W., & Milkman, H. B. (1996b). *The Thinking Errors Check List (TECL)*. Arvada, CO: Center for Addictions Research and Evaluation.

Wanberg, K. W., Milkman, H. B., & Harrison, S. (1992). *The Personal Pleasure Inventory*. Denver, CO: The Center for Interdisciplinary Studies.

Wanberg, K. W., & Timken, D. (1991). *The Driving Assessment Survey (DAS)*. Arvada, CO: Center for Addictions Research and Evaluation.

Wanberg, K. W., Tjaden, C. D., Embree, J., & Garrett, C. J. (1986). *A multiple construct approach for the assessment of drug use and deviant behavior among committed juvenile offenders*. Paper presented at the meeting of the Annual International Differential Treatment Association, Estes Park, CO.

Wanberg, K. W., Tjaden, C. D., & Garrett, C. J. (1990). *Dimensions of deviant behavior and personal adjustment problems in sentenced juvenile offenders*. Paper presented at the annual meeting of the Academy of Criminal Justice Sciences, Denver, CO.

Warren, M. Q. (1971). Classification of offenders as an aid to efficient management and effective treatment. *Journal of Criminal Law, Criminology, and Police Science, 60*, 239-258.

Watson, J. B. (1913). Psychology as the behaviorist views it. *Psychological Review, 20*, 158-177.

Weekes, J. R. (1997). Substance abuse treatment for offenders. *Corrections Today, 59*, 12-14.

Weekes, J. R., Moser, A. E., & Langevin, C. M. (1997). *Assessing substance abusing offenders for treatment. In What Works: Critical Issues Research and Best Practices in Community Corrections*. International Community Corrections Association Conference, Cleveland, OH (October 5-8, 1997).

Weibel-Orlando, J. (1987). Culture-specific treatment modalities: Assessing client-treatment fit in Indian Alcoholism programs. In W. Cox (Ed.), *Treatment and prevention of alcohol problems: A resource manual* (pp. 261-281). New York: Academic Press.

Weibel-Orlando, J. (1989). Treatment and prevention of Native American alcoholism. In T. D. Watts & R. Wright (Eds.), *Alcoholism in minority populations* (pp. 121-139). Springfield, IL: Charles C Thomas.

Weisner, T. S., Weibel-Orlando, J. C., & Long, J. (1984). Serious drinking, white man's drinking and teetotaling: Predictors of drinking level differences in an urban American Indian population. *Journal of Studies on Alcohol, 45*, 237-250.

Werner, H. (1957). The concept of development from a comparative and organismic point of view. In D. B. Harris (Ed.), *The concept of development*. Minneapolis: University of Minnesota Press.

Westermeyer, J. (1992). Cultural perspectives: Native Americans, Asians, and new immigrants. In J. H. Lowinson, P. Ruiz, R. B. Millman, & J. G. Langrod (Eds.), *Substance abuse: A comprehensive textbook* (pp. 890-896). Baltimore, MD: Williams & Wilkins.

Wexler, H. K., Falkin, G. P., & Lipton, D. S. (1990). Outcome evaluation of a prison therapeutic community for substance abuse treatment. *Criminal Justice and Behavior, 17*, 71-92.

White, J. E. (1994, October 10). The beauty of Black art. *Time,* pp. 66-73.

Williams, G. D., Grant, B. F., Harford, T. C., & Noble, J. (1989). Population projections using DSM-III criteria, alcohol abuse and dependence, 1990-2000. *Alcohol Research World, 13*, 366-470.

Wilson, J. Q., & Hernstein, R. J. (1985). *Crime and human nature*. New York: Simon & Schuster.

Witkin, H. A., Dyk, R. B., Fatterson, H. F., Goodenough, D. R., & Karp, S. A. (1962). *Psychological differentiation*. New York: Wiley.

Wolpe, J. (1958). *Psychotherapy by reciprocal inhibition*. Stanford, CA: Stanford University Press.

World Health Organization. (1964). *Expert committee report on mental health* (Technical Report Series No. 273). Geneva: Author.

Wright, F. D., Beck, A. T., Newman, C. F., & Liese, B. S. (1993). Cognitive therapy of substance abuse: Theoretical rationale. In L. S. Onken, J. D. Blaine, & J. J. Boren (Eds.), *Behavioral treatments for drug abuse and dependence* (NIDA Research Monograph 137). Rockville, MD: National Institute on Drug Abuse.

Yochelson, S., & Samenow, S. E. (1976). The criminal personality: Vol. I. *A profile for change*. New York: Jason Aronson.

Yochelson, S., & Samenow, S. (1977). The criminal personality: Vol. 2. *The change process*. Northvale, NJ: Jason Aronson.

Zeiner, A. R., Paredes, A., & Cowden, I. (1976). Physiologic responses to ethanol among the Tarahumara Indians. *Annals of the New York Academy of Science, 273*, 151-158.

Zinberg, N. (1990). Prologue. In H. Milkman & L. Sederer (Eds.), *Treatment choices for alcoholism and substance abuse*. New York: Lexington Books.

ABOUT THE AUTHORS

Kenneth W. Wanberg, Ph.D.

Kenneth W. Wanberg, Th.D, Ph.D. has academic concentrations in psychology, psychometrics and quantitative analysis, interpersonal communication and the psychology of spoken language. He has worked as a clinician and researcher in the alcohol and drug abuse field for over 35 years.

Dr. Wanberg worked as a counselor and clinical psychologist with the Alcoholism Division at the Fort Logan Mental Health Center for 15 years and as a clinical psychologist with the division of Youth Corrections, State of Colorado, for 17 years. He has been author, principal investigator and project evaluator of a number of federal research and demonstration projects. He has served as a consultant to the Colorado Alcohol and Drug Abuse Division for 23 years, as a consultant to more than 15 community mental health or substance abuse agencies and as a faculty member of six different universities and colleges. He is the author of the *Colorado Alcoholism and Drug Abuse Basic Counseling Skills* manual, has published numerous scholarly articles, and is the author or co-author of several widely used alcohol and drug use assessment instruments. His research focus has been in the area of identifying different patterns and dimensions of substance use and addictive behaviors.

Currently, Dr. Wanberg is a licensed psychologist in a private practice and is the director of the Center for Addictions Research and Evaluation — CARE.

Harvey Milkman, Ph.D.

Harvey B. Milkman, Ph.D., is Professor of Psychology at Metropolitan State College of Denver (1974–present); licensed psychologist in Colorado; founder and director of the Center for Interdisciplinary Studies; and Project Director and Principal Investigator for Project Self Discovery.

Dr. Milkman began his research on "Preferential Abuse of Heroin or Amphetamine" with William Frosch at Bellevue Psychiatric Hospital, New York City (1969–1972). In 1980–81, he studied addictive behaviors in Africa, India and southeast Asia; in 1985–86 he was recipient of a Fulbright-Hays Lectureship award at the National University of Malaysia. He has represented the United States Information Agency as a consultant and featured speaker in Iceland, Turkey, Yugoslavia, Austria, The Netherlands, and Brazil.

He is editor with Howard Shaffer of *The Addictions: Multidisciplinary Perspectives and Treatments*, Lexington Books, 1985, and editor with Lloyd Sederer of *Treatment Choices for Alcoholism and Substance Abuse*, Lexington Books, 1990. He is author with Stanley Sunderwirth of *Craving for Ecstasy: The Consciousness and Chemistry of Escape*, Lexington Books, 1987, and *Pathways to Pleasure: The Consciousness and Chemistry of Optimal Living*, Lexington Books, 1993. Dr. Milkman is author with Kenneth Wanberg and Cleo Parker Robinson of *Project Self Discovery: Artistic Alternatives for High-Risk Youth*, Clinical Psychology Publishing Company, 1996.

APPENDIX A

CLIENT SCREENING, ASSESSMENT AND OUTCOME EVALUATION INSTRUMENTS

Addiction Severity Index (ASI)

Adult Self Assessment Questionnaire (AdSAQ)

Adult Substance Use Survey (ASUS)

Alcohol Use Inventory (AUI) Profile Hand Scoring

Alcohol Use Inventory (AUI) Sample Computer Profile Report

Driving Assessment Survey (DAS)

Drug Use Self Report (DUSR) Profile

Follow-up Assessment Questionnaire - FAQ

Life Situation Questionnaire (LSQ)

Mood Appraisal Questionnaire (MAQ)

Program Interest Questionnaire (PIQ)

Provider Treatment Closure Questionnaire - PTCQ

Substance Use History Matrix - SUHM

Thinking Errors Check List (TECL)

Thinking Errors Rating Scale (TERS)

ADDICTIONS SEVERITY INDEX (ASI)

ADDICTION SEVERITY INDEX

SEVERITY RATINGS

The severity ratings are interviewer estimates
of the patient's need for additional treatment in
each area. The scales range from 0 (no treatment necessary) to 9 (treatment needed to
intervene in life-threatening situation). Each
rating is based upon the patient's history of
problem symptoms, present condition and subjective assessment of his treatment needs in a
given area. For a detailed description of severity ratings' derivation procedures and conven-
tions, see manual. **Note: These
severity ratings are optional.**

Fifth Edition/1997 Version

SUMMARY OF PATIENTS RATING SCALE

0 - Not at all
1 - Slightly
2 - Moderately
3 - Considerably
4 - Extremely

---

1. I.D. NUMBER

2. LAST 4 DIGITS OF SSN

3. PROGRAM NUMBER

4. DATE OF ADMISSION

5. DATE OF INTERVIEW

6. TIME BEGUN

7. TIME ENDED

8. CLASS:
   1 - Intake
   2 - Follow-up

9. CONTACT CODE:
   1 - In Person
   2 - Phone

10. GENDER:
    1 - Male
    2 - Female

11. INTERVIEWER CODE NUMBER

12. SPECIAL:
    1 - Patient terminated
    2 - Patient refused
    3 - Patient unable to respond

GENERAL INFORMATION

NAME _____

CURRENT ADDRESS _____

_____

_____

G13. GEOGRAPHIC CODE

G14. How long have you lived at this address?
      YRS.   MOS.

G15 Is this residence owned by you or your family?

    0 - No   1 - Yes

G16. DATE OF BIRTH

G17. RACE

    1 - White (Not of Hispanic Origin)
    2 - Black (Not of Hispanic Origin)
    3 - American Indian
    4 - Alaskan Native
    5 - Asian or Pacific Islander
    6 - Hispanic - Mexican
    7 - Hispanic - Puerto Rican
    8 - Hispanic - Cuban
    9 - Other Hispanic

G18. RELIGIOUS PREFERENCE

    1 - Protestant 4 - Islamic
    2 - Catholic   5 - Other
    3 - Jewish   6 - None

G19. Have you been in a controlled environment in the past 30 days?

    1 - No
    2 - Jail
    3 - Alcohol or Drug Treatment
    4 - Medical Treatment
    5 - Psychiatric Treatment
    6 - Other _____

G20. How many days?

ADDITIONAL TEST RESULTS

G21. Shipley C.Q.

G22. Shipley I.Q.

G23. Beck Total Score

G24. SCL-90 Total

G25. MAST

G26. _____

G27. _____

G28. _____

SEVERITY PROFILE

	9							
	8							
	7							
	6							
	5							
	4							
	3							
	2							
	1							
	0							

PROBLEMS MEDICAL EMP/SUP ALCOHOL DRUG LEGAL FAM/SOC PSYCH

MEDICAL STATUS

* **M1.** How many times in your life have you been hospitalized for medical problems? *(Include o.d.'s, d.t.'s, exclude detox.)*

M2. How long ago was your last hospitalization for a physical problem — YRS. MOS.

M3. Do you have any chronic medical problems which continue to interfere with your life?
0 - No
1 - Yes _____
Specify

M4. Are you taking any prescribed medication on a regular basis for a physical problem?
0 - No   1 - Yes

M5. Do you receive a pension for a physical disability? *(Exclude psychiatric disability.)*
0 - No
1 - Yes _____
Specify

M6. How many days have you experienced medical problems in the past 30?

FOR QUESTIONS M7 & M8 PLEASE ASK PATIENT TO USE THE PATIENT'S RATING SCALE

M7. How troubled or bothered have you been by these medical problems in the past 30 days?

Comments

M8. How important to you now is treatment for these medical problems?

INTERVIEWER SEVERITY RATING

M9. How would you rate the patient's need for medical treatment?

CONFIDENCE RATINGS

Is the above information significantly distorted by:

M10 Patient's misrepresentation?
0 - No   1 - Yes

M11 Patient's inability to understand?
0 - No   1 - Yes

EMPLOYMENT/SUPPORT STATUS

* **E1.** Education completed *(GED = 12 years)* — YRS. MOS.

* **E2.** Training or technical education completed — MOS.

E3. Do you have a profession, trade or skill?
0 - No
1 - Yes _____
Specify

E4. Do you have a valid driver's license?
0 - No   1 - Yes

E5. Do you have an automobile available for use?
(Answer No if no valid driver's license.)
0 - No   1 - Yes

E6. How long was your longest full-time job? — YRS. MOS.

* **E7.** Usual (or last) occupation.
_____
(Specify in detail)

E8. Does someone contribute to your support in any way?
0 - No   1 - Yes

E9. (ONLY IF ITEM E8 IS YES) Does this constitute the majority of your support?
0 - No   1 - Yes

E10. Usual employment pattern, past 3 years.
1 - full time (40 hrs/wk)
2 - part time (reg. hrs)
3 - part time (irreg., daywork)
4 - student
5 - service
6 - retired/disability
7 - unemployed
8 - in controlled environment

E11. How many days were you paid for working in the past 30? (include "under the table" work.)

How much money did you receive from the following sources in the past 30 days?

E12. Employment (net income)

E13. Unemployment compensation

E14. DPA

E15. Pension, benefits or social security

E16. Mate, family or friends (Money for personal expenses).

E17. Illegal

Comments

E18. How many people depend on you for the majority of their food, shelter, etc.?

E19. How many days have you experienced employment problems in the past 30?

FOR QUESTIONS E20 & E21 PLEASE ASK PATIENT TO USE THE PATIENT'S RATING SCALE

E20. How troubled or bothered have you been by these employment problems in the past 30 days?

E21. How important to you now is counseling for these employment problems?

INTERVIEWER SEVERITY RATING

E22. How would you rate the patient's need for employment counseling?

CONFIDENCE RATINGS

Is the above information significantly distorted by:

E23. Patient's misrepresentation?
0 - No   1 - Yes

E24. Patient's inability to understand?
0 - No   1 - Yes

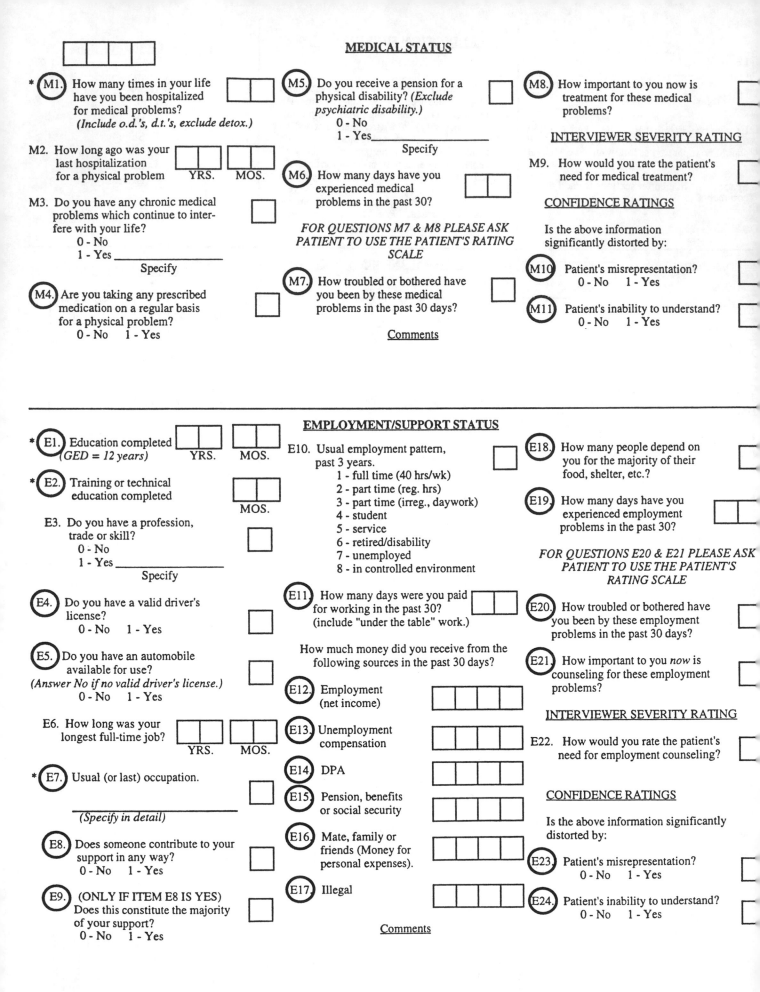

DRUG/ALCOHOL USE

	PAST 30 Days	LIFETIME USE Yrs.	Rt of adm.
D1 Alcohol - Any use at all			
D2 Alcohol - To Intoxication			
D3 Heroin			
D4 Methadone			
D5 Other opiates/ analgesics			
D6 Barbiturates			
D7 Other sed/ hyp/tranq.			
D8 Cocaine			
D9 Amphetamines			
D10 Cannabis			
D11 Hallucinogens			
D12 Inhalants			

D13 More than one substance per day (Incl. alcohol).

Note: See manual for representative examples for each drug class

* Route of Administration: 1 = Oral, 2 = Nasal
3 = Smoking, 4 = Non IV inj., 5 = IV inj.

D14 Which substance is the major problem? *Please code as above or 00-No problem; 15-Alcohol & Drug (Dual addiction); 16-Polydrug; when not clear, ask patient.*

D15. How long was your last period of voluntary abstinence from this major substance? *(00 - never abstinent)*

D16. How many months ago did this abstinence end? *(00 - still abstinent)*

How many times have you:

* D17 Had alcohol d.t.'s

* D18 Overdosed on drugs

How many times in your life have you been treated for:

* D19 Alcohol Abuse:

* D20 Drug Abuse:

How many of these were detox only?

* D21 Alcohol

* D22 Drug

How much would you say you spent during the past 30 days on:

* D23 Alcohol

* D24 Drugs

Comments

D25 How many days have you been treated in an outpatient setting for alcohol or drugs in the past 30 days *(Include NA, AA).*

How many days in the past 30 have you experienced:

D26 Alcohol Problems

D27 Drug Problems

FOR QUESTIONS D28-D31 PLEASE ASK PATIENT TO USE THE PATIENT'S RATING SCALE

How troubled or bothered have you been in the past 30 days by these:

D28 Alcohol Problems

D29 Drug Problems

How important to you now is treatment for these:

D30 Alcohol Problems

D31 Drug Problems

INTERVIEWER SEVERITY RATING
How would you rate the patient's need for treatment for:

D32 Alcohol Abuse

D33 Drug Abuse

CONFIDENCE RATINGS
Is the above information significantly distorted by:

D34 Patient's misrepresentation?
0 - No   1 - Yes

D35 Patient's inability to understand?
0 - No   1 - Yes

LEGAL STATUS

L1. Was this admission prompted or suggested by the criminal justice system (judge, probation/ parole officer, etc.)

0 - No   1 - Yes ☐

L2. Are you on probation or parole?

0 - No   1 - Yes ☐

How many times in your life have you been arrested and charged with the following:

* L3 - shoplifting/vandalism
* L4 - parole/probation violations
* L5 - drug charges
* L6 - forgery
* L7 - weapons offense
* L8 - burglary. larceny, B & E
* L9 - robbery
* L10 - assault
* L11 - arson
* L12 - rape
* L13 - homicide, manslaughter
* L14 - prostitution
* L15 - contempt of court
* L16 - other

* L17 How many of these charges resulted in convictions? ☐☐

How many times in your life have you been charged with the following:

* L18 Disorderly conduct, vagrancy public intoxication ☐☐
* L19 Driving while intoxicated ☐☐
* L20 Major driving violations (reckless driving, speeding, no license, etc.) ☐☐
* L21 How many months were you incarcerated in your life? ☐☐ MOS.

L22. How long was your last incarceration? ☐☐ MOS.

L23. What was it for? (Use code 3-16, 18-20. If multiple charges, code most severe) ☐☐

L24 Are you presently awaiting charges, trial or sentence?
0 - No   1 - Yes ☐

L25 What for (If multiple charges, use most severe). ☐☐

L26 How many days in the past 30 were you detained or incarcerated? ☐☐

L27 How many days in the past 30 have you engaged in illegal activities for profit? ☐☐

FOR QUESTIONS L28 & L29 PLEASE ASK PATIENT TO USE THE PATIENT'S RATING SCALE

L28 How serious do you feel your present legal problems are? (*Exclude civil problems*) ☐

L29 How important to you *now* is counseling or referral for these legal problems? ☐

INTERVIEWER SEVERITY RATING

L30. How would you rate the patient's need for legal services or counseling? ☐

CONFIDENCE RATINGS

Is the above information significantly distorted by:

L31 Patient's misrepresentation?
0 - No   1 - Yes ☐

L32 Patient's inability to understand?
0 - No   1 - Yes ☐

Comments

FAMILY HISTORY

Have any of your relatives had what you would call a significant drinking, drug use or psych problem- one that did or should have led to treatment?

Mother's Side	Alc	Drug	Psych
H1. Grandmother	☐	☐	☐
H2. Grandfather	☐	☐	☐
H3. Mother	☐	☐	☐
H4. Aunt	☐	☐	☐
H5. Uncle	☐	☐	☐

Father's Side	Alc	Drug	Psych
H6. Grandmother	☐	☐	☐
H7. Grandfather	☐	☐	
H8. Father	☐	☐	☐
H9. Aunt	☐	☐	☐
H10. Uncle	☐	☐	☐

Siblings	Alc	Drug	Psych
H11. Brother	☐	☐	☐
H12. Sister	☐	☐	☐

Direction: Place "0" in relative category where the answer is clearly <u>no for all relatives in the category</u>; "1" where the answer is clearly <u>yes for any relative within the category</u>; "X" where the answer is <u>uncertain or "I don't know"</u> and "N" where there <u>never was a relative from that category</u>. Code most problematic relative in cases of multiple members per category.

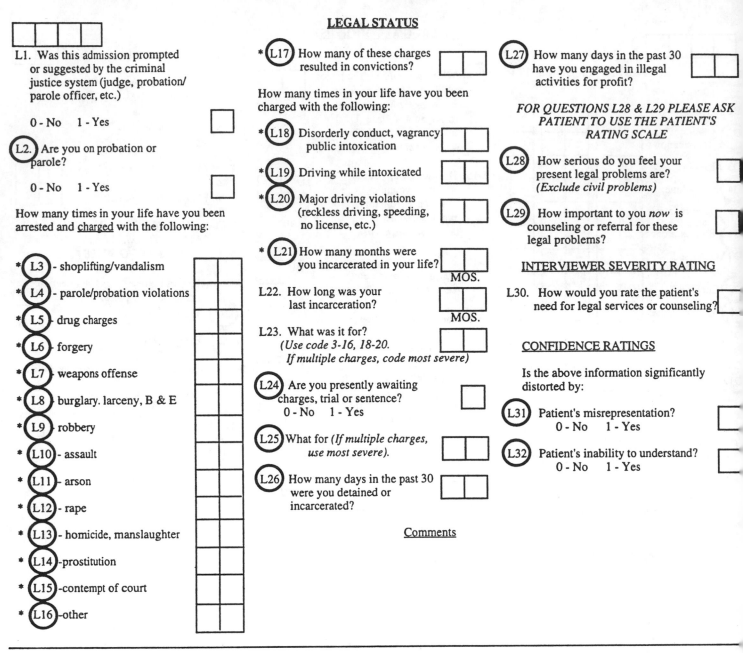

FAMILY/SOCIAL RELATIONSHIPS

F1) Marital Status

1 - Married   4 - Separated
2 - Remarried   5 - Divorced
3 - Widowed   6 - Never Married

F2 How long have you been in this marital status? YRS. MOS.
(If never married, since age 18).

F3. Are you satisfied with this situation?
0 - No
1 - Indifferent
2 - Yes

F4. Usual living arrangements (past 3 yr.)
1 - With sexual partner and children
2 - With sexual partner alone
3 - With children alone
4 - With parents
5 - With family
6 - With friends
7 - Alone
8 - Controlled environment
9 - No stable arrangements

F5. How long have you lived in these arrangements. YRS. MOS.
(If with parents or family, since age 18).

F6. Are you satisfied with these living arrangements?
0 - No
1 - Indifferent
2 - Yes

Do you live with anyone who:
0 = No   1 = Yes

F7. Has a current alcohol problem?

F8. Uses non-prescribed drugs?

F9. With whom do you spend most of your free time:
1 - Family   3 - Alone
2 - Friends

F10. Are you satisfied with spending your free time this way?
0 - No   1 - Indifferent   2 - Yes

F11. How many close friends do you have?

Direction for F12-F26: Place "0" in relative category where the answer is clearly <u>no for all relatives in the category</u>; "1" where the answer is clearly <u>yes for **any** relative within the category</u>; "X" where the answer is <u>uncertain or "I don't know"</u> and "N" where there <u>never was a relative from that category.</u>

Would you say you have had close, long lasting, personal relationships with any of the following people in your life:

F12. Mother
F13. Father
F14. Brothers/Sisters
F15. Sexual Partner/Spouse
F16. Children
F17. Friends

Have you had significant periods in which you have experienced serious problems getting along with:

0 - No   1 - Yes   PAST 30 DAYS   IN YOUR LIFE

F18 Mother
F19 Father
F20 Brothers/Sisters
F21 Sexual partner/spouse
F22 Children
F23 Other significant family_____
F24 Close friends
F25 Neighbors
F26 Co-Workers

Did any of these people (F18-F26) abuse you: 0 = No, 1 = Yes   30 DAYS   LIFE

F27 Emotionally (make you feel bad through harsh words)?
F28 Physically (cause you physical harm)?
F29 Sexually (force sexual advances or sexual acts)?

How many days in the past 30 have you had serious conflicts:

F30 with your family?

F31 with other people? (excluding family)

FOR QUESTIONS F32-F35 PLEASE ASK PATIENT TO USE THE PATIENT'S RATING SCALE

How troubled or bothered have you been in the past 30 days by these:

F32 Family problems

F33 Social problems

How important to you now is treatment or counseling for these:

F34 Family problems

F35 Social problems

INTERVIEWER SEVERITY RATING

F36. How would you rate the patient's need for family and/or social counseling?

<u>CONFIDENCE RATINGS</u>

Is the above information significantly distorted by:

F37 Patient's misrepresentation?
0 - No   1 - Yes

F38 Patient's inability to understand?
0 - No   1 - Yes

<u>Comments</u>

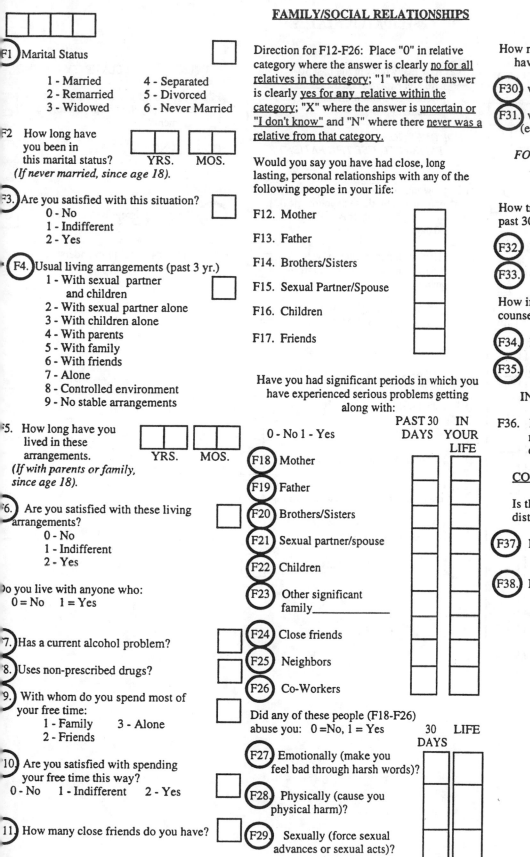
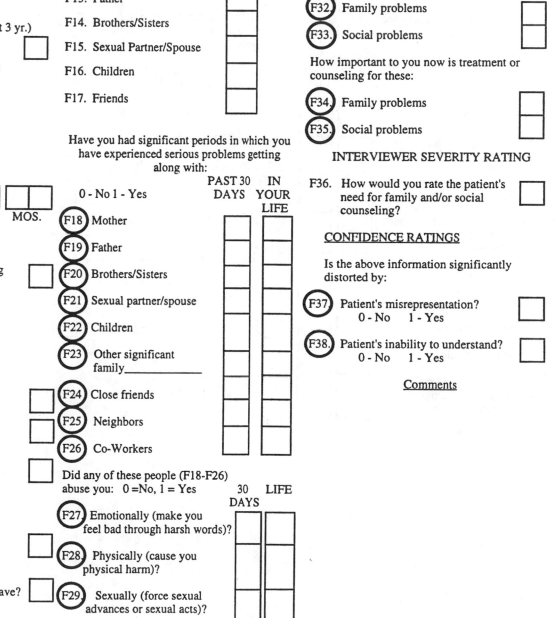

PSYCHIATRIC STATUS

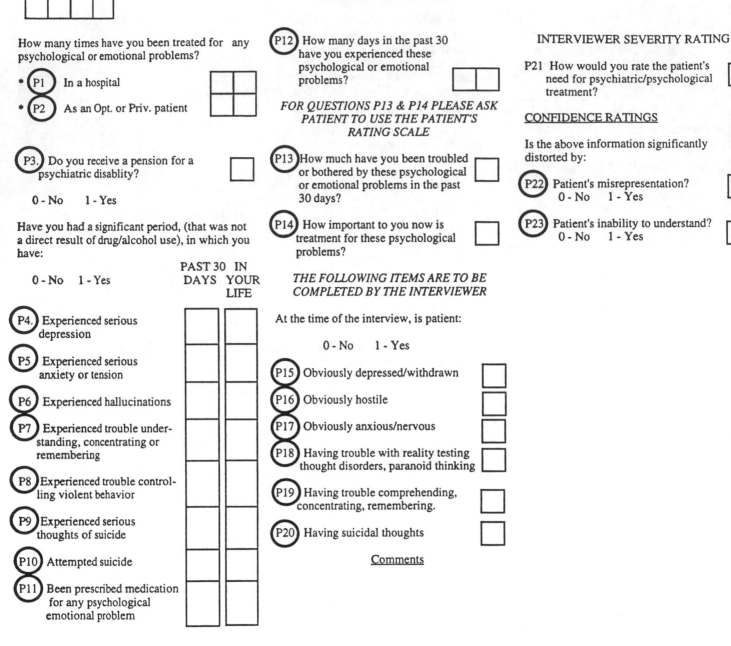

How many times have you been treated for any psychological or emotional problems?

* (P1) In a hospital

* (P2) As an Opt. or Priv. patient

(P3.) Do you receive a pension for a psychiatric disablity?

0 - No   1 - Yes

Have you had a significant period, (that was not a direct result of drug/alcohol use), in which you have:

0 - No   1 - Yes

PAST 30 DAYS | IN YOUR LIFE

(P4.) Experienced serious depression

(P5) Experienced serious anxiety or tension

(P6) Experienced hallucinations

(P7) Experienced trouble understanding, concentrating or remembering

(P8) Experienced trouble controlling violent behavior

(P9) Experienced serious thoughts of suicide

(P10) Attempted suicide

(P11) Been prescribed medication for any psychological emotional problem

(P12) How many days in the past 30 have you experienced these psychological or emotional problems?

FOR QUESTIONS P13 & P14 PLEASE ASK PATIENT TO USE THE PATIENT'S RATING SCALE

(P13) How much have you been troubled or bothered by these psychological or emotional problems in the past 30 days?

(P14) How important to you now is treatment for these psychological problems?

THE FOLLOWING ITEMS ARE TO BE COMPLETED BY THE INTERVIEWER

At the time of the interview, is patient:

0 - No   1 - Yes

(P15) Obviously depressed/withdrawn

(P16) Obviously hostile

(P17) Obviously anxious/nervous

(P18) Having trouble with reality testing thought disorders, paranoid thinking

(P19) Having trouble comprehending, concentrating, remembering.

(P20) Having suicidal thoughts

Comments

INTERVIEWER SEVERITY RATING

P21 How would you rate the patient's need for psychiatric/psychological treatment?

CONFIDENCE RATINGS

Is the above information significantly distorted by:

(P22) Patient's misrepresentation?
0 - No   1 - Yes

(P23) Patient's inability to understand?
0 - No   1 - Yes

ADULT SELF ASSESSMENT QUESTIONNAIRE (ADSAQ)

ADULT SELF ASSESSMENT QUESTIONNAIRE - ADSAQ

Kenneth W. Wanberg
Harvey B. Milkman
Authors

DESCRIPTIVE INFORMATION
(To be completed by test taker)

NAME_____ DATE OF BIRTH_____ TODAY'S DATE_____

DATE _____ AGE_____ GENDER: [ ] Male [ ] Female YEARS OF SCHOOLING _____

ETHNICITY: [ ] Anglo [ ] Black [ ] Hispanic [ ] Native American [ ] Other

PREVIOUS ALCOHOL OR OTHER DRUG SERVICES:

Outpatient: [ ] None   Inpatient: [ ] None
            [ ] 1-2 times   [ ] 1-2 times
            [ ] 3-5 times   [ ] 3-5 times
            [ ] more than 6 times   [ ] more than 6 times

INFORMATION AND INSTRUCTIONS ON THE USE OF THIS QUESTIONNAIRE

This booklet has some questions about how you see and think about yourself at this time. The answers you give will be treated as confidential according to the laws of the State of Colorado. Your answers will help us in working with you. Be as honest as you can. This will help those working with you around your concerns and questions about yourself and your current situation. Choose the answers that best fit you and then mark them with a check mark. **NOW YOU MAY TURN THE PAGE AND BEGIN TO ANSWER THE QUESTIONS.**

TO BE COMPLETED BY STAFF		
AGENCY NAME	TEST ADMINISTRATOR	CLIENT I.D. NUMBER

CURRENT SETTING (Check only one)   STATUS (Check all that apply)

[ ] Inpatient treatment - private   [ ] Voluntary self referred admission
[ ] Inpatient treatment - public   [ ] Voluntary agency/professional referred
[ ] Intensive outpatient   [ ] Voluntary other referred
[ ] Traditional outpatient   [ ] Probation
[ ] Juvenile corrections   [ ] Commitment
[ ] Criminal justice/corrections   [ ] Other court

ASAQ Profile Summary

SCALE NAME	RAW SCORE	Low First Quartile	Low-medium Second Quartile	High-medium Third Quartile	High Fourth Quartile	NUMBER IN NORM SAMPLE*
1.CONTEMPLATE		0 4 6 10¦11 12 ¦13 ¦ 14 ¦ 15 ¦ ¦ 16 ¦ ¦ ¦ 17 ¦ 18				302
2.PSYCHSOCIAL		0 ¦ 1 ¦ ¦2 ¦ 3 4¦ 5 ¦ 6 7 ¦ 8 9 ¦10 ¦ 11¦12 13 14¦15 17 18				302
3.COMMUNITY		0 1 2 3 ¦ 4 5 ¦ ¦ 6 ¦ 7 ¦ 8 9 ¦ 10 ¦ 11 ¦ ¦12 ¦13 14 15¦16 17 18				302
4.COLLATERAL		0 1 3 5 ¦ 6 ¦ 7¦ 8 ¦ 9 ¦ 10 ¦ 11 ¦ 12 ¦ ¦13 ¦ 14 ¦ 15 16				302
5.HELPACKNOW		0 2 3 4¦ 5 6 7 8¦9 ¦ 10 ¦12 13 14¦15 16 17¦ 18 19 ¦ 20 21 ¦ 22¦ 23 ¦24 25 26¦27 28 31				302
6.CHANGED		0 ¦ 1 ¦ 2 ¦ 3 ¦ 4 5¦ 6 ¦ 7 8 ¦ 9 ¦ 10 ¦ 11¦ 12 ¦ 13 14				302
A.READINESS		0 1 4 6 ¦ 7 9 10¦ 11¦ 12 ¦14 16 18¦ 19 20 ¦21 22 23¦24 25 26¦ 27¦ 28 ¦30 31 33¦34 37 42				302
B.ACTION		3 8 9 12¦13 14 15¦ ¦ 16 ¦17 18 19¦ 20 ¦ 21 22 ¦ 23 24 ¦ 25¦ ¦ 26 27 ¦ 28 29				302

	25	50	75	99
		PERCENTILE RANGE		Older Adolescent Juvenile Offenders

Version 995

1. Have you been giving some thought about making some changes in your life?

_____ a. No, not really.
_____ b. Yes, I have thought a little about making some changes.
_____ c. Yes, I have thought a lot about making some changes.
_____ d. Yes, making some changes in my life has been on my mind every day.

2. Do you feel that you need to make some changes in your life at this time?

_____ a. No, not at all.
_____ b. Yes, maybe a few changes, but I'm not sure what.
_____ c. Yes, there are few changes that I know I need to make.
_____ d. Yes, there are many changes that I need to make.

3. Do you want to stop using alcohol?

_____ a. No, not at all.
_____ b. Maybe I do.
_____ c. Yes, I want to stop using alcohol.

4. Do you plan to stop using alcohol?

_____ a. No, not at all.
_____ b. Maybe I do.
_____ c. Yes, I do intend to stop using alcohol.

5. Do you want to stop using drugs other than alcohol?

_____ a. No, not at all.
_____ b. Maybe I do.
_____ c. Yes, I want to stop using drugs other than alcohol.

6. Do you plan to stop using drugs other than alcohol?

_____ a. No, not at all.
_____ b. Maybe I do.
_____ c. Yes, I do intend to stop using drugs other than alcohol.

7. What would you say as to your hope of making changes in your life?

_____ a. I don't really have to make any changes.
_____ b. I have little hope I can make changes in my life.
_____ c. I have some hope I can make some changes.
_____ d. I have a lot of hope I can make some changes.
_____ e. I am very hopeful I can make changes.

1 ☐

Now, do you feel you need to change anything in any of the following areas:

	No changes necessary	Maybe a few changes	Quite a few changes	I need to make many changes
8. Alcohol or other drug use	___ a	___ b	___ c	___ d
9. Emotional health	___ a	___ b	___ c	___ d
10. Education or training	___ a	___ b	___ c	___ d
11. Job or employment problems	___ a	___ b	___ c	___ d
12. Problems with the law	___ a	___ b	___ c	___ d
13. Family problems	___ a	___ b	___ c	___ d
14. Problems with friends	___ a	___ b	___ c	___ d
15. Getting along with people	___ a	___ b	___ c	___ d

2 ☐

Now, do you feel you need help in any of these areas below:

	I do not need any help	I need a little help	I need quite a bit of help	I need all the help I can get	
16. Alcohol or other drug use	___a	___b	___c	___d	
17. Emotional health	___a	___b	___c	___d	
18. Education or training	___a	___b	___c	___d	
19. Job or employment problems	___a	___b	___c	___d	
20. Problems with the law	___a	___b	___c	___d	
21. Family problems	___a	___b	___c	___d	
22. Problems with friends	___a	___b	___c	___d	
23. Getting along with people	___a	___b	___c	___d	3 ☐

Do any of the following persons think that you need to make changes in your life?

	No	Yes, somewhat	Yes, for sure	
24. Parent	___a.	___b.	___c.	
25. Spouse/boyfriend or girlfriend or intimate partner	___a.	___b.	___c.	
26. Your child, brother or sister	___a.	___b.	___c.	
27. Other relative	___a.	___b.	___c.	
28. Friend(s)	___a.	___b.	___c.	
29. Employer or supervisor	___a.	___b.	___c.	
30. Counselor or therapist	___a.	___b.	___c.	
31. Probation officer, parole office or client manager	___a.	___b.	___c.	4 ☐

32. Do you feel you need help with an alcohol problem at this time?

    ___a. No, not at all.
    ___b. Maybe not, but I would like to check to see if I do have a problem.
    ___c. Maybe I need some help.
    ___d. Yes, I feel I need help.

33. Do you feel you need help with problems having to do with the use of drugs other than alcohol?

    ___a. No, not at all.
    ___b. Maybe not, but I would like to check to see if I do have a problem.
    ___c. Maybe I need some help.
    ___d. Yes, I feel I need help.

34. Would it be hard for you to give up using alcohol?

    ___a. No, I can stop using alcohol at any time.
    ___b. Yes, it would be kind of hard.
    ___c. Yes, it would be very hard to give up using alcohol.

35. Would it be hard for you to give up using drugs other than alcohol?

    ___a. No, I can stop using drugs at any time.
    ___b. Yes, it would be kind of hard.
    ___c. Yes, it would be very hard to give up using drugs.

36. Would you be willing to come to a program where people get help for problems having to do with the use of alcohol and other drugs?
    ___a. No, not at all.
    ___b. Yes, maybe I would.
    ___c. Yes, most likely.
    ___d. Yes, for sure.

37. How many times a week would you be willing to come to such a program?
    ___a. I am not willing to come at all.
    ___b. Probably once a week for an hour or two.
    ___c. Two or three times a week for an hour or two.
    ___d. Every day for an hour or two.

38. How important would it be to you to make changes in your life around the use of alcohol or other drugs?
    ___a. Not important at all.
    ___b. Somewhat important.
    ___c. Very important.
    ___d. Probably the most important thing in my life right now.

Do any of the following persons think that you need help with alcohol or other drug use problems?

		No	Yes, somewhat	Yes, for sure
39.	Spouse/boyfriend or girlfriend or intimate partner	___a.	___b.	___c.
40.	Parent or other relative	___a.	___b.	___c.
41.	Employer or supervisor	___a.	___b.	___c.
42.	Counselor or therapist	___a.	___b.	___c.
43.	Probation officer, parole office or client manager	___a.	___b.	___c.

5 ☐

44. In the past six months, have you taken action to change your life?
    ___a. No, not really.
    ___b. I have done a few things to make some changes.
    ___c. I have done a lot of things to make changes.
    ___d. I have been doing some things every day to make changes.

45. In the past six months, have you taken action to make changes in your use of alcohol or other drugs?
    ___a. No, not really.
    ___b. I have done a few things to make some changes.
    ___c. I have done a lot of things to make changes.
    ___d. I have been doing some things every day to make changes.

46. In the past six months, have you made changes in the amount or number of times you have used alcohol?
    ___a. No, I haven't made any changes.
    ___b. I have cut down on the amount or number of times I drank.
    ___c. I have stopped drinking for a few days.
    ___d. I have stopped drinking for up to a week.
    ___e. I have stopped drinking up to a month or more.

47. In the past six months, have you made changes in the amount or number of times you have used drugs other than alcohol?
    ___a. No, I haven't made any changes or I don't use drugs other than alcohol.
    ___b. Yes, I have cut down on the amount or number of times I use drugs.
    ___c. Yes, I have stopped using drugs for a few days.
    ___d. Yes, I have stopped using drugs for up to a week.
    ___e. I have stopped using drugs for up to a month or more.

6 ☐

48. Would you like to talk with a counselor at this time about your use of alcohol or other drugs?
    ___a. No. ___b. Yes, I think so. ___c. Yes, for sure.

A ☐

B ☐

THANK YOU FOR COMPLETING THIS QUESTIONNAIRE

ADULT SELF ASSESSMENT QUESTIONNAIRE (ADSAQ)

SCORING PROCEDURES

1. CONTEMPLATE (put raw score in box 1):

    Items 1 through 7
    (a=0, b=1, c=2, d=3, e=4).

2. PSYCHSOCIAL (raw score in box 2):

    Items 9, 13, 14, 15, 17, 21, 22 and 23
    (a=0, b=1, c=2, d=3).

3. COMMUNITY (raw score in box 3):

    Items 10, 11, 12, 18, 19 and 20
    (a=0, b=1, c=2, d=3).

4. COLLATERAL (raw score in box 4):

    Items 24 through 31
    (a=0, b=1, c=2).

5. HELP ACKNOWLEDGE (put raw score in box 5):

    Items 16, 32 through 43
    (a=0, b=1, c=2, d=3).

6. CHANGED (put score in box 6):

    Items 44 through 47.
    (a=0, b=1, c=2, d=3, e=4).

A. READINESS (score in box A):

    Items 8, 9, 13, 16, 17, 21, 32 through 39, 41 and 42
    (a=0, b=1, c=2, d=3).

B. ACTION (put score in box B):

    Items 1, 3 through 7, 44 through 47.
    (a=0, b=1, c=2, d=3, e=4).

Current norms on profile are based on 302 committed juvenile offenders. Adult norms are currently being developed. Use broad quartile scores to interpret profile to suggest scoring ranges as low, low-medium, high-medium and high.

ADULT SUBSTANCE USE SURVEY (ASUS)

ADULT SUBSTANCE USE SURVEY - ASUS

Kenneth W. Wanberg
Author

TO BE COMPLETED BY CLIENT

NAME:	DATE OF BIRTH:	DATE:

AGE:	GENDER: [ ] Female　　[ ] Male	YEARS OF SCHOOLING COMPLETED:

ETHNICITY: [ ] Anglo/White　　[ ] Black　　[ ] Hispanic　　[ ] Native American　　[ ] Other

MARITAL STATUS: [ ] Single　　[ ] Married　　[ ] Separated　　[ ] Divorced　　[ ] Widowed

EMPLOYMENT:　[ ] Employed　[ ] Unemployed 1-3 months　[ ] Unemployed more than 3 months

PRIOR ALCOHOL/OTHER DRUG OUTPATIENT TREATMENT: [ ] None　[ ] 1-2 times　[ ] more 2 times

PRIOR ALCOHOL/OTHER DRUG INPATIENT TREATMENT:　[ ] None　[ ] 1-2 times　[ ] more 2 times

INFORMATION AND INSTRUCTIONS ON THE USE OF THIS SURVEY

This booklet contains questions about how you see yourself.　Some questions have to do with your feelings and emotions and others have to do with the use of alcohol and drugs. The information you provide will be treated as confidential and will be released only upon your signed consent. Be as honest as you can. This will help those working with with you to understand your concerns and questions about yourself and about your use of alcohol and other drugs. For each question in this survey, circle the letter under the answer that best fits you. Please answer every question. Give only one answer to each each question. **YOU MAY NOW TURN THE PAGE AND BEGIN THE SURVEY.**

FOR EVALUATOR USE ONLY

EVALUATOR:	AGENCY:	DISTRICT:	CLIENT I.D.:

1. AOD use involvement?	Minimal Low Moderate High 0　1　2　3　4　5　6　7　8　9	4. Referral Basis　5. Referral Level
2. AOD use disruption?	Minimal Low Moderate High 0　1　2　3　4　5　6　7　8　9	[ ] ADS Score____　[ ] 1) None [ ] DAST Score____　[ ] 2) Education [ ] SSI Score____　[ ] 3) Weekly OP [ ] UA　[ ] 4) IOP
3. AOD service readiness?	Minimal Low Moderate High 0　1　2　3　4　5　6　7　8　9	[ ] Override　[ ] 5) IRT 　[ ] 6) TC 　[ ] 7) Add. Assess

ASUS SUMMARY PROFILE

SCALE NAME	RAW SCORE	Low			Low-medium		High-medium			High			NUMBER IN NORM SAMPLE*
		1	2	3	4	5	6	7	8	9	10		
1. INVOLVEMENT1		0	1	2　3	4	5	6	7　8	9　10　11	12　13　14	15　17　20	21　26　40	645*
2. DISRUPTION1			0	1　2	3　4	5	6	7　8　9　10	11　15　18	19　26　32	33　39　46	47　58　77	609*
3. SOCIAL		0　1　3　4	5	6	7　8	9	10	11　12	13　14	15　17　18	19　22　31		613*
4. MOOD		0	1	2　3	4	5	6　7	8	9	10　11	12　13　14	15　18　30	643*
5. DEFENSIVE		0　1　2	3	4	5		6	7	8	9	10　11　12　15		602*
6. GLOBAL		0　4　8　11	12　14　16	17　19　21	22　24　25	26　29　30	32　35　40	41　48　55	56　64　72	73　83　92	93　163		602*
7. INVOLVEMENT2		0　1　2　3	4	5	6　7　8	9	10　11　12	13　15　16	17　18　19	20　22　23	24　25　26	27　30　32　33　36　40	668**
8. DISRUPTION2		0　1　3	5　6	11　15	16　21　26	27　30　34	35　38　41	42　45　47	48　50　53	54　57　59	60　63　65	66　70　80	635**

1	10	20	30	40	50	60	70	80	90	99

PERCENTILE　*Adult Criminal Justice　**Public outpt/inpt

ADULT SUBSTANCE USE SURVEY (ASU

Below is a list of several kinds of drugs that people use. Circle "a" if you have never used the drug. For alcohol, it is the number of times in your lifetime that you have been intoxicated. For all other drugs, it is the number of times in your lifetime that you have used the drug. *Then, on the line on the right side of the page* opposite the drug, indicate the number of times in the past *six months* you have been intoxicated on alcohol or you have used the other drugs. Put an "a" on the line if you did not use alcohol or the other drugs in the past six months. Put a "b" if you used the drug from one to 10 times, put a "c" if you used the drug from 11 to 25 times, etc.

	Total Number of Times in Lifetime					Times used drug in the past six months
	Never used	One to 10 times	11-25 times	26-50 times	More than 50 times	
1. Number of times intoxicated or drunk on alcohol (beer, wine, hard liquor, mixed drinks).	a	b	c	d	e	_____
2. Marijuana (pot, hashish, hash, THC).	a	b	c	d	e	_____
3. Cocaine (coke, snow, crack, rock, blow).	a	b	c	d	e	_____
4. Amphetamines/stimulants (speed, uppers, bennies, diet pills, crystal, black beauties, white crosses, pep pills).	a	b	c	d	e	_____
5. Hallucinogens (LSD, acid, peyote, mushrooms, mescaline, PCP, angel dust).	a	b	c	d	e	_____
6. Inhalants (rush, gasoline, paint, glue, lighter fluid, nitrous oxide).	a	b	c	d	e	_____
7. Heroin (horse, H, smack, junk)	a	b	c	d	e	_____
8. Other opiates or pain killers used for nonmedical reasons (codeine, opium, morphine, percodans, dilaudid, demerol, methadone).	a	b	c	d	e	_____
9. Barbiturates/sedatives used for nonmedical reasons (seconal, nembutal, amytal, doriden, quaaludes, dalmane, placidyl, sleeping medicines, blues, reds, yellows, ludes, etc.)	a	b	c	d	e	_____
10. Tranquilizers used for non-medical reasons (librium, valium, ativan, xanax, serax, miltown, equanil, meprobamates).	a	b	c	d	e	_____ _____

	Never smoked	Do not smoke now	Up to half pack a day	About a pack a day	More than a pack a day
11. Cigarettes (tobacco)	a	b	c	d	e

2

As a result of using or coming off of alcohol or any of the other above drugs, indicate how often any of the following have happened to you in your lifetime. Then, for each of the following statements, on the line on the right side of the page, indicate how many times it has happened to you in the past six months. Put an "a" if it did not happen to you, put a "b" if it happened to you 1-3 times, a "c" if it happened to you 4-6 times, etc.

		Total Number of Times in Lifetime				Number of times in the past six months
	Never	1-3 times	4-6 times	7-10 times	More than 10 times	
12. Had a blackout (forgot what you did but were still awake).	a	b	c	d	e	_____
13. Became physically violent.	a	b	c	d	e	_____
14. Staggered and stumbled around.	a	b	c	d	e	_____
15. Passed out (became unconscious).	a	b	c	d	e	_____
16. Tried to take your own life.	a	b	c	d	e	_____
17. Saw or heard things not there.	a	b	c	d	e	_____
18. Became mentally confused.	a	b	c	d	e	_____
19. Thought people were out to get you or wanted to harm you.	a	b	c	d	e	_____
20. Had physical shakes or tremors.	a	b	c	d	e	_____
21. Became physically sick or nauseated.	a	b	c	d	e	_____
22. Had a seizure or a convulsion.	a	b	c	d	e	_____
23. Had rapid or fast heart beat.	a	b	c	d	e	_____
24. Became very anxious, nervous and tense.	a	b	c	d	e	_____
25. Were very feverish, hot, sweaty.	a	b	c	d	e	_____
26. Did not eat or sleep.	a	b	c	d	e	_____
27. Were weak, tired and fatigued.	a	b	c	d	e	_____
28. Unable to go to work or school.	a	b	c	d	e	_____
29. Neglected your family.	a	b	c	d	e	_____
30. Broke the law or committed a crime.	a	b	c	d	e	_____
31. Could not pay your bills.	a	b	c	d	e	_____

Please choose the answer that best fits you for the following questions or statements.

	Never	1-2 times	3-4 times	5 or more times
32. When I was in my teen years, I got into trouble with the law.	a	b	c	d
33. I was suspended or expelled from school when I was child or teenager.	a	b	c	d
34. I have been in fights or brawls.	a	b	c	d
35. I have been charged with driving under the influence of alcohol or other drugs.	a	b	c	d
36. As an adult, I have been in trouble with the law other than driving a motor vehicle.	a	b	c	d

	Not true	Somewhat true	Usually true	Always true
37. I have had trouble because I don't follow the rules.	a	b	c	d
38. I don't like police officers.	a	b	c	d
39. There are too many laws in society.	a	b	c	d
40. It is all right to break the law if it doesn't hurt anyone.	a	b	c	d
41. Usually, no one tells me what to do.	a	b	c	d ____

	Hardly at all	Yes sometimes	Yes A lot	Yes, all the time
42. Have you felt down and depressed?	a	b	c	d
43. Have you been nervous and tense?	a	b	c	d
44. Have you been irritated and angry?	a	b	c	d
45. Have your moods been up and down – from very happy to very depressed?	a	b	c	d
46. Do you tend to worry about things?	a	b	c	d
47. Have you felt like not wanting to live or like taking your life?	a	b	c	d
48. Have you had problems sleeping?	a	b	c	d
49. Have you had disturbing thoughts?	a	b	c	d
50. Are you discouraged about your future?	a	b	c	d ____

	No never	Hardly at all	A few times	Yes a lot
51. Have you ever gotten angry at someone?	a	b	c	d
52. Have you lied about something or not told the truth?	a	b	c	d
53. Do you ever find yourself unhappy?	a	b	c	d
54. Have you felt frustrated about a job?	a	b	c	d
55. Do you hold things in and not tell others what you think or feel?	a	b	c	d ____
56. Have you been unkind or rude to someone?	a	b	c	d
57. Have you ever cried about someone or something?	a	b	c	d

	No not at all	Yes maybe	Yes most likely	Yes for sure
58. Have you felt you needed to make changes around the use of alcohol *or* other drugs?	a	b	c	d
59. Do you want to *stop or continue to not use alcohol*?	a	b	c	d
60. Do you want to *stop or continue to not use other drugs*?	a	b	c	d
61. Have you felt the need for help with problems having to do with alcohol use?	a	b	c	d
62. Have you felt the need for help with problems with the use of other drugs?	a	b	c	d
63. Is it important for you to make changes around the use of alcohol or other drugs?	a	b	c	d
64. Would you be willing to go to *(or continue in)* a program where people get help for alcohol or other drug use problems?	a	b	c	d ____

END OF SURVEY

ADULT SUBSTANCE USE SURVEY - ASUS

SCORING PROCEDURES

1. INVOLVEMENT1:

   a. Score items 1 through 10.
   b. a=0, b=1, c=2, d=3, e=4.

2. DISRUPTION1:

   a. Score items 12 through 31.
   b. a=0, b=1, c=2, d=3, e=4.

3. SOCIAL:

   a. Score items 32 through 41, 51 and 52.
   b. a=0, b=1, c=2, d=3.

4. EMOTIONAL:

   a. Score items 42 through 50 and 53.
   b. a=0, b=1, c=2, d=3.

5. DEFENSIVE:

   a. Score items 51 through 55.
   b. a=3, b=2, c=1, d=0.

6. INVOLVEMENT2:

   a. Score items 1 through 10.
   b. a=0, b=1, c=2, d=3, e=4.

7. DISRUPTION2:

   a. Score items 12 through 31.
   b. a=0, b=1, c=2, d=3, e=4.

The normative reference group is indicated at the bottom of the profile. The normative reference group for INVOLVEMENT2 and DISRUPTION2 is a sample of alcohol and other drug abuse clients from both intensive outpatient and inpatient treatment settings.

The standard score is either a percentile score or decile score. Interpret these scores as you would any percentile type score: e.g., a raw score of 7 on INVOLVEMENT indicates that the individual scores higher on this scale than 50 percent of a representative sample of criminal justice clients referred for alcohol and other drug use outpatient treatment and higher than 20 percent of clients referred for either intensive outpatient or inpatient treatment in a public alcohol and other drug treatment facility.

The Adult Substance Use Survey (ASUS) is copyrighted. The instrument and user's guide are distributed by the Center for Addictions Research and Evaluation (CARE), 5640 Ward Road, Suite 140, Arvada, Colorado 80002, (303) 421-1261.

HAND SCORING
ALCOHOL USE INVENTORY (AUI)

AUI
J. L. Horn
K. W. Wanberg
F. M. Foster

ALCOHOL USE INVENTORY

Name _____ Date _____

Gender F _____ M _____ Age _____ I.D. _____

Agency _____ Education _____

Hand-Scored Profile

DECILE RANK

		Scale	RAW SCORE	1	2	3	4	5	6	7	8	9	10
PRIMARY SCALES	BENEFITS	1 SOCIALIM		0	1 2	3	4	5	6	7		8	9
		2 MENTALIM				0		1		2		3	4 5
		3 MANGMOOD		0	1 2	3	4	5	6		7		8
		4 MARICOPE				0		1	2	3	4	5	6 8
	STYLES	5 GREGARUS		0 1	2	3	4	5	6		7	8	10
		6 COMPULSV			0	1	2	3	4	5	6	7	8
		7 SUSTAIND		0 1	2	3	4	5	6	7	8	9 10	11 12
	CONSEQUENCES	8 LCONTROL		0 1	2 3 4	5	6	7	8	9	10 11	12 13	14 18
		9 ROLEMALA		0	1	2	3	4	5	6	7	8	9 10	11 13
		10 DELIRIUM			0		1	2	3	4	5 6 7	8 9	10 12 13
		11 HANGOVER		0	1	2 3	4	5	6		7	8	9 11
		12 MARIPROB			0 1		2	3	4		5		6
	CONCERNS AND ACKNOWLEDGMENTS	13 QUANTITY		0 1	2	3	4	5	6	7	8	9 10	11 12
		14 GUILTWOR		0	1 2 3	4	5	6	7		8		9
		15 HELPBEFR			0		1		2	3	4	5	6 9
		16 RECEPTIV	6	12 13	14	15	16	17		18	19	20	21
		17 AWARENES	2	4 5	6 8	9 10	11	12	13	14	15	16	17

SECOND ORDER FACTOR SCALES

	Scale	1	10	20	30	40	50	60	70	80	90	99
A	ENHANCED	1 2	3 4	5	6	7	8	9	10 11	12	13 14	17
B	OBSESSED	1 2	3 4	5	6 7	8	9	10 11	12 13 14	15	16 17	19
C	DISRUPT 1	2 4 6	7 8 10	11 12 13	14 15 16	17 18 19	20 21 22	23 24 25 26	27 28 29 30	32 34	35 37 39	48
D	DISRUPT 2	0 1 2	3 4	5	6 7	8	9	10	11	12	13 14	17
E	ANXCONCN	0 1 3	4 7 8	9 10 11	12 13	14	15 16 17	18	19	20	21	23
F	RECPAWAR	10 14	17 18 19 21 22	23 24 25	26 27	28	29	30	31	32 33	34 35 36	38
GENERAL G	ALCINVOL	1 5	9 10 14	20 21 24 25	27 28 30	32 33 34	36 37	39 40 41	43 44 45 46	49 50 53	55 56 58 60	68

PERCENTILE: 1 10 20 30 40 50 60 70 80 90 99

NCS™

Product Number 48014

CD

ALCOHOL USE INVENTORY (AUI)
SAMPLE COMPUTER PROFILE REPORT

AUI

Alcohol Use Inventory

Profile Report

ID Number 10101011

Sample

Female

Age 32

Married

13 Years of Education

Outpatient (Public, incl. VA)

1/01/97

DEMOGRAPHIC INFORMATION

ID No:	10101011	Ethnic group:	white
Date:	1/01/97	Years of education:	13
Age:	32	Marital status:	Married
Gender:	Female	Employment status:	Unemployed

Employed during the last 6 months:	No
Usual occupation:	Clerical Worker
Alcohol treatment in immediate family:	Yes
Age drinking interfered with daily living:	20-29
Treatment setting:	Outpatient (public, incl. VA)
Clinician Reported DSM code:	303.90
No. of previous inpatient treatments:	1-2
No. of previous outpatient treatments:	3-5

DURATION AND FREQUENCY OF USE OF ALCOHOL

Alcohol consumed:	Beer	Wine	Liquor
last 24 hr. period	11 - 15 cans	None	None
usual 24 hr. period	11 - 15 cans	None	None
most in 24 hr. period	16 or more cans	1 - 3 glasses	1 pint - 1 quart

No. of days/month alcohol used in past 3 months: 20
No. of days/month alcohol used when using alcohol most: 30

REPORTED USE AND PROBLEMS WITH DRUGS

Drugs	Use Over Past 12 Months	Problem With Recent Use
Caffeine	Very much use	Minor problem
Nicotine	Very much use	Moderate problem
Alcohol	Much use	Major problem
Marijuana/Hashish	No use	No use or no problem
Tranquilizers	Some use	Minor problem
Barbiturates	No use	No use or no problem
Amphetamines	No use	No use or no problem
Cocaine	No use	No use or no problem
Opiates	No use	No use or no problem
Hallucinogens	No use	No use or no problem

	No. Omit	Raw Score	Decile Rank
			1　2　3　4　5　6　7　8　9　10
PRIMARY SCALES			
Benefits			
1. SOCIALIM	0	8	
2. MENTALIM	0	1	
3. MANGMOOD	0	6	
4. MARICOPE	0	6	
Styles			
5. GREGARUS	0	7	
6. COMPULSV	0	1	
7. SUSTAIND	0	4	
Consequences			
8. LCONTROL	0	12	
9. ROLEMALA	0	6	
10. DELIRIUM	0	2	
11. HANGOVER	0	6	
12. MARIPROB	0	4	
Concerns and Acknowledgements			
13. QUANTITY	0	4	
14. GUILTWOR	0	8	
15. HELPBEFR	0	6	
16. RECEPTIV	0	11	
17. AWARENES	0	12	
SECOND ORDER FACTOR SCALES			
A. ENHANCED	0	12	
B. OBSESSED	0	4	
C. DISRUPT1	0	16	
D. DISRUPT2	0	7	
E. ANXCONCN	0	19	
F. RECPAWAR	0	23	
GENERAL ALCOHOL INVOLVEMENT SCALE			
G. ALCINVOL	0	33	

	No. Omit	Raw Score	Percentile
			10　20　30　40　50　60　70　80　90　100

The client did not omit or double-mark any responses to the administered items.

Critical Items
The following items were answered in a way that is often considered to be critical for understanding extreme conditions or particular circumstances.

Item No.	Response	Critical Information

Duration Of Drinking

28	B	Binge drinking--goes on wagon
66	B	Alternates between heavy use and no use

Disruption(s) In Behavioral Control

11	D	Unemployed more than three months in past year due to drinking
87	C	Reports several citations for drunken driving
199	C	Have smashed/broken objects when drinking several times

Disruption(s) In Mentation

29	D	Reports having had blackouts
143	C	Reports long, severe blackouts

Physical Withdrawal Symptom(s)

89	C	Reports history of drinking-related tachycardia
108	C	Reports history of diaphoresis after drinking several times
165	B	Reports history of chills or sweats when sobering up

Physical Problem(s) Related To Drinking Or When Sober

52	B	Reports history of numbness or tingling of hands, fingers, feet, toes more than a couple of times for a day or more at a time
71	D	Difficulty keeping balance when sober
109	B	Reports history of coughing up blood or blood in stools
127	D	Reports history of drinking-related gastrointestinal symptoms

Prior Treatment

112	B	Has been attending Alcoholics Anonymous
190	B	Has been in a detoxification center to sober up

ITEM RESPONSES

1: 1	2: 1	3: 2	4: 2	5: 1	6: 1	7: 1	8: 2	9: 1	10: 3
11: 4	12: 3	13: 1	14: 4	15: 1	16: 1	17: 2	18: 4	19: 4	20: 2
21: 2	22: 1	23: 1	24: 2	25: 1	26: 1	27: 1	28: 2	29: 4	30: 2
31: 1	32: 2	33: 2	34: 5	35: 2	36: 1	37: 3	38: 2	39: 2	40: 1
41: 2	42: 1	43: 2	44: 2	45: 1	46: 2	47: 4	48: 2	49: 1	50: 1
51: 2	52: 2	53: 1	54: 2	55: 2	56: 3	57: 3	58: 2	59: 1	60: 2
61: 1	62: 2	63: 1	64: 1	65: 2	66: 2	67: 2	68: 2	69: 1	70: 1
71: 4	72: 1	73: 2	74: 1	75: 3	76: 1	77: 2	78: 1	79: 2	80: 1
81: 2	82: 1	83: 1	84: 1	85: 2	86: 2	87: 3	88: 1	89: 3	90: 1
91: 1	92: 2	93: 2	94: 2	95: 3	96: 2	97: 1	98: 2	99: 2	100: 2
101: 2	102: 1	103: 1	104: 2	105: 2	106: 1	107: 1	108: 3	109: 2	110: 1
111: 2	112: 2	113: 3	114: 3	115: 2	116: 2	117: 2	118: 1	119: 1	120: 4
121: 2	122: 2	123: 1	124: 2	125: 1	126: 1	127: 4	128: 1	129: 3	130: 2
131: 3	132: 2	133: 4	134: 2	135: 3	136: 2	137: 2	138: 3	139: 1	140: 3
141: 2	142: 2	143: 3	144: 1	145: 1	146: 2	147: 2	148: 2	149: 2	150: 2
151: 2	152: 2	153: 2	154: 2	155: 3	156: 2	157: 1	158: 2	159: 2	160: 1
161: 2	162: 1	163: 1	164: 4	165: 2	166: 3	167: 1	168: 2	169: 1	170: 2
171: 2	172: 4	173: 2	174: 4	175: 2	176: 2	177: 2	178: 2	179: 4	180: 1
181: 1	182: 3	183: 4	184: 2	185: 3	186: 1	187: 3	188: 4	189: 1	190: 2
191: 4	192: 4	193: 4	194: 2	195: 1	196: 1	197: 1	198: 3	199: 3	200: 3
201: 2	202: 3	203: 4	204: 3	205: 1	206: 2	207: 1	208: 3	209: 2	210: 2
211: 2	212: 2	213: 2	214: 1	215: 2	216: 2	217: 3	218: 2	219: 2	220: 2
221: 2	222: 1	223: 1	224: 2	225: 3	226: 2	227: 2	228: 2		

End of Report.

DRIVING ASSESSMENT SURVEY (DAS)

DRIVING ASSESSMENT SURVEY (DAS)

Kenneth W. Wanberg and David Timken
Authors

PART I: PERSONAL DATA
(To be Completed by Test Taker)

NAME:	DATE:	PROGRAM:

GENDER: [ ] Female   [ ] Male   AGE   YEARS OF SCHOOLING COMPLETED

MARITAL STATUS: [ ] Never Married   [ ] Married   [ ] Remarried   [ ] Separated
[ ] Divorced   [ ] Widowed

EMPLOYMENT STATUS: [ ] Full Time   [ ] Part Time   [ ] Student   [ ] Housespouse
[ ] Retired   [ ] Disabled   [ ] Unemployed   [ ] Other_____

USUAL OCCUPATION: [ ] Skilled Laborer   [ ] Clerical and Office Worker
[ ] Skilled Craftsperson   [ ] Manager   [ ] Professional
[ ] Salesperson   [ ] Other_____

ETHNICITY: [ ] African American   [ ] Anglo American   [ ] Asian American
[ ] Hispanic American   [ ] Native American   [ ] Other_____

PART II: INFORMATION AND INSTRUCTIONS ON THE USE OF THIS SURVEY

This survey contains a number of statements that describe the various approaches that people take, and the attitudes that people have, towards driving a motor vehicle. You are asked to read each question carefully and then choose the answer that best describes how the statement applies to you. You are asked to be as accurate in your answers as you can - that is, choose the answer that best fits you. In this way, the results of this survey can be used to provide you with information most helpful to you. Once you have chosen the answer of your choice, circle the letter corresponding to your choice. IN ORDER FOR YOUR RESULTS TO BE VALID, YOU ARE ASKED TO ANSWER ALL QUESTIONS.

Your responses will be kept strictly confidential, and any information release about your responses must be only upon your written consent.

You may now begin to complete this survey by beginning with question one below.

PART III: DRIVING ASSESSMENT SURVEY QUESTIONS

1. I like driving in heavy heavy traffic.
   a. Never
   b. Seldom
   c. Often
   d. Very often

2. When driving at high speeds I feel powerful.
   a. Never
   b. Seldom
   c. Often
   d. Very often

3. I have owned vehicles with high horsepower engines.
   a. Never
   b. Seldom
   c. Often
   c. Very often

4. I have chased drivers who annoy me.
   a. Never
   b. Seldom
   c. Often
   d. Very often

5. I feel powerful behind the wheel.
   a. Never
   b. Seldom
   c. Often
   d. Very often

6. I have participated in sports such as auto racing, or hang gliding or sky driving.
   a. Never
   b. A few times
   c. Often
   d. Very often

7. High speed driving gives me a sense of power.
   a. Never
   b. Sometimes
   c. Often
   d. Very often

8. I have driven motor-cycles at high speed.
   a. Never
   b. Sometimes
   c. Often
   d. Very often

9. Beating other drivers away from intersections is fun.
   a. Never
   b. Sometimes
   c. Often
   d. Very often

Please go to the next page

1

1

10. I am a driver who likes to stay ahead of or out in front of traffic.
    a. Not true
    b. Somewhat true
    c. Usually true
    d. Always true

11. I exceed the speed limit if road conditions are safe.
    a. Not true
    b. Sometimes true
    c. Usually true
    d. Always true

12. I have tried to beat a red light.
    a. Never
    b. Seldom
    c. Often
    d. Very often.

13. When other drivers do stupid things, I lose my temper.
    a. Never
    b. Seldom
    c. Often
    d. Very often

14. I am easily provoked by other drivers when I am driving.
    a. Never
    b. Seldom
    c. Often
    d. Very often

15. I give the finger to other drivers
    a. Never
    b. Seldom
    c. Often
    d. Very often

16. I have received a traffic ticket when I have been emotionally upset.
    a. Never
    b. Once
    c. Twice
    d. Three or more times

17. I have a hard time thinking about my driving when I am upset.
    a. Never
    b. Once in a while
    c. Quite often
    d. All the time

18. I have tried to beat trains at crossings.
    a. Never
    b. Seldom
    c. Often
    d. Very often

19. I drive fast and take my chances on getting caught.
    a. Never
    b. Sometimes
    c. Often
    d. Very Often

20. I dodge and weave through traffic.
    a. Never
    b. Seldom
    c. Often
    d. Very often

21. There are times when I have felt that I could easily kill another driver.
    a. Never
    b. Seldom
    c. Often
    d. Very often

22. I swear out loud or cuss under my breath at other drivers.
    a. Never
    b. Seldom
    c. Often
    d. Very often

23. It is hard to control my temper when driving.
    a. Never
    b. Seldom
    c. Often
    d. Very often

24. It annoys me when the light turns red just as I get to the intersection.
    a. Never
    b. Sometimes
    c. Often
    d. Very often

25. I find myself in a hurry when I drive.
    a. Never
    b. Seldom
    c. Often
    d. Very often

26. I pass other drivers when not in a hurry.
    a. Never
    b. Seldom
    c. Often
    d. Very often

27. I have taken a risk when driving just for the sake of it.
    a. Never
    b. Seldom
    c. Often
    d. Very often

28. I have outrun other drivers.
    a. Never
    b. Seldom
    c. Often
    d. Very often

2

29. I retaliate if the driver behind me has his bright lights in my rear view mirror.
    a. Never
    b. Seldom
    c. Often
    d. Very often

30. When angry, I have flashed my lights at drivers.
    a. Never
    b. Seldom
    c. Often
    d. Very often

31. I honk the horn when I am angry.
    a. Never
    b. Sometimes
    c. Often
    d. Very often

3

32. I have had accidents or received tickets when under stress.
    a. Never
    b. Once
    c. Two to three times
    d. More than three times

33. I tend to pay less attention when driving while I am angry.
    a. Incorrect
    b. Partly correct
    c. Usually correct
    d. Always correct

Please go to the next page

2

34. When I have had a bad day, I will drive to unwind.
   a. Never
   b. Seldom
   c. Often
   d. Very often

35. When I have problems such as marriage, job, finances, I find myself taking a drive.
   a. Never
   b. Seldom
   c. Often
   d. Very often

36. I have passed on a double yellow line.
   a. Never
   b. A few times
   c. Quite often
   d. Often

37. How many traffic citations have you received in your lifetime?
   a. Only one
   b. Two to three
   c. Four to five
   d. More than five

38. Driver's training should be required in order to get a drivers license.
   a. Do not agree
   b. Somewhat agree
   c. Mostly agree
   d. Completely agree

39. Driving skills are important when it comes to safety.
   a. Do not agree
   b. Somewhat agree
   c. Mostly agree
   d. Completely agree

40. Better driving training and skills would reduce accidents.
   a. Do not agree
   b. Somewhat agree
   c. Mostly agree
   d. Completely agree

41. I could benefit from a driving skills and safety class.
   a. No, not at all
   b. Maybe a little bit
   c. Yes, most likely
   d. Yes, definitely

42. When I am upset, I am less cautious when driving.
   a. Never
   b. Sometimes
   c. Often
   d. Very often

43. I have found myself driving fast without realizing it.
   a. Never
   b. Seldom
   c. Often
   d. Very often

44. It calms me down if I am able to drive when I am upset.
   a. Never
   b. Seldom
   c. Often
   d. Very often

45. I am able to relax and reduce tension while driving.
   a. Never
   b. Sometimes
   c. Often
   d. Very often

46. I leave extra early for work or other destinations when the roads are bad.
   a. Hardly ever
   b. Sometimes
   c. Usually I do
   d. I always do

47. I keep a safe distance from cars in front of me.
   a. Some of the time
   b. Much of the time
   c. Almost always
   d. Always

48. I use my turn signal.
   a. Sometimes
   b. Quite often
   c. Almost always
   d. Every time I turn

49. I rebel against authority.
   a. Never
   b. Once in awhile
   c. Quite often
   d. Often

50. When mad while driving, I am less cautious
   a. Never
   b. Sometimes
   c. Often
   d. Very often

[ ] 4

51. I forget about pressures when I am driving.
   a. Never
   b. Seldom
   c. Often
   d. Very often

52. I have driven to "blow off steam" after having an argument.
   a. Never
   b. Sometimes
   c. Often
   d. Very often

53. I go driving when I feel depressed.
   a. Never
   b. Sometimes
   c. Often
   d. Very often

[ ] 5

54. When driving long distances, I take breaks for safety reasons.
   a. I usually do not
   b. Sometimes
   c. Quite often
   d. Routinely

55. I come to a complete stop at stop signs.
   a. Sometimes I do
   b. Usually I do
   c. I almost always do
   d. I always do

56. I use seat belts.
   a. Hardly ever
   b. Sometimes
   c. Usually I do
   d. Every time I drive or ride

57. I don't follow rules which I think are silly or don't make sense.
   a. No, not at all
   b. Yes, sometimes
   c. Yes, quite often
   d. Yes, often

Please go to the next page

58. At school or at work I break the rules in order to finish quicker.
   a. Never
   b. Sometimes
   c. Often
   d. Very often

59. I don't like police officers.
   a. Not true
   b. Somewhat true
   c. Usually true
   d. Always true

60. I have driven after drinking if I really had to get home.
   a. Never
   b. Sometimes
   c. Often
   d. Very often

61. I drink at bars.
   a. Never
   b. Sometimes
   c. Often
   d. Very often

62. When it comes to parties, I really like to live it up.
   a. No, not at all
   b. Yes, at times
   c. Usually
   d. Almost always

63. When it comes to the bottom line, nobody tells me what to do.
   a. Not true
   b. Somewhat true
   c. Usually true
   d. Always true

64. I have been in fights or brawls.
   a. Never
   b. Once or twice
   c. Several times
   d. Many times

65. After participating in sports, I will drink beer with my friends.
   a. Never
   b. Sometimes
   c. Often
   d. Very often

66. I enjoy going to parties where no one makes a big deal about heavy drinking.
   a. Never
   b. Sometimes
   c. Often
   d. Very often

67. I have had trouble because I don't follow rules.
   a. Never
   b. Seldom
   c. Often
   d. Very often

68. I have been tattooed.
   a. Never
   b. Once
   c. Twice
   d. Three or more times

☐ 6

69. I stay out all night and drink.
   a. Never
   b. Seldom
   c. Often
   d. Very often

70. I have been going to parties such as keggers on weekends.
   a. No, never
   b. Less than one weekend a month
   c. One to two weekends a month
   d. Three or more weekends a month

☐ 7   ☐ G

PART IV: PROFILE

SCALE NAME	RAW SCORE	Low			Low-medium		High-medium			High			NUMBER IN NORM SAMPLE
		1	2	3	4	DECILE RANK 5	6	7	8	9	10		
1. POWER			0		1	2	3	4	5	6 7 8 9 19			392
2. HAZARD		0	1	2	3	4 5	6	7	8 9 10 11 13 21				393
3. IMPULSE		0	1	2	3	4	5	6	7 8 9 10 18				393
4. STRESS		0	1	2	3	4	5	6	7 8 9 11 15				395
5. RELAX		0	1 2	3	4	5	6	7 8 9 10 15					395
6. REBEL		0	1	2	3	4	5 6 7 8 17						393
7. CONVIVIAL		0 1 2	3	4	5	6	7	8 9 10 11 12 22					395
G. GENRISK		0 1 2 3 4 5 6 7	8 9	10 11	12 13 14 15 16 17 18 19 21 22 23 27 42								385

0   10   20   30   40   50   60   70   80   90   100
PERCENTILE

Authors: K. W. Wanberg and D. Timken   0195   Copyright (c) 1991   K. W. Wanberg and D. Timken

4

DRIVING ASSESSMENT SURVEY - DAS

SCORING PROCEDURES

1. General Scoring Scheme:

    a = 0,   b = 1, c = 2,   d = 3.

2. Scoring procedure for scales:

    Scale 1: Power - Items: 1 - 8.

    Scale 2: Hazard - Items: 10-12, 18-20 and 26-28.

    Scale 3: Impulse - Items: 13-14, 21-23, 29-31.

    Scale 4: Stress - Items: 24-25, 32-33, 42, 50.

    Scale 5: Relax - Items: 43-45, 51-53.

    Scale 6: Rebel - Items 58-59, 63-64, 67-68.

    Scale 7: Convivial - Items: 60-62, 65-66, 69-70.

    Genrisk: Items: Those items highlighted on the instrument - 2, 5, 7, 9, 10, 11, 12, 13, 14,

    15, 19, 20, 22, 24, 26, 27, 28, 43, 62.

POWER: measures the extent to which the respondent reports feeling power when driving a motor vehicle.

HAZARD: indicates the degree to which an individual takes part in hazardous or high-risk driving behavior.

IMPULSE: indicates impulsive and temperamental driving behaviors and attitudes.

STRESS: indicates the person feels irritability, stress and anger when driving.

RELAX: indicates that driving is used as a means to relax and calm down.

REBEL: measures rebellion toward authority and rules.

CONVIVIAL: measures convivial and gregarious drinking.

GENRISK: is a general and overall measure of driving risk and hazard.

The normative reference group is a sample of 395 alcohol and other drug related driving offenders being evaluated for treatment services. There are several different normative samples available for the DAS.

The Driving Assessment Survey is copyrighted. The instrument and user's guide are distributed by the Center for Addictions Research and Evaluation (CARE), 5640 Ward Road, Suite 140, Arvada, Colorado 80002, (303) 421-1261.

DRUG USE SELF REPORT (DUSR) PROFILE

DRUG USE SELF REPORT INDIVIDUAL PROFILE

Name_____   Date_____   I. D. Number_____

Agency: _____   Gender: [ ] Female   [ ] Male   Age:_____

Ethnic Group:

[ ] African American   [ ] Anglo American   [ ] Asian American   [ ] Hispanic American   [ ] Other _____

SCALE NAME	RAW SCORE	DECILE RANK	IN NORM SAMPLE
		Low 1 ¦ 2 ¦ 3 ¦ Low Medium 4 ¦ 5 ¦ High Medium 6 ¦ 7 ¦ 8 ¦ High 9 ¦ 10	
1. ALCOHOL		1 2 3 5¦ 6 7 8¦ 9 10 11¦12 14 15¦16 17 18¦19 20 21¦22 23 24¦ 25 ¦26 28 29¦30 31 34	655
2. MARIJUANA		1 2 3¦ 4 5 ¦ 6 7 ¦ 8 9 10¦ 11 12¦ 13 ¦14 15 16¦ 17 18¦19 20 21¦22 25 33	566
3. COCAINE		1 2 ¦ 3 4 ¦ 5 6 ¦ 7 8 10¦11 12 13¦14 15 16¦17 18 ¦19 20 22¦23 25 26¦27 29 34	517
4. AMPHETAME		1 ¦ 2 3 ¦ 4 ¦ 5 6 ¦ 7 8 ¦ 9 10 ¦11 12 13¦14 15 17¦18 21 24¦25 28 34	454
5. HALLUCIGN		1 ¦ 2 ¦ 3 ¦ 4 ¦ 5 6¦ 7 ¦8 9 ¦10 11 ¦12 13 14¦15 18 32	410
6. INHALANTS		¦ 1 ¦ 2 ¦ ¦ 3 ¦ 4 ¦ 5 6 ¦ 7 8 ¦ 9 11 13¦14 17 34	256
7. HEROIN		1 2 3 ¦ 4 5 6 8¦ 9 13 15¦16 19 20¦21 22 23¦ 24 25 ¦ 26 27¦ 28 29 ¦ 30 31 ¦32 33 34	372
8. OPIATES		1 2 ¦ 3 4 ¦4 6 ¦ 7 8 9¦ 10 11 ¦12 13 15¦ 16 17¦18 20 22¦23 25 28¦29 31 34	412
9. BARBITUAT		1 2 ¦ 3 ¦ 4 ¦ 5 ¦ 6 7¦ 8 ¦ 9 10 11¦12 14 16¦17 19 21¦22 27 34	377
10. TRANQUIL		1 ¦ 2 3¦ 4 ¦ 5 6 ¦ 7 8 ¦ 9 10¦11 12 14¦15 16 18¦19 20 23¦24 29 34	376
11. EXTENT		0 1 2 3 ¦ 4 5 ¦6 7 8 9¦10 11 12¦13 15 16¦17 18 19¦20 22 23¦24 25 26¦27 30 32¦33 36 40	668
12. SUSTAINED		0 1 2 3¦4 5 6 7¦8 9 11¦12 13 15¦16 17 18¦19 21 23¦24 25 27¦28 30 33¦34 36 40¦41 47 80	661
13. RECENTUSE		0 1 2 3¦ 4 5 ¦ 6 7 ¦ 8 9 10¦11 12 ¦ 13 14 ¦15 16 17¦18 19 20¦21 22 24¦25 28 40	663
14. BENEFITS		0 1 ¦ 2 3 ¦ 4 5 ¦ 6 7¦ 8 9 ¦10 11 12¦13 14 15¦16 18 19¦20 23 25¦30 33 60	663
15. PROBLEMS		0 1 2 ¦ 3 4 5¦ 6 7 ¦ 8 9 10¦11 12 13¦14 16 19¦20 22 26¦27 29 34¦35 41 48¦49 120	633
16. DISRUPT		0 1 3 5¦6 11 15¦16 21 26¦27 30 34¦35 38 41¦42 45 47¦48 50 53¦54 57 59¦60 63 65¦66 70 80	635
17. DEPENDENT		0 1 2 ¦ 3 5 6 ¦7 8 ¦ 9 10¦ 11 ¦12 13 ¦ 14 ¦15 16¦ 17 ¦ 18	652
		10 20 30 40 50 60 70 80 90 99	
		PERCENTILE	

Normative group: 670 adult admissions into a public intensive outpatient or inpatient residential care for problems related to alcoholism and drug abuse. Norms on the drug category scales (Scales 1 through 1)) are based only on patients that use drugs in the respective category.

FOLLOW-UP ASSESSMENT QUESTIONNAIRE - FAQ

FOLLOW-UP ASSESSMENT QUESTIONNAIRE - FAQ
STRATEGIES FOR SELF-IMPROVEMENT AND CHANGE
(To be completed in an interview with clients)

Authors
Kenneth W. Wanberg and Harvey B. Milkman

Name of Client:	Date interview completed:
Age: Gender:[ ] M [ ] F	Ethnic Group: [ ] A [ ] B [ ] H [ ] NA [ ] Asian
Provider Name:	Agency:
Date Admitted to SCC:	Discharge Date:
Location of interview:	Interviewer name:

INFORMATION TO THE RESPONDENT

The following questions have to do with the Strategies for Self-Improvement and Change (SSC) that you participated in during this past year. Some questions have do with what you remember about the program and what you think was most helpful to you in the program. Other questions have to do with your use of substances before and after the program. Still other questions have to do with how you see yourself, your family and your friends. Your answers to these questions are very important in helping us to understand how our program is doing. Please be as honest as you can in answering these questions. What you tell us will be treated as strictly confidential according to the laws of the State in which you live. Thank you.

As you answer the following questions, remember that **SSC refers to the Strategies for Self-Improvement and Change** Program that you attended during this past year.

1. As to drug and alcohol treatment you received before you took part in the Strategies for Self-Improvement and Change:

    a. How many different treatment programs all together have you been in_____?

    b. During your life-time:

        Total number of individual drug/alcohol treatment sessions_____.

        Total number of group drug/alcohol treatment sessions_____.

        Total number of inpatient or residential drug/alcohol treatment days_____.

        Longest time in months that you went without using alcohol_____.

        Longest time in months that you went without using other drugs_____.

    b. During the time that you were in SSC:

        Longest time in months that you went without using alcohol_____.

        Longest time in months that you went without using other drugs_____.

2. Did your relationship with your family (spouse, children, parents, etc.)

    ___a. get worse during the SSC program.
    ___b. stayed the same as it was before SSC.
    ___c. get better during SSC.

3. Was support from your family members

    ___a. less during SSC.
    ___b. the same as before SSC.
    ___c. much more during SSC.

4. Did your control over your feelings and emotions

    ___a. get worse during SSC.
    ___b. stay the same as before SSC.
    ___c. get much better during SSC.

5. As to your thoughts of wanting to drink or use drugs,

    ___a. they increased during SSC.
    ___b. they stayed about the same as before SSC.
    ___c. they definitely decreased during SSC.

6. As to your thoughts of wanting to commit a crime,

    ___a. they increased during SSC.
    ___b. they stayed about the same as before SSC.
    ___c. they definitely decreased during SSC.

7. Did your control over your thoughts about wanting to drink or use drugs

    ___a. get worse during SSC.
    ___b. stay the same as before SSC.
    ___c. get much better during SSC.

8. Did your control over your thoughts about wanting to take part in criminal conduct

    ___a. get worse during SSC.
    ___b. stay the same as before SSC.
    ___c. get much better during SSC.

9. As to your urges or cravings to drink or use drugs,

    ___a. they increased during SSC.
    ___b. they stayed about the same as before SSC.
    ___c. they definitely decreased during SSC.

10. As to your desires to commit a crime,

    ___a. they increased during SSC.
    ___b. they stayed about the same as before SSC.
    ___c. they definitely decreased during SSC.

11. Did your control over your actions and behavior

    ___a. get worse during SSC.
    ___b. stay about the same as before SSC.
    ___c. get much better during SSC.

12. Did the time you spent with friends who get into trouble with the law

    ___a. increase or was more during SSC.
    ___b. stay about the same as before SSC.
    ___c. decrease or was less during SSC.

13. Did the time you spent with friends who use alcohol or other drugs

    ___a. increase or was more during SSC.
    ___b. stay about the same as before SSC.
    ___c. decrease or was less during SSC.

14. Was staying out of trouble with the law

    ___a. harder for you during SSC.
    ___b. about the same as before SSC.
    ___c. much easier during SSC during SSC.

15. Did you find staying away from using alcohol or other drugs

    ___a. much harder during SSC.
    ___b. no more difficult than before SSC.
    ___c. much easier during SSC.

16. Did your problems with alcohol use

    ___a. increase or got worse during SSC.
    ___b. stay the same as before SSC.
    ___c. decrease or got better during SSC.

17. As to being satisfied with your job and work,

    ___a. I was less satisfied with my job and work during SSC.
    ___b. My satisfaction with my job was about the same as before SSC.
    ___c. I was more satisfied with my job during SSC.

18. During the time that you were in the SSC program, did you use alcohol?

    ___a. No, not at all.
    ___b. A few times.
    ___c. Many times.
    ___d. Almost all of the time.

19. During the time that you were in SSC, did you use marijuana (pot)?

    ___a. No, not at all.
    ___b. A few times.
    ___c. Many times.
    ___d. Almost all of the time.

20. During the time that you were in SSC, did you use drugs other than alcohol or marijuana (pot)?

    ___a. No, not at all.
    ___b. A few times.
    ___c. Many times.
    ___d. Almost all of the time.

21. During the time you were in SSC, did you violate your probation, parole or the rules of your prison facility?

    ___a. No, not once.
    ___b. One or two times.
    ___c. Three or four times.
    ___d. More than four times.

22. During the time that you were in SSC, did you do things that would be considered as violating or breaking the law?

    ___a. No, not once.
    ___b. One.
    ___c. Two or more.

Please answer these questions as to your use of these drugs DURING THE PAST THREE MONTHS.

	Never used	One to 10 times	11-25 times	than 26-50 times	More than 50 times
23. Number of times intoxicated or drunk on alcohol (beer, wine, hard liquor, mixed drinks).	a	b	c	d	e
24. Marijuana (pot, hashish, hash, THC).	a	b	c	d	e
25. Cocaine (coke, snow, crack, rock, blow).	a	b	c	d	e
26. Amphetamines/stimulants (speed, uppers, bennies, diet pills, crystal, black beauties, white crosses, pep pills).	a	b	c	d	e
27. Hallucinogens (LSD, acid, peyote, mushrooms, mescaline, PCP, angel dust).	a	b	c	d	e
28. Inhalants (rush, gasoline, paint, glue, lighter fluid, nitrous oxide).	a	b	c	d	e
29. Heroin (horse, H, smack, junk).	a	b	c	d	e
30. Other opiates or pain killers used for non-medical reasons (codeine, opium, morphine, percodans, dilaudid, demerol, methadone).	a	b	c	d	e
31. Barbiturates/sedatives used for non-medical reasons (seconal, nembutal, amytal, doriden, quaaludes,dalmane, placidyl, sleeping medicines, blues, reds, yellows, ludes, etc.).	a	b	c	d	e
32. Tranquilizers used for non-medical reasons (librium, valium, ativan, xanax, serax, miltown, equanil, meprobamates).	a	b	c	d	e

	Did not smoke	Up to half pack a day	About a pack a day	More than a pack a day
33. Cigarettes (tobacco)	a	b	c	d

Now as to your plans in the future:	For sure No	Maybe no	Maybe yes	For sure yes
34. Do you want to use alcohol?	a	b	c	d
35. Do you want to use drugs other than alcohol?	a	b	c	d
36. Do you plan to use alcohol?	a	b	c	d
37. Do you plan to use drugs other than alcohol?	a	b	c	d

4

How do you see each of the following sessions or parts of the SSC program as to how they have been helpful to you in making positive changes in your alcohol and drug use problems and your criminal conduct.

	Do not remember	Not helpful	Somewhat helpful	Helpful	Very helpful
38. Sessions on building trust and harmony.	a	b	c	d	e
39. Sessions on understand how we change.	a	b	c	d	e
40. Understanding the role of thinking in making improvement and change.	a	b	c	d	e
41. Understanding the role of acting or behaving in making improvement and change.	a	b	c	d	e
42. Learning about alcohol and drugs.	a	b	c	d	e
43. Sessions on the cycles of alcohol and drug addiction.	a	b	c	d	e
44. Learning communication tools and skills.	a	b	c	d	e
45. Sessions on self-disclosure and sharing.	a	b	c	d	e
46. Sessions on relapse and recidivism prevention.	a	b	c	d	e
47. The sessions on assessment and building your Master Assessment Plan.	a	b	c	d	e
48. Involving your spouse and/or family.	a	b	c	d	e
49. Coping and social skills training.	a	b	c	d	e
50. Recognizing and handling your negative thoughts.	a	b	c	d	e
51. Session on errors in logic and thinking.	a	b	c	d	e
52. Sessions on managing cravings and urges.	a	b	c	d	e
53. Sessions on learning about high-risk situations that lead to alcohol/drug use and criminal conduct.	a	b	c	d	e
54. Session on assertiveness skills training.	a	b	c	d	e
55. Sessions on problem solving.	a	b	c	d	e
56. Sessions on handling anger, aggression and violence.	a	b	c	d	e
57. Sessions on handling guilt.	a	b	c	d	e
58. Sessions on developing close relationships.	a	b	c	d	e
59. Sessions on values and moral development.	a	b	c	d	e
60. Understanding and practicing empathy.	a	b	c	d	e
61. Being responsible in your community	a	b	c	d	e
62. Sessions on using critical reasoning.	a	b	c	d	e
63. Sessions on resolving conflicts.	a	b	c	d	e
64. Sessions on play and leisure time.	a	b	c	d	e
65. Sessions on role modeling and be a mentor for others.	a	b	c	d	e
66. Session on work and job issues.	a	b	c	d	e
67. The exercises in your workbook.	a	b	c	d	e

Now, please choose the answer that best fits the following questions.

		No not at all	Yes somewhat	Yes for sure
68.	Did you feel comfortable with your SSC provider or group leader?	a	b	c
69.	Did you feel your provider or group leader was understanding of your situation?	a	b	c
70.	Did you feel that your provider or group leader respected your cultural values?	a	b	c
71.	Was your provider or group leader there when you needed him or her?	a	b	c
72.	Do you think that some of your friends could be helped by the SSC program?	a	b	c

Now, overall..........

		No not at all	Somewhat helpful	Helpful	Very helpful
73.	Was the SSC program helpful to you?	a	b	c	d
74.	Was your Provider helpful to you?	a	b	c	d

Now at this time.................

		For sure No	Maybe no	Maybe yes	For sure yes
75.	Did you make life changes as a result of the SSC program?	a	b	c	d
76.	Do you have problems with alcohol or drug use?	a	b	c	d
77.	Do you need help with drug or alcohol problems at this time?	a	b	c	d

78. Rate the progress that you think you made while in the SSC program:

No Progress   Some Progress   Much Progress

1   2   3   4   5   6   7   8   9   10   11   12

79. Rate how you see your overall improvement.

No Improvement   Some Improvement   Much Improvement

1   2   3   4   5   6   7   8   9   10   11   12

Now, we want your opinion as to the SSC treatment program itself. Please answer each question by circling the letter under the answer of your choice.

		No	Sometimes	Most of the time	All the time
80.	Were the groups delivered on time?	a	b	c	d
81.	Did the leader follow the workbook?	a	b	c	d
82.	Were you satisfied with the program?	a	b	c	d
83.	Were you satisfied with your leader?	a	b	c	d
84.	Were your homework assignments helpful?	a	b	c	d

	No	Sometimes	Most of the time	All the time
85. Were the assignments difficult?	a	b	c	d
86. Overall, did you understand the ideas presented in the sessions?	a	b	c	d
87. Did the leader ask you things about yourself in the group?	a	b	c	d
88. Did you feel comfortable talking about your-self in the group?	a	b	c	d
89. Did you practice the coping and social skills in your group?	a	b	c	d
90. Did your leader build up your efforts to make changes in your life?	a	b	c	d
91. Did the leader follow the workbook?	a	b	c	d

92. What part of the program helped you the most?

_____

_____

93. What part of the program helped you the least?

_____

_____

94. What would you change about the program?

_____

_____

How?_____

END OF QUESTIONNAIRE

Follow-up Assessment Questionnaire - FAQ
Copyright (c) 1998, K. W. Wanberg and H. B. Milkman

LIFE SITUATION QUESTIONNAIRE (LSQ)

LIFE SITUATION QUESTIONNAIRE

Kenneth W. Wanberg
Author

NAME_____	DATE_____	BIRTH DATE_____	
AGE_____ GENDER: [ ] Female [ ] Male	YEARS OF SCHOOLING_____		
ETHNICITY: [ ] Anglo [ ] Black [ ] Hispanic [ ] Native Am. [ ] Asian			

INSTRUCTIONS ON THE USE OF THIS QUESTIONNAIRE

This questionnaire contains statements about how you see yourself. Part I of the questionnaire will ask you questions about your childhood and adolescence. Part II asks you questions about how you see yourself in the past six months. Be as honest as you can. This will help those who are working with you to understand your concerns and questions about yourself. For each question circle the letter under the answer that best fits you. The information that you give will be treated as strictly confidential and will only be used by the staff member or counselor working with you.

PART I: For each of the following statements, choose the answer that best fits how you see your childhood and adolescent years.

	No	A few times	A lot of times	All the time
1. Childhood family had money problems.	a	b	c	d
2. Was unhappy during childhood.	a	b	c	d
3. Parents had marital problems.	a	b	c	d
4. Problems getting along with parents.	a	b	c	d
5. Had problems in school.	a	b	c	d
6. Broke the law or had problems with the law.	a	b	c	d
7. Had emotional problems as a child.	a	b	c	d
8. Used alcohol or other drugs during your adolescent years.	a	b	c	d

PART II. Now choose the answer that best fits how each of the following statements applies to you during the past six months.

	No	Sometimes	A lot	All the time
9. Have had relationship problems.	a	b	c	d
10. Conflict with your spouse or intimate partner?	a	b	c	d
11. Have had family problems and conflicts.	a	b	c	d
12. Spouse or intimate partner has been unhappy?	a	b	c	d
13. Have been unhappy with your living situation.	a	b	c	d
14. Have been depressed or down in the dumps.	a	b	c	d
15. Have been anxious, stressed or tense.	a	b	c	d

1

		No	Sometimes	A lot	All the time
16.	Difficulty controlling your emotions.	a	b	c	d
17.	Have felt alone and isolated?	a	b	c	d
18.	Have had emotional problems.	a	b	c	d
19.	Problems with controlling your anger.	a	b	c	d
20.	Problems paying bills.	a	b	c	d
21.	Unhappy with your job or your work.	a	b	c	d
22.	Have had financial problems.	a	b	c	d
23.	Have been out of work.	a	b	c	d
24.	Have felt need for more education.	a	b	c	d
25.	Have lied or been untruthful.	a	b	c	d
26.	Have had problems with the law.	a	b	c	d
27.	Have been rebelling against authority.	a	b	c	d
28.	Have had difficult following rules.	a	b	c	d
29.	Have broken the law.	a	b	c	d
30.	Have argued or fought with others.	a	b	c	d
31.	Have been unable to control amount of alcohol used.	a	b	c	d
32.	Have used drugs other than alcohol.	a	b	c	d
33.	Have had problems with alcohol use.	a	b	c	d
34.	Have had problems with other drug use.	a	b	c	d
35.	People have been unhappy with my drinking.	a	b	c	d
36.	Need help for problems with alcohol or other drug use.	a	b	c	d
37.	Have felt tired and exhausted.	a	b	c	d
38.	Have had some minor health problems.	a	b	c	d
39.	Have had some major health problems.	a	b	c	d
40.	Have had medical help in past six months.	a	b	c	d
41.	Am worried about my health or medical condition.	a	b	c	d

42. Check any of the following areas that you feel you need help with at this time:

[ ] Marital relationships   [ ] Problems with the law   [ ] Parenting problems
[ ] Family relationships   [ ] More education/training   [ ] Finding a job
[ ] Job or work skills   [ ] Emotional problems   [ ] Managing anger
[ ] Finding social outlets   [ ] Managing depression   [ ] Managing stress
[ ] Problems with alcohol use [ ] Problems with drug use   [ ] Medical problems

END OF QUESTIONNAIRE. THANK YOU.

MOOD APPRAISAL QUESTIONNAIRE (MAQ)

MOOD APPRAISAL QUESTIONNAIRE (MAQ)
Author: Kenneth W. Wanberg

PERSONAL DATA INFORMATION

Name:_____ Date:_____ I.D.:_____

Gender: [ ] Male　[ ] Female　Age: _____　Years of Education:_____

Ethnic Group: [ ] Anglo　[ ] Black　[ ] Hispanic　[ ] Native America　[ ] Asian

Marital Status:　[ ] Never Married　[ ] Married　[ ] Separated
　　　　　　　　　[ ] Divorced　　　 [ ] Widowed

Number Times Married_____　Past counseling or therapy [ ] No　[ ] Yes

INSTRUCTIONS

This inventory contains a number of statements which will help you evaluate how you see yourself thinking, feeling and acting in various areas of your life. Please read each statement and then circle the letter under the response that best describes how the statement applies to you at this particular time in your life. Here is an example of a question:

A. How do you find answering questions about yourself?

Very difficult	difficult		easy	Very easy
a	b	c	d	e

Note that in some cases the middle response "c" has no particular description above it. In these cases, the "c" represents an "in between" response. In the question above, the "c" response would mean that is in between difficult and easy to answer questions about yourself. Choose only one answer for each statement. **Be sure you answer all questions in the questionnaire.**

LIFE PROBLEM SELF AREAS

RATE YOURSELF ON THE FOLLOWING AREAS AS TO HOW YOU SEE YOURSELF AT THIS TIME:

	No problems	Minor problems	Moderate problems	Serious problems	Very serious problems
1. Physical health	a	b	c	d	e
2. Getting along with others	a	b	c	d	e
3. Alcohol use	a	b	c	d	e
4. Use of other drugs	a	b	c	d	e
5. Areas of work or your job	a	b	c	d	e
6. Marriage or marriage type relationship	a	b	c	d	e
7. Emotional and mental health	a	b	c	d	e
8. Your physical health	a	b	c	d	e
9. Relationship with the law	a	b	c	d	e

NOW, PLEASE ANSWER THE QUESTIONS ON THE NEXT TWO PAGES

1

1. Regarding my basic life concerns, I am.....

Very worried	Worried		Carefree	Very carefree
a	b	c	d	e

2. With respect to my nerves, I am.....

Very tense	Tense		Relaxed	Very Relaxed
a	b	c	d	e

3. When I leave my home or house, I most often am.....

Very panicky	Panicky		In control	Very much in control
a	b	c	d	e

4. With regard to handling my life problems, I am.....

Very fearful	Fearful		Self-assured	Very self-assured
a	b	c	d	e

5. When I relate to or am talking with people, I am.....

Very uncomfortable	Uncomfortable		Comfortable	Very comfortable
a	b	c	d	e

6. When I am in crowds or groups of people, I am.....

Very uneasy	Uneasy		Unconcerned	Very Unconcerned
a	b	c	d	e

7. When I am without something to do, I find myself.....

Very restless	Restless		Satisfied	Very satisfied
a	b	c	d	e

8. With respect to focusing on a task or my job, I am.....

Easily distracted	Distracted		Attentive	Very Attentive
a	b	c	d	e

9. When I wake up in the morning, I am............

Very anxious	Anxious		Relaxed	Very Relaxed
a	b	c	d	e

____   ____   ____   ____   ____

PLEASE GO TO THE NEXT PAGE

10. Regarding my thoughts about the future, I am feeling.....

Very Discouraged	Discouraged		Hopeful	Very Hopeful
a	b	c	d	e

11. With regard to performing my work, I am feeling.....

Very incapable	Incapable		Capabale	Very Capable
a	b	c	d	e

12. As to my appetite, it is.....

Much less than usual	Less than usual	The same as usual	Higher than usual	Much higher than usual
a	b	c	d	e

13. My energy level at this time is.....

Much lower than usual	Lower than usual	The same as usual	Higher than usual	Much higher than usual
a	b	c	d	e

14. My sexual drive at this time is.....

Much lower than usual	Lower than usual	The same as usual	Higher than usual	Much higher than usual
a	b	c	d	e

15. With regard to my desire for living, I feel like.....

Not wanting to live	Somewhat not wanting to live		Wanting to live	Very much wanting to live
a	b	c	d	e

16. I would describe my emotions at this time as.....

Very sad	Sad		Happy	Very happy
a	b	c	d	e

17. Compared to my normal sleeping pattern, I am sleeping.....

Much less	Less	About the same	More	Much more
a	b	c	d	e

18. With respect to my feelings about myself, I feel.....

Very negative	Negative		Positive	Very Positive
a	b	c	d	e

____   ____   ____   ____   ____

END OF QUESTIONNAIRE

3

MOOD APPRAISAL WINDOW

NAME _____

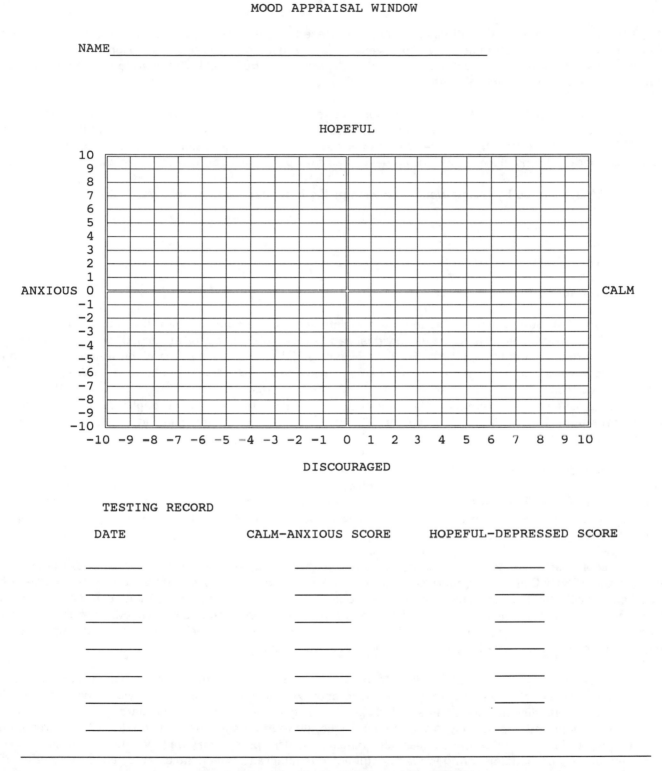

HOPEFUL

ANXIOUS

CALM

DISCOURAGED

TESTING RECORD

DATE	CALM-ANXIOUS SCORE	HOPEFUL-DEPRESSED SCORE
_____	_____	_____
_____	_____	_____
_____	_____	_____
_____	_____	_____
_____	_____	_____
_____	_____	_____
_____	_____	_____

Mood Appraisal Questionnaire (MAQ)
Copyright (c) 1989, 1998 K. W. Wanberg

Distributed by the Center for Addictions Research and Evaluation - CARE
5460 Ward Road, Suite 140, Arvada, Colorado 80002

BRIEF USERS GUIDE FOR THE MOOD APPRAISAL QUESTIONNAIRE
Kenneth W. Wanberg
Author

The Mood Appraisal Questionnaire (MAQ) is based on the measurement of two self-adjustment dimensions: calmness versus anxiety and hope versus discouragement. The first dimension is a measurement of anxiety and stress; the second is a measurement of depression. The MAQ is designed to provide a quick and crisp measurement of these two dimensions of adjustment.

Interpretation of the results of the questionnaire is based on scores which depart from the mid-range response for the particular items. The mid range response, a "c" for each question, indicates that the person falls in the middle of the items which measure calmness or stress, hope or depression. There are no current norms for this instrument. Norms are currently being developed for non-clinical and clinical samples.

The MAQ is scored by giving weights to each of the item responses as follows:

"a" response is given a -2 score;
"b" response is given a -1 score;
"c" response given a zero score;
"d" response given a +1 score;
"e" response given a +2 score.

For items 1 through 9, the "a" responses are summed and the sum placed in the scoring line the under the column of "a" responses. Thus, if the individual had two "a" responses for items 1 through 9, that would amount to a score of a negative 4 (-4). For the column of "b" responses, each is given a negative 1 score. Thus, if a person circled four "b" responses for items 1 through 9, that person would have a negative 4 score (-4). For the "c" responses, the person receives a zero for each c response; a positive 1 for each "d" response and a positive 2 for each "e" response. The same procedure is used for items 10 through 18. The columns are thus scored for items 1 through 9 and 10 through 18, and the sum of scores are placed at the bottom of the page on the designated lines.

The final scores are derived by algebraic summation. For items 1 through 9, the negative scores are added and the sum of the negative scores are subtracted from the positive scores. For example, for items 1 through 9, if the respondent had a sum of minus 2 (-2) on the "a" responses, a sum of minus 1 (-1) on the "b" responses, a positive 2 (+2) on the "d" responses and a positive 4 (+4) on the "e" responses, the total score for items 1 through 9 would be a positive 3 (+3).

The scores are summed for both sets of items (1 through 9) and (10 through 18). These scores are entered on the TESTING RECORD chart on page 4 of the test booklet. It is suggested that a testing date be recorded along with the calm-anxious score and the hopeful-depressed. Then, the examiner can plot the scores. If a respondent has a positive 3 on calm-anxious, and a positive 4 on hopeful-discouraged, then the examiner starts at the center of the grid, goes to the right of center to the 3 line on the abscissa and then up 4 on the ordinate. This places the score in the hopeful-calm quadrant of the grid.

The interpretation of the results of the plotting of the two scores of calm-anxious and hopeful-discouraged depends what quadrant the respondent falls in. One common clinical type is the individual who falls in the extreme of the anxious-discouraged quadrant. Individuals falling in the extreme of this quadrant should be further evaluated for anxiety and depression. Another type frequently found is the person who falls in the extreme end of discouraged but in calm end of the calm-anxious dimension. This person may be low anxious, but depressed. It is not unusual to find people scoring in the hopeful-anxious quadrant, which indicates a sense of hopefulness but also anxiety and apprehension. Individuals in the extreme component of the anxious-discouraged quadrant of the grid would indicate a significant if not serious level of anxiety and depression. If the respondent is in the higher of either the anxious or discouraged dimension, or both, it is recommended that the person be referred for further assessment of anxiety and/or depression problems. Again, the results of the MAQ must be used in conjunction with other test and interview data.

Center for Addictions Research and Evaluation
5460 Ward Road, Suite 140, Arvada, CO 80007

PROGRAM INTEREST QUESTIONNAIRE (PIQ)

PROGRAM INTEREST QUESTIONNAIRE - PIQ

To be Completed by the Program Candidate

Name_____ Date_____ Age_____

Referring Agency or Department_____

Referring Individual _____

You have been referred to **The Strategies for Self-Improvement and Change** Program by a counselor, probation or parole worker or another staff member representing the Adult Criminal Justice System. The program has been described to you. You have been told what we expect of you in this program. You are now asked to complete the following questions regarding whether you would like to be involved in this program. Please be as honest as you can in answering these questions.

---

1. From your understanding, is attending this program a requirement or a condition of your current status?

   _____ a. No.   _____ a. Yes.

2. Does your situation at this time make it impossible for you to attend this program as it was described to you?

   _____ a. Yes.   _____ a. Yes, maybe to some extent.   _____ No.

3. From what you now know about this program, do you think it will be of help to you?

   _____ a. Not at all.
   _____ b. Yes, I think so.
   _____ c. Yes, for sure.

4. Do you feel you need help to keep you from going back to using alcohol?

   _____ a. No, not at all.
   _____ b. Yes, I think so.
   _____ c. Yes, for sure.

5. Do you feel you need help to keep you from going back to using drugs other than alcohol?

   _____ a. No, not at all.
   _____ b. Yes, I think so.
   _____ c. Yes, for sure.

6. Do you feel you need help to keep you from taking part in further criminal acts or behavior?

   _____ a. No, not at all.
   _____ b. Yes, I think so.
   _____ c. Yes, for sure.

7. Now, how do you feel about attending this program?

   _____ a. I do not want to attend this program.
   _____ b. I am not sure if I want to attend.
   _____ c. For sure, I want to attend this program.

RATING OF THE CLIENT BY THE EVALUATOR

1. How would you rate the severity of this candidate's alcohol and other drug problem?
    _____a. Low   _____b. Moderate   _____c. High   _____d. Very high.

2. Do you think this candidate can benefit from this program?
    _____a. No.   _____b. Yes, to some extent.   _____c. Yes, definitely.

3. Is this candidate motivated to attend this program?
    _____a. No.   _____b. Yes, to some extent.   _____c. Yes, definitely.

4. Now, rate the candidate's level of appropriateness for this program.

    _____a. Low.   _____b. Moderate.
    _____c. High.   _____d. Very High.

SCREENING INSTRUMENT SCALE	Raw Score	Weighted Value	Client Score
ASUS - INVOLVEMENT SCALE	0 - 3	0	
ASUS - INVOLVEMENT SCALE	4 - 10	1	
ASUS - INVOLVEMENT SCALE	11 - 19	2	
ASUS - INVOLVEMENT SCALE	> 19	3	
ASUS - DISRUPTION	0 - 8	0	
ASUS - DISRUPTION	9 - 16	1	
ASUS - DISRUPTION	17 - 25	2	
ASUS - DISRUPTION	> 25	3	
ASUS - SOCIAL	0 - 9	0	
ASUS - SOCIAL	10 - 14	1	
ASUS - SOCIAL	> 14	2	
LSI - OVERALL SCORE	0 - 13	0	
LSI - OVERALL SCORE	14 - 20	1	
LSI - OVERALL SCORE	21 - 27	2	
LSI - OVERALL SCORE	> 27	3	
PIQ - SELF REPORT	0 - 4	0	
PIQ - SELF REPORT	5 - 8	1	
PIQ - SELF REPORT	> 8	2	
PIQ - RATER SCALE	0 - 3	0	
PIQ - RATER SCALE	4 - 6	1	
PIQ - RATER SCALE	> 6	2	
FITS SELF-SELECTION CRITERIA	Yes	1	
FITS IMPAIRED CONTROL CYCLE	Yes	1	
REQUIRED TO TAKE TREATMENT	Yes	1	
TOTAL WEIGHTED PRIORITY SCORE FOR CLIENT (SUM RIGHT COLUMN)			

SCORING DIRECTIONS: For all items, a=0, b=1, c=2, d=3.

PROVIDER TREATMENT CLOSURE QUESTIONNAIRE (PTCQ)

PROVIDER TREATMENT CLOSURE QUESTIONNAIRE - PTCQ
STRATEGIES FOR SELF-IMPROVEMENT AND CHANGE - SSC

Name of Client:	Date:	Gender: [ ] F [ ] M

Age:	Ethnic Gp: [ ] Anglo [ ] Black [ ] Hispanic [ ] Nat. Am. [ ] Asian

Provider Name:	Agency:
Date Admitted to SCC:	Discharge Date:

Legal status at admission: [ ] Probation [ ] Parole [ ] Community Corrections
[ ] Prison [ ] DUI Referral [ ] Other_____

Admission Status (check all that apply): [ ] Voluntary [ ] Court ordered
[ ] condition of probation [ ] Condition of parole [ ] Required by P.O.
[ ] Other_____

SSC structure: [ ] Twice a week for phase I and once a week for Phases II and III.
[ ] Once a week for all 50 sessions [ ] Phase I only
[ ] Other_____

1. How well do you recall this client? [ ] Not at all. [ ] Vaguely recall.

   [ ] Fairly remember client. [ ] Good recall of client. [ ] Very good recall.

2. Summary of Program Involvement and Attendance:

   Number of months in SSC _____   Number of sessions attended SSC _____

3. Check all that apply as to client's involvement in program:

   [ ] Completed Phase I   [ ] Client refused to continue program
   [ ] Completed Phase II   [ ] Did not complete because time ran out in system
   [ ] Completed Phase III   [ ] Reoffended and returned to incarceration
   [ ] Went AWOL   [ ] Left program in good standing
   [ ] Terminated by Provider [ ] Other_____

RATE YOUR CLIENT ON THE FOLLOWING SCALES BASED ON THE TIME OF DISCHARGE:

	Very poor	Poor	Fair	Good	Very good
4. Relationship with family/spouse.	a	b	c	d	e
5. Support by family/spouse.	a	b	c	d	e
6. Effort to relate to family/spouse.	a	b	c	d	e
7. Emotional adjustment.	a	b	c	d	e
8. Ability to control acting out behavior.	a	b	c	d	e
9. Mood stability.	a	b	c	d	e
10. Adjustment at work or at school.	a	b	c	d	e
11. Relationship with employer/boss/teachers.	a	b	c	d	e
12. Job attendance.	a	b	c	d	e
13. Compliance with the law.	a	b	c	d	e
14. Responsibility toward the community.	a	b	c	d	e
15. Attitude toward authority and police.	a	b	c	d	e

1

		Very poor	Poor	Fair	Good	Very good
16.	Control over not using drugs/alcohol.	a	b	c	d	e
17.	Abstinence from drug/alcohol use.	a	b	c	d	e
18.	Ability to say no to drugs.	a	b	c	d	e
19.	Overall relationship with family/spouse.	a	b	c	d	e
20.	Overall ability to handle life problems.	a	b	c	d	e
21.	Overall ability to respect and follow the law.	a	b	c	d	e
22.	Overall response to job or work or school.	a	b	c	d	e
23.	Overall ability to remain drug/alcohol free.	a	b	c	d	e

		None	Probably Some	Probably a lot
24.	Use of alcohol during SSC.	a	b	c
25.	Use of other drugs during SSC.	a	b	c
26.	Disruption from alcohol/drug use during SSC.	a	b	c

		No	Possibly	Definitely
27.	Did Client reoffend during SSC?	a	b	c

		No	One	Two	Three or more
28.	Did Client have positive UAs?	a	b	c	d

		None	Low	Moderate	High	Very High
29.	Awareness of problem with drug/alcohol use.	a	b	c	d	e
30.	Degree of improvement in prosocial behavior.	a	b	c	d	e
31.	Willingness to be involved in SSC program.	a	b	c	d	e
32.	Degree to which client tried to stop using alcohol or other drugs.	a	b	c	d	e
33.	Degree of involvement in program.	a	b	c	d	e
34.	Degree to which program helped client.	a	b	c	d	e
35.	Degree to which client changed in program.	a	b	c	d	e
36.	Degree of problem with alcohol use at the time client last attended program.	a	b	c	d	e
37.	Degree of problem with other drugs use at the time client last attended program.	a	b	c	d	e

38. Rate progress that client made during his or her involvement in the program.

No Progress					Some Progress				Much Progress		
1	2	3	4	5	6	7	8	9	10	11	12

39. Rate client's overall improvement

No improvement					Some improvement				Much improvement		
1	2	3	4	5	6	7	8	9	10	11	12

NOW RATE CLIENT ON EACH OF THE FOLLOWING AS TO HER OR HIS RESPONSE TO THE SSC PROGRAM:

		Low degree	Moderate degree	High degree	Very high degree
40.	Interaction with group members/peers.	a	a	c	d
41.	Interaction with staff/provider.	a	a	c	d
42.	Resistance and opposition to program.	a	a	c	d
43.	Follow-through with homework/readings.	a	b	c	d
44.	Participation in group discussions.	a	a	c	d
45.	Support and understanding shown to other clients in program.	a	b	c	d
46.	Degree of disruptive behavior in group.	a	b	c	d
47.	Degree of negative attitude in program.	a	b	c	d
48.	Degree to which client took part in classroom activities.	a	b	c	d
49.	Degree to which client understood program ideas and concepts.	a	b	c	d

		Poor	Fair	Good	Very good
50.	Overall program attendance.	a	a	c	d
51.	Overall program participation.	a	a	c	d
52.	Overall cooperation with program.	a	a	c	d

53. Where do you see this client on the continuum of change based on the three stages of change upon which the SCC program was built:

Challenge to Change   Commitment to Change   Ownership of Change

1   2   3   4   5   6   7   8   9   10   11   12

		Poor	Fair	Good	Very good
54.	Rate client as to overall prognosis regarding future problems with alcohol use.	a	a	c	d
55.	Rate client as to overall prognosis regarding future problems with other drug use.	a	a	c	d
56.	Rate client as to overall prognosis regarding future involvement in criminal conduct or behavior.	a	a	c	d

57. Make a brief statement as to the client's overall response to this program.

_____

_____

END OF RATING SCALE

Providers Treatment Closure Questionnaire - PTCQ
Authors: Kenneth W. Wanberg and Harvey B. Milkman
Copyright (c) K. W. Wanberg and H. B. Milkman

SUBSTANCE USE HISTORY MATRIX (SUHM)

SUBSTANCE USE HISTORY MATRIX

OFFENDER LAST NAME:	FIRST	MI	ID#:	GENDER: □ M □ F	RACE: □ W □ B □ H □ Other ( )

ASSESSMENT DATE: (mm/dd/yy)	ASSESSOR NAME:	LOCATION:	DOB: (mm/dd/yy)

ADS:	DAST:	INVLV:	DISRPT:	SOCIAL:	EMOTN:	DEFNS:	LSI:

INSTR. DERIVED TX LEVEL:	CLINICAL RECOMMENDATION LEVEL:	REASON: (See back)

NUMBER OF MOS. OF TX AT EACH LEVEL: 2 ___ 3 ___ 4 ___ 5 ___ 6 ___

Pattern Typifying Most Recent "Normal" Use of Client (During last 90-180 Days of Using Specific Drug Indicated) - Select Only One for Each Area

Drug Type	Age at First Use / Date of Last Use	Pos. UA & BA Dates	Duration of Use (Yrs.) / Length of Current Abstin. (Mos.)	Frequency 0 = 0/Life 6 = 4+/Mo. 1 = 1-3/Life 7 = 1-3/Wk. 2 = 4+/Life 8 = 4+/Wk. 3 = 1-3/Yr. 9 = 1-3/Day 4 = 4+/Yr. 10 = 4+/Day 5 = 1-3/Mo.	Intensity Typical Amount in One Day's Use	Ingestion 1 = Swallow 2 = Nasal 3 = Inhale 4 = Intrav.	Style 1 = Weekend 2 = Daily 3 = Maint. 4 = Binge	Setting 1 = Home 2 = FrndHme 3 = Bar 4 = Work 5 = Public Plc. (incld. car)	Social Context 1 = Alone 2 = W/Rltv. 3 = W/Frnds. 4 = W/Cowk. 5 = W/Acqnt.	Past Use by Immed. Fam 1 = Yes 2 = No	Longest reported abstinence - once consistent use established & while on streets (use dates)
Alcohol					(drinks)						
Marijuana					(joints)						
Cocaine					(grams)						
Amphetamines					(grams)						
Hallucinogens					(hits)						
Inhalants					(huffs)						
Opiates					(bags)						
Sedatives					(pills)						
Tranquilizers					(pills)						
Other					( )						

THINKING ERRORS CHECK LIST (TECL)

THINKING ERRORS CHECK LIST- TECL

Below is a list of errors in thinking that people tend to use. Rate yourself on each of these thinking errors by checking one of the four possible responses. Then add up your scores for each column and put your total score in the box at the bottom of the page.

ERRORS IN THINKING LIST	Do not use 0	Use sometimes 1	Use a lot 2	Use all the time 3
Power thrust: put people down				
Seeing things only your way				
Blaming others: Victim stance				
Feel superior to others				
Lack concern how others affected				
Think; can't trust anybody				
Refuse something don't want to do				
Want what want right now				
Take what want from others				
Refuse to lean on other people				
Put off things to tomorrow				
I don't have to do that				
Won't change your ideas				
Think in black and white terms				
Mountains out of molehills				
Feel singled out				
Think: They deserve it				
Think: I feel screwed				
Tune out what should hear				
Think about forbidden things				
Demand from others but don't give				
Thinking about criminal things				
Lying or exaggerating the truth				
TOTAL SCORE FOR EACH COLUMN				

TOTAL SCORE _____

Authors: Kenneth W.Wanberg and Harvey B. Milkman

THINKING ERRORS RATING SCALE (TERS)

THINKING ERRORS RATING SCALE - TERS

Below is a list of errors in thinking that people tend to use. Please rate your client on each of these thinking errors by checking one of the four possible responses. Then add up your client's scores for each column and put his or her total score in the box at the bottom of the page.

ERRORS IN THINKING LIST	Do not use 0	Use sometimes 1	Use a lot 2	Use all the time 3
Power thrust: put people down				
Seeing things only your way				
Blaming others: Victim stance				
Feel superior to others				
Lack concern how others affected				
Think; can't trust anybody				
Refuse something don't want to do				
Want what want right now				
Take what want from others				
Refuse to lean on other people				
Put off things to tomorrow				
I don't have to do that				
Won't change your ideas				
Think in black and white terms				
Mountains out of molehills				
Feel singled out				
Think: They deserve it				
Think: I feel screwed				
Tune out what should hear				
Think about forbidden things				
Demand from others but don't give				
Thinking about criminal things				
Lying or exaggerating the truth				
TOTAL SCORE FOR EACH COLUMN				

TOTAL SCORE _____

Authors: Kenneth W.Wanberg and Harvey B. Milkman
Copyright (c) 1996 K. W. Wanberg and H. B. Milkman

APPENDIX B

ADMISSION, INTAKE AND SESSION EVALUATION FORMS

Behavioral Rating Form (BFR)

Client Rights Statement

Client Session Evaluation Summary (CSES)

Consent for Program Involvement

Consent for Release of Confidential Information

Full Disclosure Statement Sample

Notice of Federal Requirements Regarding Confidentiality

Personal Data Questionnaire (PDQ)

Provider Session Evaluation Summary (PSES)

Referral Evaluation Summary (RES)

BEHAVIORAL RATING FORM (BRF)

Following designated sessions, rate the client on the items in the BRF and calculate the raw score. Provider may want to plot the scores across sessions to look for changes. It is expected that for clients responding to the program in a positive manner, the raw BRF score will plateau and remain constant.

CLIENT NAME:		DATE:		SESSION NO:	
RATE CLIENT ON THE FOLLOWING AS TO DEGREE OF RESPONSE DURING SESSION	NONE 0	LOW 1	MODERATE 2	HIGH 3
1. Interaction with group members				
2. Interaction with provider/staff				
3. Completion of homework/readings				
4. Participation in group discussion				
5. Support shown to other members				
6. Cooperation and compliance				
7. Participation in class activities				
8. Understood program concepts/ideas				
9. Willing to share/self-disclose				
10.Resistance/opposition to program*				
*(REVERSE NO. 10: 0=3; 1=2; 2=1; 3=0)			TOTAL:	

CLIENT NAME:		DATE:		SESSION NO:	
RATE CLIENT ON THE FOLLOWING AS TO DEGREE OF RESPONSE DURING SESSION	NONE 0	LOW 1	MODERATE 2	HIGH 3
1. Interaction with group members				
2. Interaction with provider/staff				
3. Completion of homework/readings				
4. Participation in group discussion				
5. Support shown to other members				
6. Cooperation and compliance.				
7. Participation in class activities				
8. Understood program concepts/ideas				
9. Willing to share/self-disclose				
10.Resistance/opposition to program*				
*(REVERSE NO. 10: 0=3; 1=2; 2=1; 3=0)			TOTAL:	

CLIENT RIGHTS STATEMENT

As a client in the Cognitive-Behavioral Program for Substance Abusing Offenders, you have certain rights.

First, you need to know that a qualified provider may consult with other experts on treatment issues. You are encouraged to discuss your progress in this program at any time with your provider. Unless you are a court ordered client in this program, you may end treatment at any time.

You are entitled to receive information about the methods and approaches of the program you are enrolling in. You will be an active participant in the development of your treatment service plan. You may also seek consultation from another expert regarding the appropriateness of this program for you.

You need to know that the information you give us during your treatment is legally confidential except as required by law. This confidentiality is regulated by state law, and for individuals in substance abuse programs, also by Federal law. Information about your treatment and your case can only be release upon your written request. It may be that you have been ordered to attend this program or that attendance is part of the conditions of your status in the criminal justice system (e.g., a condition of probation, parole or community corrections placement). If this is the case, and if there is a condition that a progress report must be sent to your criminal justice supervisor (e.g., probation worker), then you still must sign a written consent for such information to be released. Your provider will provide a consent form for you.

There are also exceptions to the law of confidentiality. These exceptions are as follows: if there is a "threat of harm to self or others," the person is of imminent danger to self or others, there is a suspicion of child abuse or if an individual is considered to be gravely mentally disabled. In these cases, a provider, by professional ethics and State Statutes, is obligated to protect the individual or others. In any situation where child abuse is suspected by a provider or other profession person, that suspicion must be reported to the Department of Social Services in the county where the abuse is suspected.

You need to know that sexual contact between a client and provider is not a part of any recognized therapy or rehabilitation and is never seen as acceptable under any circumstance or condition. Sexual intimacy between client and provider is illegal and should be reported to the appropriate grievance or professional licensing authority.

I have been informed of my provider's professional credentials, training and experience. I have also read the above information and understand my rights as a client.

_____   _____
Client Signature   Date

_____   _____
Provider name   Date

CLIENT SESSION EVALUATION SUMMARY (CSES)

YOUR NAME_____ DATE _____ SESSION NUMBER_____

Rate this session using the following questions. Please feel free to make any comments or notes regarding this session.

1. Overall, did you understand the ideas and material presented in this session?

   [ ] No, not at all.
   [ ] Yes, somewhat.
   [ ] Yes, most of the ideas and material.
   [ ] All of the ideas and material.

2. Will you be able to apply what you learned in this session to your daily living?

   [ ] No, not at all.
   [ ] Yes, somewhat.
   [ ] Most of what I learned.
   [ ] All of what I learned.

3. Will this session be helpful to you in avoiding problems with alcohol or other drug use?

   [ ] No, probably not.
   [ ] Somewhat helpful.
   [ ] Yes, helpful.
   [ ] Yes, very helpful.

4. Will this session be helpful in preventing you from becoming involved in further criminal actions?

   [ ] No, probably not.
   [ ] Somewhat helpful.
   [ ] Yes, helpful.
   [ ] Yes, very helpful.

5. Now, rate your group leader on the following:

Started session on time	[ ] No	[ ] Yes, somewhat	[ ] Yes, for sure.
Was prepared for the session	[ ] No	[ ] Yes, somewhat	[ ] Yes, for sure.
Used examples to get ideas across	[ ] No	[ ] Yes, somewhat	[ ] Yes, for sure.
Used exercises to get ideas across	[ ] No	[ ] Yes, somewhat	[ ] Yes, for sure.
Presented session in clear manner	[ ] No	[ ] Yes, somewhat	[ ] Yes, for sure.
Helped group to talk and share	[ ] No	[ ] Yes, somewhat	[ ] Yes, for sure.
Listened to group members	[ ] No	[ ] Yes, somewhat	[ ] Yes, for sure.
Showed respect to group members	[ ] No	[ ] Yes, somewhat	[ ] Yes, for sure.
Expects group members to change	[ ] No	[ ] Yes, somewhat	[ ] Yes, for sure.

6. Comments and notes:

_____

_____

_____

CONSENT FOR PROGRAM INVOLVEMENT

John Smith, M.A.
Certified Addictions Counselor III
Probation Officer

CONSENT TO TREATMENT

I agree to take part in the Strategies for Self-Improvement and Change Program, which as been fully described to me. I understand that this program is between nine months and one year in length, but that I will be reviewed for continued participation in the program after completing Phase I or after two months of taking part in the program.

You also need to know that service programs such as the one you are enrolling in are not exact sciences, and that not everyone is helped by these programs. Yet, we do know that such programs, which are set up for helping people with substance abuse problems and problems with criminal conduct, have a greater chance of being successful when the client is willing to fully take part in the program.

I have been fully informed about my right to confidentiality and the exceptions to that right. I have also been informed of the ground rules and guidelines of this program and I have gone over these with my provider. My signature below is my seal for consent to be part of this program.

_____   _____
Client Signature   Date

_____   _____
Provider signature   Date

CONSENT FOR RELEASE OF CONFIDENTIAL INFORMATION

I,_____ hereby consent to communication between
      (Name of Client)

_____and
      (agency providing Strategies for Self-Improvement and Change)

_____
      (court, probation, parole, and/or other agency)

the following information:

_____

_____

The purpose of and need for the disclosure is to inform the above named agency(ies) of my attendance and progress in the program. The extent of information to be disclosed is information about my assessment, attendance at sessions, my cooperation with the program, prognosis and other information as follows:

_____

_____

_____

I understand that this consent will remain in effect and cannot be revoked by me until:

_____   There has been a formal and effective termination or revocation of my release from confinement, probation, or parole, or other proceedings under which I was referred into the program, or

_____   Consent can be revoked and/or expires on the following date:_____

I also understand that any disclosure made is bound by Part 2 of Title 42 of the Code of Federal Regulations governing confidentiality of alcohol and drug abuse records and that recipients of this information may redisclose it only in connection with their official duties. I also release the agency disclosing this information from any and all liability with respect to the release of this information. My signature below provides the authority to release such information.

Name of Client_____

Address of Client_____

Client Signature_____ Date_____

Witness Signature_____ Date_____

FULL DISCLOSURE STATEMENT SAMPLE

John Smith, M.A.
Certified Addictions Counselor III
Probation Officer

Mr. Smith is a probation worker with the 10th District Court, State of Texas. He has a Bachelor's Degree in Criminal Justice from the University of Maine and a Master's Degree in Counseling from Northern Colorado University. He has worked as a probation worker for 20 years and has done special work with criminal justice clients in the area of alcohol and other drug addictions for the past five years. Although he works full time as a probation worker, he also does special drug and alcohol groups for a Day Reporting service which services criminal justice clients who are on parole and probation.

Mr. Smith takes a client centered and cognitive behavioral orientation in counseling. He sees alcoholism and drug addiction as having many causes, including social, psychological and physical. He also feels that the social and biological genetics are important factors in the development of a substance abuse problem.

Mr. Smith has also had special training in the areas of stress management, relaxation therapy, working with depression, the counseling of offenders with substance abuse problems and cognitive behavioral approaches to working with the substance abusing offender. He also has specialized training and experience in working with juvenile justice clients.

He is a member of the association of Substance Abuse Counselors of Texas and of the American Corrections Association.

NOTICE OF FEDERAL REQUIREMENTS REGARDING
CONFIDENTIALITY OF ALCOHOL AND DRUG ABUSE PATIENT RECORDS

The confidentiality of alcohol and drug abuse patient records maintained by this program is protected by Federal Law and Regulations. Generally, the program may not say to a person outside the program that a client attends the program, or disclose any information identifying a client as an alcohol or drug abuser unless:

1) The client consents in writing;

2) The disclosure is allowed by a court order, or;

3) The disclosure is made to medical personnel in a medical emergency or to qualified personnel for research, audit or program evaluation.

Violation of the federal law and regulations by a program is a crime. Suspected violations may be reported to appropriate authorities in accordance with federal regulations.

Federal law and regulations do not protect any information about a crime committed by a client either at the program or against any person who works for the program or about any threat to commit such a crime.

Federal laws and regulations do not protect any information about suspected child abuse or neglect from being reported under State law to appropriate State or local authorities (See 42 U.S.C. 290dd-3 and 42 U.S.C 290ee-3 for Federal laws and 42 CFR Part 2 for Federal regulations).

Client Name_____

Client Address_____

Client Signature_____ Date_____

Witness Signature_____ Date_____

PERSONAL DATA QUESTIONNAIRE (PDQ)

(TO BE COMPLETED IN AN INTERVIEW SETTING WITH CLIENT)

Last Name_____ First Name_____ MN_____ Age_____ Gender: [ ] Male [ ] Female

Address_____ City_____ County_____ ZIP_____ Phone_____

DOB_____ SSN_____ DACOD NO._____ JUDICIAL NUMBER:_____

[ ] Rent [ ] Own [ ] Apartment [ ] House   Months at Current Residence _____   Total Number in Household_____

Ethnic Group: [ ] Anglo [ ] Black [ ] Hispanic [ ] Native Am. [ ] Asian   Years of Education _____

Employment: [ ] Full time [ ] Part-time [ ] Student [ ] Disabled [ ] Homemaker [ ] Unemployed No. Months_____

Name of Employer_____ Name of School Attending_____

Months Employed in Past Year_____ Total Family Monthly Income $_____ Client's Monthly Income $_____

Marital Status: [ ] Never married [ ] Married [ ] Separated [ ] Divorced [ ] Widowed   No. Times Married_____

General Health: [ ] Good [ ] Fair [ ] Poor   Medical Problems [ ] No [ ] Yes (Explain)_____

On Medications: [ ] No [ ] Yes_____ Physical Limitations _____

Name of Medical Clinic/Doctor_____ Phone_____ Last Visit_____ Last Physical_____

No. DUI/DWAI Arrests_____   No. Non-DUI Misdemeanors _____   No. Felonies_____   On Probation [ ] No   [ ] Yes

Committed as a Juvenile Offender: [ ] No [ ] Yes Age Committed_____ Involved in Gang [ ] No [ ] Yes Months_____

Months Incarcerated _____   On Parole: [ ] No [ ] Yes Current Charges Pending [ ] No   [ ] Yes Hearing Date_____

Prior Alcohol/Drug Treatment: Outpatient Sessions_____ Residential Days_____ Facilities_____

Prior Mental Health Treatment: Outpatient Sessions_____ Residential Days_____ Facilities_____

Self Help Groups Attended: [ ] AA [ ] NA/CA [ ] Al-Anon/Alateen [ ] Rational Recovery [ ] Other _____

Attend Community groups: [ ] No [ ] Yes List _____ Attend Church/Synagogue: [ ] No [ ] Yes _____

Staff Rating of Client Problems

		None	Slight	Moderate	Severe	Very Severe
1.	Family disruption and problems	0	1	2	3	4
2.	Marital or relationship problems	0	1	2	3	4
3.	Mental health and emotional problems	0	1	2	3	4
4.	School adjustment problems	0	1	2	3	4
5.	Employment problems	0	1	2	3	4
6.	Job adjustment problems	0	1	2	3	4
7.	Deviant or antisocial problems	0	1	2	3	4
8.	Involvement in criminal behavior	0	1	2	3	4
9.	Physical health and medical problems	0	1	2	3	4
10.	Involvement with negative peers	0	1	2	3	4
11.	Involvement in alcohol use	0	1	2	3	4
12.	Life disruption due to alcohol use	0	1	2	3	4
13.	Involvement in other drugs	0	1	2	3	4
14.	Life disruption due to other drugs	0	1	2	3	4

Motivation for Treatment

Low   Moderate   High
0 1 2 3 4 5 6 7 8 9

Admission Summary

Referral Source_____

Referral date: Year_____ Mo_____ Day____

Admit date: Year_____ Mo_____ Day____

Type: [ ] Volunteer [ ] Court ordered

Admitting Staff_____

Staff Assigned_____

Judicial District_____

Treatment Agency_____

Probation/Parole Worker_____

Staff Signature_____

Date_____ Time_____

Form ADMIT 0995

PROVIDER SESSION EVALUATION SUMMARY (PSES)

PROVIDER NAME_____ DATE _____ SESSION NUMBER_____

Rate this session using the following questions.

1.   Overall, did clients understand the ideas and material presented in this session?

[ ] No, not at all.
[ ] Yes, somewhat.
[ ] Yes, most of the ideas and material.
[ ] All of the ideas and material.

2.   Will clients be able to apply what they learned in this session to their daily lives?

[ ] No, not at all.
[ ] Yes, somewhat.
[ ] Most of what they learned.
[ ] All of what they learned.

3.   Now, rate yourself on the following:

Started session on time	[ ] No	[ ] Yes, somewhat [ ] Yes, definitely.
Was prepared for the session	[ ] No	[ ] Yes, somewhat [ ] Yes, definitely.
Used examples to get ideas across	[ ] No	[ ] Yes, somewhat [ ] Yes, definitely.
Used exercises to get ideas across	[ ] No	[ ] Yes, somewhat [ ] Yes, definitely.
Presented session in clear manner	[ ] No	[ ] Yes, somewhat [ ] Yes, definitely.
Helped group to talk and share	[ ] No	[ ] Yes, somewhat [ ] Yes, definitely.
Listened to group members	[ ] No	[ ] Yes, somewhat [ ] Yes, definitely.
Satisfied with your performance	[ ] No	[ ] Yes, somewhat [ ] Yes, definitely.

4.   Now, rate the group's response to the session:

Group was attentive	[ ] No	[ ] Yes, somewhat [ ] Yes, definitely.
Was good group interaction	[ ] No	[ ] Yes, somewhat [ ] Yes, definitely.
Most members participated	[ ] No	[ ] Yes, somewhat [ ] Yes, definitely.
Members had a positive attitude	[ ] No	[ ] Yes, somewhat [ ] Yes, definitely.
Materials were appropriate for group	[ ] No	[ ] Yes, somewhat [ ] Yes, definitely.

5.   Now, rate the session as to how difficult versus how easy it was to present:

[ ] Very difficult   [ ] Somewhat difficult   [ ] Somewhat easy   [ ] Very easy.

6.   Comments and notes. Reflect on any questions presented to the provider in the *Client and Session Evaluation* section at the end of this session.

_____

_____

_____

_____

_____

8081

REFERRAL EVALUATION SUMMARY (RES)
STRATEGIES FOR SELF-IMPROVEMENT AND CHANGE - SSC

REFERRAL SOURCE

Name of Referring Individual _____ Phone_____ Date_____

Agency Name and Address_____

CLIENT DATA

Name of Client:_____ Address_____

City_____State_____Zip_____Phone_____ Judicial No:_____

DOB_____ Age_____ Gender: [ ] Male [ ] Female

Ethnic Group: [ ] Anglo [ ] Black [ ] Hispanic [ ] American Indian [ ] Asian

Currently Employed: [ ] No [ ] Yes   In School: [ ] No [ ] Yes

Criminal Justice Status: [ ] Probation [ ] Parole [ ] Community Corrections

[ ] Department of Corrections [ ] Other_____

RATING OF CLIENT PROBLEMS

Referring individual is asked to rate the client on the degree of severity in each of the following areas:

	None	Slight	Moderate	Severe	Very Severe
1. Family disruption and problems	1	2	3	4	5
2. Marital or relationship problems	1	2	3	4	5
3. Mental health and emotional problems	1	2	3	4	5
4. School adjustment problems	1	2	3	4	5
5. Employment problems	1	2	3	4	5
6. Job adjustment problems	1	2	3	4	5
7. Deviant or antisocial problems	1	2	3	4	5
8. Involvement in criminal behavior	1	2	3	4	5
9. Physical health and medical problems	1	2	3	4	5
10. Involvement with negative peers	1	2	3	4	5
11. Involvement in alcohol use	1	2	3	4	5
12. Life disruption due to alcohol use	1	2	3	4	5
13. Involvement in other drugs	1	2	3	4	5
14. Life disruption due to other drugs	1	2	3	4	5

TO BE COMPLETED BY SSC PROVIDER

Name of Staff Handling Referral_____ Final Screening Date_____

Disposition: [ ] No Show [ ] Intake Deferred [ ] Referred _____

[ ] Client Refused Admission [ ] Client Admitted to SSC program

Name of provider case manager_____